Srīmad Bhagavad Gītā Bhāṣya
of Sri Saṁkarācārya

SRĪMAD BHAGAVAD GĪTĀ BHĀṢYA OF SRI SAṀKARĀCĀRYA

WITH TEXT IN DEVANAGIRI & ENGLISH RENDERING, AND INDEX OF FIRST LINES OF VERSES

Translation by
DR. A. G. KRISHNA WARRIER

SRI RAMAKRISHNA MATH
Madras-600004 INDIA

Published by
The President
Sri Ramakrishna Math
Mylapore, Chennai-4

VII-2M 3C-4-2002
ISBN 81-7120-269-1

Printed in India at
Sri Ramakrishna Math Printing Press
Mylapore, Chennai-4

CONTENTS

PREFACE

There has been a persistent demand from our readers for an edition of Śrīmad Bhagavad Gītā containing Śrī Saṁkarācārya's commentary on it in the original with a lucid translation in English. We have, therefore, great pleasure in presenting this volume with the Sanskrit original edited and translated into English by Dr. A.G. Krishna Warrier, Curator, Adayar Library, Madras. Dr. Warrier, who is an accomplished Sanskrit scholar and also well versed in philosophy both Eastern and Western, has worked in several centres of learning and has to his credit a number of outstanding works like '*God in Advaita*', '*Concept of Mukti in Advaita*', and a Malayalam rendering of Śrī Śaṅkara's *Brahmasūtra Bhāṣhya*. The discerning reader will note how the English translation in this book makes pleasant reading without loss of precision or fidelity to the original. We are extremely grateful to Dr. Warrier for this labour of love.

A charming feature of the Sanskrit language consists in the linked sweetness of its Saṁdhis—words run together euphoniously to form long rolling phrases. This, however, poses a problem to most of the readers who cannot be expected to be familiar with the intricacies of Sanskrit grammar and so are put to the trouble of having to delink the words carefully in order to understand their purport. We have, therefore, thought it expedient to split the long phrases, so that each word stands by itself as in English and other modern languages. We crave the indulgence of the sticklers for Pāṇinian grammar for this innovation meant for the convenience of the many.

May Śri Śaṁkara's dauntless exposition of the nature of the Ultimate Reality strengthen in us the conviction that man is essentially Spirit and it is the forgetfulness of this truth that causes all our misery.

Sri Ramakrishna Math, Publisher.
Mylapore, Madras 600 004.
May, 1983.

INTRODUCTION

Śaṁkara's commentary on the Bhagavad Gītā, more than even his commentaries on the Upaniṣads and the Brahma-sūtras, has aroused heated controversy among commentators, interpreters, and thinkers all the world over. After long-fought battles among them, there is a sort of consensus among scholars today that the text of the Bhagavad Gītā, Śaṁkara fixed long ago, viz: 700 verses—is a unitary work.[1] Some modern scholars, both Indian and foreign, as a matter of course, pay tribute to Śaṁkara's scholarship, intellectual power, and supreme insight; they hope thus to make their attack on his commentary look as if it is their scrupulous regard for objective facts that has obliged them to indulge in it. For instance, Tilak observes: "Srī Śaṁkara was an extraordinary scholar and sage, who by virtue of his supernatural powers . . . established the system of Advaitic thought on the firm foundation of the Religion of the Vedas."[2] "It is no exaggeration to say that the world has not known a sage and philosopher as eminent as Śaṁkara."[3] He remarks that Jñānesvara has written his celebrated commentary on the Bhagavad Gītā in Marathi in the light of Śaṁkara's Advaitic doctrines. Nevertheless, Tilak rejects Śaṁkara's interpretation of it as sectarian and deems as objective his own view that the Gītā establishes the pre-eminence of Karma as an independent means to win *mokṣa* or the *summum bonum*.

In like fashion W. D. P. Hill, a much-admired translator of the Gītā, writes: "The famous founder of the Advaita school of Vedanta philosophy, Śaṁkara, was a brilliant scholar, gifted with one of the acutest intellects in history. His Gītā-bhāṣya is full of keen argument; but not even the subtlety of a Śaṁkara can conceal the fact that the Advaita and the Gītā

[1] R.C.Zaehner writes: "After teaching the Gītā for a number of years it appeared to me to be a far more unitary work than most modern scholars . . . concede." *The Bhagavad Gītā*, Oxford, 1969, Introduction, p.2.

[2] B.G.Tilak, *The Gītā Rahasya*, Hindi Translation, Puna, 1917; *Viṣayapraveśa*, p.13.

[3] Ibid; p.19.

systems are not at one. Nor is he able, in face of plain texts to the contrary, to make good his claim that the Gītā severs action from knowledge, the latter alone qualifying the aspirant for release."[4] Hill speaks of undue emphasis on the power of knowledge. But it may be noted that Hill refuses to face the force of texts[5] like BG.4.37 and 38. He concludes his critical remarks thus: The Philosophy of the Bhagavad Gītā more nearly approximates to that of the Viśiṣṭādvaita, though he demurely protests in the words, 'Rāmanuja errs perhaps in excessive emphasis on *Bhakti*'.[6]

We may also note at this juncture a very recent and subtle attempt to extol Rāmanuja's interpretation of the Gītā—that of R.C. Zaehner, Spalding professor, who succeeded Dr. Radhakrishnan in that chair. He talks of the founder of the extreme school of Vedantic non-dualism, Śaṁkara, and of the commentary of the "modified non-dualist Rāmanuja, so much nearer in spirit to the Gītā."[7] Zaehner however has his own fears that he may be taken as "trying to read only his own interpretation into the Gītā." A careful reader of his own voluminous work may easily find out that his object is to find a common ground between the Bhagavad Gītā and the Catholic theology on the basis of personal mysticism—eternal *Jīvas* and a Personal God being the basis of love or *Bhakti*.

In the confusion naturally caused by this multiplicity of interpretations, the independent reader who seeks to understand the Gītā as a well-knit text based on reasoning and spiritual insights has no other alternative than to study Śaṁkara's commentary in its entirety. The present situation as regards Gītā scholarship is intriguingly paralleled by the one which confronted Śaṁkara when he took up for explication this universal text of religious philosophy.[8] Witness Śaṁkara's

[4] *The Bhagavadgītā*, London, 1928; pp.273 ff.

[5] Jñānāgniḥ sarvakarmāṇi bhasmasātkurute. . . .
na hi jñānena sadṛśam pavitramiha vidyate.

[6] Hill, Ibid; p.274.

[7] Ibid; p.3.

[8] cf: A.Huxley, Introduction, *The Song of God* =BG) Translated by Swami Prabhavananda; p.13: "*The Bhagavad Gītā* is one of the clearest and most comprehensive

remarks in the Introduction to his commentary on the Gītā: ". . . but its sense is difficult to grasp. Many have striven to elucidate its words, their imports and their totality as a reasoned treatise. The public, however, has got it as a mass of self-contradictory ideas. Noting their plight, I shall set forth its contents, briefly elucidating the text with due discrimination." Therefore now, as in Śaṁkara's days, the discriminating student has no option but to turn to the guidance offered by him. Hence it is of the utmost importance to follow Śaṁkara's subtle arguments as painstakingly and loyally as possible to get at the heart of the perennial philosophy embodied in the Gītā.

The aim of the Gītā is not to exalt the way of Karma, as Tilak would have us believe, over the ways of *Jñāna* and *Bhakti*. Śaṁkara makes this clear at the very out-set:—"Succinctly, the purpose of the science of the Gītā is to set forth (the nature of) the *summum bonum* consisting in the total cessation of transmigratory life and its causes."[9] Note that, in contrast, Tilak writes that the aim of the Gītā is to set forth Karmayoga which is rooted in Jñāna, in which Bhakti is dominant and which ultimately leads to *mokṣa*—*Jñānamūlaka-bhaktipradhāna-Karmayoga*.[10] Tilak does not seem to have attempted a formal definition of *mokṣa*, though he has devoted several pages in his *Gītārahasya* to the repudiation of Śaṁkara's ideas on this pivotal concept. We shall examine briefly, in due course, Śaṁkara's attempts to substantiate his well thought-out doctrine of *mokṣa* in the light of Gītā's statements on it.

In this connection, it is of the utmost importance to remember the Advaitic emphasis on the doctrine of *adhikāra* or eligibility and competence. An elaborate elucidation of it may be found in B.S.B., 1.1.1 whose upshot is that he alone is

---

summaries of the Perennial Philosophy ever to have been made. Hence its enduring value, not only for Indians, but for all mankind." It is perhaps the most systematic scriptural statement of the Perennial Philosophy." p.22.

[9] BGB, Introduction.

[10] Tilak, Ibid; p.12.

eligible for *mokṣa* who is equipped with the *sādhana catuṣṭayam.*[11] or fourfold discipline. In its briefest form *adhikāra* is that state of mind which wholeheartedly prays, "*asato mā sadgamaya, tamaso mā jyotirgamaya, mṛtyormā amṛtam gamaya.*"[12]—"lead me from the false to the true, from darkness to light and from death to immortality." That the Gītā seeks to liberate man, to make him free, by revealing the light of Truth, is indisputably clear from its *carama-śloka* or valedictory verse[13] whose climax is *mokṣayiṣyāmi*—'I shall liberate you.' Whether this verse is taken to stress *bhakti* or *jñāna* is a matter of detail; it points to emancipation, or *Brahmabhāva* or attaining the nature of Brahman.

Equally important and decisive is the pre-eminence of *Jñāna* in the Gītā's scheme of *mokṣa*: "Nothing exists here as purifying as knowledge, whose content is *Vāsudeva sarvamiti*—Vāsudeva is all existence.[14] Here is Gītā's style of affirming *sarvaṁ khalvidaṁ brahma*—all this is Brahman.[15] The function of this saving knowledge is to reduce all activities to ashes, to lift the *mukta* or liberated above the sphere of space, time, and causes.[16] The *mukta* can no longer work in the way the empirical man works—i.e. with a sense of egoistic agency. This is the core of Śaṁkara's phrase in his Introduction to his commentary—*saṁsārasyātyantoparamalakṣaṇam,*[17] i.e., characterized by the utter subsidence of the transmigratory cycle.

The concept of the saving knowledge may be elucidated a little more. As has just been said it is the knowledge of God in the Gītā, who has, at once, "the attributes of a full-fledged monotheistic deity and those of the Upaniṣadic[18] Absolute". Verses like 13.12-17 leave no legitimate room for doubt on

[11] BSB 1.1.1.
[12] BU 1.3.28.
[13] BG 18.66
[14] BG 7.19
[15] CU 3.14.1.
[16] BSB 1.1.4.
[17] BGB, Introduction.
[18] Edgerton, BG Translation, London, 1977; p. 132.

this score. So much so that an objective scholar like Edgerton is obliged to set down his well-considered view in the following words: "Thus through its God the Gītā seems after all to arrive at an ultimate monism."[19] The impersonal Brahman in the Bhagavad Gītā is granted all the dignity which the Upaniṣads claim for It, while, of course, Kṛṣṇa representing the *saguṇa* Brahman is claimed to be Its *pratiṣṭhā* or ground.[20] Śaṁkara says Brahman is the *paramātmā* (Supreme Self) that abides in the *pratyagātmā* (percipient Self). So by right knowledge the identity of the two is perceived. Alternatively, he adds: Brahman may also be taken as conditioned or *savikalpakam*. "I am the ground of that Brahman and am Myself the unconditioned or *nirvikalpakam*."

To explain the saving power of Brahmajñāna, it is vital to note that He is not, being hidden[21] by the power of Māyā, known to the *non-adhikārins* (the unqualified). Māyā, of course, is the power by which the Absolute appears as the world in space-time which is neither non-existent nor immutable.[22] Tilak apparently accepts this Śaṁkarite view.[23] When he goes on to identify that power with the divine play or *līlā*, he seems to be in accord with Śaṁkara's explication of Māyā. In varying degrees does Māyā delude *jīvas* according to the dominance in them of *sattva*, *rajas* and *tamas*, or, in other words, to their different *adhikāra*. This decisive Advaitic doctrine has been lucidly expressed in the *Pañcadaśī* in the verse,

tucchā'nirvacanīyā ca vāstavī cetyasau tridhā |
jñeyā māyā tribhirbodhaiḥ śrautayauktikalaukikaiḥ ||[24]

Therefore when the Gītā says that the fire of knowledge reduces the empirical realm of works to ashes making it neither possible nor necessary for the knower of God to work any more,

[19] Ibid; pp.146–47.
[20] BG 14.27.
[21] BG 7.13, etc.
[22] BSB 2.1.14.
[23] Vide his commentary on BG 7.24.
[24] PD. 6.130:- Māyā is the object of three kinds of knowledge: according to revealed knowledge it is unreal; according to reasoning it is indescribable; according to the perceptions of the empirical man, it is real.

it has the *uttamādhikārin* (the most competent aspirant) in view, for whom nothing is real except God.

Tilak's contention that the Gītā never envisages a situation in which all work drops off, that its final teaching is the continuation of *Karma* till death, violates *śruti*, *smṛti* and the experience of the perfected sage or *vidvadanubhava.*[25] What about formulations like, *tasmādasaktaḥ satataṁ kāryaṁ karma samācara*; *karmaṇaiva hi samsiddhimāsthitā janakādaya*, etc.[26] (Therefore, ever perform unattached action that has to be done; by action alone Janaka and others attained perfection)? A point of utmost importance in Advaitic theory and practice in solving the problems of *pravṛtti* (work) and *nivṛtti* (withdrawal) has to be adverted to here. Śaṁkara writes:—In the case of the knower who has, after purifying his mind through the performance of Karmayoga, won the knowledge of the primal Reality, the knowledge whose content is "all this is Brahman, the non-agent", there is no more work to do; nothing remains for him to gain through it. Still he is diligently active for the welfare of the world. This, apparently, is activity on his part. But with this kind of activity, knowledge can't be combined. An instance of this kind of activity and agency is the Lord Kṛṣṇa and His activity as a Kṣatriya. Combination is ruled out; for, His activity is not a means of realizing *mokṣa*; He is already perfect. The knower of God is like Him, since common to the two are the absence of the desire for perfection and the egoistic sense. A Karmayogin works without craving for work's fruits, or by dedicating the fruits to God for mental purification. Karmayoga is never an end in itself: it is only the first step towards gaining the knowledge that liberates.[27] Arjuna has been exhorted, as his nature is largely *rājasic*, to work without craving for fruit, without *kāma*, to achieve *cittaśuddhi* (purity of heart) and the ultimate saving knowledge. That achievement of *kaivalyam*, the flight of the 'alone' to the Alone,

[25] cf. BG 2.69; 6.3-4, etc.
[26] BG 3.19,20 etc.
[27] BGB 2.11.

can be achieved only through *saṁnyāsa*, undivided consecration to God. Gītā itself affirms:

asaktabuddhiḥ sarvatra jitātmā vigataspṛhaḥ |
naiṣkarmyasiddhiṁ paramāṁ saṁnyāsenādhigacchati || [28]

—He, whose understanding is unattached throughout, whose mind is under control, who is devoid of craving, attains through renunciation that supreme state of freedom from action. Tilak's mockery of the Advaitin who insists on exclusive consecration to God for gaining the saving knowledge is misconceived. In view of the theory of *adhikāra*, not every worker is called upon to renounce;[29] Gītā itself underscores this truth.[30]

Śaṁkara's detailed discussion on the *purvamīmāṁsa's* claim on behalf of its scheme of works alone as leading to liberation, without full-fledged renunciation at any stage, is set forth in his Gītā commentary on 13.2 and 18.66; it serves to disillusion the unwary student regarding the possibility of achieving liberation without *Jñāna*. Another point however has to be noticed in this brief Introduction—the way Śaṁkara deals with *bhakti* and *Jñāna* in the Gītā's scheme of liberation. Those who talk of Rāmānuja being nearer to the intention of the Gītā conveniently forget that the Bhagavad Gītā is a unified work that has arrived at an ultimate Monism; that its God is personal-impersonal combining the attributes of a monotheistic deity and those of the Upaniṣadic Absolute. Devotion to the God of the Gītā is logically capable of being synthesized with Knowledge of *nirguṇa* Brahman. Devotion[31] is only a means, may be an indispensable means, to the winning of the saving knowledge. The two, devotion and knowledge, have been intimately blended as means and end in the Gītā. Among the four kinds of devotees or *bhaktas*, *Jñānī* has been singled out as the very Self of the Lord—*Jñānī tvātmaiva me matam*.[32] Thus

[28] BG 18.49.
[29] KU 4.1.
[30] BG 7.3.
[31] Edgerton, Ibid, p.168; p.173. "Devotion to God is an auxilliary means of gaining knowledge of Him."
[32] BG 7.18.

when the contents of the Bhagavad Gītā are logically synthesized and integrated, the paths and the goal, Yogas and salvation, fall into harmony; the paths lead the *uttamādhikārin* (one of full competency) out of the realm of *saṁsāra* or empirical life to the realization of unitary consciousness as stated in *Vāsudevaḥ sarvamiti* or *sarvaṁ khalvidaṁ brahma* . . . Let it be noted and assimilated that it is *Jñānadīpena bhāsvatā*[33]—by the lighted lamp of knowledge—that *ajñānajaṁ tamaḥ* or the darkness born of ignorance is destroyed, and not by *karmayoga* or *bhaktiyoga*.[34]

Once this basic stand of Śaṁkara is grasped, the interpretation he gives to the most controversial verses of the Gītā will be seen to be inevitable. For instance in 4.18, both *karma* and *akarma* according to Śaṁkara are acts of super-imposition, due to *avidyā* on the ineffable ground or Absolute, of perceptions like "I am the agent" and "I am no agent". The seeker after liberation is instructed to perceive the peaceful Ground as behind and beyond all forms of empirical activities. "I am no agent" is an egoistic ascription of actionlessness to the transphenomenal Ground that is strictly connoted only as *neti neti*.[35] This perception alone yields *kaivalyam*, the supreme goal of life. Equally intelligible becomes the exhortation in 5.8.—"*naiva kiṁcit karomīti yukto manyeta tattvavit*—The knower of Truth should have the conviction, 'I am not doing anything'. The metaphysical Truth is that, being timeless and spaceless, the Self or the Ground cannot and does not act.[36]

Before concluding these introductory observations it should be added that in the Sanskrit text of Śaṁkara's commentary printed in the present edition the laws of euphonious combinations or *saṁdhi* have not all been strictly followed according

[33] BG 10.11.

[34] BG 10.11.

[35] BU 2.3.6; 3.9.26, etc.

[36] Those who talk of the Viśiṣṭādvaita as nearer to the spirit of BG do not ask how there can be a multiplicity of 'selves' or *cits*. Multiplicity can pertain only to things in space-time. *cit* is spirit, timeless and spaceless; that is why it is non-dual, and not even one. cf. Russell, H.W.P. 1946, p.783. How can action such as Kaiṁkarya, etc, pertain to the timeless and spaceless spirit?

to Pāṇini's aphorisms. The aim has rather been to enable the readers, not so well vẹrsed in the intricacies of Sanskrit grammar, to get familiar with the original text of the commentary.

It may also be noted that none of the intricacies of Śaṁkara's subtle arguments have been ignored. A conscientious effort has been made in the translation here offered to put his subtle arguments in intelligible English; some notes and summaries have also been appended to give the readers an insight into the Master's mind. Perhaps this fact may serve as an adequate reason for translating anew Śaṁkara's *Gītābhāṣya* despite the availability of Sri Mahādeva Śāstri's well-known translation.

A. G. KRISHNA WARRIER

The abbreviations used:

1. BG The Bhagavadgītā
2. BGB Śaṁkara's Commentary on BG.
3. BS The Brahmasūtras
4. BSB Śaṁkara's Commentary on BS
5. BU The Bṛhadāraṇyaka Upaniṣad.
6. CU The Chāndogya Upaniṣad.
7. KU The Kaṭhopaniṣad.
8. PD The Pañcadaśī.
9. HWP Bertrand Russell's History of Western Philosophy, 1946.

* * *

THE LIST OF ABBREVIATIONS

Ait. Ā.	Aitareya Āraṇyaka
Anu G.	Anu Gītā
A.P.S.	Āpastaṃbasūtra
Aśva	Aśvamedhaparva
B.D.S.	Baudhāyanadharmasūtra
B.G.	Bhagavadgītā
B.G.B.	Śaṁkara's Bhagavadgītābhāṣya
B.S.	Brahmasūtras
B.U.	Bṛhadāraṇyaka Upaniṣad
C.U.	Chāndogya Upaniṣad
G.D.S.	Gautamadharmasūtras
H.W.P.	B. Russell's History of Western Philosophy, London, 1946.
I.U.B.	Śaṁkara's Iśāvāsya Upaniṣad Bhāṣya
Jal.U.	Jābāla Upaniṣad
K.U.	Kaṭha Upaniṣad
Kai.U.	Kaivalya Upaniṣad
Ke.U.	Kena Upaniṣad
Manu.	Manu Smṛti
M.B.	Mahābhārata
M.U.	Muṇḍaka Upaniṣad
Nar.Pari.U.	Nārada Parivrājaka Upaniṣad
P.D.	Pañcadaśī
P.U.	Praśna Upaniṣad
R.V.	Ṛg Veda
Śānti.	Śāntiparva
Ś.U.	Śvetaśvatara Upaniṣad
Sk.	Skandha
T.A.	Taittirīya Āraṇyaka
T.B.	Taittirīya Upaniṣad Bhāṣya of Śaṁkara
T.S.	Taiṭṭirīya Saṁhitā
T.U.	Taittirīya Upaniṣad
Vana	Vanaparva
V.P.	Viṣṇu Purāṇa

ॐ

।। गीताध्यानम् ।।

पार्थाय प्रतिबोधितां भगवता नारायणेन स्वयं
व्यासेन ग्रथितां पुराणमुनिना मध्येमहाभारतम् ।
अद्वैतामृतवर्षिणीं भगवतीमष्टादशाध्यायिनीं
अम्ब त्वामनुसंदधामि भगवद्गीते भवद्वेषिणीम् ।।१।।
नमोऽस्तु ते व्यास विशालबुद्धे फुल्लारविंदायतपत्रनेत्र ।
येन त्वया भारततैलपूर्णः प्रज्वालितो ज्ञानमयः प्रदीपः ।।२।।
प्रपन्नपारिजाताय तोत्रवेत्रैकपाणये ।
ज्ञानमुद्राय कृष्णाय गीतामृतदुहे नमः ।।३।।
सर्वोपनिषदो गावो दोग्धा गोपालनन्दनः ।
पार्थो वत्सः सुधीर्भोक्ता दुग्धं गीतामृतं महत् ।।४।।
वसुदेवसुतं देवं कंसचाणूरमर्दनम् ।
देवकीपरमानंदं कृष्णं वन्दे जगद्गुरुम् ।।५।।
भीष्मद्रोणतटा जयद्रथजला गांधारनीलोत्पला
शल्यग्राहवती कृपेण वहनी कर्णेन वेलाकुला ।
अश्वत्थामविकर्णघोरमकरा दुर्योधनावर्तिनी ।
सोत्तीर्णा खलु पांडवै रणनदी कैवर्तकः केशवः ।।६।।
पाराशर्यवचःसरोजममलं गीतार्थगन्धोत्कटं ।
नानाख्यानककेसरं हरिकथासद्वासनावासितम् ।
लोके सज्जनषट्पदैरहरहः पेपीयमानं मुदा ।
भूयाद्भारतपंकजं कलिमलप्रध्वंसि नः श्रेयसे ।।७।।
मूकं करोति वाचालं पंगुं लंघयते गिरिम् ।
यत्कृपा तमहं वंदे परमानंदमाधवम् ।।८।।
यं ब्रह्मा वरुणेंद्ररुद्रमरुतः स्तुन्वन्ति दिव्यैः स्तवैः
वेदैः सांगपदक्रमोपनिषदैर्गायन्ति यं सामगाः ।
ध्यानावस्थिततद्गतेन मनसा पश्यन्ति यं योगिनो
यस्यान्तं न विदुः सुरासुरगणा देवाय तस्मै नमः ।।९।।

श्रीमच्छंकराचार्यविरचितं

श्रीमद्भगवद्गीताभाष्यम् ।

ॐ नमो भगवते वासुदेवाय

उपाद्धातः

THE COMMENTATOR'S INTRODUCTION

नारायणः परोऽव्यक्तात् अण्डमव्यक्तसम्भवम् ।
अण्डस्यान्तस्त्विमे लोकाः सप्तद्वीपा च मेदिनी ॥

"Nārāyaṇa is beyond the Unmanifest (Prakṛti); the Cosmic Egg is born of the Unmanifest. Within the Cosmic Egg are these worlds as also the earth with its seven isles[1]."

1. स भगवान् सृष्ट्वेदं जगत्, तस्य च स्थितिं चिकीर्षुः, मरीच्यादीन् अग्रे सृष्ट्वा प्रजापतीन्, प्रवृत्तिलक्षणं धर्मं ग्राहयामास वेदोक्तम् । ततः अन्यान् च सनकसनन्दनादीन् उत्पाद्य, निवृत्तिलक्षणं धर्मं ज्ञानवैराग्यलक्षणं ग्राहयामास । द्विविधो हि वेदोक्तो धर्मः — प्रवृत्तिलक्षणः, निवृत्तिलक्षणश्च, जगतः स्थितिकारणम् । प्राणिनां साक्षात् अभ्युदयनिःश्रेयसहेतुः यः स धर्मः ब्राह्मणाद्यैः वर्णिभिः आश्रमिभिः श्रेयोर्थिभिः अनुष्ठीयमानः । दीर्घेण कालेन अनुष्ठातॄणां कामोद्भवात् हीयमानविवेकविज्ञानहेतुकेन अधर्मेण अभिभूयमाने धर्मे, प्रवर्धमाने च अधर्मे, जगतः स्थितिं परिपिपालयिषुः सः आदिकर्ता नारायणाख्यः विष्णुः भौमस्य ब्रह्मणः ब्राह्मणत्वस्य रक्षणार्थं देवक्यां वसुदेवात् अंशेन कृष्णः किल सम्बभूव । ब्राह्मणत्वस्य हि रक्षणे रक्षितः स्यात् वैदिको धर्मः, तदधीनत्वात् वर्णाश्रमभेदानाम् ॥

1. Having created the cosmos and seeking to ensure its existence, the Lord brought forth in the beginning the Progenitors

[1] At the beginning of his commentary, instead of composing a verse of benediction or Mangala, Saṁkara quotes an ancient verse extolling Nārāyaṇa, "the Indweller immortal" (*antaryāmī*) who is also the supreme source of the world (vide Anandagiri on 'Saṁkara's Introduction to his Gītā Bhāṣya'). The seven isles constituting the earth are known as Jambu, Plakṣa, Kuśa, Krauñca, Śāka, Śālmala, and Puṣkara.

(Prajāpatīs)[2] Marīci and the rest. Then he imparted to them the Vedic law of works. Later, bringing forth others like Sanaka and Sanandana[3], He imparted to them the law of cessation of work (nivṛtti), marked by knowledge and detachment. Indeed, the Vedic law making for the world's stability is two-fold: (i) embracing works; (ii) embracing cessation. The law of righteousness (Dharma) is what directly promotes the prosperity and emancipation of living beings. It is cultivated in the pursuit of progress by classes of men, set in different stations of life. Due to the lapse of long periods of time, the practitioners of the law of righteousness came to be dominated by cravings. Then lawlessness, arising from the decline of discriminative knowledge, overcame righteousness and became dominant. Therefore, with a view to ensuring the well-being of the world, the primal and all-pervading Agent, celebrated as Nārāyaṇa, is held to have been born of Vasudeva from Devaki's womb by an aspect of Himself as Kṛṣṇa in order to safeguard the spiritual power in the world or the state of Brāhmanhood. Once the dominance of spirituality is assured, the survival of the Vedic law of righteousness is guaranteed; for, on it depends the multiplicity of the human classes and life-stations.

2. स च भगवान् ज्ञानैश्वर्यशक्तिबलवीर्यतेजोभिः सदा सम्पन्नः त्रिगुणात्मिकां वैष्णवीं स्वां मायां मूलप्रकृतिं वशीकृत्य, अजः अव्ययः भूतानां ईश्वरः नित्यशुद्धबुद्धमुक्तस्वभावोऽपि सन्, स्वमायया देहवान् इव जातः इव च लोकानुग्रहं कुर्वन् लक्ष्यते । स्वप्रयोजनाभावेऽपि भूतानुजिघृक्षया वैदिकं धर्मद्वयं अर्जुनाय शोकमोहमहोदधौ निमग्नाय उपदिदेश, गुणाधिकैः हि गृहीतः अनुष्ठीयमानश्च धर्मः

[2] Prajāpatis are the progenitors of living beings. Manu applies the names to ten sages, the mind-born sons of Brahma. They are Marīci, Atri, Aṅgira, Pulastya, Pulaha, Kratu, Vasiṣṭha, Pracetas or Dakṣa, Bhṛgu, and Nārada. According to some authorities there are only seven Prajapatis identified with the Saptarṣis. The *Śatapathabrāhmaṇa* names them as follows: Gotama, Bharadvāja, Viśvamitra, Jamadagni, Vasiṣṭha, Kaśyapa, Atri. The list in the Mahābharata is: Marīcī, Atri, Aṅgira, Pulaha, Kratu, Pulastya, Vasiṣṭha. Saṁkara seems to follow the Mahābhārata list.

[3] The reference is to the eternal Kumāras, the non-procreating sages who remain in eternal and holy adolescence. They are Sanaka, Sanandana, Sanātana, and Sanatkumāra.

प्रचयं गमिष्यतीति । तं धर्मं भगवता यथोपदिष्टं वेदव्यासः सर्वज्ञः भगवान् गीताख्यैः सप्तभिः श्लोकशतैः उपनिबबन्ध ॥

2. The Lord is in eternal possession of knowledge, lordliness, executive power, strength, energy and splendour. He has under His control His all-pervasive Māyā (Illusive Power) or material Nature, whose essence is the three constituents.[4] Thus, though unborn, immutable, Lord of beings, and, in essence, eternally pure, conscious and free, He appears, by virtue of His Māyā, to be embodied and born as man, for ensuring the welfare of the world. Though he has no private end of His own to promote, in order to further the well-being of all living beings, He imparted to Arjuna, submerged in a sea of grief and delusion, the two-fold Vedic law of righteousness; for, when espoused and practised by men rich in excellences, it is bound to flourish. The Vedic Dharma, as it was imparted by the Lord, has been set forth by the omniscient and venerable Vedavyāsa in seven hundred verses, celebrated as the Gītā.

3. तत् इदं गीताशास्त्रं समस्तवेदार्थसारसङ्ग्रहभूतं दुर्विज्ञेयार्थं, तदर्थाविष्करणाय अनेकैः विवृतपदपदार्थवाक्यार्थन्यायम् अपि अत्यन्तविरुद्धानेकार्थत्वेन लौकिकैः गृह्यमाणं उपलभ्य अहं विवेकतः अर्थनिर्धारणार्थं संक्षेपतः विवरणं करिष्यामि ॥

3. This science of the Gītā is the quintessence of all that goes under the name of the Vedas, but its sense is difficult to grasp. Many have striven to elucidate its words, their imports, and their totality as a reasoned treatise. Men in general, however, have got it as a mass of self-contradictory ideas. Noting this predicament, I shall set forth its contents, briefly explicating the text with due discrimination.

4. तस्य अस्य गीताशास्त्रस्य संक्षेपतः प्रयोजनं परं निःश्रेयसं सहेतुकस्य संसारस्य अत्यन्तोपरमलक्षणम् । तच्च सर्वकर्मसंन्यासपूर्वकात् आत्मज्ञाननिष्ठारूपात् धर्मात्

[4] The three Guṇas, Sattva, Rajas and Tamas, constituting the Sāṁkhyan Prakṛti, are referred to vide SK, verses 11–13.

भवति । तथा इमं एव गीतार्थं धर्मं उद्दिश्य भगवता एव उक्तम् —
"स हि धर्मः सुपर्याप्तो ब्रह्मणः पदवेदने" ॥ [म.भा.अश्व.१६.१२.], इति अनुगीतासु । तत्रैव च उक्तम् —
"नैव धर्मी न चाधर्मी न चैव हि शुभाशुभी ।" [म. भा. अश्व. १९.७.],
"यः स्यादेकासने लीनः तूष्णीं किञ्चिदचिन्तयन् ।" [म. भा. अश्व. १९.१.],
"ज्ञानं संन्यासलक्षणम्" [म. भा. अश्व. ४३.२५.] इति च ।
इहापि च अन्ते उक्तं अर्जुनाय—
"सर्वधर्मान् परित्यज्य मामेकं शरणं व्रज ।" [१८. ६६.] इति ।

4. Succinctly, the purpose of the science of the Gītā is to set forth the *summum bonum*, which consists in the total cessation of the transmigratory life and its causes. This is brought about by the law of implementation of Self-knowledge, preceded by the renunciation of all works. Pointing to this sense of the Gītā —the law of life which it inculcates—the Lord Himself has declared: "This Dharma is indeed adequate to lead one to the status of Brahman" (MB. Aśva. 16. 12). The same context says: "Neither pursuing Dharma nor Adharma, neither good nor evil" (Ibid. 19. 7); "Whoever is quiescent, firmly seated, silent, not thinking any thought" (Ibid. 19. 1); also, "Knowledge marked by renunciation" (Ibid. 43. 25). In the Gītā itself, at the end, Arjuna is bidden: "Giving up all disciplines, seek refuge in Me alone" (18. 66).

5. अभ्युदयार्थोऽपि यः प्रवृत्तिलक्षणः धर्मः वर्णान् आश्रमांश्च उद्दिश्य विहितः स देवादिस्थानप्राप्तिहेतुः अपि सन्, ईश्वरार्पणबुद्ध्या अनुष्ठीयमानः सत्त्वशुद्धये भवति फलाभिसन्धिवर्जितः । शुद्धसत्त्वस्य च ज्ञाननिष्ठायोग्यताप्राप्तिद्वारेण ज्ञानोत्पत्ति-हेतुत्वेन च निःश्रेयसहेतुत्वम् अपि प्रतिपद्यते । तथा चेमम् एव अर्थम् अभिसंधाय वक्ष्यति—'ब्रह्मण्याधाय कर्माणि' [५.१०.], 'योगिनः कर्म कुर्वन्ति सङ्गं त्यक्त्वात्मशुद्धये' [५.११.] इति ॥

5. The Vedic law of works, promoting prosperity in the world, and enjoined on the classes and life-stations, promotes the purification of the mind when it is observed with a sense of dedication to God and without expectation of rewards; though normally i.e., when done with desire for fruits, it leads its practitioners to the higher stations of heavenly beings and

so forth. It also, indirectly, subserves the attainment of emancipation (when performed without desire for fruits), since such work purifies the mind and the purified mind becomes fit for practising the discipline of knowledge which, in due course, generates the liberating knowledge itself. Keeping this idea in mind, the Lord declares in BG 5. 10 and 11: "The Yogins work without attachment for purifying the mind."

6. इमं द्विप्रकारं धर्मं निःश्रेयसप्रयोजनं, परमार्थतत्त्वं च वासुदेवाख्यं परब्रह्माभिधेयभूतं विशेषतः अभिव्यञ्जयत् विशिष्टप्रयोजनसम्बन्धाभिधेयवत् गीताशास्त्रम् । यतः तदर्थविज्ञाने समस्तपुरुषार्थसिद्धिः, अतः तद्विवरणे यत्नः क्रियते मया ॥

अत्र च धृतराष्ट्र उवाच — "धर्मक्षेत्रे" इत्यादि ।

6. The science of the Gītā, thus elucidating especially the two-fold law of the Vedas, is aimed at emancipation; also, it sets forth the ultimate Truth that is synonymous with Vāsudeva, the content of Supreme Brahman. Hence it is equipped with a specific goal, relation and content.[5] Since its mastery yields all values of life, I am endeavouring to explicate it.

[5] The four *anubhandhas* entailed by a *śāstra* are *viṣaya*, *prayojana*, *adhikāri*, and *sambandha*—subject matter, necessity for its study, competency of the student, connection of subject matter with the book (cf the *Vedāntasāra*).

प्रथमोऽध्यायः

CHAPTER I

ARJUNA'S DESPONDENCY

धृतराष्ट्र उवाच:

धर्मक्षेत्रे कुरुक्षेत्रे समवेता युयुत्सवः ।
मामकाः पाण्डवाश्चैव किमकुर्वत सञ्जय ॥१॥

Dhṛtarāṣṭra said:

1. On the field of Righteousness, on the grounds of Kurukṣetra, marshalled for war, what did my men and Pāṇḍavas do, O Sañjaya!

सञ्जय उवाच:

दृष्ट्वा तु पाण्डवानीकं व्यूढं दुर्योधनस्तदा ।
आचार्यमुपसङ्गम्य राजा वचनमब्रवीत् ॥२॥

Sañjaya said:

2. Then seeing the marshalled army of the Pāṇḍavas, King Duryodhana approached the preceptor (Drona) and spoke the following words:

पश्यैतां पाण्डुपुत्राणामाचार्य महतीं चमूम् ।
व्यूढां द्रुपदपुत्रेण तव शिष्येण धीमता ॥३॥

3. O Preceptor! Observe the immense army of Pāṇḍu's sons, marshalled by your perceptive disciple, the son of Drupada.

अत्र शूरा महेष्वासा भीमार्जुनसमा युधि ।
युयुधानो विराटश्च द्रुपदश्च महारथः ॥४॥

4. In this army are present brave and mighty bowmen, equal to Bhīma and Arjuna in battle. There are Yuyudhāna, Virāṭa and the mighty car-warrior Drupada.

धृष्टकेतुश्चेकितानः काशिराजश्च वीर्यवान् ।
पुरुजित् कुन्तिभोजश्च शैब्यश्च नरपुङ्गवः ॥५॥

5. Dhṛṣṭaketu; Cekitāna; the heroic King Purujit of Kāśi, Kuntibhoja and Saibya, a hero among men;

युधामन्युश्च विक्रान्त उत्तमौजाश्च वीर्यवान् ।
सौभद्रो द्रौपदेयाश्च सर्व एव महारथाः ॥६॥

6. The valiant Yudhāmanyu; the formidable Uttamaujāḥ; the son of Subhadrā and the sons of Draupadī —all indeed great lords of mighty chariots.

अस्माकं तु विशिष्टा ये तान्निबोध द्विजोत्तम ।
नायका मम सैन्यस्य संज्ञार्थं तान् ब्रवीमि ते ॥७॥

7. As for the distinguished leaders on our side, note them, thou, best of the twice-born! I mention the leaders of my army to bring them to your notice.

भवान् भीष्मश्च कर्णश्च कृपश्च समितिञ्जयः ।
अश्वत्थामा विकर्णश्च सौमदत्तिर्जयद्रथः ॥८॥

8. Yourself; Bhīṣma; Karṇa; Kṛpa, victorious in battles; Asvatthāmā; Vikarṇa; as well as Jayadratha, the son of Somadatta,

अन्ये च बहवः शूरा मदर्थे त्यक्तजीविताः ।
नानाशस्त्रप्रहरणाः सर्वे युद्धविशारदाः ॥९॥

9. Many other brave warriors, too, there are who have staked their lives for my sake and are armed in manifold ways—all adepts in war.

अपर्याप्तं तदस्माकं बलं भीष्माभिरक्षितम् ।
पर्याप्तं त्विदमेतेषां बलं भीमाभिरक्षितम् ॥१०॥

10. This force of ours, under the protection of Bhīṣma, is inadequate; but the Pāṇḍava force, protected by Bhīma, is quite adequate.

अयनेषु च सर्वेषु यथाभागमवस्थिताः ।
भीष्ममेवाभिरक्षन्तु भवन्तः सर्व एव हि ॥११॥

11. Stationed at all points of entry and exit, with due regard to order, all of you must provide protection to Bhīṣma.

तस्य संजनयन् हर्षं कुरुवृद्धः पितामहः ।
सिंहनादं विनद्योच्चैः शङ्खं दध्मौ प्रतापवान् ॥१२॥

12. Delighting him, the grand old man of the Kurus, the mighty grandfather (Bhīṣma) roaring aloud like a lion, blew his conch.

ततः शङ्खाश्च भेर्यश्च पणवानकगोमुखाः ।
सहसैवाभ्यहन्यन्त स शब्दस्तुमुलोऽभवत् ॥१३॥

13. Then conchs, kettle-drums, cymbals, double-drums and trumpets were sounded together. That din was tumultuous.

ततः श्वेतैर्हयैर्युक्ते महति स्यन्दने स्थितौ ।
माधवः पाण्डवश्चैव दिव्यौ शङ्खौ प्रदध्मतुः ॥१४॥

14. Then stationed in a large chariot, yoked with white steeds, Kṛṣṇa and Arjuna blew their divine conchs.

पाञ्चजन्यं हृषीकेशो देवदत्तं धनञ्जयः ।
पौण्ड्रं दध्मौ महाशङ्खं भीमकर्मा वृकोदरः ॥१५॥

15. Kṛṣṇa blew the Pāñcajanya; Arjuna the Devadatta; Bhīma, of formidable action, blew the mighty Pauṇḍra.

अनन्तविजयं राजा कुन्तीपुत्रो युधिष्ठिरः ।
नकुलः सहदेवश्च सुघोषमणिपुष्पकौ ॥१६॥

16. King Yudhiṣṭhira, son of Kuntī, blew his conch the Anantavijaya, while Nakula and Sahadeva blew the Sughoṣa and the Maṇipuṣpaka.

काश्यश्च परमेष्वासः शिखण्डी च महारथः ।
धृष्टद्युम्नो विराटश्च सात्यकिश्चापराजितः ॥१७॥

17. The supreme bowman King of Kāśi, the great charioteer Śikhaṇḍi, Dhṛṣṭadyumna, Virāta and the unsurpassed Sātyaki;

द्रुपदो द्रौपदेयाश्च सर्वशः पृथिवीपते ।
सौभद्रश्च महाबाहुः शङ्खान् दध्मुः पृथक् पृथक् ॥१८॥

18. Drupada, the sons of Draupadī, the mighty son of Subhadrā—these, O King! from all sides, severally blew their several shells.

स घोषो धार्तराष्ट्राणां हृदयानि व्यदारयत् ।
नभश्च पृथिवीं चैव तुमुलो व्यनुनादयन् ॥१९॥

19. That uproar tore up the hearts of the Kauravas and resounded on earth and in the sky.

अथ व्यवस्थितान् दृष्ट्वा धार्तराष्ट्रान् कपिध्वजः ।
प्रवृत्ते शस्त्रसंपाते धनुरुद्यम्य पाण्डवः ॥२०॥
हृषीकेशं तदा वाक्यमिदमाह महीपते ।

20-21. Then, seeing the followers of Dhṛtarāṣṭra in battle-array, when the missiles started to fly, the monkey-bannered Arjuna lifted his bow, and spoke, O King! as follows to Sri Kṛṣṇa.

अर्जुन उवाच :
सेनयोरुभयोर्मध्ये रथं स्थापय मेऽच्युत ॥२१॥
यावदेतान्निरीक्षेहं योद्धुकामानवस्थितान् ।
कैर्मया सह योद्धव्यमस्मिन् रणसमुद्यमे ॥२२॥

Arjuna said:

21-22. Station the chariot, Kṛṣṇa! between the two armies, that I may behold them standing, bent on doing battle—those with whom I have to fight in this warlike endeavour.

योत्स्यमानानवेक्षेऽहं य एतेऽत्र समागताः ।
धार्तराष्ट्रस्य दुर्बुद्धेर्युद्धे प्रियचिकीर्षवः ॥२३॥

23. I shall observe them who have massed here and are about to commence the war, eager to please the wicked Duryodhāna in this enterprise of war.

सञ्जय उवाच :
एवमुक्तो हृषीकेशो गुडाकेशेन भारत ।
सेनयोरुभयोर्मध्ये स्थापयित्वा रथोत्तमम् ॥२४॥

Sañjaya said:
24. Thus bidden, O King! by Arjuna, Kṛṣṇa stationed that best of chariots between those two armies,

भीष्मद्रोणप्रमुखतः सर्वेषां च महीक्षिताम् ।
उवाच पार्थ पश्यैतान् समवेतान् कुरूनिति ।।२५।।

25. In front of Bhīṣma and Droṇa as well as of all those rulers, and said: Behold, Arjuna! those massed Kauravas here.

तत्रापश्यत् स्थितान् पार्थः पितॄनथ पितामहान् ।
आचार्यान् मातुलान् भ्रातॄन् पुत्रान् पौत्रान् सखींस्तथा ।।२६।।
श्वशुरान् सुहृदश्चैव सेनयोरुभयोरपि ।

26-27. There Arjuna saw standing, fathers, grandfathers, teachers, uncles, brothers, sons, grandsons and comrades, as well as fathers-in-law and friends in the ranks of the two armies.

तान् समीक्ष्य स कौन्तेयः सर्वान् बन्धूनवस्थितान् ।।२७।।
कृपया परयाऽऽविष्टो विषीदन्निदमब्रवीत् ।

अर्जुन उवाच :

दृष्ट्वेमं स्वजनं कृष्ण युयुत्सुं समुपस्थितम् ।।२८।।

27-28. Seeing them, his kith and kin, Arjuna was overwhelmed by supreme compassion, and sorrowing, he said:
Arjuna said:
Beholding these relations of mine, in battle posture, ready to fight,

सीदन्ति मम गात्राणि मुखं च परिशुष्यति ।
वेपथुश्च शरीरे मे रोमहर्षश्च जायते ।।२९।।

29. My limbs droop, my mouth dries up, my body trembles, and hairs stand on end.

गाण्डीवं स्रंसते हस्तात् त्वक्चैव परिदह्यते ।
न च शक्नोम्यवस्थातुं भ्रमतीव च मे मनः ॥३०॥

30. My bow, Gāṇḍīva, slips from my grip; my skin is afire; I cannot stand steady and my mind wanders, as it were;

निमित्तानि च पश्यामि विपरीतानि केशव ।
न च श्रेयोऽनुपश्यामि हत्वा स्वजनमाहवे ॥३१॥

31. Also I see contrary portents. In killing one's kin in a war, I can see no good at all.

न काङ्क्षे विजयं कृष्ण न च राज्यं सुखानि च ।
किं नो राज्येन गोविन्द किं भोगैर्जीवितेन वा ॥३२॥

32. I don't seek victory, Kṛṣṇa! I want neither kingdom nor pleasures, O Govinda! How can kingdom, enjoyments or even life profit us?

येषामर्थे काङ्क्षितं नो राज्यं भोगाः सुखानि च ।
त इमेऽवस्थिता युद्धे प्राणांस्त्यक्त्वा धनानि च ॥३३॥

33. Those for whose sakes are the kingdom, enjoyments and pleasures sought—those very persons stand here to fight, surrendering life and possessions.

आचार्याः पितरः पुत्रास्तथैव च पितामहाः ।
मातुलाः श्वशुराः पौत्राः श्यालाः संबन्धिनस्तथा ॥३४॥

34. Preceptors, fathers, sons, grandfathers, uncles, fathers-in-law, grandsons, brothers-in-law, relatives.

एतान्न हन्तुमिच्छामि घ्नतोऽपि मधुसूदन ।
अपि त्रैलोक्यराज्यस्य हेतोः किं नु महीकृते ॥३५॥

35. These I do not wish to slay, though they may slay, O Kṛṣṇa; nay, not even for dominion over the three worlds, much less for this earthly kingdom.

निहत्य धार्तराष्ट्रान्नः का प्रीतिः स्याज्जनार्दन ।
पापमेवाश्रयेदस्मान् हत्वैतानाततायिनः ॥३६॥

36. What pleasure shall be ours in killing Dhṛtarāṣṭra's sons? O Kṛṣṇa! only sin will accrue to us in killing these lawless foes.

तस्मान्नार्हा वयं हन्तुं धार्तराष्ट्रान् स्वबान्धवान् ।
स्वजनं हि कथं हत्वा सुखिनः स्याम माधव ॥३७॥

37. Therefore, we ought not to slay our kinsmen, the sons of Dhṛtarāṣṭra. How can we, Kṛṣṇa! be happy, once we kill them?

यद्यप्येते न पश्यन्ति लोभोपहतचेतसः ।
कुलक्षयकृतं दोषं मित्रद्रोहे च पातकम् ॥३८॥

38. Blinded by greed, though they do not see the evil that threatens our family with decay, or the sin in being treacherous to relations,

कथं न ज्ञेयमस्माभिः पापादस्मान्निवर्तितुम् ।
कुलक्षयकृतं दोषं प्रपश्यद्भिर्जनार्दन ॥३९॥

39. How can we fail to turn away from sin—we who recognise the evil that threatens our family with downfall, O Kṛṣṇa?

कुलक्षये प्रणश्यन्ति कुलधर्माः सनातनाः ।
धर्मे नष्टे कुलं कृत्स्नमधर्मोऽभिभवत्युत ॥४०॥

40. With the downfall of the family, the eternal laws of righteousness fostered in the family will perish. When righteousness perishes, unrighteousness will overwhelm the entire family.

अधर्माभिभवात्कृष्ण प्रदुष्यन्ति कुलस्त्रियः ।
स्त्रीषु दुष्टासु वार्ष्णेय जायते वर्णसङ्करः ॥४१॥

41. Due to the sway of unrighteousness, Kṛṣṇa! the women of the family will be ruined. From their ruination, confusion of classes is bound to ensue.

सङ्करो नरकायैव कुलघ्नानां कुलस्य च ।
पतन्ति पितरो ह्येषां लुप्तपिण्डोदकक्रियाः ॥४२॥

42. Such confusion will land in hell the wreckers of the family and the family itself. Then the ancestral spirits must indeed fall, robbed of the obsequial rites due to them.

दोषैरेतैः कुलघ्नानां वर्णसङ्करकारकैः ।
उत्साद्यन्ते जातिधर्माः कुलधर्माश्च शाश्वताः ॥४३॥

43. By these flaws of the wreckers of the family causing confusion of classes, the eternal laws of the community and the family are nullified.

उत्सन्नकुलधर्माणां मनुष्याणां जनार्दन ।
नरके नियतं वासो भवतीत्यनुशुश्रुम ॥४४॥

44. O Kṛṣṇa! We have been told that men whose family principles are nullified have necessarily to dwell in hell.

अहो बत महत्पापं कर्तुं व्यवसिता वयम् ।
यद्राज्यसुखलोभेन हन्तुं स्वजनमुद्यताः ॥४५॥

45. Alas! we seem determined to commit a grievous sin, since due to greed for a kingdom and its pleasures, we are up in arms to slaughter our kinsmen.

यदि मामप्रतीकारमशस्त्रं शस्त्रपाणयः ।
धार्तराष्ट्रा रणे हन्युस्तन्मे क्षेमतरं भवेत् ॥४६॥

46. If in battle the sons of Dhṛtarāṣṭra, weapons in hand, were to kill me unarmed and undefending, it will be better for me.

सञ्जय उवाच :

एवमुक्त्वाऽर्जुनः सङ्ख्ये रथोपस्थ उपाविशत् ।
विसृज्य सशरं चापं शोकसंविग्नमानसः ॥४७॥

Sañjaya said:

47. Throwing away his bow and arrows, his mind consumed with grief, Arjuna spoke thus in battle, and sank into the seat of the chariot.

इति श्रीमहाभारते शतसाहस्र्यां संहितायां वैयासिक्यां भीष्मपर्वणि
श्रीमद्भगवद्गीतासु उपनिषत्सु ब्रह्मविद्यायां योगशास्त्रे श्रीकृष्णार्जुनसंवादे
अर्जुनविषादयोगः नाम प्रथमोऽध्यायः ॥१॥

द्वितीयोऽध्यायः

CHAPTER II

THE SĀMKHYA YOGA

सञ्जय उवाच :

तं तथा कृपयाऽऽविष्टमश्रुपूर्णाकुलेक्षणम् ।
विषीदन्तमिदं वाक्यमुवाच मधुसुदनः ॥१॥

Sañjaya said:

1. To him thus overpowered by compassion, tearful, distressed and desponding, Kṛṣṇa spoke (the following) words:

श्रीभगवानुवाच :

कुतस्त्वा कश्मलमिदं विषमे समुपस्थितम् ।
अनार्यजुष्टमस्वर्ग्यमकीर्तिकरमर्जुन ॥२॥

The blessed Lord said:

2. Whence, Arjuna! has this timidity, unwelcome to noble spirits, unheavenly, and disgraceful, come upon you in this crisis?

क्लैब्यं मा स्म गमः पार्थ नैतत्त्वय्युपपद्यते ।
क्षुद्रं हृदयदौर्बल्यं त्यक्त्वोत्तिष्ठ परंतप ॥३॥

3. Yield not to unmanliness, O Arjuna! It does not become you. Shake off this petty weakness of the heart and stand up, O terror of your foes!

अर्जुन उवाच :

कथं भीष्ममहं सङ्ख्ये द्रोणं च मधुसूदन ।
इषुभिः प्रतियोत्स्यामि पूजार्हावरिसूदन ॥४॥

Arjuna said:

4. How shall I, Kṛṣṇa! fight back with shafts, in war, Bhīṣma and Droṇa who deserve my reverence?

गुरूनहत्वा हि महानुभावान्
श्रेयो भोक्तुं भैक्ष्यमपीह लोके ।
हत्वार्थकामांस्तु गुरूनिहैव
भुञ्जीय भोगान् रुधिरप्रदिग्धान् ॥५॥

5. Indeed it were better for me to live on alms in the world and avoid slaying my honoured elders. Killing these people who seek to gain ends of their own, I should be tasting blood-stained enjoyments.

न चैतद्विद्मः कतरन्नो गरीयो
यद्वा जयेम यदि वा नो जयेयुः ।
यानेव हत्वा न जिजीविषाम-
स्तेऽवस्थिताः प्रमुखे धार्तराष्ट्राः ॥६॥

worried abt the outcome

6. Nor do we know which is better for us—victory over them, or their victory over us. The very persons, destroying whom we should not care to live, are standing in front of us—the followers of Dhṛtarāṣṭra.

king.

कार्पण्यदोषोपहतस्वभावः
पृच्छामि त्वां धर्मसम्मूढचेताः ।
यच्छ्रेयः स्यान्निश्चितं ब्रूहि तन्मे
शिष्यस्तेऽहं शाधि मां त्वां प्रपन्नम् ॥७॥

7. My inborn nature has been overwhelmed by the bane of faintheartedness, and I am confused as regards

the law of righteousness. So I am asking you: Tell me for certain what shall prove beneficial. I am your disciple. Teach me who have surrendered myself to you.

न हि प्रपश्यामि ममापनुद्याद्
यच्छोकमुच्छोषणमिन्द्रियाणाम् ।
अवाप्य भूमावसपत्नमृद्धं
राज्यं सुराणामपि चाधिपत्यम् ॥८॥

8. I do not see that an unrivalled and prosperous kingdom on earth and overlordship over the denizens of heaven will dispel the grief that has scorched my senses.

सञ्जय उवाच
एवमुक्त्वा हृषीकेशं गुडाकेशः परन्तपः ।
न योत्स्य इति गोविन्दमुक्त्वा तूष्णीं बभूव ह ॥९॥

Sañjaya said:
9. Having spoken thus to Kṛṣṇa, the valiant Arjuna added, "I shall never fight." Then he maintained silence.

तमुवाच हृषीकेशः प्रहसन्निव भारत ।
सेनयोरुभयोर्मध्ये विषीदन्तमिदं वचः ॥१०॥

10. To him, who sat despondent between the two armies, spoke Kṛṣṇa mockingly, as it were, O King!

11.0.a अत्र 'दृष्ट्वा तु पाण्डवानीकम्' [१.२.] इति आरभ्य यावत् 'न योत्स्य इति गोविन्दमुक्त्वा तूष्णीं बभूव ह ।' [२.९.] इत्येतदन्तः प्राणिनां शोकमोहादिसंसारबीजभूतदोषोद्भवकारणप्रदर्शनार्थत्वेन व्याख्येयः ग्रन्थः । तथा हि — अर्जुनेन राज्यगुरुपुत्रमित्रसुहृत्स्वजनसंबन्धिबान्धवेषु 'अहं एषां', 'मम एते' इत्येवं

भ्रान्तिप्रत्ययनिमित्तस्नेहविच्छेदादिनिमित्तौ आत्मनः शोकमोहौ प्रदर्शितौ 'कथं भीष्ममहं संख्ये' [२.४.] इत्यादिना । शोकमोहाभ्यां हि अभिभूतविवेकविज्ञानः स्वतः एव क्षत्रधर्मे युद्धे प्रवृत्तोऽपि तस्मात् युद्धात् उपरराम, परधर्मं च भिक्षाजीवनादिकं कर्तुं प्रववृते । तथा च सर्वप्राणिनां शोकमोहादिदोषाविष्टचेतसां स्वभावतः एव स्वधर्मपरित्यागः प्रतिषिद्धसेवा च स्यात् । स्वधर्मे प्रवृत्तानाम् अपि तेषां वाङ्मनःकायादीनां प्रवृत्तिः फलाभिसन्धिपूर्विका एव साहङ्कारा च भवति । तत्र एवं सति धर्माधर्मोपचयात् इष्टानिष्टजन्मसुखदुःखप्राप्तिलक्षणः संसारः अनुपरतः भवति । इत्यतः संसारबीजभूतौ शोकमोहौ । तयोश्च सर्वकर्मसंन्यासपूर्वकात् आत्मज्ञानात् नान्यतः निवृत्तिः इति तत् उपदिदिक्षुः सर्वलोकानुग्रहार्थं अर्जुनं निमित्तीकृत्य आह भगवान् वासुदेवः — अशोच्यान् [२.११.] इत्यादि ॥

11.0.a. The text beginning from "Seeing the army of the Pāṇḍavās" (1.2) and ending with "Telling Govinda 'I shall not fight', he remained silent" (2.9)—must be explained as designed to elucidate the origin of flaws like grief and delusion, which form the defects constituting the seed of the transmigratory life of all living beings. This may be explained as follows: In regard to the kingdom, teachers, descendants, allies, friends, kinsmen and relatives, both remote and intimate, Arjuna displayed his grief and delusion, born of the fear of a breakdown of his affection. This affection itself was a product of the illusory cognitions, "I belong to them" and "they are mine". Vide: "How shall I (oppose) Bhīṣma in battle?" (2.4) etc. It was because his discrimination and practical knowledge were undermined by grief and delusion that Arjuna refrained from fighting, though he had voluntarily undertaken to fight his opponents as the duty of the Kṣatriya, and instead got ready to live a mendicant's life, conforming to an alien law of life (*paradharma*). Thus all living beings, whose minds are gripped by defects like grief and delusion, might readily forsake the law (of their life) and embrace forbidden courses of action. Even when they live according to the proper law of their life (*svadharma*), the activities of their speech, mind and body are surely impelled by their desire for the fruits of those very activities which emanate from egoism. In these circumstances, owing to an accumulation of righteousness and unrighteousness, transmigratory life continues unabated. *There-*

fore, the seeds of the transmigratory life are grief and delusion. They can be exhausted only by the knowledge of the Self, preceded by the renunciation of all activities, and not by any other means. Therefore, in order to impart that knowledge for the well-being of the entire world, Lord Kṛṣṇa says, making Arjuna but an occasion for it: "Those for whom one should not grieve" (2.11).

11.0.b. अत्र केचित् आहुः—सर्वकर्मसंन्यासपूर्वकात् आत्मज्ञाननिष्ठामात्रात् एव केवलात् कैवल्यं न प्राप्यते एव । किं तर्हि ? अग्निहोत्रादिश्रौतस्मार्तकर्मसहितात् ज्ञानात् कैवल्यप्राप्तिः इति सर्वासु गीतासु निश्चितः अर्थः इति । ज्ञापकं च आहुः अस्य अर्थस्य — 'अथ चेत्त्वमिमं धर्म्यं संग्रामं न करिष्यसि' [२.३३.], 'कर्मण्येवाधिकारस्ते' [२.४७.] 'कुरु कर्मैव तस्मात्त्वम्' [४.१५.] इत्यादि । हिंसादियुक्तत्वात् वैदिक कर्म अधर्माय इति इयम् अपि आशङ्का न कार्या । कथम्? क्षात्रं कर्म युद्धलक्षणं गुरुभ्रातृपुत्रादिहिंसालक्षणं अत्यन्तक्रूरम् अपि स्वधर्मः इति कृत्वा न अधर्माय; तदकरणे च — 'ततः स्वधर्मं कीर्तिं च हित्वा पापमवाप्स्यसि ।' [२.३३.] इति ब्रुवता यावज्जीवादिश्रुतिचोदितानां पश्वादिहिंसालक्षणानां च कर्मणां प्रागेव न अधर्मत्वमिति सुनिश्चितं उक्तं भवति — इति ।

11.0.b. In regard to this matter, some argue as follows: *Objection:* Aloneness (*kaivalyam*) is surely not won by mere adherence to unaided Self-knowledge preceded by the renunciation of activities; on the contrary, the indubitable sense of the entire BG is that aloneness has to be won by means of knowledge combined with the system of activities like the fire-sacrifice (*agnihotra*) ordained by Śruti and Smṛti. They also point out the following passages that indicate this sense of the BG: "On the other hand, if you do not wage this righteous war" (2.33); "To perform action alone have you the obligation" (2.47); "Therefore, perform action alone" (4.15) and so forth. It need not be apprehended that Veda-enjoined actions entailing infliction of pain and so forth will promote unrighteousness. Why not? War, the activity of the Kṣatriya entailing the slaughter of even one's teachers, brothers, children, etc., though cruel in the extreme, will nevertheless not make for unrighteousness, because it is the proper law of a Kṣatriya's life. On the other hand, it is declared that by refusing to fight "sacrificing both the law of your life and your reputation, you will incur sin" (2.33). Therefore, making these affirmations, the

Lord emphatically asserts that the Veda-oriented, life-long activities, though they entail the slaughter of animals and so forth, cannot conceivably be sinful; for they are obligatory in their nature.

11.0.c. तत् असत्; ज्ञानकर्मनिष्ठयोः विभागवचनात् बुद्धिद्वयाश्रययोः । 'अशोच्यान्' [२.११.] इत्यादिना भगवता यावत् 'स्वधर्ममपि चावेक्ष्य' [२.३१.] इत्येतदन्तेन ग्रन्थेन यत्परमार्थात्मतत्त्वनिरूपणं कृतम्, तत् सांख्यम् । तद्विषया बुद्धिः आत्मनः जन्मादिषड्विक्रियाभावात् अकर्ता आत्मा इति प्रकरणार्थनिरूपणात् या जायते, सा सांख्यबुद्धिः । सा येषां ज्ञानिनां उचिता भवति, ते सांख्याः । एतस्याः बुद्धेः जन्मनः प्राक् आत्मनः देहादिव्यतिरिक्तत्वकर्तृत्वभोक्तृत्वाद्यपेक्षः धर्माधर्मविवेकपूर्वकः मोक्षसाधनानुष्ठानलक्षणः योगः । तद्विषया बुद्धिः योगबुद्धिः । सा येषां कर्मिणा उचिता भवति ते योगिनः । तथा च भगवता विभक्ते द्वे बुद्धी निर्दिष्टे 'एषा तेऽभिहिता सांख्ये बुद्धिर्योगे त्विमां शृणु ।' [२.३९.] इति । तयोश्च साङ्ख्यबुद्ध्याश्रयां ज्ञानयोगेन निष्ठां साङ्ख्यानां विभक्तां वक्ष्यति 'पुरा वेदात्मना मया प्रोक्ता' [३.३.] इति । तथा च योगबुद्ध्याश्रयां कर्मयोगेन निष्ठां विभक्तां वक्ष्यति—'कर्मयोगेन योगिनाम्' [३.३.] इति । एवं साङ्ख्यबुद्धिं योगबुद्धिं च आश्रित्य द्वे निष्ठे विभक्ते भगवता एव उक्ते ज्ञानकर्मणोः कर्तृत्वाकर्तृत्वैकत्वानेकत्वबुद्ध्याश्रययोः युगपत् एकपुरुषाश्रयत्वासंभवं पश्यता ।

11.0.c. *Reply:* All that has been said above is vacuous. For, the discipline of knowledge and that of action, rooted in two kinds of understanding, have been clearly distinguished from each other. The content of the text beginning from—"Those who should not be grieved for" (2.11) and ending with "And in view of the law of one's life" (2.31), where the Lord elucidates the eternal Truth of the Self—is the Sāṁkhya. This teaches that the Self, being free from the six-fold transformation like birth and so on, is a non-agent. This knowledge, generated by the study of the relevant context (*prakaraṇa*), is the Sāṁkhya knowledge. Those for whom this knowledge is appropriate are the Sāṁkhyas. Prior to the birth of this knowledge is the state of Yoga characterised by the performance of activities instrumental to liberation. Such peformance is based on the discrimination between righteousness and unrighteousness; it depends on the notion that the Self is other than the body, etc., and is an agent of actions, a reaper of the fruits thereof and so forth. This kind of knowledge is the Yoga-knowledge. Those for whom it is appropriate are the Yogins. Accordingly, the Lord has made a clear distinction between these two kinds of knowledge—the knowledge of the Sāṁkyas rooted in the understanding of the Sāṁkhya, and that of the Yogins rooted in the understanding of the Yoga. Thus realising the incompatibility, at one and the same time in one and the same person, of Jñāna (knowledge) and Karma (action), and also with due regard to the understanding of Sāṁkhya and Yoga, the Lord has discriminated between the two disciplines. The incompatibility (above referred to) is due to the fact that knowledge and action are rooted respectively in the notions of the non-agency and of the agency of the Self, and in the perception of unity and of plurality in the world.

11.0.d. यथा एतत् विभागवचनं तथैव दर्शितं शातपथीये ब्राह्मणे—“एतमेव प्रव्राजिनो लोकमिच्छन्तो ब्राह्मणाः प्रव्रजन्ति” इति सर्वकर्मसंन्यासं विधाय तच्छेषेण “किं प्रजया करिष्यामो येषां नोऽयमात्माऽयं लोकः” [बृ. उ. ४.४.२२.] इति । तत्रैव च प्राक् दारपरिग्रहात् ‘पुरुषः’ ‘आत्मा’ प्राकृतः धर्मजिज्ञासोत्तरकालं लोकत्रयसाधनं—पुत्रं, द्विप्रकारं च वित्तं—‘मानुषं,’ ‘दैवं’ च; तत्र मानुषं कर्मरूपं पितृलोकप्राप्तिसाधनं, विद्यां च दैवं वित्तं देवलोकप्राप्तिसाधनं ‘सोऽकामयत’ इति अविद्याकामवतः एव सर्वाणि कर्माणि श्रौतादीनि दर्शितानि । तेभ्यः (व्युत्थाय, प्रव्रजन्ति इति) व्युत्थानं आत्मानं एव लोकं इच्छतः अकामस्य विहितम् । तदेतत् विभागवचनं अनुपपन्नं स्यात्, यदि श्रौतकर्मज्ञानयोः समुच्चयः अभिप्रेत स्यात् भगवतः ॥

11.0.d. This declaration of distinction between knowledge and action in the BG corresponds to the following demonstration of the same in the *Śatapathabrāhmaṇa*: “Desiring only this world of the Self, mendicant Brāhmaṇas wander forth.” Here, having laid down the renunciation of all actions, to it has been affiliated the idea contained in the following passage: “Of what profit is progeny to us, who have this Self, this world?” (*BU* 4.4.22). In the very same text has also been highlighted the fact that all actions pertain only to those who are subject to nescience and desire; for, before marriage the human self is ‘unregenerate’ (*prākṛta*). After an investigation into the science of Veda-enjoined actions, man, becoming 'regenerate', desired (*akāmayata*) the means to secure the three worlds viz., a son and the two-fold wealth, human and divine. The 'human wealth' consists in activities by which the world of the manes is attained. The 'divine wealth' is knowledge by which the world of the gods is attained. The transcending of the sphere of all activities and the pursuit of a life of mendicancy have been laid down for one who seeks only the world of the Self and who is rid of all cravings. Now this pronouncement on the distinction between knowledge and action will be illogical, if the Lord had intended to combine Vedic activities and knowledge of the Self.

11.0.e. न च अर्जुनस्य प्रश्नः उपपन्नः भवति 'ज्यायसी चेत्कर्मणस्ते' [३.१.] इत्यादिः । एकपुरुषानुष्ठेयत्वासंभवं बुद्धिकर्मणोः भगवता पूर्वं अनुक्तं कथं अर्जुनः अश्रुतं बुद्धेश्च कर्मणः ज्यायस्त्वं भगवति अध्यारोपयेत् मृषैव 'ज्यायसी चेत्कर्मणस्ते मता बुद्धिः' [३.१.] इति ॥

11.0.e. Nor in that case could Arjuna's question—"If, according to You, knowledge is superior to action etc. . .?" (*BG*.3.1)—be logical. How could Arjuna super-impose on the Lord, falsely, what He has never so far affirmed, viz., the impossibility of combining knowledge and action? Again, how could he ascribe to Him what He had never *clearly* stated viz, the superiority of knowledge to action? The fact that Arjuna ascribes both these views to the Lord shows that he had understood the Lord as affirming both.

11.0.f. किञ्च—यदि बुद्धिकर्मणोः सर्वेषां समुच्चयः उक्तः स्यात्, अर्जुनस्यापि सः उक्तः एव इति, 'यच्छ्रेय एतयोरेकं तन्मे ब्रूहि सुनिश्चितम्' [५.१.] इति कथमुभयोः उपदेशे सति अन्यतरविषयः एव प्रश्नः स्यात् ? न हि पित्तप्रशमनार्थिनः वैद्येन मधुरं शीतं च भोक्तव्यम् इति उपदिष्टे 'तयोरन्यतरत्पित्तप्रशमनकारणं ब्रूहि' इति प्रश्नः संभवति । अथ अर्जुनस्य भगवदुक्तवचनार्थविवेकानवधारणनिमित्तः प्रश्नः कल्प्यते, तथाऽपि भगवता प्रश्नानुरूपं प्रतिवचनं देयं, 'मया बुद्धिकर्मणोः समुच्चयः उक्तः, किमर्थम् इत्थं त्वं भ्रान्तोऽसि' इति । न तु पुनः प्रतिवचनमननुरूपं पृष्टात् अन्यत् एव 'द्वे निष्ठे मया पुरा प्रोक्ते' [३.३.] इति वक्तुं युक्तम् ।

11.0.f. Again, if the combination of knowledge and action

had been universally laid down, it would of course have been valid for Arjuna also. How then, when both were taught, could he make a request regarding only one of the two, in the words, "Tell me, for certain, that one of these two, which is superior to the other" (5.1)? When, for instance, a doctor has prescribed a diet, which is both sweet and cooling, for a patient suffering from biliousness, the patient's request, "Please tell which of these two will cure my malady", is clearly impossible. Even if Arjuna's query is supposed to be due to his inability to grasp the distinction stated by the Lord, the latter should have given a reply like this suited to that query: "I bade you combine knowledge and action. Why are you confused in regard to it?" It is not proper for Him to have given an unsuitable reply, unrelated to the query, in the words "Of old, two disciplines were laid down by Me" (3.3).

11.0.g. नापि स्मार्तेनैव कर्मणा बुद्धेः समुच्चयेऽभिप्रेते विभागवचनादि सर्वम् उपपन्नं किंच क्षत्रियस्य युद्धं स्मार्तं कर्म स्वधर्म इति जानतः 'तत्किं कर्मणि घोरे मां नियोजयसि' [३.१.] इति उपालम्भः अनुपपन्नः ।

11.0.g. Nor is the distinction in its totality reasonable if the combination proposed related only to knowledge and action enjoined by Smṛtis. Besides, knowing as he did that fighting is the law of the Kṣatriyas according to Smṛtis, Arjuna's complaint, "Why do you bid me plunge into this dreadful action?" is not in order.

11.0.h. तस्माद्गीताशास्त्रे ईषन्मात्रेणापि श्रौतेन स्मार्तेन वा कर्मणाऽऽत्मज्ञानस्य समुच्चयः न केनचिद्दर्शयितुं शक्यः ।

11.0.h. *Therefore, none can possibly demonstrate that in the science of the Gītā there is the slightest proposal to combine knowledge of the Self with action laid down by* Śruti *or* Smṛti.

11.0.i. यस्य तु अज्ञानाद्रागादिदोषतो वा कर्मणि प्रवृत्तस्य यज्ञेन, दानेन, तपसा वा विशुद्धसत्त्वस्य ज्ञानमुत्पन्नं परमार्थतत्त्वविषयं 'एकमेवेदं सर्वं ब्रह्म अकर्तृ च' इति, तस्य कर्मणि कर्मप्रयोजने च निवृत्तेऽपि लोकसंग्रहार्थं यत्नपूर्वं यथा प्रवृत्तिः

तथैव कर्मणि प्रवृत्तस्य यत्प्रवृत्तिरूपं दृश्यते न तत्कर्म येन बुद्धेः समुच्चयः स्यात्; यथा भगवतः वासुदेवस्य क्षात्रधर्मचेष्टितं न ज्ञानेन समुच्चीयते पुरुषार्थसिद्धये; तद्वत्तत्फलाभिसंध्यहंकाराभावस्य तुल्यत्वात् विदुषः। तत्त्ववित्तु न 'अहं करोमि' इति मन्यते, न च तत्फलम् अभिसंधत्ते। यथा च स्वर्गादिकामार्थिनः अग्निहोत्रादिकामसाधनानुष्ठानाय आहिताग्नेः काम्ये एव अग्निहोत्रादौ प्रवृत्तस्य सामिकृते विनष्टेऽपि कामे तदेव अग्निहोत्रादि अनुतिष्ठतोऽपि न तत्काम्यम् अग्निहोत्रादि भवति। तथा च दर्शयति भगवान् 'कुर्वन्नपि न लिप्यते' [५.७.], 'न करोति न लिप्यते' [१३.३१.] इति तत्र तत्र। यच्च 'पूर्वैः पूर्वतरं कृतम्' [४.१५.], 'कर्मणैव हि संसिद्धिमास्थिता जनकादयः' [३.२०.] इति, तत्तु प्रविभज्य विज्ञेयम्। तत्कथम्? यदि तावत्पूर्वे जनकादयः तत्त्वविदः अपि प्रवृत्तकर्माणः स्युः, ते लोकसंग्रहार्थं 'गुणा गुणेषु वर्तन्ते' [३.२८.] इति ज्ञानेनैव संसिद्धिम् आस्थिताः। कर्मसंन्यासे प्राप्ते अपि कर्मणा सहैव संसिद्धिम् आस्थिताः न कर्मसंन्यासं कृतवन्तः इत्यर्थः। अथ न ते तत्त्वविदः—ईश्वरसमर्पितेन कर्मणा साधनभूतेन संसिद्धिं सत्त्वशुद्धिं, ज्ञानोत्पत्तिलक्षणां वा संसिद्धिमास्थिताः जनकादयः इति व्याख्येयम्। एतमेव अर्थं वक्ष्यति भगवान् 'सत्त्वशुद्धये कर्म कुर्वन्ति' [५.११.] इति। 'स्वकर्मणा तमभ्यर्च्य सिद्धिं विन्दति मानवः' [१८.४६.] इत्युक्त्वा सिद्धिं प्राप्तस्य च पुनः ज्ञाननिष्ठां वक्ष्यति 'सिद्धिं प्राप्तो यथा ब्रह्म' [१८.५०.] इत्यादिना।

तस्मात् गीताशास्त्रे केवलात् एव तत्त्वज्ञानात् मोक्षप्राप्तिः, न कर्मसमुच्चितात् इति निश्चितः अर्थः। यथा च अयं अर्थः तथा प्रकरणशः विभज्य तत्र तत्र दर्शयिष्यामः॥

11.0.i. On the other hand, when either due to nescience or flaws like attachment, a person proceeds to act and his mind is in the course of it purified by means of sacrificial rites, the giving of gifts, austerities etc., then the knowledge of the supreme Truth dawns. The content of that knowledge is 'All this world is the one Brahman, a non-agent.' For him both activity and its goal cease to operate. Still, for the well-being of the world, that Brahman-knower may be observed to persist in his activity, purposefully, as of old. The form of activity observed in his case is not real action with which Self-knowledge (*buddhi*) can be combined. An instance is the warrior-like activity of the divine Kṛṣṇa. This is not action combined with Self-knowledge for winning the *summum bonum*. The same is the case with any knower of the Self, as he, like the Lord Himself, is free from the egoistic sense and the desire for the fruits of activities. On the contrary, the knower of the Truth of the Self maintains: "I act not"; and he does not seek the fruits of his actions. His position is similar to what happens to a householder who commences the fire-sacrifice for winning the desired objects, namely heaven and the like, but who, after going through half of the rite, ceases to desire them and yet carries the ceremony through. Now, of course, the sacrificial rite ceases to be desire-prompted. Accordingly does the Lord, in different contexts, affirm: "Though working, the agent is not stained" (5.7), "He neither works nor gets stained" (13.31) etc. As for utterances such as the following: "As your progenitors performed of old" (4.15), "Janaka and others achieved perfection by means of action alone" (3.20)—these have to be distinguished and grasped. How? If, at the outset, it is held that enlightened people like Janaka performed action in bygone days, they did so, aiming at perfection and to promote the world's well-being; for they knew that "Gunas operate in the medium of Guṇas" (3.28). That is, it was appropriate for them to renounce all action; nevertheless, they sought that perfection through the medium of action; they did not renounce action. Such is the import of this passage. On the other hand, if it is held that they were not enlightened, the passage may be explained to mean that Janaka and others like him achieved *saṁsiddhi*, purity of mind, by means of actions dedicated to God; or, *saṁsiddhi* here denotes the dawn of Self-knowledge. The same idea will be conveyed by the Lord in the words: "They act to purify the mind" (5.11). Having stated, "Worshipping Him by means of his own actions, man achieves *siddhi* or *pre-eminence*" (18.46), for one who has (thus) achieved pre-eminence, He prescribes the discipline of knowledge or *jñānaniṣṭhā* saying, "The way that the pre-eminent one attains Brahman" and so on (18.50). *Therefore, according to the science of the Gītā, the attainment of liberation is by means of the unaided knowledge of Truth alone. This is the indubitable doctrine.* That this is the (the right) doctrine, we shall demonstrate with reference to the various contexts of the *Bhagavadgītā*.

11.0.j. तत्र एवं धर्मसम्मूढचेतसः मिथ्याज्ञानवतः महति शोकसागरे निमग्नस्य अर्जुनस्य अन्यत्र आत्मज्ञानात् उद्धरणं अपश्यन् भगवान् वासुदेवः ततः कृपया अर्जुनं उद्दिधारयिषुः आत्मज्ञानाय अवतारयन् आह —

11.0.g. Convinced that the redemption of Arjuna, whose mind was confused in regard to the law of righteousness, swayed by nescience, and sunk in a vast sea of sorrow, is impossible except through the knowledge of the Self, Lord Kṛṣṇa, seeking to save him, introduces to him the theme of Self-knowledge.

श्रीभगवानुवाच :

अशोच्यानन्वशोचस्त्वं प्रज्ञावादांश्च भाषसे ।
गतासूनगतासूंश्च नानुशोचन्ति पण्डिताः ॥११॥

The blessed Lord said:

11. You grieve for those who call for no grief; at the same time, you utter words of wisdom. The wise grieve neither for the dead nor for the living.

11.1. अशोच्यान् इत्यादि ॥ न शोच्याः अशोच्याः भीष्मद्रोणादयः, सद्वृत्तत्वात्, परमार्थस्वरूपेण च नित्यत्वात् । तान् अशोच्यान् अन्वशोचः अनुशोचितवान् असि 'ते म्रियन्ते मन्निमित्तं, अहं तैः विनाभूतः किं करिष्यामि राज्यसुखादिना ?' इति । त्वं प्रज्ञावादान् प्रज्ञावतां बुद्धिमतां वादान् च वचनानि च भाषसे । तदेतत् मौढ्यं पाण्डित्यं च विरुद्धं आत्मनि दर्शयसि उन्मत्तः इव इति अभिप्रायः । यस्मात् गतासून् गतप्राणान् मृतान्, अगतासून् अगतप्राणान् जीवतः च न अनुशोचन्ति पण्डिताः आत्मज्ञाः । पण्डा आत्मविषया बुद्धिः येषां ते हि पण्डिताः, 'पाण्डित्यं निर्विद्य' [बृ. उ. ३.५.१.] इति श्रुतेः । परमार्थतस्तु तान् नित्यान् अशोच्यान् अनुशोचसि, अतः मूढः असि इति अभिप्रायः ॥

11.1. Not meriting grief (*aśocyān*) are Bhīṣma, Droṇa, etc; for, their conduct is virtuous. From the point of view of transcendental Truth, they are eternal. For them, who call for no grief, you have grieved, thinking, "They will die on account of me; what shall I, deprived of them, do with the happiness that the possession of kingdom, etc., will bring me?" And at the same time, you utter words befitting the wise—those who have wisdom (*prajñā*) or intellect. Thus at once combining an air of wisdom with misplaced grief, you display in yourself, like one demented, confusion and wisdom that are mutually contradictory. This is the idea of the Lord. For, both for those whose vital airs have departed (the dead), and for those whose vital airs have not, (the living), the knowers of the Self (*ātmajñāḥ*) do not grieve. *Paṇḍā* is knowledge of the Self. Those who have it are *paṇḍitāḥ*. Vide the *śruti*: "Securing the status of Self-knowers" (*BU*.3.5.1). Transcendentally speaking, you grieve for those who are eternal, and, as such, do not call for grief. Therefore you are demented. This is the Lord's idea.

12.0. कुतः ते अशोच्या ? यतः नित्याः । कथम् ? —

12.0. Why do they not call for grief? Because they are eternal. How?

न त्वेवाहं जातु नासं न त्वं नेमे जनाधिपाः ।
न चैव न भविष्यामः सर्वे वयमतः परम् ॥१२॥

12. Never, at any time, have I been not; neither you nor these rulers of men. And never shall we all cease to be.

12.1. न तु इति ॥ न तु एव, जातु कदाचित् अहं न आसम्, किन्तु आसम् एव ॥ अतीतेषु देहोत्पत्तिविनाशेषु घटादिषु वियद् इव नित्यः एव अहं आसं इति अभिप्रायः । तथा — न त्वं न आसीः, किं तु आसीः एव । तथा — न इमे, जनाधिपाः न आसन्, किं तु आसन् एव । तथा — न च एव न भविष्यामः, किं तु भविष्यामः एव सर्वे वयं अतः अस्मात् देहविनाशात् परं उत्तरकालेऽपि । त्रिष्वपि कालेषु नित्याः आत्मस्वरूपेण इत्यर्थः । देहभेदानुवृत्त्या बहुवचनम्, न आत्मभेदाभिप्रायेण ।

12.1. Never, at any time, was I not; on the contrary, I certainly ever was. Though My bodies originated and perished in the past, in them all, like space in pots and the like, I remained an eternal entity. This is the idea. Similarly you were not non-existent; on the contrary, surely, you too existed. So also these rulers of men were not non-existent; they too existed, to be sure. So, too, we all shall not cease to exist, but continue to be in the future as well, after the disintegration of the body. The idea is that in all the three divisions of time we are eternal as identical with the Self. The plural number in verse 12 refers to differences in respect of bodies; it does not point to a plurality of Selves.

13.0. तत्र कथमिव नित्यः आत्मा इति ? दृष्टान्तं आह —

13.0. In what manner is the Self eternal? An example is offered:

देहिनोऽस्मिन् यथा देहे कौमारं यौवनं जरा ।
तथा देहान्तरप्राप्तिर्धीरस्तत्र न मुह्यते ॥१३॥

13. Just as the embodied Self has, in the body, childhood, youth, and old age, so does it win another body. An intelligent man is not bewildered by it.

13.1. देहिनः इति ॥ देहः अस्य अस्ति इति देही तस्य देहिनः देहवतः आत्मनः अस्मिन् वर्तमाने देहे यथा येन प्रकारेण कौमारं कुमारभावः बाल्यावस्था, यौवनं यूनः भावः मध्यमावस्था, जरा वयोहानिः जीर्णावस्था, इति एताः तिस्रः अवस्थाः अन्योन्यविलक्षणाः । तासां प्रथमावस्थानाशे न नाशः, द्वितीयावस्थोपजनने न उपजननं आत्मनः । किं तर्हि ? अविक्रियस्य एव एकस्य द्वितीयतृतीयावस्थाप्राप्तिः आत्मनः दृष्टा । तथा तद्वत् एव देहात् अन्यः देहः देहान्तरं, तस्य प्राप्तिः देहान्तरप्राप्तिः अविक्रियस्य एव आत्मनः इत्यर्थः । धीराः धीमान्, तत्र एवं सति, न मुह्यति न मोहं आपद्यते ॥

13.1. The embodied Self, *dehī*, is what owns a body. For the embodied Self, in the present body, there are childhood, the condition of a child, or the early stage of life; youth, the condition of a young man, the middle stage; and old age or decline due to age, the stage of disintegration. These three stages are different among themselves. When the first among them ends, the Self does not end. When the second comes into being, the Self is not born. On the contrary, it is observed that to the one immutable Self the second and the third stages accrue. Just as in the example cited, so the undoubtedly immaterial Self wins another body, different from the present one. This is the sense. An intelligent person, *dhīraḥ*, is not bewildered in these circumstances.

14.0. यद्यपि आत्मविनाशनिमित्तः मोहः न संभवति नित्यः आत्मा इति विजानतः तथापि शीतोष्णसुखदुःखप्राप्तिनिमित्तः मोहः लौकिकः दृश्यते, सुखवियोगनिमित्तो मोहः दुःखसंयोगनिमित्तश्च शोकः । इत्येतत् अर्जुनस्य वचनं आशङ्क्य भगवान् आह —

14.0. Though for one who knows the Self to be eternal, it is impossible to be bewildered by the notion that the Self perishes, still bewilderment due to cold and heat, pleasure and pain, is commonly noticed. So too is noticed bewilderment due to separation from the joys of life and grief arising from contact with pain. The Lord anticipates that Arjuna may raise this question and says:

मात्रास्पर्शास्तु कौन्तेय शीतोष्णसुखदुःखदाः ।
आगमापायिनोऽनित्यास्तांस्तितिक्षस्व भारत ॥१४॥

14. O son of Kuntī! Contacts of senses with their objects cause cold and heat, pleasure and pain. These come and go—they are fleeting, O Bhārata prince! Endure them.

14.1. मात्रास्पर्शाः इति ॥ मात्राः आभिः मीयन्ते शब्दादयः इति श्रोत्रादीनि इन्द्रियाणि । मात्राणां स्पर्शाः शब्दादिभिः संयोगाः । ते शीतोष्णसुखदुःखदाः शीतं उष्णं सुखं दुःखं च प्रयच्छन्तीति । अथवा — स्पृश्यन्ते इति स्पर्शाः विषयाः शब्दादयः मात्राश्च स्पर्शाश्च शीतोष्णसुखदुःखदाः — शीतं कदाचित् सुखं, कदाचित् दुःखम् । तथा उष्णम् अपि अनियतस्वरूपम् । सुखदुःखे पुनः नियतरूपतां न व्यभिचरतः । अतः ताभ्यां पृथक् शीतोष्णयोः ग्रहणम् । यस्मात् ते मात्रास्पर्शादयः आगमापायिनः

आगमापायशीलाः तस्मात् अनित्याः । अतः तान् शीतोष्णादीन् तितिक्षस्व प्रसहस्व । तेषु हर्षं विषादं वा मा कार्षीः इत्यर्थः ॥

14.1. *Mātras* are the senses like the ears etc., by which are measured, i.e. determined, objects like sounds. Touches (*sparśāḥ*) of these senses are their contacts with objects like sounds. They generate cold and heat, pleasure and pain. The root *dā* in the text refers to the idea of giving rise to cold, etc. Alternatively, what are "touched" are the objects like sound and so forth. The senses and their objects, *mātrāḥ* and *sparśāḥ*, are the yielders of cold and heat, pleasure and pain. Cold is sometimes pleasant, sometimes unpleasant. So heat, too, has no stable form of its own. Pleasure and pain, on the contrary, never lose their identity. Hence they have been mentioned apart from the former two. As these senses, objects, etc., by their very nature, appear and disappear, they are impermanent. Therefore, endure these objects, cold, heat and so forth. The sense of the verse is: Feel neither pleasure nor pain in respect of them.

15.0. शीतोष्णादीन् सहतः किं स्यात् इति ? शृणु —

15.0. What happens to one who endures cold, heat, etc.? Listen:

यं हि न व्यथयन्त्येते पुरुषं पुरुषर्षभ ।
समदुःखसुखं धीरं सोऽमृतत्वाय कल्पते ॥१५॥

15. O hero! The man whom these do not agitate, who is the same in pain and pleasure, and who is wise, becomes fit indeed for immortality.

15.1. यं हि इति ॥ यं हि पुरुषं समदुःखसुखं समे दुःखसुखे यस्य तं समदुःखसुखं सुखदुःखप्राप्तौ हर्षविषादरहितं धीरं धीमन्तं न व्यथयन्ति न चालयन्ति नित्यात्मदर्शनात् एते यथोक्ताः शीतोष्णादयः, सः नित्यात्मस्वरूपदर्शननिष्ठः द्वन्द्वसहिष्णुः

अमृतत्वाय अमृतभावाय मोक्षाय कल्पते समर्थः भवति ॥

15.1. Wise, indeed, is the man to whom pain and pleasure are the same, who is devoid of elation and dejection when pleasure and pain accrue. These do not agitate him; he is not jolted out of the perception of the Self. Devoted to the vision of the essence of the eternal Self, enduring all dualities, he becomes fit for liberation, *mokṣa*, the state of immortality.

16.0. इतश्च शोकमोहौ अकृत्वा शीतोष्णादिसहनं युक्तं, यस्मात् —

16.0. What happens to one who endures cold, heat, etc? Listen:

नासतो विद्यते भावो नाभावो विद्यते सतः ।
उभयोरपि दृष्टोऽन्तस्त्वनयोस्तत्त्वदर्शिभिः ॥१६॥

16. The unreal comes not into being, the real never lapses into non-being. The truth about both these has been perceived by the seers of Reality.

16.1. नासतः इति ॥ न असतः अविद्यमानस्य शीतोष्णादेः सकारणस्य न विद्यते नास्ति भावो भवनं अस्तिता ॥

न हि शीतोष्णादि सकारणं प्रमाणैः निरूप्यमाणं वस्तु सत् भवति । विकारो हि सः, विकारश्च व्यभिचरति । यथा घटादिसंस्थानं चक्षुषा निरूप्यमाणं मृद्व्यतिरेकेण अनुपलब्धेः असत्, तथा सर्वो विकारः कारणव्यतिरेकेण अनुपलब्धेः असन् । जन्मप्रध्वंसाभ्यां प्राक् ऊर्ध्वं च अनुपलब्धेः कार्यस्य घटादेः मृदादिकारणस्य च तत्कारणव्यतिरेकेण अनुपलब्धेः असत्त्वम् ॥

तदसत्त्वे सर्वाभावप्रसङ्गः इति चेत् — न; सर्वत्र बुद्धिद्वयोपलब्धेः, सद्बुद्धिः असद्बुद्धिः इति । यद्विषया बुद्धिः न व्यभिचरति, तत् सत्, यद्विषया व्यभिचरति, तत् असत् — इति सदसद्विभागे बुद्धितन्त्रे स्थिते, सर्वत्र द्वे बुद्धी सर्वैः उपलभ्येते समानाधिकरणे — न नीलोत्पलवत्, — सन् घटः, सन् पटः, सन् हस्ती, इति । एवं सर्वत्र । तयोः बुद्ध्योः घटादिबुद्धिः व्यभिचरति । तथा च दर्शितम् । न तु सद्बुद्धिः । तस्माद् घटादिबुद्धिविषयः असन्, व्यभिचारात्, न तु सद्बुद्धिविषयः, अव्यभिचारात् ॥

16.1. The unreal i.e. that which has no being, such as cold

and heat as well as their cause, has no true existence. Effected states like cold and heat are observed to be unreal in themselves when tested by means of valid cognition. They are only inconstant transformations. Take, as an example, effected entities like a pot. When scrutinised, they are not seen apart from clay and the like, their material causes. Therefore, as effects, they are unreal. In the same way, all transformations, not being cognizable apart from their causes, are unreal. Unreal are effects like pots, for they are unknown before their origination and after their destruction. The same holds good for things like clay, the cause of pots and the like, for these causes too are not known apart from *their* causes.

Objection: If the totality of causes and effects be unreal there arises the contingency of an absolute vacuum.

Answer: No; throughout the sphere of cognitive experience we have to deal with two cognitions: (1) the cognition of the real and (ii) the cognition of the unreal. That alone is real whose cognition is not mutable, and that is unreal whose cognition proves mutable. Thus the distinction between the real and the unreal rests on cognitions. Throughout the sphere of experience the two cognitions with an identical substratum are available to one and all. Note that this case is different in nature from the cognition of "a blue lotus". Right examples are "the pot is", "the cloth is", "the elephant is" and so on throughout the whole sphere of cognitive experience. Of these two cognitions, the one whose content is the pot and the like, is mutable. And so it is demonstrated. Not so the cognition of reality or *sat*. Therefore, being mutable the objects of the cognitions of pot and the like are unreal; not so, the object of the cognition of the "real", it being immutable.

16.2. घटे विनष्टे घटबुद्धौ व्यभिचरन्त्यां सद्बुद्धिः अपि व्यभिचरति इति चेत् — न; पटादौ अपि सद्बुद्धिदर्शनात् । विशेषणविषया एव सा सद्बुद्धिः ॥ सद्बुद्धिवत् घटबुद्धिः अपि घटान्तरे दृश्यते इति चेत् — न; पटादौ अदर्शनात् ॥

सद्बुद्धिः अपि नष्टे घटे न दृश्यते इति चेत् – न; विशेष्याभावात् । सद्बुद्धिः विशेषणविषया सती विशेष्याभावे विशेषणानुपपत्तौ किंविषया स्यात् ? न तु पुनः सद्बुद्धेः विषयाभावात् ।

16.2. *Objection:* When the pot perishes and the cognition of the pot proves mutable, the cognition of the real, *sat*, too proves mutable.

Answer: No, the cognition of the real is still available in regard to other objects like the cloth. The cognition of the real has, as its content, only the adjective.[1]

Objection: Like the cognition of the real, that of the pot also is available in regard to another existent pot.

Answer: No; it is not available in regard to the cloth.

Objection: The cognition of the real, too, does not occur in regard to the pot that has perished.

[1] *Viśeṣaṇaviṣayā eva sā sadbuddhiḥ.*

The question being discussed dialectically, both from the points of Sanskrit grammar and metaphysics, relates to the status of "is" in cognitions like "the pot is", "the cloth is" etc. Para 15 cited these examples. The metaphysical proposition is: when the content of a cognition does not change, it is *sat* or real. What changes is either empirical or illusory. The distinction between *sat* and *asat*, thus depends on the concerned cognitions. Cognitions of pot etc., change; not so the cognitions of *sat* or being. The reference of the cognition of *isness* in the compound cognition "pot is" does not change.

Even when the pot perishes, *isness*, qualifying it, does not, for, it manifests itself with reference, say, to a cloth, *vide* "*Paṭaḥ san*". In the examples, *isness* is grammatically an adjective, as it refers to what qualifies substantives or nouns like pot and cloth. Its cognition is not on a par with that of pot and cloth. For, though the cognition of a given pot may perish with reference to other pots, the cognition of the pot may very well continue. On the other hand, the cognition of a pot is impossible with reference to objects like cloth. But the cognition of *isness—sadbuddhiḥ*—does not perish even when the given pot has perished; it may be had in relation to a cloth, for example. True, the cognition of *isness* is ruled out in relation to the pot that has perished; yet the fact that it may be had in relation to cloth etc., shows that it is imperishable, unlike the individual pots. The answer to the objection that *isness* is not experienced with reference to the individual that has perished, is that it nevertheless continues to be available with reference to surviving pots and non-pots like cloth etc. *Isness* appears as an adjective only (in the grammatical sense) in cognitions relating to individual objects. Whereas the substantives perish, the adjective, *isness*, just ceases to be experienced; it does not perish. Only, being an adjective qualifying individuals, in the absence of the latter, it cannot manifest itself.

There is the further question: Can the cognition of a real entity and that of an unreal entity inhere in a common ground? Look at the cognition 'this is water' with reference to a mirage, where 'this' alone is given, while the water is absent. The entire world of dualities is like the water in the mirage; it inheres in the Eternal Ground, the ultimate Reality or Brahman that timelessly persists unsublated, unlike the world that inheres in it.

Answer: No; your remark sounds plausible only because the substantive is absent. The cognition of the real, whose content is the adjective *sat*, will not have *that* as its referent; for, an adjective without a substantive is illogical. The non-occurence of the cognition of the real, then, is not due to the absence of the real.

16.3. एकाधिकरणत्वं घटादिविशेष्याभावे न युक्तमिति चेत् – न; 'इदं उदकम्' इति मरीच्यादौ अन्यतराभावेऽपि सामानाधिकरण्यदर्शनात् ।

तस्मात् देहादेः द्वन्द्वस्य च सकारणस्य असतः न विद्यते भावः इति । तथा सतः च आत्मनः अभावः अविद्यमानता न विद्यते, सर्वत्र अव्यभिचारात् इति अवोचाम । एवं आत्मानात्मनोः सदसतोः उभयोः अपि दृष्टः उपलब्धः अन्तः निर्णयः, सत् सदेव असत् असदेव इति तु अनयोः यथोक्तयोः तत्त्वदर्शिभिः ।

16.3. *Objection:* Dependence on the same substratum of both the cognitions is illogical, since the substantives like the pot are, in truth, not there at all.

Answer: No; in fact one observes that the cognitions of light and so forth expressed in the proposition, 'there is water' refer to an identical substratum, though one of the two component elements, water, is not there at all. Therefore, on the one hand, unreal and caused entities like the body and dual entities like heat and cold do not come into being; on the other hand, a real entity like the Self never lapses into non-being. For, as we observed, it is everywhere present. Thus has the unshakable truth about the Self and the non-Self—the real and the unreal—namely, that the real is ever real and the unreal ever unreal, been perceived by the seers of Reality.

16.4. तत् इति सर्वनाम; सर्वं च ब्रह्म; तस्य नाम तत् इति तद्भावः तत्त्वं, ब्रह्मणः याथात्म्यम् । तत् द्रष्टुं शीलं येषां ते तत्त्वदर्शिनः, तैः तत्त्वदर्शिभिः । त्वमपि तत्त्वदर्शिनां दृष्टिं आश्रित्य शोकं मोहं च हित्वा शीतोष्णादीनि नियतानियतरूपाणि द्वन्द्वानि, विकारोऽयमसन् एव मरीचिजलवत् मिथ्या अवभासते — इति मनसि निश्चित्य तितिक्षस्व इति अभिप्रायः ॥

16.4. *Tat* in the word *tattva* is the name of the 'all', and the all is Brahman. Those who habitually perceive it are the seers of Reality. By them has the above Truth been perceived. Relying on this perception of the seers of Reality, you must endure grief and delusion. Giving up both grief and delusion and firmly holding that uncertain dualities like cold and heat are unreal transformations or effects that, like a mirage, illusorily appear, you should endure them. This is the idea.

17.0. किं पुनः तत् यत् सत् एव सर्वदा इति ? उच्यते —

17.0. What then is that which is eternally real? Listen:

अविनाशि तु तद्विद्धि येन सर्वमिदं ततम् ।
विनाशमव्ययस्यास्य न कश्चित्कर्तुमर्हति ॥१७॥

17. On the contrary, know that to be imperishable by which all this is pervaded. None can destroy that which is immutable.

17.1. अविनाशि इति ॥ अविनाशि न विनष्टुं शीलं अस्य इति । तु शब्दः असतः विशेषणार्थः । तत् विद्धि विजानीहि । किम् ? येन सर्वं इदं जगत् ततं व्याप्तं सदाख्येन ब्रह्मणा साकाशं, आकाशेन इव घटादयः । विनाशं अदर्शनं, अभावम् । अव्ययस्य न व्येति उपचयापचयौ न याति इति अव्ययं, तस्य अव्ययस्य ।

17.1. What does not habitually perish is the imperishable. *Tu*, on the contrary, distinguishes It from the unreal. Know *that*. What? Brahman or *Sat*, i.e. Being, by which the whole world, together with the sky, is pervaded, just as pots and the like are pervaded by the sky. Destruction is non-perception or non-being. The immutable is that which neither increases nor decreases.

17.2. न एतत् सदाख्यं ब्रह्म स्वेन रूपेण व्येति, व्यभिचरति निरवयवत्वात्, देहादिवत् । नापि आत्मीयेन, आत्मीयाभावात् । यथा देवदत्तः धनहान्या व्येति, न तु एवं ब्रह्म व्येति । अतः अव्ययस्य अस्य ब्रह्मणः विनाशं न कश्चित् कर्तुं अर्हति, न कश्चित् आत्मानं विनाशयितुं शक्नोति ईश्वरोऽपि । आत्मा हि ब्रह्म; स्वात्मनि च क्रियाविरोधात् ॥

17.2. This Brahman known as *sat* does not change Its own nature, i.e. does not forfeit it; for, It is partless, unlike the body, etc. Neither in respect of Its properties does It change; for, It has no property. For example, Devadatta decays through loss of his wealth; but Brahman does not. Therefore, none can bring about the destruction of this immutable Brahman. None, not even God, may destroy the Self. Indeed the Self is Brahman and any transitive activity of the Self (the Self acting on Itself) is inconceivable.

18.0. किं पुनः तत् असत् यत् स्वात्मसत्तां व्यभिचरति इति ? उच्यते—

18.0. Again what is that which, being unreal, has but an inconstant existence? It is thus set forth:

अन्तवन्त इमे देहा नित्यस्योक्ताः शरीरिणः ।
अनाशिनोऽप्रमेयस्य तस्माद्युध्यस्व भारत ॥१८॥

18. These bodies that perish are said to pertain to the eternal Self that is embodied—the eternal Self, that is imperishable and indeterminable. Therefore, fight, O scion of the Bharatas!

18.1. अन्तवन्तः इति ॥ अन्तः विनाशः विद्यते येषां ते अन्तवन्तः । यथा मृगतृष्णिकादौ सद्बुद्धिः अनुवृत्ता प्रमाणनिरूपणान्ते विच्छिद्यते, स तस्य अन्तः; तथा इमे देहाः स्वप्नमायादेहादिवच्च अन्तवन्तः नित्यस्य शरीरिणः शरीरवतः अनाशिनः अप्रमेयस्य आत्मनः अन्तवन्त इति उक्ताः विवेकिभिः इत्यर्थः । 'नित्यस्य' अनाशिनः इति न पुनरुक्तम्; नित्यत्वस्य द्विविधत्वात् लोके, नाशस्य च । यथा देहः भस्मीभूतः अदर्शनं गतः नष्टः उच्यते । विद्यमानोऽपि यथा अन्यथा परिणतः व्याध्यादियुक्तः जातः नष्टः उच्यते । तत्र 'नित्यस्य' 'अनाशिनः' इति द्विविधेनापि नाशेन असंबद्धस्य इत्यर्थः । अन्यथा पृथिव्यादिवत् अपि नित्यत्वं स्यात् आत्मनः, तत् मा भूत् इति 'नित्यस्य' 'अनाशिनः' इत्याह ।

18.1. The perishables are things which have an end or *anta*. For instance, the idea of reality, associated with things like a mirage, snaps when tested by means of right cognition. This is its 'end'. Likewise, these bodies of the eternal and indeterminable Self are as perishable as the bodies seen in a dream or projected by a magician. Men of discrimination affirm this truth. The expressions 'eternal' and 'imperishable' (*nityasya, anāśinaḥ*) are not tautologous; for, eternity and perishability are of two types. For instance, a body, reduced to ashes and no longer perceptible, is said to have perished. It is also said to have perished when, though existent, it has undergone a great transformation due to diseases, etc. The two expressions *nityasya* and *anāśinaḥ* rule out both these forms of destruction as regards the Self. Otherwise, the eternity of the Self may be held to be similar to that of objects like the earth. To exclude this possibility the text says, "of the eternal" and "of the imperishable."

18.2. अप्रमेयस्य न प्रमेयस्य प्रत्यक्षादिप्रमाणैः अपरिच्छेद्यस्य इत्यर्थः ॥ ननु आगमेन आत्मा परिच्छिद्यते, प्रत्यक्षादिना च पूर्वम् । न, आत्मनः स्वतःसिद्धत्वात् । सिद्धे हि आत्मनि प्रमातरि प्रमित्सोः प्रमाणान्वेषणा भवति । न हि पूर्वं 'इत्थं अहं' इति आत्मानं अप्रमाय पश्चात् प्रमेयपरिच्छेदाय प्रवर्तते । न हि आत्मा नाम कस्यचित् अप्रसिद्धः भवति । शास्त्रं तु अन्त्यं प्रमाणं अतद्धर्माध्यारोपणमात्रनिवर्तकत्वेन प्रामाण्यं आत्मनः प्रतिपद्यते, न तु अज्ञातार्थज्ञापकत्वेन । तथा च श्रुतिः— 'यत् साक्षादपरोक्षाद् ब्रह्म य आत्मा सर्वान्तरः' [बृ. उ. ३.४.१.] इति ॥

18.2. "Of the indeterminable" means "of that which is not measurable by the means of right cognition like perception and so forth."

Objection: The Self is measured or determined by Revelation, and, earlier, by perception and so forth.

Answer: No; for the Self is self-established. Indeed it is only when the knower, the Self, is given, that there arises the search for the means of right cognition on the part of the seeker after knowledge. Without knowing the Self earlier as "such and such am I", none attempts to secure determinate knowledge of the object of knowledge. To none at all is the Self altogether unknown. The final means of right cognition, the *śāstra* or scripture, acquires validity as regards the Self by setting aside the non-attributes of the Self superimposed on It, and not by revealing what was altogether unknown. Thus the *śruti* declares: "That which is immediately present is Brahman, the Self in all" (*BU*.3.4.1).

18.3. यस्मात् एवं नित्यः अविक्रियश्च आत्मा तस्मात् युध्यस्व, युद्धात् उपरमं मा कार्षीः इत्यर्थः ॥

न हि अत्र युद्धकर्तव्यता विधीयते, युद्धे प्रवृत्तः एव हि असौ शोकमोहप्रतिबद्धः तूष्णीं आस्ते । अतः तस्य कर्तव्यप्रतिबन्धापनयनमात्रं भगवता क्रियते । तस्मात् 'युध्यस्व' इति अनुवादमात्रं, न विधिः ॥

18.3. Since the Self is thus eternal and immutable, you must fight, and not withdraw from battle—this is the sense. Here fighting is not enjoined as a duty. For, Arjuna has already addressed himself to fight. But he remains immobilised due to grief and delusion. Therefore, the Lord removes the impediment in his path to the performance of his duty. Hence the term "fight" is only a restatement of a given position and not an original injunction.

19.0. शोकमोहादिसंसारकारणनिवृत्त्यर्थं गीताशास्त्रं, न प्रवर्तकं, इति एतस्य अर्थस्य साक्षिभूते ऋचौ [कठ. उ. २.१८.१९.] आनिनाय भगवान् ॥

यत्तु मन्यसे 'युद्धे भीष्मादयः मया हन्यन्ते, अहम् एव तेषां हन्ता' इति एषा बुद्धिः मृषैव ते । कथम् ? —

19.0. The Lord has cited two *mantras* (*KU*.2.18.19) that testity to the fact that the science of the Gītā purports to remove the cause of transmigratory life consisting of grief, delusion etc., and not to compel anyone to initiate action of any kind. It tells Arjuna: Your notion that people like Bhīṣma are slain by you in battle—that you are their slayer—is indeed false. How?

य एनं वेत्ति हन्तारं यश्चैनं मन्यते हतम् ॥
उभौ तौ न विजानीतो नायं हन्ति न हन्यते ॥१९॥

19. Both he who takes It for the slayer and he who

takes It to be the slain know not (the truth); It neither slays nor is slain.

19.1. य एनं इति ॥ यः एनं प्रकृतं देहिनं वेत्ति विजानाति हन्तारं हननक्रियायाः कर्तारं, यः च एनं अन्यः मन्यते हतं देहहननेन 'हतः अहम्' इति हननक्रियायाः कर्मभूतं, तौ उभौ न विजानीतः न ज्ञातवन्तौ अविवेकेन आत्मानम् । 'हन्ता अहम्', 'हतः अस्मि अहम्' इति देहहननेन आत्मानं अहंप्रत्ययविषयं यौ विजानीतः तौ आत्मस्वरूपानभिज्ञौ इत्यर्थः । यस्मात् न अयं आत्मा हन्ति न हननक्रियायाः कर्ता भवति, न हन्यते न च कर्म भवतीत्यर्थः, अविक्रियत्वात् ॥

19.1. He who takes the embodied Self in question for the slayer or the agent of the action of slaying and he who deems It the slain or the object of that action, crying out "I am slain" when the body is slain—both these do not know aright the Self due to their lack of discrimination. The sense is that both these are ignorant of the proper nature of the Self, because this Self is neither the agent nor the object of the action of slaying. The reason is that the Self is immutable.

20.0. कथं अविक्रियः आत्मा इति द्वितीयः मन्त्रः —

20.0. The second *mantra* (from *KU.*) explains how the Self is immutable.

न जायते म्रियते वा कदाचिन्
नायं भूत्वाऽभविता वा न भूयः ।
अजो नित्यः शाश्वतोऽयं पुराणो
न हन्यते हन्यमाने शरीरे ॥२०॥

20. This Self is never born; It never dies either. Having been born, It never ceases to be, again. Unborn, eternal and everlasting, this ancient One is not slain when the body is slain.

20.1. न जायते इति । न जायते न उत्पद्यते, जनिलक्षणा वस्तुविक्रिया न आत्मनः विद्यते इत्यर्थः । तथा न म्रियते वा । वाशब्दः चार्थे । न म्रियते च इति अन्त्या

विनाशलक्षणा विक्रिया प्रतिषिद्धयते । कदाचित् शब्दः सर्वविक्रियाप्रतिषेधैः संबद्धयते — न कदाचित् जायते, न कदाचित् म्रियते, इत्येवम् । यस्मात् अयं आत्मा भूत्वा भवनक्रियां अनुभूय पश्चात् अभविता अभावं गन्ता न भूयः पुनः, तस्मात् न म्रियते । यो हि भूत्वा न भविता स म्रियते इति उच्यते लोके । वाशब्दात् नशब्दाच्च अयं आत्मा अभूत्वा वा भविता देहवत् न भूयः पुनः । तस्मात् न जायते । यो हि अभूत्वा भविता स जायते इति उच्यते । नैवं आत्मा । अतः न जायते । यस्मात् एवं तस्मात् अजः । यस्मात् न म्रियते तस्मात् नित्यः च ।

20.1. This Self is not born i.e., It does not come into being. The sense is that the transformation of things known as birth does not happen to the Self. Similarly It does not die either. 'Either', *vā*, has the sense of 'and'. And It does not die. The final transformation known as destruction is negated of the Self. The phrase "at any time" (*kadācit*) is associated with the negation of all transformation. It means : at no time whatsoever is It born, at no time whatsoever does It die and so on. Because, having been, i.e. having experienced the state of being, this Self does not again reach the state of non-being. Therefore, It does not die. In the world one who, having been, ceases to be, is said to die. Due to the force of words "either" and "not", it follows also that the Self, having ceased to be, does not again come into being, like the body. Therefore "It is not born". That which, having been non-existent, comes into being, is said to be born. The Self is not an entity like that. Hence It is not born. Since, It is such, therefore, It is unborn. Since It does not die, therefore, It is eternal also.

20.2. यद्यपि आद्यन्तयोः विक्रिययोः प्रतिषेधे सर्वाः विक्रियाः प्रतिषिद्धाः भवन्ति, तथापि मध्यभाविनीनां विक्रियाणां स्वशब्दैः एव तदर्थैः प्रतिषेधः कर्तव्यः इति अनुक्तानां अपि यौवनादिसमस्तविक्रियाणां प्रतिषेधः यथा स्यात् इत्याह—शाश्वतः इत्यादिना । शाश्वतः इति अपक्षयलक्षणा विक्रिया प्रतिषिद्धयते । शश्वद्भवः शाश्वतः । न अपक्षीयते स्वरूपेण, निरवयवत्वात् । निर्गुणत्वात् च नापि गुणक्षयेण अपक्षयः । अपक्षयविपरीता अपि वृद्धिलक्षणा विक्रिया प्रतिषिद्धयते पुराणः इति । यो हि अवयवागमेन उपचीयते स वर्धते, अभिनवः इति च उच्यते । अयं तु आत्मा निरवयवत्वात् पुरा अपि नवः एव इति पुराणः; न वर्धते इत्यर्थः । तथा— न हन्यते । हन्तिः अत्र विपरिणामार्थो द्रष्टव्यः अपुनरुक्ततायै । न विपरिणम्यते इत्यर्थः । हन्यमाने विपरिणम्यमानेऽपि शरीरे । अस्मिन् मन्त्रे षड् भावविकाराः

लौकिकवस्तुविक्रियाः आत्मनि प्रतिषिद्धयन्ते । सर्वप्रकारविक्रियारहितः आत्मा इति वाक्यार्थः । यस्मात् एवं तस्मात् 'उभौ तौ न विजानीतः' [२. १९.] इति पूर्वेण मन्त्रेण अस्य संबन्धः ॥

20.2. Though by the negation of the first and the last transformations, all transformations are in effect negated in regard to the Self, still it is meet that the intermediate transformations also are negated specifically. Therefore, to negate transformations like youth, not specifically mentioned, expressions like 'everlasting' are used in the text. By the term 'everlasting' is negated the transformation consisting in decay. What exists for ever is everlasting. In Itself the Self does not decay; for It is impartite. Being devoid of attributes, It does not suffer decay through that of the attributes, either. The term 'ancient' denies also the transformation of growth, the opposite of decay. What develops through the accession of parts is said to grow. It is also called new. But this Self, being impartite, was new even in times of yore. So it is ancient, *purāṇa*, i.e. It grows not. Similarly It is not slain. The root *han* in this context must be taken in the sense of decay, to avoid redundancy. The sense is that the Self does not decay, though the body is slain i.e., undergoes decay. In this *mantra* are repudiated, in respect of the Self, the six transformations which affect empirical objects. The sense of the proposition is that the Self is free from all kinds of transformation. Such being the case, this verse must be understood in conjunction with the previous one (2.19), "both of them know not".

21.0. 'य एनं वेत्ति हन्तारम्' [२.१९.] इत्यनेन मन्त्रेण हननक्रियायाः कर्ता कर्म च न भवति इति प्रतिज्ञाय, 'न जायते' इत्यनेन अविक्रियत्वे हेतुं उक्त्वा प्रतिज्ञातार्थं उपसंहरति —

21.0. Having affirmed, in verse 2.19, that "the Self is neither the agent nor the object of the action of slaying" and pointed out in 2.20 the reason for Its freedom from mutability, the Lord concludes the argument already set forth:

वेदाविनाशिनं नित्यं य एनमजमव्ययम् ।
कथं स पुरुषः पार्थ कं घातयति हन्ति कम् ॥२१॥

21. How can a man, O Arjuna! who knows It as the imperishable, the eternal, the unborn, the undecaying, cause anyone to be slain? Whom can he slay?

21.1. वेदाविनाशिनं इति । वेद विजानाति अविनाशिनं अन्त्यभावविकाररहितं नित्यं विपरिणामरहितं यः वेद इति सम्बन्धः । एनं पूर्वेण मन्त्रेण उक्तलक्षणं अजं जन्मरहितं अव्ययं अपक्षयरहितं कथं केन प्रकारेण सः विद्वान् पुरुषः अधिकृतः हन्ति, हननक्रियां करोति ? कथं वा घातयति हन्तारं प्रयोजयति ? न कथंचित् कंचित् हन्ति, न कथंचित् कंचित् घातयति इति उभयत्र आक्षेपः एव अर्थः, प्रश्नार्थासंभवात् । हेत्वर्थस्य च अविक्रियत्वस्य तुल्यत्वात् विदुषः सर्वकर्मप्रतिषेधः एव प्रकरणार्थः अभिप्रेतः भगवतः । हन्तेः तु आक्षेपः उदाहरणार्थत्वेन कथितः ॥

21.1. He who knows the Self as imperishable, i.e., as free from the last transformation, and as eternal, i.e., as free from decay—thus are these two words, *anāśinam*, *nityam*, to be construed—how can such a knower of the unborn and imperishable Self slay or cause to be slain when he fights as a matter of duty? In no manner does he slay; in no manner does he cause to slay. The upshot is the repudiation of the two suggestions of slaying and causing to slay. The idea that two questions are here being asked is impossible in this context. The reason, namely, the immutability of the Self, being the same for negating all actions on its part, the Lord here conveys the idea of negation of all actions by a knower of the Self. The negation of slaying has been chosen as an example.

21.2. विदुषः कं कर्मासंभवे हेतुविशेषं पश्यन् कर्माणि आक्षिपति भगवान् 'कथं स पुरुषः' इति । ननु उक्तः एव आत्मनः अविक्रियत्वं सर्वकर्मासंभवकारणविशेषः । सत्यं उक्तः । न तु सः कारणविशेषः अन्यत्वात् विदुषः अविक्रियात् आत्मनः इति । न हि अविक्रियं स्थाणुं विदितवतः कर्म न सम्भवति इति चेत्—न; विदुषः आत्मत्वात् । न देहादिसंघातस्य विद्वत्ता । अतः पारिशेष्यात् असंहतः आत्मा विद्वान् अविक्रियः इति तस्य विदुषः कर्मासंभवात् आक्षेपः युक्तः 'कथं स पुरुषः' इति ।

21.2. In the light of what specific reason for ruling out all activities, does the Lord negate them in the words, "How can a man who knows. . . . ?" That has been mentioned already. It is the immutability of the Self. This is the reason that makes all action impossible for the Self-knower. True, it has been mentioned; but it cannot be the specific reason; for, the knower of the Self is different from the immutable Self. For example, action is not impossible for one who has known that a post is actionless. The case in question, however, is different, because the Ātman is the Self of the knower. The state of being a knower does not, of course, pertain to the conglomerate of the body, senses, etc. Therefore, after their elimination whatever remains—the non-composite Self—is the knower, free from all actions. Thus actions being impossible for the knower, it is appropriate to negate all of them in the words, "How can a man who knows. . . . ?"

21.3. यथा बुद्ध्याद्याहृतस्य शब्दाद्यर्थस्य अविक्रियः एव सन् बुद्धिवृत्त्यविवेकविज्ञानेन अविद्यया उपलब्धा आत्मा कल्प्यते, एवम् एव आत्मानात्मविवेकज्ञानेन बुद्धिवृत्त्या विद्यया—असत्यरूपया एव परमार्थतः अविक्रियः एव आत्मा विद्वान् उच्यते । विदुषः कर्मासंभववचनात् यानि कर्माणि शास्त्रेण विधीयन्ते तानि अविदुषः विहितानि इति भगवतः निश्चयोऽवगम्यते ॥

21.3. Through nescience the immutable Self is deemed a knower both of the sense-objects and of the Self itself. In the former case, the immutable Self is supposed to know objects like sound presented to the intellect and so forth, because there is a lack of discrimination of the Self from the modifications of the intellect. In the latter case, the Self is said to know by virtue of the intellect's modification of discrimination between the Self and the non-Self. This knowledge by discrimination, too, is unreal, metaphysically. On the basis of the Lord's teaching that it is impossible for the Self-knower to act, whatever actions have been enjoined by the Śāstras have reference only to the non-knower. This may be taken to be the settled doctrine of the Lord.

21.4. ननु विद्यापि अविदुषः एव विधीयते, विदितविद्यस्य पिष्टपेषणवत् विद्याविधानानर्थक्यात् । तत्र अविदुषः कर्माणि विधीयन्ते न विदुषः इति विशेषः न उपपद्यते इति चेत् — न । अनुष्ठेयस्य भावाभावविशेषोपपत्तेः । अग्निहोत्रादिविध्यर्थज्ञानोत्तरकालं अग्निहोत्रादिकर्म अनेकसाधनोपसंहारपूर्वकं अनुष्ठेयं 'कर्ता अहं, मम कर्तव्यम्' इत्येवंप्रकारकविज्ञानवतः अविदुषः यथा अनुष्ठेयं भवति न तु तथा 'न जायते' इत्याद्यात्मस्वरूपविध्यर्थज्ञानोत्तरकालभावि किञ्चित् अनुष्ठेयं भवति, किन्तु 'नाहं कर्ता, नाहं भोक्ता' इत्याद्यात्मैकत्वाकर्तृत्वादिविषयज्ञानात् अन्यत् न उत्पद्यते इति एषः विशेषः उपपद्यते । यः पुनः 'कर्ता अहं' इति वेत्ति आत्मानं, तस्य 'मम इदं कर्तव्यम्' इति अवश्यंभाविनी बुद्धिः स्यात्; तदपेक्षया सः अधिक्रियते इति तं प्रति कर्माणि संभवन्ति । स च अविद्वान्, 'उभौ तौ न विजानीतः' [२.१९.] इति वचनात्, विशेषितस्य च विदुषः कर्माक्षेपवचनात् च 'कथं स पुरुषः' इति । तस्मात् विशेषितस्य अविक्रियात्मदर्शिनः विदुषः मुमुक्षोश्च सर्वकर्मसंन्यासे एव अधिकारः । अतः एव भगवान् नारायणः सांख्यान् विदुषः, अविदुषश्च कर्मिणः प्रविभज्य द्वे निष्ठे ग्राहयति — 'ज्ञानयोगेन सांख्यानां कर्मयोगेन योगिनाम्' [३.३.] इति । तथा च पुत्राय आह भगवान् व्यासः— 'द्वाविमावथ पन्थानौ' [म. भा. शांति. २४०.६.] इत्यादि । तथाच 'क्रियापथश्चैव पुरस्तात् पश्चात् संन्यासश्च' [तै. आ. १०.६२.१२. तात्पर्यानुवादः । तुलय—ई. उ. २. भाष्यं, तथा के. उ. १. भाष्यम्] इति । एतमेव विभागं पुनः पुनः दर्शयिष्यति भगवान्— अतत्त्ववित् 'अहंकारविमूढात्मा कर्ताहमिति मन्यते,' 'तत्त्ववित् तु न अहं करोमि' [३.२७-२८] इति । तथा च 'सर्वकर्माणि मनसा संन्यस्यास्ते' [५.१३.] इत्यादि ॥

21.4. *Objection:* But knowledge also has been enjoined on the non-knower only. On one who has acquired knowledge, the enjoining of knowledge is pointless like the grinding of corn already ground. Therefore the distinction that actions have been enjoined only on the non-knower and not on the knower is not logical.

Answer: No; the distinction between existence and non-existence is sound only as regards what has to be accomplished. After knowing the sense of an injunction regarding rites like *agnihotra* (fire-sacrifice), which require the assemblage of numerous accessories, they have to be performed by the non-knowers of the Self, each of whom thinks, "I am an agent; I have to perform this." But different is the case of one who masters the sense of propositions like "This Self is never born", which set forth the real nature of the Self. After acquiring the knowledge he has no ritualistic act to perform. On the dawn of knowledge that the Self is one, a non-agent, a non-experiencer and so forth, no action supervenes. A distinction like this is thus logical. On the other hand, for him who thinks of his Self as "I am an agent", the inevitable thought follows: "I must perform this." As regards such actions, he is obliged to play the role of the agent. In respect of him actions are performable. And he is a non-knower in the light of the verse 2.19: "Both of them fail to know." Besides, the words, "How can a man. . .?" (2.21) repudiate actions in respect of the knower, who has been distinguished from the non-knower. Therefore, both the Self-knower perceiving the immutability of the Self, and the seeker after liberation, are called upon exclusively to renounce all Veda-enjoined works. It is for this reason that the Lord Kṛṣṇa, distinguishing the Sāṁkyas, who are Self-knowers, from the ritualists, who are non-knowers of the Self, enjoins on each group a distinctive discipline—by the Yoga of knowledge for the Sāṁkhyas, and by that of works for the Yogins (3.3). Accordingly Vyāsa tells his son: "Two are the paths here" (*MB*.12.240.6). Also, "First the paths of works, then renunciation" (*TA*.10.62.12; cf.*IUB*.2; *KeUP*.1). The same distinction will be drawn by the Lord repeatedly: the non-knower of the Self, with a mind confounded by egoism, deems, "I am an agent", but the Self-knower holds "I act not" (*BG*.3.27.28). Again, "He, the Self-knower, is seated, mentally renouncing all works" (5.13), and so on.

21.5. तत्र केचित् पण्डितंमन्याः वदन्ति — 'जन्मादिषड्भावविक्रियारहितः अविक्रियः अकर्ता एकः अहं आत्मा' इति न कस्यचित् ज्ञानं उत्पद्यते, यस्मिन् सति सर्वकर्मसंन्यासः उपदिश्यते, इति । तत् न; 'न जायते' इत्यादिशास्त्रोपदेशानर्थक्यप्रसङ्गात् । यथा च शास्त्रोपदेशसामर्थ्यात् धर्माधर्मास्तित्वविज्ञानं कर्तुश्च देहान्तरसंबन्धविज्ञानं उत्पद्यते, तथा शास्त्रात् तस्य एव आत्मनः अविक्रियत्वाकर्तृत्वैकत्वादिविज्ञानं कस्मात् न उत्पद्यते इति प्रष्टव्याः ते । करणागोचरत्वात् इति चेत् — न, 'मनसैवानुद्रष्टव्यम्' [बृ. उ. ४.४.१९.] इति श्रुतेः । शास्त्राचार्योपदेशशमदमादिसंस्कृतं मनः आत्मदर्शने करणम् । तथा च तदधिगमाय अनुमाने आगमे च सति ज्ञानं न उत्पद्यते इति साहसमात्रं एतत् ॥

21.5. In this context some self-styled scholars affirm: None can acquire the knowledge "I am the Self", that is, the one who is a non-agent, is immutable, and free from the six transformations like birth and so forth—the knowledge by virtue of which the renunciation of all works is enjoined. This affirmation is untenable; for, it will stultify the Śāstraic (scriptural) teaching regarding the Self that "It is not born etc." (2.20). If, on the strength of Śāstraic teaching, the knowledge of the existence of righteousness and unrighteousness and of the relation of the agent's self with future bodies can arise, why will not, similarly from the *śāstra*, arise the knowledge of Self's immutability, non-agency, unity and so forth? When this question is put to these so-called scholars, they reply, "Because the Self is beyond the range of the senses." But this won't do. For, the *śruti* teaches that 'by the mind alone is the Self to be perceived' (BU.4.4.19). The mind, purified by the teachings of the *Śāstra* and the teacher, and by the control of itself and of the senses, is the means of Self-perception. Also, when inference and scripture are available for winning Self-knowledge, the bare assertion that such knowledge won't arise is merely presumptuous.

21.6. ज्ञानं च उत्पद्यमानं तद्विपरीतं अज्ञानं अवश्यं बाधते इति अभ्युपगन्तव्यम् । तत् च अज्ञानं दर्शितं 'हन्ता अहं, हतः अस्मि' इति, 'उभौ तौ न विजानीतः' [२.१९.] इति । अत्र च आत्मनः हननक्रियायाः कर्तृत्वं, कर्मत्वं, हेतुकर्तृत्वं च अज्ञानकृतं दर्शितम् । तत् च सर्वक्रियासु अपि समानं कर्तृत्वादेः अविद्याकृतत्वं, अविक्रियत्वात् आत्मनः । विक्रियावान् हि कर्ता आत्मनः कर्मभूतं अन्यं प्रयोजयति 'कुरु' इति — तत् एतत् अविशेषेण विदुषः सर्वक्रियासु कर्तृत्वं हेतुकर्तृत्वं च प्रतिषेधति भगवान् वासुदेवः विदुषः कर्माधिकाराभावप्रदर्शनार्थं 'वेदाविनाशिनं.....कथं स पुरुषः' इत्यादिना ।

21.6. It must be granted that the dawn of knowledge of the Self is bound to sublate its opposite, namely, ignorance. The content of that ignorance, "I am the slayer, I am the slain. . ." (2.19), has already been set forth. It was elucidated there that the states of the Self as agent, object and causal agent in regard to the action of slaying are the products of ignorance. The fact of the agency etc., as products of ignorance applies to all actions, because the Self is immutable. Only a mutable agent can cause another, its object, to act. To clarify the absence of any obligation to act for a Self-knower, in verses like 2.21 the Lord repudiates alike the agency, direct and causal, of the knower in respect of all actions.

21.7. क्व पुनः विदुषः अधिकारः इति ? एतत् उक्तं पूर्वमेव 'ज्ञानयोगेन सांख्यानाम्' [३.३.] इति । तथा च सर्वकर्मसंन्यासं वक्ष्यति 'सर्वकर्माणि मनसा' [५.१३.] इत्यादिना ।

ननु 'मनसा' इति वचनात् न वाचिकानां कायिकानां च संन्यासः इति चेत् — न, सर्वकर्माणि इति विशेषितत्वात् । मानसानां एव सर्वकर्मणां इति चेत् — न, मनोव्यापारपूर्वकत्वात् वाक्कायव्यापाराणां, मनोव्यापाराभावे तदनुपपत्तेः । शास्त्रीयाणां वाक्कायकर्मणां कारणानि मानसानि कर्माणि वर्जयित्वा अन्यानि सर्वकर्माणि मनसा संन्यस्य इति चेत् — न, 'नैव कुर्वन्न कारयन्' [५.१३.] इति विशेषणात् । सर्वकर्मसंन्यासः अयं भगवता उक्तः मरिष्यतः, न जीवतः इति चेत् — न, 'नवद्वारे पुरे देही...आस्ते' [५.१३.] इति विशेषणानुपपत्तेः । न हि सर्वकर्मसंन्यासेन मृतस्य तद्देहे आसनं संभवति । अकुर्वतः अकारयतश्च देहे संन्यस्य इति संबन्धः, न देहे आस्ते इति चेत् — न, सर्वत्र आत्मनः अविक्रियत्वावधारणात्, आसनक्रियायाः च अधिकरणापेक्षत्वात्, तदनपेक्षत्वात् च संन्यासस्य । संपूर्वस्तु न्यासशब्दः अत्र त्यागार्थः, न निक्षेपार्थः । तस्मात् गीताशास्त्रे आत्मज्ञानवतः संन्यास एव अधिकारः, न कर्मणि इति तत्र तत्र उपरिष्टात् आत्मज्ञानप्रकरणे दर्शयिष्यामः ॥

21.7. *Objection:* In regard to what, then, is there an obligation on the part of the knower of the Self? The answer has already been stated thus: "By means of the discipline of knowledge as regards the Sāṁkhyas" (*BG*.3.3). Accordingly the Lord enjoins the renunciation of all works in 5.13: 'Renouncing all works, mentally, etc." It may be objected: The term 'mentally' shows that the renunciation in question does not apply to the activities of speech and body. "No; for the term 'works' is qualified by the word 'all'". "But this may mean only 'all mental activities'". "No, the activities of speech and body also are preceded by those of the mind in the absence of which the former are inconceivable." "The verse, then, may be construed thus: renouncing mentally all activities other than the mental causes of the *śāstraic* activities of speech and body." "No, the Lord's statement has been qualified as follows: 'Neither performing nor causing to perform.'" A new objection may be raised: "The Lord enjoins renunciation of all works on one about to breathe his last, and not on the living." "No, in that case, the description, 'the embodied Self is seated in the nine-gated city' (5.13), will prove incompatible. One who dies after renunciation of all works cannot possibly be seated in his body." It may be objected: "The way the words are to be construed is not 'seated in the body', but 'depositing (*saṁnyasya*) in the body the sense of acting and causing to act.'"

Reply: "Not so; for both in the *BG* and the Upaniṣads the Self has been determined to be immutable. The act of sitting requires a place while that of renunciation does not. The term *nyāsa* preceded by the preposition *sam* means abandonment and not depositing. *Therefore, in the science of the* Gītā, *the Self-knower is obliged to renounce and not to perform works of all kinds.*" This doctrine will be further demonstrated wherever the topic of Self-knowledge is discussed.

22.0. प्रकृतं तु वक्ष्यामः । तत्र आत्मनः अविनाशित्वं प्रतिज्ञातम् । तत् किमिव इति ? उच्यते —

22.0. Let us however discuss what is immediately relevant. What has been asserted is the imperishability of the Self. What is it like? The answer follows:

वासांसि जीर्णानि यथा विहाय
नवानि गृह्णाति नरोऽपराणि ।
तथा शरीराणि विहाय जीर्णा-
न्यन्यानि संयाति नवानि देही ॥२२॥

22. Just as a man puts on fresh clothes after discarding worn-out ones, so does the embodied Self, discarding worn-out bodies, proceed to take up new ones.

22.1. वासांसि इति ॥ वासांसि वस्त्राणि जीर्णानि दुर्बलतां गतानि यथा लोके विहाय परित्यज्य नवानि अभिनवानि गृह्णाति उपादत्ते नरः पुरुषः अपराणि अन्यानि, तथा तद्वत् एव शरीराणि विहाय जीर्णानि अन्यानि संयाति संगच्छति नवानि देही आत्मा पुरुषवत् अविक्रियः एव इत्यर्थः ॥२२॥

22.1. As in the world, discarding worn-out clothes a man puts on new ones, so, discarding worn-out bodies, the 'embodied Self'—the immutable Spirit—proceeds to take up fresh bodies. This is the meaning.

23.0. कस्मात् अविक्रिय एवेति ? आह—

23.0. Why qualify the Spirit as 'immutable'? Answer:

नैनं छिन्दन्ति शस्त्राणि नैनं दहति पावकः ।
न चैनं क्लेदयन्त्यापो न शोषयति मारुतः ॥२३॥

23. Weapons do not cut It; fire does not burn It. Neither does water wet It; nor does the wind dry It.

23.1. नैनं छिन्दन्ति इति ॥ एनं प्रकृतं देहिनं न छिन्दन्ति शस्त्राणि, निरवयवत्वात् न अवयवविभागं कुर्वन्ति । शस्त्राणि अस्यादीनि । तथा न एनं दहति पावकः, अग्निः अपि न भस्मीकरोति । तथा—न च एनं क्लेदयन्ति आपः । अपां हि सावयवस्य वस्तुनः आर्द्रीभावकरणेन अवयवविश्लेषापादने सामर्थ्यम् । तत् न निरवयवे आत्मनि संभवति । तथा स्नेहवत् द्रव्यं स्नेहशोषणेन नाशयति वायुः । एनं तु आत्मानं न शोषयति मारुतः अपि ॥
यतः एवं तस्मात्—

23.1. 'It' means the embodied Self under discussion. Weapons do not cut It. Being impartite, It has no parts to be severed. Weapons—swords and so forth. Similarly, fire does not burn It, i.e., even fire does not reduce It to ashes. So, too, water does not wet It. Water has the power to wet or decompose only objects having parts. This process cannot apply to the partless Self. Likewise the wind destroys an oil-soaked material by drying up that oil. But this Self even the wind cannot dry up.

Therefore,

अच्छेद्योऽयमदाह्योऽयमक्लेद्योऽशोष्य एव च ।
नित्यः सर्वगतः स्थाणुरचलोऽयं सनातनः ॥२४॥

24. This Self cannot be cut, burned, wetted or dried. Eternal, all-pervasive, stable, immovable and everlasting is It.

24.1. अच्छेद्योऽयं इति ॥ यस्मात् अन्योन्यनाशहेतूनि भूतानि एनं आत्मानं नाशयितुं न उत्सहन्ते तस्मात् नित्यः । नित्यत्वात् सर्वगतः । सर्वगतत्वात् स्थाणुः इव स्थिरः इत्येतत् । स्थिरत्वात् अचलः अयं आत्मा, अतः सनातनः चिरन्तनः, न कारणात् कुतश्चित् निष्पन्नः, अभिनवः इत्यर्थः ।

24.1. As the elements that ruin one another cannot destroy this Self, therefore It is eternal. Being eternal, It is all-pervasive. Being all-pervasive, It is stable like a pillar. Being stable, this Self is immovable. As such It is everlasting, i.e. ancient, and not produced by any cause whatsoever. The sense is—It is ever new.

24.2. न एतेषां श्लोकानां पौनरुक्त्यं चोदनीयम्, यतः एकेन एव श्लोकेन आत्मनः नित्यत्वं अविक्रियत्वं चोक्तम् 'न जायते म्रियते वा' इत्यादिना । तत्र यदेव आत्मविषयं किंचित् उच्यते तत् एतस्मात् श्लोकार्थात् न अतिरिच्यते, किंचित् शब्दतः पुनरुक्तं किंचित् अर्थतः इति । दुर्बोधत्वात् आत्मवस्तुनः पुनः पुनः प्रसङ्गं आपाद्य शब्दान्तरेण तदेव वस्तु निरूपयति भगवान् वासुदेवः कथं नु नाम अव्यक्तं संसारिणां [असंसारित्व-] बुद्धिगोचरतां आपन्नं सत् संसारनिवृत्तये स्यात् इति ॥
किञ्च —

24.2. No objection may be raised against the verses (21-24) on the score of their redundancy, though it may be said that the eternality and immutability of the Self are affirmed in 2.20. Repetitions are obvious in 2.24. The explanation is that the Lord recurs to the theme of the recondite Self in order to elucidate it still more; for, He is anxious that even the empirical man should grasp the abstract truth about the Self and overcome the state of transmigratory life.

Further,

अव्यक्तोऽयमचिन्त्योऽयमविकार्योऽयमुच्यते ।
तस्मादेवं विदित्वैनं नानुशोचितुमर्हसि ॥२५॥

25. This Self is said to be unmanifest, imponderable and immutable. Knowing It to be such, you ought not to grieve for It.

25.1. अव्यक्तोऽयं इति ॥ सर्वकरणाविषयत्वात् न व्यज्यते इति अव्यक्तः अयं आत्मा । अतः एव अचिन्त्यः अयम् । यत् हि इन्द्रियगोचरः तत् चिन्ताविषयत्वं आपद्यते । अयं तु आत्मा अनिन्द्रियगोचरत्वात् अचिन्त्यः अविकार्यः अयम्, यथा क्षीरं दध्यातञ्चनादिना विकारि, न तथा अयं आत्मा । निरवयवत्वात् च अविक्रियः । न हि निरवयवं किञ्चित् विक्रियात्मकं दृष्टम् । अविक्रियत्वात् अविकार्यः अयं आत्मा उच्यते । तस्मात् एवं यथोक्तप्रकारेण एनं आत्मानं विदित्वा त्वं न अनुशोचितुं अर्हसि 'हन्ता अहं एषां, मया एते हन्यन्ते' इति ॥

25.1. Being beyond the ken of all the senses, the Self is not manifest; so It is unmanifest. For the same reason, one cannot ponder on It. Only what is accessible to the senses becomes an object of thought. Being beyond their ken, the Self is imponderable. It is immutable also. Unlike things like milk that change into curds, the Self does not undergo changes. Also because It is impartite, It is immutable. Nothing partless is known to mutate. As impartite, the Self is said to be immutable. Knowing the Self thus, you ought not to grieve thinking, "I am their slayer, by me are they slain."

26.0. आत्मनः अनित्यत्वं अभ्युपगम्य इदं उच्यते —

26.0. Granting for argument's sake the non-eternality of the Self, the following observation is made:

अथ चैनं नित्यजातं नित्यं वा मन्यसे मृतम् ।
तथापि त्वं महाबाहो नैवं शोचितुमर्हसि ॥२६॥

26. Even if you think that the Self is perpetually born

and perpetually dies, still, O hero! you ought not to grieve for It thus.

26.1. अथ चैनं इति ॥ अथ च इति अभ्युपगमार्थः । एनं प्रकृतं आत्मानं नित्यजातं लोकप्रसिद्धचा प्रत्यनेकशरीरोत्पत्ति जातो जातः इति वा मन्यसे, तथा प्रतितत्तद्विनाशं नित्यं वा मन्यसे मृतं मृतो मृतः इति; तथापि तथाभावेऽपि आत्मनि त्वं महाबाहो न एवं शोचितुं अर्हसि, जन्मवतः नाशः नाशवतः जन्म च इति एतौ अवश्यंभाविनौ इति यस्मात् ॥

तथा च सति —

26.1. The words *atha ca* have the sense, 'granted'. On the basis of popular notion if you think that this Self is perpetually born with the birth of the bodies It indwells, and that It perpetually dies with their destruction, still, O hero! you ought not to grieve with regard to It, because what takes birth undergoes destruction and what is destroyed necessarily takes birth.

Therefore:

जातस्य हि ध्रुवो मृत्युर्ध्रुवं जन्म मृतस्य च ।
तस्मादपरिहार्येऽर्थे न त्वं शोचितुमर्हसि ॥२७॥

27. Death is indeed certain for one who is born; and for one who dies, birth, too, is certain. Therefore, as regards this unavoidable sequence, you ought not to grieve.

27.1. जातस्य इति । जातस्य हि लब्धजन्मनः ध्रुवः अव्यभिचारी मृत्युः मरणं ध्रुवं जन्म मृतस्य च । तस्मात् अपरिहार्योऽयं जन्ममरणलक्षणः अर्थः [यस्मात् — तस्मात् अपरिहार्ये अर्थे न त्वं शोचितुं अर्हसि । जन्मवतो नाशः नाशवतो जन्म इति च स्वाभाविकश्चेत् अपरिहार्यः सः अर्थः ।] तस्मिन् अपरिहार्ये अर्थे न त्वं शोचितुं अर्हसि ॥

27.1. For one who is born, i.e. who has taken birth, death is an inevitable concomitant; so too is birth for one who dies. Therefore the sequence of birth and death is unavoidable, and is a matter of course. Hence you ought not to grieve for it.

28.0. कार्यकरणसङ्घातात्मकानि अपि भूतानि उद्दिश्य शोकः न युक्तः कर्तुं, यतः —

28.0. It is not reasonable to grieve for beings who are mere bundles of causes and effects, because,

अव्यक्तादीनि भूतानि व्यक्तमध्यानि भारत ।
अव्यक्तनिधनान्येव तत्र का परिदेवना ॥२८॥

28. The beginning of beings is unmanifest, O Bhārata prince! Their middle state is manifest. Their end, too, is unmanifest. In these circumstances, why lament?

28.1. अव्यक्तादीनि इति ॥ अव्यक्तादीनि अव्यक्तं अदर्शनं, अनुपलब्धिः आदिः येषां भूतानां पुत्रमित्रादिकार्यकरणसंघातात्मकानां तानि अव्यक्तादीनि भूतानि प्राक् उत्पत्तेः । उत्पन्नानि च प्राक् मरणात् व्यक्तमध्यानि । अव्यक्तनिधनानि एव पुनः अव्यक्तं अदर्शनं, निधनं, मरणं येषां तानि अव्यक्तनिधनानि । मरणात् ऊर्ध्वं अव्यक्तताम्, एव प्रतिपद्यन्ते इत्यर्थः । तथा चोक्तम्—"अदर्शनादापतितः पुनश्चादर्शनं गतः । नासौ तव न तस्य त्वं वृथा का परिदेवना" ॥ [स्त्रीपर्व. २. १३.] इति ॥ तत्र का परिदेवना को वा प्रलापः अदृष्टदृष्टप्रनष्टभ्रान्तिभूतेषु भूतेषु इत्यर्थः ॥

28.1. 'Unmanifest', i.e., unperceived or unknown, is the beginning of beings such as one's sons, friends, etc. These seem to be nothing but bundles of means and effects, organs and bodies. Before their appearance in time, these beings are unmanifest. Having appeared, their intermediate state, till their death, is manifest. Again, their end in death is 'unmanifest', unperceived. The idea is that after death they arrive at a state of unmanifestedness. So it has been affirmed in the MB (*Strī*, 2.13): "He has come from an unseen state and has returned to that state again. He does not belong to you nor do you, to him. Why, then, this vain lament?" In these circumstances where is the room for lamentation or vain speech as regards beings whose very essence is a delusion—who are unseen, then seen, and finally wiped out? This is the idea.

29.0. दुर्विज्ञेयः अयं प्रकृतः आत्मा; किं त्वाम् एव एकं उपालभे साधारणे भ्रान्तिनिमित्ते ? कथं दुर्विज्ञेयः अयं आत्मा इति ? अतः आह—

29.0. The Self in question is hard to comprehend. Why should I blame you alone when the cause of the delusion is universal? For, how hard it is to comprehend the Self! The Lord affirms:

आश्चर्यवत्पश्यति कश्चिदेन-
माश्चर्यवद्वदति तथैव चान्यः ।
आश्चर्यवच्चैनमन्यः शृणोति
श्रुत्वाप्येनं वेद न चैव कश्चित् ॥२९॥

29. One beholds It as a marvel. Similarly, another talks of it as a marvel. Yet another hears of It as a marvel. Even after hearing, none indeed knows It aright.

29.1. आश्चर्यवत् इति ॥ आश्चर्यवत् आश्चर्यं अदृष्टपूर्वं अद्भुतं अकस्मात् दृश्यमानं तेन तुल्यं आश्चर्यवत् आश्चर्यमिव एनं आत्मानं पश्यति कश्चित् । आश्चर्यवत् एनं वदति तथैव च अन्यः, आश्चर्यवत् च एनं अन्यः शृणोति । श्रुत्वा दृष्ट्वा उक्त्वा अपि एनं आत्मानं वेद न चैव कश्चित् ।

29.1. As a marvel: a marvel is what is unseen before, a wonder, that is unexpectedly seen. So, as a marvel, one beholds the Self. Similarly another talks of It as a marvel and yet another hears of It as a marvel. Having heard, seen, and spoken, too, none at all comprehends this Self.

29.2. अथवा—यः अयं आत्मानं पश्यति स आश्चर्यतुल्यः । यः वदति यः च शृणोति, सः अनेकसहस्रेषु कश्चिदेव भवति । अतः दुर्बोधः आत्मा इत्यभिप्रायः ॥

29.2. Or, he who sees the Self is, as it were, marvellous, He who speaks and he who hears about the Self is but one in in many thousands. Therefore the idea is that the Self is hard to comprehend.

30.0. अथ इदानी प्रकरणार्थं उपसहरति—

30.0. Now the theme in hand is wound up:

देही नित्यमवध्योऽयं देहे सर्वस्य भारत ।
तस्मात्सर्वाणि भूतानि न त्वं शोचितुमर्हसि ॥३०॥

30. This embodied Self (dwelling) in the bodies of all, O Bharata prince! is eternally indestructible. Therefore you ought not to grieve for any being at all.

30.1. देही इति ॥ देही शरीरी नित्यं सर्वदा सर्वावस्थासु अवध्यः निरवयवत्वात् नित्यत्वात् च तत्र अवध्योऽयं देहे शरीरे सर्वस्य सर्वगतत्वात् स्थावरादिषु स्थितोऽपि । सर्वस्य प्राणिजातस्य देहे वध्यमानेऽपि अयं देही न वध्यः यस्मात् तस्मात् भीष्मादीनि सर्वाणि भूतानि उद्दिश्य न त्वं शोचितुं अर्हसि ॥

30.1. 'Eternally'—at all times and in all states—the embodied Self is indestructible, because It is impartite and everlasting. The Self dwelling in no body may be slain. Being all-pervasive, the Self present even in stationary objects like trees is indestructible. Even when the bodies are slain, the Self remains indestructible; so you ought not to grieve for beings like Bhīṣma and the rest.

31.0. इह [२.३०.] परमार्थतत्त्वापेक्षायां शोको वा मोहो वा न संभवति इत्युक्तम् । न केवलं परमार्थतत्त्वापेक्षायाम् एव किंतु—

31.0. In 2.30 it is stated that in the light of the ultimate Truth neither grief nor delusion is possible. Not only in the light of ultimate Truth is this so, but also,

स्वधर्ममपि चावेक्ष्य न विकम्पितुमर्हसि ।
धर्म्याद्धि युद्धाच्छ्रेयोऽन्यत् क्षत्रियस्य न विद्यते ॥३१॥

31. Having regard to the law of your own life, you ought not to be perturbed. A Kṣatriya cannot have a greater good than a righteous battle.

31.1. स्वधर्मं इति ॥ स्वधर्मं अपि स्वः धर्मः क्षत्रियस्य धर्मः युद्धं तमपि अवेक्ष्य त्वं न विकम्पितुं प्रचलितुं अर्हसि धर्म्यात् क्षत्रियस्य स्वाभाविकात् धर्मात् आत्मस्वाभाव्यात् इत्यभिप्रायः । तच्च युद्धं पृथिवीजयद्वारेण धर्मार्थं प्रजारक्षणार्थं च इति परमं धर्म्यम् । धर्मात् अनपेतं धर्म्यम् । तस्मात् धर्म्यात् युद्धात् श्रेयः अन्यत् क्षत्रियस्य न विद्यते हि यस्मात् ॥

31.1. 'The law of your life'—your law is the Kṣatriya's law of battle. With due regard to that, you ought not to be perturbed or upset. The righteous law of battle is what is natural to, is the very nature of, a Kṣatriya. Such is the purport. And battle is for the sake of righteousness and people's security, through the conquest of the world. Hence it is eminently righteous, *dharmya*, which means what is not divorced from righteousness. Than a righteous battle, no greater good can accrue to a Kṣatriya. This is the reason for the assertion in 2.31.

32.0. कुतश्च तत् युद्धं कर्तव्यं इति ? उच्यते—

32.0. What additional reason is there for fighting? Answer:

यदृच्छया चोपपन्नं स्वर्गद्वारमपावृतम् ।
सुखिनः क्षत्रियाः पार्थ लभन्ते युद्धमीदृशम् ॥३२॥

32. An open gateway to heaven has, by a happy chance, offered itself to you. O Arjuna! For, fortunate Kṣatriyas alone gain an occasion to wage a war like this.

32.1. यदृच्छया इति । यदृच्छया च अप्रार्थितया उपपन्नं आगतं स्वर्गद्वारं अपावृतं उद्घाटितं ये एतत् ईदृशं युद्धं लभन्ते क्षत्रियाः हे पार्थ ! किं न सुखिनः ते ? ॥

32.1. 'By chance', i.e., what has come unsought. An open

gateway to heaven is this war. Are not Kṣatriyas happy to get a chance to wage a war like this?

33.0. एवं कर्तव्यताप्राप्तम् अपि —

33.0. This war has offered itself to you as your duty; still,

अथ चेत्त्वमिमं धर्म्यं संग्रामं न करिष्यसि ।
ततः स्वधर्मं कीर्तिं च हित्वा पापमवाप्स्यसि ॥३३॥

33. On the other hand, if you refuse to fight this righteous war, sacrificing both the law of your life and renown, you will incur sin.

33.1. अथ इति ॥ अथ चेत् त्वं इमं धर्म्यं धर्मादनपेतं विहितं संग्रामं युद्धं न करिष्यसि चेत्, ततः तदकरणात् स्वधर्मं कीर्तिं च महादेवादिसमागमनिमित्तां हित्वा केवलं पापं अवाप्स्यसि ॥

33.1. 'On the other hand' if you do not fight this war that is righteous, i.e. the war that conforms with the rules of righteousness, for that very reason, abandoning the 'law of your life' and forfeiting the 'renown' gained in your duel with Siva and the like, you will incur sin.

34.0. न केवलं स्वधर्मकीर्तिपरित्यागः—

34.0. Not only will you have given up the righteous law of your life and renown—

अकीर्तिं चापि भूतानि कथयिष्यन्ति तेऽव्ययाम् ।
संभावितस्य चाकीर्तिर्मरणादतिरिच्यते ॥३४॥

34. All will recount your everlasting infamy! For one honoured, infamy is worse than death.

34.1. अकीर्तिं इति ॥ अकीर्तिं च अपि भूतानि कथयिष्यन्ति ते तव अव्ययां दीर्घकालाम् । धर्मात्मा शूरः इत्येवमादिभिः गुणैः संभावितस्य च अकीर्तिः मरणात्

अतिरिच्यते, संभावितस्य च अकीर्तेः वरं मरणं इत्यर्थः ॥
किंच —

34.1. All will recount your everlasting 'infamy' for a long time to come. For one honoured so far for virtues like righteousness, bravery and so forth, infamy is worse than death. The sense is that for an honourable man death is preferable to infamy.

Besides,

भयाद्रणादुपरतं मंस्यन्ते त्वां महारथाः ।
येषां च त्वं बहुमतो भूत्वा यास्यसि लाघवम् ॥३५॥

35. Great heroes will deem that out of fear you withdrew from battle. You will fall in the esteem of those very heroes who have honoured you (so far).

35.1. भयात् इति ॥ भयात् कर्णादिभ्यः रणात् युद्धात् उपरतं निवृत्तं मंस्यन्ते चिन्तयिष्यन्ति न कृपया इति त्वां महारथाः दुर्योधनप्रभृतयः । [के मंस्यन्ते ? इति आह—] येषां च त्वं दुर्योधनादीनां बहुमतः बहुभिः गुणैः युक्तः इत्येवं मतः, बहुमतः भूत्वा पुनः त्वं यास्यसि लाघवं लघुभावम् ॥
किंच —

35.1. Due to fear of Karna and others you have withdrawn from battle and not due to compassion—so will mighty heroes like Duryodhana think. Who will think so ? Those very heroes, Duryodhana etc., who esteemed you as very rich in virtues. Now you will become light in their esteem.

Also,

अवाच्यवादांश्च बहून् वदिष्यन्ति तवाहिताः ।
निन्दन्तस्तव सामर्थ्यं ततो दुःखतरं नु किम् ॥३६॥

36. Your foes will hurl many unmentionable insults at you—foes bent on downgrading your competence. What can be more painful than that ?

36.1. अवाच्यवादान् इति ॥ अवाच्यवादान् अवक्तव्यान् वादान् च बहून् अनेकप्रकारान् वदिष्यन्ति तव अहिताः शत्रवः निन्दन्तः कुत्सयन्तः तव त्वदीयं सामर्थ्यम् निवातकवचादियुद्धनिमित्तम् । ततः तस्मात् निन्दाप्राप्तेः दुःखात् दुःखतरं नु किं ? ततः कष्टतरं दुःखं नास्ति इत्यर्थः ॥

36.1. 'Many unmentionable insults'—they are of many sorts that your foes will hurl at you, pouring scorn over your competence, established by your encounters with Nivāta-kavaca and others. Is there any pain worse than suffering such insults? That no pain can be more miserable is the sense.

37.0. युद्धे पुनः क्रियमाणे कर्णादिभि :—

37.0. On the other hand in the battle with Karṇa and the rest,

हतो वा प्राप्स्यसि स्वर्गं जित्वा वा भोक्ष्यसे महीम् ।
तस्मादुत्तिष्ठ कौन्तेय युद्धाय कृतनिश्चयः ॥३७॥

37. Getting slain, you will gain heaven; victorious, you will enjoy this world. Therefore, O son of Kunti! stand up, determined to fight.

37.1. हतो वा इति ॥ हतः वा प्राप्स्यसि स्वर्गं, हतः सन् स्वर्गं प्राप्स्यसि । जित्वा वा कर्णादीन् शूरान् भोक्ष्यसे महीम् । उभयथापि तव लाभः एव इत्यभिप्रायः । यतः एवं तस्मात् उत्तिष्ठ कौन्तेय ! युद्धाय कृतनिश्चयः 'जेष्यामि शत्रून्, मरिष्यामि वा' इति निश्चयं कृत्वा इत्यर्थः ॥

37.1. If you are slain you will win heaven. Victorious over heroes like Karṇa and others, you will enjoy this world. In either case, you stand only to gain—this is the Lord's idea. Such being the case, O son of Kunti! Get up, determined to fight i.e., having resolved, "I shall either conquer my foes or perish." This is the idea.

38.0. तत्र युद्धं स्वधर्मः इत्येवं युध्यमानस्य उपदेशम् इमं शृणु—

38.0. Listen to this instruction of Mine addressed to one who fights with the idea, 'fighting is the law of my life'.

सुखदुःखे समे कृत्वा लाभालाभौ जयाजयौ।
ततो युद्धाय युज्यस्व नैवं पापमवाप्स्यसि ॥३८॥

38. Looking with an equal eye on pleasure and pain, gain and loss, victory and defeat, strive to fight; thus will you incur no sin.

38.1. सुखदुःखे इति ॥ सुखदुःखे समे तुल्ये कृत्वा, रागद्वेषौ [अपि] अकृत्वा इत्येतत्। तथा लाभालाभौ जयाजयौ च समौ कृत्वा ततः युद्धाय युज्यस्व घटस्व। न एवं युद्धं कुर्वन् पापं अवाप्स्यसि [इति] एषः उपदेशः प्रासङ्गिकः ॥

38.1. 'Looking with an equal eye' on pleasure and pain, i.e., without attachment to the former or aversion to the latter. Similarly in respect of gain and loss, victory and defeat. Thus strive to fight. Fighting thus, you will not incur sin. This counsel is incidental.

39.0. शोकमोहापनये [नयनाय] लौकिकः न्यायः 'स्वधर्ममपि चावेक्ष्य' इत्याद्यैः श्लोकैः उक्तः, न तु तात्पर्येण। परमार्थदर्शनं तु इह प्रकृतम्। तच्च उक्तं उपसंह्रियते—एषा ते अभिहिता इति शास्त्रविषयविभागप्रदर्शनाय। इह हि प्रदर्शिते पुनः शास्त्रविषयविभागे उपरिष्ठात् 'ज्ञानयोगेन सांख्यानां कर्मयोगेन योगिनाम्' [३.३.] इति निष्ठाद्वयविषयं शास्त्रं सुखं प्रवर्तिष्यते, श्रोतारश्च विषयविभागेन सुखं ग्रहीष्यन्ति इति—अतः आह—

39.0. Considerations of worldly wisdom in (2.31-36) were cited with a view to dispelling grief and delusion, and not as ends in themselves. But what is relevant in this context is the perception of the ultimate Reality. What has already been remarked about it is concluded here (2.39) in order to set forth clearly the valid divisions of the Śāstra. For, once this division is set forth here, the later recurrence to it in 3.3 will easily make this Śāstra, comprising the two disciplines, fully operative, and the listeners will grasp it smoothly in all its details. Hence the Lord says:

एषा तेऽभिहिता सांख्ये बुद्धिर्योगे त्विमां शृणु।
बुद्ध्या युक्तो यया पार्थ कर्मबन्धं प्रहास्यसि ॥३९॥

39. This knowledge of the Sāṁkhya has so far been imparted to you. Now, listen to (a statement of) the knowledge of Yoga by acquiring which, O Arjuna! you will discard the bondage of works.

39.1. एषा ते इति ॥ एषा ते तुभ्यं अभिहिता उक्ता सांख्ये परमार्थवस्तुविवेकविषये बुद्धिः ज्ञानं साक्षात् शोकमोहादिसंसारहेतुदोषनिवृत्तिकारणम्, योगे तु तत्प्राप्त्युपाये निःसङ्गतया द्वन्द्वप्रहाणपूर्वकं ईश्वराराधनार्थे कर्मयोगे कर्मानुष्ठाने समाधियोगे च इमां अनन्तरम् एव उच्यमानां बुद्धिं शृणु । तां च बुद्धिं स्तौति प्ररोचनार्थम् — बुद्ध्या यया योगविषयया युक्तः हे पार्थ ! कर्मबन्धं कर्म एव धर्माधर्माख्यः बन्धः कर्मबन्धः तं प्रहास्यसि ईश्वरप्रसादनिमित्तज्ञानप्राप्त्या एव इत्यभिप्रायः ॥

किंच अन्यत् —

39.1. This knowledge of the Sāṁkhya or discrimination of metaphysical reality has been imparted to you. It is the cause of the removal of that flaw, attachment, aversion and so forth, which engenders the transmigratory life. Yoga leads to the knowledge of the Sāṁkhya. Yoga is Karma Yoga whose immediate purpose is the worship of God. It is to be performed after discarding, by the force of detachment, the pairs of opposites like heat and cold. Also it includes the achievement of *samādhi* or concentration. Now listen to the immediately following exposition of the knowledge of Yoga. This knowledge of Yoga is lauded to heighten the interest of the listeners. Acquiring this knowledge, O Arjuna! you will surely cast off the bondage of works. Note that action, righteous or unrighteous, is bondage and that Arjuna was to discard their bondage by virtue of knowledge attained through God's grace. This is the idea.

Moreover,

नेहाभिक्रमनाशोऽस्ति प्रत्यवायो न विद्यते ।
स्वल्पमप्यस्य धर्मस्य त्रायते महतो भयात् ॥४०॥

40. Here in the sphere of Karma Yoga there is no loss of

good beginnings; nor is there any sin involved. Even a little of this righteous law delivers one from great peril.

40.1. नेह इति ॥ न इह मोक्षमार्गे कर्मयोगे अभिक्रमनाशः अभिक्रमणं अभिक्रमः प्रारम्भः तस्य नाशः न अस्ति यथा कृष्यादेः । योगविषये प्रारम्भस्य न अनैकान्तिकफलत्वं इत्यर्थः । किं च — न अपि चिकित्सावत् प्रत्यवायः विद्यते । किं तु स्वल्पम् अपि अस्य धर्मस्य योगधर्मस्य अनुष्ठितं त्रायते रक्षति महतः भयात् संसारभयात् जन्ममरणादिलक्षणात् ॥

40.1. Here, in Karma Yoga, the path leading to liberation, there is no loss of the good beginnings one makes; unlike in the case of agriculture etc., the effects of these beginnings are conserved. And unlike what may happen in undergoing a medical treatment adverse reactions will not result from the practice of Karma Yoga. On the other hand, even a little of this Yogic discipline delivers one from the great peril of transmigratory life with its births, deaths and so forth.

41.0. या इयं सांख्ये बुद्धिः उक्ता योगे च वक्ष्यमाणलक्षणा सा —

41.0. In regard to the knowledge of Sāṁkhya already set forth, and of Yoga about to be set forth, note the following:

व्यवसायात्मिका बुद्धिरेकेह कुरुनन्दन ।
बहुशाखा ह्यनन्ताश्च बुद्धयोऽव्यवसायिनाम् ॥४१॥

41. The conviction as regards this (twofold Yoga), marked by resolution, is single; the convictions of the irresolute are indeed many-branched and endless, O Arjuna!

41.1. व्यवसाय इति ॥ व्यवसायात्मिका निश्चयस्वभावा एका एव बुद्धिः इतरविपरीतबुद्धिशाखाभेदस्य बाधिका, सम्यक् प्रमाणजनितत्वात्, इह श्रेयोमार्गे हे कुरुनन्दन । याः पुनः इतराः विपरीतबुद्धयः यासां शाखाभेदप्रचारवशात् अनन्तः अपारः अनुपरतः संसारः नित्यप्रततः विस्तीर्णः भवति, प्रमाणजनितविवेकबुद्धिनिमित्तवशाच्च उपरतासु अनन्तभेदबुद्धिषु संसारोऽपि उपरमते ताः बुद्धयः बहुशाखाः

बह्व्यः शाखाः यासां ताः बहुशाखाः, बहुभेदाः इत्येतत् । प्रतिशाखाभेदेन हि अनन्ताश्च बुद्धयः । केषाम् ? अव्यवसायिनां, प्रमाणजनितविवेकबुद्धिरहितानां इत्यर्थः ॥

41.1. Regarding the path to the supreme good, know O Arjuna! that there is only one conviction, marked by a firm resolution. It abolishes the plurality of other and opposed notions, because this conviction has been engendered by the right means of cognition. Many-branched are these opposed notions. Because of the pursuit of this play of multiplicity has arisen the infinite, shoreless, and ceaseless transmigratory life perpetually spread out before us. But upon their cessation, due to the discrimination that the right means of cognition engenders, transmigratory life comes to a halt. The differences among them being a legion, those opposed notions are many-branched. Each branch gives rise to infinite notions. For whom does this hold good? For the irresolute, who lack the conviction marked by discrimination and born of the means of right cognition.

42.0. येषां व्यवसायात्मिका बुद्धिः नास्ति ते —

42.0. Regarding those who lack resolute conviction:

यामिमां पुष्पितां वाचं प्रवदन्त्यविपश्चितः ।
वेदवादरताः पार्थ नान्यदस्तीति वादिनः ॥४२॥

42. They are the unwise who utter flowery speeches, O Arjuna! They revel in the letter of the Vedas and declare, "There is nothing else."

42.1. यामिमां इति ॥ यां इमां वक्ष्यमाणां पुष्पितां पुष्पितवृक्षः इव शोभमानां श्रूयमाणरमणीयां वाचं वाक्यलक्षणां प्रवदन्ति । के ? अविपश्चितः अल्पमेधसः अविवेकिनः इत्यर्थः । वेदवादरताः बह्वर्थवादफलसाधनप्रकाशकेषु वेदवाक्येषु रताः हे पार्थ ! न अन्यत् स्वर्गपश्वादिफलसाधनेभ्यः कर्मभ्यः अस्ति इति एवं वादिनः वदनशीलाः ॥

ते च —

42.1. They utter speech pleasant to hear and splendid like a tree in flower. Who are they? The unwise, men of feeble minds who lack in discrimination. They are addicted to the Vedic words which glorify or condemn and set forth works as well as modes of their implementation. They maintain there is nothing in the Vedas other than rites which promise heaven, cattle, wealth and the like.

And further:

कामात्मानः स्वर्गपरा जन्मकर्मफलप्रदाम् ।
क्रियाविशेषबहुलां भोगैश्वर्यगतिं प्रति ॥४३॥

43. Desire-ridden, heaven-bent, they utter words which lead to births and actions replete with specific rites that yield enjoyments and power.

43.1. कामात्मानः इति ॥ कामात्मानः कामस्वभावाः, कामपराः इत्यर्थः । स्वर्गपराः, स्वर्गः परः पुरुषार्थः येषां ते स्वर्गपराः स्वर्गप्रधानाः । जन्मकर्मफलप्रदां, कर्मणः फलं कर्मफलं, जन्म एव कर्मणः फलं जन्मकर्मफलं तत् प्रददाति इति जन्मकर्मफलप्रदा, तां वाचम्—प्रवदन्ति इति अनुषज्यते । क्रियाविशेषबहुलां, क्रियाणां विशेषाः क्रियाविशेषाः, ते बहुला यस्यां वाचि तां, स्वर्गपशुपुत्राद्यर्थाः यया वाचा बाहुल्येन प्रकाश्यन्ते । भोगैश्वर्यगतिं प्रति, भोगश्च ऐश्वर्यं च भोगैश्वर्ये, तयोः गतिः प्राप्तिः भोगैश्वर्यगतिः, तां प्रति साधनभूताः ये क्रियाविशेषाः, तद्बहुलां तां वाचं प्रवदन्तः मूढाः संसारे परिवर्तन्ते इत्यभिप्रायः ॥

तेषां च—

43.1. They are 'desire-ridden', i.e., they are embodiments of cravings. That they are enslaved by cravings is the sense. They are "heaven-bent", for their supreme goal in life is heaven. Heaven comes first in their scheme of things. Their speech points to 'births' which are the fruits of Veda-enjoined actions. That speech enjoins specific acts by which are won things like heaven, progeny and animal wealth. Again these specific acts are the means by which enjoyments and power are won. The idea is that these deluded persons, who utter Vedic words laying down rites, flounder in transmigratory life.

The fact is:

भोगैश्वर्यप्रसक्तानां तयाऽपहृतचेतसाम् ।
व्यवसायात्मिका बुद्धिः समाधौ न विधीयते ॥४४॥

44. In the case of those who have given themselves up to pleasures and power and whose minds have been enslaved by the words of the Vedas that command rites, there is no chance of the resolute mind addressing itself to concentration.

44.1. भोग इति ॥ भोगैश्वर्यप्रसक्तानां, भोगः कर्तव्यं ऐश्वर्यं च इति भोगैश्वर्ययोः एव प्रणयवतां तदात्मभूतानां । तया क्रियाविशेषबहुलया वाचा अपहृतचेतसां आच्छादितविवेकप्रज्ञानां व्यवसायात्मिका सांख्ये योगे वा या बुद्धिः, सा समाधौ समाधीयते अस्मिन् पुरुषोपभोगाय सर्वं इति समाधिः अन्तःकरणं — बुद्धिः, तस्मिन् समाधौ न विधीयते न भवति इत्यर्थः ॥

44.1. Of those who love enjoyments and power that constitute the very substance of their selves, over whose sense of discrimination has fallen the shroud of Vedic words enjoining specific rites, the resolute mind or the conviction in respect of Sāṁkhya or Yoga does not influence the inner sense (*antaḥkaraṇa*). *Samādhi* in the text means the inner sense, since all things are reflected therein for promoting the experience of the self.

45.0. ये एवं विवेकबुद्धिरहिताः तेषां कामात्मनां यत् फलं तत् आह —

45.0. Next is set forth the fruit accruing to these desire-ridden people devoid of discrimination:

त्रैगुण्यविषया वेदा निस्त्रैगुण्यो भवार्जुन ।
निर्द्वन्द्वो नित्यसत्त्वस्थो निर्योगक्षेम आत्मवान् ॥४५॥

45. The scope of the Vedas embraces the three-fold force of nature, O Arjuna! Go beyond these three forces. He who has mastered the self rises beyond all dualities,

beyond acquisition and all states of welfare, and rests in eternal placidity.

45.1. त्रैगुण्य इति ।। त्रैगुण्यविषयाः— त्रैगुण्यं संसारः विषयः प्रकाशयितव्यः येषां ते वेदाः त्रैगुण्यविषयाः । त्वं तु निस्त्रैगुण्यः भव अर्जुन, निष्कामः भव इत्यर्थः निर्द्वन्द्वः, सुखदुःखहेतू सत्प्रतिपक्षौ पदार्थौ द्वन्द्वशब्दवाच्यौ, ततः निर्गतः निर्द्वन्द्वः भव। नित्यसत्त्वस्थः सदा सत्त्वगुणाश्रितः भव । तथा निर्योगक्षेमः अनुपात्तस्य उपादानं योगः, उपात्तस्य रक्षणं क्षेमः । योगक्षेमप्रधानस्य श्रेयसि प्रवृत्तिः दुष्करा इति अतः निर्योगक्षेमः भव । आत्मवान् अप्रमत्तः च भव । एष तव उपदेशः स्वधर्मं अनुतिष्ठतः ।।

45.1. The scope of the *guṇas* (Nature's forces or constituents) covers all transmigratory life. It is what the Vedas set forth. On the other hand, you, Arjuna, must go beyond their scope i.e., rise above all desires. Dualities are mutually opposed to each other, causing pleasure and pain. Go beyond them all. He who always resorts to the Sattva-constituent of nature rests in eternal placidity. *Yoga* here means the securing of what has not been made one's own, and *kṣema* the securing and guarding of what has been acquired. Bent upon acquiring and preserving, one will find it hard to strive for spiritual well-being. Therefore go beyond seizing and guarding. Master the self, and be vigilant. This is the instruction for you who are to discharge your duty.

46.0. सर्वेषु वेदोक्तेषु कर्मसु यानि उक्तानि अनन्तानि फलानि तानि न अपेक्ष्यन्ते चेत्, किमर्थं तानि ईश्वराय इति अनुष्ठीयन्ते इति ? उच्यते, शृणु —

46.0. If the countless fruits of actions laid down by all the Vedas are not to be gathered by the agent, why should those actions be performed at all as offerings to God? Listen to the answer:

यावानर्थ उदपाने सर्वतः संप्लुतोदके ।
तावान् सर्वेषु वेदेषु ब्राह्मणस्य विजानतः ।।४६।।

46. For a knower of Brahman who has realised the

ultimate Truth, there is as much profit from all the Vedas as there is profit from reservoirs when all around there is an inundation.

46.1. यावान् इति ॥ यथा लोके कूपतडागाद्यनेकस्मिन् उदपाने परिच्छिन्नोदके यावान् यावत्परिमाणः स्नानपानादिः अर्थः फलं प्रयोजनं सः सर्वः अर्थः सर्वतः संप्लुतोदके तावान् एव संपद्यते, तत्र अन्तर्भवति इत्यर्थः । एवं तावान् तावत्परिमाणः एव संपद्यते सर्वेषु वेदेषु वेदोक्तेषु कर्मसु यः अर्थः यत् कर्मफलं सः अर्थः ब्राह्मणस्य संन्यासिनः परमार्थतत्त्वं विजानतः यः अर्थः यत् विज्ञानफलं सर्वतः संप्लुतोदकस्थानीयं तस्मिन् तावान् एव संपद्यते — तत्रैव अन्तर्भवतीत्यर्थः । 'सर्वं तत् अभिसमेति यत् किञ्च प्रजाः साधु कुर्वन्ति यस्तद्वेद यत् स वेद' [छा. उ. ४. १. ४.] इति श्रुतेः । 'सर्वं कर्माखिलम्' [४. ३३.] इति च वक्ष्यति । तस्मात् प्राक् ज्ञाननिष्ठाधिकारप्राप्तेः कर्मणि अधिकृतेन कूपतडागाद्यर्थस्थानीयं अपि कर्म कर्तव्यम् ॥

तव च —

46.1. Just as in the world, various purposes like bathing and drinking are served by reservoirs of water like a well, a tank and so forth, and they are all, in the same measure, served by a widespread flood, so too is the case as regards the purpose of the Vedas. Here 'Vedas' means the actions enjoined by them. The fruits of such actions are all included in the fruit of the realization of Truth won by an all-renouncing mendicant, a Brāhmaṇa. This latter fruit corresponds to the wide-spread flood of waters. Vide the *śruti*: So whatever good thing creatures do, all that goes to him who knows what he knows (*CU*.4.1.4). *BG* (4.33) also declares "All works in their totality. . . ." Therefore, before acquiring the fitness for practising the discipline of knowledge those who are called upon to work, must do such works as promote limited ends, like those served by wells, tanks, and so forth.

As for you:

कर्मण्येवाधिकारस्ते मा फलेषु कदाचन ।
मा कर्मफलहेतुर्भूर्मा ते सङ्गोऽस्त्वकर्मणि ॥४७॥

47. To work alone have you the right and never to the fruits (of works). Don't be impelled by the fruits of works; (at the same time) don't be tempted to withdraw from works.

47.1. कर्मणि इति ।। कर्मणि एव अधिकारः, न ज्ञाननिष्ठायां ते तव । तत्र च कर्म कुर्वतः मा फलेषु अधिकारः अस्तु, कर्मफलतृष्णा मा भूत् कदाचन कस्यांचित् अपि अवस्थायां इत्यर्थः । यदा कर्मफले तृष्णा ते स्यात् तदा कर्मफलप्राप्तेः हेतुः स्याः, एवं मा कर्मफलहेतुः भूः । यदा हि कर्मफलतृष्णाप्रयुक्तः कर्मणि प्रवर्तते तदा कर्मफलस्य एव जन्मनः हेतुः भवेत् । यदि कर्मफलं न इष्यते, किं कर्मणा दुःखरूपेण ? इति मा ते तव सङ्गः अस्तु अकर्मणि अकरणे प्रीतिः मा भूत् ।।

47.1. You have right only to perform work and not to undertake the discipline of knowledge. While doing works, do not think you have the right to claim their fruits. Never, in any state of life whatsoever, should you crave for the fruits of your works—this is the idea. When you crave for the fruits of your works, you make yourselves liable to reap those fruits; (but) you should never be the cause of such fruit-gathering, for when one works, impelled by the craving for fruits, one has to reap the fruits of such works, namely, birth in the world. 'If the fruits of works are not to be desired, why should painful works be undertaken at all?' This thought should not tempt you, Arjuna, to withdraw from all works, either.

48.0. यदि कर्मफलप्रयुक्तेन न कर्तव्यं कर्म, कथं तर्हि कर्तव्यं इति ? उच्यते —

48.0. If work, impelled by the desire for its fruit, is not to be performed, how should it, then, be performed? Listen:

योगस्थः कुरु कर्माणि सङ्गं त्यक्त्वा धनञ्जय ।
सिद्ध्यसिद्ध्योः समो भूत्वा समत्वं योग उच्यते ।।४८।।

48. Giving up attachment and established in Yoga, with evenness of mind in success and failure, perform works, O Arjuna. This evenness is Yoga.

48.1. योगस्थः इति ॥ योगस्थः सन् कुरु कर्माणि केवलं ईश्वरार्थं; तत्रापि 'ईश्वरो मे तुष्यतु' इति सङ्गं त्यक्त्वा धनञ्जय । फलतृष्णाशून्येन क्रियमाणे कर्मणि सत्त्वशुद्धिजा ज्ञानप्राप्तिलक्षणा सिद्धिः, तद्विपर्ययजा असिद्धिः, तयोः सिद्ध्यसिद्ध्योः अपि समः तुल्यः भूत्वा कुरु कर्माणि । कोऽसौ योगः यत्रस्थः कुरु इति उक्तम् ? इदं एव तत् — सिद्ध्यसिद्ध्योः समत्वं योगः उच्यते ॥

48.1. Established in Yoga, do works, O Arjuna! just for the sake of God. Give up even the desire to please God with such work. 'Success' here is the attainment of knowledge born of mental purity, which, performance of works without craving for their fruits produces. 'Failure' is due to works of the opposite sort. As regards both these, let there be evenness of mind and then do works. What is this Yoga, established in which Arjuna is asked to do works? It is this very same thing—evenness of mind, both in success and in failure.

49.0. यत् पुनः समत्वबुद्धियुक्तं ईश्वराराधनार्थं कर्म [उक्तं] एतस्मात् कर्मणः—

49.0. Compared with this sort of work, performed with evenness of mind, as an act of worship of God.

दूरेण ह्यवरं कर्म बुद्धियोगाद्धनञ्जय ।
बुद्धौ शरणमन्विच्छ कृपणाः फलहेतवः ॥४९॥

49. Work impelled by the desire for the fruit is indeed far inferior, evenness of mind being far above it. O Arjuna! Take refuge in the evenness of intelligence. Pitiful are those impelled by the desire for the fruits of works.

49.1. दूरेण इति ॥ दूरेण अतिविप्रकर्षेण हि अवरं अधमं निकृष्टं कर्म फलार्थिना क्रियमाणं बुद्धियोगात् समत्वबुद्धियुक्तात् कर्मणः, जन्ममरणादिहेतुत्वात् । हे धनञ्जय, यतः एवं ततः योगविषयायां बुद्धौ तत्परिपाकजायां वा सांख्यबुद्धौ शरणं आश्रयं अभयप्राप्तिकारणं अन्विच्छ प्रार्थयस्व, परमार्थज्ञानशरणः भव इत्यर्थः । यतः अवरं कर्म कुर्वाणाः कृपणाः दीनाः फलहेतवः फलतृष्णाप्रयुक्ताः सन्तः 'यो वा

एतदक्षरं गार्ग्यविदित्वाऽस्माल्लोकात्प्रैति स कृपणः' [बृ. उ. ३.८.१०.] इति श्रुतेः ॥

49.1. Indeed, far inferior is work done by one impelled by desire for its fruit, compared with work inspired by the intelligence of evenness (Karma Yoga), because the former is the cause of birth, death and so forth. Therefore, Arjuna! resort to the intelligence of this Yoga of evenness, or to that of Sāṁkhya, the mature form of the former. It will produce fearlessness. "Seek refuge in the knowledge of the supreme Reality"—this is the idea. Those who do inferior work are pitiful. Impelled by cravings for the fruits of works, they have to reap them i.e., undergo transmigratory life. *Vide*: "Gārgi! Pitiful is he who departs from this world before knowing that imperishable Ātman" (*BU*.3.8.10).

50.0. समत्वबुद्धियुक्तः सन् स्वधर्मं अनुतिष्ठन् यत् फलं प्राप्नोति तत् शृणु —

50.0. Know what fruit is gained by him who conforms to the law of his life with the intelligence of mind's evenness:

बुद्धियुक्तो जहातीह उभे सुकृतदुष्कृते ।
तस्माद्योगाय युज्यस्व योगः कर्मसु कौशलम् ॥५०॥

50. With the intelligence of evenness one discards (in this world) both good and evil works (i.e. the merits and demerits of works). Therefore strive to secure this Yoga; Yoga is skill in works.

50.1. बुद्धि इति ॥ बुद्धियुक्तः समत्वविषयया बुद्ध्या युक्तः बुद्धियुक्तः सः जहाति परित्यजति इह अस्मिन् लोके उभे सुकृतदुष्कृते पुण्यपापे सत्त्वशुद्धिज्ञानप्राप्तिद्वारेण यतः, तस्मात् समत्वबुद्धियोगाय युज्यस्व घटस्व । योगः हि कर्मसु कौशलं स्वधर्माख्येषु कर्मसु वर्तमानस्य या सिद्ध्यसिद्ध्योः समत्वबुद्धिः ईश्वरार्पितचेतस्तया तत् कौशलं कुशलभावः । तद्धि कौशलं यत् बन्धस्वभावानि अपि कर्माणि समत्वबुद्ध्या स्वभावात् निवर्तन्ते । तस्मात् समत्वबुद्धियुक्तः भव त्वम् ॥

यस्मात् —

50.1. Rich in the intelligence of evenness, one discards in this world both good and evil works, i.e. merit and demerit, by the process of purifying the mind and attaining knowledge. Therefore, strive to win this intelligence of evenness. Yoga is skill in the performance of works. That skill consists in maintaining the evenness of mind in success and failure in the performance of works as one's duty, with the mind dedicated to God. With such dedication should one work, conforming to the law of one's life. That indeed is skill by which works that bind cease to do so due to the intelligence of evenness. Therefore, unite with the intelligence of evenness.

For,

कर्मजं बुद्धियुक्ता हि फलं त्यक्त्वा मनीषिणः ।
जन्मबन्धविनिर्मुक्ताः पदं गच्छन्त्यनामयम् ॥५१॥

51. Wise men, united with the intelligence of evenness, discard, indeed, the fruits of works; they are liberated from the bondage of birth and attain the status which is free from all sufferings.

51.1. कर्मजं इति ॥ 'कर्मज फलं त्यक्त्वा' इति व्यवहितेन संबन्धः इष्टानिष्ट-देहप्राप्तिः कर्मजं फलं कर्मभ्यः जातं बुद्धियुक्ताः समत्वबुद्धियुक्ताः सन्तः हि यस्मात् फलं त्यक्त्वा परित्यज्य मनीषिणः ज्ञानिनः भूत्वा, जन्मबन्धविनिर्मुक्ताः जन्म एव बन्धः जन्मबन्धः, तेन विनिर्मुक्ताः जीवन्तः एव जन्मबन्धात् विनिर्मुक्ताः सन्तः, पदं परमं विष्णोः मोक्षाख्यं गच्छन्ति अनामयम्, सर्वोपद्रवरहितं इत्यर्थः ।

51.1. "Discarding the fruits of works"—thus these separate words (in the verse) have to be construed. The fruit of works is pleasant or unpleasant embodiment; *karmaja* (born of works) means that which works yield. "Wise men" are those who possess the intelligence of evenness; they discard the fruits of works, and, liberated from the bondage of birth—for birth is bondage—attain the supreme status of Viṣṇu, i.e., emancipation. This status is free from all kinds of sufferings.

51.2. अथवा — 'बुद्धियोगाद्धनञ्जय' इत्यारभ्य परमार्थदर्शनलक्षणा एव सर्वतः संप्लुतोदकस्थानीया कर्मयोगजसत्त्वशुद्धिजनिता बुद्धिः दर्शिता, साक्षात् सुकृतदुष्कृतप्रहाणादिहेतुत्वश्रवणात् ॥

51.2. Alternatively, in verses from 49 onwards, what is set forth is knowledge, the realization of the metaphysical Reality, consequent on the purification of the mind through Karma Yoga. This knowledge corresponds to "the inundation all around" (2.46), because it is held to obliterate all deeds, good and evil, alike.

52.0. योगानुष्ठानजनितसत्त्वशुद्धिजा बुद्धिः कदा प्राप्यते इति ? उच्यते —

52.0. When shall this intelligence (or knowledge), born of mind's purification, be won, mental purification itself being the product of Karma Yoga? Listen:

यदा ते मोहकलिलं बुद्धिर्व्यतितरिष्यति ।
तदा गन्तासि निर्वेदं श्रोतव्यस्य श्रुतस्य च ॥५२॥

52. When your intellect goes beyond the mist of delusion, you will win detachment from both what is to be heard and what has been heard.

52.1. यदा इति ॥ यदा यस्मिन् काले ते तव मोहकलिलं मोहात्मकं अविवेकरूपं कालुष्यं, येन आत्मानात्मविवेकबोधं कलुषीकृत्य विषयं प्रति अन्तःकरणं प्रवर्तते, तत् तव बुद्धिः व्यतितरिष्यति व्यतिक्रमिष्यति, अतिशुद्धभावं आपत्स्यते इत्यर्थः । तदा तस्मिन् काले गन्तासि प्राप्स्यसि निर्वेदं वैराग्यं श्रोतव्यस्य श्रुतस्य च, तदा श्रोतव्यं श्रुतं च ते निष्फलं प्रतिभाति [प्रतिपद्यते] इत्यभिप्रायः ॥

52.1. When your intellect goes beyond the mist of non-discrimination, whose essence is the delusion obscuring the distinction between the Self and the non-Self, and drives the inner sense towards the sphere of objects, i.e., when your intellect is thoroughly cleansed, you will reach detachment from both 'what is to be heard and what has been heard'. In other words, both knowledge already gained and that which remains to be gained will strike you as unprofitable. This is the idea.

53.0. मोहकलिलात्ययद्वारेण लब्धात्मविवेकजप्रज्ञः कदा कर्मयोगजं फलं परमार्थयोगं अवाप्स्यामि इति चेत्, तत् शृणु —

53.0. If you ask when, having won the discriminative knowledge of the Self through the destruction of the mist of delusion, you will attain to Yoga proper (*paramārthayoga*), which attainment is the real fruit of Karma Yoga—here is the answer:

श्रुतिविप्रतिपन्ना ते यदा स्थास्यति निश्चला ।
समाधावचला बुद्धिस्तदा योगमवाप्स्यसि ॥५३॥

53. You will win this supreme Yoga when your intellect, bewildered by Vedic texts, becomes firm and unwavering in concentration.

53.1. श्रुतिविप्रतिपन्ना इति ॥ श्रुतिविप्रतिपन्ना अनेकसाध्यसाधनसंबन्धप्रकाशनश्रुतिभिः श्रवणैः प्रवृत्तिनिवृत्तिलक्षणैः विप्रतिपन्ना नानाप्रतिपन्ना [श्रुतिविप्रतिपन्ना] विक्षिप्ता सती ते तव बुद्धिः यदा यस्मिन् काले स्थास्यति स्थिरीभूता भविष्यति निश्चला विक्षेपचलनवर्जिता सती समाधौ — समाधीयते चित्तम् अस्मिन् इति समाधिः आत्मा, तस्मिन् आत्मनि इत्येतत् । [सा अपि] अचला, तत्रापि विकल्पवर्जिता इत्येतत् । बुद्धिः अन्तःकरणम् । तदा तस्मिन् काले योगं अवाप्स्यसि विवेकप्रज्ञां समाधिं प्राप्स्यसि ॥

53.1. 'Bewildered by Vedic Texts' refers to the intellect distracted by the manifold directions of the Vedic texts. These elucidate the links between the various ends and means, involving activities and abstention therefrom. Becoming stable and stirless, it rests in concentration (*samādhi*). Concentration is the Spirit, the Self, in which the mind is concentrated. It (the concentrated mind) is unwavering or free from all distractions. Intellect (*buddhi*) is the inner sense. Then will you win union, the wisdom born of discrimination. This is concentration, the content of the Spirit.

54.0. प्रश्नबीजं प्रतिलभ्य अर्जुनः उवाच लब्धसमाधिप्रज्ञस्य लक्षणबुभुत्सया—

54.0. Here arose an occasion for a question. Wishing to know the characteristics of (the sage) who has won the wisdom that concentration yields.

अर्जुन उवाच :

स्थितप्रज्ञस्य का भाषा समाधिस्थस्य केशव ।
स्थितधीः किं प्रभाषेत किमासीत व्रजेत किम् ॥५४॥

Arjuna said :

54. How can a man of stable wisdom, anchored in concentration, be described, O Kṛṣṇa? How does a man of steadfast intelligence speak? How does he sit? How walk?

54.1. स्थितप्रज्ञस्य इति ॥ स्थिता प्रतिष्ठिता 'अहं अस्मि परं ब्रह्म' इति प्रज्ञा यस्य स स्थितप्रज्ञः, तस्य का भाषा भाषणं वचनं, कथं असौ परैः भाष्यते समाधिस्थस्य समाधौ स्थितस्य हे केशव । स्थितधीः स्थितप्रज्ञः स्वयं वा किं प्रभाषेत ? किं आसीत ? व्रजेत किं ? आसनं व्रजनं वा तस्य कथं ? इत्यर्थः । स्थितप्रज्ञस्य लक्षणं अनेन श्लोकेन पृच्छ्यते ॥

54.1. A man of stable *prajñā* (wisdom) is he who has the assured wisdom born of the experience, "I am the Supreme Brahman." Of such a man, what is the description? How is he spoken of by others? O Kṛṣṇa! How would he himself speak? How would he walk? In what manner does he sit or move about? What is requested in this verse is a definition (of the sage) of stable wisdom.

55.0. यो हि आदितः एव संन्यस्य कर्माणि ज्ञानयोगनिष्ठायां प्रवृत्तः, यश्च कर्मयोगेन, तयोः 'प्रजहाति' इति आरभ्य आ अध्यायपरिसमाप्तेः स्थितप्रज्ञलक्षणं साधनं च उपदिश्यते । सर्वत्रैव हि अध्यात्मशास्त्रे कृतार्थलक्षणानि यानि तान्येव साधनानि उपदिश्यन्ते, यत्नसाध्यत्वात् । यानि यत्नसाध्यानि साधनानि लक्षणानि च भवन्ति तानि श्रीभगवान् उवाच —

55.0. In the verses from 2.55 to the end of the chapter are taught the characteristics of, and the means employed by, the sage of stable wisdom who concerns himself with the discipline of knowledge. He does so either after renouncing actions right from the beginning, or he may have become a sage practising Karma Yoga. For, in all texts on the science of the Spirit, the very characteristics of the perfected sage have been set forth as means, too, to be cultivated by the practitioner of the life of the Spirit. Thus, indeed, are these characteristics acquired through directed effort. The blessed Lord recounted these characteristics that are at once the means, demanding efforts on the part of the aspirant, and also the marks of the accomplished sage. So the Lord said:

श्रीभगवानुवाच :

प्रजहाति यदा कामान् सर्वान् पार्थ मनोगतान् ।
आत्मन्येवात्मना तुष्टः स्थितप्रज्ञस्तदोच्यते ॥५५॥

The blessed Lord said:

55. When one wholly discards desires of the heart and becomes exclusively content with the Self, one is called a sage of stable wisdom. O Arjuna!

55.1. प्रजहाति इति ॥ प्रजहाति प्रकर्षेण जहाति परित्यजति यदा यस्मिन् काले सर्वान् समस्तान् कामान् इच्छाभेदान् हे पार्थ, मनोगतान्, मनसि प्रविष्टान् हृदि प्रविष्टान् । सर्वकामपरित्यागे तुष्टिकारणाभावात् शरीरधारणनिमित्तशेषे च सति उन्मत्तप्रमत्तस्य इव प्रवृत्तिः प्राप्ता, इत्यतः उच्यते — आत्मनि एव प्रत्यगात्मस्वरूपे एव आत्मना स्वेनैव बाह्यलाभनिरपेक्षः तुष्टः परमार्थदर्शनामृतरसलाभेन अन्यस्मात् अलंप्रत्ययवान् स्थितप्रज्ञः स्थिता प्रतिष्ठिता आत्मानात्मविवेकजा प्रज्ञा यस्य सः स्थितप्रज्ञः विद्वान् तदा उच्यते । त्यक्तपुत्रवित्त-

लोकैषणः संन्यासी आत्मारामः — आत्मक्रीडः — स्थितप्रज्ञः इत्यर्थः ॥
किञ्च —

55.1. One "wholly discards" when, in an eminent degree, one gives up all desires, i.e. all forms of desire which fill the heart. It may be objected: "But when all desires are discarded, causes of satisfaction dry up, still there would remain the need to sustain the body. What follows then may well be aimless movements as of a person deranged." So it is stated: "Content with the Self." The idea is that contentment should be due to the Self alone, independently of external gains. Since he has tasted the immortalizing nectar of the knowledge of supreme Reality, he is indifferent to everything else. His wisdom, born of discrimination between the Self and the non-Self, has become stabilized. Such a sage is said to have stable wisdom. The idea is that the monk, who has renounced the desire for progeny, wealth, and reputation, who rejoices and revels in the Self, is the sage of stable wisdom.

Besides,

दुःखेष्वनुद्विग्नमनाः सुखेषु विगतस्पृहः ।
वीतरागभयक्रोधः स्थितधीर्मुनिरुच्यते ॥५६॥

56. The silent sage is said to have stable wisdom when sufferings no longer perturb his mind, when he ceases to cling to pleasures, and he is rid of attachment, fear and wrath.

56.1. दुःखेषु इति ॥ दुःखेषु आध्यात्मिकादिषु [प्राप्तेषु] अनुद्विग्नं न प्रक्षुभितं दुःखप्राप्तौ मनः यस्य सोऽयं अनुद्विग्नमनाः । तथा सुखेषु प्राप्तेषु विगता स्पृहा तृष्णा यस्य, न अग्निः इव इन्धनाद्याधाने, सुखानि अनुविवर्धते स विगतस्पृहः । वीतरागभयक्रोधः रागश्च भयं च क्रोधश्च वीताः विगताः यस्मात् सः वीतरागभयक्रोधः स्थितधीः स्थितप्रज्ञः मुनिः संन्यासी तदा उच्यते ॥
किञ्च —

56.1. He whose mind, even amidst the threefold suffering,

stays unperturbed is the *anudvignamanāḥ*. When pleasures come, he does not crave for them, his mind being unlike the fire fed on fuel. From him have departed attachment, fear and wrath. He, the silent sage and renouncer, is said to be the man of stable wisdom.

Moreover:

यः सर्वत्रानभिस्नेहस्तत्तत्प्राप्य शुभाशुभम् ।
नाभिनन्दति न द्वेष्टि तस्य प्रज्ञा प्रतिष्ठिता ॥५७॥

57. His wisdom is stable who clings to nothing good or evil when these occur to him; he neither seeks nor shuns them.

57.1. यः सर्वत्र इति ॥ यः मुनिः सर्वत्र देहजीवनादिषु अपि अनभिस्नेहः अभिस्नेहवर्जितः तत् तत् प्राप्य शुभाशुभं तत् तत् शुभं अशुभं वा लब्ध्वा न अभिनन्दति न द्वेष्टि, शुभं प्राप्य न तुष्यति न हृष्यति, अशुभं च प्राप्य न द्वेष्टि इत्यर्थः । तस्य एवं हर्षविषादवर्जितस्य विवेकजा प्रज्ञा प्रतिष्ठिता ॥

किञ्च —

57.1. The silent sage does not care even for his own body, life-style and so forth. He is devoid of all attachment and aversion when good and evil occur to him. He neither seeks the one nor shuns the other. The discriminating wisdom of such a sage, free from gaiety and depression, is stable.

Also:

यदा संहरते चायं कूर्मोऽङ्गानीव सर्वशः ।
इन्द्रियाणीन्द्रियार्थेभ्यस्तस्य प्रज्ञा प्रतिष्ठिता ॥५८॥

58. When he wholly withdraws his senses from their objects, just as a tortoise does his limbs from all sides, his wisdom is stable.

58.1. यदा संहरते इति ॥ यदा संहरते सम्यक् उपसंहरते च अयं ज्ञाननिष्ठायां

प्रवृत्तः यतिः, कूर्मः अङ्गानि इव — यथा कूर्मः भयात् स्वानि अङ्गानि उपसंहरति सर्वशः सर्वतः, एवं ज्ञाननिष्ठः इन्द्रियाणि इन्द्रियार्थेभ्यः सर्वविषयेभ्यः उपसंहरते । तस्य प्रज्ञा प्रतिष्ठिता इति उक्तार्थं वाक्यम् ॥

58.1. Actively engaged in the discipline of the Yoga of knowledge, when he withdraws aright his senses from their objects, just as a tortoise tucks up, due to fear, its limbs on all sides, his wisdom is stabilised. This idea has already been explained.

59.0. तत्र विषयान् अनाहरतः आतुरस्य अपि इन्द्रियाणि [निवर्तन्ते कूर्माङ्गानीव] संहियन्ते, न तु तद्विषयः रागः । स कथं संहियते इति ? उच्यते—

59.0. The senses even of a sick man who does not react to objects become indrawn; but his attachment to them does not cease. How can that attachment be withheld? Answer:

विषया विनिवर्तन्ते निराहारस्य देहिनः ।
रसवर्जं रसोऽप्यस्य परं दृष्ट्वा निवर्तते ॥५९॥

59. Objects, but not the taste for them, fall off as regards the man who feeds not on them. When he intuits the supreme (Reality), even this taste wanes.

59.1. विषया इति ॥ यद्यपि विषयाः विषयोपलक्षितानि विषयशब्दवाच्यानि इन्द्रियाणि [अथवा विषयाः एव] निराहारस्य अनाह्रियमाणविषयस्य कष्टे [काष्ठ-] तपसि स्थितस्य मूर्खस्य अपि विनिवर्तन्ते देहिनः देहवतः रसवर्जं रसः रागः विषयेषु यः तं वर्जयित्वा । रसशब्दः रागे प्रसिद्धः 'स्वरसेन प्रवृत्तः,' 'रसिकः', 'रसज्ञः' इत्यादिदर्शनात् । सः अपि रसः रञ्जनरूपः सूक्ष्मः अस्य यतेः परं परमार्थतत्त्वं ब्रह्म दृष्ट्वा उपलभ्य 'अहमेव तत्' इति वर्तमानस्य निवर्तते निर्बीजं विषयविज्ञानं संपद्यते इत्यर्थः । न असति सम्यग्दर्शने रसस्य उच्छेदः । तस्मात् सम्यग्दर्शनात्मिकायाः प्रज्ञायाः स्थैर्यं कर्तव्यं इति अभिप्रायः ॥

59.1. Though the objects, meaning the senses related to them (or the very objects themselves) cease to operate as regards the man who rejects tbem—and this happens even if the practitioner of severe austerities be but a fool—the taste or joy in the objects may, nevertheless persist. This taste or *rasa* is the attachment to the objects concerned, *vide* usages such as "active due to specific attachment", 'enjoyer', 'knower of taste' etc. Even that subtle joy which makes objects attractive retreats from the disciplined sage, once he realises the supreme Reality as "I am verily That". The sense is that, then, the source of objective awareness dries up. In the absence of this realization, "the taste" won't be obliterated. The import is that the stability of wisdom whose essence is right knowledge must be secured.

60.0. सम्यग्दर्शनलक्षणप्रज्ञास्थैर्यं चिकीर्षता आदौ इन्द्रियाणि स्ववशे स्थापयितव्यानि, यस्मात् तदनवस्थापने दोषम् आह —

60.0. One who seeks stability of wisdom, defined as right knowledge, must, first, control the senses. Otherwise evil may ensue:

यततो ह्यपि कौन्तेय पुरुषस्य विपश्चितः ।
इन्द्रियाणि प्रमाथीनि हरन्ति प्रसभं मनः ॥६०॥

60. The impetuous senses, Arjuna! of even a learned man who strives, forcibly drive the mind astray.

60.1. यततः इति ॥ यततः प्रयत्नं कुर्वतः हि यस्मात् कौन्तेय, पुरुषस्य विपश्चितः मेधाविनः 'अपि' इति व्यवहितेन संबन्धः । इन्द्रियाणि प्रमाथीनि प्रमथनशीलानि विषयाभिमुखं हि पुरुषं विक्षोभयन्ति आकुलीकुर्वन्ति, आकुलीकृत्य च हरन्ति प्रसभं प्रसह्य प्रकाशम् एव पश्यतः विवेकविज्ञानयुक्तं मनः ॥
यतः तस्मात् —

60.1. "Since the impetuous senses of even a learned man, intelligent man, who strives"—this is how these separately placed words have to be construed. The impetuous senses drive him towards objects and agitate his mind. Thus, perforce, they carry it away, though he has clear perception or the right knowledge of discrimination.

Therefore,

तानि सर्वाणि संयम्य युक्त आसीत मत्परः ।
वशे हि यस्येन्द्रियाणि तस्य प्रज्ञा प्रतिष्ठिता ॥६१॥

61. Controlling them all, one should sit integrated, deeming Me supreme. Stable is his wisdom who has brought his senses under control.

61.1. तानि इति ॥ तानि सर्वाणि संयम्य संयमनं वशीकरणं कृत्वा युक्तः समाहितः सन् आसीत मत्परः अहं वासुदेवः सर्वप्रत्यगात्मा परः यस्य स मत्परः, 'न अन्योऽहं तस्मात्' इति आसीत इत्यर्थः । एवं आसीनस्य यतेः वशे हि यस्य इन्द्रियाणि वर्तन्ते अभ्यासवशात् [बलात्] तस्य प्रज्ञा प्रतिष्ठिता ॥

61.1. "Controlling them all", establishing dominion over all of them, "integrated" i.e. concentrated, one should sit. "Deeming Me supreme", means that for him Vāsudeva, the inner Self of all, is supreme. The idea is that he should sit, thinking, "I am not different from Vāsudeva." The wisdom of that Yogin, seated thus, is stable. Through the force of repeated efforts he has brought his senses under control.

62.0. अथ इदानीं पराभविष्यतः सर्वानर्थमूलं इदं उच्यते—

62.0. Now is pointed out the root of all disaster betiding one who fails in his efforts at self-control.

ध्यायतो विषयान् पुंसः सङ्गस्तेषूपजायते ।
सङ्गात्सञ्जायते कामः कामात्क्रोधोऽभिजायते ॥६२॥

62. Attachment to objects is born when one ponders on them. Of attachment is born desire, and of desire, wrath.

62.1. ध्यायतः इति ॥ ध्यायतः चिन्तयतः विषयान् शब्दादीन् विषयविशेषान् आलोचयतः पुंसः पुरुषस्य सङ्गः आसक्तिः प्रीतिः तेषु विषयेषु उपजायते उत्पद्यते । सङ्गात् प्रीतेः सञ्जायते समुत्पद्यते कामः तृष्णा । तस्मात् कामात् कुतश्चित् प्रतिहतात् क्रोधः अभिजायते ॥

62.1. In the case of the man who "ponders on" i.e., who thinks of or contemplates, particular objects like sounds, "attachment to them", pleasure in them, arises. Of that pleasure is born desire or craving. From this craving, when obstructed somehow, wrath arises.

क्रोधाद्भवति संमोहः संमोहात्स्मृतिविभ्रमः ।
स्मृतिभ्रंशाद्बुद्धिनाशो बुद्धिनाशात्प्रणश्यति ॥६३॥

63. From wrath arises delusion; from delusion, failure of memory. Due to this latter, intelligence perishes, and from its loss total destruction ensues.

63.1. क्रोधात् इति ॥ क्रोधात् भवति संमोहः अविवेकः कार्याकार्यविषयः । क्रुद्धो हि संमूढः सन् गुरुम् अपि आक्रोशति । संमोहात् स्मृतिविभ्रमः शास्त्राचार्योपदेशाहितसंस्कारजनितायाः स्मृतेः स्यात् विभ्रमः भ्रंशः स्मृत्युत्पत्तिनिमित्तप्राप्तौ अनुत्पत्तिः । ततः स्मृतिभ्रंशात् बुद्धिनाशः बुद्धिनाशः बुद्धेः नाशः । कार्याकार्यविषयविवेकायोग्यता अन्तःकरणस्य बुद्धेः नाशः उच्यते । बुद्धिनाशात् प्रणश्यति । तावदेव हि पुरुषः यावत् अन्तःकरणं तदीयं कार्याकार्यविषयविवेकयोग्यम् । तदयोग्यत्वे नष्ट एव पुरुषः भवति । अतः तस्यान्तःकरणस्य बुद्धेः नाशात् प्रणश्यति पुरुषार्थायोग्यः भवति इत्यर्थः ॥

63.1. From wrath arises delusion or lack of discrimination between what ought and what ought not to be done. Indeed an angry man, being deluded, rails even at his teacher. Due to delusion confusion of memory reuslts, i.e. the fading of those impressions constituting memory which the *śāstras* and the instructions of teachers have engendered. In other words even when the causes of its appearance are present, that memory fails to arise. Due to this failure, Buddhi, the competence of the mind to discriminate between right and wrong, perishes.

Through the loss of this discrimination, one is wholly destroyed; for a man retains self-identity only as long as he retains his power to discriminate between right and wrong. Where this power fails, the man in question perishes, indeed. The sense is that with the destruction of the organ of discrimination man perishes; he becomes unfit to realise the ends of life.

64.0. सर्वानर्थस्य मूलं उक्तं विषयाभिध्यानम् । अथ इदानीं मोक्षकारणं इदं उच्यते —

64.0. The contemplation of objects (of desire) has been pointed out as the root of all evil. Now is pointed out the cause of liberation:

रागद्वेषवियुक्तैस्तु विषयानिन्द्रियैश्चरन् ।
आत्मवश्यैर्विधेयात्मा प्रसादमधिगच्छति ॥६४॥

64. Approaching objects with senses free from attachment and aversion, and controlled by the mind, the man who has mastered his mind wins serenity.

64.1. रागद्वेष इति ॥ रागद्वेषवियुक्तैः रागश्च द्वेषश्च रागद्वेषौ, तत्पुरःसरा हि इद्रियाणां प्रवृत्तिः स्वाभाविकी । तत्र यः मुमुक्षुः भवति सः ताभ्यां वियुक्तैः श्रोत्रादिभिः इन्द्रियैः विषयान् अवर्जनीयान् चरन् उपलभमानः आत्मवश्यैः आत्मनः वश्यानि वशीकृतानि [—भूतानि] इन्द्रियाणि तैः आत्मवश्यैः विधेयात्मा इच्छातः आत्मा अन्तःकरणं यस्य सः अयं प्रसादं अधिगच्छति । प्रसादः प्रसन्नता, स्वास्थ्यम् ॥

64.1. Indeed, the normal activities of the senses are impelled by 'attachment and aversion'. One who seeks liberation, however, approaches unavoidable objects by means of his senses, ear, eye, etc., which are free from attachment and aversion. Besides, these senses are under the sway of the disciplined mind. He whose self, the inner sense or mind, has been disciplined, attains serenity, which is placidity or Self-abidance.

65.0. प्रसादे सति किं स्यात् इति ? उच्यते —

65.0. What happens when serenity is won? Listen:

प्रसादे सर्वदुःखानां हानिरस्योपजायते ।
प्रसन्नचेतसो ह्याशु बुद्धिः पर्यवतिष्ठते ॥६५॥

65. Serenity won, sufferings come to an end; the reason of that man, whose mind is serene, soon becomes steadfast.

65.1. प्रसादे इति ॥ प्रसादे सर्वदुःखानां आध्यात्मिकादीनां हानिः विनाशः अस्य यतेः उपजायते । किञ्च प्रसन्नचेतसः शुद्धा- [स्वस्था-] न्तःकरणस्य हि यस्मात् आशु शीघ्रं बुद्धिः पर्यवतिष्ठते आकाशम् इव परि समन्तात् अवतिष्ठते, आत्मस्वरूपेण एव निश्चलीभवति इत्यर्थः ॥ एवं प्रसन्नचेतसः अवस्थितबुद्धेः कृतकृत्यता यतः, तस्मात् रागद्वेषविमु[यु]क्तैः इन्द्रियैः शास्त्राविरुद्धेषु अवर्जनीयेषु युक्तः समाचरेत् इति वाक्यार्थः ॥

सा इयं प्रसन्नता स्तूयते —

65.1. In serenity the three kinds of sufferings of the disciplined sage come to an end. Also, the reason of the sage, whose inner sense has been purified, soon becomes steady like the sky in all circumstances. The sense is that it becomes immutable, having been assimilated to the Self. Since he, whose mind is serene and reason immutable, has achieved his life's goal, he may approach the unavoidable sense-objects, permitted by the *śāstras*, with senses free from attachment and aversion. This is the upshot of the verse as a whole.

This serenity is lauded:

नास्ति बुद्धिरयुक्तस्य न चायुक्तस्य भावना ।
न चाभावयतः शान्तिरशान्तस्य कुतः सुखम् ॥६६॥

66. The unintegrated mind has no wisdom; nor can such a person have yearning (for Self-knowledge). Without such yearning, no peace (is possible). For one lacking peace, how can there be happiness?

66.1. नास्ति इति ॥ न अस्ति न विद्यते न भवति इत्यर्थः । बुद्धिः आत्म-

स्वरूपविषया अयुक्तस्य असमाहितान्तःकरणस्य । न च अस्ति अयुक्तस्य भावना आत्मज्ञानाभिनिवेशः । तथा न च अस्ति अभावयतः आत्मज्ञानाभिनिवेशम् अकुर्वतः शान्तिः उपशमः । अशान्तस्य कुतः सुखम् ? इन्द्रियाणां हि विषयसेवातृष्णातः निवृत्तिः या तत् सुखं, न विषयविषया तृष्णा । दुःखम् एव हि सा । न तृष्णायां सत्यां सुखस्य गन्धमात्रम् अपि उत्प[-पप]द्यते इत्यर्थः ॥

66.1. There is not, i.e., there cannot exist *buddhi* or Wisdom born of the perception of the real Self, for one whose inner sense is 'unintegrated', or unconcentrated. Neither can such a one have yearning for Self-knowledge. Without this yearning one cannot gain peace or quietude. How can there be happiness without quietude? The turning away of the senses from the craving for enjoyment of object is happiness; it is not the craving for objects. The latter indeed is pain. So long as there is craving, there cannot be even the remotest semblance of happiness. This is the sense of the passage.

67.0. अयुक्तस्य कस्मात् बुद्धिः नास्ति इति ? उच्यते —

67.0. Why can't the unintegrated man gain wisdom? Listen:

इन्द्रियाणां हि चरतां यन्मनोऽनुविधीयते ।
तदस्य हरति प्रज्ञां वायुर्नावमिवाम्भसि ॥६७॥

67. The mind that conforms to the roving senses robs (one) of perception, just as the wind sweeps the boat off its course at sea.

67.1. इन्द्रियाणां इति ॥ इन्द्रियाणां हि यस्मात् चरतां स्वस्वविषयेषु प्रवर्तमानानां यत् मनः अनुविधीयते अनुप्रवर्तते तत् इन्द्रियविषयविकल्पनेन प्रवृत्तं मनः अस्य यतेः हरति प्रज्ञां आत्मानात्मविवेकजां नाशयति । कथं ? वायुः नावम् इव अम्भसि उदके जिगमिषतां सांयात्रिकाणां मार्गात् उद्धृत्य उन्मार्गे यथा वायुः नावं प्रवर्तयति, एवं आत्मविषयां प्रज्ञां हृत्वा मनो विषयविषयां करोति ॥

67.1. The mind that follows the senses in their pursuit of their proper objects destroys the ascetic's perception, born of discrimination between Self and non-Self; for, it is a slave to these senses and their objects. How? As the wind blows off its course a boat (at sea), so the mind, suppressing Self-perception, causes one to hurry after objects.

68.0. 'यततो ह्यपि' [२.६०.] इत्युपन्यस्तस्य अर्थस्य अनेकधा उपपत्तिं उक्त्वा तं च अर्थं उपपाद्य उपसंहरति —

68.0. Having discoursed in manifold ways on the rightness of the view advanced in verse II.60 and supported it with reasoning, the Lord winds it up:

तस्माद्यस्य महाबाहो निगृहीतानि सर्वशः ।
इन्द्रियाणीन्द्रियार्थेभ्यस्तस्य प्रज्ञा प्रतिष्ठिता ॥६८॥

68. Therefore, O hero! his wisdom is stable whose senses have been withdrawn on all sides from their (respective) objects.

68.1. तस्माद् इति ॥ इन्द्रियाणां प्रवृत्तौ दोषः उपपादितः यस्मात् तस्मात् यस्य यतेः हे महाबाहो ! निगृहीतानि सर्वशः सर्वप्रकारैः मानसादिभेदैः इन्द्रियाणि इन्द्रियार्थेभ्यः शब्दादिभ्यः तस्य प्रज्ञा प्रतिष्ठिता ॥

68.1. The evil caused by the activities of the senses has been set forth. Therefore, O hero! that ascetic's wisdom becomes stable, whose senses have been withdrawn totally from their objects such as sounds etc., on all planes of activity.

69.0. योऽयं लौकिकः वैदिकश्च व्यवहारः सः उत्पन्नविवेकज्ञानस्य स्थितप्रज्ञस्य अविद्याकार्यत्वात् अविद्यानिवृत्तौ निवर्तते, अविद्यायाः च विद्याविरोधात् निवृत्तिः, इत्येतं अर्थं स्फुटीकुर्वन् आह —

69.0. For the sage of stable wisdom who has won the knowledge of discrimination, all works, secular and Vedic, cease, since nescience, their cause, has been sublated. Nescience, too, is sublated as it is opposed to knowledge. Clarifying this idea, the Lord says:

या निशा सर्वभूतानां तस्यां जागर्ति संयमी ।
यस्यां जाग्रति भूतानि सा निशा पश्यतो मुनेः ॥६९॥

69. The restrained ascetic (the sage) is awake in what is night for all living beings, while, when these latter are awake, it is night for the silent sage who perceives.

69.1. या निशा इति ॥ या निशा रात्रिः सर्वपदार्थानां अविवेककरी तमःस्वभावत्वात् सर्वभूतानां सर्वेषां भूतानाम् । किं तत् ? परमार्थतत्त्वं स्थितप्रज्ञस्य विषयः । यथा नक्तंचराणां अहः एव सत् अन्येषां निशा भवति, तद्वत् नक्तंचरस्थानीयानां अज्ञा[नि]नां सर्वभूतानां निशा इव निशा परमार्थतत्त्वं, अगोचरत्वात् अतद्बुद्धीनाम् । तस्यां परमार्थतत्त्वलक्षणायां अज्ञाननिद्रायाः प्रबुद्धः जागर्ति संयमी संयमवान्, जितेन्द्रियः योगी इत्यर्थः । यस्यां ग्राह्यग्राहक [-भेद-] लक्षणायां अविद्यानिद्रा[-शा]यां प्रसुप्तानि एव भूतानि जाग्रति इति उच्यन्ते [-ते], यस्यां निशायां प्रसुप्ता इव स्वप्नदृशः, सा निशा अविद्यारूपत्वात् परमार्थतत्त्वं पश्यतः मुनेः इति ॥

69.1. The supreme Truth, the sphere of the sage of stable wisdom, is night for the rest of the world. At night things cannot be distinguished because of darkness. Just as what is day to nocturnal creatures is night for others, so the supreme Truth is, as it were, 'night' for all ignorant beings who correspond to these nocturnal creatures. The supreme Truth, of course, does not fall within the range of their understanding. Into that (day of) ultimate Truth, the ascetic sage, the Yogin who has mastered his senses, wakes up from the sleep of nescience. Sunk in the sleep of nescience, marked by the plurality of subjects and objects, the rest of the world is said to be awake like dreamers in their sleep. But this is night for the sage who has grasped the ultimate Truth.

69.2. अतः कर्माणि अविद्यावस्थायां एव चोद्यन्ते, न विद्यावस्थायाम् । विद्यायां हि सत्यां उदिते सवितरि शार्वरं इव तमः प्रणाशं उपगच्छति अविद्या । प्राक् विद्योत्पत्तेः अविद्या प्रमाणबुद्ध्या गृह्यमाणा क्रियाकारकफलभेदरूपा च सती सर्वकर्महेतुत्वं प्रतिपद्यते । न अप्रमाणबुद्ध्या गृह्यमाणायाः कर्महेतुत्वोपपत्तिः । 'प्रमाणभूतेन वेदेन मम चोदितं कर्तव्यं कर्म' इति हि कर्मणि कर्ता प्रवर्तते, न 'अविद्यामात्रमिदं सर्वं निशा इव' इति । यस्य तु पुनः 'निशेवाविद्यामात्रमिदं सर्वं भेदजातम्' इति

ज्ञानं तस्याऽऽत्मज्ञस्य सर्वकर्मसन्यासे एवाधिकारः न प्रवृत्तौ । तथा च दर्शयिष्यति 'तद्बुद्धयस्तदात्मानः' [५.१७] इत्यादिना ज्ञाननिष्ठायाम् एव तस्य अधिकारम् ।

69.2. Therefore, works are enjoined (on man) only in his state of nescience and not in that of knowledge. When knowledge dawns, nescience perishes like the darkness of the night when the sun rises. Before the dawn of knowledge, the deliverances of nescience in its varied forms of action, accessories and fruits are entertained as valid. When known to be invalid, nescience stops its operations. An agent acts under the impression that valid Vedic injunctions have enjoined actions on him; he cannot do so when he judges the world to be (a sort of night)—a mere structure of nescience. On the other hand, he who knows the whole sphere of objects to be nothing but nescience is the knower of the Self. What is incumbent on him is to renounce all actions and not to perform them. This the Lord will elucidate in the verse 5.17: 'Their intellect anchored in It, having That as their Self' etc. The exclusive obligation of the sage is the pursuit of knowledge.

69.3. तत्रापि प्रवर्तकप्रमाणाभावे प्रवृत्त्यनुपपत्तिः इति चेत्—न, स्वात्मविषयत्वात् आत्मविज्ञानस्य । न हि आत्मनः स्वात्मनि प्रवर्तकप्रमाणापेक्षा, आत्मत्वात् एव तदन्तत्वात् च सर्वप्रमाणानां प्रमाणत्वस्य । न हि आत्मस्वरूपाधिगमे सति पुनः प्रमाणप्रमेयव्यवहारः संभवति । प्रमातृत्वं हि आत्मनः निवर्तयति अन्त्यं प्रमाणम् । निवर्तयत् एव च अप्रमाणीभवति स्वप्नकालप्रमाणम् इव प्रबोधे । लोके च वस्त्वधिगमे प्रवृत्तिहेतुत्वादर्शनात्प्रमाणस्य । तस्मात् न आत्मविदः कर्मणि अधिकारः इति सिद्धम् ॥

69.3. *Objection:* He cannot address himself even to the discipline of knowledge in the absence of a valid source of knowledge that prescribes it.

Reply: No, for Self-knowledge is directed to one's own Self. The Self does not need an (alien) source of knowledge to initiate activity in regard to Itself, the goal being the realization of the Self. Once Self-realization is won, it is no longer possible to discuss the distinctions between the means of knowledge and their objects. The last means of knowledge indeed liberates the Self from Its status as a knower. Doing this, it ceases to be a valid means, resembling in this respect the means of knowledge in a dream. In the state of supreme enlightenment and in the empirical world, once the reality is known, the means of knowledge is not experienced as leading to further activity of any kind. In this world, too, means of right cognition yielding right knowledge ceases to cause any further activity. Therefore it follows that the Self-knower is under no further obligation to perform work.

70.0. विदुषः त्यक्तैषणस्य स्थितप्रज्ञस्य यतेः एव मोक्षप्राप्तिः न तु असंन्यासिनः कामकामिनः इत्येतम् अर्थं दृष्टान्तेन प्रतिपादयिष्यन् आह —

70.0. In order to elucidate with the help of a simile the idea that emancipation can be won only by the ascetic sage of stable wisdom who has renounced all desires, and not by a non-renouncer pursuing objects of desires, the Lord affirms:

आपूर्यमाणमचलप्रतिष्ठं
समुद्रमापः प्रविशन्ति यद्वत् ।
तद्वत्कामा यं प्रविशन्ति सर्वे
स शान्तिमाप्नोति न कामकामी ॥७०॥

70. He wins peace into whose mind objects of desires enter as waters flow into a full and stable sea that is being filled; and not he who yearns after objects of desire.

70.1. आपूर्य इति । आपूर्यमाणं अद्भिः अचलप्रतिष्ठं अचलतया प्रतिष्ठा अवस्थितिः यस्य तम् अचलप्रतिष्ठं समुद्रम् आपः सर्वतो गताः प्रविशन्ति स्वात्मस्थं अविक्रियम् एव सन्तं यद्वत् तद्वत्कामाः विषयसंनिधौ अपि सर्वतः इच्छाविशेषाः यं पुरुषं [-मुनिं], समुद्रम् इव आपः, अविकुर्वन्तः प्रविशन्ति सर्वे आत्मनि एव प्रलीयन्ते न स्वात्मवशं कुर्वन्ति सः शान्तिं मोक्षं आप्नोति, न इतरः कामकामी — काम्यन्ते इति कामाः विषयाः तान् कामयितुं शीलं यस्य स कामकामी, सः नैव प्राप्नोति इत्यर्थः ॥

यस्मात् एवं तस्मात्—

70.1. Though being filled on all sides by waters, the sea remains unchanged; for it is stable. These waters flow into it from all sides, while the sea abides in itself, unaltered. Thus all forms of desire, all around, like the waters into the sea, enter the sage's mind. He contains them all, and is not enslaved by them. Only he wins peace or liberation, and not any other who habitually yearns after objects of desire.

Such being the case,

विहाय कामान् यः सर्वान् पुमांश्चरति निःस्पृहः ।
निर्ममो निरहंकारः स शान्तिमधिगच्छति ॥७१॥

71. The man who, giving up all objects of desires, moves about seeking nothing, and rid of all sense of 'mine' and 'I', wins peace.

71.1. विहाय इति ॥ विहाय परित्यज्य कामान् यः संन्यासी पुमान् सर्वान् अशेषतः कात्स्न्र्येन चरति जीवनमात्रचेष्टाशेषः पर्यटति इत्यर्थः । निःस्पृहः शरीरजीवनमात्रेऽपि निर्गता स्पृहा यस्य सः निःस्पृहः सन् निर्ममः शरीरजीवनमात्राक्षिप्तपरिग्रहेऽपि 'मम इदं' इति अभिनिवेशवर्जितः, निरहंकारः विद्यावत्त्वादिनिमित्तात्मसंभावनारहितः इत्येतत् । सः एवंभूतः स्थितप्रज्ञः ब्रह्मवित् शान्तिं सर्वसंसारदुःखोपरमलक्षणां निर्वाणाख्यां अधिगच्छति प्राप्नोति ब्रह्मभूतः भवति इत्यर्थः ॥

सा एषा ज्ञाननिष्ठा स्तूयते —

71.1. Giving up, i.e. having renounced objects of desires in their totality, the renouncer moves about. His efforts have been reduced to securing just what sustains life—this is the sense. 'Seeking nothing'—he does not desire even to keep the body alive. So he is free from all sense of 'mine'—he has no sense of possessions even in regard to those few things needed to maintain his body alive. Neither has he egoism, being free from all feelings of self-esteem based on his scholarship etc. So circumstanced, the sage of stable wisdom, the knower of Brahman, attains peace—the cessation of all forms of transmigratory sufferings. This is Nirvāṇa. He becomes assimilated to Brahman.

This discipline of knowledge is eulogised.

एषा ब्राह्मी स्थितिः पार्थ नैनां प्राप्य विमुह्यति ।
स्थित्वाऽस्यामन्तकालेऽपि ब्रह्मनिर्वाणमृच्छति ॥७२॥

72. This is the status of Brahman, Arjuna!; attaining it, none gets deluded (any more). Abiding in it, at least at the hour of death, one gains super-consciousness in Brahman.

इति श्रीमहाभारते शतसाहस्र्यां संहितायां वैयासिक्यां भीष्मपर्वणि श्रीमद्भगवद्गीतासु उपनिषत्सु ब्रह्मविद्यायां योगशास्त्रे श्रीकृष्णार्जुनसंवादे सांख्ययोगो नाम द्वितीयोऽध्यायः ॥

72.1. एषा ब्राह्मी इति ॥ एषा यथोक्ता ब्राह्मी ब्रह्मणि भवा इयं स्थितिः सर्वं कर्म संन्यस्य ब्रह्मस्वरूपेण एव अवस्थानं इत्येतत् । हे पार्थ ! न एनां स्थितिं प्राप्य लब्ध्वा विमुह्यति मोहं प्राप्नोति । स्थित्वा अस्यां स्थितौ ब्राह्म्यां यथोक्तायां अन्तकालेऽपि अन्त्ये वयस्यपि ब्रह्मनिर्वाणं ब्रह्मनिर्वृतिं मोक्षम् ऋच्छति गच्छति । किमु वक्तव्यं ब्रह्मचर्यात् एव संन्यस्य यावज्जीवं यः ब्रह्मणि एव अवतिष्ठते सः ब्रह्मनिर्वाणं ऋच्छति इति ?

72.1. The status engendered in Brahman is *brāhmī*. It is the status as Brahman, won after renouncing all works, O Arjuna! Having won it, one is no longer deluded. Stationing oneself in it, as described above, at least in the final stage of one's life, one achieves super-consciousness in Brahman—the bliss of Brahman. It goes without saying that he who renounces works right from the station of celibacy (a *Brahmacārin*) and remains anchored in Brahman throughout his life, attains Brahmic super-consciousness.

इति श्रीमत्परमहंसपरिव्राजकाचार्यगोविन्दभगवत्पूज्यपादशिष्यश्रीमच्छंकरभगवतः कृतौ श्रीमद्भगवद्गीताभाष्ये सांख्ययोगो नाम द्वितीयोऽध्यायः ॥

अथ तृतीयोऽध्यायः

CHAPTER III
KARMA YOGA

0.1. शास्त्रस्य प्रवृत्तिनिवृत्तिविषयभूते द्वे बुद्धी भगवता निर्दिष्टे, सांख्ये बुद्धिः योगे बुद्धिः इति च । तत्र 'प्रजहाति यदा कामान्' [२.५५.] इति आरभ्य आ अध्यायपरिसमाप्तेः सांख्यबुद्ध्याश्रितानां संन्यासं कर्तव्यं उक्त्वा तन्निष्ठतया एव च कृतार्थता उक्ता—'एषा ब्राह्मी स्थितिः' [२.७२] इति । अर्जुनाय च 'कर्मण्येवाधिकारस्ते...मा ते सङ्गोऽस्त्वकर्मणि' [२.४७] इति कर्मैव कर्तव्यं उक्तवान् योगबुद्धिं आश्रित्य, न ततः एव श्रेयःप्राप्तिं उक्तवान् । तदेतत् आलक्ष्य पर्याकुलीकृ[भू]तबुद्धिः अर्जुनः उवाच । कथं भक्ताय श्रेयोर्थिने यत् साक्षात् श्रेयःप्राप्तिसाधनं सांख्यबुद्धिनिष्ठां श्रावयित्वा मां कर्मणि दृष्टानेकानर्थयुक्ते पारम्पर्येण अपि अनैकान्तिकश्रेयःप्राप्तिफले नियुञ्ज्यात् इति युक्तः पर्याकुलीभावः अर्जुनस्य, तदनुरूपश्च प्रश्नः 'ज्यायसी चेत्' [३.१.] इत्यादिः । प्रश्नापाकरणवाक्यं च भगवतः यु[-उ-]क्तं यथोक्तविभागविषये शास्त्रे ॥

0.1. In the science of the Gītā the Lord has pointed out, as causes of action and abstention from it, two kinds of intelligence pertaining to Yoga and Sāṁkhya. Now, beginning from the verse 2.55 upto the end of the second Chapter, the duty of renunciation has been laid down for those who resort to the intelligence of Sāṁkhya and it has been taught that they achieve life's goal; *vide* verse 2.72. The Lord told Arjuna to perform works as a matter of duty depending on the intelligence of Yoga; *vide* verse 2.47, but He did not affirm that through such performance alone, he would secure the highest good. Noticing this, in a dejected state of mind, Arjuna spoke. Arjuna's dejection was in place: having introduced to him the subject of the discipline of the intelligence of Sāṁkhya, the direct cause of the highest good for a devotee and seeker after the highest good, which Arjuna admittedly was, the Lord bade him plunge into works, the well-known source of numerous evils, which, at the same time, was no certain means to the achievement of the highest good. The question Arjuna raised has been appropriate; *vide* 3.1; and equally appropriate has also been the Lord's answer to that question, once the two-fold division of this science is given.

0.2. केचित्तु—अर्जुनस्य प्रश्नार्थं अन्यथा कल्पयित्वा तत्प्रतिकूलं भगवतः प्रतिवचनं वर्णयन्ति, यथा च आत्मना संबन्धग्रन्थे गीतार्थः निरूपितः तत्प्रतिकूलं च इह पुनः प्रश्नप्रतिवचनयोः अर्थं निरूपयन्ति । कथं ? तत्र संबन्धग्रन्थे तावत्—सर्वेषां आश्रमिणां ज्ञानकर्मणोः समुच्चयः गीताशास्त्रे निश्चितः [निरूपितः] अर्थः इत्युक्तम्; पुनः विशेषितं च यावज्जीवं श्रुतिचोदितानि कर्माणि परित्यज्य केवलात् एव ज्ञानात् मोक्षः प्राप्यते इत्येतत् एकान्तेन एव प्रतिषिद्धं इति । इह तु आश्रमविकल्पं दर्शयता यावज्जीवं श्रुतिचोदितानां एव कर्मणां परित्यागः उक्तः । तत् कथं ईदृशं विरुद्धं अर्थं अर्जुनाय ब्रूयात् भगवान्, श्रोता वा कथं विरुद्धं अर्थं अवधारयेत् ?

0.2. However, some commentators put a different construction on Arjuna's question and make it out that the Lord's response is contrary to its spirit. Further, they contradict themselves, as their explanation of Arjuna's question, as also of the Lord's response thereto, does not harmonise with the sense of the *BG* as set forth by themselves at the beginning of their commentary while discussing the structure of that sense. How? They said that in the analysis of that structure, the firm doctrine of the science of the Gītā is the synthesis of knowledge and works as regards all people occupying the various stations of life. Again, they have specially asserted that the Gītā absolutely repudiates the view that emancipation may be attained through knowledge alone, once the rites prescribed as valid for the entire life-period of a man have been renounced. Here, on the contrary, pointing to optional courses (of renunciation or performance of works), what is taught is the renunciation of those very rites taught as valid for the whole of the life-period. How can the Lord impart instruction riddled with such contradictions to Arjuna? How can the latter comprehend such contradictory notions?

0.3. तत्र एतत् स्यात् — गृहस्थानाम् एव श्रौतस्मार्तकर्मपरित्यागेन केवलात् एव ज्ञानात् मोक्षः प्रतिषिध्यते, न तु आश्रमान्तराणां इति । एतदपि पूर्वोत्तरविरुद्धमेव । कथं ? सर्वाश्रमिणां ज्ञानकर्मणोः समुच्चयः गीताशास्त्रे निश्चितः अर्थः इति प्रतिज्ञाय इह कथं तद्विरुद्धं केवलात् एव ज्ञानात् मोक्षं ब्रूयात् आश्रमान्तरणाम् ?

अथ मतं — श्रौतकर्मापेक्षया एतद्वचनं — 'केवलादेव ज्ञानात् श्रौतकर्मरहितात् गृहस्थानां मोक्षः प्रतिषिध्यते' इति; तत्र गृहस्थानां विद्यमानम् अपि स्मार्तं कर्म अविद्यमानवत् उ [अन-] पेक्ष्य 'ज्ञानादेव केवलात्' इति उच्यते इति । एतदपि विरुद्धम् । कथं ? गृहस्थस्य एव स्मार्तकर्मणा समुच्चितात् ज्ञानात् मोक्षः प्रतिषिध्यते, न तु आश्रमान्तराणां इति कथं विवेकिभिः शक्यं अवधारयितुम् ? किञ्च—यदि मोक्षसाधनत्वेन स्मार्तानि कर्माणि ऊर्ध्वरेतसां समुच्चीयन्ते, तथा गृहस्थस्य अपि इष्यतां स्मार्तैः एव समुच्चयः, न श्रौतैः ॥

0.3. An explanation may be advanced as follows: the repudiation of the view that the way to emancipation is through mere knowledge preceded by the renunciation of works prescribed by *śruti* and *smṛti*, is applicable to householders alone. But even this position involves a contradiction between what had been affirmed and what is now being affirmed. How? Having already stated that the indisputable doctrine of the Gītā is the synthesis of knowledge and works, a synthesis valid for the occupants of all stations of life, can it be stated here that the non-householders may win emancipation through knowledge alone? Perhaps you may argue as follows: Emancipation cannot accrue to the householders through knowledge alone, divorced from the rites enjoined by the Śruti. The phrase 'through knowledge alone' is not to be literally understood; it has been used, ignoring the fact that these householders have, nevertheless, to perform works enjoined by the *Smṛti*. Even this argument is self-contradictory. How can men of discrimination accept the position that to householders alone emancipation won't accrue from knowledge though combined with Smṛti-enjoined works, but not so to the non-householders? Besides, if, as means to emancipation, Smṛti-enjoined works are to be combined with knowledge in the case of celibate aspirants, in the case of householders, too, let only such works be combined with knowledge and not Śruti-enjoined works also.

0.4. अथ श्रौतैः स्मार्तैः च गृहस्थस्य एव समुच्चयः मोक्षाय, ऊर्ध्वरेतसां तु स्मार्तकर्ममात्रसमुच्चितात् ज्ञानात् मोक्षः इति । तत्र एवं सति गृहस्थस्य आयास-बाहुल्यं — श्रौतं स्मार्तं च बहुदुःखरूपं कर्म शिरसि आरोपितं स्यात् ॥

अथ गृहस्थस्य एव आयासबाहुल्यकारणात् मोक्षः स्यात्, न आश्रमान्तराणां श्रौतनित्यकर्मरहितत्वात् इति । तदपि असत्, सर्वोपनिषत्सु इतिहासपुराणयोगशास्त्रेषु च ज्ञानाङ्गत्वेन मुमुक्षोः सर्वकर्मसंन्यासविधानात्, आश्रमविकल्पसमुच्चयविधानाच्च श्रुतिस्मृत्योः ॥

सिद्धः तर्हि सर्वाश्रमिणां ज्ञानकर्मणोः समुच्चयः — न, मुमुक्षोः सर्वकर्मसंन्यासविधानात् । 'पुत्रैषणायाश्च वित्तैषणायाश्च लोकैषणायाश्च व्युत्थायाथ भिक्षाचर्यं चरन्ति' [बृ. ३.५.१.] 'तस्मात् न्यासं एषां तपसां अतिरिक्तं आहुः' [महाना उ. २४.१.] 'न्यास एवात्यरेचयत्' [महाना. उ. २१.२.] इति । 'न कर्मणा न प्रजया धनेन त्यागेनैके अमृतत्वमानशुः' [महाना उ. १०.५, कै. उ. २.] इति च, 'ब्रह्मचर्यादेव प्रव्रजेत्' [जाबा. उ. ४] इत्याद्याः श्रुतयः ॥

त्यज धर्ममधर्मं च उभे सत्यानृते त्यज ।
उभे सत्यानृते त्यक्त्वा येन त्यजसि तत् त्यज ॥
[शांतिपर्व ३२९.४०, ३३१.४४.]

संसारमेव निःसारं दृष्ट्वा सारदिदृक्षया ।
प्रव्रजन्त्यकृतोद्वाहाः परं वैराग्यमाश्रिताः ॥
इति बृहस्पतिः [? नारदपरि. उ. ३.१५.],

कर्मणा बध्यते जन्तुः विद्यया च विमुच्यते ।
तस्मात् कर्म न कुर्वन्ति यतयः पारदर्शिनः ॥
इति शुकानुशासनम् । [शान्तिपर्व २४१.७.]

इहापि च 'सर्वकर्माणि मनसा संन्यस्य' [५. १३.] इत्यादि ॥

0.4. If, however, the emancipation of the householders alone calls for a synthesis of knowledge and works, both Sruti-enjoined and Smṛti-enjoined, while that of the celibates may leave out Śruti-enjoined works, the result would be a heavier burden of painful labour for the householders to bear. This latter position may not be readily accepted, because in all the *Upaniṣads*, *Itihāsas*, *Purāṇas* and *Yoga-texts* renunciation of works, as such, has been laid down as obligatory on all who seek liberation, and because *śruti* and *smṛti* teach either a combination of, or choice among, the various stations of life. It does not follow from this that the occupants of all stations of life must combine knowledge and works; for, the seeker after liberation must needs renounce all forms of works, Śruti-enjoined or Smṛti-enjoined: *vide*: "Overcoming the desire for sons, wealth, and worlds, they take to a life of mendicancy" *B.U.*3.5.1; "Therefore they say that renunciation exceeds these austerities''; *Maha.Nar.U.*24.1; "Renunciation alone excelled'' *Ibid.* 21.2; "Not by works, not by progency and wealth, (but) by renunciation, they say, some won immortality'' *Ibid.* 10.5; *Kai.U.*2; "One shall renounce from the station of celibacy itself'' *Jal.U.*4.; "Give up (works) righteous and unrighteous; give up the true and the false; having given up the true and the false, give up *that* which prompted you to give up'' *Śānti parvan*, 329.40, 331.44; "Beholding the transmigratory life as void of all contents, and desiring to vision the Essence, the celibates, in a mood of supreme detachment, go forth into a life of mendicancy'' *Nāradapari. U.*3.15; "Work binds the living being; knowledge liberates. Therefore the ascetics, the beholders of the Supreme, refrain from work'' *śānti parvan* 241.7. Here, in *BG* also occurs, in 5.13 etc., "Renouncing all works, mentally.''

0.5. मोक्षस्य च अकार्यत्वात् मुमुक्षोः कर्मानर्थक्यम् । नित्यानि प्रत्यवायपरिहारार्थम् अनुष्ठेयानि इति चेत्—न, असंन्यासिविषयत्वात्प्रत्यवायप्राप्तेः न हि अग्निकार्याद्यकरणात् संन्यासिनः प्रत्यवायः कल्पयितुं शक्यः, यथा ब्रह्मचारिणाम् असंन्यासिनाम् अपि [कर्मिणाम्] । न तावन्नित्यानां अकरणात् अभावात् एव भावरूपस्य प्रत्यवायस्य उत्पत्तिः कल्पयितुं शक्या, 'कथमसतः सज्जायेत' [छा. उ. ६. २.२.] इति असतः सज्जन्मासंभवश्रुतेः । यदि विहिताकरणात् असंभाव्यम् अपि प्रत्यवायं ब्रूयाद्वेदः तदाऽनर्थकरः वेदोऽप्रमाणम् इत्युक्तं स्यात्, विहितस्य करणाकरणयोः दुःखमात्रफलत्वात् । तथा च कारकं शास्त्रं न ज्ञापकम् इति अनुपपन्नार्थं कल्पितं स्यात् । न च एतत् इष्टम् । तस्मात् न संन्यासिनां कर्माणि । अतः ज्ञानकर्मणोः समुच्चयानुपपत्तिः ।

0.5. Also because emancipation is not an effect, its seeker stands to gain nothing from works. The argument that works have to be done to avoid the sin of omission is futile; for only the non-renouncers may incur that sin. The sin of omission may not be ascribed to a renouncer who omits the performance of the fire sacrifice and so forth; while the matter is different as regards the non-renouncing celibate students who will incur that sin due to non-performance of enjoined works. Again it is impossible to assume that a positive entity like the sin of omission will spring from a state of non-existence, namely the non-performance of obligatory Vedic works. Witness the *ChU.* 6.2.2: "How can being arise from non-being?" This authoritatively denies the birth of aught positive from a state of non-being. If, however, the Veda were to assert the birth of the inconceivable sin of omission from the non-performance of Veda-enjoined work, it would be tantamount to the assertion that the troublesome Veda is no source of valid knowledge; for, what it prescribes, whether carried out or omitted, is a source of pain only. Further, there would result the false doctrine that the authoritative scripture forces one to work, and does not merely supply information. This is not acceptable. Therefore, ritualistic works are not binding on the renouncers. So, the plea for the synthesis of knowledge and works is untenable.

0.6. 'ज्यायसी चेत्कर्मणस्ते मता बुद्धिः' [३.१.] इति अर्जुनस्य प्रश्नानुपपत्तेश्च। यदि हि भगवता द्वितीयेऽध्याये ज्ञानं कर्म च समुच्चित्य त्वया एकेन अनुष्ठेयम् इति उक्तं स्यात्, ततोऽर्जुनस्य प्रश्नोऽनुपपन्नः 'ज्यायसी चेत्कर्मणस्ते मता बुद्धिः' इति। अर्जुनाय चेद्बुद्धिकर्मणी त्वयाऽनुष्ठेये इत्युक्ते, या च कर्मणः ज्यायसी बुद्धिः साऽपि उक्ता एव इति 'तत्किं कर्मणि घोरे मां नियोजयसि केशव' [३. १.] इति उपालंभो वा प्रश्नो वा न कथंचन उपपद्यते। न चार्जुनस्यैव ज्यायसी बुद्धिः न अनुष्ठेया इति भगवता उक्तं पूर्वम् इति कल्पयितुं युक्तं, येन 'ज्यायसी चेत्' इति प्रश्नः स्यात्।

0.6. Again, this conclusion is strengthened by the unreasonableness of Arjuna's question formulated in *BG* 3.1; "If, in your view, knowledge is superior to work." In chapter II, if the the Lord had affirmed that Arjuna should practise synthesized knowledge and work, his question would obviously be unreasonable. If Arjuna was personally bidden to practise synthesized knowledge and work, the knowledge that is superior to work has also to be practised, of course. There is thus no room for the reproach expressed in the words, "Why, Kṛṣṇa! do you bid me do this dreadful work?" *BG* 3.1. Nor is this question itself reasonable. To make this question reasonable, it is not to be supposed that the Lord had asked Arjuna alone not to practise this knowledge, so superior to works.

0.7. यदि पुनः एकस्य पुरुषस्य ज्ञानकर्मणोः विरोधात् युगपदनुष्ठानं न संभवतीति भिन्नपुरुषानुष्ठेयत्वं भगवता पूर्वम् उक्तं स्यात्, ततोऽयं प्रश्नः उपपन्नः 'ज्यायसी चेत्' इत्यादिः । अविवेकतः प्रश्नकल्पनायाम् अपि भिन्नपुरुषानुष्ठेयत्वेन ज्ञान-कर्मनिष्ठयोः भगवतः प्रतिवचनं न उपपद्यते । न च अज्ञाननिमित्तं भगवत्प्रतिवचनं कल्पनीयम् । अस्माच्च भिन्नपुरुषानुष्ठेयत्वेन ज्ञानकर्मनिष्ठयोः भगवतः प्रति-वचनदर्शनात् ज्ञानकर्मणोः समुच्चयानुपपत्तिः ।

तस्मात् केवलात् एव ज्ञानात् मोक्ष इति एषोऽर्थो निश्चितः गीतासु सर्वोपनिषत्सु च ॥

0.7. To make the question reasonable, the Lord may be taken to have stated that the opposing disciplines of knowledge and works cannot be practised by one and the same person simultaneously; only different persons may practise them. Even if the question of Arjuna is held to have sprung from lack of discrimination, the Lord's reply that the disciplines of knowledge and works pertain to different agents does not stand to reason. Nor may the Lord's reply be set down to His ignorance. Also from the nature of His reply that different agents should practise the two disciplines, the incompatibility of the synthesis of knowledge and works follows. Therefore, the indubitable doctrine of the Gītā and the Upaniṣads is that emancipation ensues from the self-sufficient knowledge alone.

0.8. ज्ञानकर्मणोः 'एकं वद निश्चित्य' [३.२.] इति च एकविषया एव प्रार्थ-नाऽनुपपन्ना, उभयोः समुच्चयसंभवे । 'कुरु कर्मैव तस्मात्त्वम्' [४. १५] इति च ज्ञाननिष्ठाऽसंभवमर्जुनस्य अवधारणेन दर्शयिष्यति ।

0.8. If knowledge and works could possibly be synthesized, the request in verse 3.2 'to point out the one sure means' would be inconsistent with reason. In 4.15 the Lord will emphatically rule out the discipline of knowledge as far as Arjuna is concerned: "Therefore you must perform work."

अर्जुन उवाच :

ज्यायसी चेत्कर्मणस्ते मता बुद्धिर्जनार्दन ।
तत्किं कर्मणि घोरे मां नियोजयसि केशव ॥१॥

Arjuna said:

1. O Kṛṣṇa! If your view is that knowledge is superior to work, why do you bid me undertake this fearful work of war?

1.1. ज्यायसी चेत् इति ॥ ज्यायसी श्रेयसी चेत् यदि कर्मणः सकाशात् ते तव मता अभिप्रेता बुद्धिः ज्ञानं हे जनार्दन । यदि बुद्धिकर्मणी समुच्चिते इष्टे तदा एकं श्रेयःसाधनम् इति कर्मणः ज्यायसी बुद्धिः इति कर्मणोऽतिरिक्तकरणं बुद्धेः अनुपपन्नं अर्जुनेन कृतं स्यात्; न हि तदेव तस्मात् फलतः अतिरिक्तं स्यात् । तथा च, कर्मणः श्रेयस्करी भगवता उक्ता बुद्धिः, अश्रेयस्करं च कर्म कुरु इति मां प्रतिपादयति, तत् किं कारणं इति भगवतः उपालम्भमिव कुर्वन् तत् किं कस्मात् कर्मणि घोरे क्रूरे हिंसालक्षणे मां नियोजयसि केशव इति च यत् आह तत् च न उपपद्यते ॥

अथ स्मार्तेनैव कर्मणा समुच्चयः सर्वेषां भगवता उक्तः अर्जुनेन च अवधारितश्चेत्, 'तत् किं कर्मणि घोरे मां नियोजयसि' इत्यादि कथं युक्तं वचनम् ? किञ्च

1.1. "In relation to works, if your view or opinion is that knowledge is superior to works . . . O Kṛṣṇa." If knowledge and works were sought to be combined, the means of the supreme good or emancipation would be just one only; and Arjuna would be unreasonable in treating knowledge as something over and above works. Indeed, one and the same thing cannot exceed itself with reference to the effect it produces. Therefore, what the Lord had declared was that knowledge contributes to a greater good in comparison with works. Still, He tells Arjuna to perform works that produce but little good. Reproaching, as it were, the Lord for doing it, Arjuna asks: why do you bid me do this fearful work—this cruel slaughter? This procedure of Arjuna is unreasonable. On the other hand, had the Lord taught, and Arjuna clearly understood, that the synthesis is with works enjoined by Smṛti, how can his reproach, "Why do you bid me, etc.," be deemed reasonable?

Moreover,

**व्यामिश्रेणेव वाक्येन बुद्धिं मोहयसीव मे ।
तदेकं वद निश्चित्य येन श्रेयोऽहमाप्नुयाम् ॥२॥**

2. By words that seem confused, You bewilder my intelligence, as it were. Therefore set forth one sure course by which I may attain the highest good.

2.1. व्यामिश्रेण इति ॥ व्यामिश्रेण इव, यद्यपि विविक्ताभिधायी भगवान् तथापि मम मन्दबुद्धेः व्यामिश्रम् इव भगवद्वाक्यं प्रतिभाति । तेन मम बुद्धिं मोहयसि इव, मम मन्दबुद्धेः व्यामोहापनयाय हि प्रवृत्तः त्वं तु कथं मोहयसि? अतः ब्रवीमि बुद्धिं मोहयसि इव मे मम इति । त्वं तु भिन्नकर्तृकयोः ज्ञानकर्मणोः एकपुरुषानुष्ठानासंभवं यदि मन्यसे, तत्र एवं सति तत् तयोः एकं बुद्धिं कर्म वा इदम् एव अर्जुनस्य योग्यं बुद्धिशक्त्यवस्थानुरूपम् इति निश्चित्य वद ब्रूहि, येन ज्ञानेन कर्मणा वा अन्यतरेण श्रेयः अहं आप्नुयां प्राप्नुयाम् इति [यदुक्तं तदपि नोपपद्यते] ॥

2.1. Though the Lord spoke distinctly to 'me', Arjuna, who am feeble in intelligence, His words seem to be confused. With them, "You bewilder my intelligence, as it were." How can you, who sought to dispel the confusion of my dull wits, bewilder me, instead? So I say, "You bewilder my intelligence, as it were." But if You think that the disciplines of knowledge and works, meant for different agents, cannot be observed by one and the same person, then affirm with certitude which one of these two would suit me, i.e. be in accordance with the power of my intelligence and my standing in life. Thus by either knowledge or works I shall achieve the highest good." (Even this plea is not reasonable.)

2.2. यदि हि कर्मनिष्ठायां गुणभूतम् अपि ज्ञानं भगवता उक्तं स्यात्, तत् कथं तयोः "एकं वद" इति एकविषया एव अर्जुनस्य शुश्रूषा स्यात्? न हि भगवता पूर्वं उक्तं "अन्यतरत् एव ज्ञानकर्मणोः वक्ष्यामि, नैव द्वयं" इति, येन उभयप्राप्त्यसंभवं आत्मनः मन्यमानः एकमेव प्रार्थयेत् ॥

2.2. Had the Lord assigned to knowledge even a subordinate place in the discipline of works, how could Arjuna seek instruction in 'one of these two'? Surely He did not say earlier that He would speak only about one of the two disciplines of knowledge and works, and not about both of them. Were that the case, thinking that instruction on both was impossible, Arjuna might request instruction in one

3.0. प्रश्नानुरूपम् एव प्रतिवचनं श्रीभगवान् उवाच–

3.0. In conformity with the question the Lord replied:

श्रीभगवानुवाच :

लोकेऽस्मिन् द्विविधा निष्ठा पुरा प्रोक्ता मयाऽनघ।
ज्ञानयोगेन सांख्यानां कर्मयोगेन योगिनाम् ॥३॥

The blessed Lord said:

3. O sinless one! Two kinds of disciplines in this world were set forth by Me in times of yore—for the Sāṁkhyas the discipline of knowledge, and for the Yogins, that of works.

3.1. लोके अस्मिन् इति ॥ लोके अस्मिन् शास्त्रार्थानुष्ठानाधिकृतानां त्रैवर्णिकानां द्विविधा द्विप्रकारा निष्ठा स्थितिः अनुष्ठेयतात्पर्यं पुरा पूर्वं सर्गादौ प्रजाः सृष्ट्वा तासां अभ्युदयनिःश्रेयसप्राप्तिसाधनं वेदार्थसंप्रदायम् आविष्कुर्वता प्रोक्ता मया सर्वज्ञेन ईश्वरेण हे अनघ अपाप। तत्र का सा द्विविधा निष्ठा इति ? आह— तत्र ज्ञानयोगेन ज्ञानम् एव योगः तेन सांख्यानां आत्मानात्मविषयविवेकविज्ञानवतां ब्रह्मचर्याश्रमात् एव कृतसंन्यासानां वेदान्तविज्ञानसुनिश्चितार्थानां परमहंसपरिव्राजकानां ब्रह्मणि एव अवस्थितानां निष्ठा प्रोक्ता। कर्मयोगेन कर्म एव योगः कर्मयोगः तेन कर्मयोगेन योगिनां कर्मिणां निष्ठा प्रोक्ता इत्यर्थः।

3.1. In this world, in times of yore, i.e., at the beginning of creation, after bringing forth mankind, a two-fold discipline was promulgated by Me for the members of the first three classes, who are entitled to carry out the injunctions of the *śāstras*,—by Me, the omniscient Lord. O sinless prince! I sought to reveal a tradition for implementing the Vedic scheme of life whose goals are worldly prosperity and emancipation. What is this two-fold discipline? Listen: (i) The discipline of knowledge. Knowledge of the Self itself is the Yoga or discipline meant here. This has been promulgated for the followers of Sāṁkhya who have the discriminative knowledge between Self and non-self. From the stage of celibacy itself, they have embraced the life of renunciation. Through their mastery of the Vedānta they have acquired an unshakable grip over the principles of that *śāstra.* They are the renouncers of the Paramahamsa order who have established themselves in the ultimate Reality. (ii) The discipline of works, wherein works constitute Yoga, has been promulgated for the Yogins or the performers of works.

3.2. यदि च एकेन पुरुषेण एकस्मै पुरुषार्थाय ज्ञानं कर्म च समुच्चित्य अनुष्ठेयं भगवता इष्टं उक्तं वक्ष्यमाणं वा गीतासु वेदेषु चोक्तम् कथं इह अर्जुनाय उपसन्नाय प्रियाय विशिष्टभिन्नपुरुषकर्तृके एव ज्ञानकर्मनिष्ठे ब्रूयात् ? यदि पुनः 'अर्जुनः ज्ञानं कर्म च द्वयं श्रुत्वा स्वयम् एव अनुष्ठास्यति, अन्येषां तु भिन्नपुरुषानुष्ठेयतां वक्ष्यामि' इति मतं भगवतः कल्प्येत, तदा रागद्वेषवान् अप्रमाणभूतो भगवान् कल्पितः स्यात् । तत् च अयुक्तम् । तस्मात् कयापि युक्त्या न समुच्चयः ज्ञान-कर्मणोः ॥

3.2. If, according to the Lord, both knowledge and work are to be practised in combination by one and the same person and therefore have been set forth or are going to be set forth in the Vedas and the Gītā, how can He say to Arjuna here, His beloved and confiding disciple, that these disciplines are meant for differently qualified agents? It may be suggested that the Lord's idea is as follows: After listening to Me, of his own accord, Arjuna will practise both knowledge and works; for others, I shall teach that they are to be practised by different agents. A suggestion like this, however, makes the Lord guilty of partiality and antipathy; He can no longer be an authoritative teacher. Of course, this is an unreasonable procedure. Therefore, by no line of reasoning whatsoever, is it possible to combine knowledge and works.

4.0. यत् अर्जुनेन उक्तं कर्मणः ज्यायस्त्वं बुद्धेः, तत् च स्थितं, अनिराकरणात् । तस्याश्च ज्ञाननिष्ठायाः संन्यासिनाम् एव अनुष्ठेयत्वं, भिन्नपुरुषानुष्ठेयत्ववचनात् । भगवतः एवमेव अनुमतम् इति गम्यते ।

'मां च बन्धकारणे कर्मण्येव नियोजयसि' इति विषण्णमनसं अर्जुनं 'कर्म नारभे'

इति एवं मन्वानं आलक्ष्य आह भगवान् — न कर्मणां अनारम्भात् इति । अथवा — ज्ञानकर्मनिष्ठयोः परस्परविरोधात् एकेन पुरुषेण युगपत् अनुष्ठातुं अशक्यत्वे सति इतरेतरानपेक्षयोः एव पुरुषार्थहेतुत्वे प्राप्ते कर्मनिष्ठायाः ज्ञाननिष्ठाप्राप्तिहेतुत्वेन पुरुषार्थहेतुत्वं, न स्वातन्त्र्येण; ज्ञाननिष्ठा तु कर्मनिष्ठोपायलब्धात्मिका सती स्वातन्त्र्येण पुरुषार्थहेतुः अन्यानपेक्षा, इति एतं अर्थं प्रदर्शयिष्यन् आह भगवान् —

4.0. The superiority of knowledge to works that Arjuna affirmed remains, since it has not been repudiated by the Lord. The world-renouncers alone may practise the discipline of knowledge, since the Lord has stated that the two are to be practised by different agents. That this position alone has the Lord's sanction may be understood. To Arjuna who grieves, saying to the Lord, "You enjoin on me work alone that binds", and who, therefore, proposes to avoid works, the Lord says, "not by refusing to work at all" (*BG* 3.4). Alternatively, since one and the same person cannot address himself to the opposed disciplines of knowledge and works at the same time, it should follow that they can promote the ends of life only independently of each other. Even so, the discipline of works may promote life's ends by endowing the agent with the fitness to adopt the disciplines of knowledge, and not independently, by itself, whereas the discipline of knowledge, generated by that of works, is a totally independent means to life's supreme end. In order to elucidate this view, the Lord says:

न कर्मणामनारम्भान्नैष्कर्म्यं पुरुषोऽश्नुते ।
न च संन्यसनादेव सिद्धिं समधिगच्छति ॥४॥

4. Man does not achieve freedom from works by abstention from them. None attains perfection through the mere renunciation of works, either.

4.1. न कर्मणां इति ॥ न कर्मणां अनारम्भात् अप्रारम्भात् कर्मणां क्रियाणां यज्ञादीनां इह जन्मनि जन्मान्तरे वा अनुष्ठितानां उपात्तदुरितक्षयहेतुत्वेन सत्त्वशुद्धिकारणानां तत्कारणत्वेन च ज्ञानोत्पत्तिद्वारेण ज्ञाननिष्ठाहेतूनां,

'ज्ञानमुत्पद्यते पुंसां क्षयात् पापस्य कर्मणः ।
यथादर्शतलप्रख्ये पश्यत्यात्मानमात्मनि' ॥ [शां. प. २०४. ८.]

इत्यादिस्मरणात्, अनारम्भात् अननुष्ठानात् नैष्कर्म्यं निष्कर्मभावं कर्मशून्यतां ज्ञानयोगेन निष्ठा निष्क्रियात्मस्वरूपेणैव अवस्थानं इति यावत्, पुरुषः न अश्नुते न प्राप्नोति इत्यर्थः ।

4.1. By abstention from—the mere non-initiation of—works like sacrifices, man cannot achieve freedom from them i.e., the discipline of knowledge or existence as pure Self. Works performed in this life or past lives serve to attenuate the sins incurred and to purify the mind; thus they give a start to the discipline of knowledge by generating knowledge. *Vide*, the Smṛti: "Due to the exhaustion of evil deeds there springs up knowledge. As in a mirror, in the mind one perceives the Self (*Śānti-parvan*, 204.8). 'Abstention' means non-initiation. Freedom from works is the state of one who performs no works; it is the utter absence of works or the discipline of knowledge. It is restful being, the very essence of the Self that works not. Man may not achieve this state by merely abstaining from works. This is the sense of the verse.

4.2. 'न कर्मणां अनारम्भात् नैष्कर्म्यं पुरुषोऽश्नुते' इति वचनात् तद्विपर्ययात् तेषां आरम्भात् नैष्कर्म्यं अश्नुते गम्यते । कस्मात्पुनः कारणात् अनारम्भात् नैष्कर्म्यं न अश्नुते इति ? उच्यते—नैष्कर्म्योपायत्वात् कर्मारम्भस्य । न हि उपायमन्तरेण उपेयप्राप्तिः अस्ति । कर्मयोगोपायत्वं च नैष्कर्म्यलक्षणस्य ज्ञानयोगस्य, श्रुतौ इह च प्रतिपादनात् । श्रुतौ तावत् प्रकृतस्य आत्मलोकस्य वेद्यस्य वेदनोपायत्वेन 'तमेतं वेदानुवचनेन ब्राह्मणा विविदिषन्ति यज्ञेन' [बृ. उ. ४. ४. २२.] इत्यादिना कर्मयोगस्य ज्ञानयोगोपायत्वं प्रतिपादितम् । इहापि च —

संन्यासस्तु महाबाहो दुःखमाप्तुमयोगतः [५.६.]
योगिनः कर्म कुर्वन्ति संगं त्यक्त्वाऽऽत्मशुद्धये [५.११.]
यज्ञो दानं तपश्चैव पावनानि मनीषिणाम् [१८.५.]

इत्यादि प्रतिपादयिष्यति । ननु च —

'अभयं सर्वभूतेभ्यो दत्वा नैष्कर्म्यमाचरेत्' । [आश्वमे. प. ४६. १८.] इत्यादौ कर्तव्यकर्मसंन्यासात् अपि नैष्कर्म्यप्राप्तिं दर्शयति । लोके च कर्मणां अनारम्भात् नैष्कर्म्यं इति प्रसिद्धतरम् । अतश्च नैष्कर्म्यार्थिनः किं कर्मारम्भेण ? — इति प्राप्तम् । अतः आह — न च संन्यसनादेव इति । नापि संन्यसनात् एव केवलात् कर्मपरित्यागमात्रात् एव ज्ञानरहितात् सिद्धिं नैष्कर्म्यलक्षणां — ज्ञानयोगेन निष्ठां — समधिगच्छति न प्राप्नोति ॥

4.2. "Man does not attain freedom from works by abstention from them," these words suggest that by its opposite i.e., by the performance of works man may attain such freedom. Why does he fail to attain freedom by abstention from works? Because, the means to such freedom is the performance of works. An end cannot be attained without the employment of means. To the discipline of knowledge, whose characteristic is freedom from works, Karma Yoga is the means. So has it been taught both in the *śruti* and in the *Gītā*. The *śruti* states the means of knowing the sphere of the Self, the contextual object of knowledge, thus: "Brāhmaṇas seek to know this sphere of the Self through the study of the Vedas, through sacrifice." (*B.U.*4.4.22), which makes the Karma Yoga instrumental to the discipline of knowledge. Here in *B.G.*5.6 too, this idea will be set forth thus: "It is hard, O mighty armed! to achieve renunciation without Karma Yoga." "Unattached, the Yogins perform works for purifying the mind" 5.11; "Sacrifice, gift-giving, and penance purify the intelligent" 18.5. But the attainment of freedom from works through the renunciation of works has also been laid down, *Vide*: "Ensuring freedom from fear to all living beings, practise abstention from all works" (*Aśvamedha-parvan* 46.18). Besides, the world is more familiar with the freedom from works resulting from the non-commencement of works. Therefore, why should one perform works at all, when the aim is freedom from works? "Because, none attains perfection through renunciation alone." That is, through the non-performance of works alone, without knowledge, none attains perfection, freedom from work, establishment in the discipline of knowledge.

5.0. कस्मात् पुनः कारणात् कर्मसंन्यासमात्रात् एव केवलात् ज्ञानरहितात् सिद्धिं नैष्कर्म्यलक्षणां पुरुषः न अधिगच्छति ? इति हेत्वाकाङ्क्षायां आह —

5.0. Due to what reason does a man fail to attain perfection or freedom from the obligation to work, by renunciation of works, sans knowledge? The answer to this demand for reason follows:

न हि कश्चित् क्षणमपि जातु तिष्ठत्यकर्मकृत् ।
कार्यते ह्यवशः कर्म सर्वः प्रकृतिजैर्गुणैः ॥५॥

5. None indeed, even for a moment, remains without doing work. All, being dependent, are made to work by the constituents of Prakṛti.

5.1. न हि इति ॥ न हि यस्मात् क्षणमपि कालं जातु कदाचित् कश्चित् तिष्ठति अकर्मकृत् सन् । कस्मात् ? कार्यते प्रवर्त्यते हि यस्मात् अवशः एव अस्वतन्त्रः एव कर्म सर्वः प्राणी प्रकृतिजैः प्रकृतितः जातैः सत्त्वरजस्तमोभिः गुणैः । अज्ञः इति वाक्यशेषः, यतः वक्ष्यति 'गुणैर्यो न विचाल्यते' [१४. २३.] इति । सांख्यानां पृथक्करणात् [३. ३.] अज्ञानाम् एव हि कर्मयोगः, न ज्ञानिनाम् । ज्ञानिनां तु गुणैः अचाल्यमानानां स्वतः चलनाभावात् कर्मयोगः न उपपद्यते । तथा च व्याख्यातं 'वेदाविनाशिनं' [२. २१.] इत्यत्र ॥

5.1. Because, not even for a moment, does anyone remain without doing work. Why? Being dependent, all living beings are made to work by Prakṛti's constituents, *sattva*, *rajas* and *tamas*. This applies to the ignorant only, for in 14.23, a reference is made to "one who is not pushed about by the constituents'. The verse 3.3 places the Sāṁkhyas, the followers of the discipline of knowledge, in a separate class. So Karma Yoga is prescribed for the ignorant alone, and not for those who know. These latter, not subject to Prakṛti's constituents, stir not of their own accord; so Karma Yoga would not suit them. Thus has it been elucidated in the commentary on 2.21.

6.0. यस्तु अनात्मज्ञः चोदितं कर्म नारभते इति तत् असत् इति आह—

6.0. The non-knowers of the Self, who refuse to do work prescribed by the scripture, are in error. This is pointed out here:

कर्मेन्द्रियाणि संयम्य य आस्ते मनसा स्मरन् ।
इन्द्रियार्थान् विमूढात्मा मिथ्याचारः स उच्यते ॥६॥

6. Controlling the organs of action, he who lets his mind dwell on their objects has a confounded mind; he is said to be a hyprocrite.

6.1. कर्मेन्द्रियाणि इति ॥ कर्मेन्द्रियाणि हस्तादीनि संयम्य संहृत्य यः आस्ते तिष्ठति मनसा स्मरन् चिन्तयन् इन्द्रियार्थान् विषयान् विमूढात्मा विमूढान्तःकरणः मिथ्याचारः मृषाचारः पापाचारः सः उच्यते ॥

6.1. The organs of action are the hands etc., 'Controlling them' i.e., immobilizing them, 'he who lets his mind dwell or think of their objects'—his 'mind' or inner sense, is confounded. His conduct is false; he is said to sin.

यस्त्विन्द्रियाणि मनसा नियम्यारभतेऽर्जुन ।
कर्मेन्द्रियैः कर्मयोगमसक्तः स विशिष्यते ॥७॥

7. Controlling the sense organs with the mind, he who commences the Yoga of action with the organs of action, unattached, is held to excel, O Arjuna!

7.1. यस्तु इति ॥ यस्तु पुनः कर्मणि अधिकृतः अज्ञः बुद्धीन्द्रियाणि मनसा नियम्य आरभते अर्जुन, कर्मेन्द्रियैः वाक्पाण्यादिभिः । किं आरभते ? इत्याह — कर्मयोगं असक्तः सन् फलाभिसन्धिवर्जितः सः विशिष्यते इतरस्मात् मिथ्याचारात् ॥

7.1. But, Arjuna! the ignorant man, called upon to act, who mentally controls the organs of cognition and begins the Yoga of action with the organs of action, i.e., tongue, hands, etc. 'unattached' or without desire for fruits of actions, is superior to the hypocrite (*vide* verse 6).

8.0. यतः एवं अतः—

8.0. Such being the case,

नियतं कुरु कर्म त्वं कर्म ज्यायो ह्यकर्मणः ।
शरीरयात्रापि च ते न प्रसिद्ध्येदकर्मणः ॥८॥

8. Always do prescribed work; work is superior to inaction. Indeed, even life in the body is impossible without working.

8.1. नियतं इति ॥ नियतं नित्यं [शास्त्रोपदिष्टं], यो यस्मिन् कर्मणि अधिकृतः फलाय च अश्रुतं तत् नियतं कर्म, तत् कुरु त्वं हे अर्जुन, यतः कर्म ज्यायः अधिकतरं फलतः, हि यस्मात् अकर्मणः अकरणात् अनारम्भात् । कथं ? शरीरयात्रा शरीरस्थितिः अपि च ते तव न प्रसिद्धयेत् प्रसिद्धिं न गच्छेत् अकर्मणः अकरणात् । अतः दृष्टः कर्माकर्मणोः विशेषः लोके ॥

8.1. Work prescribed by the *śāstras* is obligatory, is to be done always by one called upon to do it; no fruit is associated with it. That work, Arjuna! you must do, because work is superior to inaction or non-doing as regards consequences. How? 'Life in the body', even its continuance, cannot be secured without working. Thus has the distinction between working and non-working been marked in this world.

9.0. यच्च मन्यसे बन्धार्थत्वात् कर्म न कर्तव्यं इति तत् अपि असत् । कथम् ?

9.0. Also your notion that work makes for bondage and so must not be done is wrong. How?

यज्ञार्थात्कर्मणोऽन्यत्र लोकोऽयं कर्मबन्धनः ।
तदर्थं कर्म कौन्तेय मुक्तसङ्गः समाचर ॥९॥

9. This world is bound by works other than those done as sacrifice, O son of Kuntī. Free from attachment, do work as sacrifice.

9.1. यज्ञार्थात् इति ॥ 'यज्ञो वै विष्णुः' [तै. सं. १. ७. ४.] इति श्रुतेः यज्ञः ईश्वरः, तदर्थं यत् क्रियते तत् यज्ञार्थं कर्म । तस्मात् कर्मणः अन्यत्र अन्येन कर्मणा लोकः अयं अधिकृतः कर्मकृत् कर्मबन्धनः कर्म बन्धनं यस्य सः अयं लोकः, न तु यज्ञार्थात् । अतः तदर्थं यज्ञार्थं कर्म कौन्तेय, मुक्तसङ्गः कर्मफलसङ्गवर्जितः सन् समाचर निर्वर्तय ॥

9.1. 'Sacrifice is indeed Viṣṇu' (*TS* 1.7.4)—this makes sacrifice equivalent to God. What is done for Him is work as sacrifice; through works other than those done as sacrifice are people called upon to work, bound by works. Through non-sacrificial works this world is bound, such works proving a bondage; but never through sacrificial works. Therefore,

Arjuna! free from attachment to the fruits of works, perform works as sacrifice.

10.0. इतश्च अधिकृतेन कर्म कर्तव्यम्—

10.0. For the following reason also work has to be done by one entitled to do it.

सहयज्ञाः प्रजाः सृष्ट्वा पुरोवाच प्रजापतिः ।
अनेन प्रसविष्यध्वमेष वोऽस्त्विष्टकामधुक् ॥१०॥

10. Bringing forth creatures together with sacrifice, the Lord of creatures said of old: Multiply by means of sacrifice; let it yield whatever you seek.

10.1. सह इति ॥ सहयज्ञाः यज्ञसहिताः प्रजाः त्रयः वर्णाः ताः सृष्ट्वा उत्पाद्य पुरा पूर्वं सर्गादौ उवाच उक्तवान् प्रजापतिः प्रजानां स्रष्टा अनेन यज्ञेन प्रसविष्यध्वं प्रसवः वृद्धिः उत्पत्तिः तां कुरुध्वम् । एष यज्ञः वः युष्माकं अस्तु भवतु इष्टकामधुक् इष्टान् अभिप्रेतान् कामान् फलविशेषान् दोग्धि इति इष्टकामधुक् ॥
कथम् ? —

10.1. 'Together with sacrifice' i.e., the creatures were brought forth together with sacrifices. 'Creatures' point to the classes. 'Bringing them forth' or generating them, 'of old', at the beginning of creation, 'the Lord of creatures', the creator, said: By means of the sacrifice do you multiply or increase. Let this sacrifice prove to be the cow that yields all that you seek, the specific fruits you seek.
How?

देवान् भावयतानेन ते देवा भावयन्तु वः ।
परस्परं भावयन्तः श्रेयः परमवाप्स्यथ ॥११॥

11. By means of this sacrifice nourish the Devas; let the Devas nourish you. Mutually nourishing, may you win the supreme good.

11.1. देवान् इति ॥ देवान् इन्द्रादीन् भावयत वर्धयत अनेन यज्ञेन । ते देवाः

भावयन्तु वृष्ट्यादिना आप्याययन्तु वः युष्मान् । एवं परस्परं अन्योन्यं भावयन्तः श्रेयः परं मोक्षलक्षणं ज्ञानप्राप्तिक्रमेण अवाप्स्यथ । स्वर्गं वा परं श्रेयः अवाप्स्यथ ॥

किञ्च —

11.1. 'Nourish the Devas' i.e., Indra and others, by means of sacrifice, and let the Devas, by means of rains etc., 'nourish' you, i.e. cause you to flourish. Thus, mutually nourishing, achieve the 'supreme good' or emancipation by gaining knowledge.

Besides,

इष्टान् भोगान् हि वो देवा दास्यन्ते यज्ञभाविताः ।
तैर्दत्तानप्रदायैभ्यो यो भुङ्क्ते स्तेन एव सः ॥१२॥

12. The Devas nourished by sacrifices will give you the enjoyments you seek. Verily he is a thief who enjoys without giving back to the Devas (a share of) the gifts given by them.

12.1. इष्टान् भोगान् इति ॥ इष्टान् अभिप्रेतान् भोगान् हि वः युष्मभ्यं देवाः दास्यन्ते वितरिष्यन्ति स्त्रीपशुपुत्रादीन् यज्ञभाविताः यज्ञैः वर्धिताः तोषिताः इत्यर्थः । तैः देवैः दत्तान् भोगान् अप्रदाय अदत्वा, आनृण्यं अकृत्वा इत्यर्थः, एभ्यः देवेभ्यः, यः भुङ्क्ते स्वदेहेन्द्रियाण्येव तर्पयति स्तेनः एव तस्करः एव सः देवादिस्वापहारी ॥

ये पुनः —

12.1. The Devas will give you the enjoyments you seek—wives, cattle, children etc., that you seek, since they have been 'nourished' or pleased, by you through sacrifice. Without giving back a share of these enjoyments granted by the Devas i.e., without discharging the debts owed to them, whoso enjoys or pleases his body and sense organs, is verily a thief; he has misappropriated the wealth of the Devas.

On the contrary those

यज्ञशिष्टाशिनः सन्तो मुच्यन्ते सर्वकिल्बिषैः ।
भुञ्जते ते त्वघं पापा ये पचन्त्यात्मकारणात् ॥१३॥

13. Good men who partake of what remains after offering sacrifices are liberated from all sins; whereas the sinners who cook for their own sake live on their sins.

13.1. यज्ञ इति ॥ देवयज्ञादीन् निर्वर्त्य तच्छिष्टं अशनं अमृताख्यं अशितुं शीलं येषां ते यज्ञशिष्टाशिनः सन्तः मुच्यन्ते सर्वकिल्बिषैः सर्वैः पापैः चुलचादिपञ्च-सूनाकृतैः प्रमादकृतहिंसादिजनितैः च अन्यैः । ये तु आत्मरयः, भुञ्जते ते तु अघं पापं स्वयमपि पापाः—ये पचन्ति पाकं निर्वर्तयन्ति आत्मकारणात् आत्महेतोः ॥

13.1. Those who habitually feed on the ambrosial food that remains after sacrificing to the Devas are partakers of the sacrificial leavings. These good men are liberated from all the sins involved in the five-fold killing, connected with the hearth etc., and also from other sins incurred through heedless slaughter, etc. On the contrary, those sinful self-seekers eat sin who cook only for feeding themselves.

14.0. इतश्च अधिकृतेन कर्म कर्तव्यं, जगच्चक्रप्रवृत्तिहेतुः हि कर्म । कथं इति ? उच्यते—

14.0. For the following reason, too, work must be done by one called upon to do it; for, work is what operates the wheel of the universe. How? Listen:

अन्नाद्भवन्ति भूतानि पर्जन्यादन्नसंभवः ।
यज्ञाद्भवति पर्जन्यो यज्ञः कर्मसमुद्भवः ॥१४॥

14. Living beings are born of food; food is produced by rain. Rain is due to sacrifice. Sacrifice is the offspring of work.

14.1. अन्नात् इति ॥ अन्नात् भुक्तात् लोहितरेतःपरिणतात् प्रत्यक्षं भवन्ति जायन्ते भूतानि । पर्जन्यात् वृष्टेः अन्नस्य संभवः अन्नसंभवः । यज्ञात् भवति पर्जन्यः, 'अग्नौ प्रास्ताहुतिः सम्यगादित्यमुपतिष्ठते । आदित्याज्जायते वृष्टिः वृष्टेरन्नं ततः प्रजाः' ॥ इति स्मृतेः [मनु ३.७६.] । यज्ञः अपूर्वम् । स च यज्ञः कर्मसमुद्भवः ऋत्विग्यजमानयोश्च व्यापारः कर्म, ततः समुद्भवः यस्य यज्ञस्य अपूर्वस्य सः यज्ञः कर्मसमुद्भवः ॥

14.1. Living beings, obviously, are born of the consumed food that is transformed into blood and semen. Food is produced by rain which is a product of sacrifice; *vide Manu*, 3.76. The oblation, properly placed in the fire, goes up to the sun. Rain is due to the sun, and food due to the rain. Of food are born living beings. 'Sacrifice' means the unique power engendered by the activity of the priests and the sacrificer. This activity is the work whence the 'unique power' the *apūrva*, is born.

15.0. तच्च एवंविधं कर्म कुतः जातमित्याह—

15.0. Whence is this sort of 'work' or energy born? Answer:

कर्म ब्रह्मोद्भवं विद्धि ब्रह्माक्षरसमुद्भवम् ।
तस्मात्सर्वगतं ब्रह्म नित्यं यज्ञे प्रतिष्ठितम् ॥१५॥

15. Know that this work is born of the Vedas, and that the Vedas are born of the imperishable Reality. Therefore, the all-pervading Veda is eternally rooted in sacrificial work.

15.1. कर्म इति ॥ कर्म ब्रह्मोद्भवं ब्रह्म वेदः सः उद्भवः कारणं प्रकाशकः यस्य तत् कर्म ब्रह्मोद्भवं विद्धि विजानीहि । ब्रह्म पुनः वेदाख्यं अक्षरसमुद्भवं अक्षरं ब्रह्म परमात्मा समुद्भवः यस्य तत् अक्षरसमुद्भवम् । ब्रह्म वेदः इत्यर्थः । यस्मात् साक्षात् परमात्माख्यात् अक्षरात् पुरुषात् निश्वासवत् समुद्भूत ब्रह्म तस्मात् सर्वार्थप्रकाशकत्वात् सर्वगतं; सर्वगतं अपि सत् नित्यं सदा यज्ञविधिप्रधानत्वात् यज्ञे प्रतिष्ठितम् ॥

15.1. Work is born of Brahman, Brahman is the Veda. 'Born of Veda' means revealed by the Veda. Work, in this context, is of this description. Again, Brahman or Veda is born of the Imperishable or Brahman, the supreme Self. That Brahman here means the Veda is the sense. Since Brahman, the Veda, is directly derived from the supreme Self—the imperishable Spirit—like the vital breath, therefore, the all-revealing and eternal Veda is established for all times in sacrificial work, the latter being a dominant theme of the Vedas.

So,

एवं प्रवर्तितं चक्रं नानुवर्तयतीह यः ।
अघायुरिन्द्रियारामो मोघं पार्थ स जीवति ॥१६॥

16. He who fails to conform to the cycle of functions thus established is, Arjuna! a sinner; he revels in the sphere of sense-life; he lives in vain.

16.1. एवं इति ॥ एवं इत्थं ईश्वरेण वेदयज्ञपूर्वकं जगच्चक्रं प्रवर्तितं न अनुवर्तयति इह लोके यः कर्मणि अधिकृतः सन् अघायुः अघं पापं आयुः जीवनं यस्य सः अघायुः, पापजीवनः इति यावत् इन्द्रियारामः इन्द्रियैः आरामः आरमणं आक्रीडा विषयेषु यस्य सः इन्द्रियारामः मोघं वृथा हे पार्थ, सः जीवति ॥

16.1. The cycle of cosmic functions, preceded by the Vedas and sacrifices, has been set in motion by God. In the world, he who, being competent only to do work, fails to conform to this cycle of functions, leads a life of sin. He delights in sense-contacts with objects, Arjuna! He lives in vain.

16.2. तस्मात् अज्ञेन अधिकृतेन कर्तव्यम् एव कर्म इति प्रकरणार्थः (३. ४–१६) प्राक् आत्मज्ञाननिष्ठायोग्यताप्राप्तेः तादर्थ्येन कर्मयोगानुष्ठानं अधिकृतेन अनात्मज्ञेन कर्तव्यम् एव इत्येतत् 'न कर्मणामनारम्भात्' [३. ४.] इत्यत आरभ्य 'शरीरयात्रापि च ते न प्रसिद्ध्येदकर्मणः' [३. ८.] इत्येवमन्तेन प्रतिपाद्य 'यज्ञार्थात् कर्मणोऽन्यत्र' [३. ९.] इत्यादिना 'मोघं पार्थ स जीवति' [३. १६.] इत्येवमन्तेन अपि ग्रन्थेन प्रासंगिकं अधिकृतस्य अनात्मविदः कर्मानुष्ठाने बहु कारणं उक्तम्, तदकरणे च दोषसंकीर्तनं कृतम् ॥

16.2. Therefore the upshot of this context in this *BG* 3.4-16, is that the ignorant man, called upon to work, must do it. Before gaining competence to address oneself to the discipline of Self-knowledge, one, who is ignorant of the Self and called upon to work, must undertake the discipline of Karma Yoga. This idea has been elucidated in the *BG* from 3.4 to 3.8. A variety of reasons in support of it has been advanced in the verses 3.9 to 3.15—reasons that are valid for one ignorant of the Self and called upon to work. The errors involved in ignoring the call to work have also been stated.

17.0. एवं स्थिते किं एवं प्रवर्तितं चक्रं सर्वेण अनुवर्तनीयं ? आहोस्वित् पूर्वोक्तकर्मयोगानुष्ठानोपायप्राप्यां अनात्मविदा [-दः] ज्ञानयोगेनैव निष्ठां आत्मविद्भिः सांख्यैः अनुष्ठेयां अप्राप्तेनैव ? —इत्येवमर्थं अर्जुनस्य प्रश्नं आशङ्क्य स्वयमेव शास्त्रार्थस्य विवेकप्रतिपत्त्यर्थं 'एतं वै तमात्मानं विदित्वा निवृत्तमिथ्याज्ञानाः सन्तो ब्राह्मणा मिथ्याज्ञानवद्भिरवश्यं कर्तव्येभ्यः पुत्रैषणादिभ्यो व्युत्थायाथ भिक्षाचर्यं शरीरस्थितिमात्रप्रयुक्त चरन्ति न तेषां आत्मज्ञाननिष्ठाव्यतिरेकेणान्यत् कार्यं अस्ति' [बृ. उ. ३. ५. १ अर्थानुवादमात्रम्] इत्येवं श्रुत्यर्थं इह गीताशास्त्रे प्रतिपिपादयिषितं आविष्कुर्वन् आह भगवान् —

17.0. In this context is raised the question whether all should conform to the established cycle of activities or only he who is ignorant of the Self and has failed to rise to the level of the discipline of knowledge i.e., the sphere of the Sāṁkhyas who know the Self, the performance of Karma Yoga, set forth earlier, being but the means to attain this discipline of knowledge. In anticipation of this question on Arjuna's part, and in order to facilitate a discriminating grasp of the contents of the śāstra, the Lord unfolds the imports of the śāstra which the Gītā also seeks to convey.

The following is that teaching:

यस्त्वात्मरतिरेव स्यादात्मतृप्तश्च मानवः ।
आत्मन्येव च संतुष्टस्तस्य कार्यं न विद्यते ॥१७॥

17. For the man who delights solely in the Self, who is content with the Self, who finds satisfaction alone in the Self, there is no duty to perform.

17.1. यस्तु इति ॥ यस्तु सांख्यः आत्मज्ञाननिष्ठः आत्मरतिः आत्मनि एव रतिः न विषयेषु यस्य सः आत्मरतिः एव स्यात् भवेत् आत्मतृप्तः च आत्मना एव तृप्तः न अन्नरसादिना सः मानवः मनुष्यः संन्यासी आत्मनि एव च सन्तुष्टः । संतोषः हि बाह्यार्थलाभे सर्वस्य भवति, तं अनपेक्ष्य आत्मनि एव च संतुष्टः सर्वतः वीततृष्णः इत्येतत् । यः ईदृशः आत्मवित् तस्य कार्यं करणीयं न विद्यते नास्ति इत्यर्थः ॥

किञ्च —

17.1. That Sāṁkhya or man of knowledge, devoted to

Self-knowledge, who delights solely in the Self, and not in objects; who is content exclusively with the Self and not with pleasing the palate etc.,—that man is the renouncer who finds satisfaction in the Self. All people are generally pleased with external possessions. Disregarding them, the renouncer finds satisfaction in the Self alone; he is detached from all else—this is the import. The idea is that for such a Self-knower there is no duty to perform.

Moreover,

नैव तस्य कृतेनार्थो नाकृतेनेह कश्चन ।
न चास्य सर्वभूतेषु कश्चिदर्थव्यपाश्रयः ॥१८॥

18. He has nothing to gain from work done or left undone. On no beings does he depend as regards any interests of his own.

18.1. नैव इति ॥ न एव तस्य परमात्मरतेः कृतेन कर्मणा अर्थः प्रयोजनं अस्ति । अस्तु तर्हि अकृतेन अकरणेन प्रत्यवायाख्यः अनर्थः ? न अकृतेन इह लोके कश्चन कश्चिदपि प्रत्यवायप्राप्तिरूपः आत्महानिलक्षणः वा नैव अस्ति । न च अस्य सर्वभूतेषु ब्रह्मादिस्थावरान्तेषु भूतेषु कश्चित् अर्थव्यपाश्रयः प्रयोजननिमित्त-क्रियासाध्यः व्यपाश्रयः व्यपाश्रयणं [आलंबनं] कंचित् भूतविशेषं आश्रित्य न साध्यः कश्चित् अर्थः अस्ति येन तदर्था क्रिया अनुष्ठेया स्यात् ॥

18.1. He who is in love with the supreme Self has no purpose of his own to accomplish through any work done. Does he, then, incur the sin of omission or *pratyavāya* by not doing any work? Here in this world, surely, he does not incur the sin of omission by his failure to do work, either—a sin entailing a loss to his Self. Again, on no particular being, from Brahmā to stocks and stones, does he depend for gaining any end through his activity. Only if he did so, would he have had to perform such activity.

18.2. न त्वं एतस्मिन् सर्वतः संप्लुतोदकस्थानीये [२.४६.] सम्यग्दर्शने वर्तसे यत एवं—

18.2. However, you have not won this status, comparable

to the all-round inundation' (*vide BG* 2.46), namely the height of right perception.

This being the case,

तस्मादसक्तः सततं कार्यं कर्म समाचर ।
असक्तो ह्याचरन् कर्म परमाप्नोति पूरुषः ॥१९॥

19. Therefore, unattached, always do the work that has to be done; for, doing work with detachment, man attains the Supreme.

19.1. तस्मात् इति ॥ तस्मात् असक्तः सङ्गवर्जितः सततं सर्वदा कार्यं कर्तव्यं नित्यं कर्म समाचर निर्वर्तय । असक्तः हि यस्मात् समाचरन् ईश्वरार्थं कर्म कुर्वन् परं मोक्षं आप्नोति पूरुषः सत्त्वशुद्धिद्वारेण इत्यर्थः ॥

यस्माच्च—

19.1. Therefore, unattached, i.e. without clinging to the fruits of works, always do the work that calls for the doing—the obligatory work. Because, by doing works for the sake of God, man attains supreme liberation, through the purification of the mind.

Also because,

कर्मणैव हि संसिद्धिमास्थिता जनकादयः ।
लोकसंग्रहमेवापि संपश्यन् कर्तुमर्हसि ॥२०॥

20. Janaka and others achieved perfection through works alone. At least, to promote the welfare of the world, you ought to do works.

20.1. कर्मणैव इति । कर्मणा एव हि पूर्वे क्षत्रियाः विद्वांसः संसिद्धिं मोक्षं गन्तुं आस्थिताः प्रवृत्ताः । के ? जनकादयः जनकाश्वपतिप्रभृतयः । यदि ते प्राप्तसम्यग्दर्शनाः, तत् लोकसंग्रहार्थं प्रारब्धकर्मत्वात् कर्मणा सहैव असंन्यस्य एव कर्म संसिद्धिं आस्थिताः इत्यर्थः । अथ अप्राप्तसम्यग्दर्शनाः जनकादयः, तदा कर्मणा सत्त्वशुद्धिसाधनभूतेन क्रमेण संसिद्धिम् आस्थिता इति व्याख्येयः श्लोकः ॥

20.1. It is well known that wise Kṣatriyas in the past sought perfection or liberation by means of works alone. Who were they? Janaka and others like him, for example, Aśvapati. If they are held to have attained right perception due to their past operative works (Prārabdha-Karma), directed to world's welfare, they attained perfection while still doing works i.e., without renouncing them. This is the sense of this verse. If, however, Janaka etc., had not attained right perception, the verse may be taken to mean that they sought perfection through the process of working, the means of mental purification.

20.2. अथ मन्यसे—पूर्वैः अपि [जनकादिभिः] अजानद्भिः एव कर्तव्यं कर्म कृतं, तावता न अवश्यं अन्येन कर्तव्यं सम्यग्दर्शनवता कृतार्थेन इति ? तथापि प्रारब्धकर्मायत्तः त्वं लोकसंग्रहं एव अपि लोकस्य उन्मार्गप्रवृत्तिनिवारणं लोकसंग्रहः, तमेव अपि प्रयोजनं संपश्यन् कर्तुं अर्हसि ॥

20.2. Now you may think that even these ancient Kṣatriyas, Janaka and so forth, discharged their duties because they were ignorant of Self, and, therefore, that another, a perfect man with the right perception, need not follow suit. Still, being subject to operative past works, you ought to work in order to promote world's welfare i.e., to safeguard people from falling into wrong paths of conduct.

21.0. लोकसंग्रहः किमर्थं कर्तव्यः इति ? उच्यते—

21.0. Why should world's welfare be promoted? Listen:

यद्यदाचरति श्रेष्ठस्तत्तदेवेतरो जनः ।
स यत्प्रमाणं कुरुते लोकस्तदनुवर्तते ॥२१॥

21. Whatever is done by the best of men, others also do; the world conforms to the standard that he sets.

21.1. यद्यत् इति ॥ यद्यत् कर्म आचरति करोति श्रेष्ठः प्रधानः तत् एव कर्म आचरति इतरः जनः तदनुगतः । किं च सः श्रेष्ठः यत् प्रमाणं कुरुते लौकिकं वैदिकं वा लोकः तत् अनुवर्तते तदेव प्रमाणीकरोति इत्यर्थः ॥

21.1. Whatever work the best, the foremost man, does, other

men also, following him, do. Again only the standard the best man sets up, secular or Vedic, the world accepts as authoritative.

22.0. यदि अत्रापि लोकसंग्रहकर्तव्यतायां ते विप्रतिपत्तिः, तर्हि मां किं न पश्यसि ?

22.0. If you question even this obligation to promote world's welfare, why don't you observe the example I set?

न मे पार्थास्ति कर्तव्यं त्रिषु लोकेषु किंचन ।
नानवाप्तमवाप्तव्यं वर्त एव च कर्मणि ॥२२॥

22. I have, Arjuna! no duty whatever to discharge in all the three worlds; there is nothing I have not won, and nothing remains to be won by Me; still I ceaselessly work.

22.1. न इति ॥ मे मम पार्थ न अस्ति न विद्यते कर्तव्यं त्रिषु अपि लोकेषु किंचन किंचिदपि । कस्मात् ? न अनवाप्तं अप्राप्तं अवाप्तव्यं प्रापणीयं, तथापि वर्ते एव च कर्मणि अहम् ॥

22.1. In all the three worlds, Arjuna! no duty whatsoever exists for Me to discharge. Why? 'There is nothing unobtained, and nothing yet to be obtained, by Me. Nevertheless I ceaselessly work.

Still,

यदि ह्यहं न वर्तेयं जातु कर्मण्यतन्द्रितः ।
मम वर्त्मानुवर्तन्ते मनुष्याः पार्थ सर्वशः ॥२३॥

23. Indeed O Arjuna! if at any time, I do not work tirelessly, men will in all possible ways, tread that path of Mine.

23.1. यदि इति ॥ यदि हि पुनः अहं न वर्तेयं जातु कदाचित् कर्मणि अतन्द्रितः अनलसः सन् मम श्रेष्ठस्य सतः वर्त्म मार्गं अनुवर्तन्ते मनुष्याः हे पार्थ, सर्वशः सर्वप्रकारैः ॥

23.1. Again, if at any time, Arjuna! I do not tirelessly, without indolence, work, men will follow, in all possible ways, that path of the best of men, namely of Myself.

24.0. तथा च कः दोषः इति ? आह—

24.0. What harm is there if they do so? Answer:

उत्सीदेयुरिमे लोका न कुर्यां कर्म चेदहम् ।
सङ्करस्य च कर्ता स्यामुपहन्यामिमाः प्रजाः ॥२४॥

24. If I don't work the worlds will perish; I may cause confusion, and may ruin these living beings.

24.1. उत्सीदेयुः इति ॥ उत्सीदेयुः विनश्येयुः इमे सर्वे लोकाः लोकस्थितिनिमित्तस्य कर्मणः अभावात् न कुर्यां कर्म चेत् अहम् । किंच सङ्करस्य च कर्ता स्याम् । तेन कारणेन उपहन्यां इमाः प्रजाः । प्रजानाम् अनुग्रहाय प्रवृत्तः तदुपहतिं [उपहननं] कुर्यां इति मम ईश्वरस्य अननुरूपं आपद्येत ॥

24.1. If I work not, all the worlds 'will perish'—will be ruined, in the absence of the work that maintains their equilibrium. Also I shall cause confusion, and thus destroy these living beings. Seeking to confer a blessing on them, I might work their ruin. It will ill accord with My character as God.

25.0. यदि पुनः अहमिव त्वं कृतार्थबुद्धिः, आत्मवित् अन्यः वा, तस्यापि आत्मनः कर्तव्याभावेऽपि परानुग्रहः एव कर्तव्यः इत्याह —

25.0. Like Me, if you think you have reached life's goal of being a knower of Self in your own right, you may have no duty to perform; still you should work to promote others' well-being. Says the Lord:

सक्ताः कर्मण्यविद्वांसो यथा कुर्वन्ति भारत ।
कुर्याद्विद्वांस्तथाऽसक्तश्चिकीर्षुर्लोकसंग्रहम् ॥२५॥

25. Prince of the Bharata line! just as the ignorant work with attachment to that work, so should the wise work, unattached, seeking the world's integration.

25.1. सक्ताः इति ॥ सक्ताः कर्मणि "अस्य कर्मणः फलं मम भविष्यति" इति केचित् अविद्वांसः यथा कुर्वन्ति भारत, कुर्यात् विद्वान् आत्मवित् तथा असक्तः सन् । तद्वत् किमर्थं करोति ? तत् शृणु — चिकीर्षुः कर्तुं इच्छुः लोकसंग्रहम् ॥

25.1. 'With attachment to that work' the ignorant work, thinking that the fruit of the work will accrue to them; so, the wise man, a knower of the Self, should work 'unattached'. Why should he do so? Listen! Out of eagerness to work for the world's integration.

26.0. एवं लोकसंग्रहं चिकीर्षोः न मम आत्मविदः कर्तव्यं अस्ति, अन्यस्य वा, लोकसंग्रहं मुक्त्वा । [ततः] तस्य आत्मविदः इद उपदिश्यते —

26.0. For Me, the Self-knower, thus eager to promote the world's well-being or for any other like Me, there is no duty other than the promotion of that well-being. Hence is this instruction addressed to the knower of the Self:

न बुद्धिभेदं जनयेदज्ञानां कर्मसङ्गिनाम् ।
जोषयेत्सर्वकर्माणि विद्वान् युक्तः समाचरन् ॥२६॥

26. The integrated man of wisdom should not bewilder the mind of the ignorant attached to works; performing them all, let him cause them (also) to do so.

26.1. न इति ॥ बुद्धेः भेदः बुद्धिभेदः "मया इदं कर्तव्यं भोक्तव्यं चास्य कर्मणः फलं" इति निश्चयरूपायाः बुद्धेः भेदनं चालनं बुद्धिभेदः तं न जनयेत् न उत्पादयेत् अज्ञानां अविवेकिनां कर्मसङ्गिनां कर्मणि आसक्तानां आसङ्गवताम् । किन्नु कुर्यात् ? जोषयेत् कारयेत् सर्वकर्माणि विद्वान् स्वयं तदेव अविदुषां कर्म युक्तः अभियुक्तः समाचरन् ॥

26.1. Bewilderment of the mind is a split in, a jolt to, the conviction, "I must do this work and enjoy its fruit". The man of wisdom should not cause it to the ignorant who do not discriminate and are attached to works. What then should he do? He should cause them to do all works by doing them himself, integratedly.

27.0. अविद्वान् अज्ञः कथं कर्मसु सज्जते इति ? आह—

27.0. How does the unwise man, ignorant of the Self, get attached to works? Answer:

प्रकृतेः क्रियमाणानि गुणैः कर्माणि सर्वशः ।
अहङ्कारविमूढात्मा कर्ताऽहमिति मन्यते ॥२७॥

27. Works are being done in all ways by the constituents of Prakṛti. He whose mind is deluded by egoism thinks, 'I am the agent.'

27.1. प्रकृतेः इति ॥ प्रकृतेः प्रकृतिः प्रधानं सत्त्वरजस्तमसां गुणानां साम्यावस्था तस्याः प्रकृतेः गुणैः विकारैः कार्यकरणरूपैः क्रियमाणानि कर्माणि लौकिकानि शास्त्रीयाणि च सर्वशः सर्वप्रकारैः अहङ्कारविमूढात्मा कार्यकरणसंघातात्मप्रत्ययः अहङ्कारः तेन विविधं नानाविधं मूढः आत्मा अन्तःकरणं यस्य सः अयं कार्यकरणधर्मा कार्यकरणाभिमानी अविद्यया कर्माणि आत्मनि मन्यमानः तत्तत्कर्मणां अहं कर्ता इति मन्यते ॥

27.1. *Prakrti* is *Pradhāna* the state of equilibrium of the constituents, *sattva*, *rajas* and *tamas*. These constituents are transformations of *Prakṛti* as effects and instruments. By these are works, secular and scriptural, done in all possible ways. Egoism is the conceit of self in the complex of effects and instruments—the body and sense-organs. He whose inner sense is deluded in manifold ways by egoism, who identifies himself with the body and its instruments due to ignorance, ascribes works to the Self, thinking, "I am the doer of works."

28.0. यः पुनः विद्वान्—

28.0. As for the wise man:

तत्त्ववित्तु महाबाहो गुणकर्मविभागयोः ।
गुणा गुणेषु वर्तन्ते इति मत्वा न सज्जते ॥२८॥

28. O Hero! on the contrary, the knower of the truth of the distinction between constituents of Prakṛti and their operations does not attach himself to works knowing that constituents operate amidst constituents.

28.1. तत्त्ववित् इति ॥ तत्त्ववित् तु महाबाहो । कस्य तत्त्ववित् ? गुणकर्मविभागयोः — गुणविभागस्य कर्मविभागस्य च तत्त्ववित् इत्यर्थः । गुणाः करणात्मकाः गुणेषु विषयात्मकेषु वर्तन्ते, न आत्मा, इति मत्वा न सज्जते सक्तिं न करोति ॥

ये पुनः —

28.1. On the contrary, O hero! 'the knower of the truth' i.e.,—the distinction between Prakṛti's constituents and their works. The idea refers to the knower of the truth of the class of constituents and the class of works. The constituents of *Prakṛti* are the essence of the instruments of works; the same constituents operate amidst themselves as objects. The Self does not operate at all. So deeming, the truth-knower does not get attached.

Again,

प्रकृतेर्गुणसंमूढाः सज्जन्ते गुणकर्मसु ।
तानकृत्स्नविदो मन्दान् कृत्स्नविन्न विचालयेत् ॥२९॥

29. Those who are deluded by Prakṛti's constituents cling to the works of these constituents. The knower of the whole ought not to destabilize the dull and partial knowers.

29.1. प्रकृतेः इति ॥ प्रकृतेः गुणैः मूढाः संमोहिताः सन्तः सज्जन्ते गुणानां कर्मसु गुणकर्मसु "वयं कर्म कुर्मः फलाय" इति तान् कर्मसङ्गिनः अकृत्स्नविदः कर्मफलमात्रदर्शिनः मन्दान् मन्दप्रज्ञान् कृत्स्नवित् आत्मवित् स्वयं न विचालयेत् — बुद्धिभेदकरणं एव चालनं, तत् न कुर्यात् इत्यर्थः ॥

29.1. Those who are wholly deluded by Prakṛti's constituents cling to the works of these constituents, thinking, "We work for the fruits of works." The knower 'of the Whole', of the Self, should not destabilize the dull-witted, partial knowers who cling thus to works. The splitting of their understanding is destabilization. That this ought not to be attempted is the idea.

30.0. कथं पुनः कर्मणि अधिकृतेन अज्ञेन मुमुक्षुणा कर्म कर्तव्यं इति ? उच्यते—

30.0. How should work be done by the ignorant who seeks liberation and who is called upon to work? Answer:

मयि सर्वाणि कर्माणि संन्यस्याध्यात्मचेतसा ।
निराशीर्निर्ममो भूत्वा युध्यस्व विगतज्वरः ॥३०॥

30. Surrendering all works to Me in a spiritual frame of mind that craves naught, and free from all sense of possessions, fight with unconcern.

30.1. मयि इति ॥ मयि वासुदेवे परमेश्वरे सर्वज्ञे सर्वात्मनि सर्वाणि कर्माणि संन्यस्य निक्षिप्य अध्यात्मचेतसा विवेकबुद्धचा "अहं कर्ता ईश्वराय भृत्यवत् करोमि" इति अनया बुद्धचा । किञ्च—निराशीः त्यक्ताशीः, निर्ममः ममभावश्च निर्गतः यस्य तव सः त्वं निर्ममो भूत्वा युध्यस्व विगतज्वरः विगतसन्तापः, विगतशोकः सन् इत्यर्थः ॥

30.1. Surrendering or offering all works to Me, Vāsudeva, the supreme and omniscient Lord and Self of all, 'in a spiritual frame of mind' i.e., with the discriminating perception, 'I, the agent, work for the Lord as His servant'; and also, 'craving naught' i.e., giving up all desires, being free from all sense of possessions, or ownership—you should fight, 'with unconcern', or free from worry or sorrow.

31.0. यत् एतत् मम मतं "कर्म कर्तव्यं" इति सप्रमाणं उक्तं तत् तथा—

31.0. This doctrine of Mine, based on scriptural authority, that work must be done, remains valid:

ये मे मतमिदं नित्यमनुतिष्ठन्ति मानवाः ।
श्रद्धावन्तोऽनसूयन्तो मुच्यन्ते तेऽपि कर्मभिः ॥३१॥

31. Those men who invariably conform to this doctrine of Mine—men faithful, unenvious—are also liberated from works.

31.1. ये मे इति ॥ ये मे मदीयं इदं मतं नित्यं अनुतिष्ठन्ति अनुवर्तन्ते मानवाः मनुष्याः श्रद्धावन्तः श्रद्दधानाः अनसूयन्तः असूयां च मयि परमगुरौ वासुदेवे अकुर्वन्तः, मुच्यन्ते ते अपि एवंभूताः कर्मभिः धर्माधर्माख्यैः ॥

31.1. Those men who invariably conform to this doctrine of Mine—men 'faithful' or confiding, and 'unenvious' or not envying Me, the supreme teacher Vāsudeva—are also liberated from the sway of works righteous and unrighteous.

On the contrary,

ये त्वेतदभ्यसूयन्तो नानुतिष्ठन्ति मे मतम् ।
सर्वज्ञानविमूढांस्तान् विद्धि नष्टानचेतसः ॥३२॥

32. Know them to be an inert and a ruined lot, who, deluded in respect of all knowledge, carp at this doctrine of Mine and refuse to conform to it.

32.1. ये तु इति ॥ ये तु तद्विपरीताः एतत् मे मम मतं अभ्यसूयन्तः निन्दन्तः न अनुतिष्ठन्ति नानुवर्तन्ते [मे मतं] सर्वेषु ज्ञानेषु विविधं मूढाः ते सर्वज्ञानविमूढाः तान् विद्धि जानीहि नष्टान् नाशं गतान् अचेतसः अविवेकिनः ॥

32.1. But, in contrast, those who carp at or scorn this doctrine of Mine and fail to conform to it are variously deluded in respect of all forms of knowledge. Know them to be a ruined lot lacking in discrimination.

33.0. कस्मात् पुनः कारणात् त्वदीयं मतं नानुतिष्ठन्तः [-न्ति] परधर्मान् अनुतिष्ठन्ति, स्वधर्मं च न अनुवर्तन्ते, त्वत्प्रतिकूलाः कथं न बिभ्यति त्वच्छासनातिक्रमदोषात् ? तत्राह—

33.0. Why do they fail to conform to Your doctrine and follow alien laws of conduct, rejecting those proper to their nature? Why don't these opponents of Yours shrink from the sin of transgressing Your commandments?

सदृशं चेष्टते स्वस्याः प्रकृतेः ज्ञानवानपि ।
प्रकृतिं यान्ति भूतानि निग्रहः किं करिष्यति ॥३३॥

33. Even a man of knowledge behaves according to his nature. All living beings conform to nature. What can repression avail?

33.1. सदृशं इति ॥ सदृशं अनुरूपं चेष्टते चेष्टतां करोति । कस्य? स्वस्याः स्वकीयायाः प्रकृतेः । प्रकृतिः नाम पूर्वकृतधर्माधर्मादिसंस्काराः वर्तमानजन्मादौ अभिव्यक्ताः, सा प्रकृतिः । तस्याः सदृशम् एव सर्वः जन्तुः ज्ञानवान् अपि चेष्टते, कि पुनः मूर्खः ? तस्मात् प्रकृतिं यान्ति अनुगच्छन्ति भूतानि प्राणिनः । निग्रहः निषेधरूपः किं करिष्यति मम वा अन्यस्य वा ? [दुर्निग्रहा प्रकृतिः इति वाक्यशेषः] ॥

33.1. 'Behaves accordingly'—according to what? One's own nature. Nature means impressions of work, righteous and unrighteous, done already, which manifest themselves in the present life and later. According to that nature, every living being—even one who has knowledge—behaves; let alone the foolish. Therefore, all living beings conform to nature. What will repression or prohibition, either by Me or by someone else, avail? It follows that nature is hard to repress.

34.0. यदि सर्वः जन्तुः आत्मनः प्रकृतिसदृशम् एव चेष्टते — न च प्रकृतिशून्यः कश्चित् अस्ति — ततः पुरुषकारस्य विषयानुपपत्तेः शास्त्रानर्थक्यप्राप्तौ इदं उच्यते —

34.0. The following objection may be raised: If all living beings behave according to nature—and there is none devoid of his own special nature—there remains no scope for individual initiative, and the *śāstra* is thus reduced to futility. Answer:

इन्द्रियस्येन्द्रियस्यार्थे रागद्वेषौ व्यवस्थितौ ।
तयोर्न वशमागच्छेत्तौ ह्यस्य परिपन्थिनौ ॥३४॥

34. Senses have attachment and aversion to their respective objects; none should be swayed by them. They indeed are obstacles in man's path.

34.1. इन्द्रियस्य इति ॥ इन्द्रियस्य इन्द्रियस्य अर्थे सर्वेन्द्रियाणां अर्थे शब्दादिविषये — इष्टे रागः, अनिष्टे द्वेषः — इत्येवं प्रतीन्द्रियार्थं रागद्वेषौ अवश्यंभाविनौ तत्र अयं पुरुषकारस्य शास्त्रार्थस्य च विषयः उच्यते । शास्त्रार्थे प्रवृत्तः पूर्वमेव रागद्वेषयोः वशं नागच्छेत् । या हि पुरुषस्य प्रकृतिः सा रागद्वेषपुरःसरा एव

स्वकार्ये पुरुषं प्रवर्तयति; तदा स्वधर्मपरित्यागः परधर्मानुष्ठानं च भवति। यदा पुनः रागद्वेषौ तत्प्रतिपक्षेण नियमयति तदा शास्त्रदृष्टिः एव पुरुषः भवति, न प्रकृतिवशः। तस्मात् तयोः रागद्वेषयोः वशं न आगच्छेत्, यतः तौ हि अस्य पुरुषस्य परिपन्थिनौ श्रेयोमार्गस्य विघ्नकर्तारौ तस्करौ इव पथि इत्यर्थः ॥३४॥

34.1. The senses have attachment and aversion in respect of their objects such as sound—attachment to what pleases and aversion to what repels. Thus attachment and aversion are inevitable for each sense. In this context, the scope of individual initiative and that of the mandate of the *śāstra* are being indicated. Submitting to the mandate of the *śāstra* at the very outset, one should refuse to be swayed by attachment and aversion. Human nature indeed forces man to work under the urges of his attachment and aversion. Thus result the abandonment of the laws of one's conduct and conformity with those of alien conduct. On the other hand when attachment and aversion are restrained by countervailing forces, man's vision becomes that of the *śāstra*; he ceases to be Nature's thrall. Therefore none should submit to attachment and aversion; for those are stumbling blocks on the path to betterment, like robbers infesting the public road.

35.0. तत्र रागद्वेषप्रयुक्तः मन्यते शास्त्रार्थम् अपि अन्यथा 'परधर्मः अपि धर्मत्वात् अनुष्ठेयः एव' इति, तत् असत् —

35.0. Moved by attachment and aversion, man may misconstrue the contents of the *śāstras* and maintain that even an alien law of conduct, being a law, after all, has to be observed. This is wrong. How?

श्रेयान् स्वधर्मो विगुणः परधर्मात् स्वनुष्ठितात्।
स्वधर्मे निधनं श्रेयः परधर्मो भयावहः ॥३५॥

35. Superior is the law of one's own nature, though lacking in merits, to that of another even though well-observed. Death in working out the law of one's nature is superior; but an alien law is fraught with risk.

35.1. श्रेयान् इति ॥ श्रेयान् प्रशस्यतरः स्वः धर्मः स्वधर्मः विगुणः अपि विगत-गुणः अपि अनुष्ठीयमानः परधर्मात् स्वनुष्ठितात् साद्गुण्येन संपादितात् अपि । स्वधर्मे स्थितस्य निधनं मरणं अपि श्रेयः परधर्मे स्थितस्य जीवितात् । कस्मात्? परधर्मः भयावहः नरकादिलक्षणं भयं आवहति इति [यतः] ॥३५॥

35.1. Superior—more admirable—is the law of one's own nature, though wanting in merits, if it is worked out aright, to the law of another's nature, however meritoriously worked out. Death while adhering to the laws of one's own nature is superior to a life devoted to the law of another's nature. Why? An alien law brings fear in its train—the fear of hell, etc.

36.0. यद्यपि अनर्थमूलं 'ध्यायतो विषयान् पुंसः' [२. ६२.] इति 'रागद्वेषौ ह्यस्य परिपन्थिनौ' [३. ३४.] इति च उक्तं; विक्षिप्तं अनवधारितं च तत् उक्तं; तत् संक्षिप्तं निश्चितं च इदम् एव इति ज्ञातुं इच्छन् अर्जुनः उवाच, 'ज्ञाते हि तस्मिन् तदुच्छेदाय यत्नं कुर्यां' इति —

36.0. Though the root of all evil has been pin-pointed in *BG*.2.62 and 3.34, there have been both diffusion and lack of emphasis there. Seeking to know it concisely and with certitude, Arjuna asked as follows, in order to extirpate it wholly:

अर्जुन उवाच :

अथ केन प्रयुक्तोऽयं पापं चरति पूरुषः ।
अनिच्छन्नपि वार्ष्णेय बलादिव नियोजितः ॥३६॥

Arjuna said:

36. Now, impelled by what does man commit sin? O Kṛṣṇa!, though loath to sin, he is driven to it forcibly, as it were.

36.1. अथ इति ॥ अथ केन हेतुभूतेन प्रयुक्तः सन् राज्ञा इव भृत्यः अयं पापं कर्म चरति आचरति पूरुषः पुरुषः स्वयं अनिच्छन् अपि हे वार्ष्णेय वृष्णिकुलप्रसूत, बलात् इव नियोजितः राज्ञा इव इति उक्तः दृष्टान्तः ॥

36.1. Impelled by what cause, O Kṛṣṇa, does a man sin, compelled as a servant is by his master the king, though, left to himself, he is loath to do so? It is as if he were bidden, as by a king, to do it. This is a simile.

37.0. शृणु त्वं तं वैरिणं सर्वानर्थकरं यं त्वं पृच्छसि इति भगवान् उवाच—

37.0. Hear who that foe, the author of all mischief, is, of whom you ask—the Lord spoke giving him the required information:

श्रीभगवानुवाच :

काम एष क्रोध एष रजोगुणसमुद्भवः ।
महाशनो महापाप्मा विद्ध्येनमिह वैरिणम् ॥३७॥

The blessed Lord said:

37. This is craving, this is wrath, born of the constituent Rajas. He is voracious, a great sinner; know him to be the foe in this context.

37.1. ऐश्वर्यस्य समग्रस्य वीर्यस्य यशसः श्रियः ।
वैराग्यस्याथ मोक्षस्य षण्णां भग इतीरणा ॥ [विष्णुपु. ६.५.७४.]
ऐश्वर्यादिषट्कं यस्मिन् वासुदेवे नित्यं अप्रतिबन्धेन सामस्त्येन च वर्तते —
उत्पत्तिं प्रलयं चैव भूतानामागतिं गतिम् ।
वेत्ति विद्यामविद्यां च स वाच्यो भगवानिति ॥ [विष्णुपु. ६.५.७८.]
उत्पत्त्यादिविषयं च विज्ञानं यस्य स वासुदेवः वाच्यः भगवान् इति —

37.1. *Bhagavān* is the Lord. *Bhaga*, according to *VP*.6.5.74, denotes the six attributes—full lordliness, energy, renown, glory, detachment, and emancipation. Vāsudeva in whom those six exist eternally, unimpeded, and in full measure, is the *Bhagavān*. Or, according to *VP*.6.5.78, He is the blessed Lord as He knows 'the origin, dissolution, appearance and disappearance of living beings, and is aware also of knowledge and ignorance'.

37.2. कामः इति ॥ काम एषः सर्वलोकशत्रुः यन्निमित्ता सर्वानर्थप्राप्तिः प्राणिनाम् ।

स एष कामः प्रतिहतः केनचित् क्रोधत्वेन परिणमते । अतः क्रोधः अपि एषः एव । रजोगुणसमुद्भवः रजश्च तत् गुणश्च रजोगुणः समुद्भवः । यस्य सः कामः रजोगुणसमुद्भवः रजोगुणस्य वा समुद्भवः कामः हि उद्भूतः रजः प्रवर्तयन् पुरुषं प्रवर्तयति; 'तृष्णया हि अहं कारितः' इति दुःखितानां रजःकार्ये सेवादौ प्रवृत्तानां प्रलापः श्रूयते । महाशनः महत् अशनं यस्य इति महाशनः; अतः एव महापाप्मा; कामेन हि प्रेरितः जन्तुः पापं करोति । अतः विद्धि एनं कामं इह संसारे वैरिणम् ॥

37.2. The foe of the whole world is this craving that proves disastrous to all living beings. Craving, impeded by some one or other, changes into wrath. So wrath, too, is this very thing born of *rajas*. When it arises it activates *rajas* and drives man to act. Those who suffer, busy in servitude, due to *rajas*, lament, "We are made to work due to craving." It consumes much, and is a great sinner. Incited by *rajas* man sins. Therefore know craving to be the foe in this empirical life.

38.0. कथं वैरी ? इति दृष्टान्तैः प्रत्याययति —

38.0. By means of analogies, how craving is the foe is inculcated:

धूमेनाव्रियते वह्निर्यथाऽऽदर्शो मलेन च ।
यथोल्बेनावृतो गर्भस्तथा तेनेदमावृतम् ॥३८॥

38. Just as fire is obscured by smoke, a mirror by dirt and embryo by the womb, so is knowledge by craving.

38.1. धूमेन इति ॥ धूमेन सहजेन आव्रियते वह्निः प्रकाशात्मकः अप्रकाशात्मकेन यथा वा आदर्शः मलेन च, यथा उल्बेन च जरायुणा गर्भवेष्टनेन आवृतः आच्छादितः गर्भः तथा तेन इदं आवृतम् ॥

38.1. Just as luminous fire is obscured by the non-luminous smoke, born together with fire; or a mirror by dirt; or the embryo by a sheathing membrane—so is this knowledge by it i.e., by craving.

39.0. किं पुनः तत् इदंशब्दवाच्यं यत् कामेन आवृतं इति ? उच्यते—

39.0. What is the thing denoted by the word 'this' and obscured by craving? Answer:

आवृतं ज्ञानमेतेन ज्ञानिनो नित्यवैरिणा ।
कामरूपेण कौन्तेय दुष्पूरेणानलेन च ॥३९॥

39. Knowledge, O son of Kuntī, is obscured by this persistent foe of the knower, i.e. by craving, as by an insatiable fire.

39.1. आवृतं इति ॥ आवृतं एतेन ज्ञानं ज्ञानिनः नित्यवैरिणा, ज्ञानी हि पूर्वम् एव जानाति 'अनेन अहं अनर्थे प्रयुक्तः' इति । अतः दुःखी च भवति नित्यम् एव । तेन असौ ज्ञानिनः नित्यवैरी, न तु मूर्खस्य । सः हि कामं तृष्णाकाले मित्रं इव पश्यन् तत्कार्ये दुःखे प्राप्ते जानाति 'तृष्णया अहं दुःखित्वं आपादितः' इति, न पूर्वम् एव । अतः ज्ञानिनः एव नित्यवैरी । किंरूपेण ? कामरूपेण काम इच्छा एव रूपं अस्य इति कामरूपः तेन, दुष्पूरेण दुःखेन पूरणं अस्य इति दुष्पूरः तेन, अनलेन न अस्य अलं पर्याप्तिः विद्यते इति अनलः तेन च ॥

39.1. Knowledge is obscured by this persistent foe of the man of knowledge. The man of knowledge already knows: "I have been flung into this trouble by this craving." So he always suffers. Thus is it the persistent foe of the knower, and not of the ignorant. The latter, in the grip of craving, indeed may look upon it as a friend. But when its effect, pain, overtakes him, he realizes: "I have been made to suffer through craving"; but not till then. So it is the persistent foe of the knower alone. What form does this foe assume? Of craving or desire. It is hard to satisfy, being a fire that nothing can quench.

40.0. किमधिष्ठानः च पुनः कामः ज्ञानस्य आवरणत्वेन वैरी सर्वस्य लोकस्य ? इति अपेक्षायां आह, ज्ञाते हि शत्रोः अधिष्ठाने सुखेन निबर्हणं कर्तुं शक्यते इति —

40.0. Abiding in what does craving, obscuring knowledge, prove a foe of the whole world? The reply follows. Once the base of the foe is known he may be easily destroyed.

इन्द्रियाणि मनो बुद्धिरस्याधिष्ठानमुच्यते ।
एतैर्विमोहयत्येष ज्ञानमावृत्य देहिनम् ॥४०॥

40. His abode is said to be the senses, mind, and intellect. By means of these he obscures knowledge and deludes the embodied man.

40.1. इन्द्रियाणि इति ॥ इन्द्रियाणि मनः बुद्धिः च अस्य कामस्य अधिष्ठानं आश्रयः उच्यते । एतैः इन्द्रियादिभिः आश्रयैः विमोहयति विविधं मोहयति एषः कामः ज्ञानं आवृत्य आच्छाद्य देहिनं शरीरिणम् ॥४०॥
यतः एवम् —

40.1. Senses, mind and intellect are said to be the abode of this craving. By means of these abodes obscuring knowledge, this foe deludes the embodied Spirit in manifold ways.

Such being the case,

तस्मात्त्वमिन्द्रियाण्यादौ नियम्य भरतर्षभ ।
पाप्मानं प्रजहिह्येनं ज्ञानविज्ञाननाशनम् ॥४१॥

41. Therefore, mighty prince! first controlling the senses, give up this wicked craving that destroys knowledge and realization.

41.1. तस्मात् इति ॥ तस्मात् त्वं इन्द्रियाणि आदौ पूर्वमेव नियम्य वशीकृत्य भरतर्षभ, पाप्मानं पापाचारं कामं प्रजहीहि परित्यज एनं प्रकृतं वैरिणं ज्ञानविज्ञाननाशनं, ज्ञानं शास्त्रतः आचार्यतश्च आत्मादीनां अवबोधः, विज्ञानं विशेषतः तदर्थानुभवः, तयो; ज्ञानविज्ञानयोः श्रेयःप्राप्तिहेत्वोः नाशनं नाशकरं प्रजहीहि आत्मनः परित्यज इत्यर्थः ॥

41.1. Therefore, at the outset, controlling the senses, O mighty prince! give up, this wicked craving, this foe, who destroys knowledge won from the *śāstras* and the teacher and also the specific realization thereof. These two lead to supreme well-being. This is the idea.

42.0. इन्द्रियाणि आदौ नियम्य कामं शत्रुं जहीहि इति उक्तम् । तत्र किमाश्रयः काम जह्यात् इति ? उच्यते —

42.0. It has been stated that, first, controlling senses, the foe craving, must be given up. Resorting to what may one give it up? Answer:

इन्द्रियाणि पराण्याहुरिन्द्रियेभ्यः परं मनः ।
मनसस्तु परा बुद्धिर्यो बुद्धेः परतस्तु सः ॥४२॥

42. They say that the senses are noble; nobler than the senses is mind. Intellect is even nobler than the mind. What is nobler, still, than the intellect is He, the Self.

42.1. इन्द्रियाणि इति ॥ इन्द्रियाणि श्रोत्रादीनि पञ्च देहं स्थूलं बाह्यं परिच्छिन्नं च अपेक्ष्य सौक्ष्म्यान्तरस्थितत्वव्यापित्वाद्यपेक्षया पराणि प्रकृष्टानि आहुः पण्डिताः । तथां—इन्द्रियेभ्यः परं मनः सङ्कल्पविकल्पात्मकम् । तथा—मनसः तु परा बुद्धिः निश्चयात्मिका । तथा—यः सर्वदृश्येभ्यः बुद्ध्यन्तेभ्यः आभ्यन्तरः, यं देहिनं इन्द्रियादिभिः आश्रयैः युक्तः कामः ज्ञानावरणद्वारेण मोहयति इत्युक्तं, 'बुद्धेः परतः तु सः' । सः बुद्धेः द्रष्टा पर आत्मा ॥

ततः किम् ? —

42.1. The senses, ear etc., in relation to the gross and finite external body, are held by the sages to be noble; for, they are subtle, internal, and wider in scope. Similarly mind, imaginative and analytic, is nobler than the senses. So too the intellect, whose essence is discrimination, is nobler than the mind. Finally He (the embodied self) who is inner to every object and instrument of perception up to the intellect, whom 'craving', resorting to those instruments, namely, the senses, mind and intellect, deludes by obscuring knowledge—He is nobler than even the intellect. He, the beholder of the intellect, is the supreme Self.

What follows?

एवं बुद्धेः परं बुद्ध्वा संस्तभ्यात्मानमात्मना ।
जहि शत्रुं महाबाहो कामरूपं दुरासदम् ॥४३॥

43. Thus knowing Him as nobler than the intellect, and restraining the inner senses through the Self, O mighty

armed! destroy the enemy—the craving, so hard to reach.

इति श्रीमहाभारते शतसाहस्र्यां संहितायां वैयासिक्यां भीष्मपर्वणि श्रीमद्भगवद्गीतासूपनिषत्सु ब्रह्मविद्यायां योगशास्त्रे श्रीकृष्णार्जुनसंवादे कर्मयोगो नाम तृतीयोऽध्यायः ॥३॥

43.1. एवं इति ॥ एवं बुद्धेः परं आत्मानं बुद्ध्वा ज्ञात्वा संस्तभ्य सम्यक् स्तम्भनं कृत्वा आत्मानं स्वेनैव आत्मना संस्कृतेन मनसा सम्यक् समाधाय इत्यर्थः । जहि एनं शत्रुं हे महाबाहो, कामरूपं दुरासदं दुःखेन आसदः आसादनं प्राप्तिः यस्य तं दुरासदं दुर्विज्ञेयानेकविशेषं इति ॥

43.1. Thus knowing the Self beyond the intellect, and controlling the inner sense by means of the purified mind, i.e. by properly concentrating it, O mighty-armed! destroy the enemy, craving, that is so hard to reach; for it assumes numerous forms that are scarcely intelligible.

इति श्रीमत्परमहंसपरिव्राजकाचार्यगोविंदभगवत्पूज्यपादशिष्यश्रीमच्छंकरभगवतः कृतौ श्रीभगवद्गीताभाष्ये कर्मप्रशंसायोगो नाम तृतीयोऽध्यायः ॥३॥

चतुर्थोऽध्यायः

CHAPTER IV

JNANA KARMA SAMNYASA YOGA

0.1. यः अयं योगः अध्यायद्वयेन उक्तः ज्ञाननिष्ठालक्षणः, ससंन्यासः कर्मयोगोपायः, यस्मिन् वेदार्थः परिसमाप्तः, प्रवृत्तिलक्षणः निवृत्तिलक्षणश्च, गीतासु च सर्वासु अयं एव योगो विवक्षितः भगवता । अतः परिसमाप्तं वेदार्थं मन्वानः तं वंशकथनेन स्तौति श्रीभगवान् —

0.1. The Yoga set forth in the two previous chapters, characterized by dedication to the discipline of knowledge accompanied by renunciation and implemented by the Yoga of Action—a teaching in which the contents of the Vedas, both activistic and quietistic, culminate—is the same that the Lord seeks to inculcate in *BG* as a whole. Therefore, deeming that the sense of the Vedas has already been set forth in its entirety, the Lord lauds the same with reference to the line of teachers through whom it has been handed down to posterity.

श्रीभगवानुवाच :

इमं विवस्वते योगं प्रोक्तवानहमव्ययम् ।
विवस्वान्मनवे प्राह मनुरिक्ष्वाकवेऽब्रवीत् ॥१॥

The blessed Lord said:

1. This immutable Yoga I imparted to the Sun (Vivasvān) who declared it to Manu. Manu proclaimed it to Ikṣvāku.

1.1. इमं इति ॥ इमं अध्यायद्वयेन उक्तं योगं विवस्वते आदित्याय सर्गादौ प्रोक्तवान् अहं जगत्परिपालयितॄणां क्षत्रियाणां बलाधानाय । तेन हि योगबलेन युक्ताः समर्थाः भवन्ति ब्रह्म परिरक्षितुम् । ब्रह्मक्षत्रे परिपालयितुं अलम् । अव्ययं अव्ययफलत्वात् । न हि अस्य योगस्य सम्यग्दर्शननिष्ठालक्षणस्य मोक्षाख्यं फलं व्येति । स च विवस्वान् मनवे प्राह । मनुः इक्ष्वाकवे स्वपुत्राय आदिराजाय अब्रवीत् ॥

1.1. This Yoga or way of life set forth in the two previous chapters I imparted to the Sun in the beginning of creation in order to confer strength on the Kṣatriyas, the rulers of the world. With the strength of this Yoga they became competent to protect the Brāhmaṇa class. The Brāhmaṇas and Kṣatriyas are competent to protect the whole world. This Yoga is immutable as its fruit does not decline; for, the fruit of this Yoga, namely, emancipation characterized by the discipline of right perception, is unfailing. And the Sun declared it to Manu, who, in his turn, proclaimed it to his son, the first king, Ikṣvāku.

Further:

एवं परम्पराप्राप्तमिमं राजर्षयो विदुः ।
स कालेनेह महता योगो नष्टः परंतप ॥२॥

2. Royal sages have known this Yoga thus traditionally transmitted. O valiant prince! Due to lapse of long time, this Yoga has perished in this world.

2.1. एवं इति ॥ एवं क्षत्रियपरम्पराप्राप्तं इमं राजर्षयः राजानश्च ते ऋषयः च इति ते राजर्षयः विदुः इमं योगम् । सः योगः कालेन इह महता दीर्घेण नष्टः विच्छिन्नसंप्रदायः संवृत्तः । हे परंतप, आत्मनः विपक्षभूताः पराः इति उच्यन्ते, तान् शौर्यतेजोगभस्तिभिः भानुः इव तापयति इति परंतपः शत्रुतापनः इत्यर्थः ॥

2.1. The royal sages came to know this Yoga, thus traditionally handed down. Due to lapse of a long stretch of time, the tradition of its transmission has perished in this world. *Para* in *Paramtapa* denotes adversaries. By means of the rays of courage and energy, like the sun, Arjuna scorches them; he is the scourge of his foes.

3.0. दुर्बलान् अजितेन्द्रियान् प्राप्य नष्टं योगं इमं उपलभ्य लोकं च अपुरुषार्थसंबन्धिनम् —

3.0. Noting that this Yoga has perished, since its practitioners have been weak and sensuous, and that the world is severed from life's supreme values:

स एवायं मया तेऽद्य योगः प्रोक्तः पुरातनः ।
भक्तोऽसि मे सखा चेति रहस्यं ह्येतदुत्तमम् ॥३॥

3. The same ancient Yoga has now been proclaimed to you by Me; for, you are a devotee and My comrade. Knowledge of this Yoga, indeed, is the highest mystery.

3.1. सः इति ॥ सः एव अयं मया ते तुभ्यं अद्य इदानीं योगः प्रोक्तः पुरातनः, भक्तः असि मे सखा च असि इति । रहस्यं हि यस्मात् एतत् उत्तमं योगज्ञानं इत्यर्थः ॥

3.1. That same ancient Yoga has been related to you now by me; because you are my devotee and friend. As it is secret, knowledge of this Yoga is the highest.

4.0. भगवता विप्रतिषिद्धं उक्तं इति मा भूत् कस्यचित् बुद्धिः इति परिहारार्थं चोद्यं इव कुर्वन् अर्जुनः उवाच—

4.0. "Let none deem that the Lord is guilty of self-contradiction"—as if to drive home this point, Arjuna spoke, posing a question, as it were.

अर्जुन उवाच :

अपरं भवतो जन्म परं जन्म विवस्वतः ।
कथमेतद्विजानीयां त्वमादौ प्रोक्तवानिति ॥४॥

Arjuna said:

4. Your birth has been later; that of the Sun (Vivasvān) earlier. How then am I to take it that You imparted this Yoga in the beginning?

4.1. अपरं इति ॥ अपरं अर्वाक् वसुदेवगृहे भवतः जन्म । परं पूर्वं सर्गादौ जन्म उत्पत्तिः विवस्वतः आदित्यस्य । तत् कथं एतत् विजानीयां अविरुद्धार्थतया, यः त्वमेव आदौ प्रोक्तवान् इमं योगं सः एव इदानीं मह्यं प्रोक्तवान् असि इति ॥

4.1. Later in time, in the house of Vasudeva, your birth took place. Earlier, in the beginning of creation, was Vivasvān (the Sun) born. Therefore, how am I to understand, as free from contradiction, the assertion that You, who in the beginning of creation imparted this Yoga, have now proclaimed it to me?

5.0. या वासुदेवे अनीश्वरासर्वज्ञाशङ्का मूर्खाणां, तां परिहरन् श्रीभगवानुवाच, यदर्थः हि अर्जुनस्य प्रश्नः—

5.0 In order to remove the scepticism of the dull-witted as regards the power and omniscience of Vāsudeva, the Lord spoke. Indeed, this is the purpose served by Arjuna's question:

श्रीभगवानुवाच:

बहूनि मे व्यतीतानि जन्मानि तव चार्जुन ।
तान्यहं वेद सर्वाणि न त्वं वेत्थ परंतप ॥५॥

The blessed Lord said:

5. Numerous births of Mine have already taken place, as also those of yours, Arjuna! I know them all, but O scourge of foes! you do not.

5.1. बहूनि इति ॥ बहूनि मे मम व्यतीतानि अतिक्रान्तानि जन्मानि तव च हे अर्जुन । तानि अहं वेद जाने सर्वाणि न त्वं वेत्थ न जानीषे, धर्माधर्मादिप्रतिबद्धज्ञानशक्तित्वात् । अहं पुनः नित्यशुद्धबुद्धमुक्तस्वभावत्वात् अनावरणज्ञानशक्तिः इति वेद अहं हे परंतप ॥

5.1. Numerous births of Mine have already taken place, occurred, as also those of yours, O Arjuna! I know them all, you don't, as your powers of cognition have been impeded by merits, demerits, etc. On the contrary, being eternally pure, awake and free, and endowed with unimpaired cognitive powers, I know them all, O scourge of foes!

6.0. कथं तर्हि तव नित्येश्वरस्य धर्माधर्माभावे अपि जन्म इति? उच्यते—

6.0. If so, even in the absence of merit and demerit, how is it that You, the Lord eternal, have birth at all? Answer:

अजोऽपि सन्नव्ययात्मा भूतानामीश्वरोऽपि सन् ।
प्रकृतिं स्वामधिष्ठाय संभवाम्यात्ममायया ॥६॥

6. Though unborn and though the immutable Self and

the Lord of all living beings, resorting to My power of becoming, through My Māyā, I take birth.

6.1. अजोऽपि इति ॥ अजः अपि जन्मरहितः अपि सन्, तथा अव्ययात्मा अक्षीणज्ञानशक्तिस्वभावः अपि सन्, तथा भूतानां ब्रह्मादिस्तम्बपर्यन्तानां ईश्वरः ईशनशीलः अपि सन् प्रकृतिं स्वां मम वैष्णवीं मायां त्रिगुणात्मिकां, यस्याः वशे सर्वं [इदं] जगत् वर्तते, यया मोहितं जगत् सत् स्वं आत्मानं वासुदेवं न जानाति, तां प्रकृतिं स्वां अधिष्ठाय वशीकृत्य संभवामि देहवान् इव भवामि जातः इव आत्ममायया आत्मनः मायया, न परमार्थतः लोकवत् ॥

6.1. Though I am the unborn and immutable Self, i.e., though My cognitive power never wanes and I am the master of all beings from Brahmā down to a tuft of grass, resorting to, i.e. mastering, My 'power of becoming', I take birth or appear to become embodied. My power of becoming is all-pervasive; it consists of the three constituents. The entire world is subject to it. Deluded by it, the world does not know its own Self, Vāsudeva. Thus am I born, as it were, by virtue of My power of becoming and not in fact, as is the case with the world.

7.0. तत् च जन्म कदा किमर्थं च इति ? उच्यते—

7.0. When, for what purpose, does that birth of the Lord occur? Listen:

यदा यदा हि धर्मस्य ग्लानिर्भवति भारत ।
अभ्युत्थानमधर्मस्य तदाऽऽत्मानं सृजाम्यहम् ॥७॥

7. Whenever, scion of Bharatas! righteousness declines and unrighteousness prevails, I project Myself.

7.1. यदा इति ॥ यदा यदा हि धर्मस्य ग्लानिः हानिः वर्णाश्रमादिलक्षणस्य प्राणिनां अभ्युदयनिःश्रेयससाधनस्य भवति भारत, अभ्युत्थानं उद्भवः अधर्मस्य तदा तदा आत्मानं सृजामि अहं मायया ॥

किमर्थम् ? —

7.1. Whenever righteousness declines or withers—righteousness as embodied in the order of classes, life-stations etc., which promotes the prosperity and makes for the emancipation of all living beings—and unrighteousness prevails, 'flourishes', then, through Māyā, I project Myself. Wherefore?

परित्राणाय साधूनां विनाशाय च दुष्कृताम् ।
धर्मसंस्थापनार्थाय संभवामि युगे युगे ॥८॥

8. For the protection of the virtuous, the destruction of the wicked, and to secure establishment of righteousness, I am born in every age.

8.1. परित्राणाय इति ॥ परित्राणाय परिरक्षणाय साधूनां सन्मार्गस्थानां, विनाशाय च दुष्कृतां पापकारिणाम्, किंच, धर्मसंस्थापनार्थाय धर्मस्य सम्यक् स्थापनं धर्मसंस्थापनं तदर्थं संभवामि युगे युगे प्रतियुगम् ॥

8.1. For the all-round protection of the virtuous—i.e., of those who tread the path of morality—for the destruction of sinners, and also for the secure establishment of righteousness, I am born in every age.

Further:

जन्म कर्म च मे दिव्यमेवं यो वेत्ति तत्त्वतः ।
त्यक्त्वा देहं पुनर्जन्म नैति मामेति सोऽर्जुन ॥९॥

9. Whosoever thus truthfully knows My divine birth and work, is not reborn after giving up his body; he reaches Me, O Arjuna!

9.1. जन्म इति ॥ तत् जन्म मायारूपं, कर्म च साधूनां परित्राणादि मे मम दिव्यं अप्राकृतं ऐश्वरं — एवं यथोक्तं यः वेत्ति तत्त्वतः तत्त्वेन यथावत् त्यक्त्वा देहं इमं पुनः जन्म पुनरुत्पत्तिं न एति प्राप्नोति । मां एति आगच्छति — सः मुच्यते हे अर्जुन ॥

9.1. My birth, having the nature of an appearance, and My work, viz., the protection of the virtuous, etc., both of which are divine and lordly, and not material,—whosoever knows these truly, as set forth by Me, is no more reborn; he reaches Me, he is liberated, O Arjuna!

10.0. न एषः मोक्षमार्गः इदानीं प्रवृत्तः, किं तर्हि ? पूर्वमपि —

10.0. This path to emancipation has not been opened up just now; on the contrary, it existed in the past, too.

वीतरागभयक्रोधा मन्मया मामुपाश्रिताः ।
बहवो ज्ञानतपसा पूता मद्भावमागताः ॥१०॥

10. Free from passion, fear, and wrath, filled with My power, dependent on Me, and purged by the austerity of knowledge, many have attained My status.

10.1. वीतराग इति ॥ वीतरागभयक्रोधाः रागश्च भयं च क्रोधश्च वीताः विगताः येभ्यः ते मन्मयाः ब्रह्मविदः ईश्वराभेददर्शिनः मां एव च परमेश्वरं उपाश्रिता केवलज्ञाननिष्ठाः इत्यर्थः । बहवः अनेके ज्ञानतपसा ज्ञानं एव च परमात्मविषयं तपः तेन ज्ञानतपसा पूताः परां शुद्धिं गताः सन्तः मद्भावं ईश्वरभावं मोक्षं आगताः समनुप्राप्ताः । इतरतपोनिरपेक्षज्ञाननिष्ठाः इत्यस्य लिङ्गम् 'ज्ञानतपसा' इति विशेषणम् ॥

10.1. Those whom passion, fear and wrath have left free, filled with My power—i.e., those who are knowers of Brahman, who perceive their non-difference from the Lord, who depend solely on Me, the Lord supreme, who are affiliated to the discipline of knowledge—many such men, purged through the austerity consisting in the knowledge of the supreme Self and raised to the highest level of purity, have won emancipation or the status of the Lord. The qualifying expression, 'through the austerity of knowledge', points to the fact that these emancipated men need no other austerity than knowledge.

11.0. 'तव तर्हि रागद्वेषौ स्तः, येन केभ्यश्चिदेव आत्मभावं प्रयच्छसि न सर्वेभ्यः इति' ? उच्यते—

11.0. "Then You have attachment and aversion; for, to some only You vouchsafe the status as Yourself; not to all". Listen:

ये यथा मां प्रपद्यन्ते तांस्तथैव भजाम्यहम् ।
मम वर्त्मानुवर्तन्ते मनुष्याः पार्थ सर्वशः ॥११॥

11. Whatsoever the manner in which they approach Me, in that very manner I resort to them; for, O Arjuna! on all sides, men tread paths leading to Me.

11.1. ये यथा इति । ये यथा येन प्रकारेण येन प्रयोजनेन यत्फलार्थितया मां प्रपद्यन्ते तान् तथैव तत्फलदानेन भजामि अनुगृह्णामि अहम्, तेषां मोक्षं प्रति अनर्थित्वात् । न हि एकस्य मुमुक्षुत्वं फलार्थित्वं च युगपत् सम्भवति । अतः ये यत्फलार्थिनः तान् तत्फलदानेन, ये यथोक्ताधिकारिणः तु अफलार्थिनः मुमुक्षवश्च तान् ज्ञानप्रदानेन, ये ज्ञानिनः संन्यासिनः मुमुक्षवश्च तान् मोक्षप्रदानेन, तथा आर्तान् आर्तिहरणेन — इत्येवं यथा प्रपद्यन्ते ये तान् तथैव भजामि इत्यर्थः । न पुना रागद्वेषनिमित्तं मोहनिमित्तं वा कंचित् भजामि । सर्वथा अपि सर्वावस्थस्य मम ईश्वरस्य वर्त्म मार्गं अनुवर्तन्ते मनुष्याः — यत्फलार्थितया यस्मिन् कर्मणि अधिकृताः ये प्रवर्तन्ते ते मनुष्याः अत्र उच्यन्ते—हे पार्थ, सर्वशः सर्वप्रकारैः ॥

11.1. Whatsoever the manner in which men approach Me, and whatever fruits they have in view to gain, in that very manner I resort to them, i.e., I bless them granting them those very fruits, for they do not seek emancipation. Indeed one cannot at once seek a finite fruit and emancipation together. So in view of their varying aims, I sanction their gains. To the eligible few, on the other hand, who cherish no other aims, and seek emancipation, I grant knowledge; to the knowers who have renounced the world for winning emancipation, I grant emancipation. To those who suffer, I grant relief by removing their sufferings. Thus do I resort to My devotees in the very way they approach Me—this is the idea. I resort to no one due to attachment, aversion, or delusion. In all conceivable ways, men tread paths leading to Me, the Lord, in My countless states. Here the reference is to men called upon to work with various goals in view.

12.0. यदि तव ईश्वरस्य रागादिदोषाभावात् सर्वप्राणिषु अनुजिघृक्षायां तुल्यायां सर्वफलप्रदानसमर्थे च त्वाय सति "वासुदेवः सर्वम्" [७. १९.] इति ज्ञानेनैव

मुमुक्षवः सन्तः कस्मात् त्वाम् एव सर्वे न प्रतिपद्यन्ते इति ? शृणु तत्र कारणम् —

12.0. If You, the Lord, free from flaws like attachment etc., are ready to bless all alike and are thus competent to vouchsafe all forms of success, why don't all devotees, aiming at liberation through the knowledge "all is Vāsudeva" (*BG* 7.19), approach You alone? Listen to the reason thereof:

कांक्षन्तः कर्मणां सिद्धिं यजन्त इह देवताः ।
क्षिप्रं हि मानुषे लोके सिद्धिर्भवति कर्मजा ॥१२॥

12. People in the world offer sacrifices to gods, desiring the success of their works. For, in this human world, quick is the success born of works.

12.1. कांक्षन्तः इति ॥ कांक्षन्तः प्रार्थयन्तः [अभीप्सन्तः] कर्मणां सिद्धिं फलनिष्पत्तिं यजन्ते इह अस्मिन् लोके देवताः इंद्राग्नचाद्याः; 'अथ यः अन्यां देवतां उपास्ते — अन्यः असौ, अन्यः अहं अस्मि इति न स वेद, यथा पशुः, एवं स देवानां' [बृ. उ. १. ४. १०.] इति श्रुतेः । तेषां हि भिन्नदेवतायाजिनां फलाकांक्षिणां क्षिप्रं शीघ्रं हि यस्मात् मानुषे लोके — मनुष्यलोके हि शास्त्राधिकारः । 'क्षिप्रं हि मानुषे लोके' इति विशेषणात् अन्येषु अपि कर्मफलसिद्धिं दर्शयति भगवान्। मानुषे लोके वर्णाश्रमादिकर्माधिकारः इति विशेषः — तेषां च वर्णाश्रमाधिकारिणां कर्मणां फलसिद्धिः भवति कर्मजा कर्मणो जाता ॥

12.1. 'Desiring' i.e., praying for, seeking to obtain, success in their works, people offer sacrifices in the world to Devas like Indra and Agni. "Now one who worships a different Deva, thinking, 'that Deva is other than Myself' and 'I am different from that Deva,' does not know; he is like a sacrificial animal for those Devas" (*B.U.* 1.410). In this world of men, success is quickly gained in respect of the works done by men who offer sacrifices to alien deities, prompted by desire for their fruits. The special feature of this world of men is the eligibility to undertake works prescribed by scriptures for those who conform to the order, classes and life-stations. This points to the fact that, in other worlds also, works yield their fruits. 'Born of works' means fruits resulting from works.

13.0. मानुष एव लोके वर्णाश्रमादिकर्माधिकारः, न अन्येषु लोकेषु इति नियमः किंनिमित्तः इति ? अथवा – वर्णाश्रमादिप्रविभागोपेताः मनुष्याः मम वर्त्म अनुवर्तन्ते सर्वशः इत्युक्तम् । कस्मात्पुनः कारणात् नियमेन तवैव वर्त्म अनुवर्तन्ते न अन्यस्य इति ? उच्यते —

13.0. "Why is competence to work, based on the order of classes and life-stations, confined to this human world? Why should it not prevail in other realms as well?" Or, it was remarked that members of the classes in various life-stations tread the Lord's paths in all possible ways. Why do they tread only His paths and those of none else? Answer:

चातुर्वर्ण्यं मया सृष्टं गुणकर्मविभागशः ।
तस्य कर्तारमपि मां विद्ध्यकर्तारमव्ययम् ॥१३॥

13. The fourfold class-system according to the divisions of Prakṛti's constituents and works, has been ordained by Me. Though I am its author, know Me to be the immutable non-agent.

13.1. चातुर्वर्ण्यं इति ॥ चत्वारः एव वर्णाः चातुर्वर्ण्यं मया ईश्वरेण सृष्टं उत्पादितं "ब्राह्मणोऽस्य मुखमासीत्" [ऋ. सं. १०.९०.१२, तै. आ. ३.१२.१३. इत्यादिश्रुतेः] गुणकर्मविभागशः गुणविभागशः कर्मविभागशश्च । गुणाः सत्त्वरजस्तमांसि । तत्र सात्त्विकस्य सत्त्वप्रधानस्य ब्राह्मणस्य 'शमो दमस्तपः' [१८.४२.] इत्यादीनि कर्माणि, सत्त्वोपसर्जनरजः प्रधानस्य क्षत्रियस्य 'शौर्यतेजः' प्रभृतीनि कर्माणि [१८.४३.], तमउपसर्जनरजःप्रधानस्य वैश्यस्य 'कृष्यादीनि' कर्माणि [१८.४४.], रजउपसर्जनतमःप्रधानस्य शूद्रस्य शुश्रूषा एव कर्म [१८.४४.], इत्येवं गुणकर्मविभागशः चातुर्वर्ण्यं मया सृष्टं इत्यर्थः । तत् च इदं चातुर्वर्ण्यं न अन्येषु लोकेषु, अतः मानुषे लोके [४. १२.] इति विशेषणम् ।

13.1. The fourfold class comprises the four Varṇas. They have been ordained by Me, the Lord, vide: "The Brāhmaṇa was His face etc." (*RV*.10.90.12, *TA*.3.12.13), 'according to the divisions of Prakṛti's constituents and works', or in keeping with the divisions of constituents and works—the constituents being *sattva*, *rajas* and *tamas*. The works of the Brāhmaṇas, in whom *sattva* dominates, are quiescence of mind, control of senses, austerity and so forth (*BG*.18.42); those of the Kṣatriyas, in whom *rajas* dominates subordinating *sattva*, are heroism, power, and so forth (*BG*.18.43); those of the Vaiśyas, in whom *rajas* dominates subordinating *tamas*, are tilling and so forth (*BG*.18.44); and those of the Śūdras, in whom *tamas* dominates subordinating *rajas*, are forms of menial service (*BG*.18.44). The order of classes has been established by Me according to the division of constituents and works detailed above. In other realms the order of classes does not exist; hence the qualified expression 'in the human world' (*BG*.4.12).

13.2. हन्त ! तर्हि चातुर्वर्ण्यस्य सर्गादेः कर्मणः कर्तृत्वात् तत्फलेन युज्यसे, अतः न त्वं नित्यमुक्तः नित्येश्वरश्च इति ? उच्यते — यद्यपि मायासंव्यवहारेण तस्य कर्मणः कर्तारम् अपि सन्तं मां परमार्थतः विद्धि अकर्तारम् । अतः एव अव्ययं असंसारिणं च मां विद्धि ॥

13.2. *Objection:* "Well, then: You being the author of actions like the ordering of the classes, etc., their fruits will accrue to You. Therefore, You are not eternally free; nor are You the Lord eternal."

Answer: Though, according to the usage current in the sphere of Māyā, I am the author of all this work, metaphysically, know that I am no agent; for the same reason know that I am immutable, or trans-empirical.

14.0. येषां तु कर्मणां कर्तारं मन्यसे परमार्थतः तेषां अकर्ता एव अहं, यतः —

14.0. Metaphysically, I am not the agent of those works of which you deem Me the agent; for,

न मां कर्माणि लिम्पन्ति न मे कर्मफले स्पृहा ।
इति मां योऽभिजानाति कर्मभिर्न स बध्यते ॥१४॥

14. Works do not taint Me; I desire not their fruits. Whoso knows Me to be such, is not bound by works.

14.1. न इति ॥ न मां तानि कर्माणि लिम्पन्ति देहाद्यारम्भकत्वेन, अहङ्का-

राभावात् । न च तेषां कर्मणां फले मे मम स्पृहा तृष्णा । येषां तु संसारिणां "अहं कर्ता" इत्यभिमानः कर्मसु, स्पृहा च तत्फलेषु, तान् कर्माणि लिम्पन्ति इति युक्तम्, तदभावात् न मां कर्माणि लिम्पन्ति—इति एवं यः अन्यः अपि मां आत्मत्वेन अभिजानाति "न अहं कर्ता, न मे कर्मफले स्पृहा" इति सः कर्मभिः न बद्धयते, तस्यापि न देहाद्यारम्भकाणि कर्माणि भवन्ति इत्यर्थः ॥

14.1. Those works do not taint Me by originating a body etc., for Me, as I am not egoistic. Nor have I any desire or yearning for their fruits. It stands to reason that those transmigrating persons, who have the conceit of being agents in respect of their works, and who yearn for their fruits, are tainted by them. But in the absence of both these, works taint Me not. Even another, who knows Me to be the Self of all, a non-agent without yearning for the fruits of works, is not bound by works. In his case, too, works do not originate a psycho-physical organism.

15.0. "न अहं कर्ता न मे कर्मफले स्पृहा" इति —

15.0. 'How? I am not an agent; I desire not the fruits of works'—

एवं ज्ञात्वा कृतं कर्म पूर्वैरपि मुमुक्षुभिः ।
कुरु कर्मैव तस्मात्त्वं पूर्वैः पूर्वतरं कृतम् ॥१५॥

15. Knowing thus was work done by ancient seekers after liberation. Therefore you too do only work, as was done by the ancients in bygone days.

15.1. एवं इति ॥ एवं ज्ञात्वा कृतं कर्म पूर्वैः अपि अतिक्रान्तैः मुमुक्षुभिः । कुरु तेन एव त्वं, न तूष्णीं आसनं, नापि संन्यासः कर्तव्यः, तस्मात् त्वं पूर्वैः अपि अनुष्ठितत्वात्, यदि अज्ञः [अनात्मज्ञः] तदा आत्मशुद्धयर्थं तत्त्ववित् चेत् लोकसंग्रहार्थं पूर्वैः जनकादिभिः पूर्वतरं कृतं, न अधुना [तनं] कृतं निर्वर्तितम् ॥

15.1. Knowing thus was work done even by the ancients, who have passed away and who sought liberation. Therefore do only work. Don't sit inactive; neither renounce. So, since even the ancients worked, work for mind's purification if you are ignorant of the Self; but if you know the Truth, work for the world's well-being, as was done by the ancients such as Janaka in excellent style.

16.0. तत्र कर्म चेत् कर्तव्यं त्वद्वचनात् एव करोमि अहम् । किं विशेषितेन 'पूर्वैः पूर्वतरं कृतम्' इति ? उच्यते — यस्मात् महत् वैषम्यं कर्मणि । कथम् ? —

16.0. *Objection:* If work is to be done, I shall do it at Your bidding. Why recommend it in the words 'done by the ancients in by-gone days'?

Answer: Because, great confusion prevails as regards work. How?

किं कर्म किमकर्मेति कवयोऽप्यत्र मोहिताः ।
तत्ते कर्म प्रवक्ष्यामि यज्ज्ञात्वा मोक्ष्यसेऽशुभात् ॥१६॥

16. What is work? What is non-work? In respect of these questions the sages even are deluded. Therefore, I shall elucidate the nature of work, by knowing which you will be delivered from evil.

16.1. किं कर्म इति ॥ किं कर्म किं च अकर्म इति कवयः मेधाविनः अपि अत्र अस्मिन् कर्मादिविषये मोहिताः मोहं गताः । तत् अतः ते तुभ्यं अहं कर्म अकर्म च प्रवक्ष्यामि, यत् ज्ञात्वा विदित्वा कर्मादि मोक्ष्यसे अशुभात् संसारात् ॥

16.1. Even the sages of powerful intellects are deluded in respect of the questions what work is and what non-work is. Therefore, I shall elucidate for you work and non-work, by knowing which you will be delivered from 'evil' or the empirical life.

17.0. न च एवं त्वया मन्तव्यं — कर्म नाम देहादिचेष्टा लोकप्रसिद्धं, अकर्म नाम तदक्रिया तूष्णीं आसनं; किं तत्र बोद्धव्यं ? — इति । कस्मात् ? उच्यते —

17.0. Don't think: "Work is well-known in the world.

Exertion of body etc., is work, while non-work is its absence or immobility. What is there to know about them?" Why? Listen:

कर्मणो ह्यपि बोद्धव्यं बोद्धव्यं च विकर्मणः ।
अकर्मणश्च बोद्धव्यं गहना कर्मणो गतिः ॥१७॥

17. Indeed you ought to know about work; also you ought to know about bad work; and, besides, you ought to know about non-work. Profound is the course of work.

17.1. कर्मणः इति ॥ कर्मणः शास्त्रविहितस्य हि यस्मात् अपि अस्ति बोद्धव्यं, बोद्धव्यं च अस्त्येव विकर्मणः प्रतिषिद्धस्य, तथा अकर्मणः च तूष्णींभावस्य बोद्धव्यं अस्ति इति त्रिष्वपि अध्याहारः कर्तव्यः । यस्मात् गहना विषमा दुर्ज्ञेया — कर्मणः इति उपलक्षणार्थं कर्मादिनाम्—कर्माकर्मविकर्मणां—गतिः याथात्म्यं तत्त्वं इत्यर्थः ॥

17.1. Indeed, one ought to know about the work enjoined by the Śāstra and also of 'bad' or forbidden work. Similarly of non-work, or immobility, also one ought to know. 'Is' has to be understood after the expression *boddhavya* used thrice in the verse. Because, the course of work is 'profound'—hard to understand. 'Work' connotes the three—work, bad work and non-work. 'Course' means the truth.

18.0. किं पुनः तत्त्वं कर्मादेः यत् बोद्धव्यं वक्ष्यामि इति प्रतिज्ञातं ? उच्यते—

18.0. What is the truth about work etc., that has to be known, and which the Lord has promised to elucidate? Answer:

कर्मण्यकर्म यः पश्येदकर्मणि च कर्म यः ।
स बुद्धिमान् मनुष्येषु स युक्तः कृत्स्नकर्मकृत् ॥१८॥

18. Whoso beholds non-work in work and work in non-work is wise among men; he is integrated; he does all works.

18.1. कर्मणि इति ॥ कर्मणि, क्रियते इति कर्म व्यापारमात्रम्, तस्मिन् कर्मणि अकर्म कर्माभावं यः पश्येत्, अकर्मणि च कर्माभावे कर्तृतन्त्रत्वात् प्रवृत्तिनिवृत्त्योः —वस्तु अप्राप्य एव हि सर्वः एव क्रियाकारकादिव्यवहारः अविद्याभूमौ एव— कर्म यः पश्येत् पश्यति, सः बुद्धिमान् मनुष्येषु, सः युक्तः योगी च, कृत्स्नकर्मकृत् समस्तकर्मकृत् च सः, इति स्तूयते कर्माकर्मणोः इतरेतरदर्शी ॥

18.1. Any action done is work; whoso beholds in it 'non-work or absence of work', and in 'non-work or absence of work', work—is wise among men. Action and cessation therefrom depend on the agent. All references to action, its accessories and so forth take place on the plane of nescience before Reality is attained. A man of such attainment is not only wise but also integrated, a Yogi; he does the totality of works. Thus is extolled the one who beholds work in non-work and non-work in work reciprocally.

18.2. ननु किं इदं विरुद्धं उच्यते 'कर्मणि अकर्म यः पश्येत्' इति, 'अकर्मणि च कर्म' इति ? न हि कर्म अकर्म स्यात्, अकर्म वा कर्म । तत्र विरुद्धं कथं पश्येत् द्रष्टा ? — न, अकर्म एव परमार्थतः सत् कर्मवत् अवभासते मूढदृष्टेः लोकस्य, तथा कर्म एव अकर्मवत् । तत्र यथाभूतदर्शनार्थं आह भगवान् — 'कर्मण्यकर्म यः पश्येत्' इत्यादि । अतः न विरुद्धम् । बुद्धिमत्त्वाद्युपपत्तेश्च । 'बोद्धव्यं' [१७] इति च यथाभूतदर्शनं उच्यते । न च विपरीतज्ञानात् अशुभात् मोक्षणं स्यात्; 'यत् ज्ञात्वा मोक्ष्यसेऽशुभात्' [१६] इति च उक्तम् । तस्मात् कर्माकर्मणी विपर्ययेण गृहीते प्राणिभिः तद्विपर्ययग्रहणनिवृत्त्यर्थं भगवतः वचनं 'कर्मण्यकर्म यः' इत्यादि ।

18.2. *Objection:* What is the sense of this self-contradictory proposition about the perception of non-work in work and vice versa? Work, of course, can't be non-work, nor non-work, work. How can the beholder see contradictory states?

Answer: Not so. What in truth is non-work appears, to a deluded man, as work; and, similarly, work appears as non-work. The Lord is pleading for veridical perception in 4.18. So no self-contradiction is entailed. This follows also because it alone would make sense of the claim of wisdom on behalf of such a beholder. The passage 4.17 also speaks of veridical perception in the expression 'it ought to be known'. Contradictory perception cannot deliver any from evil; *vide* 4.16. Therefore the Lord's utterance in 4.18 seeks to abolish the contradictory perception, by the ignorant, of work and non-work.

18.3. न च अत्र कर्माधिकरणं अकर्म अस्ति, कुण्डे बदराणि इव । नापि अकर्माधिकरणं कर्म, कर्माभावत्वात् अकर्मणः । अतः विपरीतगृहीते एव कर्माकर्मणी लौकिकैः, यथा मृगतृष्णिकायां उदकं, शुक्तिकायां वा रजतम् ।

18.3. Note that there is no non-work contained in work as Jujube fruits (Badari) are contained in a bowl. Nor is there work in the container, non-work; for this latter means the absence of work. Therefore, the empiricists mistakenly apprehend work and non-work as water is apprehended in the mirage or silver in nacre.

18.4. ननु कर्म कर्मैव सर्वेषां न क्वचित् व्यभिचरति—तत् न, नौस्थस्य नावि गच्छन्त्यां तटस्थेषु अगतिषु नगेषु प्रतिकूलगतिदर्शनात्, दूरेषु चक्षुषाऽसन्निकृष्टेषु गच्छत्सु गत्यभावदर्शनात्, एवं इहापि अकर्मणि कर्मदर्शनं कर्मणि च अकर्मदर्शनं, येन तन्निराकरणार्थं उच्यते 'कर्मण्यकर्म यः पश्येत्' इत्यादि ॥

18.4. *Objection:* Is not work just work for all alike? It never forfeits its nature.

Answer: No. To a man in a moving boat, the stationary trees on the banks seem to move in the opposite direction; remote moving objects seem to be stationary. Similarly in this context, too, must be understood the perception of work in non-work and vice-versa. Therefore, to correct this mistake is advanced the proposition in IV.18.

18.5. तत् एतत् उक्तप्रतिवचनमपि असकृत् अत्यन्तविपरीतदर्शनभाविततया मोमुह्यमानो लोकः श्रुतमपि असकृत् तत्त्वं विस्मृत्य विस्मृत्य मिथ्याप्रसङ्गं अवतार्य अवतार्य चोदयति इति पुनः पुनः उत्तरं आह भगवान्, दुर्विज्ञेयत्वं च आलक्ष्य वस्तुनः । 'अव्यक्तोऽयमचिन्त्योऽयम्,' 'न जायते म्रियते' [२.२०, २५.] इत्यादिना आत्मनि कर्माभावः श्रुतिस्मृतिन्यायप्रसिद्धः उक्तः वक्ष्यमाणश्च । तस्मिन् कर्माभावे अकर्मणि कर्मविपरीतदर्शनं अत्यन्तनिरूढम्, यतः— "किं कर्म किमकर्मेति कवयोऽप्यत्र मोहिताः" (१६) । देहाद्याश्रयं कर्म आत्मनि अध्यारोप्य "अहं कर्ता, मम एतत् कर्म, मया अस्य कर्मणः फलं भोक्तव्यं" इति च, तथा "अहं तूष्णीं भवामि, येन अहं निरायासः अकर्मा सुखी स्याम्" इति कार्यकरणाश्रयं व्यापारोपरमं तत्कृतं च

सुखित्वं आत्मनि अध्यारोप्य "न करोमि किञ्चित्, तूष्णीं सुखं आसे इति अभिमन्यते लोकः । तत्र इदं लोकस्य विपरीतदर्शनापनयनाय आह भगवान् — 'कर्मण्यकर्म यः पश्येत्' इत्यादि ॥

18.5. The same objection has been often stated and answered. But due to the impact of repeated and inveterate misapprehension, the plain man is totally deluded. He forgets the truth, though he has often heard it affirmed. So he erroneously repeats the objection and demands an answer. In view of the inherent difficulty of this truth, the Lord repeatedly answers the objection. The negation of work as regards the Self, established by Śruti, Smṛti and reasoning is stated in *BG*.2.20 and 25; and it will be stated again. In that negation of work in respect of the Self, the perception of its opposite, namely work, has become an inveterate habit. Hence the statement in *BG*. IV.16 'even the sages are deluded'. The plain man superimposes on the Self the work of the psycho-physical organism and maintains, "I am the agent, this work is mine; its fruit must be reaped by me." Similarly he superimposes on the Self the cessation from work of the same organism, and the resultant satisfaction and maintains, 'I do nothing; I rest comfortably.' In order to correct this contrary perception of the plain man of the world, the Lord affirms, 'Whoso beholds non-work in work' and so forth.

18.6. अत्र च कर्म कर्मैव सत् कार्यकरणाश्रयं कर्मरहिते अविक्रिये आत्मनि सर्वैः अध्यस्तं, यतः पण्डितः अपि "अहं करोमि" इति मन्यते । अतः आत्मसमवेततया सर्वलोकप्रसिद्धे कर्मणि नदीकूलस्थेषु इव वृक्षेषु गतिप्रातिलोम्येन अकर्म कर्माभावं (यथाभूतं) गत्यभावम् इव वृक्षेषु यः पश्येत्, अकर्मणि च कार्यकरणव्यापारोपरमे कर्मवत् आत्मनि अध्यारोपिते — "तूष्णीं अकुर्वन् सुखं आसे" इति अहङ्काराभिसन्धिहेतुत्वात् — तस्मिन् अकर्मणि च कर्मः यः पश्येत्, यः एवं कर्माकर्मविभागज्ञः सः बुद्धिमान् पण्डितः मनुष्येषु, सः युक्तः योगी कृत्स्नकर्मकृत् च, सः अशुभात् मोक्षितः कृतकृत्यः भवति इत्यर्थः ॥

18.6. Also note in this context that the work of the psycho-physical organism of course remains as such; but it is superimposed by all on the immutable Self that works not; for, even the learned man thinks, 'I work'. Therefore, the wise man is he who perceives non-work in what all the world believes to be work inherent in the self, even as he is aware of the non-movement of the trees on the river-bank despite their apparent movement. Contrariwise, he perceives work where the world superimposes non-work on the self mistaking the psycho-physical organism itself for the self, when the psycho-physical organism ceases to work. The consequence of the second superimposition is the egoistic affirmation, 'I am happy, doing nothing.' He is wise among men as he grasps the real distinction between work and non-work; he is the discriminator, the integrated Yogi, who accomplishes all work. He is delivered from all evil. He has discharged all his duties. This is the upshot of this verse.

18.7. अयं श्लोकः अन्यथा व्याख्यातः कैश्चित् । कथम् ? नित्यानां किल कर्मणां ईश्वरार्थत्वेन अनुष्ठीयमानानां फलाभावात् अकर्माणि तानि उच्यन्ते गौण्या वृत्त्या । तेषां च अकरणं अकर्म; तच्च प्रत्यवायफलत्वात् कर्म उच्यते गौण्यैव वृत्त्या । तत्र नित्ये कर्मणि अकर्म यः पश्येत् फलाभावात्; यथा धेनुः अपि गौः अगौः इति उच्यते क्षीराख्यं फलं न प्रयच्छति इति, तद्वत् । तथा नित्याकरणे तु अकर्मणि च कर्म यः पश्येत् नरकादिप्रत्यवायफलं प्रयच्छति इति —

18.7. This verse has been interpreted differently by others. How? In a secondary sense, obligatory works enjoined by the scriptures, done for the sake of God, may be styled non-works, since they yield no fruits of their own. Their non-performance is non-work, which entails the sin of omission or *pratyavāya*. As such, this non-performance may be, secondarily, styled work. In this context, whosoever beholds non-work in obligatory work on account of its fruitlessness, is wise (work being non-work), just as a milch cow that yields no milk is a 'no-cow', as it yields not the reward namely, the milk for which it is kept. Similarly, whoso sees work in 'non-work', the non-performance of the obligatory work due to which results hell—the fruit of the sin of omission—is wise.

18.8. न एतत् युक्तं व्याख्यानम् । एवंज्ञानात् अशुभात् मोक्षानुपपत्तेः 'यज्ज्ञात्वा

मोक्ष्यसेऽशुभात्' (१६) इति भगवता उक्तं वचनं बाध्येत । कथं ? नित्यानां अनुष्ठानात् अशुभात् स्यात् नाम मोक्षणं, न तु तेषां फलाभावज्ञानात् ? न हि नित्यानां फलाभावज्ञानं अशुभमुक्तिफलत्वेन चोदितम्, नित्यकर्मज्ञानं वा । न च भगवता एव इह उक्तम् । एतेन अकर्मणि कर्मदर्शनं प्रत्युक्तम् । न हि अकर्मणि "कर्म" इति दर्शनं कर्तव्यतया इह चोद्यते नित्यस्य तु कर्तव्यतामात्रम् । न च 'अकरणात् नित्यस्य प्रत्यवायः भवति' इति विज्ञानात् किञ्चित् फलं स्यात् । नापि नित्याकरणं ज्ञेयत्वेन चोदितम् । नापि "कर्म अकर्म" इति मिथ्यादर्शनात् अशुभात् मोक्षणं, बुद्धिमत्त्वं, युक्तता, कृत्स्नकर्मकृत्त्वादि च फलं उपपद्यते, स्तुतिर्वा । मिथ्याज्ञानम् एव हि साक्षात् अशुभस्वरूपम् । कुतः अन्यस्मात् अशुभात् मोक्षणम् ? न हि तमः तमसः निवर्तकं भवति ॥

18.8. The above interpretation is not rational; for release from evil cannot reasonably come from this kind of knowledge. It runs counter to the Lord's utterance in *BG* 4.16. How? From performing obligatory works release from evil may, conceivably, result, but not from knowing that 'they yield no fruits'. *Śruti* has not decreed that the knowledge of the fruitlessness of obligatory works, or that of the latter, shall release one from evil, nor has the Lord maintained that position in the Gītā. This should refute this theory of the perception of work in non-work. What has been enjoined here is not the duty of perceiving work in non-work; but only the duty of performing the obligatory work. No worthwile result may follow from the knowledge that the non-performance of obligatory work entails the sin of omission. The non-performance of obligatory work has not been enjoined as something to be known. From the erroneous perception 'work is non-work' there cannot follow release from evil, wisdom, Yogic integration and the state of being a performer of all works; it deserves no laudation. Erroneous cognition itself is an obvious evil. How can it release one from other evils? Darkness cannot dispel darkness.

18.9. ननु कर्मणि यत् अकर्मदर्शनं, अकर्मणि वा कर्मदर्शनं, न तत् मिथ्याज्ञानं, किं तर्हि ? गौणं फलभावाभावनिमित्तं — न, कर्माकर्मविज्ञानात् अपि गौणात् फलस्य अश्रवणात् । नापि श्रुतहान्यश्रुतपरिकल्पनायां कश्चित् विशेषः उपलभ्यते । स्वशब्देन अपि शक्यं वक्तुं " नित्यकर्मणां फलं नास्ति, अकरणात्

च तेषां नरकपातः स्यात्'' इति; तत्र व्याजेन परव्यामोहरूपेण 'कर्मण्यकर्म यः पश्येत्' इत्यादिना किम् ? तत्र एवं व्याचक्षाणेन भगवतः वाक्यं लोकव्यामोहार्थं इति व्यक्तं कल्पितं स्यात् । न च एतत् छद्मरूपेण वाक्येन रक्षणीयं वस्तुः नापि शब्दान्तरेण पुनःपुनः उच्यमानं सुबोधं स्यात् इत्येवं वक्तुं युक्तम् । 'कर्मण्येवाधिकारः' [२.४७.] इत्यत्र हि सः स्फुटतर उक्तः अर्थः न पुनः वक्तव्यः भवति । सर्वत्र च प्रशस्तं बोद्धव्यं च कर्तव्यम् एव । न च निष्प्रयोजनं बोद्धव्यं इति उच्यते । न च मिथ्याज्ञानं बोद्धव्यं भवति, तत्प्रत्युपस्थापितं वा वस्त्वाभासम् ।

18.9. It may be urged that the perception of non-work in work or of work in non-work is no erroneous cognition but a form of secondary knowledge, due to the fruitlessness or fruitfulness of the obligatory work and its non-performance. But this is unavailing; for the *śruti* does not teach any result as accruing from a secondary knowledge of work and non-work. No merit may be claimed for a supposition that rejects what has been positively stated and sets up what has not even been alluded to. The view now being repudiated could very well have been directly stated as follows: Obligatory works yield no fruits; their non-performance entails fall into hell. Why then, was a misleading subterfuge adopted in the expressions, "Whoso beholds non-work in work" etc? An interpretation like the objector's amounts to the statement that the Lord's words are intended to confound the world. The truth conveyed by Him is not anything to be concealed in deceptive words. Nor are they in order just because what they convey will become easy to grasp when repeatedly restated in other words. The idea conveyed in *BG* 2.47 is extremely lucid; it calls for no repetition at all. Everywhere what is lauded and what offers itself as the object of knowledge calls for performance. Nothing unprofitable may be said to be worth knowing. No erroneous cognition needs to be known; neither its content, which is but an appearance.

18.10. नापि नित्यानां अकरणात् अभावात् प्रत्यवायभावोत्पत्तिः 'नासतो विद्यते भावः' [२. १६.] इति, 'कथं असतः सज्जायेत' [छां. उ. ६. २. २.] इति च दर्शितं असतः सज्जन्मप्रतिषेधात् । असतः सदुत्पत्तिं ब्रुवता — असदेव सत् भवेत्, स च अपि असत् भवेत् — इत्युक्तं स्यात् । तत् च अयुक्तम्, सर्वप्रमाणविरोधात् ।

न च निष्फलं विदध्यात् कर्म शास्त्रं, दुःखस्वरूपत्वात्, दुःखस्य च बुद्धिपूर्वकतया कार्यत्वानुपपत्तेः । तदकरणे च नरकपाताभ्युपगमात् अनर्थाय एव उभयथा अपि करणे च अकरणे च शास्त्रं निष्फलं कल्पितं स्यात्; स्वाभ्युपगमविरोधश्च "नित्यं निष्फलं कर्म" इति अभ्युपगम्य 'मोक्षफलाय' इति ब्रुवतः । तस्मात् यथाश्रुतः एव अर्थः 'कर्मण्यकर्म' इत्यादेः । तथा च व्याख्यातः अस्माभिः श्लोकः ॥१८॥

18.10. From a mere negation like the non-performance of obligatory works a positive entity like the sin of omission cannot arise, *vide BG* II.16 and *CU* VI.2.2, which deny the birth of a positive entity from non-being. To affirm the birth of aught positive from non-being is equivalent to saying that non-being may become positive being and being non-being. This is unreasonable, as it repudiates all means of right cognition. A Śāstra may not enjoin futile work as this is but pain. Pain may not be consciously striven for. Since the non-performance of obligatory work is held to lead to a fall into hell, both its performance and non-performance promote only evil. The Śāstra that teaches it is construed as unprofitable. This position also implies self-contradiction on the part of its sponsor. Having maintained that obligatory work yields no fruit, he is now driven to hold that it makes for liberation. Therefore the verse IV. 18 means what we have explained.

19.0. तत् एतत् कर्मादौ अकर्मादिदर्शनं स्तूयते —

19.0. The perception of non-work etc., in work and the like, is extolled:

यस्य सर्वे समारम्भाः कामसंकल्पवर्जिताः ।
ज्ञानाग्निदग्धकर्माणं तमाहुः पण्डितं बुधाः ॥१९॥

19. Him the wise call a man of discrimination, all of whose undertakings are free from desire-prompted imaginations and all of whose works have been consumed in the fire of knowledge.

19.1. यस्य इति ॥ यस्य यथोक्तदर्शिनः सर्वे यावन्तः समारम्भाः सर्वाणि

कर्माणि, समारभ्यन्ते इति समारम्भाः, कामसंकल्पवर्जिताः कामैः तत्कारणैश्च सङ्कल्पैः वर्जिताः मुधैव चेष्टामात्राः अनुष्ठीयन्ते; प्रवृत्तेन चेत् लोकसंग्रहार्थं निवृत्तेन चेत् जीवनमात्रार्थम् । तं ज्ञानाग्निदग्धकर्माणं कर्मादौ अकर्मादिदर्शनं ज्ञानं तदेव अग्निः तेन ज्ञानाग्निना दग्धानि शुभाशुभलक्षणानि कर्माणि यस्य तं आहुः परमार्थतः पण्डितं बुधाः ब्रह्मविदः ॥

19.1. All his undertakings or works of him who has the perception set forth in IV.18 are free from desires and imaginations prompted by them. They are performed without egoistic motives, being mere motions. If the agent is an activist his works promote the world's welfare. If he is a quietist they just keep him alive. The knowledge or the perception of non-work in work etc., is like a fire. He, all of whose works, good as well as evil, are consumed in this fire, is the real man of discrimination—so think the wise, the knowers of Brahman.

20.0. यस्तु कर्मादौ अकर्मादिदर्शी सः अकर्मादिदर्शनात् एव निष्कर्मा संन्यासी जीवनमात्रार्थचेष्टः सन् कर्मणि न प्रवर्तते; यद्यपि प्राक् विवेकतः प्रवृत्तः । यस्तु प्रारब्धकर्मा सन् उत्तरकालं उत्पन्नात्मसम्यग्दर्शनः स्यात्, स सर्वकर्मणि प्रयोजनमपश्यन् ससाधनं कर्म परित्यजति एव। स कुतश्चित् कर्मपरित्यागासम्भवे सति कर्मणि तत्फले च संगरहिततया स्वप्रयोजनाभावात् लोकसंग्रहार्थं पूर्ववत् कर्मणि प्रवृत्तोऽपि नैवं किंचित् करोति, ज्ञानाग्निदग्धकर्मत्वात् तदीयं कर्म अकर्म एव संपद्यते इति एतम् अर्थं दर्शयिष्यन् आह —

20.0. He who habitually perceives non-work, etc., in work and so forth is, for that very reason, beyond all works; he is a renouncer and his stirrings are meant just to maintain life in the body. He does not work though, before the dawn of discrimination, he was an activist. But he whose operative works have begun to bear fruits and who, later, achieves the right perception of the Self will, of course, renounce works with all their auxiliaries; he sees no profit in any work whatsoever. If, for some reason or other, works have not been wholly renounced by such a sage, due to his detachment from works and their fruits, his persistent performance of works is for the world's welfare. He has no private end to serve. In truth, he works not at all. All his works have been burnt up in the fire of knowledge and so his work has become non-work. To set forth this idea, says the Lord:

त्यक्त्वा कर्मफलासङ्गं नित्यतृप्तो निराश्रयः ।
कर्मण्यभिप्रवृत्तोऽपि नैव किञ्चित् करोति सः ॥२०॥

20. Giving up attachment to the fruits of works, eternally content, independent, the man, engaged in works as he is, does nothing at all.

20.1. त्यक्त्वा इति ॥ त्यक्त्वा कर्मसु अभिमानं फलासङ्गं च यथोक्तेन ज्ञानेन नित्यतृप्तः निराकांक्षो विषयेषु इत्यर्थः । निराश्रयः आश्रयरहितः, आश्रयः नाम यत् आश्रित्य पुरुषार्थं सिसाधयिषति, दृष्टादृष्टेष्टफलसाधनाश्रयरहितः इत्यर्थः । विदुषा क्रियमाणं कर्म परमार्थतः अकर्म एव, तस्य निष्क्रियात्मदर्शनसंपन्नत्वात् । तेन एवंभूतेन स्वप्रयोजनाभावात् ससाधनं कर्म परित्यक्तव्यम् एव इति प्राप्ते, ततः निर्गमासम्भवात् लोकसंग्रहचिकीर्षया शिष्टविगर्हणापरिजिहीर्षया वा पूर्ववत् कर्मणि अभिप्रवृत्तोऽपि निष्क्रियात्मदर्शनसंपन्नत्वात् नैव किंचित् करोति सः ॥

20.1. He does nothing who gives up conceit in all works and attachment to their fruits; who is ever content by virtue of the knowledge already set forth. The idea is that he does not desire objects of any kind. He is free from all dependence. Dependence refers to the external means, relying on which, goals are sought to be reached. The sense is that he has no reliance on means to ends, seen and unseen. Work done by the knower is, in reality, non-work; for he has already achieved the realization of the Self that acts not. What ought to follow is that such a sage, having no private ends to serve, should give up all work and their auxiliaries. But due to the desire to promote world's welfare, he finds no way out of activity. Or, may be, he wants to avoid the censure of righteous folk. So he may, as was his wont before Self-realization, continue to work. Still, he works not; for he knows his identity with the work-free Self.

21.0. यः पुनः पूर्वोक्तविपरीतः प्रागेव कर्मारम्भात् ब्रह्मणि सर्वान्तरे प्रत्यगात्मनि निष्क्रिये सञ्जातात्मदर्शनः स दृष्टादृष्टेष्टविषयाशीर्विवर्जिततया दृष्टादृष्टार्थे

कर्मणि प्रयोजनम् अपश्यन् ससाधनं कर्म संन्यस्य शरीरयात्रामात्रचेष्टः यतिः ज्ञाननिष्ठः मुच्यते इति एतम् अर्थं दर्शयितुं आह —

21.0. On the contrary, the ascetic who, prior to any undertaking, has had the realization, as his Self, of the work-free Brahman that is the innermost indweller, remains loyal to the discipline of knowledge; he desires no objective good, seen or unseen, and notes that all work directed to ends, seen or unseen, is unprofitable. He renounces all actions while maintaining a bare bodily existence, and is liberated. To elucidate this idea, the Lord says:

निराशीर्यतचित्तात्मा त्यक्तसर्वपरिग्रहः ।
शारीरं केवलं कर्म कुर्वन्नाप्नोति किल्बिषम् ॥२१॥

21. Free from expectations, controlling mind and self, renouncing all possessions, one who does but an exclusive form of bodily work incurs no sin.

21.1. निराशीः इति ॥ निराशीः निर्गताः आशिषः यस्मात् सः निराशीः, यतचित्तात्मा चित्तं अन्तःकरणं आत्मा बाह्यः कार्यकरणसंघातः तौ उभौ अपि यतौ संयतौ येन सः, त्यक्तसर्वपरिग्रहः त्यक्तः सर्वः परिग्रहः येन सः, शारीरं शरीरस्थितिमात्रप्रयोजनं, केवलं तत्रापि अभिमानवर्जितं, कर्म कुर्वन् न आप्नोति न प्राप्नोति किल्बिषं पापं अनिष्टरूपं धर्मं च । धर्मोऽपि मुमुक्षोः किल्बिषम् एव बन्धापादकत्वात् । तस्मात् ताभ्यां मुक्तः भवति, संसारात् मुक्तः भवति इत्यर्थः ॥

21.1. He from whom all expectations have departed is 'free from expectations'. The 'mind' is the inner sense. Here 'self' means the external psycho-physical organism as a whole. He who has controlled both these is referred to here. He has given up all possessions. The sole aim of his bodily work is the maintenance of his body, and he has no conceit in that work even. He incurs no sin that is adverse to his interests; he reaps no merit. Even merit, for the seeker of deliverance, is a sort of sin; for it will entail bondage. So he is delivered from sin and merit or in other words, delivered from empirical life.

21.2. किंच 'शारीरं केवलं कर्म' इत्यत्र किं शरीरनिर्वर्त्यं शारीरं कर्म अभिप्रेतं ? आहोस्वित् शरीरस्थितिमात्रप्रयोजनं शारीरं कर्म इति ? किं च अतः — यदि शरीरनिर्वर्त्यं शारीरं कर्म, यदि वा शरीरस्थितिमात्रप्रयोजनं शारीरं इति ? उच्यते — यदा शरीरनिर्वर्त्यं कर्म शारीरं अभिप्रेतं स्यात्, तदा दृष्टादृष्टप्रयोजनं कर्म प्रतिषिद्धम् अपि शरीरेण कुर्वन् न आप्नोति किल्बिषं इति ब्रुवतः विरुद्धाभिधानं प्रसज्येत । शास्त्रीयं च कर्म दृष्टादृष्टप्रयोजनं शरीरेण कुर्वन् नाप्नोति किल्बिषं इत्यपि ब्रुवतः अप्राप्तप्रतिषेधप्रसङ्गः । 'शारीरं कर्म कुर्वन्' इति विशेषणात् केवलशब्दप्रयोगात् च वाङ्मनसाभ्यां निर्वर्त्यं कर्म विधिप्रतिषेधविषयं धर्माधर्मशब्दवाच्यं कुर्वन् प्राप्नोति किल्बिषं इति उक्तं स्यात् । तत्रापि वाङ्मनसाभ्यां विहितानुष्ठानपक्षे किल्बिषप्राप्तिवचनं विरुद्धं आपद्येत । प्रतिषिद्धसेवापक्षे अपि भूतार्थानुवादमात्रं अनर्थकं स्यात् । यदा तु शरीरस्थितिमात्रप्रयोजनं शारीरं कर्म अभिप्रेतं भवेत्, तदा दृष्टादृष्टप्रयोजनं कर्म विधिप्रतिषेधगम्यं शरीरवाङ्मनोनिर्वर्त्यं अन्यत् अकुर्वन् तैः एव शरीरादिभिः शरीरस्थितिमात्रप्रयोजनं केवलशब्दप्रयोगात् 'अहं करोमि' इत्यभिमानवर्जितः शरीरादिचेष्टामात्रं लोकदृष्ट्या कुर्वन् न आप्नोति किल्बिषम् । एवंभूतस्य पापशब्दवाच्यकिल्बिषप्राप्त्यसम्भवात् किल्बिषं संसारं न प्राप्नोति; ज्ञानाग्निदग्धसर्वकर्मत्वात् अप्रतिबन्धेन मुच्यते एव इति पूर्वोक्तसम्यग्दर्शनफलानुवादः एव एषः । एवं 'शारीरं केवलं कर्म' इत्यस्य अर्थस्य परिग्रहे निरवद्यं भवति ॥

21.2. By the expression 'an exclusive form of bodily work' what is meant? Is it work to be accomplished by the body only or is it work whose sole aim is the maintenance of the body? What does the distinction between these two interpretations amount to? Listen: The first interpretation will involve a contradiction. Though even a prohibited bodily work is done leading to results seen or unseen, no sin will be incurred, according to the Lord. Further, it will have to be maintained that any course of work, prescribed by scriptures to be performed physically, with seen or unseen ends in view, cannot entail a sin. This is a position not maintained even by the opponent and therefore needs no refutation. The qualification in the expressions, 'doing a bodily form of work' and 'exclusive' implies that works, enjoined or prohibited, righteous or unrighteous, when performed by word or in thought entails sin. In this case is involved the further contradiction that an enjoined work, verbally or mentally performed, entails sin. Even as regards the performance of a forbidden work, the statement of the entailment of sin is futile, being too obvious to require it. On the other hand, when the expression 'a bodily form of work' is taken to denote work aimed at the maintenance of the body, the passage means as follows: Working from the point of view of the plain man, with the body, words or mind, without the conceit of agency and according to injunctions and prohibitions, in order to keep up bodily existence and avoiding all other similar works, one incurs no sins. Such a person cannot possibly sin at all; he won't come by 'sin' or sink into empirical life. For all his works have been consumed in the fire of knowledge. Of course he is delivered without obstacles of any kind. This is but a restatement of the fruit of perfect perception already set forth. Such an interpretation of the expression, 'an exclusive form of bodily work' is faultless.

22.0. त्यक्तसर्वपरिग्रहस्य यतेः अन्नादेः शरीरस्थितिहेतोः परिग्रहस्य अभावात् याचनादिना शरीरस्थितिकर्तव्यतायां प्राप्तायाम् — 'अयाचितमसंक्ल्प्तमुपपन्नं यदृच्छया' [बौधा. ध. २१. ८. १२, अनुगीता ४५. १९.] इत्यादिना वचनेन अनुज्ञातं यतेः शरीरस्थितिहेतोः अन्नादेः प्राप्तिद्वारं आविष्कुर्वन् आह —

22.0. An ascetic who has renounced all possessions will not have the food etc., needed to maintain his body; this requires that he lead a mendicant's life. Utterances like *BDS*.22.8.19 and *Anugītā* 45.19 'what chance brings, unasked, uncontrived', permit certain sources of food and so forth for the maintenance of the ascetic's body. The Lord prescribes the same in the verse that follows:

यदृच्छालाभसन्तुष्टो द्वन्द्वातीतो विमत्सरः ।
समः सिद्धावसिद्धौ च कृत्वाऽपि न निबध्यते ॥२२॥

22. Content with what is gained by chance, beyond dualities, rid of competitive spirit, equanimous in gain and loss, one is not bound in spite of working.

22.1. यदृच्छा इति ॥ यदृच्छालाभसन्तुष्टः अप्रार्थितोपनतः लाभः यदृच्छालाभः तेन सन्तुष्टः सञ्जातालंप्रत्ययः द्वन्द्वातीतः द्वन्द्वैः शीतोष्णादिभिः हन्यमानोऽपि अविषण्णचित्तः द्वन्द्वातीतः उच्यते । विमत्सरः विगतमत्सरः निर्वैरबुद्धिः समः तुल्यः यदृच्छालाभस्य सिद्धौ असिद्धौ च । यः एवंभूतो यतिः अन्नादेः शरीरस्थितिहेतोः लाभालाभयोः समः हर्षविषादवर्जितः कर्मादौ अकर्मादिदर्शी यथाभूतात्मदर्शननिष्ठः सन् शरीरस्थितिमात्रप्रयोजने भिक्षाटनादिकर्मणि शरीरादिनिर्वर्त्ये "नैव किञ्चित् करोम्यहम्" [५. ८.], "गुणा गुणेषु वर्तन्ते" [३. २८.] इत्येवं सदा [यदा] संपरिचक्षाणः आत्मनः कर्तृत्वाभावं पश्यन् नैव किञ्चित् भिक्षाटनादिकं कर्म करोति, लोकव्यवहारसामान्यदर्शनेन तु लौकिकैः आरोपितकर्तृत्वे भिक्षाटनादौ कर्मणि कर्ता भवति । स्वानुभवेन तु शास्त्रप्रमाणजनितेन अकर्ता एव । सः एवं पराध्यारोपितकर्तृत्वः शरीरस्थितिमात्रप्रयोजनं भिक्षाटनादिकं कर्म कृत्वा अपि न निबद्ध्यते बन्धहेतोः कर्मणः सहेतुकस्य ज्ञानाग्निना दग्धत्वात् इति उक्तानुवादः एव एषः [४. १९, २१.] ॥

22.1. What is gained by 'chance' is what comes unsought. 'Content with that' means that one feels he has had enough. When the mind is untroubled, though assailed by dualities like cold and heat, and so on, one is said to be 'beyond all dualities'. 'Rid of the competitive spirit' is he who is not competitive, who sets himself against none. 'Equanimous' refers to the sameness of mind whether one gains what chance brings or fails to bring. An ascetic who is 'the same', is devoid of elation and depression, whether he gains or fails to gain food, etc., to support his life. He perceives non-work in work and so forth. He is established in the vision of the real Self. In respect of work like mendicancy involving the psycho-physical organism, he is always convinced, "I do nothing" *BG* V.8; "The constituents subsist among constituents" *BG* III.28. Perceiving the non-agency of the Self he knows that he performs no work such as mendicancy etc. Only men of the world, when they note the usual forms of worldly activities, ascribe agency to him. Only thus a sage 'becomes' an agent *vis-a-vis* mendicancy, etc. His own experience, occasioned by the *śāstras*, the source of right cognition, is that he is but a non-agent. Seeing him apparently working as a mendicant with the sole aim of the up-keep of the bodily life, others may ascribe agency to him, but the sage is not bound. For, the source of bondage, namely, work along with its cause, has been consumed in the fire of knowledge. Thus this verse affirms what has already been declared in *BG* 4.19.21.

23.0. 'त्यक्त्वा कर्मफलासंगं [४.२०.] इति अनेन श्लोकेन यः प्रारब्धकर्मा सन् यदा निष्क्रियब्रह्मात्मदर्शनसंपन्नः स्यात् तदा तस्य आत्मनः कर्तृकर्मप्रयोजनाभाव-दर्शिनः कर्मपरित्यागे प्राप्ते कुतश्चित् निमित्तात् तदसम्भवे सति पूर्ववत् तस्मिन् कर्मणि अभिप्रवृत्तस्य अपि 'नैव किंचित् करोति सः' [४.२०.] इति कर्माभावः प्रदर्शितः । यस्य एवं कर्माभावः दर्शितः तस्यैव—

23.0. 'Giving up attachment to the fruits of works' (IV.20) —in this verse is set forth 'the absence of work' for one who, due to operative work, continues to work as some occasion or other for it arises. He does this in spite of his realization that the inactive Brahman is his Self and, as such, renunciation of all works is appropriate for him. In fact he has had the perception that there is neither a real agent, nor work, nor purpose to be served by it. In spite of his continuing to work, 'he does nothing at all' (*BG* IV.20). Of such a sage as this:

गतसङ्गस्य मुक्तस्य ज्ञानावस्थितचेतसः ॥
यज्ञायाचरतः कर्म समग्रं प्रविलीयते ॥२३॥

23. Whose attachment has vanished, who has been liberated, whose mind has been established in knowledge and who works as a sacrifice, all works are dissolved.

23.1. गतसङ्गस्य इति ॥ गतसङ्गस्य सर्वतः निवृत्तासक्तेः, मुक्तस्य निवृत्त-धर्माधर्मादिबन्धनस्य, ज्ञानावस्थितचेतसः ज्ञाने एव अवस्थितं चेतः यस्य सोऽयं ज्ञानावस्थितचेताः तस्य, यज्ञाय यज्ञनिवृत्त्यर्थं आचरतः निर्वर्तयतः कर्म समग्रं सह अग्रेण फलेन वर्तते इति समग्रं कर्म तत् समग्रं प्रविलीयते-विनश्यति इत्यर्थः ॥

23.1. 'Whose attachment has vanished' means of one who is attached to nothing whatsoever. He has been liberated, all bondage due to righteousness and unrighteousness having fallen off. His mind has been established in knowledge. He works as a sacrifice. Hence together with 'ends' or fruits all his works 'are dissolved'—they perish. This is the idea.

24.0. कस्मात् पुनः कारणात् क्रियमाणं कर्म स्वकार्यारंभं अकुर्वन् समग्रं प्रविलीयते इति उच्यते ? यतः —

24.0. Why does the work that is done fail to produce its result, and instead get wholly dissolved? Because,

ब्रह्मार्पणं ब्रह्म हविर्ब्रह्माग्नौ ब्रह्मणा हुतम् ।
ब्रह्मैव तेन गन्तव्यं ब्रह्मकर्मसमाधिना ॥२४॥

24. The means of the sacrificial offering is Brahman; Brahman is the oblation placed in the fire of Brahman and by Brahman is the sacrifice made. This sacrificer, who concentrates on the act that is Brahman, reaches Brahman alone.

24.1. ब्रह्म इति ॥ ब्रह्म अर्पणं येन करणेन ब्रह्मवित् हविः अग्नौ अर्पयति तत् ब्रह्मैव इति पश्यति, तस्य आत्मव्यतिरेकेण अभावं पश्यति, यथा शुक्तिकायां रजताभावं पश्यति; तदुच्यते ब्रह्मैव अर्पणमिति, यथा यत् रजतं तत् शुक्तिका एव इति । 'ब्रह्म अर्पणं' इति असमस्ते पदे । यत् अर्पणबुद्ध्या गृह्यते लोके तत् अस्य ब्रह्मविदः ब्रह्मैव इत्यर्थः । ब्रह्म हविः तथा यत् हविर्बुद्ध्या गृह्यमाणं तत् ब्रह्मैव अस्य । तथा ब्रह्माग्नौ इति समस्तं पदम् । अग्निः अपि ब्रह्मैव; यत्र हूयते ब्रह्मणा कर्त्रा, ब्रह्मैव कर्ता इत्यर्थः । यत् तेन हुतं हवनक्रिया तत् ब्रह्मैव । यत् तेन गन्तव्यं फलं तदपि ब्रह्मैव । ब्रह्मकर्मसमाधिना — ब्रह्मैव कर्म ब्रह्मकर्म तस्मिन् समाधिः यस्य स ब्रह्मकर्मसमाधिः — तेन ब्रह्मकर्मसमाधिना ब्रह्मैव गन्तव्यम् ॥

24.1. The means by which the Brahman-knower offers the oblation in the fire, is seen by him to be Brahman only. He sees it as nothing but Brahman, just as in the nacre one sees the total absence of silver. Thus is affirmed the fact that the instrument of offering is Brahman alone, as one may say that what seems to be silver is only nacre. The words Brahman and *arpaṇa* are uncompounded. The sense is: that which the plain man takes to be the instrument is Brahman only for the Brahman-knower. So is oblation Brahman—i.e., what is taken to be oblation is only Brahman for him. 'Brahman-fire' is a compound. The fire in which the oblation is offered by the agent is also Brahman. That agent, the sacrificer, too is Brahman. His action, namely, the sacrifice or *hutam*, is also Brahman. The fruit he has to reap too is Brahman. The action of offering is Brahman. He who concentrates thereon, is the agent who repairs to Brahman.

24.2. एवं लोकसंग्रहचिकीर्षुणा अपि क्रियमाणं कर्म परमार्थतः अकर्म, ब्रह्मबुद्ध्युपमृदितत्वात् । निवृत्तकर्मणोऽपि सर्वकर्मसंन्यासिनः सम्यग्दर्शनस्तुत्यर्थं यज्ञत्वसम्पादनं ज्ञानस्य सुतरां उपपद्यते; यत् अर्पणादि अधियज्ञे प्रसिद्धं तत् अस्य अध्यात्मं ब्रह्मैव परमार्थदर्शिनः इति । अन्यथा सर्वस्य ब्रह्मत्वे अर्पणादीनामेव विशेषतः ब्रह्मत्वाभिधानं अनर्थकं स्यात् । तस्मात् ब्रह्मैव इदं सर्वम् इति जानतः विदुषः कर्माभावः, कारकबुद्ध्यभावाच्च । न हि कारकबुद्धिरहितं यज्ञाख्यं कर्म दृष्टम् । सर्वम् एव अग्निहोत्रादिकं कर्म शब्दसमर्पितदेवताविशेषसम्प्रदानादिकारकबुद्धिमत् कर्त्रभिमानफलाभिसन्धिमत् च दृष्टं; न उपमृदितक्रियाकारकफलभेदबुद्धिमत् कर्तृत्वाभिमानफलाभिसन्धिरहितं वा ।

24.2. Thus even the work performed by one seeking the world's welfare is, metaphysically, no work at all; for, the knowledge of Brahman has wiped out all his Karma. The picturing of knowledge as a sacrifice, even in regard to the renouncer of all works, all of whose works have ceased to be, is eminently in order. Its object is the laudation of right perception. This laudation takes the form of identifying auxiliaries, well-known in the context of sacrificial rites, with Brahman in the spiritual context of the sage who has won the realization of the supreme Truth. Otherwise, the exclusive description of these auxiliaries alone as Brahman will be pointless since all things, in reality, are Brahman. Therefore, for the sage who knows all the world to be Brahman there is no work to perform. All ideas of auxiliaries of work have ceased to hold good for him. A work like sacrifice is unthinkable in the absence of ideas relating to auxiliaries. The normal experience is that works like the fire-sacrifice are invariably preceded by notions conveyed by *Śruti*, of deities to whom offerings are made, and also by the conceit of agency and the desire for the fruits of works. They are not preceded by the dissolution of these distinctive ideas or the absence of the conceit and the desire referred to.

24.3. इदं तु ब्रह्मबुद्ध्युपमृदितार्पणादिकारकक्रियाफलभेदबुद्धि कर्म । अतः अकर्म एव तत् । तथा च दर्शितं 'कर्मण्यकर्म यः पश्येत्' [४.१८.], 'कर्मण्यभिप्रवृत्तोऽपि नैव किञ्चित्करोति सः' [४.२०.], 'गुणा गुणेषु वर्तन्ते' [६.२८.], 'नैव किञ्चित्करोमीति युक्तो मन्येत तत्त्ववित्' [५.८.] इत्यादिभिः । तथा च दर्शयन् तत्र तत्र क्रियाकारकफलभेदबुद्ध्युपमर्दनं करोति । दृष्टा च काम्याग्निहोत्रादौ कामोपमर्देन काम्याग्निहोत्रादिहानिः । तथा मतिपूर्वकामतिपूर्वकादीनां कर्मणां कार्यविशेषस्य आरम्भकत्वं दृष्टम् । तथा इहापि ब्रह्मबुद्ध्युपमृदितार्पणादिकारकक्रियाफलभेदबुद्धेः । बाह्यचेष्टामात्रेण कर्म अपि विदुषः अकर्म संपद्यते । अतः उक्तं 'समग्रं प्रविलीयते' [२३] इति ॥

24.3. But the text refers to work marked by the disappearance of ideas relating to fruit, work, and auxiliaries due to all-dissolving Brahman-knowledge. Therefore this is no work at all. Thus has it been elucidated in 4.18, 20; 3.28; 5.8; etc. To demonstrate this, the Lord dissolves in these texts the ideas of difference among work, auxiliaries, and fruit. And in the context of the fire-sacrifice prompted by desire, its character as 'desire-prompted' is seen to be wiped out when the desire in question is dissolved. Also, it is a matter of experience that deliberate or spontaneous works produce distinctive results. In the present context also, for the sage whose sense of difference among auxiliaries, work, and fruit has been dissolved by Brahman-knowledge, work or apparent movements of limbs cease to be work. Hence the statement 'all works are dissolved' (4.23).

24.4. अत्र केचित् आहुः—यत् ब्रह्म तत् अर्पणादीनि; ब्रह्मैव किल अर्पणादिना पञ्चविधेन कारकात्मना व्यवस्थितं सत् तदेव कर्म करोति । तत्र न अर्पणादिबुद्धिः निवर्त्यते; किं तु अर्पणादिषु ब्रह्मबुद्धिः आधीयते, यथा प्रतिमादौ विष्णवादिबुद्धिः, यथा वा नामादौ ब्रह्मबुद्धिः — एवमिति [छां. उ. ७. १. ५.] ॥

24.4. Some interpreters assert: Brahman is the auxiliaries of sacrifice. It seems that Brahman alone assumes a five-fold character as the auxiliaries and performs work. The idea of being instrument etc., of work does not cease; rather the idea of being Brahman is instilled into them, just as in an image the idea of being Viṣṇu is instilled, or in a name, the idea of being Brahman (*vide CU.*7.1.5).

24.5. सत्यं, एवम् अपि स्यात् यदि ज्ञानयज्ञस्तुत्यर्थं प्रकरणं न स्यात् । अत्र तु सम्यग्दर्शनं ज्ञानयज्ञशब्दितं अनेकान् यज्ञशब्दितान् क्रियाविशेषान् उपन्यस्य 'श्रेयान् द्रव्यमयाद्यज्ञात् ज्ञानयज्ञः' [४.३३.] इति ज्ञानं स्तौति । अत्र च समर्थं इदं वचनं 'ब्रह्मार्पणम्' इत्यादि ज्ञानस्य यज्ञत्वसम्पादने इत्युक्तम् । ये तु अर्पणादिषु प्रतिमायां विष्णुदृष्टिवत् ब्रह्मदृष्टिः क्षिप्यते नामादिषु इव च इति ब्रुवते न तेषां ब्रह्मविद्या उक्ता इह विवक्षिता स्यात्, अर्पणादिविषयत्वात् ज्ञानस्य ।

24.5. Well, this might have been the case, if the context had not, as its theme, the glorification of knowledge as sacrifice. Of course here knowledge as sacrifice refers to right perception, and relatively to numerous activities as sacrifice. The Lord lauds knowledge in the words, "Knowledge as sacrifice is superior to material sacrifice" (4.33). The articulation in 4.24 secures the character of sacrifice for knowledge as already explained. But, for those who hold that just as in the case of the idea of Viṣṇu vis-a-vis an image, the idea of Brahman too has to be instilled into the sacrificial auxiliaries, the theme of the context will cease to be Brahman-knowledge either expressly or by implication; for them knowledge will refer only to sacrificial auxiliaries.

24.6. न च दृष्टिसंपादनज्ञानेन मोक्षफलं प्राप्यते । 'ब्रह्मैव तेन गन्तव्यम्' इति च उच्यते । विरुद्धं च सम्यग्दर्शनं अन्तरेण मोक्षफलं प्राप्यते इति । प्रकृतविरोधश्च; सम्यग्दर्शनं च प्रकृतं 'कर्मण्यकर्म यः पश्येत्']१८.] इत्यत्र, अन्ते च सम्यग्दर्शनस्य एव उपसंहारात् । 'श्रेयान् द्रव्यमयाद्यज्ञात् ज्ञानयज्ञः परंतप' [३३.], 'ज्ञानं लब्ध्वा परां शान्तिम्' [३९.] इत्यादिना सम्यग्दर्शनस्तुतिम् एव कुर्वन् उपक्षीणः अध्यायः । तत्र अकस्मात् अर्पणादौ ब्रह्मदृष्टिः अप्रकरणे, प्रतिमायाम् इव विष्णुदृष्टिः, उच्यते इति अनुपपन्नम् । तस्मात् यथाव्याख्यातार्थः एव अयं श्लोकः ॥

24.6. Nor can the fruit of emancipation be secured by means of a cognitive construction. On the other hand the text asserts, "By him will Brahman be attained." The achievement of emancipation without right perception is self-contradictory. This stance also runs counter to the contextual theme which is right perception, *vide* 4.18. The conclusion, too, rests on this theme. This chapter concludes with the laudation of right perception in 4.33 and 39. Therefore it is illogical to argue that, all of a sudden, the instilling of the ideas of Brahman in sacrificial auxiliaries is taught as that of Viṣṇu in an image. Hence the meaning of the verse 4.24 is as set forth by us.

25.0. तत्र अधुना सम्यग्दर्शनस्य यज्ञत्वं सम्पाद्य तत्स्तुत्यर्थं अन्ये अपि यज्ञाः उपक्षिप्यन्ते दैवमेव इत्यादिना—

25.0. Now having high-lighted right perception as sacrifice, other sacrifices too are introduced for belauding that perception in the verses that follow:

दैवमेवापरे यज्ञं योगिनः पर्युपासते ।
ब्रह्माग्नावपरे यज्ञं यज्ञेनैवोपजुह्वति ॥२५॥

25. Some Yogins offer sacrifices to deities; others sacrifice in the fire of Brahman by means of the sacrifice itself.

25.1. दैवमेव इति ॥ दैवमेव देवा इज्यन्ते येन यज्ञेन असौ दैवो यज्ञः तमेव अपरे यज्ञं योगिनः कर्मिणः पर्युपासते कुर्वन्तीत्यर्थः । ब्रह्माग्नौ 'सत्यं ज्ञानमनन्तं ब्रह्म' [तै. उ. २. १.], 'विज्ञानमानन्दं ब्रह्म' [बृ. उ. ३. ९. २८.] 'यत् साक्षादपरोक्षात् ब्रह्म य आत्मा सर्वान्तरः' [बृ. उ. ३. ४. १.] इत्यादिवचनोक्तं अशनायापिपासादिसर्वसंसारधर्मवर्जितं [बृ. उ. ३. ५. १.] 'नेति नेति' [बृ. उ. ४. ४. २२.] इति निरस्ताशेषविशेषं ब्रह्मशब्देन उच्यते । ब्रह्म च तत् अग्निश्च सः होमाधिकरणत्वविवक्षया ब्रह्म अग्निः तस्मिन् ब्रह्माग्नौ अपरे अन्ये ब्रह्मविदः यज्ञम् — यज्ञशब्दवाच्यः आत्मा आत्मनामसु यज्ञशब्दस्य पाठात् — तं आत्मानं यज्ञं परमार्थतः परमेव ब्रह्म सन्तं बुद्धयाद्युपाधिसंयुक्तं अध्यस्तसर्वोपाधिधर्मकं आहुतिरूपं यज्ञेन एव आत्मनैव उक्तलक्षणेन उपजुह्वति प्रक्षिपन्ति, सोपाधिकस्य आत्मनः निरुपाधिकेन परब्रह्मस्वरूपेण एव यत् दर्शनं स तस्मिन् होमः तं कुर्वन्ति ब्रह्मात्मैकत्वदर्शननिष्ठाः संन्यासिनः इत्यर्थः ॥

25.1. 'Sacrifice offered to deities' is that by means of which the deities are propitiated. To that alone some 'Yogins' or activists attend. This is the sense. 'In the fire of Brahman'—Brahman being what the following passages affirm: Truth, knowledge, the Infinite is Brahman (*TU* 2.1); experiential knowledge, bliss, is Brahman (*BU*.3.9.28); that direct and immediate entity is Brahman, the Self innermost (Ibid.3.4.1). These and similar passages affirm that Brahman is beyond all empirical attributes like hunger and thirst (*BU*.3.5.1)—"Not so, not so" (*BU*.4.4.22). That which is Brahman the fire—the receptacle of oblation—is Brahmanfire, in which 'some' Brahman-knowers offer 'sacrifice'. Sacrifice here means the Self. Metaphysically this Self is the supreme Brahman. But it is conjoined to adjuncts like the intellect. On it are superimposed the attributes of all these adjuncts. It takes on the character of an oblation. Some activists deliberately cast it in 'that fire'. The sacrifice in that fire means the perception of the self with adjuncts as the supreme Brahman devoid of all adjuncts. This sacrifice they perform. The idea is that the renouncers devote themselves to the perception of the identity of Brahman and Atman.

26.0. सोऽयं सम्यग्दर्शनलक्षणः यज्ञः दैवयज्ञादिषु यज्ञेषु उपक्षिप्यते 'ब्रह्मार्पणम्' [४.२४.] इत्यादिश्लोकैः प्रस्तुतः 'श्रेयान् द्रव्यमयात् यज्ञात् ज्ञानयज्ञः परंतप' [४.३३.] इत्यादिना स्तुत्यर्थम्—

26.0. This sacrifice of right perception introduced in verse 4.24 etc., is subsumed under sacrifices to deities in order to glorify it in the verse 4.33: "Scourage of foes! the sacrifice by knowledge is superior to material sacrifice."

श्रोत्रादीनीन्द्रियाण्यन्ये संयमाग्निषु जुह्वति ।
शब्दादीन्विषयानन्य इन्द्रियाग्निषु जुह्वति ॥२६॥

26. Others sacrifice the senses, hearing, etc., in the fires of restraints; yet others sacrifice objects like sound in the fires of the senses.

26.1. श्रोत्रादीनि इति ॥ श्रोत्रादीनि इन्द्रियाणि अन्ये योगिनः संयमाग्निषु — प्रतीन्द्रियं संयमो भिद्यते इति बहुवचनम् — संयमा एव अग्नयः तेषु जुह्वति इन्द्रियसंयमम् एव कुर्वन्ति इत्यर्थः । शब्दादीन् विषयान् अन्ये इन्द्रियाग्निषु इन्द्रियाणि एव अग्नयः तेषु इन्द्रियाग्निषु जुह्वति — श्रोत्रादिभिः अविरुद्धविषयग्रहणं होमं मन्यन्ते ॥

किञ्च —

26.1. Some Yogins sacrifice senses, hearing etc., in restraints. The plural is used because each sense has a corresponding restraint. The restraints are the fires. The meaning is that they practise restraint alone. Others sacrifice objects, sound and so forth, in the fires of the senses. Cognition of objects by means of senses they deem a sacrifice.

And,

सर्वाणीन्द्रियकर्माणि प्राणकर्माणि चापरे ।
आत्मसंयमयोगाग्नौ जुह्वति ज्ञानदीपिते ॥२७॥

27. Yet others sacrifice all sense-activities and all activities of vital breaths in the fire of self-restraint, kindled by knowledge.

27.1. सर्वाणि इति ॥ सर्वाणि इन्द्रियकर्माणि इन्द्रियाणां कर्माणि, इन्द्रियकर्माणि, तथा प्राणकर्माणि प्राणः वायुः आध्यात्मिकः तत्कर्माणि आकुञ्चनप्रसारणादीनि तानि च अपरे आत्मसंयमयोगाग्नौ आत्मनि संयमः आत्मसंयमः स एव योगाग्निः तस्मिन् आत्मसंयमयोगाग्नौ जुह्वति प्रक्षिपन्ति ज्ञानदीपिते स्नेहेन इव प्रदीपे विवेकविज्ञानेन उज्ज्वलभावं आपादिते जुह्वति प्रविलापयन्ति इत्यर्थः ॥

27.1. 'Activities of the senses and those of vital breaths'—the vital breath is air in the living body. Its activities are bending, extending and so forth. A set of Yogins, sacrifice i.e., offer these in the Yoga-fire of self-restraint, self-restraint being deemed the Yoga-fire. As a lamp of light is kindled with oil, so is the Yoga-fire by discriminative knowledge. 'Offering there' means total dissolution.

द्रव्ययज्ञास्तपोयज्ञा योगयज्ञास्तथाऽपरे ।
स्वाध्यायज्ञानयज्ञाश्च यतयः संशितव्रताः ॥२८॥

28. Other ascetics, subject to severe disciplines, sacrifice their material possessions, their penances, spiritual exercises, prescribed lessons, and knowledge.

28.1. द्रव्य इति ॥ द्रव्ययज्ञाः तीर्थेषु द्रव्यविनियोगं यज्ञबुद्धया कुर्वन्ति ये ते द्रव्ययज्ञाः । तपोयज्ञाः तपः यज्ञः येषां तपस्विनां ते तपोयज्ञाः । योगयज्ञाः प्राणायामप्रत्याहारादिलक्षणः योगः यज्ञः येषां ते योगयज्ञाः । तथा अपरे स्वाध्यायज्ञानयज्ञाः च स्वाध्यायः यथाविधि ऋगाद्यभ्यासः यज्ञः येषां ते स्वाध्याययज्ञाः । ज्ञानयज्ञाः ज्ञानं शास्त्रार्थपरिज्ञानं यज्ञः येषां ते ज्ञानयज्ञाः च । यतयः यतनशीलाः मंशितव्रताः सम्यक् शितानि तनूकृतानि तीक्ष्णीकृतानि व्रतानि येषां ते संशितव्रताः ॥

28.1. 'Those who sacrifice materials' expend, in the spirit of sacrifice, their wealth in holy places. The ascetics who deem their penances as sacrifice constitute the next group. Those who deem breath-restraints, withdrawals etc., as sacrifices, sacrifice their spiritual exercises. Similarly others deem their methodical prescribed study of the *Rg Veda* and so forth as a sacrifice. Those reckon knowledge a sacrifice who deem their masterly knowledge of *śāstras* itself as such. They are tireless in application; their disciplines are 'sharp', i.e. sharpened to the utmost severity.

Besides,

अपाने जुह्वति प्राणं प्राणेऽपानं तथाऽपरे ।
प्राणापानगती रुद्ध्वा प्राणायामपरायणाः ॥२९॥

29. Some intent on breath-control, blocking the movement of the in-breath and out-breath, sacrifice the in-breath in the out-breath, and, similarly, sacrifice the out-breath in the in-breath.

29.1. अपाने इति ॥ अपाने अपानवृत्तौ जुह्वति प्रक्षिपन्ति प्राणं प्राणवृत्तिं, पूरकाख्यं च प्राणायामं कुर्वन्ति इत्यर्थः । प्राणे अपानं तथा अपरे जुह्वति, रेचकाख्यं च प्राणायामं कुर्वन्ति इत्यर्थः । प्राणापानगती मुखनासिकाभ्यां वायोः निर्गमनं प्राणस्य गतिः, तद्विपर्ययेण अधोगमनं अपानस्य गतिः, ते प्राणापानगती एते रुद्ध्वा

निरुद्धच प्राणायामपरायणाः प्राणायामतत्पराः कुम्भकाख्यं प्राणायामं कुर्वन्ति इत्यर्थः ॥

किञ्च —

29.1. In 'the out-breath', in its movements, they 'sacrifice'—cast—the movements of the in-breath; they practise a phase of breath-control, called the in-filling. So in the in-breath they sacrifice the out-breath, they practise the phase called the emptying out. The movement of in-breath refers to its exit through mouth and nostrils. In contrast, the downward movement is that of the out-breath. Restraining these two movements, those who are devoted to the practice of breath control perform the *kumbhaka*, the immobilization of breath. This is the idea.

Also,

अपरे नियताहाराः प्राणान् प्राणेषु जुह्वति ।
सर्वेऽप्येते यज्ञविदो यज्ञक्षपितकल्मषाः ॥३०॥

30. Yet others, with strictly regulated diet, sacrifice vital breaths in vital breaths. All those are conversant with sacrifice, having destroyed their sins by acts of sacrifice.

30.1. अपरे इति ॥ अपरे नियताहाराः नियतः परिमितः आहारः येषां ते नियताहाराः सन्तः प्राणान् वायुभेदान् प्राणेषु एव जुह्वति, यस्य यस्य वायोः जयः क्रियते इतरान् वायुभेदान् तस्मिन् तस्मिन् जुह्वति, ते तत्र प्रविष्टाः इव भवन्ति । सर्वेऽपि एते यज्ञविदः यज्ञक्षपितकल्मषाः यज्ञैः यथोक्तैः क्षपितः नाशितः कल्मषः येषां ते यज्ञक्षपितकल्मषाः ॥

एवं यथोक्तान् यज्ञान् निर्वर्त्य —

30.1. Those who have strictly restricted their diet, sacrifice vital breaths in those very breaths. In the breath that is mastered, other vital breaths are 'sacrificed.' i.e., these appear as though they entered into it. All these whose sins have been attenuated by these sacrifices are conversant with sacrifices.

Having performed the sacrifices thus enumerated,

यज्ञशिष्टामृतभुजो यान्ति ब्रह्म सनातनम् ।
नायं लोकोऽस्त्ययज्ञस्य कुतोऽन्यः कुरुसत्तम ॥३१॥

31. They partake of the ambrosial remains of these sacrifices and repair to the eternal Brahman. The non-performer of sacrifices does not own (even) this world; why then, O best of Kuru princes! speak of another?

31.1. यज्ञ इति ॥ यज्ञशिष्टामृतभुजः यज्ञानां शिष्टं यज्ञशिष्टं, यज्ञशिष्टं च तत् अमृतं च यज्ञशिष्टामृतं, तत् भुञ्जत इति यज्ञशिष्टामृतभुजः । यथोक्तान् यज्ञान् कृत्वा तच्छिष्टेन कालेन यथाविधिचोदितं अन्नं अमृताख्यं भुञ्जते ये ते यज्ञशिष्टामृतभुजः यान्ति गच्छन्ति ब्रह्म सनातनं चिरन्तनं मुमुक्षवः चेत्; कालातिक्रमापेक्षया इति सामर्थ्यात् गम्यते । न अयं लोकः सर्वप्राणिसाधारणोऽपि अस्ति यथोक्तानां यज्ञानां एकोऽपि यज्ञः यस्य नास्ति सः अयज्ञः तस्य । कुतः अन्यः विशिष्टसाधनसाध्यः कुरुसत्तम ? ॥

31.1. The remains of sacrifices are what is left over; it is ambrosia. The sacrificers partake of it. Having performed the sacrifices enumerated above, they eat, according to Vedic injunctions, the ambrosial food and they repair to the eternal Brahman, in case they seek liberation. From the logic of the situation it follows that this happens in course of time. Even this world of human beings is not won by him who performs not even one of these sacrifices. How then, O the best of the Kuru princes, can he win the other world, to win which special causal collocations are called for?

एवं बहुविधा यज्ञा वितता ब्रह्मणो मुखे ।
कर्मजान्विद्धि तान् सर्वानेवं ज्ञात्वा विमोक्ष्यसे ॥३२॥

32. Thus have many sacrifices been spread out in the pages of the Veda. Know them all to be born of works. Knowing thus will you be liberated.

32.1. एवं इति ॥ यथोक्ताः बहुविधाः बहुप्रकाराः यज्ञाः वितताः विस्तीर्णाः ब्रह्मणः वेदस्य मुखे द्वारे । वेदद्वारेण अवगम्यमानाः ब्रह्मणः मुखे विततः उच्यन्ते; तद्यथा 'वाचि हि प्राणान् जुहुमः' [ऐ. आ. ३.२.६.] इत्यादयः । कर्मजान् कायि-

कवाचिकमानसकर्मोद्भवान् विद्धि तान् सर्वान् अनात्मजान्, निर्व्यापारः हि आत्मा । अतः एवं ज्ञात्वा विमोक्ष्यसे अशुभात् । न मद्व्यापाराः एते, निर्व्यापारोऽहं उदासीनः इत्येवं ज्ञात्वा अस्मात् सम्यग्दर्शनात् मोक्ष्यसे अशुभात् संसारबन्धनात् इत्यर्थः ॥

32.1. As stated, many sorts of sacrifice have been 'spread out'—set-forth—in the Vedic path. Those which are known by means of the Vedas are said to be 'spread out' in 'the face' of the Vedas; for example, "we sacrifice the vital breaths in speech" (*Ait.A*.3.26). Know all of them to be born of works—born of the exertions of the body, word and mind, and not of the Self. For the Self works not. Therefore, thus knowing, you will be released from evil. Knowing "these are not my activities; I exert not, I am indifferent"—due to this right perception, you will be released from 'evil' or the bondage of empirical life. This is the idea.

33.0. 'ब्रह्मार्पणम्' इत्यादिश्लोकेन सम्यग्दर्शनस्य यज्ञत्वं संपादितम् । यज्ञाश्च अनेके उपदिष्टाः । तैः सिद्धपुरुषार्थप्रयोजनैः ज्ञानं स्तूयते । कथम् ? —

33.0. In verse 4.24 right perception has been identified with sacrifice; and many sacrifices have been laid down. By means of them all, which help man to secure his goal, knowledge is extolled. How?

श्रेयान् द्रव्यमयाद्यज्ञात् ज्ञानयज्ञः परंतप ।
सर्वं कर्माखिलं पार्थ ज्ञाने परिसमाप्यते ॥३३॥

33. The sacrifice of knowledge, O scourge of foes! is superior to the sacrifice of materials. All works, without exception, Arjuna! culminate in knowledge.

33.1. श्रेयान् इति ॥ श्रेयान् द्रव्यमयात् द्रव्यसाधनसाध्यात् यज्ञात् ज्ञानयज्ञः हे परंतप । द्रव्यमयः हि यज्ञः फलस्य आरम्भकः, न ज्ञानयज्ञः फलस्य आरंभकः, अतः श्रेयान् प्रशस्यतरः । कथं ? यतः सर्वं कर्म समस्तं अखिलं अप्रतिबद्धं पार्थ ! ज्ञाने मोक्षसाधने सर्वतः संप्लुतोदकस्थानीये [२. ४६.] परिसमाप्यते अन्तर्भवति इत्यर्थः । 'यथा कृताय विजितायाधरेयाः संयन्त्येवमेनं सर्वं तदभिसमेति यत् किञ्च प्रजाः साधु कुर्वन्ति यस्तद्वेद यत् स वेद' [छां. उ. ४. १. ४.] इति श्रुतेः ॥

33.1. Superior to 'the sacrifice of materials'—sacrifices done with materials—is the sacrifice of knowledge. For, a material sacrifice engenders fruit; not so the sacrifice of knowledge. Hence its superiority. How? All works, unobstructedly 'culminate' i.e., are included in, knowledge that leads to liberation and that corresponds to the 'inundation all around' (2.46); *Vide* the *Śruti*: "As the lower throws of dice go to the highest throw, to the winner, so whatever good creatures do all go to him, who knows what he knows" (*CU*.4.1.4).

34.0. तत् एतत् विशिष्टं ज्ञानं तर्हि केन प्राप्यते इति ? उच्यते—

34.0. By what means, then, is this superior knowledge won? Listen:

तद्विद्धि प्रणिपातेन परिप्रश्नेन सेवया ।
उपदेक्ष्यन्ति ते ज्ञानं ज्ञानिनस्तत्त्वदर्शिनः ॥३४॥

34. Know it by means of obeisance, exhaustive questionings, service to the (teacher). Knowers who have realised the truth will impart to you that knowledge.

34.1. तद्विद्धि इति ॥ तत् विद्धि विजानीहि येन विधिना प्राप्यते इति । आचार्यान् अभिगम्य, प्रणिपातेन प्रकर्षेण नीचैः पतनं प्रणिपातः दीर्घनमस्कारः तेन, "कथं बन्धः ? कथं मोक्षः ? का विद्या ? का च अविद्या ?" इति परिप्रश्नेन, सेवया गुरुशुश्रूषया एवमादिना । प्रश्रयेण आवर्जिताः आचार्याः उपदेक्ष्यन्ति कथयिष्यन्ति ते ज्ञानं यथोक्तविशेषणं ज्ञानिनः । ज्ञानवन्तोऽपि केचित् यथावत् तत्त्वदर्शनशीलाः, अपरे न; अतः विशिनष्टि तत्त्वदर्शिनः इति । ये सम्यग्दर्शिनः तैः उपदिष्टं ज्ञानं कार्यक्षमं भवति, न इतरत् इति भगवतः मतम् ॥

34.1. Know it—the procedure by which knowledge is won. Approaching teachers, lowly prostrating the whole body before them—this is obeisance—and exhaustively questioning them, learn it. Learn it by putting questions such as these. 'How comes bondage? How, liberation? What is knowledge? And what, nescience?' The teachers, the knowers of Brahman, thus won over through humility, will instruct or impart the knowledge described above. Some among them alone are well-established in truth as it is; others are not. Hence the qualification 'who have realised the truth'. Only the knowledge imparted by those who have realised the truth is effective, not aught else. Such is the Lord's doctrine.

35.0. तथा च सति इदम् अपि समर्थं वचनम्—

35.0. In these circumstances, the following utterance becomes significant:

यत् ज्ञात्वा न पुनर्मोहमेवं यास्यसि पाण्डव ।
येन भूतान्यशेषेण द्रक्ष्यस्यात्मन्यथो मयि ॥३५॥

35. By grasping that knowledge, O Pāṇḍava prince! you will no longer be deluded as you now are; and through that, you will behold all beings in the Self and then in Me.

35.1. यत् इति ॥ यत् ज्ञात्वा यत् ज्ञानं तैः उपदिष्टं अधिगम्य पुनः भूयः मोहं एवं यथा इदानीं मोहं गतः असि पुनः एवं न यास्यसि हे पाण्डव । किंच — येन ज्ञानेन भूतानि अशेषेण ब्रह्मादीनि स्तम्बपर्यन्तानि द्रक्ष्यसि साक्षात् आत्मनि प्रत्यगात्मनि 'मत्संस्थानि' इति; अथो अपि मयि वासुदेवे "परमेश्वरे च इमानि" इति; क्षेत्रज्ञेश्वरैकत्वं सर्वोपनिषत्प्रसिद्धं द्रक्ष्यसि इत्यर्थः ॥

35.1. By grasping—mastering—that knowledge imparted by them, you will no longer be deluded as you now are. Further, by virtue of it you will behold all beings, from the creator down to stocks and stones, directly in the inner Self. 'They all dwell in Me,' will be your realization. Also you will see them in Me, Vāsudeva; i.e., you will realise: 'They also are in the supreme Lord.' The idea is that Arjuna will realise the identity of Self and God, which all Upaniṣads have established.

36.0. किञ्च—एतस्य ज्ञानस्य माहात्म्यम्—

36.0. Also note the majesty of this knowledge:

अपि चेदसि पापेभ्यः सर्वेभ्यः पापकृत्तमः ।
सर्वं ज्ञानप्लवेनैव वृजिनं सन्तरिष्यसि ॥३६॥

36. Even if, among all sinners, you are the very worst, by this raft of knowledge you will go beyond sin.

36.1. अपि इति ॥ अपि चेत् असि पापेभ्यः पापकृद्भ्यः सर्वेभ्यः अतिशयेन पापकृत् पापकृत्तमः सर्वं ज्ञानप्लवेन एव ज्ञानम् एव प्लवं कृत्वा वृजिनं वृजिनार्णवं पापं सन्तरिष्यसि । धर्मो अपि इह मुमुक्षोः पापं उच्यते ॥

36.1. Even if, among all sinners, you are the worst sinner, you will cross the sea of sins by means of this raft of knowledge alone. This knowledge is the raft. Even religious merit, for the seeker after liberation, is said to be a form of sin (as it, too, causes bondage).

37.0. ज्ञानं कथं नाशयति पापमिति ? सदृष्टान्तं उच्यते—

37.0. How does knowledge destroy sin? The answer is proffered with an example.

यथैधांसि समिद्धोऽग्निर्भस्मसात्कुरुतेऽर्जुन ।
ज्ञानाग्निः सर्वकर्माणि भस्मसात्कुरुते तथा ॥३७॥

37. As a kindled fire reduces all fuel to ashes, so, Arujuna! does the fire of knowledge reduce all works to ashes.

37.1. यथा इति ॥ यथा एधांसि काष्ठानि समिद्धः सम्यक् इद्धः दीप्तः अग्निः भस्मसात् भस्मीभावं कुरुते हे अर्जुन, ज्ञानमेव अग्निः ज्ञानाग्निः सर्वकर्माणि भस्मसात् कुरुते तथा निर्बीजीकरोति इत्यर्थः । न हि साक्षात् एव ज्ञानाग्निः कर्माणि इन्धनवत् भस्मीकर्तुं शक्नोति । तस्मात् सम्यग्दर्शनं सर्वकर्मणां निर्बीजत्वकारणं इति अभिप्रायः । सामर्थ्यात् येन कर्मणा शरीरं आरब्धं तत् प्रवृत्तफलत्वात् उपभोगेन एव क्षीयते, 'तस्य तावदेव चिरं यावन्न विमोक्ष्येऽथ संपत्स्ये' [छां. उ. ६. १४. २.] इति श्रुतेः । अतः यानि अप्रवृत्तफलानि ज्ञानोत्पत्तेः प्राक् कृतानि ज्ञानसहभावीनि च अतीतानेकजन्मकृतानि च तानि एव सर्वाणि भस्मसात् कुरुते ॥

यतः एव अतः—

37.1. Just as fire well-kindled reduces faggots to ashes, O Arjuna! so the fire of knowledge reduces all works to ashes, i.e., robs them of their power to produce effects. Of course, literally, the fire of knowledge does not reduce works to ashes as though works constituted fuel. Hence the idea is that right perception robs all works of their power to generate effects. Propriety suggests that the works that have effected the present body of the knower are exhausted through experience of the fruits they have borne; *vide* the *Sruti*: 'He has to wait only as long as he is unreleased; then, he attains perfection' (*CU*.6.14.2). Hence only those works, which were done in countless prior lives before the dawn of knowledge, and which have not begun to bear fruits, as well as those which coexist with knowledge, are burnt up.

On account of this,

न हि ज्ञानेन सदृशं पवित्रमिह विद्यते ।
तत्स्वयं योगसंसिद्धः कालेनात्मनि विन्दति ॥३८॥

38. Nothing exists here as purifying as knowledge. Perfected in Yoga, in course of time, one wins it in one's own Self.

38.1. न हि इति ॥ न हि ज्ञानेन सदृशं तुल्यं पवित्रं पावनं शुद्धिकरं इह विद्यते । तत् ज्ञानं स्वयम् एव योगसंसिद्धः योगेन कर्मयोगेन समाधियोगेन च संसिद्धः संस्कृतः योग्यतां आपन्नः सन् मुमुक्षुः कालेन महता आत्मनि विन्दति लभते इत्यर्थः ॥

38.1. There is nothing here comparable to knowledge as purifier. One 'perfected', i.e. purified and made competent and intent on liberation through the practice of Yoga, meaning Karma Yoga and the Yoga of concentration, wins it (this knowledge) in the Self after the lapse of a long time. This is the idea.

39.0. येन एकान्तेन ज्ञानप्राप्तिः भवति सः उपायः उपदिश्यते—

39.0. The means by which knowledge is won unfailingly is pointed out:

श्रद्धवाँल्लभते ज्ञानं तत्परः संयतेन्द्रियः ।
ज्ञानं लब्ध्वा परां शान्तिमचिरेणाधिगच्छति ॥३९॥

39. The man of faith, who has mastered his senses and who is intent on it, wins knowledge. Winning knowledge, he attains without delay the peace supreme.

39.1. श्रद्धावान् इति ॥ श्रद्धावान् श्रद्धालुः लभते ज्ञानम् । श्रद्धालुत्वेऽपि भवति कश्चित् मन्दप्रस्थानः, अतः आह—तत्परः गुरूपसदनादौ [-पासनादौ] अभियुक्तः ज्ञानलब्ध्युपाये श्रद्धावान् । तत्परः अपि अजितेन्द्रियः स्यात् इत्यतः आह—संयतेन्द्रियः संयतानि विषयेभ्यः निवर्तितानि यस्य इन्द्रियाणि स संयतेन्द्रियः । यः एवंभूतः श्रद्धावान् तत्परः संयतेन्द्रियश्च सः अवश्यं ज्ञानं लभते । प्रणिपातादिस्तु [३४] बाह्योऽनैकान्तिकोऽपि भवति, मायावित्वादिसम्भवात्; न तु तत् श्रद्धावत्त्वादौ इत्येकान्ततः ज्ञानलब्ध्युपायः ।

39.1. The 'man of faith' or one endowed with faith wins knowledge. Though faithful one may proceed slowly; hence the qualification, 'intent on it'. He applies himself to the means of winning knowledge such as approaching a teacher etc. Though 'intent', his senses may not have been mastered; hence the further qualification, 'who has mastered his senses' i.e., who has withdrawn his senses from their objects. Such a man, faithful, intent on knowledge and master of his senses, is bound to gain knowledge. Prostration and so forth (4.34) may very well be external and uncertain of result as he may be hypocritical. This however is out of question where faith etc., are present. They constitute the unfailing means to knowledge.

39.2. किं पुनः ज्ञानलाभात् स्यात् इति ? उच्यते — ज्ञानं लब्ध्वा परां मोक्षाख्यां शान्तिं उपरतिं अचिरेण क्षिप्रम् एव अधिगच्छति । सम्यग्दर्शनात् क्षिप्रमेव मोक्षः भवति इति सर्वशास्त्रन्यायप्रसिद्धः सुनिश्चितः अर्थः ॥

39.2. What follows from the gain of knowledge? Winning

knowledge, the peace supreme, liberation or withdrawal is attained 'without delay', immediately. That liberation immediately follows from right perception is the unshakable doctrine established by all the *śāstras*.

40.0. अत्र संशयः न कर्तव्यः, पापिष्ठो हि संशयः। कथं इति ? उच्यते—

40.0. No doubt is admissible in this respect; doubt is most despicable, indeed. How?

अज्ञश्चाश्रद्दधानश्च संशयात्मा विनश्यति ।
नायं लोकोऽस्ति न परो न सुखं संशयात्मनः ।।४०।।

40. The ignorant, the unfaithful, the doubting self perishes. Neither this world nor the next nor happiness accrues to the doubter.

40.1. अज्ञश्च इति ।। अज्ञश्च अनात्मज्ञश्च अश्रद्दधानश्च गुरुवाक्यशास्त्रेषु अविश्वासवान् च संशयात्मा च संशयचित्तश्च विनश्यति । अज्ञाश्रद्दधानौ यद्यपि विनश्यतः न तथा, यथा संशयात्मा । स तु पापिष्ठः सर्वेषाम् । कथं ? नायं साधारणोऽपि लोकोऽस्ति । तथा न परः लोकः अस्ति । न सुखं, तत्रापि संशयोत्पत्तेः संशयात्मनः संशयचित्तस्य । तस्मात् संशयः न कर्तव्यः ।।
कस्मात् ? [यस्मात्] —

40.1. He is ignorant who knows not his Self. 'The unfaithful' reposes no faith in the words of the teacher and in the *śāstras*. The doubter has a mind that entertains doubts. All these perish. Though the ignorant and the unfaithful perish, they do not do so to the same extent as the doubter. He is the worst sinner. How? Even this work-a-day world he can't claim; so, too, the next world to come. Neither is happiness his, about which also his mind may doubt. Therefore, doubt must be discarded. Why?

योगसंन्यस्तकर्माणं ज्ञानसंछिन्नसंशयम् ।
आत्मवन्तं न कर्माणि निबध्नन्ति धनञ्जय ।।४१।।

41. Arjuna! works bind not him who is vigilant, who, through Yoga, has renounced works and who has slain doubts with knowledge.

41.1. योग इति ॥ योगसंन्यस्तकर्माणं परमार्थदर्शनलक्षणेन योगेन संन्यस्तानि कर्माणि येन परमार्थदर्शिना धर्माधर्माख्यानि तं योगसंन्यस्तकर्माणम् । कथं योग-संन्यस्तकर्मा इति ? आह — ज्ञानसंछिन्नसंशयं ज्ञानेन आत्मेश्वरैकत्वदर्शनलक्षणेन संछिन्नः संशयः यस्य सः ज्ञानसंछिन्नसंशयः । यः एवं योगसंन्यस्तकर्मा तं आत्मवन्तं अप्रमत्तं गुणचेष्टारूपेण दृष्टानि कर्माणि न निबध्नन्ति अनिष्टादिरूपं फलं न आरभन्ते, हे धनञ्जय ! ॥

41.1. Works do not bind him, who, through the Yoga of realisation of the supreme Reality, has renounced all works, righteous and unrighteous. How does he renounce works through Yoga? By means of knowledge—by the perception of the identity of Self and God—he has cut through all doubts. This renouncer of works, who is vigilant, works not, as the operation of the constituents does not bind in his case; i.e., they do not generate for him effects adverse, favourable, etc.

42.0. यस्मात् कर्मयोगानुष्ठानात् अशुद्धिक्षयहेतुकज्ञानसंछिन्नसंशयः न निबध्यते कर्मभिः ज्ञानाग्निदग्धकर्मत्वादेव, यस्माच्च ज्ञानकर्मानुष्ठानविषये संशयवान् विनश्यति–

42.0. Since he, whose doubts have been slain with knowledge caused by the attenuation of impurities due to the practice of Karma Yoga, is not bound by the works consumed in the fire of knowledge and since the doubter of the efficiency of knowledge and works perishes,

तस्मादज्ञानसम्भूतं हृत्स्थं ज्ञानासिनाऽऽत्मनः ।
छित्त्वैनं संशयं योगमातिष्ठोत्तिष्ठ भारत ॥४२॥

42. Therefore, O Bhārata prince! with the sword of knowledge slay the doubt in the heart born of nescience; resort to Yoga and stand up.

इति श्रीमहाभारते शतसाहस्त्र्यां संहितायां वैयासिक्यां भीष्मपर्वणि श्रीमद्भगवद्गीतासूपनिषत्सु ब्रह्मविद्यायां योगशास्त्रे श्रीकृष्णार्जुनसंवादे ज्ञान-कर्मसंन्यासयोगो नाम चतुर्थोऽध्यायः ॥

42.1. तस्मात् इति ॥ तस्मात् पापिष्ठं अज्ञानसम्भूतं अज्ञानात् अविवेकात् जातं हृत्स्थं हृदि बुद्धौ स्थितं ज्ञानासिना शोकमोहादिदोषहरं सम्यग्दर्शनं ज्ञानं तदेव असिः खड्गः तेन ज्ञानासिना आत्मनः स्वस्य, आत्मविषयत्वात् संशयस्य । न हि परस्य संशयः अपरेण छेत्तव्यतां प्राप्तः, येन स्वस्य इति विशेष्येत । अतः आत्मविषयोऽपि स्वस्यैव भवति । छित्त्वा एनं संशयं स्वविनाशहेतुभूतं, योगं सम्यग्दर्शनोपायं कर्मानुष्ठानं आतिष्ठ कुरु इत्यर्थः । उत्तिष्ठ च इदानीं युद्धाय, हे भारत इति ॥

42.1. Therefore slay this most wicked doubt in the heart or intellect, born of nescience or lack of discrimination. Slay it with the sword of knowledge or right perception. Knowledge of the Self is the sword, and doubt has the Self for its object. None may slay another's doubt. He who doubts about the Self is the slayer thereof. Destroying this doubt that may work one's destruction, practise Karma Yoga, the means of right perception. Stand up to wage this battle, O Bhārata Prince.

इति श्रीमत्परमहंसपरिव्राजकाचार्यगोविन्दभगवत्पूज्यपादशिष्यश्रीमच्छंकरभगवतः कृतौ श्रीभगवद्गीताभाष्ये ज्ञान-कर्म-संन्यासयोगो [ब्रह्मयज्ञप्रशंसा] नाम चतुर्थोऽध्यायः ॥४॥

पञ्चमोऽध्यायः

CHAPTER V

YOGA OF RENUNCIATION

0.1. 'कर्मण्यकर्म यः पश्येत्' [४.१८.] इत्यारभ्य 'स युक्तः कृत्स्नकर्मकृत्' [४.१८.], 'ज्ञानाग्निदग्धकर्माणम्' [४.१९.], 'शारीरं केवलं कर्म कुर्वन्' [४.२१.], 'यदृच्छालाभसन्तुष्टः' [४.२२.], 'ब्रह्मार्पणं ब्रह्म हविः' [४.२४.], 'कर्मजान् विद्धि तान् सर्वान्' [४.३२.], 'सर्वं कर्माखिलं पार्थ' [४.३३.], 'ज्ञानाग्निः सर्वकर्माणि' [४.३७.], 'योगसंन्यस्तकर्माणं' [४.४१.]—इत्येतैः वचनैः सर्वकर्मणां संन्यासं अवोचत् भगवान्। 'छित्त्वैनं संशयं योगमातिष्ठ' [४.४२.] इति अनेन वचनेन योगं च कर्मानुष्ठानलक्षणं अनुतिष्ठ इति उक्तवान्। तयोः उभयोश्च कर्मानुष्ठानकर्मसंन्यासयोः स्थितिगतिवत् परस्परविरोधात् एकेन सह कर्तुं अशक्यत्वात्, कालभेदेन च अनुष्ठानविधानाभावात्, अर्थात् एतयोः अन्यतरकर्तव्यताप्राप्तौ सत्यां यत् प्रशस्यतरं एतयोः कर्मानुष्ठानकर्मसंन्यासयोः तत् कर्तव्यं, न इतरत् इत्येवं मन्यमानः प्रशस्यतरबुभुत्सया अर्जुनः उवाच—संन्यासं कर्मणां कृष्ण [५.१.] इत्यादिना॥

0.1. In the utterances beginning from 4.18, including 4.19, 21, 22, 24, 32, 33, 37 and 41, the Lord has taught the renunciation of all works. In 4.42 He also teaches Yoga whose characteristic is the performance of works. These two mutually contradictory courses, the performance and the renunciation of works, like rest and movement, cannot be undertaken at once by one and the same person. Nor have they been prescribed for pursuit at different times. In other words, only one of the two courses may be practically pursued. Of these that which is better must be taken up and not the other. So thinking, and desiring to know which of the two is the better, Arjuna said: "Renunciation of works, Kṛṣṇa, etc." (5.1).

0.2. ननु च आत्मविदः ज्ञानयोगेन निष्ठां प्रतिपिपादयिष्यन् पूर्वोदाहृतैः वचनैः भगवान् सर्वकर्मसंन्यासं अवोचत्, न तु अनात्मज्ञस्य। अतश्च कर्मानुष्ठानकर्मसंन्यासयोः भिन्नपुरुषविषयत्वात् अन्यतरस्य प्रशस्यतरत्वबुभुत्सया अयं प्रश्नः अनुपपन्नः। सत्यमेव त्वदभिप्रायेण प्रश्नः न उपपद्यते, प्रष्टुः स्वाभिप्रायेण पुनः प्रश्नः युज्यते एव इति वदामः। कथम्? पूर्वोदाहृतैः वचनैः भगवता कर्मसंन्यासस्य कर्तव्यतया

विवक्षितत्वात् प्राधान्यम्, अन्तरेण च कर्तारं तस्य कर्तव्यत्वासम्भवात्, अनात्मवित् अपि कर्ता पक्षे प्राप्तः अनूद्यते एव; न पुनः आत्मवित्कर्तृकत्वम् एव संन्यासस्य विवक्षितं, इत्येवं मन्वानस्य अर्जुनस्य कर्मानुष्ठानकर्मसंन्यासयोः अविद्वत्पुरुषकर्तृकत्वम् अपि अस्ति इति पूर्वोक्तेन प्रकारेण तयोः परस्परविरोधात् अन्यतरस्य कर्तव्यत्वे प्राप्ते प्रशस्यतरं च कर्तव्यम्, न इतरत् इति प्रशस्यतरविविदिषया प्रश्नः न अनुपपन्नः ॥

0.2. *Objection:* "Now, in the utterances cited above, the Lord has enjoined renunciation of all works in order to teach the discipline of knowledge for the Self-knower, and not for one who is not a Self-knower. Therefore, since the performance of works and their renunciation refer to different types of persons it is irrational to ask which of these two courses is better." *Reply*: "True, according to your thinking, the query may be irrational; but in the light of the enquirer's own thinking, it is quite rational, we should say. How? The affirmations quoted above show that the Lord teaches the importance of the renunciation of all works as a necessary duty. Without an agent, of course, it cannot be performed. So it is implied that even a non-knower of the Self may conceivably renounce works. It is not as though only a Self-knower can do it."

Thinking on these lines, Arjuna felt that the renunciation of works and their performance may very well be undertaken by a non-knower of the Self also. Therefore, as has been pointed out, a contradiction is involved: only one of these lines of conduct is practicable and, of course, the more meritorious of the two must be adopted. Hence the question, prompted by the desire to know the more meritorious course, is not irrational.

0.3. प्रतिवचनवाक्यार्थनिरूपणेन अपि प्रष्टुः अभिप्रायः एवम् एव इति गम्यते। कथम् ? "संन्यासकर्मयोगौ निःश्रेयसकरौ तयोस्तु कर्मयोगो विशिष्यते" [५. २.] इति प्रतिवचनम् । एतत् निरूप्यम् — किं अनेन आत्मवित्कर्तृकयोः संन्यासकर्मयोगयोः निःश्रेयसकरत्वं प्रयोजनं उक्त्वा तयोरेव कुतश्चित् विशेषात् कर्मसंन्यासात् कर्मयोगस्य विशिष्टत्वं उच्यते ? आहोस्वित् अनात्मवित्कर्तृकयोः संन्यासकर्मयोगयोः तत् उभयं उच्यते ? इति । किञ्च अतः — यदि आत्मवित्कर्तृकयोः कर्मसंन्यासकर्मयोगयोः निःश्रेयसकरत्वम्, तयोस्तु कर्मसंन्यासात् कर्मयोगस्य

विशिष्टत्वं उच्यते; यदि वा अनात्मवित्कर्तृकयोः संन्यासकर्मयोगयोः तत् उभयं उच्यते ? — इति । अत्र उच्यते — आत्मवित्कर्तृकयोः संन्यासकर्मयोगयोः असम्भवात् तयोः निःश्रेयसकरत्ववचनं, तदीयाच्च कर्मसंन्यासात् कर्मयोगस्य विशिष्टत्वाभिधानं इत्येतत् उभयं अनुपपन्नम् । यदि अनात्मविदः कर्मसंन्यासः, तत्प्रतिकूलश्च कर्मानुष्ठानलक्षणः कर्मयोगः संभवेतां, तदा तयोः निःश्रेयसकरत्वोक्तिः कर्मयोगस्य च कर्मसंन्यासात् विशिष्टत्वाभिधानं इत्येतत् उभयं उपपद्येत । आत्मविदस्तु संन्यासकर्मयोगयोः असम्भवात् तयोः निःश्रेयसकरत्वाभिधानं, कर्म सन्यासाच्च कर्मयोगः विशिष्यते इति च अनुपपन्नम् ॥

0.3. An analysis of the reply, too, shows that this idea prompted the questioner. To explain: "Both renunciation and Karma Yoga promote liberation; of the two, Karma Yoga is better," (5.2)—this is the Lord's reply. This demands critical analysis. Does this reply affirm that, while renunciation of works and Karma Yoga, performed by a Self-knower, promote liberation, Karma Yoga is for some reason or other, the better of the two? Or, do these two features pertain to the renunciation and Karma Yoga performed by the non-Self-knower? "Pray, what follows from these alternatives? Irrational is the affirmation that the renunciation of works and Karma Yoga each has the power to promote liberation, and yet Karma Yoga is superior to the renunciation of works. This affirmation is irrational. For, it is impossible for the Self-knower to renounce and, at the same time, to perform works. Only if both renunciation and performance of works together were possible would such a statement become rational. Incredible is the proposition that the Self-knower may either renounce works or perform them, i.e. practise Karma Yoga. Were this possible, it might have been rational to maintain that both courses subserve liberation and that still Karma Yoga is superior. But since the Self-knower cannot undertake both renunciation of works and Karma Yoga, it is irrational to hold that liberation may be won by either the one or the other, and that the latter is the better of the two.

0.4. अत्र आह — किं आत्मविदः संन्यासकर्मयोगयोः उभयोः अपि असम्भवः ? आहोस्वित् अन्यतरस्य असम्भवः ? यदा च अन्यतरस्य असम्भवः तदा किं कर्म-

संन्यासस्य ? उत कर्मयोगस्य ? इति, असम्भवे कारणं च वक्तव्यम् इति । अत्र उच्यते—आत्मविदः निवृत्तमिथ्याज्ञानत्वात् विपर्ययज्ञानमूलस्य कर्मयोगस्य असंभवः स्यात् । जन्मादिसर्वविक्रियारहितत्वेन निष्क्रियं आत्मानं आत्मत्वेन यः वेत्ति तस्य आत्मविदः सम्यग्दर्शनेन अपास्तमिथ्याज्ञानस्य निष्क्रियात्मस्वरूपावस्थानलक्षणं सर्वकर्मसंन्यासं उक्त्वा तद्विपरीतस्य मिथ्याज्ञानमूलकर्तृत्वाभिमानपुरःसरस्य सक्रियात्मस्वरूपावस्थानरूपस्य कर्मयोगस्य इह गीताशास्त्रे तत्र तत्र आत्मस्वरूपनिरूपणप्रदेशेषु सम्यग्ज्ञानमिथ्याज्ञानतत्कार्यविरोधात् अभावः प्रतिपाद्यते यस्मात्, तस्मात् आत्मविदः निवृत्तमिथ्याज्ञानस्य विपर्ययज्ञानमूलः कर्मयोगः न सम्भवति इति युक्तं उक्तं स्यात् ॥

0.4. In this context one may ask: "Are both, the renunciation of works and Karma Yoga, equally impossible for the Self-knower or only one of them? In the second alternative—is renunciation impossible or is Karma Yoga impossible? Also, the reason for the alleged impossibility must be advanced". Since the nescience of the Self-knower has been abolished, he cannot undertake Karma Yoga that is rooted in error. He is the Self-knower who knows his Self as immutable and devoid of all transformations like birth, etc. Right perception has routed his errors. It has been stated that his is the course of renunciation of all works i.e. the status as the workless Self. Now, in the science of the *BG.*, in the various contexts elucidating the nature of the Self, it has been explained that, since there is incompatibility between right knowledge and error, and among their varied consequences, for the Self-knower there can be no Karma Yoga which implies the status as the active self and conceit in Self's agency. Therefore it is rational to maintain that Karma Yoga rooted in error is out of question for the Self-knower whose nescience has been abolished.

0.5. केषु केषु पुनः आत्मस्वरूपनिरूपणप्रदेशेषु आत्मविदः कर्माभावः प्रतिपाद्यते इति ? अत्र उच्यते—'अविनाशि तु तत्' [२.१७.] इति प्रक्रुत्य 'य एनं वेत्ति हन्तारं' [२.१९.], 'वेदाविनाशिनं नित्यं' [२.२१.] इत्यादौ तत्र तत्र आत्मविदः कर्माभावः उच्यते ॥

ननु च कर्मयोगोऽपि आत्मस्वरूपनिरूपणप्रदेशेषु तत्र तत्र प्रतिपाद्यते एव; तत् यथा 'तस्मात् युध्यस्व भारत' [२.१८.], 'स्वधर्ममपि चावेक्ष्य' [२.३१.], 'कर्मण्येवाधिकारस्ते' [२.४७.] इत्यादौ, अतश्च कथं आत्मविदः कर्मयोगस्य असंभवः

स्यादिति ? अत्र उच्यते—सम्यग्ज्ञानमिथ्याज्ञानतत्कार्यविरोधात्, 'ज्ञानयोगेन सांख्यानां' [३.३.] इत्यनेन सांख्यानां आत्मतत्त्वविदां अनात्मवित्कर्तृककर्मयोगनिष्ठातः निष्क्रियात्मस्वरूपावस्थानलक्षणायाः ज्ञानयोगनिष्ठायाः पृथक्करणात्, कृतकृत्यत्वेन आत्मविदः प्रयोजनान्तराभावात् 'तस्य कार्यं न विद्यते' [३.१७.] इति कर्तव्यान्तराभाववचनाच्च, 'न कर्मणामनारम्भात्' [३.४.], 'संन्यासस्तु महाबाहो दुःखमाप्तुमयोगतः' [५.६.]—इत्यादिना च आत्मज्ञानाङ्गत्वेन कर्मयोगस्य विधानात्, 'योगारूढस्य तस्यैव शमः कारणमुच्यते' [६.३.] इत्यनेन च उत्पन्नसम्यग्दर्शनस्य कर्मयोगाभाववचनात्, 'शारीरं केवलं कर्म कुर्वन्नाप्नोति किल्बिषम्' [४.२१.] इति च शरीरस्थितिकारणातिरिक्तस्य कर्मणः निवारणात्, 'नैव किञ्चित्करोमीति युक्तो मन्येत तत्त्ववित्' [५.८.] इत्यनेन च शरीरस्थितिमात्रप्रयुक्तेषु अपि दर्शनश्रवणादिकर्मसु आत्मयाथात्म्यविदः "न अहं करोमि" इति प्रत्ययस्य समाहितचेतस्तया सदा कर्तव्यत्वोपदेशात् आत्मतत्त्वविदः सम्यग्दर्शनविरुद्धः मिथ्याज्ञानहेतुकः कर्मयोगः स्वप्नेऽपि न सम्भावयितुं शक्यते यस्मात्, तस्मात् अनात्मवित्कर्तृकयोः एव संन्यासकर्मयोगयोः निःश्रेयसकरत्ववचनं, तदीयात् च कर्मसंन्यासात् पूर्वोक्तात्मवित्कर्तृकसर्वकर्मसंन्यासविलक्षणात् सत्येव कर्तृत्वविज्ञाने कर्मैकदेशविषयात् यमनियमादिसहितत्वेन च दुरनुष्ठेयात् सुकरत्वेन च कर्मयोगस्य विशिष्टत्वाभिधानं इत्येवं प्रतिवचनवाक्यार्थनिरूपणेनापि पूर्वोक्तः प्रष्टुः अभिप्रायः निश्चीयते इति स्थितम् ॥

0.5. *Objection*: "Which are the contexts in the *BG*. referred to above where the Self-knower has been said to be workless?" *Reply*: "Starting with the affirmation, 'On the contrary know that to be imperishable' (2.17), in 2.19, 21 and so forth, work has been negated in respect of the Self-knower." *Objection*: "Now in these very contexts Karma Yoga has been enjoined also. *Vide* 2.18, 31, 47 and so forth. How then can it be maintained that Karma Yoga is impossible for the Self-knower?" *Reply*: "There is a contradiction between right perception and false cognitions as well as between the consequences of these two. In 3.3 the discipline of knowledge, abidance in the Self that works not, has been isolated, vis-a-vis the Self-knowing Sāmkhyas, from the discipline of works pertaining to the non-Self-knowers. The Self-knower, having discharged all duties, has no further purpose to fulfil. 3.17 states that he has no more duties to discharge. 3.4, 5, 6 etc., lay down Karma Yoga as an accessory of the Yoga of knowledge. 6.3 states that to one who has won right perception Karma Yoga is no longer relevant. 4.21 rules out, in regard to him, work other than what ensures the maintenance of his body. 5.8 teaches that even in regard to works like sight, hearing, etc., meant to ensure the body's maintenance, the agent who knows the truth about the Self must cherish the idea 'I work not', through mind's concentration. Since, then, the knower of the truth of the Self cannot even dream of Karma Yoga that runs counter to right perception and is rooted in false cognition, the affirmation that renunciation and Karma Yoga equally promote liberation refers to the non-Self-knower. Superior to the non-Self-knower's act of renunciation of works, which is quite distinct from the total renunciation of a Self-knower, is the former's Karma Yoga; for it is easier to accomplish. For, renunciation will be hard for him as it depends on self-restraint and discipline. Further, it is bound to be partial. Thus the analysis of the Lord's statements in reply to Arjuna reinforces what was affirmed above to be the idea inspiring Arjuna's query."

0.6. 'ज्यायसी चेत् कर्मणस्ते' [३.१.] इत्यत्र ज्ञानकर्मणोः सह असंभवात् "यत् श्रेय एतयोः तत् मे ब्रूहि" इत्येवं पृष्टोऽर्जुनेन भगवान् सांख्यानां संन्यासिनां ज्ञानयोगेन निष्ठा, पुनः कर्मयोगेन योगिनां निष्ठा प्रोक्ता इति निर्णयं चकार । "न च संन्यसनादेव केवलात् सिद्धिं समधिगच्छति" [३.४.] इति वचनात् ज्ञानसहितस्य तस्य सिद्धिसाधनत्वं इष्टं; कर्मयोगस्य च विधानात् [४.४२.] । ज्ञानरहितस्य संन्यासः श्रेयान् ? किं वा कर्मयोगः श्रेयान् ? इति एतयोः प्रशस्यतरं बुभुत्सुः—

0.6. Due to the impossibility of the co-existence of knowledge and works, Arjuna asked the Lord in 3.1, 'Say which of these two is better?' and the Lord decidedly stated that the discipline of knowledge is meant for the Sāṁkhyas, the renouncers, and that of works is for the Yogins. This was the doctrine inculcated in that context. According to the affirmation, 'By mere renunciation none attains perfection' in 3.4, it is taught (by implication) that renunciation accompained by knowledge is the means to perfection. For Karma Yoga, too, has been enjoined (4.42). In order to know which of the two, renunciation and Karma Yoga, is better for the non-knower, Arjuna said:

अर्जुन उवाच :

संन्यासं कर्मणां कृष्ण पुनर्योगं च शंससि ।
यच्छ्रेय एतयोरेकं तन्मे ब्रूहि सुनिश्चितम् ॥१॥

1. The renunciation of works, Kṛṣṇa, and again, their performance you praise. Tell me for certain which of the two is better.

1.1. संन्यासं इति ॥ संन्यासं परित्यागं कर्मणां शास्त्रीयाणां अनुष्ठेयविशेषाणां शंससि प्रशंससि, कथयसि इत्येतत् । पुनः योगं च तेषाम् एव अनुष्ठानं अवश्यं कर्तव्यं शंससि । अतः मे कतरत् श्रेयः इति संशयः — किं कर्मानुष्ठानं श्रेयः ? किं वा तद्धानं इति ? प्रशस्यतरं च अनुष्ठेयम् । अतश्च यत् श्रेयः प्रशस्यतरं एतयोः कर्मसंन्यासकर्मयोगयोः, यदनुष्ठानात् श्रेयोऽवाप्तिः मम स्यात् इति मन्यसे, तत् एकं अन्यतरत्, सह एकपुरुषानुष्ठेयत्वासम्भवात् मे ब्रूहि सुनिश्चितं अभिप्रेतं तवेति ॥१॥

1.1. Renunciation or the giving up of works enjoined by the *śāstras* to be performed, You praise or affirm. Again, Yoga or the unfailing performance of these very works is commended by you. So I wonder which of these two is the better—whether performance of works is better or their renunciation. The better ought to be done. So, of these two, the renunciation and performance of works, that which is better according to you, doing which I may attain the Good—state that for certain as Your view; for, both cannot be done together by one and the same person.

2.0. स्वाभिप्रायं आचक्षाणः निर्णयाय श्रीभगवानुवाच —

2.0. Setting forth His view definitely, the blessed Lord spoke:

श्रीभगवानुवाच :

संन्यासः कर्मयोगश्च निःश्रेयसकरावुभौ ।
तयोस्तु कर्मसंन्यासात्कर्मयोगो विशिष्यते ॥२॥

2. Both renunciation and Karma Yoga promote the supreme good; but of the two, Karma Yoga is superior to the renunciation of works.

2.1. संन्यासः इति । संन्यासः कर्मणां परित्यागः कर्मयोगः च तेषां अनुष्ठानं तौ उभौ अपि निःश्रेयसकरौ मोक्षं कुर्वाते ज्ञानोत्पत्तिहेतुत्वेन । उभौ यद्यपि निःश्रेयसकरौ, तथापि तयोः तु निःश्रेयसहेत्वोः कर्मसंन्यासात् केवलात् कर्मयोगः विशिष्यते इति कर्मयोगं स्तौति ॥

2.1. Renunciation, the giving up of works, and Karma Yoga, their performance—both these bring about the highest good or liberation, since they generate knowledge. Though both lead to the highest good, still, of these two causes of the highest Good, Karma Yoga is superior to mere renunciation

3.0. कस्मात् इति ? आह—

3.0. Thus the Lord commends Karma Yoga. Why?

ज्ञेयः स नित्यसंन्यासी यो न द्वेष्टि न कांक्षति ।
निर्द्वन्द्वो हि महाबाहो सुखं बन्धात्प्रमुच्यते ॥३॥

3. Know him to be a perpetual renouncer who neither shuns nor seeks. O mighty-armed! One who is above such contraries is easily liberated from bondage.

3.1. ज्ञेयः इति ॥ ज्ञेयः ज्ञातव्यः सः कर्मयोगी नित्यसंन्यासी इति यः न द्वेष्टि किञ्चित् न कांक्षति सुखं दुःखं वा तत्साधनं च । एवंविधः यः, कर्मणि वर्तमानोऽपि, स नित्यसंन्यासी इति ज्ञातव्यः इत्यर्थः । निर्द्वन्द्वः द्वन्द्ववर्जितः हि यस्मात् महाबाहो सुखं बन्धात् अनायासेन प्रमुच्यते ॥

3.1. Know the Karma Yogin to be a perpetual renouncer; he neither shuns nor seeks anything—whether it be pain or pleasure or the means to attain them. Such a person, though working, must be taken to be a perpetual renouncer. This is the sense. For, O mighty-armed! one who is above such contraries is released easily, i.e., without much effort.

4.0. संन्यासकर्मयोगयोः भिन्नपुरुषानुष्ठेययोः विरुद्धयोः फलेऽपि विरोधः युक्तः, न तु उभयोः निःश्रेयसकरत्वम् एव इति प्राप्ते इदं उच्यते —

4.0. "The mutually opposed renunciation and Karma Yoga, performed by different types of persons, ought to be opposed as regards their fruits, too. Normally, these ought not to produce an identical result viz., the supreme Good"—the following is affirmed negating this normal position.

सांख्ययोगौ पृथग्बालाः प्रवदन्ति न पण्डिताः ।
एकमप्यास्थितः सम्यगुभयोर्विन्दते फलम् ॥४॥

4. The thoughtless—not men of discrimination—affirm that Sāṁkhya and Yoga are different. Properly resorting to either of them, one wins the fruit of both.

4.1. सांख्ययोगौ इति । सांख्ययोगौ पृथक् विरुद्धभिन्नफलौ बालाः प्रवदन्ति न पण्डिताः । पण्डिताः तु ज्ञानिनः एकं फलं अविरुद्धं इच्छन्ति । कथं ? एकमपि सांख्ययोगयोः सम्यक् आस्थितः सम्यगनुष्ठितवान् इत्यर्थः । उभयोः विन्दते फलम् । उभयोः तदेव हि निःश्रेयसं फलं; अतः न फले विरोधः अस्ति ॥

4.1. The thoughtless affirm that Sāṁkhya and Yoga are 'different', i.e., they bear opposed and varied fruits; discriminating men don't say so. These latter are men of knowledge who maintain that these fruits are one and unopposed. How? Of Sāṁkhya and Yoga even one, properly resorted to, i.e., if even one is properly observed, the fruit of both is won. The fruit of both is indeed the same supreme Good. So there is no antagonism in regard to their results.

4.2. ननु संन्यासकर्मयोगशब्देन प्रस्तुत्य सांख्ययोगयोः फलैकत्वं कथं इह अप्रकृतं ब्रवीति ? न एष दोषः—यद्यपि अर्जुनेन संन्यासं कर्मयोगं च केवलं अभिप्रेत्य प्रश्नः कृतः, भगवांस्तु तदपरित्यागेन एव स्वाभिप्रेतं च विशेषं संयोज्य शब्दान्तरवाच्यतया प्रतिवचनं ददौ 'सांख्ययोगौ' इति । तौ एव संन्यासकर्मयोगौ ज्ञानतदुपायसमबुद्धित्वादिसंयुक्तौ सांख्ययोगशब्दवाच्यौ इति भगवतः मतम् । अतः न अप्रकृतप्रक्रिया इति ॥

4.2. *Objection:* "Beginning with the terms renunciation and Karma Yoga, why does the Lord speak of the unity of the results of Sāṁkhya and Karma Yoga. Is it not irrelevant?" *Answer:* This is no flaw; for, though Arjuna's question had only renunciation and Karma Yoga in view, without rejecting these and adding His own characteristic view, the Lord answered, using the terms Sāṁkhya and Karma Yoga. His idea is that renunciation, and Karma Yoga together with knowledge and its means, namely, equality of vision, are denoted by Sāṁkhya and Yoga. Hence this discussion is not irrelevant.

5.0. एकस्यापि सम्यगनुष्ठानात् कथं उभयोः फलं विन्दते इति ? उच्यते—

5.0. How can one win the fruit of both by performing either of them aright? Answer:

यत्सांख्यैः प्राप्यते स्थानं तद्योगैरपि गम्यते ।
एकं सांख्यं च योगं च यः पश्यति स पश्यति ॥५॥

5. The status won by the Sāṁkhyas is attained by the Yogins also. Only he perceives who perceives that Sāṁkhya and Yoga are one.

5.1. यत् इति ॥ यत् सांख्यैः ज्ञाननिष्ठैः संन्यासिभिः प्राप्यते स्थानं मोक्षाख्यं तत् योगैः अपि ज्ञानप्राप्त्युपायत्वेन ईश्वरे समर्प्य कर्माणि आत्मनः फलं अनभिसन्धाय अनुतिष्ठन्ति ये ते योगाः—योगिनः, तैः अपि परमार्थज्ञानसंन्यासप्राप्तिद्वारेण गम्यते इति अभिप्रायः । अतः एकं सांख्यं च योगं च यः पश्यति फलैकत्वात् सः पश्यति सम्यक् पश्यति इत्यर्थः ॥

5.1. The status, i.e., liberation, achieved by the all-renouncing Sāṁkhyas, established in knowledge, is reached by the Yogins, too. The Yogins are those who, without seeking fruit of works for themselves, perform them, dedicating them all to God as a means to winning knowledge. The Yogins reach the state of liberation through the knowledge of the supreme Reality and renunciation of all works. This is the idea. Therefore, only he who perceives Sāṁkhya and Yoga to be one, due to the identity of their fruits, perceives aright. This is the meaning.

6.0. एवं तर्हि योगात् संन्यासः एव विशिष्यते; कथं तर्हि इदम् उक्तं 'तयोस्तु कर्मसंन्यासात् कर्मयोगो विशिष्यते' [२] इति ? शृणु तत्र कारणम्–त्वया पृष्टं—केवलं कर्मसंन्यासं कर्मयोगं च अभिप्रेत्य तयोः अन्यतरः कः श्रेयान् — इति । तदनुरूपं प्रतिवचनं मया उक्तं कर्मसंन्यासात् कर्मयोगः विशिष्यते इति ज्ञानं अनपेक्ष्य ज्ञानापेक्षस्तु संन्यासः सांख्यमिति मया अभिप्रेतः । परमार्थयोगश्च स एव । यस्तु कर्मयोगः वैदिकः स च तादर्थ्यात् योगः — संन्यासः — इति च उपचर्यते । कथं तादर्थ्यं इति ? उच्यते —

6.0. If this is the case, renunciation is better than Yoga. Why then is it affirmed that 'of the two, Karma Yoga is superior to the renunciation of works' (5.2). Listen to the reason: "You asked with reference to mere renunciation of works and Karma Yoga, which of these two is better. Accordingly I replied, without reference to knowledge, that Karma Yoga is superior to renunciation of works. But I hold that renunciation with knowledge is Sāṁkhya. That alone is real Yoga. As regards the Vedic Karma Yoga, it is Yoga only because it leads to the real Yoga. Figuratively, it is renunciation also." How does the Vedic Karma Yoga lead to real Yoga? Answer:

संन्यासस्तु महाबाहो दुःखमाप्तुमयोगतः ।
योगयुक्तो मुनिर्ब्रह्म नचिरेणाधिगच्छति ॥६॥

6. Indeed, renunciation, mighty-armed! is hard to win without Karma Yoga. With Yoga, the silent sage attains Brahman without much delay.

6.1. संन्यासः इति ॥ संन्यासस्तु पारमार्थिकः हे महाबाहो ! दुःखं आप्तुं प्राप्तुं अयोगतः योगेन विना । योगयुक्तः वैदिकेन कर्मयोगेन ईश्वरसमर्पितरूपेण फलनिरपेक्षेण युक्तः मुनिः — मननात् ईश्वरस्वरूपस्य — मुनिः, ब्रह्म — परमात्मज्ञाननिष्ठालक्षणत्वात् प्रकृतः संन्यासः ब्रह्म उच्यते, 'न्यास इति ब्रह्मा ब्रह्मा हि परः'

[महाना. उ. २१.२.] इति श्रुतेः—ब्रह्म परमार्थसंन्यासं परमार्थज्ञाननिष्ठालक्षणं नचिरेण क्षिप्रम् एव अधिगच्छति प्राप्नोति । अतः मया उक्तं 'कर्मयोगो विशिष्यते' इति [५.२.]

6.1. Real renunciation, O mighty-armed! is hard to win 'without Yoga'. With the Vedic Karma Yoga, consisting in the dedication of works to God without craving for their fruits, the silent sage, who meditates on God's essence, wins Brahman. Renunciation relevant to this context and consisting in the discipline of knowledge of Supreme Reality is styled Brahman. *Vide*: "Renunciation is Brahman who is the Supreme" (*Mahā. Nā.U.*21.2.) This Brahman, real renunciation, the discipline of knowledge of the Supreme Reality, the silent sages win, without delay, i.e., quickly. Hence, I said, "Karma Yoga is superior" (5.2).

7.0. यदा पुनः अयं सम्यग्ज्ञानप्राप्त्युपायत्वेन—

7.0. What follows when the Yogi uses Karma Yoga as a means to attain Self-knowledge? Answer:

योगयुक्तो विशुद्धात्मा विजितात्मा जितेन्द्रियः ।
सर्वभूतात्मभूतात्मा कुर्वन्नपि न लिप्यते ॥७॥

7. Established in Yoga, his mind purified, his self and senses controlled, his Self becomes the Self of all living beings, he is not tainted though he works.

7.1. योगयुक्तः इति ॥ योगेन युक्तः योगयुक्तः, विशुद्धात्मा विशुद्धसत्त्वः, विजितात्मा विजितदेहः, जितेन्द्रियः च, सर्वभूतात्मभूतात्मा सर्वेषां ब्रह्मादीनां स्तम्बपर्यन्तानां भूतानां आत्मभूतः आत्मा प्रत्यक्चेतनः यस्य सः सर्वभूतात्मभूतात्मा सम्यग्दर्शी इत्यर्थः, स तत्र एवं वर्तमानः लोकसंग्रहाय कर्म कुर्वन् अपि न लिप्यते — न कर्मभिः बध्यते इत्यर्थः ।

7.1. Established in Yoga, his mind purified, his self, i.e., body and senses controlled, his Self identified with the Self of all beings ranging from Brahmā to clumps of grass i.e., having become the right percipient, and living and working for the world's well-being, he is not tainted or he is not bound by his works. This is the idea.

8.0. न च असौ परमार्थतः करोति इत्यतः—

8.0. And since he does not, in reality, work—

नैव किंचित्करोमीति युक्तो मन्येत तत्त्ववित् ।
पश्यञ्शृण्वन्स्पृशञ्जिघ्रन्नश्नन्गच्छन्स्वपञ्श्वसन् ॥८॥
प्रलपन् विसृजन् गृह्णन्नुन्मिषन्निमिषन्नपि ।
इन्द्रियाणीन्द्रियार्थेषु वर्तन्त इति धारयन् ॥९॥

8–9. Let the integrated sage who knows the truth think 'I work not at all' even when he sees, hears, touches, smells, eats, walks, sleeps, breathes, talks, evacuates, grasps, opens and closes the eyes, knowing that the senses operate vis-a-vis their objects.

8-9.1. नैव इति ॥ नैव किंचित् करोमि इति युक्तः समाहितः सन् मन्येत चिन्तयेत् तत्त्ववित् आत्मनः याथात्म्यं तत्त्वं वेत्ति इति तत्त्ववित् परमार्थदर्शी इत्यर्थः । कदा कथं वा तत्त्वं अवधारयन् मन्येत इति ? उच्यते—पश्यन्निति । मन्येत इति पूर्वेण सम्बन्धः ॥

तस्य एवं तत्त्वविदः सर्वकार्यकरणचेष्टासु कर्मसु अकर्म एव, पश्यतः सम्यग्दर्शिनः तस्य सर्वकर्मसंन्यासे एव अधिकारः, कर्मणः अभावदर्शनात् । न हि मृगतृष्णिकायां उदकबुद्धया पानाय प्रवृत्तः उदकाभावज्ञानेऽपि तत्र एव पानप्रयोजनाय प्रवर्तते ॥

8–9.1. 'I work not at all'—let the integrated sage, the knower of Truth, of the reality of the Self, i.e., the percipient of ultimate Reality, think so. When and in what way knowing the truth, shall he think so? Listen: when he sees etc., let him think—thus construe the words. The knower of truth who sees only non-work in all works of the psycho-physical organism, i.e., the right seer, is alone fit to renounce all works; for he he sees the negation of works. None indeed striving to drink the water in the mirage will continue to do so even after grasping the absence of water there.

10.0. यस्तु पुनः अतत्त्ववित् प्रवृत्तश्च कर्मयोगे—

10.0. However the non-knower of truth who practises Karma Yoga—

ब्रह्मण्याधाय कर्माणि संगं त्यक्त्वा करोति यः ।
लिप्यते न स पापेन पद्मपत्रमिवाम्भसा ॥१०॥

10. Reposing all works in Brahman, he operates without attachment; he is not stained by sin as a lotus is not by water.

10.1. ब्रह्मणि इति ॥ ब्रह्मणि ईश्वरे आधाय निक्षिप्य "तदर्थं कर्म करोमि" इति भृत्यः इव स्वाम्यर्थं सर्वाणि कर्माणि मोक्षेऽपि फले संगं त्यक्त्वा करोति यः सर्वकर्माणि, लिप्यते न स, पापेन न सम्बध्यते, पद्मपत्रम् इव अम्भसा उदकेन । केवलं सत्त्वशुद्धिमात्रम् एव फलं तस्य तत्कर्मणः स्यात् ॥
—यस्मात् —

10.1. Reposing all works in Brahman i.e., God, and believing, "I work for the sake of God, as a servant for the master, without attachment even to the fruit of liberation",—he who works thus is not stained by sin; he is not in touch with it. He is like the lotus leaf unstained by water. Of the works done thus the only fruit is purification. Because,

कायेन मनसा बुद्ध्या केवलैरिन्द्रियैरपि ।
योगिनः कर्म कुर्वन्ति संगं त्यक्त्वाऽऽत्मशुद्धये ॥११॥

11. With body, mind, intellect and mere senses, Yogins perform work without attachment, for the purification of the self.

11.1. कायेन इति ॥ कायेन देहेन मनसा बुद्धया च केवलैः इन्द्रियैः अपि ममत्ववर्जितैः "ईश्वरायैव कर्म करोमि, न मम फलाय" इति ममत्वबुद्धिशून्यैः इन्द्रियैः अपि केवलशब्दः कायादिभिः अपि प्रत्येकं संबध्यते — सर्वव्यापारेषु ममतावर्जनाय । योगिनः कर्मिणः कर्म कुर्वन्ति संगं त्यक्त्वा फलविषये आत्मशुद्धये सत्त्वशुद्धये इत्यर्थः । तस्मात् तत्रैव तव अधिकारः इति कुरु कर्मैव ॥

यस्माच्च—

11.1. With body, mind, intellect and mere senses, devoid of the sense of ownership, and thinking, "I work for God's sake alone and not for my profit", and thus excluding the sense of ownership, the Yogins, who are workers, work. The term 'mere' may be held to qualify all the words like body etc., in order to rule out the sense of ownership over any of them. The Yogins work without attachment to the fruits of works to win self-purification i.e. purification of the mind-stuff. Therefore, you are called upon to work only; do work. Also because:

युक्तः कर्मफलं त्यक्त्वा शान्तिमाप्नोति नैष्ठिकीम् ।
अयुक्तः कामकारेण फले सक्तो निबध्यते ॥१२॥

12. Giving up the fruits of works, the Yogin attains disciplined peace; the non-Yogin, attached to fruits by the force of cravings is bound.

12.1. युक्तः इति ॥ युक्तः "ईश्वराय कर्माणि करोमि न मम फलाय" इत्येवं समाहितः सन् कर्मफलं त्यक्त्वा परित्यज्य शान्तिं मोक्षाख्यां आप्नोति नैष्ठिकीं निष्ठायां भवां — सत्त्वशुद्धिज्ञानप्राप्तिसर्वकर्मसंन्यासज्ञाननिष्ठाक्रमेण इति वाक्यशेषः यस्तु पुनः अयुक्तः असमाहितः कामकारेण — करणं कारः, कामस्य कारः कामकारः, तेन कामकारेण कामप्रेरिततया इत्यर्थः, "मम फलाय इदं करोमि कर्म" इति एवं फले सक्तः निबध्यते । अतः त्वं युक्तः भव इत्यर्थः ॥

12.1. The Yogin, concentrating on the thought, "I work for the sake of God and not for fruits", and giving up fruits, attains the peace called liberation. This is 'disciplined peace,' being born of the discipline, whose stages are mental purification, achievement of knowledge, renunciation of works, and consecration to the discipline of knowledge. The verse 12 leads to this conclusion. The non-Yogin who is not so consecrated is swayed by the force of cravings. He thinks: "I work for its fruit", and gets attached to it, and he is bound. Therefore be a Yogin—this is the sense of the verse.

13.0. यस्तु परमार्थदर्शी सः—

13.0. On the other hand, the percipient of the supreme Reality—

सर्वकर्माणि मनसा संन्यस्यास्ते सुखं वशी ।
नवद्वारे पुरे देही नैव कुर्वन्न कारयन् ॥१३॥

13. Mentally renouncing all works, and self-controlled, the embodied being happily sits in the nine-gated city, neither working nor causing others to work.

13.1. सर्वकर्माणि इति ॥ सर्वाणि कर्माणि सर्वकर्माणि संन्यस्य परित्यज्य नित्यं नैमित्तिकं काम्यं प्रतिषिद्धं च तानि सर्वाणि कर्माणि मनसा विवेकबुद्ध्या, कर्मादौ अकर्मदर्शनेन संत्यज्येत्यर्थः, आस्ते तिष्ठति सुखं । त्यक्तवाङ्मनःकायचेष्टः निरायासः प्रसन्नचित्तः आत्मनः अन्यत्र निवृत्तसर्वबाह्यप्रयोजनः इति 'सुखं आस्ते' इत्युच्यते । वशी जितेन्द्रियः इत्यर्थः । क्व कथं आस्ते इति ? आह—नवद्वारे पुरे । सप्त शीर्षण्यानि आत्मन उपलब्धिद्वाराणि, अर्वाक् द्वे मूत्रपुरीषविसर्गार्थे, तैः द्वारैः नवद्वारं पुरं उच्यते शरीरं, पुरमिव पुरं, आत्मैकस्वामिकं, तदर्थप्रयोजनैश्च इन्द्रियमनोबुद्धिविषयैः अनेकफलविज्ञानस्य उत्पादकैः पौरैरिव अधिष्ठितम् । तस्मिन् नवद्वारे पुरे देही सर्वं कर्म संन्यस्य आस्ते ॥

13.1. "Renouncing"—giving up—all works viz., the obligatory, occasional, desire-prompted and forbidden works; "mentally"—by discriminative intelligence, by perceiving in works non-works, etc., (*Vide* 4.18)—the sage happily sits. Giving up the activities of speech, mind and body, unconstrained, peaceful, and seeking no profit outside the sphere of the Self—this is the sense of the expression, 'happily sits'. Self-controlled means that the sage has conquered his senses. Where and how does he sit ? 'In the nine-gated city.' The seven openings in the head by which objective knowledge is gained and the two below, the rectum and the urinary passage, are the nine gates of the body that resembles a city. Its Lord is the Self; it is inhabited by its subservient citizens, the objects of the senses, mind and intellect that generate knowledge and its numerous consequences. In that city the embodied being resides, having given up all works.

13.2. किं विशेषणेन ?—सर्वो हि देही संन्यासी असंन्यासी वा देहे एव आस्ते; तत्र अनर्थकं विशेषणमिति ? उच्यते—यस्तु अज्ञः देही देहेन्द्रियसंघातमात्रात्मदर्शी स सर्वोऽपि "गेहे भूमौ, आसने वा आसे" इति मन्यते । न हि देहमात्रात्मदर्शिनः गेहे इव देहे आसे इति प्रत्ययः संभवति । देहादिसंघातव्यतिरिक्तात्मदर्शिनस्तु "देहे आसे" इति प्रत्ययः उपपद्यते । परकर्मणां च परस्मिन् आत्मनि अविद्यया अध्यारोपितानां विद्यया विवेकज्ञानेन मनसा संन्यासः उपपद्यते । उत्पन्नविवेकविज्ञानस्य सर्वकर्मसंन्यासिनोऽपि गेहे इव देहे एव नवद्वारे पुरे आसनं, प्रारब्धफलकर्मसंस्कारशेषानुवृत्त्या देहे एव विशेषविज्ञानोत्पत्तेः । देहे एव आस्ते इति अस्त्येव विशेषणफलं, विद्वदविद्वत्प्रत्ययभेदापेक्षत्वात् ॥

13.2. *Objection:* "Why this qualification? For, all embodied beings, whether renouncers or otherwise, dwell in their bodies; so the qualification is otiose". *Answer*: the embodied being who is ignorant, taking the complex of body and senses alone for the self, thinks invariably "I dwell in the house here in the world; I sit on the seat". One who takes the body alone to be the Self cannot think, "I dwell in the body as in my house." On the contrary, he who desires the Self as other than the complex of body etc., may properly think 'I dwell in the body'. Proper is the mental renunciation, due to discriminative knowledge, of the works of body etc., superimposed on the Supreme Self through nescience. Also, the renouncer of all works, who has gained discriminative knolwedge, may dwell in the nine-gated city of the body as in a house; for, a specific knowledge ("I am other than the body") has accrued to him while dwelling in his body due to the force of the persistent impressions of operative works. Thus the qualification is significant viz., the sage dwells in the body; it points to the difference in the ideas entertained by the sage and an ignoramus.

13.3. यद्यपि कार्यकरणकर्माणि अविद्यया आत्मनि अध्यारोपितानि 'संन्यस्यास्ते' इत्युक्तम्, तथापि कृतसंन्यासस्य आत्मसमवायि तु कर्तृत्वं कारयितृत्वं च स्यात् इति आशङ्क्य आह—नैव कुर्वन् स्वयं, न च कार्यकरणानि कारयन् क्रियासु प्रवर्तयन् । किं यत् तत् कर्तृत्वं कारयितृत्वं च देहिनः स्वात्मसमवायि सत् संन्यासात् न संभवति, यथा गच्छतो गतिः [गमनव्यापारपरित्यागे न स्यात् तद्वत्] ? किं वा स्वतः एव आत्मनः न अस्ति इति ? अत्र उच्यते—न अस्ति आत्मनः स्वतः कर्तृत्वं कारयितृत्वं च । उक्तं हि 'अविकार्योऽयमुच्यते' [२.२५.], शरीरस्थोऽपि कौन्तेय न करोति न लिप्यते' [१३.३१.] इति, 'ध्यायतीव लेलायतीव' [बृ. उ. ४.३.७.] इति च श्रुतेः ।

किंच—

13.3. Though it was remarked that the sage "dwells", having renounced the works of the body-complex, ignorantly superimposed on the Self, one may deem that even the renouncer treats his self as either an agent or cause of agency. On this point it is said—neither working nor causing to work. *Doubt*: "Is it maintained that due to renunciation, direct agency or causative agency inherent in the self becomes impossible, as movement becomes, for one who ceases to move? Or, do these not naturally belong to the Self?" *Answer*: "Naturally, the Self has neither direct nor causative agency. Indeed it has been remarked: 'the Self is said to be immutable' 2.25; 'Though dwelling in the body, Arjuna! the Self neither acts nor gets tainted' 13.31; 'Meditates, as it were; moves, as it were' *BU*.4.3.7"

Moreover,

न कर्तृत्वं न कर्माणि लोकस्य सृजति प्रभुः ।
न कर्मफलसंयोगं स्वभावस्तु प्रवर्तते ॥१४॥

maya illusion

14. The Lord creates neither agency nor objects for the world; nor contact with the fruits of works; rather, the nature of things operates.

14.1. न कर्तृत्वं इति ॥ न कर्तृत्वं स्वतः कुरु इति न अपि कर्माणि रथघट-प्रासादादीनि ईप्सिततमानि लोकस्य सृजति उत्पादयति प्रभुः आत्मा । न अपि रथादि कृतवतः तत्फलेन संयोगं कर्मफलसंयोगं उत्पादयति । यदि किंचिदपि स्वयं न करोति न कारयति च देही, कः तर्हि कुर्वन् कारयंश्च प्रवर्तते इति ? उच्यते — स्वभावस्तु स्वो भावः स्वभावः — अविद्यालक्षणा प्रकृतिः, माया प्रवर्तते 'दैवी ह्येषा गुणमयी' [७. १४.] इत्यादिना वक्ष्यमाणा ॥

परमार्थतस्तु —

14.1. "Neither agency"—the Lord i.e., the Self, impels not the world to do work; nor does He create objects of such work, does not generate the objects that are sought after viz., chariots, pots, mansions, etc: neither the contacts of agents making chariots, etc., with the objects made. *Doubt*: If nothing whatsoever the embodied self does or causes to be done, who then operates, both as direct agent and causative agent? *Answer:* Nature, Prakṛti as nescience, Māyā, operates as will be affirmed in *BG* 7.14: "Indeed this divine Māyā consisting of the constituents."

But in reality,

नादत्ते कस्यचित्पापं न चैव सुकृतं विभुः ।
अज्ञानेनावृतं ज्ञानं तेन मुह्यन्ति जन्तवः ॥१५॥

15. The mighty Being accepts nobody's sin or merit. Knowledge is shrouded in ignorance; therefore are living beings deluded.

15.1. नादत्ते इति । न आदत्ते न च गृह्णाति भक्तस्यापि कस्यचित् पापम् । न चैव आदत्ते सुकृतं भक्तैः प्रयुक्तं विभुः । किमर्थं तर्हि भक्तैः पूजादिलक्षणं याग-दानहोमादिकं च सुकृतं प्रयुज्यते इति ? आह — अज्ञानेन आवृतं ज्ञानं विवे-कविज्ञानं, तेन मुह्यन्ति "करोमि, कारयामि, भोक्ष्ये, भोजयामि" इत्येवं मोहं गच्छन्ति अविवेकिनः संसारिणो जन्तवः ॥

15.1. The mighty Being (*Vibhu* can also mean the Atman) accepts not the sin even of a devotee, nor merits offered by devotees. *Doubt*: "Why then do devotees offer meritorious deeds like worship, sacrifice, gifts, oblations in the fire, etc.?" *Answer:* "Discriminative knowledge is shrouded in ignorance; so the non-discriminating and transmigrating beings are deluded into thinking, "We work, cause others to work, enjoy and cause others to enjoy the fruits of works."

On the contrary,

ज्ञानेन तु तदज्ञानं येषां नाशितमात्मनः ।
तेषामादित्यवज्ज्ञानं प्रकाशयति तत्परम् ॥१६॥

16. For them whose ignorance has been destroyed by knowledge, that very knowledge, like the sun, illumines the supreme Reality.

16.1. ज्ञानेन इति ॥ ज्ञानेन तु येन अज्ञानेन आवृता मुह्यन्ति जन्तवः तत् अज्ञानं येषां जन्तूनां विवेकज्ञानेन आत्मविषयेण नाशितं आत्मनः भवति, तेषां जन्तूनां आदित्यवत् यथा आदित्यः समस्तं वस्तुजातं [रूपजातं] अवभासयति, तद्वत् ज्ञानं ज्ञेयं वस्तु सर्वं प्रकाशयति तत् परं परमार्थतत्त्वम् ॥

16.1. However, for those living beings whose ignorance of Self, shrouding and deluding them, has been destroyed by the discriminative knowledge of the Self, that very knowledge, like the sun lighting up all objects, illumines all that is to be known, even that Supreme Truth.

17.0. यत् परं परमार्थतत्त्वं ज्ञानप्रकाशितम्—

17.0. That Supreme Truth beyond, illumined by knowledge, is further characterised:

तद्बुद्धयस्तदात्मानस्तन्निष्ठास्तत्परायणाः ।
गच्छन्त्यपुनरावृत्तिं ज्ञाननिर्धूतकल्मषाः ॥१७॥

17. With the intellect set on It as the Self, perceiving It as the Self, devoted to It, It being the supreme abode,

the sages, their sins routed by knowledge, proceed to that status whence there is no return.

17.1. तद्बुद्धयः इति ॥ तस्मिन् ब्रह्मणि गता बुद्धिः येषां ते तद्बुद्धयः, तदात्मानः तदेव परं ब्रह्म आत्मा येषां ते तदात्मानः, तन्निष्ठाः निष्ठा अभिनिवेशः तात्पर्यं सर्वाणि कर्माणि संन्यस्य तस्मिन् ब्रह्मण्येव अवस्थानं येषां ते तन्निष्ठाः, तत्परायणाः च तदेव परं अयनं परा गतिः येषां भवति ते तत्परायणाः केवलात्मरतयः इत्यर्थः [येषां ज्ञानेन नाशितं आत्मनः अज्ञानं] ते गच्छन्ति एवंविधाः अपुनरावृत्तिं अपुनर्देहसम्बन्धं ज्ञाननिर्धूतकल्मषाः यथोक्तेन ज्ञानेन निर्धूतः निहतः नाशितः कल्मषः पापादिसंसारकारणदोषः येषां ते ज्ञाननिर्धूतकल्मषाः यतयः इत्यर्थः ॥

17.1. With the intellect dwelling on Brahman, having that supreme Brahman as their Self, devoted to It i.e., renouncing all works, established in Brahman alone single-mindedly, It being their supreme refuge and goal—in other words, delighting solely in the Self, their ignorance of the Self having been destroyed by knowledge, these self-restrained ascetics will have no more embodiments; for, as set forth above, knowledge has destroyed the flaw—sins etc.—that engenders the transmigratory life. This is the sense.

18.0. येषां ज्ञानेन नाशितं आत्मनः अज्ञानं ते पण्डिताः कथं तत्त्वं पश्यन्ति इति ? उच्यते—

18.0. How do the sages whose ignorance of the Self has been destroyed by knowledge perceive the Truth? Answer:

विद्याविनयसंपन्ने ब्राह्मणे गवि हस्तिनि ।
शुनि चैव श्वपाके च पण्डिताः समदर्शिनः ॥१८॥

18. The sages perceive the same truth in the Brāhmaṇa, rich in knowledge and culture, a cow, an elephant, a dog and a dog-eating outcaste.

18.1. विद्या इति ॥ विद्याविनयसंपन्ने विद्या च विनयश्च विद्याविनयौ, विनयः उपशमः, ताभ्यां विद्याविनयाभ्यां संपन्नः विद्याविनयसंपन्नः विद्वान् विनीतश्च यो ब्राह्मणः तस्मिन्

ब्राह्मणे गवि हस्तिनि शुनि चैव श्वपाके च पण्डिताः समदर्शिनः—विद्याविनयसंपन्ने उत्तमसंस्कारवति ब्राह्मणे सात्त्विके, मध्यमायां च राजस्यां गवि संस्कारहीनायां, अत्यंतमेव केवलतामसे हस्त्यादौ, सत्त्वादिगुणैः तज्जैश्च संस्कारैः, तथा राजसैः तथा तामसैः च संस्कारैः, अत्यन्तमेव असंस्पृष्टं समं एकं अविक्रियं तत् ब्रह्म द्रष्टुं शीलं येषां ते पण्डिताः समदर्शिनः ।

18.1. "Knowledge and culture"—culture consists in restraint—rich in these is the *brāhmaṇa* who knows and is cultured. In him, in a cow, elephant, dog and outcaste the sages behold the same Reality. In the *sāttvika brāhmaṇa*, endowed with knowledge and culture, who has the best latent impressions of life's experiences, in an intermediate being like the cow that is *rājasic* without such impression, and in the low merely *tāmasic* beings like an elephant etc., the sages are trained to perceive the same, single, and immutable Brahman, wholly unaffected by constituents like the *sattva* and by the latent impressions they generate.

19.0. ननु अभोज्यान्नाः ते दोषवन्तः, 'समासमाभ्यां विषमसमे पूजातः' [गौ. ध. १७.२०.] इति स्मृतेः । न ते दोषवन्तः । कथम् ?—

19.0. *Objection* "Now, is not the food offered by such tainted individuals forbidden?" *Vide*, the *smṛiti*: The food should not be accepted from him who invidiously treats equals as unequals and unequals as equals *GDS*. 17.20. *Answer* "No; they are not tainted." How?

इहैव तैर्जितः सर्गो येषां साम्ये स्थितं मनः ।
निर्दोषं हि समं ब्रह्म तस्माद्ब्रह्मणि ते स्थिताः ॥१९॥

19. Even here is birth vanquished by them whose mind abides in equality. Flawless indeed is Brahman, the same; hence they abide in Brahman.

19.1. इहैव इति ॥ इह एव जीवद्भिरेव तैः समदर्शिभिः पण्डितैः जितो वशीकृतः सर्गः जन्म, येषां साम्ये सर्वभूतेषु ब्रह्मणि समभावे स्थितं निश्चलीभूतं मनः अन्तः-

करणम् । निर्दोषं — यद्यपि दोषवत्सु श्वपाकादिषु मूढैः तद्दोषैः दोषवत् इव विभाव्यते, तथापि तद्दोषैः असंस्पृष्टं इति निर्दोषं दोषवर्जितं हि यस्मात्; नापि स्वगुणभेदभिन्नं, निर्गुणत्वात् चैतन्यस्य । वक्ष्यति च भगवान् इच्छादीनां क्षेत्रधर्मत्वं [१३.६.], 'अनादित्वान्निर्गुणत्वात्' [१३.३१.] इति च । नापि अन्त्यविशेषा आत्मनो भेदकाः सन्ति, प्रतिशरीरं तेषां सत्त्वे प्रमाणानुपपत्तेः । अतः समं ब्रह्म एकं च । तस्मात् ब्रह्मणि एव ते स्थिताः । तस्मात् न दोषगन्धमात्रमपि तान् स्पृशति, देहादिसंघातात्मदर्शनाभिमानाभावात् तेषाम् ।

19.1. Birth is vanquished "even here"—while yet alive—by the sages who look on all alike. Their 'mind'—the inner sense—abides, stilled, in 'equality', in Brahman, that is identically the same in all beings. 'Flawless'—i.e., untouched by defilements, though the deluded deem Brahman defiled in tainted beings, like the dog-eaters. So flawless—free from all defilements—is Brahman. Nor is Brahman variegated due to Its own diverse attributes; for Spirit is beyond all attributes. The Lord will declare that attributes like desire pertain to the 'field', *BG* 13.6.—also "As It is without beginning and attributes" 13.31. Nor are there the ultimate pluralizers to differentiate the Self: for, there is no proof to establish their reality in respect of the Self in each body. Therefore Brahman is one and the same. So they abide in Brahman alone. Hence even a suspicion of taint cannot touch them. They are free from the conceit of Self in regard to their psycho-physical organisms.

19.2. देहादिसंघातात्मदर्शनाभिमानवद्विषयं तु तत् सूत्रं 'समासमाभ्यां विषमसमे पूजातः' इति, पूजाविषयत्वेन विशेषणात् । दृश्यते हि ब्रह्मवित्, षडङ्गवित्, चतुर्वेदवित् इति पूजादानादौ गुणविशेषसंबन्धः कारणम् । ब्रह्म तु सर्वगुणदोषसम्बन्धवर्जितं इत्यतः 'ब्रह्मणि ते स्थिताः' इति युक्तम् । कर्मविषयं च 'समासमाभ्यां' इत्यादि । इदं तु सर्वकर्मसंन्यासविषयं प्रस्तुतं, 'सर्वकर्माणि मनसा' इत्यारभ्य आ अध्यायपरिसमाप्तेः ॥

19.2. The Dharmasūtra quoted above refers to those who have such conceit; for, it refers to those who are cremoniously respected. As regards the measure of such respect offered, the determining causes are the degrees of merit of the persons concerned—one being a knower of Brahman, another, a knower of the six limbs of the Vedas, and yet another, a knower of the four Vedas etc. As for Brahman, It is unrelated to merits and demerits of all kinds. So it is affirmed—they abide in Brahman. The aphorism refers to works. On the other hand, the matter under consideration from 5.13 to the end of the chapter refers to the renunciation of works.

20.0. यस्मात् निर्दोषं समं ब्रह्म आत्मा, तस्मात्—

20.0. Since the same taintless Brahman is the Self,

न प्रहृष्येत्प्रियं प्राप्य नोद्विजेत्प्राप्य चाप्रियम् ।
स्थिरबुद्धिरसंमूढो ब्रह्मविद्ब्रह्मणि स्थितः ॥२०॥

20. With a steady intellect, undeluded, knowing and abiding in Brahman, one should neither be elated when gaining the pleasant nor shrink when meeting with the unpleasant.

20.1. न प्रहृष्येत् इति ॥ न प्रहृष्येत् प्रहर्षं न कुर्यात् प्रियं इष्टं प्राप्य लब्ध्वा । न उद्विजेत् प्राप्य च अप्रियं अनिष्टं लब्ध्वा । देहमात्रात्मदर्शिनां हि प्रियाप्रियप्राप्ती हर्षविषादौ कुर्वाते, न केवलात्मदर्शिनः, तस्य प्रियाप्रियप्राप्त्यसम्भवात् । किंच — "सर्वभूतेषु एकः समः निर्दोषः आत्मा" इति स्थिरा निर्विचिकित्सा बुद्धिः यस्य सः स्थिरबुद्धिः असंमूढः संमोहवर्जितश्च स्यात् यथोक्तब्रह्मवित् ब्रह्मणि स्थितः, अकर्मकृत् सर्वकर्मसंन्यासी इत्यर्थः ॥

20.1. One should not be elated—should not rejoice—upon gaining the pleasant; nor shrink upon meeting with the unpleasant. The incidence of the pleasant and that of the unpleasant causes pleasure and pain only for those for whom the Self is the body alone, and not for one who perceives the pure Self. The latter can't have contact with anything pleasant or unpleasant. Moreover, 'one whose intellect is steady'—free from all doubts, who is convinced that in all beings abides the flawless Self, and who is undeluded or free from all delusions, knows Brahman as already set forth, and abides in Brahman. He works not; he has renounced all works. This is the idea.

21.0. किं च, ब्रह्मणि स्थितः—

21.0. Moreover, abiding in Brahman,

बाह्यस्पर्शेष्वसक्तात्मा विन्दत्यात्मनि यत्सुखम् ।
स ब्रह्मयोगयुक्तात्मा सुखमक्षयमश्नुते ॥२१॥

21. The sage whose inner sense is unattached to objective contacts wins bliss in the Self; his inner sense is united with Brahman; he enjoys inexhaustible bliss.

21.1. बाह्य इति ॥ बाह्यस्पर्शेषु बाह्याश्च ते स्पर्शाश्च बाह्यस्पर्शाः । स्पृश्यन्ते इति स्पर्शाः शब्दादयः विषयाः,—तेषु बाह्यस्पर्शेषु असक्तः आत्मा अन्तःकरणं यस्य सः अयं असक्तात्मा विषयेषु प्रीतिवर्जितः सन् विन्दति लभते आत्मनि यत् सुखं तत् विन्दति इत्येतत् । स ब्रह्मयोगयुक्तात्मा ब्रह्मणि योगः समाधिः ब्रह्मयोगः, तेन ब्रह्मयोगेन युक्तः समाहितः तस्मिन् व्यापृतः आत्मा अन्तकरणं यस्य सः ब्रह्मयोगयुक्तात्मा सुखं अक्षयं अश्नुते व्याप्नोति । तस्मात् बाह्यविषयप्रीतेः क्षणिकायाः इन्द्रियाणि निवर्तयेत् आत्मनि अक्षयसुखार्थी इत्यर्थः ॥

21.1. "Objective contacts" are the external objects which are contacted—sounds and so forth. With an inner sense unattached to them, he does not delight in objects. Thus he wins bliss in the Self. "United with Brahman" refers to concentration on Brahman. "Contact with that" means engagement in that concentration. With an inner sense so concentrated, the sage wins inexhaustible bliss. Therefore, one should withdraw one's sense-organs from the momentary objective pleasures; for he seeks the inexhaustible bliss in the Self.

22.0. इतश्च निवर्तयेत्—

22.0. For the following reason, too, one should withdraw them:

ये हि संस्पर्शजा भोगा दुःखयोनय एव ते ।
आद्यन्तवन्तः कौन्तेय न तेषु रमते बुधः ॥२२॥

22. Enjoyments born of objective contacts, indeed, cause pain only. Son of Kuntī! they have a beginning and end; the sage does not delight in them.

22.1. ये हि इति ॥ ये हि यस्मात् संस्पर्शजाः विषयेन्द्रियसंस्पर्शेभ्यः जाताः भोगा भुक्तयः दुःखयोनयः एव ते, अविद्याकृतत्वात् । दृश्यन्ते हि आध्यात्मिकानि दुःखानि तन्निमित्तानि एव । यथा इह लोके तथा परलोकेऽपि इति गम्यते, एवशब्दात् । न संसारे सुखस्य गन्धमात्रमपि अस्ति इति बुद्ध्वा विषयमृगतृष्णिकायाः इन्द्रियाणि निवर्तयेत् । न केवलं दुःखयोनयः एव, आद्यन्तवन्तः च — आदिः विषयेन्द्रियसंयोगः भोगानां, अन्तश्च तद्वियोगः एव; अतः आद्यन्तवन्तः अनित्याः, मध्यक्षणभावित्वात् इत्यर्थः । हे कौन्तेय, न तेषु भोगेषु रमते बुधः विवेकी अवगतपरमार्थतत्त्वः; अत्यन्तमूढानां एव हि विषयेषु रतिः दृश्यते, यथा पशुप्रभृतीनाम् ॥

22.1. Because, the enjoyments born of contacts between objects and senses cause only pain, as they are brought about by nescience. Indeed bodily sufferings are seen to be exclusively occasioned by such contacts. As is the case in this world, it may be inferred, so is the case in the world to come, also. This is the sense of the expression 'only'. Knowing that in this transmigratory life there is not the remotest shadow of genuine joy, one should withdraw the senses from the mirage of objective enjoyments. Not only do 'contacts' cause pain; they also have a 'beginning and end.' The beginning of enjoyments is the contact of senses and their objects; 'the end' is their separation. So they are ephemeral—they exist only in the interval. Son of Kuntī! the sage, man of discrimination, having known the supreme Reality, does not delight in objective enjoyments. Only the extremely deluded souls are observed to delight in objects as beasts etc., do.

23.0. अयं च श्रेयोमार्गप्रतिपक्षी कष्टतमः दोषः सर्वानर्थप्राप्तिहेतुः दुर्निवारश्च इति तत्परिहारे यत्नाधिक्यं कर्तव्यं इति आह भगवान्—

23.0. And this is the most disastrous impediment in the path to the supreme Good, the cause of all sufferings that is hard to escape. Therefore, great effort must be made to avoid it. Says the Lord:

शक्नोतीहैव यः सोढुं प्राक् शरीरविमोक्षणात् ।
कामक्रोधोद्भवं वेगं स युक्तः स सुखी नरः ॥२३॥

23. The man, strong enough to resist in this world—before the fall of his body—the urge of lust and wrath, is integrated; he is happy.

23.1. शक्नोति इति ॥ शक्नोति उत्सहते इहैव जीवन्नेव यः सोढुं प्रसहितुं प्राक् पूर्वं शरीरविमोक्षणात् आ मरणात् इत्यर्थः । मरणसीमाकरणात् जीवतोऽवश्यंभावी हि कामक्रोधोद्भवो वेगः, अनन्तनिमित्तवान् हि सः इति यावत् मरणं तावत् न विस्रम्भणीय इत्यर्थः । कामः इन्द्रियगोचरप्राप्ते इष्टे विषये श्रूयमाणे स्मर्यमाणे वा, अनुभूते सुखहेतौ, या गर्धिः तृष्णा—स कामः, क्रोधश्च, आत्मनः प्रतिकूलेषु दुःखहेतुषु दृश्यमानेषु श्रूयमाणेषु स्मर्यमाणेषु वा यः द्वेषः सः क्रोधः; तौ कामक्रोधौ उद्भवः यस्य वेगस्य सः कामक्रोधोद्भवः वेगः । रोमाञ्चनप्रहृष्टनेत्रवदनादिलिङ्गः अन्तःकरणप्रक्षोभरूपः कामोद्भवः वेगः, गात्रप्रकंपप्रस्वेदसंदष्टौष्ठपुटरक्तनेत्रादिलिङ्गः क्रोधोद्भवो वेगः । तं कामक्रोधोद्भवं वेगं यः उत्सहते प्रसहते सोढुं प्रसहितुं, सः युक्तो योगी सुखी च इह लोके नरः ॥

23.1. Here, in this very life, the man who strives to resist in this world, before his body's fall, i.e. before the moment of his death, alone is integrated, etc. The limit of death implies that the urge in question is unavoidable for any living being; it is occasioned by numerous causes. The sense is that there is no room for complacency till one dies. Lust is the craving or greed for what occasions pleasure—i.e., any loved object of the senses previously experienced—when it is heard about, or remembered. Wrath is the aversion felt for things causing pain and obstructing one's interests, when they are seen, heard of, or remembered. The urge born of these two, lust and wrath, is referred to here. The lust-born urge is marked by horripilation, beaming eyes and face etc. Its essence is an agitation of the inner sense. The wrath-born urge is marked by the trembling of the body, sweat, the biting of lips, reddened eyes etc. He who strives to resist the urge born of lust and wrath is integrated; he is a happy man here below.

24.0. कथंभूतश्च ब्रह्मणि स्थितः ब्रह्म प्राप्नोति इति ? आह भगवान्—

24.0. Abiding in Brahman how does one attain It? The Lord replies:

योऽन्तःसुखोऽन्तरारामस्तथाऽन्तर्ज्योतिरेव यः ।
स योगी ब्रह्मनिर्वाणं ब्रह्मभूतोऽधिगच्छति ॥२४॥

24. With joy within, sporting within, and likewise, with light within, the Yogin becomes Brahman and wins the peace of Brahman.

24.1. यः इति ॥ यः अन्तःसुखः अन्तः आत्मनि सुखं यस्य सः अन्तःसुखः, तथा अन्तरेव आत्मनि आरामः आरमणं क्रीडा यस्य सः अन्तरारामः, तथा एव अन्तः एव आत्मन्येव ज्योतिः प्रकाशो यस्य सः अन्तर्ज्योतिरेव, यः ईदृशः सः योगी ब्रह्मनिर्वाणं ब्रह्मणि निर्वृतिं मोक्षं इह जीवन्नेव ब्रह्मभूतः सन् अधिगच्छति प्राप्नोति ॥

किंच —

24.1. The Yogin is 'with joy within', i.e. with joy in the Self, 'sporting within the Self', and likewise, 'with light within' —i.e., in the Self. While living here below he wins 'the peace of Brahman', having become Brahman.

Also,

लभन्ते ब्रह्मनिर्वाणमृषयः क्षीणकल्मषाः ।
छिन्नद्वैधा यतात्मानः सर्वभूतहिते रताः ॥२५॥

25. The seers win the peace of Brahman, their sins attenuated, doubts cut through, the inner sense controlled; they are busy promoting the welfare of all living beings.

25.1. लभन्ते इति ॥ लभन्ते ब्रह्मनिर्वाणं मोक्षं ऋषयः सम्यग्दर्शिनः संन्यासिनः क्षीणकल्मषाः क्षीणपापाः निर्दोषाः छिन्नद्वैधाः छिन्नसंशयाः यतात्मानः संयतेन्द्रियाः सर्वभूतहिते रताः सर्वेषां भूतानां हिते आनुकूल्ये रताः अहिंसका इत्यर्थः ॥
किंच —

25.1. 'The seers with right perception', i.e., the renouncers, win 'the peace of Brahman', i.e. liberation. Their sins have been 'attenuated'—they are flawless. Their doubts have been cut through. Their senses have been controlled. They are busy promoting the welfare or the good of all living beings. That they injure none, is the sense.

And,

कामक्रोधवियुक्तानां यतीनां यतचेतसाम् ।
अभितो ब्रह्मनिर्वाणं वर्तते विदितात्मनाम् ॥२६॥

26. On both sides, the peace of Brahman is there for the self-restrained ascetics, who are released from lust and wrath, and have known the Self.

26.1. काम इति ॥ कामक्रोधवियुक्तानां कामश्च क्रोधश्च कामक्रोधौ ताभ्यां वियुक्तानां यतीनां संन्यासिनां यतचेतसां संयतान्तःकरणानां अभितः उभयतः जीवतां मृतानां च ब्रह्मनिर्वाणं मोक्षो वर्तते, विदितात्मनां विदितः ज्ञातः आत्मा येषां ते विदितात्मानः तेषां विदितात्मनां सम्यग्दर्शिनां इत्यर्थः ॥

26.1. From lust and wrath those renouncers have been released. Their 'self'—the inner sense—has been disciplined. 'On both sides', both when they are alive and dead, 'the peace of Brahman' or liberation is there for them. They have known the Self—they have had the right perception. This is the idea.

27.0. सम्यग्दर्शननिष्ठानां संन्यासिनां सद्यः मुक्तिः उक्ता । कर्मयोगश्च ईश्वरार्पितसर्वभावेन ईश्वरे ब्रह्मणि आधाय क्रियमाणः सत्त्वशुद्धिज्ञानप्राप्तिसर्वकर्मसंन्यासक्रमेण मोक्षाय इति भगवान् पदे पदे अब्रवीत्, वक्ष्यति च । अथ इदानीं ध्यानयोगं सम्यग्दर्शनस्य अन्तरङ्गं विस्तरेण वक्ष्यामि इति तस्य सूत्रस्थानीयान् श्लोकान् उपदिशति स्म —

27.0. Instant liberation has been affirmed for the renouncers who are under the discipline of right perception. The Lord has also repeatedly affirmed—and He will do so again—the need for the practice of Karma Yoga dedicated to God or Brahman with total mental dedication to the Lord, the object being to win liberation through mind's purification, knowledge and renunciation of works. In this context, for elucidating the Yoga of meditation, the direct means to right perception, He utters the following verses constituting the basic aphorisms of that Yoga:

स्पर्शान् कृत्वा बहिर्बाह्यान् चक्षुश्चैवान्तरे भ्रुवोः ।
प्राणापानौ समौ कृत्वा नासाभ्यन्तरचारिणौ ॥२७॥
यतेन्द्रियमनोबुद्धिर्मुनिर्मोक्षपरायणः ।
विगतेच्छाभयक्रोधो यः सदा मुक्त एव सः ॥२८॥

27-28. Keeping out external contacts, fixing the eye between the eye-brows, and equalising the in-breath and the out-breath that move within the nostrils;

Controlling the senses, mind and intellect, and free from desire, fear and wrath, the silent sage intent on liberation is eternally emancipated, indeed.

27-28.1. स्पर्शान् इति ॥ स्पर्शान् शब्दादीन् कृत्वा बहिः बाह्यान् — श्रोत्रादिद्वारेण अन्तः बुद्धौ प्रवेशिताः शब्दादयः विषयाः, तान् अचिन्तयतः शब्दादयः बाह्याः बहिः एव कृताः भवन्ति — तान् एवं बहिः कृत्वा चक्षुश्चैव अन्तरे भ्रुवोः कृत्वा इति अनुषज्यते । तथा प्राणापानौ नासाभ्यन्तरचारिणौ समौ कृत्वा, यतेन्द्रियमनोबुद्धिः यतानि संयतानि इन्द्रियाणि मनः बुद्धिश्च यस्य सः यतेन्द्रियमनोबुद्धिः, मननात् मुनिः संन्यासी, मोक्षपरायणः एवंदेहसंस्थानः मोक्षपरायणः—मोक्षः एव

परं अयनं परा गतिः यस्य सः—अयं मोक्षपरायणः मुनिः भवेत् । विगतेच्छाभयक्रोधः इच्छा च भयं च क्रोधश्च इच्छाभयक्रोधाः ते विगताः यस्मात् सः विगतेच्छाभयक्रोधः यः एवं वर्तते सदा संन्यासी, मुक्तः एव सः—न तस्य मोक्षः अन्यः कर्तव्यः अस्ति ॥

27–28.1. 'The contacts' are the objects, sound etc., that were admitted into the intellect within via the ears and so forth. For one who dwells not on them mentally, the outer sounds etc., remain external alone. Thus expelling them, and fixing the eye between the eye-brows and likewise equalizing the in-breath and out-breath that move within the nostrils, and having controlled the senses, mind and intellect, the silent sage, the thinker and renouncer, shall become intent on liberation; for him liberation is the final refuge and goal. From him have departed desire, fear, and wrath. A practical renouncer who lives thus is indeed liberated; no other liberation is there for him to accomplish.

29.0. एवं समाहितचित्तेन किं विज्ञेयं इति ? उच्यते—

29.0. With mind thus concentrated, what ought to be known? Answer:

भोक्तारं यज्ञतपसां सर्वलोकमहेश्वरम् ।
सहृदं सर्वभूतानां ज्ञात्वा मां शान्तिमृच्छति ॥२९॥

29. He attains peace knowing Me, the partaker of sacrifices and penances, the supreme Lord of the whole world and the friend of all living beings.

इति श्रीमहाभारते शतसाहस्र्यां संहितायां वैयासिक्यां भीष्मपर्वणि
श्रीमद्भगवद्गीतासूपनिषत्सु ब्रह्मविद्यायां योगशास्त्रे श्रीकृष्णार्जुनसंवादे
संन्यासयोगो नाम पञ्चमोऽध्याय ॥५॥

29.1. भोक्तारं इति ॥ भोक्तारं यज्ञतपसां यज्ञानां तपसां च कर्तृरूपेण देवतारूपेण च सर्वलोकमहेश्वरं सर्वेषां लोकानां महान्तं ईश्वरं, सुहृदं सर्वभूतानां सर्व-

प्राणिनां प्रत्युपकारनिरपेक्षतया उपकारिणं — सर्वभूतानां हृदयेशयं सर्वकर्मफलाध्यक्षं, सर्वप्रत्ययसाक्षिणं मां नारायणं ज्ञात्वा शान्तिं सर्वसंसारोपरतिं ऋच्छति प्राप्नोति ।

29.1. 'The partaker of sacrifices and penances' i.e., both as the agent and the Deity related to sacrifices and penances, the Supreme Lord of the worlds and of all living beings—their friend and helper—, regardless of any benefit in return for services rendered. It is Myself who dwells in the hearts of all living beings, who is the superintendent of the fruits of all works and who is the witness of all ideas in the mind. Knowing Me, Nārāyaṇa thus, one attains peace or the cessation of the transmigratory life.

इति श्रीमत्परमहंसपरिव्राजकाचार्यगोविन्दभगवत्पूज्यपादशिष्यश्रीमच्छंकरभगवतः कृतौ श्रीभगवद्गीताभाष्ये संन्यासयोगो (प्रकृतिगर्भो) नाम पञ्चमोऽध्यायः ॥५॥

षष्ठोऽध्यायः

CHAPTER VI

YOGA OF MEDITATION

0.1. अतीतानन्तराध्यायान्ते ध्यानयोगस्य सम्यग्दर्शनं प्रति अन्तरङ्गस्य सूत्रभूताः श्लोकाः 'स्पर्शान् कृत्वा बहिः' (५.२७-२९) इत्यादय उपदिष्टाः । तेषां वृत्तिस्थानीयः अयं षष्ठोऽध्याय आरभ्यते । तत्र ध्यानयोगस्य बहिरङ्गं कर्म इति, यावत् ध्यानयोगारोहणासमर्थः तावत् गृहस्थेन अधिकृतेन कर्तव्यं कर्म इत्यतः तत् स्तौति—अनाश्रितः इति ॥

0.1. At the end of the preceding chapter were set forth verses 5.27–29 that constitute the basic aphorisms of the Yoga of Meditation, the direct means of right perception. Now is commenced the chapter that forms a gloss on them. Since the preliminary accessory of the Yoga of meditation is work, till one becomes fit to embark on meditation, the eligible householder must do work. So it is commended in verse 6.1.

0.2. ननु किमर्थं ध्यानयोगारोहणसीमाकरणं, यावता अनुष्ठेयं एव विहितं कर्म यावज्जीवम्? —न, 'आरुरुक्षोर्मुनेर्योगं कर्म कारणमुच्यते' [६.३.] इति विशेषणात्, आरूढस्य च शमेन एव सम्बन्धकरणात् । आरुरुक्षोः आरूढस्य च शमः कर्म च उभयं कर्तव्यत्वेन अभिप्रेतं चेत् स्यात् तदा 'आरुरुक्षोः, 'आरूढस्य' च इति शमकर्मविषयभेदेन विशेषणं विभागकरणं च अनर्थकं स्यात् ॥

तत्र आश्रमिणां कश्चित् योगम् आरुरुक्षुः भवति, आरूढश्च कश्चित्, अन्ये न आरुरुक्षवः न च आरूढाः —तान् अपेक्ष्य, 'आरुरुक्षोः', 'आरूढस्य' च इति विशेषणं विभागकरणं च उपपद्यते एव इति चेत् —न, 'तस्यैव' इति वचनात् पुनः योगग्रहणाच्च 'योगारूढस्य' इति; यः आसीत् पूर्वं योगं आरुरुक्षुः तस्यैव आरूढस्य शमः एव कर्तव्यः कारणं योगफलं प्रति उच्यते इति । अतः न यावज्जीवं कर्तव्यत्वप्राप्तिः कस्यचिदपि कर्मणः ॥

0.2. *Objection:* Why is the fitness to undertake the Yoga of meditation made the limit of the period for doing work? Work prescribed by the scriptures must be performed as long as life lasts.

Answer: No; *vide* the qualification in 6.3. Work has causal force for the ascetic who seeks to scale the peak of Yoga; he who has scaled it is concerned only with quietude. If both he who seeks to scale Yoga's peak and he who has done it have necessarily to cultivate quietude and do works, according to the Lord, pointless indeed would be the qualification and distinction based on the difference between 'seeking to scale' and, 'having scaled Yoga's peak'. It may be argued that among the occupants of life's stations, some one may seek to scale Yoga's peak and another may in fact do it, while others may neither care to scale nor succeed in scaling. In relation to these, the qualification and the distinction are applicable. But this won't do. For, the expressions *yogārūḍhasya tasyaiva* mean that the very person who sought to scale Yoga's peak is he who has achieved it: he, then, has only to cultivate that quietude which contributes to the final fruit of Yoga. Therefore no kind of work has to be performed throughout life by him.

0.3. योगविभ्रष्टवचनाच्च—गृहस्थस्य चेत् कर्मिणः योगः विहितः षष्ठे अध्याये, सः योगविभ्रष्टः अपि कर्मगतिं कर्मफलं प्राप्नोति इति तस्य नाशाशंका अनुपपन्ना स्यात् । अवश्यं हि कृतं कर्म काम्यं नित्यं वा—मोक्षस्य नित्यत्वात् अनारभ्यत्वे—स्वं फलं आरभत एव। नित्यस्य च कर्मणः वेदप्रमाणावबुद्धत्वात् फलेन भवितव्यं इति अवोचाम । [४.१८.] अन्यथा वेदस्य आनर्थक्यप्रसङ्गात् इति । न च कर्मणि सति उभयविभ्रष्टवचनं अर्थवत्, कर्मणः विभ्रंशकारणानुपपत्तेः ॥

कर्म कृतं ईश्वरे संन्यस्य इत्यतः कर्तरि कर्म फलं नारभते इति चेत्—न, ईश्वरे संन्यासस्य अधिकतरफलहेतुत्वोपपत्तेः ॥

मोक्षाय एव इति चेत्—स्वकर्मणां कृतानां ईश्वरे संन्यासः मोक्षायैव न फलान्तराय योगसहितः; योगात् च विभ्रष्टः, इत्यतः तं प्रति नाशाशङ्का युक्तैव इति चेत्—न, 'एकाकी यतचित्तात्मा निराशीरपरिग्रहः' [६.१०.], 'ब्रह्मचारिव्रते स्थितः' [६.१४.] इति च कर्मसंन्यासविधानात् । न च अत्र ध्यानकाले स्त्रीसहायत्वाशङ्का, येन एकाकित्वं विधीयते । न च गृहस्थस्य 'निराशीरपरिग्रहः' [६.१०.] इत्यादिवचनं अनुकूलम् । उभयविभ्रष्टप्रश्नानुपपत्तेश्च [६.३८.] ॥

0.3. This follows also from the reference to the lapse from Yoga in 6.38. If in Chapter VI Yoga is prescribed for the householder who has to do works, despite his lapse from Yoga, he is bound, as a matter of course, to reap the fruits of his works; the fear that he may perish does not stand to reason.

Indeed, inevitably, the works he has done have to be either desire-prompted or obligatory, which will bear their appropriate fruits. (Liberation, being eternal, is no product of work). We have already stated (*vide BGB*.4.18) that the obligatory work, prescribed by the authoritative Vedas, must bear fruit; otherwise, the Veda would prove to be merely futile. So long as there are works to the credit of the householder, all talk of his lapse from both heaven and Yoga is senseless; works cannot reasonably cause such lapse. The suggestion that the work done, having been dedicated to God, may not bear any fruit is improper; indeed such dedication should make work more fruitful. Futile is the argument that dedication of works to God promotes liberation, but won't yield other fruits. So the fear that the agent of works may perish is not in place. Verses 6.10 and 14 enjoin renunciation of works. 'Alone' in 6, 10 (*ekākī*) does not refer to the practitioner of Yoga, the Yogi being unaccompanied by his wife; there is no room for any help at the time of meditation that a wife may render. That the reference here is not to the householder follows also from the expressions 'free from yearnings' and 'rid of all possessions' in verse 6.10. This view is strengthened by the unreasonableness of Arjuna's reference in 6.38, to lapse from both the path of works and meditation.

0.4. 'अनाश्रितः' [६. १.] इत्यनेन कर्मिणः एव संन्यासित्वं योगित्वं च उक्तं, प्रतिषिद्धं च निरग्नेः अक्रियस्य च संन्यासित्वं योगित्वं चेति चेत् — न, ध्यानयोगं प्रति बहिरङ्गस्य सतः कर्मणः फलाकांक्षासंन्यासस्तुतिपरत्वात् । न केवलं निरग्निः अक्रियः एव संन्यासी योगी च । किं तर्हि ? — कर्मी अपि, कर्मफलासङ्गं संन्यस्य कर्मयोगं अनुतिष्ठन् सत्त्वशुद्ध्यर्थं, 'स संन्यासी च योगी च' भवतीति स्तूयते [६. १.] । न च एकेन वाक्येन कर्मफलासङ्गसंन्यासस्तुतिः चतुर्थाश्रमप्रतिषेधश्च उपपद्यते । न च प्रसिद्धं निरग्नेः अक्रियस्य परमार्थसंन्यासिनः श्रुतिस्मृतिपुराणेतिहासयोगशास्त्रेषु विहितं संन्यासित्वं योगित्वं च प्रतिषेधति भगवान् । स्ववचनविरोधात् च — 'सर्वकर्माणि मनसा संन्यस्य . . . नैव कुर्वन्न कारयन् आस्ते' [५. १३.], ''मौनी सन्तुष्टो येन केनचित् अनिकेतः स्थिरमतिः' [१२. १९.], 'विहाय कामान् यः सर्वान् पुमांश्चरति निःस्पृहः' [२. ७१.], 'सर्वारम्भपरित्यागी' [१२. १६.] इति च तत्र भगवता स्ववचनानि दर्शितानि; तैः विरुध्येत चतुर्थाश्रम — प्रतिषेधः । तस्मात् मुनेः योगं आरुरुक्षोः प्रतिपन्नगार्हस्थ्यस्य अग्निहोत्रादिकर्म फलनिरपक्षं

अनुष्ठीयमानं ध्यानयोगारोहणसाधनत्वं सत्त्वशुद्धिद्वारेण प्रतिपद्यतु इति 'स संन्यासी च योगी च' इति स्तूयते—

0.4. Unsound is the argument that 6.1 with its expression 'not depending on the fruits of works' refers to a householder who also renounces and meditates. Renunciation and meditation have been ruled out for one who does not maintain the household fires and who does not work, because 6.1 just commends the renunciation of cravings for the fruits of works that constitutes an external means to the Yoga of meditation. The sense is: Not he alone, who has renounced the household fires and works is a renouncer and meditator, but also he who works without attachment to the fruits of work—i.e., who performs Karmayoga in order to purify his mind. Verse 6.1 is only a commendation of such an agent. One and the same sentence cannot both praise renunciation of attachment to the fruit of works, and also repudiate the fourth station of life. The Lord does not thereby repudiate the status of being a real renouncer and Yogin to the man who has rejected the household fires and works. For, such a status has been recognised by Sruti, Smṛti, Purāṇas, Itihāsas and the authoritative texts on Yoga. Were He to do so, He would contradict His very words such as 5.13, 12.19, 2.71 and 12.16, which reveal His doctrines, and with which the repudiation of the fourth life-station will come in conflict. Therefore, in the case of the ascetic who seeks to scale Yoga's peak and who is occupying the station of the householder, works like the fire-sacrifice, performed without desire for fruit, prove, due to their power to purify the mind, to be a means to rise to the heights of the Yoga of meditation. Hence the commendation in the words: "He is a renouncer and a Yogin."

श्रीभगवानुवाच :

अनाश्रितः कर्मफलं कार्यं कर्म करोति यः ।
स संन्यासी च योगी च न निरग्निर्न चाक्रियः ॥१॥

The blessed Lord said:

1. Not depending on the fruits of it, whoever performs the work that has to be done is the renouncer and Yogin; not he who has rejected the household fires and is a non-worker.

1.1. अनाश्रित इति ॥ अनाश्रितः न आश्रितः अनाश्रितः — किं ? — कर्मफलं कर्मणां फलं यत् तत् अनाश्रितः, कर्मफलतृष्णारहितः इत्यर्थः । यो हि कर्मफले तृष्णावान् सः कर्मफलं आश्रितः भवति, अयं तु तद्विपरीतः, अतः अनाश्रितः कर्मफलम् । एवंभूतः सन् कार्यं कर्तव्यं नित्यं काम्यविपरीतं अग्निहोत्रादिकं कर्म करोति निर्वर्तयति यः कश्चित् ईदृशः कर्मी स कर्म्यन्तरेभ्यः विशिष्यते इत्येतमर्थं आह—सः संन्यासी च योगी च इति । संन्यासः परित्यागः, स यस्य अस्ति स संन्यासी च, योगी च—योगः चित्तसमाधानं, स यस्य अस्ति स योगी च—इत्येवंगुणसंपन्नः अयं मन्तव्यः, न केवलं निरग्निः अक्रियः एव संन्यासी योगी च इति मन्तव्यः । निर्गताः अग्नयः कर्माङ्गभूताः यस्मात् स निरग्निः, अक्रियश्च अनग्निसाधना अपि अविद्यमानाः क्रियाः तपोदानादिकाः यस्य असौ अक्रियः ॥

1.1. Not depending on what? 'The fruit of work', i.e. he who is free from the craving for the fruits of works. One who craves for the fruit of work depends on it. The renouncer in question is different; so he does not depend on it. As such, he does what has to be done—obligatory rites like the fire-sacrifice that are other than desire-prompted works. Such a worker excels other workers, says the Lord: he is the renouncer and the Yogin. Renunciation consists in giving up; one who gives up is the renouncer. Yoga is mind's concentration: one who has it is the Yogin. One who has such attributes as these is to be considered renouncer and Yogin, and not the person who has merely given up the sacred household fires and rituals. One 'rid of fires' is he who has given up the fires that are auxiliaries to rituals. Rid of works is he also who is free from activities like penance, charity, etc., that are not associated with the sacred fires.

2.0. ननु च निरग्नेः अक्रियस्य एव श्रुतिस्मृतियोगशास्त्रेषु संन्यासित्वं योगित्वं च प्रसिद्धम् । कथं इह साग्नेः सक्रियस्य च संन्यासित्वं योगित्वं च अप्रसिद्धं उच्यते इति—नैष दोषः, कयाचित् गुणवृत्त्या उभयस्य संपिपादयिषितत्वात् । तत् कथम् ?

कर्मफलसंकल्पसंन्यासात् संन्यासित्वं, योगाङ्गत्वेन च कर्मानुष्ठानात् कर्मफलसंकल्पस्य च चित्तविक्षेपहेतोः परित्यागात् योगित्वं च इति गौणं उभयम्; न पुनः मुख्यं संन्यासित्वं योगित्वं च अभिप्रेतं इत्येतमर्थं दर्शयितुमाह—

2.0. Now in *Śruti* and *Smṛti* and authoritative Yoga texts he only is declared to be a renouncer and Yogin who has discarded the sacred fires and who works not. Why then is declared here this unheard-of doctrine, viz., that he who maintains the sacred fires and performs works is a renouncer and Yogin? This is no flaw; for the doctrine sought to be established is secondary only. How? The renouncer is secondarily said to be one who has discarded mental clinging to works' fruits; such a person too is a Yogin, as he performs works as part of the discipline of Yoga and as he has given up the distracting addiction to the fruits of works. Thus these two are secondary; they are not to be taken in their primary signification. To set forth this idea the Lord says:

यं संन्यासमिति प्राहुर्योगं तं विद्धि पाण्डव ।
न ह्यसंन्यस्तसंकल्पो योगी भवति कश्चन ॥२॥

2. That which they call renunciation, know to be Yoga, O Pāṇḍava Prince! None indeed who has not discarded mental constructions can become a Yogin.

2.1. यं इति ॥ यं सर्वकर्मतत्फलपरित्यागलक्षणं परमार्थसंन्यासं संन्यासं इति प्राहुः श्रुतिस्मृतिविदः, योगं कर्मानुष्ठानलक्षणं तं परमार्थसंन्यासं विद्धि जानीहि हे पाण्डव । कर्मयोगस्य प्रवृत्तिलक्षणस्य तद्विपरीतेन निवृत्तिलक्षणेन परमार्थसंन्यासेन कीदृशं सामान्यं अङ्गीकृत्य तद्भावः उच्यते इति अपेक्षायां इदं उच्यते—अस्ति हि परमार्थसंन्यासेन सादृश्यं कर्तृद्वारकं कर्मयोगस्य । यो हि परमार्थसंन्यासी स त्यक्तसर्वकर्मसाधनतया सर्वकर्मतत्फलविषयं संकल्पं प्रवृत्तिहेतुकामकारणं संन्यस्यति । अयमपि कर्मयोगी कर्म कुर्वाणः एव फलविषयं संकल्पं संन्यस्यति इति एतं अर्थं दर्शयिष्यन् आह—न हि यस्मात् असंन्यस्तसङ्कल्पः असंन्यस्तः अपरित्यक्तः फलविषयः संकल्पः अभिसन्धिः येन सः असंन्यस्तसंकल्पः कश्चन कश्चिदपि कर्मी योगी समाधानवान् भवति, न सम्भवति इत्यर्थः, फलसंकल्पस्य चित्तविक्षेपहेतुत्वात् । तस्मात् यः कश्चन कर्मी संन्यस्तफलसंकल्पः भवेत् स योगी समाधानवान् अवि-

क्षिप्तचित्तः भवेत्, चित्तविक्षेपहेतोः फलसंकल्पस्य संन्यस्तत्वात् इति अभिप्रायः ।।

2.1. Know that what is genuine renunciation, according to the scholars of *Śruti* and *Smṛti*, characterized by the rejection of all works and their fruits, is Yoga, the performance of works, O Arjuna. On the basis of what common characteristic are identified these two opposed states, Karma Yoga, a state of activity, and real renunciation, a state of cessation therefrom? The answer follows: Indeed there is similarity between real renunciation and Karma Yoga in respect of the agent. The real renouncer discards craving, the cause of activity and mental constructions as regards works and their fruits. These, at the back of all works, he has discarded. The Karma Yogin, too, while performing works, gives up mental constructions as regards their fruits. This is the idea set forth in the second half of the verse; for, an agent of activity, who has not discarded mental constructions and attachment to the fruits of activity, cannot be a Yogin, a concentrated man. This is the sense of the passage. Mental clinging to the fruits of works distracts. Therefore any doer of works who has given up mental clinging to the fruits of works is a Yogin; his mind is concentrated, not being distracted. He has discarded the cause of distractions, *viz.*, mental clingings to the fruits of works. This is the idea.

3.0. एवं परमार्थसंन्यासकर्मयोगयोः कर्तृद्वारकं संन्याससामान्यं अपेक्ष्य 'यं संन्यासमिति प्राहुर्योगं तं विद्धि पाण्डव' इति कर्मयोगस्य स्तुत्यर्थं संन्यासत्वं उक्तम् । ध्यानयोगस्य फलनिरपेक्षः कर्मयोगः बहिरङ्गसाधनं इति तं संन्यासत्वेन स्तुत्वा अधुना कर्मयोगस्य ध्यानयोगसाधनत्वं दर्शयति —

3.0. Thus as a commendation of Karma Yoga, its parity with renunciation has been affirmed in 6.2 on the basis of the common element of 'rejection' by the agent—common to genuine renunciation and Karma Yoga. Now, Karma Yoga characterized by unconcern for fruits is an external auxiliary of the Yoga of meditation; so Karma Yoga has been commended and its relation to the Yoga of meditation is set forth:

आरुरुक्षोर्मुनेर्योगं कर्म कारणमुच्यते ।
योगारूढस्य तस्यैव शमः कारणमुच्यते ।।३।।

3. Work is said to be the cause in the case of the silent sage who seeks to scale the peak of Yoga; as regards this very sage who has scaled it, quiescence is said to be the cause.

3.1. आरुरुक्षोः इति ॥ आरुरुक्षोः आरोढुं इच्छतः—अनारूढस्य, ध्यानयोगे अवस्थातुं अशक्तस्य एव इत्यर्थः । कस्य तस्य आरुरुक्षोः ? मुनेः, कर्मफलसंन्यासिनः इत्यर्थः । किं आरुरुक्षोः? योगम् । कर्म कारणं साधनं उच्यते । योगारूढस्य पुनः तस्य एव शमः उपशमः सर्वकर्मभ्यः निवृत्तिः कारणं, योगारूढस्य साधनं उच्यते इत्यर्थः यावत् यावत् कर्मभ्यः उपरमते, तावत् तावत् निरायासस्य जितेन्द्रियस्य चित्तं समाधीयते । तथा सति स झटिति योगारूढः भवति । तथा चोक्तम् व्यासेन—

"नैतादृशं ब्राह्मणस्यास्ति वित्तं
यथैकता समता सत्यता च ।
शीलं स्थितिर्दण्डनिधानमार्जवं
ततस्ततश्चोपरमः क्रियाभ्यः" ॥ [शां. प. १७५.३८.] इति ।

3.1. For the sage seeking to scale—but who has, as yet, not scaled—being unable to establish himself in the Yoga of meditation—, work is the cause. Of this sage, who seeks to scale Yoga's peak and who has discarded the fruits of his works, work is said to be the cause, i.e. the means. Of the same sage who has scaled that peak, 'quiescence', cessation, or withdrawal from all works is said to be the cause or means. In the measure in which an unperturbed sage, who has conquered his senses, has withdrawn from works, to that extent his mind becomes concentrated. Quickly thus he reaches Yoga's peak. Vyāsa has affirmed this: A Brahmana has no wealth equal to unity, equality and truthfulness; character, firmness, amiability, gentleness and withdrawal from works of all kinds (*Śānti-parvan* 175.38).

4.0. अथ इदानीं कदा योगारूढः भवति इति उच्यते—

4.0. Now may be raised the question—when is the peak of Yoga scaled? Answer:

यदा हि नेन्द्रियार्थेषु न कर्मस्वनुषज्जते ।
सर्वसंकल्पसंन्यासी योगारूढस्तदोच्यते ॥४॥

4. When the sage is no longer attached to sense objects and works, he discards all mental constructions; then he is said to have scaled the peak of Yoga.

4.1. यदा इति ॥ यदा समाधीयमानचित्तो योगी हि इन्द्रियार्थेषु इन्द्रियाणां अर्थाः शब्दादयः तेषु इन्द्रियार्थेषु कर्मसु च नित्यनैमित्तिककाम्यप्रतिषिद्धेषु प्रयोजनाभावबुद्धया न अनुषज्जते अनुषङ्गं कर्तव्यताबुद्धिं न करोति इत्यर्थः । सर्वसंकल्पसंन्यासी सर्वान् संकल्पान् इहामुत्रार्थकामहेतून् संन्यसितुं शीलं अस्य इति स सर्वसंकल्पसंन्यासी योगारूढः, प्राप्तयोगः इत्येतत्, तदा तस्मिन् काले उच्यते । 'सर्वसंकल्पसंन्यासी' इति वचनात् सर्वांश्च कामान् सर्वाणि च कर्माणि संन्यसेत् इत्यर्थः । संकल्पमूलाः हि सर्वे कामाः—

"संकल्पमूलः कामो वै यज्ञाः संकल्पसंभवाः" [मनुस्मृ. २.३.]
"काम जानामि ते मूलं संकल्पात्किल जायसे ।
न त्वां संकल्पयिष्यामि समूलो न भविष्यसि" ॥ [शां. प. १७७.२५]
इत्यादिस्मृतेः ।

4.1. Concentrating his mind, when the sage ceases to be 'attached to'—gives up—the sense objects like sound etc., when he is no longer attached to works, obligatory, contingent, desire-prompted and forbidden, as he has no purpose of his own to be realised by means of them, and ceases to pursue them, then, trained to discard all mental constructions, the cause of desires here and hereafter, he has scaled the peak of Yoga. By virtue of the expression, 'discarding all mental constructions', it follows that one must discard all desires and works. Indeed all desires are rooted in mental constructions. *Vide*: "Desire is rooted in mental constructions; sacrifices are said to be born of mental constructions" (Manu 2.3). "Desire! I know in what you are rooted; you are born of mental constructions. I shall not set you up mentally; then you will have no root to support you" (*Śānti Parvan* 177.25).

4.2. सर्वकामपरित्यागे च सर्वकर्मसंन्यासः सिद्धः भवति "स यथाकामो भवति तत्क्रतुर्भवति, यत्क्रतुर्भवति तत्कर्म कुरुते" [बृ. उ. ४.४.५.] इत्यादिश्रुतिभ्यः,

"यद्यद्धि कुरुते जन्तुः तत्तत् कामस्य चेष्टितम्" [मनुस्मृ. २.४.] इत्यादिस्मृतिभ्यश्च । न्यायाश्च — न हि सर्वसंकल्पसंन्यासे कश्चित् स्पन्दितुम् अपि शक्तः । तस्मात् 'सर्वसंकल्पसंन्यासी' इति वचनात् सर्वान् कामान् सर्वाणि च कर्माणि त्याजयति भगवान् ॥

4.2. Once all desires are discarded, renunciation of works follows. *Vide*: "He wills according to his desire; he acts according to his desire; he acts according to his will" (BU.4.4.5), and similar Upaniṣadic utterances. Also, passages like the following state this:-"All that a living being does is the work of desire" (Manu 2.4). Reasoning, too, supports this view. None indeed may so much as stir, once mental constructions are discarded. Therefore, the Lord's expression 'discarding all mental constructions' obliges all to give up all desires and works.

5.0. यदा एवं योगारूढः तदा तेन आत्मा आत्मना उद्धृतः भवति संसारानर्थव्रातात् । अतः —

5.0. Thus, Yoga's peak being scaled, the self becomes lifted up by the self above all empirical turmoils. So,

उद्धरेदात्मनाऽऽत्मानं नात्मानमवसादयेत् ।
आत्मैव ह्यात्मनो बन्धुरात्मैव रिपुरात्मनः ॥५॥

5. Elevate the self by the self; do not weaken the self. Self is indeed the friend of the self. Self alone is self's foe.

5.1. उद्धरेत् इति ॥ उद्धरेत् संसारसागरे निमग्नं आत्मानं आत्मना ततः उत् ऊर्ध्वं हरेत् उद्धरेत् योगारूढतां आपादयेत् इत्यर्थः । न आत्मानं अवसादयेत् न अधः नयेत् [न अधः गमयेत्] । आत्मा एव हि यस्मात् आत्मनः बन्धुः । न हि अन्यः कश्चित् बन्धुः यः संसारमुक्तये भवति । बन्धुः अपि तावत् मोक्षं प्रति प्रतिकूलः एव, स्नेहादिबन्धनायतनत्वात् । तस्मात् युक्तं अवधारणं 'आत्मैव ह्यात्मनो बन्धुः' इति । आत्मा एव रिपुः शत्रुः । यः अन्यः अपकारी बाह्यः शत्रुः सोऽपि आत्मप्रयुक्तः एव इति युक्तम् एव अवधारणं 'आत्मैव रिपुरात्मनः' इति ॥

5.1. Elevate the self sunk in the sea of transmigratory life by means of the Self. Pull it upwards from the sea, make it scale the peak of Yoga. This is the idea. Do not weaken or push it down. For the Self alone is the self's friend; no other friend is there who may promote one's liberation from this transmigratory life. Even a relation, being the seat of emotions like attachment etc. which make for bondage, may prove adverse as regards liberation. Therefore, the stress in the expressions 'the Self *indeed* is the friend of the self, the Self *alone* is the foe' or adversary, is appropriate. Any other external adversary, too, is impelled by the self. Hence the stress in the expression "Self alone is. . ." is right.

6.0. आत्मा एव बन्धुः आत्मा एव रिपुः आत्मनः इत्युक्तम् । तत्र किंलक्षणः आत्मा आत्मनः बन्धुः ? किंलक्षणः वा आत्मा आत्मनः रिपुः इति ? उच्यते —

6.0. It has been affirmed that the self alone is the friend and the self alone is the foe, of the self. What sort of self is the friend and what sort, the foe of the self? Answer:

बन्धुरात्माऽऽत्मनस्तस्य येनात्मैवात्मना जितः ।
अनात्मनस्तु शत्रुत्वे वर्तेतात्मैव शत्रुवत् ॥६॥

6. The Self is the friend of that self by which the self has been subdued. The Self alone operates as the foe of one unsubdued by the self.

6.1. बन्धुः इति ॥ बन्धुः आत्मा आत्मनः तस्य, तस्य आत्मनः स आत्मा बन्धुः येन आत्मना आत्मा एव जितः, आत्मा कार्यकरणसंघातः येन वशीकृतः, जितेन्द्रियः इत्यर्थः । अनात्मनः तु अजितात्मनः तु शत्रुत्वे शत्रुभावे वर्तेत आत्मा एव शत्रुवत्, यथा अनात्मा शत्रुः आत्मनः अपकारी, तथा आत्मा आत्मनः अपकारे वर्तेत इत्यर्थः ॥

6.1. Self is the friend of that self which has been subdued by itself. The subdued self is the conglomerate of 'effect and instruments' (body and its organs). The reference is to the Jīva who has mastered his body and sense organs. Of the unsubdued self the foe is the self alone. As non-self is self's foe or adversary, so, this very self that is unsubdued will operate as the foe. This is the idea.

जितात्मनः प्रशान्तस्य परमात्मा समाहितः ।
शीतोष्णसुखदुःखेषु तथा मानापमानयोः ॥७॥

7. The supreme Self is concentrated for one who has subdued the self and is quiescent, in cold and heat, in pleasure and pain, and in honour and disgrace.

7.1. जितात्मनः इति ॥ जितात्मनः कार्यकरणसंघातः आत्मा जितः येन सः जितात्मा तस्य जितात्मनः, प्रशान्तस्य उपशान्तस्य [प्रसन्नान्तःकरणस्य सतः संन्यासिनः] परमात्मा समाहितः साक्षात् आत्मभावेन वर्तते इत्यर्थः । किञ्च— शीतोष्णसुखदुःखेषु तथा माने अपमाने च मानापमानयोः पूजापरिभवयोः समः स्यात् ॥

7.1. The supreme Self is 'concentrated'—exists as one's immediate Self—for one who has subdued the self or the conglomerate of 'effects and instruments', and who is quiescent. (The reference is to the renouncer whose inner sense has been tranquillized.) This is the idea. Moreover, he will be the same in states like cold and heat, pleasure and pain, as well as in honour and disgrace.

ज्ञानविज्ञानतृप्तात्मा कूटस्थो विजितेन्द्रियः ।
युक्त इत्युच्यते योगी समलोष्टाश्मकाञ्चनः ॥८॥

8. That yogin is said to be integrated whose self is content with knowledge and experience, who is immutable, who has subdued his senses and to whom clod, stone and gold are all alike.

8.1. ज्ञान इति ॥ ज्ञानविज्ञानतृप्तात्मा ज्ञानं शास्त्रोक्तपदार्थानां परिज्ञानं, विज्ञानं तु शास्त्रतः ज्ञातानां तथैव स्वानुभवकरणं, ताभ्यां ज्ञानविज्ञानाभ्यां तृप्तः संजातालंप्रत्ययः आत्मा अन्तःकरणं यस्य सः ज्ञानविज्ञानतृप्तात्मा कूटस्थः अप्रकंप्यः,

भवति इत्यर्थः, विजितेन्द्रियः च । यः ईदृशः, युक्तः समाहितः इति सः उच्यते कथ्यते योगी । सः समलोष्टाश्मकाञ्चनः लोष्टाश्मकाञ्चनानि समानि यस्य सः समलोष्टाश्मकाञ्चनः ॥

किंच—

8.1. 'Content with knowledge and experience'—'knowledge' means conversance with the principles enunciated in the *śāstras*; on the other hand, 'experience' means the exact realisation of whatever has been learned from the *śāstras*. Content with these two is the self—the inner sense—of the Yogin. He becomes immutable or unshakable; for, he has subdued the senses. Whoever answers to this description is 'integrated', is said to be concentrated. To this Yogin a clod, a stone and a piece of gold are all alike.

Moreover:

सुहृन्मित्रार्युदासीनमध्यस्थद्वेष्यबन्धुषु ।
साधुष्वपि च पापेषु समबुद्धिर्विशिष्यते ॥९॥

9. He excels whose intellect is the same in respect of good men, friends, foes, indifferent persons, neutrals, antagonists, relations, the righteous and the unrighteous.

9.1. सुहृत् इति ॥ 'सुहृत्' इत्यादिश्लोकार्धं एकं पदम् । सुहृत् इति प्रत्युपकारं अनपेक्ष्य उपकर्ता, मित्रं स्नेहवान्, अरिः शत्रुः, उदासीनः न कस्यचित् पक्षं भजते, मध्यस्थः यः विरुद्धयोः उभयोः हितैषी, द्वेष्यः आत्मनः अप्रियः, बन्धुः, सम्बन्धी । इत्येतेषु साधुषु शास्त्रानुवर्तिषु अपि च पापेषु प्रतिषिद्धकारिषु सर्वेषु एतेषु समबुद्धिः "कः किंकर्मा" इति अव्यापृतबुद्धिः इत्यर्थः । विशिष्यते—'विमुच्यते' इति वा पाठान्तरम्—योगारूढानां सर्वेषां अयं उत्तमः इत्यर्थः ॥

9.1. The first half of this verse is a single compound word. The 'good man' helps, regardless of any requital. 'The friend' is one affectionate. 'The foe' is the adversary. 'The indifferent' takes no sides. 'The neutral' seeks the well-being of both of those who oppose each other. 'The antagonist' is he whom one does not like. 'The relations' are the kith and kin.

In regard to all these, as also to the righteous who conform to the *śāstras* and the unrighteous who do evil, he excels whose intellectual attitude is the same, who does not bother about what another is and does. Another reading for 'excels' is *vimucyate*, meaning 'is liberated'. The idea is that this kind of person is the foremost among all those who have scaled Yoga's peak.

10.0. अतः एवं उत्तमफलप्राप्तये —

10.0. Therefore in order to reap the best fruits:

योगी युञ्जीत सततमात्मानं रहसि स्थितः ।
एकाकी यतचित्तात्मा निराशीरपरिग्रहः ॥१०॥

10. Living in solitude, alone, with controlled mind and self, free from cravings, owning nothing, the Yogin ought to apply himself to Yoga incessantly.

10.1. योगीति ॥ योगी ध्यायी युञ्जीत समादध्यात् सततं सर्वदा आत्मानं अन्तःकरणं रहसि एकान्ते गिरिगुहादौ स्थितः सन् एकाकी असहायः—'रहसि स्थितः एकाकी च' इति विशेषणात् संन्यासं कृत्वा इत्यर्थः — यतचित्तात्मा चित्तं अन्तःकरणं आत्मा देहश्च संयतौ यस्य सः यतचित्तात्मा, निराशीः वीततृष्णः अपरिग्रहः परिग्रहरहितश्च इत्यर्थः । संन्यासित्वेऽपि त्यक्तसर्वपरिग्रहः सन् युञ्जीत इत्यर्थः ॥

10.1. Let 'the Yogin', the meditator, ceaselessly concentrate 'the self', the inner sense, 'in solitude' i.e., stationing himself in mountain caves, etc. 'Alone'—unaccompanied. The qualifications, living in solitude and unaccompanied, mean 'having renounced'. 'With controlled mind' i.e. the inner sense, and the 'self' or the body. "Free from cravings, owning no possessions" mean without mental clingings and possessions of any kind. A true renouncer that he is, he must own literally nothing and apply himself to Yoga.

11.0. अथ इदानीं योगं युञ्जानस्य आसनाहारविहारादीनां योगसाधनत्वेन

नियमः वक्तव्यः, प्राप्तयोगस्य लक्षणं, तत्फलादि च, इत्यतः आरभ्यते । तत्र आसनम् एव तावत् प्रथमं उच्यते—

11.0. Now begins the section that lays down regulations regarding the posture, diet, recreation, etc., of the practising Yogin; for, these constitute the means to Yoga. It also enumerates the characteristics of the perfected Yogin and Yoga's fruits and so forth. First is described the posture:

शुचौ देशे प्रतिष्ठाप्य स्थिरमासनमात्मनः ।
नात्युच्छ्रितं नातिनीचं चैलाजिनकुशोत्तरम् ॥११॥

11. Setting one's firm seat in a clean spot, neither too high nor too low, covered with a cloth, or hide, and Kuśa grass, one over the other;

11.1. शुचौ इति ॥ शुचौ शुद्धे विविक्ते स्वभावतः संस्कारतः वा, देशे स्थाने प्रतिष्ठाप्य स्थिरं अचलं आत्मनः आसनं न अत्युच्छ्रितं न अतीव उच्छ्रितं न अपि अतिनीचं, तच्च चैलाजिनकुशोत्तरं चैलं अजिनं कुशाश्च उत्तरे यस्मिन् आसने तत् आसनं चैलाजिनकुशोत्तरम् । पाठक्रमात् विपरीतः अत्र क्रमः चैलादीनाम् ॥

प्रतिष्ठाप्य किम्—

11.1. 'In a clean spot', solitary, either by its very nature or made so by appropriate means; having set up one's 'firm seat' which is neither too high nor too low, and covered with cloth, hide and *kuśa* grass arranged in the reverse order to the one given in the verse;

Having set up a seat there—what follows?

तत्रैकाग्रं मनः कृत्वा यतचित्तेन्द्रियक्रियः ।
उपविश्यासने युञ्ज्याद्योगमात्मविशुद्धये ॥१२॥

12. Sitting on it, making the mind one-pointed, controlling the activities of the mind and the senses, let the practitioner apply himself to Yoga for self-purification.

12.1. तत्र इति ॥ तत्र तस्मिन् आसने उपविश्य योगं युञ्ज्यात्—कथं ? —सर्वविषयेभ्यः उपसंहृत्य एकाग्रं मनः कृत्वा यतचित्तेन्द्रियक्रियः चित्तं च इन्द्रियाणि च चित्तेन्द्रियाणि तेषां क्रियाः संयता यस्य सः यतचित्तेन्द्रियक्रियः । स किमर्थं योगं युञ्ज्यात् इति ? आह—आत्मविशुद्धये अन्तःकरणस्य विशुद्ध्यर्थं इत्येतत् ॥

12.1. There seated, one should apply oneself to Yoga. How? Withdrawing the mind from all objects, making it one-pointed, and controlling the activities of mind and senses. What is the aim of this application to Yoga? Self-purification or the purification of the inner sense.

13.0. बाह्यं आसनं उक्तम् अधुना शरीरस्य धारणं कथं इति ? उच्यते—

13.0. The external seat has been described. Now is answered the question how the body is to be held:

समं कायशिरोग्रीवं धारयन्नचलं स्थिरः ।
संप्रेक्ष्य नासिकाग्रं स्वं दिशश्चानवलोकयन् ॥१३॥

13. Holding the body, head and neck evenly and steadily, the resolute Yogin fixes his gaze on the tip of his nose, not looking around.

13.1. समं इति ॥ समं कायशिरोग्रीवं कायश्च शिरश्च ग्रीवा च कायशिरोग्रीवं तत् समं धारयन् अचलं च । समं धारयतः चलनं संभवति; अतः विशिनष्टि—अचलं इति । स्थिरः स्थिरो भूत्वा इत्यर्थः स्वं नासिकाग्रं संप्रेक्ष्य सम्यक् प्रेक्षणं दर्शनं कृत्वा इव इति; इवशब्दो लुप्तः द्रष्टव्यः । न हि स्वनासिकाग्रसंप्रेक्षणं इह विधित्सितम् । किं तर्हि ? चक्षुषो दृष्टिसंनिपातः । स च अन्तःकरणसमाधानापेक्षः विवक्षितः । स्वनासिकाग्रसंप्रेक्षणमेव चेत् विवक्षितं, मनः तत्रैव समाधीयेत, न आत्मनि । आत्मनि हि मनसः समाधानं वक्ष्यति 'आत्मसंस्थं मनः कृत्वा' [६.२५.] इति । तस्मात् इवशब्दलोपेन अक्ष्णोः दृष्टिसंनिपातः एव 'संप्रेक्ष्य' इत्युच्यते । दिशश्च अनवलोकयन् दिशां च अवलोकनं अन्तरा अकुर्वन् इत्येतत् ॥

किञ्च—

13.1. 'The body, head and neck: holding these three evenly and steadily'—there may be movement in spite of even holding; to exclude it is added the qualification 'steadily'. 'Resolute' i.e., becoming resolute and 'fixing the gaze on'—looking at—the tip of one's nose. Understand this to mean 'looking at the tip', as it were. The expression 'as it were' is understood. What is sought to be enjoined is not the gazing at the tip of the nose; rather it is the convergence of sight. This depends on the concentration of the inner sense. Were the gaze at the tip of the nose sought to be enjoined, the result would be mind's concentration thereon, and not on the Self. In 6.25 what will be enjoined is concentration on the Self—'the centering of the mind on the Self'. So by the expression 'as it were' implicit in this context what is affirmed is the convergence of sight. 'Not looking around' means not looking in various directions, every now and then.

Moreover,

प्रशान्तात्मा विगतभीः ब्रह्मचारिव्रते स्थितः ।
मनः संयम्य मच्चित्तो युक्त आसीत मत्परः ॥१४॥

14. With the inner sense tranquillized, fear gone, established in the vow of chastity, controlling the mind, thoughts anchored in Me, the integrated Yogin should sit, intent on Me.

14.1. प्रशान्त इति ॥ प्रशान्तात्मा प्रकर्षेण शान्तः आत्मा अन्तःकरणं यस्य सोऽयं प्रशान्तात्मा, विगतभीः विगतभयः, ब्रह्मचारिव्रते स्थितः ब्रह्मचारिणो व्रतं ब्रह्मचारिव्रतं ब्रह्मचर्यं गुरुशुश्रूषाभिक्षान्नभुक्तयादि तस्मिन् स्थितः, तदनुष्ठाता भवेत् इत्यर्थः । किञ्च—मनः संयम्य मनसः वृत्तीः उपसंहृत्य इत्येतत्, मच्चित्तः मयि परमेश्वरे चित्तं यस्य सोऽयं मच्चित्तो युक्तः समाहितः सन् आसीत उपविशेत् । मत्परः, अहं परो यस्य सोऽयं मत्परो भवति । कश्चित् रागी स्त्रीचित्तः, न तु स्त्रियं एव परत्वेन गृह्णाति; किं तर्हि ? राजानं, महादेवं वा। अयं तु मच्चित्तो मत्परश्च ॥

14.1. With the inner sense eminently tranquillized and fear dispelled, let the Yogin sit. The vow of chastity implies waiting upon the teacher, eating the food collected through mendicancy, etc. Let him stick to this course. Controlling the moods of the mind, thoughts directed to Me, the Supreme Lord, integrated, i.e. concentrated, let him sit, intent on Me or deeming Me the Supreme Reality. This contrasts with a man who may direct his thoughts to a woman, for example, but who may not deem her supreme; for him the king or the Deity may be supreme. Here the Yogin directs his thoughts to Me and deems Me the supreme Reality.

15.0. अथ इदानीं योगफलं उच्यते—

15.0. Now is stated the fruit of Yoga:

युञ्जन्नेवं सदाऽऽत्मानं योगी नियतमानसः ।
शान्तिं निर्वाणपरमां मत्संस्थामधिगच्छति ॥१५॥

15. Thus applying himself unintermittently, with a disciplined mind, the Yogin wins peace, which is abidance in Me, and whose climax is emancipation.

15.1. युञ्जन् इति ॥ युञ्जन् समाधानं कुर्वन् एवं यथोक्तेन विधानेन सदा आत्मानं सर्वदा योगी नियतमानसः नियतं संयतं मानसं मनः यस्य सोऽयं नियतमानसः शान्तिं उपरतिं निर्वाणपरमां निर्वाणं मोक्षः तत्परमा निष्ठा यस्याः शान्तेः सा निर्वाणपरमा तां निर्वाणपरमां मत्संस्थां मदधीनां अधिगच्छति प्राप्नोति ॥

15.1. 'Applying', concentrating, 'thus', unintermittently as stated, the Yogin with a disciplined mind wins 'peace'—withdrawal from the sphere of objects that culminates in emancipation. The discipline of 'peace' has *nirvāṇa* or emancipation as its climax; it is abidance in Me and being subject to Me.

16.0. इदानीं योगिनः आहारादिनियमः उच्यते—

16.0. Now is set forth the regulation of the Yogin's diet, etc.

नात्यश्नतस्तु योगोऽस्ति न चैकान्तमनश्नतः ।
न चातिस्वप्नशीलस्य जाग्रतो नैव चार्जुन ॥१६॥

16. He has no Yoga who eats too much or who eats not at all; who habitually sleeps too much or who keeps always awake, O Arjuna!

16.1. न इति ॥ न अत्यश्नतः आत्मसंमितं अन्नपरिमाणं अतीत्याश्नतः अत्यश्नतः न योगः अस्ति । न च एकान्तं अनश्नतः योगः अस्ति । 'यदु ह वा आत्मसंमितं अन्नं तदवति, तन्न हिनस्ति, यद्भूयो हिनस्ति तत् कनीयोऽन्नं न तदवति' [शत. ब्रा. ९.२.१.२.] इति श्रुतेः । तस्मात् योगी न आत्मसम्मितात् अन्नात् अधिकं न्यूनं वा अश्नीयात् । अथवा—योगिनः योगशास्त्रे परिपठितात् अन्नपरिमाणात् अतिमात्रं अश्नतः योगः नास्ति । उक्तं हि—

अर्धं सव्यञ्जनान्नस्य तृतीयमुदकस्य च ।
वायोः सञ्चरणार्थं तु चतुर्थमवशेषयेत् ॥ —[?]

इत्यादिपरिमाणम् । तथा—न च अतिस्वप्नशीलस्य योगो भवति, नैव च अतिमात्रं जाग्रतो योगो भवति च अर्जुन ॥

16.1. For him who 'eats too much'—who exceeds the measure of food that suffices for him, there is no Yoga; nor for one who eats not at all. "The food, in sufficient measure, protects and does not hurt. What exceeds it, hurts. What is less, protects not'' (Sat.Brā. 9.2.1.2). Therefore, the Yogin shall eat neither more nor less than what suffices for himself. Or 'the Yogin who eats more than what has been prescribed in the Yoga texts cannot have Yoga. *Vide* the following: 'Half of the stomach, fill with food and condiments; the third quarter is for water; leave the fourth for the movement of air.' So, too, there is no Yoga for him who habitually sleeps too much; nor, for him who keeps awake too long, O Arjuna!

17.0. कथं पुनर्योगो भवतीत्युच्यते—

17.0. How then is Yoga achieved? Answer:

युक्ताहारविहारस्य युक्तचेष्टस्य कर्मसु ।
युक्तस्वप्नावबोधस्य योगो भवति दुःखहा ॥१७॥

17. One who in proper measure eats and plays, applies

himself to works, sleeps and keeps awake, achieves Yoga that destroys all pains.

17.1. युक्त इति ॥ युक्ताहारविहारस्य आह्रियते इति आहारः अन्नं, विहरणं विहारः पादक्रमः, तौ युक्तौ नियतपरिमाणौ यस्य सः युक्ताहारविहारः तस्य; तथा युक्तचेष्टस्य [अन्या च] युक्ता नियता चेष्टा यस्य कर्मसु तस्य; तथा युक्तस्वप्नावबोधस्य युक्तौ स्वप्नश्च अवबोधश्च तौ नियतकालौ यस्य तस्य; युक्ताहारविहारस्य युक्तचेष्टस्य कर्मसु युक्तस्वप्नावबोधस्य योगिनो योगो भवति दुःखहा दुःखानि सर्वाणि हन्तीति दुःखहा सर्वसंसारदुःखक्षयकृत् योगः भवति इत्यर्थः ॥

17.1. What is taken in is food. Play is movement, walk. To him who has these two in proper measure, to him whose application to works is in due measure and whose sleep and wakefulness are of measured duration, accrues Yoga that destroys all pains—all the pains of empirical life. This is the idea.

18.0. अथ अधुना कदा युक्तो भवति इति ? उच्यते—

18.0. Now arises the question: When does one become integrated? Answer:

यदा विनियतं चित्तं आत्मन्येवावतिष्ठते ।
निःस्पृहः सर्वकामेभ्यो युक्त इत्युच्यते तदा ॥१८॥

18. When the well-controlled mind abides solely in the Self, rid of cravings for objects of desires, one is said to be integrated in Yoga.

18.1. यदा इति ॥ यदा विनियतं विशेषेण नियतं संयतं एकाग्रतां आपन्नं चित्तं हित्वा बाह्यार्थचिन्तां आत्मनि एव केवले अवतिष्ठते, स्वात्मनि स्थितिं लभते इत्यर्थः । निःस्पृहः सर्वकामेभ्यः निर्गता दृष्टादृष्टविषयेभ्यः स्पृहा तृष्णा यस्य योगिनः स युक्तः समाहितः इति उच्यते तदा तस्मिन् काले ॥

18.1. When the mind is marked by control and is made one-pointed, giving up all thoughts of external objects, when it abides in the pure Self alone, i.e., is anchored in the Self, at that time one is said to be integrated or concentrated, For, he has no more cravings for objects of desires, seen or unseen.

19.0. तस्य योगिनः समाहितं यत् चित्तं तस्य उपमा उच्यते —

19.0. A simile of the concentrated mind of the Yogin is offered:

यथा दीपो निवातस्थो नेङ्गते सोपमा स्मृता ।
योगिनो यतचित्तस्य युञ्जतो योगमात्मनः ॥१९॥

19. As light in a windless spot stirs not—this is the simile of the Yogin whose mind is controlled and who applies himself to Yoga.

19.1. यथा इति ॥ यथा दीपः प्रदीपः निवातस्थः निवाते वातवर्जिते स्थाने स्थितः न इङ्गते न चलति, सा उपमा उपमीयते अनया इत्युपमा योगज्ञैः चित्त-प्रचारदर्शिभिः स्मृता चिन्तिता योगिनो यतचित्तस्य संयतान्तःकरणस्य युञ्जतो योगं अनुतिष्ठतः आत्मनः समाधिं अनुतिष्ठतः इत्यर्थः ॥

19.1. As a light in a windless spot does not stir—this is the simile, the object to which the Yogin is likened by the knowers of Yoga who are conversant with the movements of the mind. The Yogin's mind—the inner sense—is controlled and he practises Yoga i.e., concentration.

20.0. एवं योगाभ्यासबलात् एकाग्रीभूतं निवातप्रदीपकल्पं सत् —

20.0. Thus the mind becomes one-pointed, very much like the light in a windless spot, due to the power of Yoga-practice.

यत्रोपरमते चित्तं निरुद्धं योगसेवया ।
यत्र चैवात्मनाऽऽत्मानं पश्यन्नात्मनि तुष्यति ॥२०॥

20. When through the practice of Yoga the motionless mind withdraws (from objects) and rejoices in the Self, beholding the Self by one's inner sense;

20.1. यत्र इति ॥ यत्र यस्मिन् काले उपरमते चित्तं उपरतिं गच्छति निरुद्धं सर्वतो निवारितप्रचारं योगसेवया योगानुष्ठानेन, यत्र च एव यस्मिंश्च काले आत्मना समाधिपरिशुद्धेन अन्तःकरणेन आत्मानं परं चैतन्यं ज्योतिःस्वरूपं पश्यन् उपलभमानः स्वे एव आत्मनि तुष्यति तुष्टिं भजते ॥

किञ्च–

20.1. When the mind withdraws, being checked from all external movements by the practice of Yoga, and when he rejoices in his own Self, beholding the Supreme Spirit—the All-pervasive Light—by means of the inner sense purified through concentration.

And,

सुखमात्यन्तिकं यत्तद्बुद्धिग्राह्यमतीन्द्रियम् ।
वेत्ति यत्र न चैवायं स्थितश्चलति तत्त्वतः ॥२१॥

21. When the Yogin experiences the endless bliss, beyond the senses, that may be grasped only by the intellect, becomes steadfast and does not move away from the Truth;

21.1. सुखं इति ॥ सुखं आत्यन्तिकं अत्यन्तम् एव भवति इत्यात्यन्तिकं अनन्तं इत्यर्थः, यत् तत् बुद्धिग्राह्यं बुद्ध्यैव इन्द्रियनिरपेक्षया गृह्यते इति बुद्धिग्राह्यं अतीन्द्रियं इन्द्रियगोचरातीतं अविषयजनितं इत्यर्थः, वेत्ति तत् ईदृशं सुखं अनुभवति यत्र यस्मिन् काले, न च एव अयं विद्वान् आत्मस्वरूपे स्थितः तस्मात् नैव चलति तत्त्वतः तत्त्वस्वरूपात् न प्रच्यवते इत्यर्थः ॥

किञ्च—

21.1. 'Endless bliss'—bliss that knows no end—is everlasting. It may be grasped by the intellect only, independent of sense organs, it being beyond the senses, i.e. since it is not generated by objects. When this kind of bliss is experienced and the Yogin is anchored in the Self's essence, he, the knower, does not move away from the Truth—does not slip from the nature of Truth.

And,

यं लब्ध्वा चापरं लाभं मन्यते नाधिकं ततः ।
यस्मिन् स्थितो न दुःखेन गुरुणापि विचाल्यते ॥२२॥

22. That prize, winning which one deems no other greater; established in which, one is not overpowered even by grievous pain;

22.1. यं इति ॥ यं लब्ध्वा यं आत्मलाभं लब्ध्वा प्राप्य च अपरं लाभं [अन्यत्] लाभान्तरं ततः अधिकं अस्ति इति न मन्यते न चिन्तयति । किंच—यस्मिन् आत्मतत्त्वे स्थितः दुःखेन शस्त्रनिपातादिलक्षणेन गुरुणा महता अपि न विचाल्यते ॥

22.1. Having won that prize—the gain of the Self—,one thinks that there is no prize greater than it. Established in the truth of the Self, one is not overpowered even by 'grievous' or great pain due to weapons etc.

23.0. 'यत्रोपरमते' [६.२०.] इत्यारभ्य यावद्भिः विशेषणैः विशिष्टः आत्मावस्था-विशेषः योगः उक्तः—

23.0. That Yoga, described in verses 6.20 etc., and consisting in a certain status of the Self, is defined:

तं विद्याद्दुःखसंयोगवियोगं योगसंज्ञितम् ।
स निश्चयेन योक्तव्यो योगोऽनिर्विण्णचेतसा ॥२३॥

23. Know that to be styled Yoga which consists in disjunction from experienced-pain. This Yoga has slowly got to be practised with an undejected mind.

23.1. तं इति ॥ तं विद्यात् विजानीयात् दुःखसंयोगवियोगं दुःखैः संयोगः दुःखसंयोगः, तेन वियोगः दुःखसंयोगवियोगः, तं दुःखसंयोगवियोगं योगः इत्येव संज्ञितं विपरीतलक्षणेन विद्यात् विजानीयात् इत्यर्थः । योगफलं उपसंहृत्य पुनः अन्वारम्भेण योगस्य कर्तव्यता उच्यते निश्चयानिर्वेदयोः योगसाधनत्वविधानार्थं — सः यथोक्तफलः योगः निश्चयेन अध्यवसायेन योक्तव्यः अनिर्विण्णचेतसा न निर्विण्णं अनिर्विण्णं किं तत्? —चेतः तेन निर्वेदरहितेन चेतसा चित्तेन इत्यर्थः ॥

किञ्च–

23.1. Know that to be styled Yoga which is a disjunction from experienced-pains. This knowledge is aimed at a process of knowing through exclusion. Having concluded the discussion on Yoga's fruit, once more is set forth the propriety of undertaking Yoga, in order to teach that determination and non-dejection are its instruments. Yoga with its fruit, as already set forth, must be pursued with determination and a mind rid of dejection.

Besides,

संकल्पप्रभवान् कामांस्त्यक्त्वा सर्वानशेषतः ।
मनसैवेन्द्रियग्रामं विनियम्य समन्ततः ॥२४॥

24. Giving up wholly all desires born of mental constructions and controlling, on all sides, the senses with the mind;

24.1. संकल्प इति ॥ संकल्पप्रभवान् संकल्पः प्रभवः येषां कामानां ते संकल्पप्रभवाः कामाः तान् त्यक्त्वा परित्यज्य सर्वान् अशेषतः निर्लेपेन । किं च — मनसा एव विवेकयुक्तेन इन्द्रियग्रामं इन्द्रियसमुदायं विनियम्य नियमनं कृत्वा समन्ततः समन्तात् ॥

24.1. 'Giving up' or renouncing desires born of mental constructions—all of them, leaving not a trace behind, and controlling with the discriminating mind itself all the senses from pursuing their objects on all sides;

शनैः शनैरुपरमेद्बुद्ध्या धृतिगृहीतया ।
आत्मसंस्थं मनः कृत्वा न किञ्चिदपि चिन्तयेत् ॥२५॥

25. Withdraw gradually, with the help of the resolute intellect; anchoring the mind in the Self, think of nothing whatsoever.

25.1. शनैः इति ॥ शनैः शनैः न सहसा उपरमेत् उपरतिं कुर्यात्—कया

—बुद्धया—किंविशिष्टया ? —धृतिगृहीतया धृत्या धैर्येण गृहीतया धृतिगृहीतया धैर्येण युक्तया इत्यर्थः । आत्मसंस्थं आत्मनि संस्थितं "आत्मैव सर्वं न ततः अन्यत् किञ्चित् अस्ति" इत्येवं आत्मसंस्थं मनः कृत्वा न किञ्चित् अपि चिन्तयेत् । एष योगस्य परमः विधिः ॥

25.1. 'Gradually', not impetuously, one should withdraw. With the aid of the resolute intellect, perceiving that Self alone is all this. This is the supreme injunction concerning Yoga.

26.0. तत्र एवं आत्मसंस्थं मनः कर्तुं प्रवृत्तो योगी—

26.0. Striving thus to anchor the mind in the Self—

यतो यतो निश्चरति मनश्चंचलमस्थिरम् ।
ततस्ततो नियम्यैतदात्मन्येव वशं नयेत् ॥२६॥

26. The Yogin should bring the fickle and unsteady mind under the sole control of the Self, withdrawing it from all causes whatever that make it sally forth.

26.1. यतः इति ॥ यतः यतः यस्मात् यस्मात् निमित्तात् शब्दादेः निश्चरति निर्गच्छति स्वाभाविकदोषात् मनः चंचलं अत्यर्थं चलं, अत एव अस्थिरं, ततः ततः तस्मात् तस्मात् शब्दादेः निमित्तात् नियम्य तत् तत् निमित्तं याथात्म्यनिरूपणेन आभासीकृत्य वैराग्यभावनया च एतत् मनः आत्मनि एव वशं नयेत् आत्मवश्यतां आपादयेत् । एवं योगाभ्यासबलात् योगिनः आत्मनि एव प्रशाम्यति मनः ॥

26.1. 'From all causes whatever', such as sounds etc. Controlling the excessively fickle and unsteady mind that sallies forth due to its innate flaws, through a rational consideration of the truth of their causes and reducing them to empty appearances and thus resorting to detachment, let him bring the mind under the control of the Self.

Thus by the strength of Yogic practice, the mind of the Yogin becomes quiescent in the Self alone.

प्रशान्तमनसं ह्येनं योगिनं सुखमुत्तमम् ।
उपैति शान्तरजसं ब्रह्मभूतमकल्मषम् ॥२७॥

27. Indeed the bliss supreme accrues to this sinless Yogin whose mind has been stilled, Rajas supressed, and who has become Brahman.

27.1. प्रशान्त इति ॥ प्रशान्तमनसं प्रकर्षेण शान्तं मनः यस्य सः प्रशान्तमनाः तं प्रशान्तमनसं हि एनं योगिनं सुखं उत्तमं निरतिशयं उपैति उपगच्छति शान्तरजसं प्रक्षीणमोहादिक्लेशरजसं इत्यर्थः, ब्रह्मभूतं जीवन्मुक्तं "ब्रह्मैव सर्वं" इत्येवं निश्चयवन्तं ब्रह्मभूतं अकल्मषं अधर्मादिवर्जितम् ॥

27.1. To the Yogin whose mind has been thoroughly stilled, the best i.e., peerless bliss accrues—to the Yogin whose *rajas*, delusion and other afflictions have dwindled away; who has become Brahman i.e., who is liberated in life; who is convinced that Brahman alone is all this; and who is 'sinless', beyond good, evil, and so forth.

युञ्जन्नेवं सदाऽऽत्मानं योगी विगतकल्मषः ।
सुखेन ब्रह्मसंस्पर्शमत्यन्तं सुखमश्नुते ॥२८॥

28. Thus integrating himself always, the sinless Yogin easily achieves contact with Brahman or infinite bliss.

28.1. युञ्जन् इति ॥ युञ्जन् एवं यथोक्तेन क्रमेण योगी योगान्तरायवर्जितः सदा सर्वदा आत्मानं विगतकल्मषः विगतपापः, सुखेन अनायासेन ब्रह्मसंस्पर्शं ब्रह्मणा परेण संस्पर्शो यस्य तत् ब्रह्मसंस्पर्शं सुखं अत्यन्तं अन्तमतीत्य वर्तते इति अत्यन्तं उत्कृष्टं निरतिशयं सुखं अश्नुते व्याप्नोति ॥

28.1. Thus integrating the Self, according to the sequence of steps already set forth, the Yogin, rid of all impediments to Yoga, and sinless, easily achieves infinite i.e., elevated and unsurpassed bliss, in which there is contact with supreme Brahman.

29.0. इदानीं योगस्य यत् फलं ब्रह्मैकत्वदर्शनं सर्वसंसारविच्छेदकारणं तत् प्रदर्श्यते —

29.0. Now is elucidated the fruit of Yoga viz., the perception of the unity of Brahman, the cause of the cessation of all empirical life:

सर्वभूतस्थमात्मानं सर्वभूतानि चात्मनि ।
ईक्षते योगयुक्तात्मा सर्वत्र समदर्शनः ॥२९॥

29. With equality of vision everywhere, he whose inner sense has been attuned to Yoga beholds the Self in all beings and all beings in the Self.

29.1. सर्व इति ॥ सर्वभूतस्थं सर्वेषु भूतेषु स्थितं स्वं आत्मानं सर्वभूतानि च आत्मनि ब्रह्मादीनि स्तम्बपर्यन्तानि च सर्वभूतानि आत्मनि एकतां गतानि ईक्षते पश्यति योगयुक्तात्मा समाहितान्तःकरणः सन् सर्वत्र समदर्शनः सर्वेषु ब्रह्मादिस्थावरान्तेषु विषमेषु सर्वभूतेषु समं निर्विशेषं ब्रह्मात्मैकत्वविषयं दर्शनं ज्ञानं यस्य सः सर्वत्र समदर्शनः ॥

29.1. He 'whose inner sense has been attuned to Yoga'—i.e., whose inner sense is concentrated—beholds his Self existing in all beings and 'all beings', from Brahmā down to a blade of grass, 'in the Self', i.e., has become one with the Self; for, he has 'equality of vision everywhere'—which means that all unequal beings from Brahmā down to a blade of grass, are to his vision or knowledge the same or undifferentiated, that vision having as its object the identity of Brahman and Atman.

30.0. एतस्य आत्मैकत्वदर्शनस्य फलं उच्यते–

30.0. The result of this vision of unity of the Self is set forth:

यो मां पश्यति सर्वत्र सर्वं च मयि पश्यति ।
तस्याहं न प्रणश्यामि स च मे न प्रणश्यति ॥३०॥

30. I am not lost to him who beholds Me everywhere and beholds everything in Me; neither is he lost to Me.

30.1. य इति ॥ यः मां पश्यति वासुदेवं सर्वस्य आत्मानं सर्वत्र सर्वेषु भूतेषु सर्वं च ब्रह्मादिभूतजातं मयि सर्वात्मनि पश्यति, तस्य एवं आत्मैकत्वदर्शिनः अहं ईश्वरः न प्रणश्यामि न परोक्षतां गमिष्यामि । स च मे न प्रणश्यति स च विद्वान् मम वासुदेवस्य न प्रणश्यति न परोक्षः भवति, तस्य च मम च आत्मैकत्वात्; स्वात्मा हि नाम आत्मनः प्रकाशः [प्रियः] एव भवति ॥

30.1. To him who beholds Me, Vāsudeva, the Self of all things, 'everywhere', i.e., in all beings, and 'everything' i.e., the multitude of entities from Brahmā downwards, in Me, the Self of all—to him, the perceiver of Self's unity, I, namely God, 'am not lost', or never cease to be immediate; and he, the knower, is not 'lost to Me,' Vāsudeva, i.e., does not cease to be immediate. For, he and I, as Self, are one. And one's Self is always dear to one.

31.0. यस्मात् च अहमेव सर्वात्मैकत्वदर्शी इत्येतत् पूर्वश्लोकार्थं सम्यग्दर्शनं अनूद्य तत्फलं मोक्षः अभिधीयते —

31. Restating the sense of the preceding verse i.e., right perception, in other words, that the perceiver of the unity of the Self of all is Myself, its consequence or liberation is now affirmed:

सर्वभूतस्थितं यो मां भजत्येकत्वमास्थितः ।
सर्वथा वर्तमानोऽपि स योगी मयि वर्तते ॥३१॥

31. Conforming to unity, the Yogin who adores Me, present in all beings, lives in Me, no matter how he appears to live.

31.1. सर्व इति ॥ सर्वथा सर्वप्रकारैः वर्तमानोऽपि सम्यग्दर्शी योगी मयि वैष्णवे परमे पदे वर्तते, नित्यमुक्तः एव सः, न मोक्षं प्रति केनचित् प्रतिबध्यते इत्यर्थः ॥

31.1. Though living in all manner of ways, the Yogin with

the right perception lives in Me, the supreme status of Viṣṇu. He is eternally liberated. Nothing can obstruct his liberation. This is the idea.

32.0. किञ्च अन्यत्—

32.0. Yet another point:

आत्मौपम्येन सर्वत्र समं पश्यति योऽर्जुन ।
सुखं वा यदि वा दुःखं स योगी परमो मतः ॥३२॥

32. Arjuna! He, who sees alike pleasure or pain in all beings, on the analogy of his own self, is deemed the supreme Yogin.

32.1. आत्मौपम्येन इति ॥ आत्मौपम्येन आत्मा स्वयमेव उपमीयते अनया इति उपमा तस्या उपमायाः भावः औपम्यम् तेन आत्मौपम्येन सर्वत्र सर्वभूतेषु समं तुल्यं पश्यति यः अर्जुन । स च किं समं पश्यति इति ? उच्यते—यथा मम सुखं इष्टं तथा सर्वप्राणिनां सुखं अनुकूलम् । वाशब्दः चार्थे । यदि वा यच्च दुःखं मम प्रतिकूलं अनिष्टं यथा, तथा सर्वप्राणिनां दुःखं अनिष्टं प्रतिकूलं इत्येवं आत्मौपम्येन सुखदुःखे अनुकूलप्रतिकूले तुल्यतया सर्वभूतेषु समं पश्यति, न कस्यचित् प्रतिकूलं आचरति, अहिंसक इत्यर्थः । यः एवं अहिंसकः सम्यग्दर्शननिष्ठः स योगी परमः उत्कृष्टः मतः अभिप्रेतः सर्वयोगिनां मध्ये ॥

32.1. 'On the analogy of the self'—one's own self is the analogue. On the basis of this analogy, he 'who sees alike'—in the same manner—in all beings, O Arjuna! Sees what? Answer: 'As I like pleasure, so do all things'. *Or* means *and*. 'As I am averse to pain and shun it, so do all living beings.' He, the real Yogin, does not act against any one, does not injure any one. Thus he who injures none, and adheres to right perception, is deemed supreme among Yogins.

33.0. एतस्य यथोक्तस्य सम्यग्दर्शनलक्षणस्य योगस्य दुःखसंपाद्यतां आलक्ष्य शुश्रूषुः [ध्रुवं] तत्प्राप्त्युपायं अर्जुनः उवाच—

33.0. Noting how hard it is to secure this Yoga of right perception and seeking a sure means of winning it, Arjuna said:

अर्जुन उवाच :

योऽयं योगस्त्वया प्रोक्तः साम्येन मधुसूदन ।
एतस्याहं न पश्यामि चञ्चलत्वात् स्थितिं स्थिराम् ॥३३॥

Arjuna said:

33. O Kṛṣṇa! Of this Yoga, elucidated by You as consisting in sameness, I do not see firm certitude, the mind being fickle.

33.1. योऽयम् इति ॥ यः अयं योगः त्वया प्रोक्तः साम्येन समत्वेन हे मधुसूदन! एतस्य योगस्य अहं न पश्यामि न उपलभे, चञ्चलत्वात् मनसः—किं?—स्थिरां अचलां स्थितिम् ॥

33.1. Of the Yoga set forth by you as consisting in sameness or equality, O Kṛṣṇa! I do not see, i.e. know, a firm certitude, because of mind's fickleness.

34.0. प्रसिद्धं एतत्—

34.0. It is well-known that

चञ्चलं हि मनः कृष्ण प्रमाथि बलवद्दृढम् ।
तस्याहं निग्रहं मन्ये वायोरिव सुदुष्करम् ॥३४॥

34. The mind is indeed fickle, O Kṛṣṇa! a tormentor, powerful and hard. I deem its control as extremely difficult as that of the wind.

34.1. चञ्चलं इति ॥ चञ्चलं हि मनः कृष्ण । 'कृष्ण' इति कृषतेः विलेखनार्थस्य रूपम् । भक्तजनपापादिदोषाकर्षणात् कृष्णः, तस्य संबुद्धिः हे कृष्ण । हि यस्मात् मनः चंचलं न केवलं अत्यर्थं चञ्चलं, प्रमाथि च प्रमथनशीलं, प्रमथ्नाति शरीरं इन्द्रियाणि च विक्षिपत् सत् परवशीकरोति । किंच—बलवत् प्रबलं, न केनचित् नियन्तुं शक्यं, दुर्निवारत्वात् । किञ्च—दृढं तन्तुनागवत् अच्छेद्यम् । तस्य एवंभूतस्य मनसः अहं निग्रहं निरोधं मन्ये वायोः इव यथा वायोः दुष्करः निरोधः ततोऽपि मनसः दुष्करं मन्ये इत्यभिप्रायः ॥

34.1. Kṛṣṇa! The mind is fickle. The word Kṛṣṇa is derived from the root *kṛṣ*, meaning to cut through. Kṛṣṇa is so styled because He cuts off taints, sins etc., of His devotees. Hence He is addressed Kṛṣṇa in the vocative case. Because the mind is fickle, and, in addition, 'a tormentor'—robs one of freedom, tormenting the body and the senses. Besides, it is 'powerful' and by no means is it possible to control it; for, it is irresistible. Also 'hard'—it can't be cut to pieces, being like a *tantunāga* (a kind of shark). The control of this mind I deem to be like that of the wind. The control of the wind is difficult; even more difficult is that of the mind—this is the idea.

35.0. श्रीभगवानुवाच—एवं एतत् यथा ब्रवीषि—

35.0. The blessed Lord said: Yes, it is as you say—

श्रीभगवानुवाच :

असंशयं महाबाहो मनो दुर्निग्रहं चलम् ।
अभ्यासेन तु कौन्तेय वैराग्येण च गृह्यते ॥३५॥

The blessed Lord said:

35. Doubtless, O hero! the mind is difficult to control and fickle. But by means of practice and detachment, son of Kuntī! it may be held in check.

35.1. असंशयं इति ॥ असंशयं नास्ति संशयः हे महाबाहो "मनः दुर्निग्रहं चलं" इत्यत्र । किन्तु—अभ्यासेन तु, अभ्यासः नाम चित्तभूमौ कस्यांचित् समानप्रत्ययावृत्तिः चित्तस्य । वैराग्येण, वैराग्यं नाम दृष्टादृष्टेष्टभोगेषु दोषदर्शनाभ्यासात् वैतृष्ण्यम् । तेन च वैराग्येण गृह्यते विक्षेपरूपः प्रचारः चित्तस्य । एवं तत् मनः गृह्यते निगृह्यते निरुध्यते इत्यर्थः ॥

35.1. There is no doubt, O hero! that the mind is difficult to control and that it is fickle. But by means of practice it can be controlled. 'Practice' means making an unchanging idea to prevail on a given plane of mind. 'By detachment'—detachment means freedom from craving, by driving out the desire for covetable experiences in the spheres of the seen and the unseen, through the practice of discovering flaws implicit in them all. By means of this detachment the distractions of the mind are arrested. Thus is mind 'held' or checked.

36.0. यः पुनः असंयतात्मा, तेन—

36.0. As regards the man without self-control:

**असंयतात्मना योगो दुष्प्राप इति मे मतिः ।
वश्यात्मना तु यतता शक्योऽवाप्तुमुपायतः ॥३६॥**

36. I hold that for the man whose self is uncontrolled, Yoga is hard to achieve. On the contrary, it can be won by him who has disciplined it by employing appropriate means.

36.1. असंयतात्मना इति ॥ असंयतात्मना अभ्यासवैराग्याभ्यां असंयत आत्मा अन्तःकरणं यस्य सः अयं असंयतात्मा तेन असंयतात्मना योगः दुष्प्रापः दुःखेन प्राप्यते इति मे मतिः । यस्तु पुनः वश्यात्मा अभ्यासवैराग्याभ्यां वश्यत्वं आपादितः आत्मा मनः यस्य सः अयं वश्यात्मा तेन वश्यात्मना तु यतता भूयोऽपि प्रयत्नं कुर्वता शक्यः अवाप्तुं योगः उपायतः यथोक्तात् उपायात् ॥

36.1. For the man whose self, i.e. the inner sense, is not controlled through application and detachment, Yoga is 'hard to win'—it is won painfully—this view I hold. On the contrary, for him who has brought the self or mind under control through application and detachment, with 'effort' or repeated exertion, Yoga may be secured, using the means already indicated.

37.0. तत्र योगाभ्यासाङ्गीकरणेन इहलोकपरलोकाप्तिनिमित्तानि कर्माणि संन्यस्तानि, योगसिद्धिफलं च मोक्षसाधनं सम्यग्दर्शनं न प्राप्तं इति, योगी योगमार्गात् मरणकाले चलितचित्तः इति तस्य नाशं आशङ्क्य अर्जुनः उवाच—

37.0. Now, in resorting to the practice of Yoga, man's activities, leading to high positions in this world or the world to come, get renounced; and at the same time right perception that is the fruit of perfected Yoga and the means to liberation is not attained. Therefore, such a Yogin's mind, at the time of death, slips from the path of Yoga, due to which he may be ruined. This fear made Arjuna ask:

अर्जुन उवाच :

अयतिः श्रद्धयोपेतो योगाच्चलितमानसः ।

अप्राप्य योगसंसिद्धिं कां गतिं कृष्ण गच्छति ॥३७॥

Arjuna said:

37. What fate, Kṛṣṇa! is in store for the lax practitioner of Yoga whose mind is rich in faith but who fails to reach perfection in Yoga?

37.1. अयतिः इति ॥ अयतिः अप्रयत्नवान् योगमार्गे श्रद्धया आस्तिक्यबुद्ध्या च उपेतः योगात् अन्तकाले च चलितं मानसं मनः यस्य सः भ्रष्टमानसः भ्रष्टस्मृतिः सः अप्राप्य योगसंसिद्धिं योगफलं सम्यग्दर्शनं कां गतिं हे कृष्ण ! गच्छति ? ॥

37.1. The lax practitioner of Yoga, who does not adequately strive after Yoga, who, yet, is rich in faith i.e., is convinced of Yoga's validity, and whose mind, at the time of death, has 'slipped from Yoga' or whose Yoga-consciousness has deserted him—what is his fate? What goal does he reach, O Kṛṣṇa! having failed to attain perfection in Yoga?

कच्चिन्नोभयविभ्रष्टश्छिन्नाभ्रमिव नश्यति ।

अप्रतिष्ठो महाबाहो विमूढो ब्रह्मणः पथि ॥३८॥

38. Having fallen off from both (Karma and Yoga), confounded and unestablished in the path of Brahman, O hero! does he not perish, like a scattered cloud?

38.1. कच्चित् इति ॥ कच्चित्–किं न उभयविभ्रष्टः कर्ममार्गात् योगमार्गात् च विभ्रष्टः सन् छिन्नाभ्रम् इव नश्यति, किंवा न नश्यति अप्रतिष्ठः निराश्रयः हे महाबाहो ! विमूढः सन् ब्रह्मणः पथि ब्रह्मप्राप्तिमार्गे ॥

38.1. 'Fallen off from both' i.e., the way of works and that of Yoga. Like a scattered cloud, does he not perish 'unestablished' or lacking a firm hold, O hero! and confounded in the 'path of Brahman'—the path leading to the attainment of Brahman.

एतन्मे संशयं कृष्ण छेत्तुमर्हस्यशेषतः ।
त्वदन्यः संशयस्यास्य छेत्ता न ह्युपपद्यते ॥३९॥

39. O Kṛṣṇa! You ought to dispel this doubt of mine in its entirety. None but You can possibly dispel this doubt.

39.1. एतत् इति ॥ एतत् मे मम संशयं कृष्ण ! छेत्तुं अपनेतुं अर्हसि अशेषतः । त्वदन्यः त्वत्तः अन्यः ऋषिः देवः वा छेत्ता नाशयिता संशयस्य अस्य न हि यस्मात् उपपद्यते न संभवति । अतः त्वमेव छेत्तुं अर्हसि इत्यर्थः ॥

39.1. This doubt of mine, O Kṛṣṇa! You ought to dispel, i.e. remove in its entirety, because, other than You, neither seer nor celestial may prove to be its dispeller. Therefore, You alone should dispel it—this is the idea.

श्रीभगवानुवाच :

पार्थ नैवेह नामुत्र विनाशस्तस्य विद्यते ।
न हि कल्याणकृत्कश्चिद्दुर्गतिं तात गच्छति ॥४०॥

The blessed Lord said:
40. Arjuna! neither in this world nor in the world to be does he come to ruin; for no evil betides the doer of good, My son!

40.1 पार्थ इति ॥ हे पार्थ ! न एव इह लोके न अमुत्र परस्मिन् वा लोके विनाशः तस्य विद्यते नास्ति । नाशो नाम पूर्वस्मात् हीनजन्मप्राप्तिः । स तस्य योगभ्रष्टस्य नास्ति । न हि यस्मात् कल्याणकृत् शुभकृत् कश्चित् दुर्गतिं कुत्सितां गतिं —हे तात ! तनोति आत्मानं पुत्ररूपेण इति पिता तातः उच्यते, पिता एव पुत्रः इति पुत्रोऽपि तातः उच्यते; शिष्योऽपि पुत्रवत् इति अपुत्रोऽपि तातः उच्यते — यतो न गच्छति ॥

40.1. O Arjuna! Neither indeed in this world nor in the next does ruin await him. 'Ruin' means the occurrence of a birth inferior to his previous one, because no doer of good comes to a deplorable course of life, My son! The term *tāta* means 'father', as the latter manifests himself in the form of the son. Thus the father is the son and the latter is called *tāta*. A disciple is like a son; so literally though not a son, he too is called 'father'.

41.0. किं तु अस्य भवति ?

41.0. What happens, then, to him?

प्राप्य पुण्यकृतां लोकान् उषित्वा शाश्वतीः समाः ।
शुचीनां श्रीमतां गेहे योगभ्रष्टोऽभिजायते ॥४१॥

41. Reaching the spheres of the meritorious, and after sojourning there long-lasting years, the one who has slipped from Yoga is born in a home of pure and prosperous householders.

41.1. प्राप्य इति ॥ योगमार्गे प्रवृत्तः संन्यासी—सामर्थ्यात्—प्राप्य गत्वा पुण्यकृतां अश्वमेधादियाजिनां लोकान् तत्र च उषित्वा वासं अनुभूय शाश्वतीः नित्याः समाः संवत्सरान् तद्भोगक्षये शुचीनां यथोक्तकारिणां श्रीमतां विभूतिमतां गेहे गृहे योगभ्रष्टः अभिजायते ॥

41.1. The renouncer, striving on the path of Yoga, due to his competence reaches the spheres of the meritorious performers of horse-sacrifice, etc. Having lived there long-lasting years, at the end of such experiences, he is born—the man who has slipped from Yoga is thus born—in a home of householders who conform to Vedic ordinances and who are rich in resources.

अथवा योगिनामेव कुले भवति धीमताम् ।
एतद्धि दुर्लभतरं लोके जन्म यदीदृशम् ॥४२॥

42. Or, he is born in a family of wise Yogins. This sort of birth, however, is far rarer in the world.

42.1. अथ इति ॥ अथवा श्रीमतां कुलात् अन्यस्मिन् योगिनाम् एव दरिद्राणां कुले भवति जायते धीमतां बुद्धिमताम् । एतत् हि जन्म, यत् दरिद्राणां योगिनां कुले, दुर्लभतरं दुःखलभ्यतरं पूर्वम् अपेक्ष्य लोके जन्म यत् ईदृशं यथोक्तविशेषणे कुले ॥

42.1. Or he is born in a family of indigent Yogins, 'wise' i.e. intelligent, as distinct from the home of the prosperous. Indeed this kind of birth in a home of poor Yogins is more difficult to gain in this world compared to what was mentioned earlier.

43.0. यस्मात् च—

43.0. Also because,

तत्र तं बुद्धिसंयोगं लभते पौर्वदेहिकम् ।
यतते च ततो भूयः संसिद्धौ कुरुनन्दन ॥४३॥

43. There he acquires memory of the ideas relating to his previous body, and he labours harder, O Bhārata prince! to achieve perfection.

43.1. तत्र इति ॥ तत्र योगिनां कुले तं बुद्धिसंयोगं बुद्ध्या संयोगं लभते पौर्वदेहिकम् पूर्वस्मिन् देहे भवं पौर्वदेहिकम् । यतते च प्रयत्नं करोति च ततः तस्मात् पूर्वकृतात् संस्कारात् भूयः बहुतरं संसिद्धौ संसिद्धिनिमित्तं हे कुरुनन्दन ! ॥

43.1. In the family of Yogins he acquires memory of ideas cultivated in his previous body. And he strives harder, due to his earlier impressions, for winning perfection, O Arjuna!

44.0. कथं पूर्वदेहबुद्धिसंयोगः इति ? तत् उच्यते—

44.0. How does the memory of ideas in his earlier body come to the Yogin? Answer:

पूर्वाभ्यासेन तेनैव ह्रियते ह्यवशोऽपि सः ।
जिज्ञासुरपि योगस्य शब्दब्रह्मातिवर्तते ॥४४॥

44. Though not a master of himself, he is attracted by his prior discipline. Even he who desires to know about Yoga goes beyond the sphere of Vedic injunctions.

44.1. पूर्वाभ्यासेन इति ॥ यः पूर्वजन्मनि कृतः अभ्यासः सः पूर्वाभ्यासः, तेन एव बलवता ह्रियते संसिद्धौ हि यस्मात् अवशः अपि सः योगभ्रष्टः; तेन कृतं चेत् योगाभ्यासजात् संस्कारात् बलवत्तरं धर्मादिलक्षणं कर्म, तदा योगाभ्यास-जनितेन संस्कारेण आह्रियते; अधर्मः चेत् बलवत्तरः कृतः, तेन योगजोऽपि संस्कारः अभिभूयते एव, तत्क्षये तु योगजः संस्कारः स्वयमेव कार्यं आरभते, न दीर्घ-कालस्थस्यापि विनाशः तस्य अस्ति इत्यर्थः । अतः जिज्ञासुः अपि योगस्य स्वरूपं ज्ञातुं इच्छन् अपि योगमार्गे प्रवृत्तः—संन्यासी योगभ्रष्टः, सामर्थ्यात्—सोऽपि शब्दब्रह्म वेदोक्तकर्मानुष्ठानफलं अतिवर्तते अतिक्रामति—अपाकरिष्यति किमुत बुद्ध्वा य यागं तन्निष्ठः अभ्यासं कुर्यात् ॥

44.1. Because of the potent Yogic discipline of his previous life, one who has slipped from Yoga is drawn towards perfection, though he is not wholly free. If he has performed righteous works, he is attracted by their impressions in his mind; if unrighteous works have been performed, indeed they will subdue his impressions of Yoga practice. When the more potent impressions weaken, the Yogic impressions assert themselves in the results they produce. The Yogic impressions do not perish even when held up for a long period—this is the idea. Therefore even he who seeks to comprehend the essence of Yoga and begins to tread the path of Yoga—i.e., the world-renouncing Yogin who has slipped, as logic implies in this context—goes beyond the sphere of the fruits of Vedic works; i.e., he sets them aside. What then to speak of one who fully understands Yoga and is devoted to its practice?

45.0. कुतश्च योगित्वं श्रेयः इति ? —

45.0. An additional reason for Yoga's superiority:

प्रयत्नाद्यतमानस्तु योगी संशुद्धकिल्बिषः ।
अनेकजन्मसंसिद्धस्ततो याति परां गतिम् ॥४५॥

45. The Yogin who strives hard and who has been perfected in the course of many lives attains the supreme goal, all his sins having been washed away.

45.1. प्रयत्नात् इति ॥ प्रयत्नात् यतमानः, अधिकतरं यतमानः इत्यर्थः । तत्र योगी विद्वान् संशुद्धकिल्बिषः विशुद्धकिल्बिषः संशुद्धपापः अनेकजन्मसंसिद्धः अनेकेषु जन्मसु किञ्चित्किञ्चित् संस्कारजातं उपचित्य तेन उपचितेन अनेकजन्मकृतेन संसिद्धः अनेकजन्मसंसिद्धः ततः लब्धसम्यग्दर्शनः सन् याति परां प्रकृष्टां गतिम् ॥

45. 'Who strives hard' i.e., who labours much. The Yogin is the knower whose sins have been washed away and who has perfected himself through the accumulation of good impressions in small measures in many lives. He has attained perfection by virtue of all these accumulated impressions that lead to right perception. Thus he achieves the supreme goal.

46.0. यस्मात् एवं तस्मात्—

46.0. Such being the case,

तपस्विभ्योऽधिको योगी ज्ञानिभ्योऽपि मतोऽधिकः ।
कर्मिभ्यश्चाधिको योगी तस्माद्योगी भवार्जुन ॥४६॥

46. The Yogin is superior to the performers of austerities; he is deemed superior even to the knower of the Vedas; he excels those who do works. Therefore, O Arjuna! be a Yogin.

46.1. तपस्विभ्यः इति ॥ तपस्विभ्यः अधिकः योगी, ज्ञानिभ्योऽपि, ज्ञानं अत्र शास्त्रार्थपाण्डित्यं, तद्वद्भ्योऽपि मतः ज्ञातः अधिकः श्रेष्ठः इति । कर्मिभ्यः, अग्निहोत्रादि कर्म, तद्वद्भ्यः अधिकः योगी विशिष्टः । यस्मात् तस्मात् योगी भव अर्जुन ॥

46.1. The Yogin is superior to the performers of austerities and even to knowers. By knowledge here is meant mastery of the *śāstras*. The Yogin is held to be superior even to those who have such mastery. The works are the Vedic rites like the fire-sacrifice. The Yogin excels those who do those works. Therefore, be a Yogin, O Arjuna!

योगिनामपि सर्वेषां मद्गतेनांतरात्मना ।
श्रद्धावान् भजते यो मां स मे युक्ततमो मतः ॥४७॥

47. Among even these Yogins, he who, full of faith, worships Me, his inner self, absorbed in Me,—him I deem the most integrated.

इति श्रीमहाभारते शतसाहस्र्यां संहितायां वैयासिक्यां भीष्म-
पर्वणि श्रीमद्भगवद्गीतासूपनिषत्सु ब्रह्मविद्यायां योगशास्त्रे
श्रीकृष्णार्जुनसंवादे ध्यानयोगो नाम षष्ठोऽध्यायः ॥६॥

47.1. योगिनाम् इति ॥ योगिनाम् अपि सर्वेषां रुद्रादित्यादिध्यानपराणां मध्ये मद्गतेन मयि वासुदेवे समाहितेन अन्तरात्मना अन्तःकरणेन श्रद्धावान् श्रद्दधानः सन् भजते सेवते यः मां, स मे मम युक्ततमः अतिशयेन युक्तः मतः अभिप्रेतः इति ॥

47.1. Among all the Yogins who meditate on Rudras, Adityas etc., he who 'worships Me'—serves Me with his inner self or whose inner self is absorbed in Me, Vāsudeva, and who is full of faith i.e., who is a believer—is considered by Me the foremost or the best of the integrated.

इति श्रीमत्परमहंसपरिव्राजकाचार्यगोविन्दभगवत्पूज्यपादशिष्य-
श्रीमच्छंकरभगवतः कृतौ श्रीमद्भगवद्गीताभाष्ये ध्यानयोगो [अभ्यासयोगो]
नाम षष्ठोऽध्यायः ॥६॥

सप्तमोऽध्यायः

CHAPTER VII

THE YOGA OF KNOWLEDGE AND REALIZATION

0.1. 'योगिनामपि सर्वेषां मद्गतेनान्तरात्मना । श्रद्धावान् भजते यो मां स मे युक्ततमो मतः [६.४७.] इति प्रश्नबीजं उपन्यस्य स्वयमेव "ईदृशं मदीयं तत्त्वं, एवं मद्गतान्तरात्मा स्यात्" इत्येतत् विवक्षुः श्रीभगवान् उवाच—

0.1. Having given room for a question in BG VI.47 and desiring to state such and such is the truth concerning Him, the blessed Lord spoke:

श्रीभगवानुवाच :

मय्यासक्तमनाः पार्थ योगं युञ्जन्मदाश्रयः ।
असंशयं समग्रं मां यथा ज्ञास्यसि तच्छृणु ॥१॥

The blessed Lord said:

1. With mind set on Me and dependent on Me and performing Yoga, O Arjuna! hear how you will know Me wholly without any doubt whatsoever.

1.1. मय्यासक्तमना इति ॥ मयि वक्ष्यमाणविशेषणे परमेश्वरे आसक्तं मनो यस्य स मय्यासक्तमनाः, हे पार्थ ! योगं युञ्जन् मनःसमाधानं कुर्वन् मदाश्रयः अहमेव परमेश्वरः आश्रयः यस्य स मदाश्रयः । यो हि कश्चित् पुरुषार्थेन केनचित् अर्थी भवति स तत्साधनं कर्म अग्निहोत्रादि तपः दानं वा किंचित् आश्रयं प्रतिपद्यते; अयं तु योगी मामेव आश्रयं प्रतिपद्यते, हित्वा अन्यत् साधनान्तरं मय्येव आसक्तमनाः भवति । यः त्वं एवंभूतः सन् असंशयं समग्रं समस्तविभूतिबलशक्त्यैश्वर्यादिगुणसंपन्नं मां यथा येन प्रकारेण ज्ञास्यसि संशयमन्तरेण "एवमेव भगवान्" इति, तत् शृणु उच्यमानं मया ॥

1.1. With the mind set firmly on Me, the Supreme Lord (who will be described later), O Arjuna! and achieving its stability through exclusive dependence on Me, hear (what I say). Whoever seeks to achieve a human goal resorts to a means to reach that goal such as the fire-sacrifice, austerity, gift-giving etc., but the Yogi here resorts exclusively to Me as his refuge. Giving up all other means he fastens his mind on Me alone. Doing thus, hear, as I state, how indubitably you will know Me 'wholly' i.e. together with My glory, power, energy, lordliness and so forth. This knowledge is a conviction that the Lord is such and such.

2.0. तच्च मद्विषयम्—

2.0. That knowledge in respect of the Lord is described:

ज्ञानं तेऽहं सविज्ञानमिदं वक्ष्याम्यशेषतः ।
यज्ज्ञात्वा नेह भूयोऽन्यज्ज्ञातव्यमवशिष्यते ॥२॥

2. Exhaustively I shall set forth that knowledge together with its realization; once it is grasped, nothing more will remain to be known.

2.1. ज्ञान इति ॥ ज्ञानं ते तुभ्यं अहं सविज्ञानं विज्ञानसहितं स्वानुभवयुक्तं इदं वक्ष्यामि कथयिष्यामि अशेषतः कात्स्न्र्येन । तत् ज्ञानं विवक्षितं स्तौति श्रोतुः अभिमुखीकरणाय—यत् ज्ञात्वा यत् ज्ञानं ज्ञात्वा न इह भूयः पुनः अन्यत् ज्ञातव्यं पुरुषार्थसाधनं अवशिष्यते न अवशिष्टं भवति—इति मत्तत्त्वज्ञो यः, स सर्वज्ञो भवतीत्यर्थः । अतो विशिष्टफलत्वात् दुर्लभतरं ज्ञानम् ॥

2.1. That knowledge together with its experience I shall set forth in its entirety. In order to secure the attention of the listener, the Lord extols that knowledge. Once it is grasped, nothing else will remain here to be known as means to any human goal. The idea is that one who knows the truth about the Lord becomes omniscient. Yielding excellent fruit, this knowledge is extremely rare.

3.0. कथं इति ? उच्यते—

3.0. How so? Listen:

मनुष्याणां सहस्रेषु कश्चिद्यतति सिद्धये ।
यततामपि सिद्धानां कश्चिन्मां वेत्ति तत्त्वतः ॥३॥

3. Just one man among thousands strives to win it; among those who know and strive, only one comes to know Me in truth.

3.1. मनुष्याणां इति । मनुष्याणां मध्ये सहस्रेषु अनेकेषु कश्चित् यतति प्रयत्नं करोति सिद्धये सिद्ध्यर्थम् । तेषां यतताम् अपि सिद्धानां — सिद्धाः एव हि ते ये मोक्षाय यतन्ते, तेषां—कश्चित् एव हि मां वेत्ति तत्त्वतः यथावत् ॥

3.1. Among men, one in many thousands strives to win (the saving knowledge). Even among those who know and strive—all those who strive for release are knowers—only one rare soul indeed comes to know Me, in truth.

4.0. श्रोतारं प्ररोचनेन अभिमुखीकृत्याह—

4.0. Securing the listener's attention by exciting his interest, the Lord says:

भूमिरापोऽनलो वायुः खं मनो बुद्धिरेव च ।
अहंकार इतीयं मे भिन्ना प्रकृतिरष्टधा ॥४॥

4. The earth, water, fire, air, space, mind, intellect and the ego-sense constitute My distinctive eight-fold nature.

4.1. भूमिः इति ॥ 'भूमिः' इति पृथिवीतन्मात्रं उच्यते, न स्थूला, 'भिन्ना प्रकृतिरष्टधा' इति वचनात् । तथा अबादयोऽपि तन्मात्राण्येव उच्यन्ते—आपः, अनलः, वायुः, खम् । 'मनः' इति मनसः कारणं अहंकारो गृह्यते । 'बुद्धिः' इति अहंकारकारणं महत्तत्त्वम् । अहंकारः इति अविद्यासंयुक्तं अव्यक्तम् ! यथा विषसंयुक्तं अन्नं विषम् इति उच्यते, एवं अहंकारवासनावत् अव्यक्तं मूलकारणं अहंकारः

इत्युच्यते, प्रवर्तकत्वात् अहंकारस्य । अहंकारः एव हि सर्वस्य प्रवृत्तिबीजं दृष्टं लोके । इतीयं यथोक्ता प्रकृतिः मे मम ऐश्वरी मायाशक्तिः अष्टधा भिन्ना भेदं आगता ॥

4.1. The earth refers to the rudimentary earth-element, and not to the gross earth, for the phrase that follows is 'the distinctive eight-fold nature'. Similarly water, etc., also refer to the rudimentary elements of water, fire, air and space. 'Mind' refers to the cause of the mind, viz., the ego-sense. 'Intellect' refers to the cause of the 'ego-sense', the *mahat* (of the Sāṁkhya philosophy). The 'ego-sense' in the verse is the unmanifest-cum-nescience. The latter is so styled even as food mixed with poison may be called poison. The root-cause, the Unmanifest, impelled by the impressions of the ego-sense, is styled the ego-sense since the ego-sense is what causes activity. In this world, the seed of activity everywhere is observed to be the ego-sense. This nature of Mine, thus described, is the divine power of God and it is eight-fold.

अपरेयमितस्त्वन्यां प्रकृतिं विद्धि मे पराम् ।
जीवभूतां महाबाहो ययेदं धार्यते जगत् ॥५॥

5. This is the lower nature; but My higher nature, know to be other than it. That constitutes, mighty armed! the living being by which this world is upheld.

5.1. अपरा इति ॥ अपरा न परा निकृष्टा अशुद्धा अनर्थकरी संसारबन्धनात्मिका इयम् । इतः अस्याः यथोक्तायाः तु अन्यां विशुद्धां प्रकृतिं मम आत्मभूतां विद्धि मे परां प्रकृष्टां जीवभूतां क्षेत्रज्ञलक्षणां प्राणधारणनिमित्तभूतां हे महाबाहो, यया प्रकृत्या इदं धार्यते जगत् अन्तःप्रविष्टया ॥

5.1. 'The lower'—inferior, impure, troublesome, whose essence is bondage. But other than it—pure—is My essential nature, the higher living being, the field-knower, the cause leading to the assumption of vital force, O hero! This world is penetrated and upheld by it.

एतद्योनीनि भूतानि सर्वाणीत्युपधारय ॥
अहं कृत्स्नस्य जगतः प्रभवः प्रलयस्तथा ॥६॥

6. Know all beings to be born of this My dual nature. I am the source of the entire world as well as that into which it is dissolved.

6.1. एतत् इति ॥ एतद्योनीनि एते परापरे क्षेत्रक्षेत्रज्ञलक्षणे प्रकृती योनिः येषां भूतानां तानि एतद्योनीनि भूतानि सर्वाणि इति एवं उपधारय जानीहि । यस्मात् मम प्रकृती योनिः कारणं सर्वभूतानां, अतः अहं कृत्स्नस्य समस्तस्य जगतः प्रभवः उत्पत्तिः, प्रलयः विनाशः तथा । प्रकृतिद्वयद्वारेण अहं सर्वज्ञः ईश्वरः जगतः कारणं इत्यर्थः ॥

यस्मात् एवं तस्मात् —

6.1. These two, the lower and the higher (natures), constituting the field and the field knower, are the womb of all beings. Do know this. Such being the case, the birth and dissolution of the entire world are due to Me. I, the omniscient Lord, am the world-cause through the medium of My two natures. Hence,

मत्तः परतरं नान्यत् किंचिदस्ति धनंजय ।
मयि सर्वमिदं प्रोतं सूत्रे मणिगणा इव ॥७॥

7. Nothing whatsoever is beyond Me. All this is strung on Me like clusters of gems on a thread.

7.1. मत्तः इति ॥ मत्तः परमेश्वरात् परतरं अन्यत् कारणान्तरं किञ्चित् न अस्ति न विद्यते, अहमेव जगत्कारणं इत्यर्थः, हे धनंजय । यस्मात् एवं तस्मात् मयि परमेश्वरे सर्वाणि भूतानि सर्वं इदं जगत् प्रोतं अनुस्यूतं अनुगतं (अनुविद्धं) ग्रथितं इत्यर्थः, दीर्घतन्तुषु पटवत्, सूत्रे च मणिगणाः इव ॥७॥

7.1. Beyond Me, the supreme Lord, there is no causal stuff. The sense is: I alone am the world-cause, O Arjuna. Such being the case, on Me the Supreme Lord, all beings, this entire world is strung—woven or held together—as a cloth on the warp or clusters of gems on a thread.

8.0. केन केन धर्मेण विशिष्टे त्वयि सर्वमिदं प्रोतं इत्युच्यते ? —

8.0. On You, distinguished by what all traits, is this entire world woven? Answer:

रसोऽहमप्सु कौन्तेय प्रभाऽस्मि शशिसूर्ययोः ।
प्रणवः सर्ववेदेषु शब्दः खे पौरुषं नृषु ॥८॥

8. I am the essence of water, O Arjuna! as also the light of the moon and the sun. (I am) the sacred syllable AUM in all the Vedas, the sound inherent in space, and the manhood in men.

8.1. रसः इति ॥ रसः अहं, अपां यः सारः सः रसः; तस्मिन् रसभूते मयि आपः प्रोताः इत्यर्थः । एवं सर्वत्र । यथा अहं अप्सु रसः, एवं प्रभा अस्मि शशिसूर्ययोः । प्रणवः ओङ्कारः सर्ववेदेषु, तस्मिन् प्रणवभूते मयि सर्वे वेदाः प्रोताः । तथा खे आकाशे शब्दः सारभूतः, तस्मिन् मयि खं प्रोतम् । तथा पौरुषं पुरुषस्य भावः पौरुषं—यतः पुंबुद्धिः—नृषु तस्मिन् मयि पुरुषाः प्रोताः ॥

8.1. The essence of water is its flavour—that I am. On Me, the essence, are the waters woven. This is the idea. The following statements also may be thus understood. Just as I am its essence in water, so I am the light of the moon and the sun. In all the Vedas I am the sacred syllable AUM. Across Me, the AUM, are all the Vedas woven. So in space its essence is sound, and across Me, as such, is the space woven. Similarly across man's being or manhood, due to which rises the idea that one is a man, are men woven.

पुण्यो गन्धः पृथिव्यां च तेजश्चास्मि विभावसौ ।
जीवनं सर्वभूतेषु तपश्चास्मि तपस्विषु ॥९॥

9. I am pure odour in the earth; splendour in the fire; life in all beings; and austerity in ascetics.

9.1. पुण्यः इति ॥ पुण्यः सुरभिः गन्धः पृथिव्यां च अहम्, तस्मिन् मयि गन्धभूते पृथिवी प्रोता । पुण्यत्वं गन्धस्य स्वभावतः एव पृथिव्यां दर्शितं अबादिषु रसादेः पुण्यत्वोपलक्षणार्थम् । अपुण्यत्वं तु गन्धादीनां अविद्याधर्माद्यपेक्षं संसारिणां भूतविशेषसंसर्गनिमित्तं भवति । तेजः दीप्तिः च अस्मि विभावसौ अग्नौ । तथा जीवनं सर्वभूतेषु, येन जीवन्ति सर्वाणि भूतानि तत् जीवनम् । तपः च अस्मि तपस्विषु, तस्मिन् तपसि मयि तपस्विनः प्रोताः ॥

9.1. 'Pure odour in the earth'—that I am. Across Me as that odour is the earth woven. As a matter of course, in the earth the purity of the odour has been pointed out in order to stress the purity of essence etc., in water and so forth. The impurity of odour etc., is contingent on nescience, demerit etc., of the transmigrating *Jīvas* and caused by contact with particular elements. 'Splendour' means the luminosity in the fire; 'life in all beings' is that by which they all are alive. Also I am the austerity in the ascetics—across Me, as such, are the ascetics 'woven'.

बीजं मां सर्वभूतानां विद्धि पार्थ सनातनम् ।
बुद्धिर्बुद्धिमतामस्मि तेजस्तेजस्विनामहम् ॥१०॥

10. Know Me, Arjuna! to be the eternal seed-power in all beings; of intellectual beings I am the intellect; of those who are splendorous, I am the splendour.

10.1. बीजं इति ॥ बीजं प्ररोहकारणं मां विद्धि सर्वभूतानां हे पार्थ सनातनं चिरन्तनम् । किञ्च—बुद्धिः विवेकशक्तिः अन्तःकरणस्य बुद्धिमतां विवेकशक्तिमतां अस्मि, तेजः प्रागल्भ्यं तद्वतां तेजस्विनां अहम् ॥

10.1. Know Me to be 'the eternal seed-power', the cause of germination, of all beings, O Arjuna! Moreover, I am also the intellect—mind's power of discrimination in respect of those who discriminate. I am 'the splendour', the power, of those who are endowed with it.

बलं बलवतामस्मि कामरागविवर्जितम् ।
धर्माविरुद्धो भूतेषु कामोऽस्मि भरतर्षभ ॥११॥

11. Also of the mighty I am the might, devoid of appetite and attachment. Foremost Bhārata prince! in beings I am appetite not opposed to righteousness.'

11.1. बलं इति । बलं सामर्थ्यं ओजः बलवतां अहं, तत् च बलं कामरागविवर्जितं, कामश्च रागश्च कामरागौ—कामः तृष्णा असन्निकृष्टेषु विषयेषु, रागः रञ्जना प्राप्तेषु विषयेषु—ताभ्यां कामरागाभ्यां विवर्जितं देहादिधारणमात्रार्थं बलं सत्त्वं अहं अस्मि; न तु यत् संसारिणां तृष्णारागकारणम् । किञ्च—धर्माविरुद्धः धर्मेण शास्त्रार्थेन अविरुद्धः यः प्राणिषु भूतेषु कामः, यथा देहधारणमात्राद्यर्थः अशनपानादिविषयः, सः कामः अस्मि हे भरतर्षभ ! ॥
किञ्च —

11.1. I am 'the might'—the force, the energy—of the mighty; that might is devoid of appetite and attachment. Appetite is the craving for objects that are not presented, and attachment is the pleasure felt once the objects become available. Devoid of both these is the might that I am, and not that which generates craving and pleasure in the *Jīvas*. It just suffices to sustain the body. Moreover, the appetite of living beings that is sufficient to sustain the body, and directed to eating and drinking, and that is unopposed to righteousness i.e., to the content of the '*sāstras*'—that appetite I am, O foremost Bhārata prince!

ये चैव सात्त्विका भावा राजसास्तामसाश्च ये ।
मत्त एवेति तान् विद्धि न त्वहं तेषु ते मयि ॥१२॥

12. Whatever things are sāttvic, rājasic and tāmasic,

know these to proceed from Me alone; I am not in them; they are in Me.

12.1. ये इति ॥ ये च एव सात्त्विकाः सत्त्वनिर्वृत्ताः भावाः पदार्थाः, राजसाः रजोनिर्वृत्ताः, तामसाः तमोनिर्वृत्ताश्च, ये केचित् प्राणिनां स्वकर्मवशात् जायन्ते भावाः तान् मत्तः एव जायमानान् इति एवं विद्धि सर्वान् समस्तान् एव । यद्यपि ते मत्तः जायन्ते तथापि न तु अहं तेषु तदधीनः तद्वशः, यथा संसारिणः । ते पुनः मयि मद्वशाः मदधीनाः ॥

12.1. Whatever objects are constituted by *sattva*, *rajas*, and *tamas*, (Vide ch.14) and generated by the Kārmic forces of living beings—know them all to be born of Me alone. Though they are born of Me, nevertheless, I am not in them—i.e., I am not subject to them as the transmigrating *Jivas* are. On the contrary, they are subject to Me.

13.0. एवंभूतमपि परमेश्वरं नित्यशुद्धबुद्धमुक्तस्वभावं सर्वभूतात्मानं निर्गुणं संसार-दोषबीजप्रदाहकारणं मां नाभिजानाति जगत् इति अनुक्रोशं दर्शयति भगवान् । तच्च किन्निमित्तं जगतः अज्ञानमिति ?
उच्यते—

13.0. The Lord evinces His pity for the world that fails to know Him intimately, the supreme Lord above described, whose nature is eternally pure, enlightened, and free, who is the Self of all beings, beyond all attributes and who burns up the seeds of evil in transmigratory life. And what is the cause of the world's nescience? Answer.

त्रिभिर्गुणमयैर्भावैरेभिः सर्वमिदं जगत् ।
मोहितं नाभिजानाति मामेभ्यः परमव्ययम् ॥१३॥

13. Due to these three (kinds of) objects, consisting of (Prakṛti's) constituents, this whole world is deluded; it fails to cognise Me, the immutable (Reality) beyond them.

13.1. त्रिभिः इति ॥ त्रिभिः गुणमयैः गुणविकारैः रागद्वेषमोहादिप्रकारैः भावैः पदार्थैः एभिः यथोक्तैः सर्वं इदं प्राणिजातं जगत् मोहितं अविवेकितां आपादितं सत् न अभिजानाति मां एभ्यः यथोक्तेभ्यः गुणेभ्यः परं व्यतिरिक्तं विलक्षणं च अव्ययं व्ययरहितं जन्मादिसर्वभावविकारवर्जितं इत्यर्थः ॥

13.1. Due to the transformation of these constituents as attachment, aversion, delusion and so forth, this entire world of living beings is 'deluded'—deprived of the power to discriminate—and so fails to cognise Me as beyond and as other than the constituents. I am immutable—devoid of states like birth that mark all contingent beings.

14.0. कथं पुनः दैवीं एतां त्रिगुणात्मिकां वैष्णवीं मायां अतिक्रामन्ति इति? उच्यते—

14.0. Now, how do people go beyond this divine all-pervasive power of delusion consisting of the three constituents? Answer:

दैवी ह्येषा गुणमयी मम माया दुरत्यया ।
मामेव ये प्रपद्यन्ते मायामेतां तरन्ति ते ॥१४॥

14. Indeed this divine delusive power of Mine is hard to cross over. Those who surrender themselves exclusively to Me pass beyond this Māyā.

14.1. दैवी इति ॥ दैवी देवस्य मम ईश्वरस्य विष्णोः स्वभावभूता हि यस्मात् एषा यथोक्ता गुणमयी मम माया दुरत्यया दुःखेन अत्ययः अतिक्रमणं यस्याः सा दुरत्यया । तत्र एवं सति सर्वधर्मान् परित्यज्य मां एव मायाविनं स्वात्मभूतं सर्वात्मना ये प्रपद्यन्ते ते मायां एतां सर्वभूतमोहिनीं तरन्ति अतिक्रामन्ति; ते संसारबंधनात् मुच्यन्ते इत्यर्थः ॥

14.1. 'Divine'—pertaining to Me, Lord Viṣṇu, being My very nature. As such, this Māyā of Mine consisting of the constituents is hard to cross over. In these circumstances, those who, renouncing all conventional norms of life, wholeheartedly surrender themselves to Me, the wielder of Māyā, and their very Self, pass beyond this all-deluding power. The idea is that they are liberated from the bondage of transmigratory life.

15.0. यदि त्वां प्रपन्नाः मायां एतां तरन्ति, कस्मात् त्वाम् एव सर्वे न प्रपद्यन्ते इति ? उच्यते—

15.0. If those who surrender themselves to You pass beyond this Māyā, why don't all surrender to You? Answer.

न मां दुष्कृतिनो मूढाः प्रपद्यन्ते नराधमाः ।
माययाऽपहृतज्ञाना आसुरं भावमाश्रिताः ॥१५॥

15. Base, deluded, evil-doers do not surrender to Me; due to Māyā, they have been robbed of knowledge and they assume a demoniac attitude.

15.1. न मां इति ॥ न मां परमेश्वरं नारायणं दुष्कृतिनः पापकारिणः मूढाः प्रपद्यन्ते नराधमाः नराणां मध्ये अधमाः निकृष्टाः ते च मायया अपहृतज्ञानाः संमुषितज्ञानाः आसुरं भावं हिंसानृतादिलक्षणं आश्रिताः ॥

15.1. To Me, the Supreme Lord Nārāyaṇa, 'the evil doers—the sinners, the deluded—don't surrender. They are 'base' or the lowest among men. 'Of knowledge' they are deprived due to Māyā. So they assume or resort to the attitude of demons marked by violence, falsehood etc.

16.0. ये पुनः नरोत्तमाः पुण्यकर्माणः—

16.0. On the contrary the best among men are those who do good.

चतुर्विधा भजन्ते मां जनाः सुकृतिनोऽर्जुन ।
आर्तो जिज्ञासुरर्थार्थी ज्ञानी च भरतर्षभ ॥१६॥

16. Arjuna! Men of righteous acts are four-fold. They resort to Me, O best of Bhāratas! They are the afflicted, the knowledge-seeker, wealth-seeker and the knower.

16.1. चतुर्विधा इति ॥ चतुर्विधाः चतुःप्रकाराः भजन्ते सेवन्ते मां जनाः सुकृतिनः पुण्यकर्माणः हे अर्जुन । आर्तः आर्तिपरिगृहीतः तस्करव्याघ्ररोगादिना अभिभूतः आपन्नः । जिज्ञासुः भगवत्तत्त्वं ज्ञातुं इच्छति यः । अर्थार्थी धनकामः । ज्ञानी विष्णोः तत्त्ववित्, च हे भरतर्षभ ॥

16.1. Of four kinds are the men who 'resort to'—serve—Me. Their acts are righteous or meritorious, O Arjuna! 'The afflicted' are those in the grip of suffering, being threatened by robbers, tigers, snakes etc. 'The knowledge-seeker' is he who desires to know the truth of the Lord. The wealth-seeker desires wealth. 'The knower' is he who knows the truth of Viṣṇu, O best of Bhāratas!

तेषां ज्ञानी नित्ययुक्त एकभक्तिर्विशिष्यते ।
प्रियो हि ज्ञानिनोऽत्यर्थमहं स च मम प्रियः ॥१७॥

17. Of them all, the knower, ever integrated and exclusively devoted, excels; for I am exceedingly dear to the knower and he is dear to Me.

17.1. तेषां इति ॥ तेषां चतुर्णां मध्ये ज्ञानी तत्त्ववित् तत्त्ववित्त्वात् नित्ययुक्तः भवति एकभक्तिश्च, अन्यस्य भजनीयस्य अदर्शनात्; अतः सः एकभक्तिः विशिष्यते विशेषं आधिक्यं आपद्यते, अतिरिच्यते इत्यर्थः । [१८.५५. भाष्ये] प्रियः हि यस्मात् अहं आत्मा ज्ञानिनः, अतः तस्य अहं अत्यर्थं प्रियः, प्रसिद्धं हि लोके 'आत्मा प्रियः भवति' इति । तस्मात् ज्ञानिनः आत्मत्वात् वासुदेवः प्रियः भवतीत्यर्थः । स च ज्ञानी मम वासुदेवस्य आत्मा एव इति मम अत्यर्थं प्रियः ॥

17.1. Of the four types, 'the knower' knows the truth and therefore is ever integrated and 'exclusively devoted'; for none else is seen deserving of devotion. So he is exclusively devoted to the Lord. He 'excels'—surpasses all others (Cf. BGB. XVIII.55). To him 'exceedingly dear I am', being the

Self of the knower. That the Self is dear is a fact established in the world. Thus Vāsudeva, being the Self of the knower, is dear. This is the idea. Again, the knower is Vāsudeva's Self, and as such, is exceedingly dear to Me.

18.0. न तर्हि आर्तादयः त्रयः वासुदेवस्य प्रियाः ? न; किं तर्हि ? —

18.0. "Then are not the first three, the afflicted, etc. dear to Vāsudeva?" Not so, yet,

उदाराः सर्व एवैते ज्ञानी त्वात्मैव मे मतम् ।
आस्थितः स हि युक्तात्मा मामेवानुत्तमां गतिम् ॥१८॥

18. All these (four) are noble; but the knower, I deem to be My very Self; for, with an integrated self, he has resorted to Me alone, the goal without parallel.

18.1. उदाराः इति ॥ उदाराः उत्कृष्टाः सर्वे एव एते, त्रयोऽपि मम प्रियाः एवेत्यर्थः । न हि कश्चित् मद्भक्तः मम वासुदेवस्य अप्रियः भवति । ज्ञानी तु अत्यर्थं प्रियः भवतीति विशेषः । तत् कस्मात् इति ? अतः आह — ज्ञानी तु आत्मा एव, न अन्यः मत्तः इति मे मम मतं निश्चयः । आस्थितः आरोढुं प्रवृत्तः सः ज्ञानी हि यस्मात् "अहमेव भगवान् वासुदेवः न अन्यः अस्मि" इत्येवं युक्तात्मा समाहितचित्तः सन् माम् एव परं ब्रह्म गन्तव्यं अनुत्तमां गतिं गन्तुं प्रवृत्तः इत्यर्थः ॥

18.1. All these are indeed noble; even the first three are dear to Me. No devotee of Mine is other than dear to Vāsudeva. But the knower is exceedingly dear. This is the distinction. Why? The answer is that the knower is the very Self— not different from Me. This is My settled doctrine. The knower seeks to ascend the peak of knowledge: "I myself am the Lord Vāsudeva, I am none else." With a mind concentrated on this knowledge, he strives to reach Me, the Supreme Brahman, the goal without parallel.

19.0. ज्ञानी पुनरपि स्तूयते—

19.0. Once more the knower is extolled:

बहूनां जन्मनामन्ते ज्ञानवान्मां प्रपद्यते ।
वासुदेवः सर्वमिति स महात्मा सुदुर्लभः ॥१९॥

19. At the end of many births, the man of knowledge directly reaches Me, realizing, "Vāsudeva is all". Such a magnanimous soul is extremely rare.

19.1. बहूनां इति ॥ बहूनां जन्मनां ज्ञानार्थसंस्काराश्रयाणां अन्ते समाप्तौ ज्ञानवान् प्राप्तपरिपाकज्ञानः मां वासदेवं प्रत्यगात्मानं प्रत्यक्षतः प्रपद्यते—कथम् ? —वासुदेवः सर्वं इति । य एवं सर्वात्मानं मां नारायणं प्रतिपद्यते, सः महात्मा; न तत्समः अन्यः अस्ति, अधिकः वा । अतः सुदुर्लभः, 'मनुष्याणां सहस्रेषु' [७.३.] इति हि उक्तम् ॥

19.1. At 'the end of many births', devoted to self-purification resulting in greater knowledge, 'the man of knowledge' gains full illumination and directly reaches Me, Vāsudeva, the inner Self of all. How? Realizing that 'Vāsudeva is all'. Whoso thus directly reaches Me, Nārāyaṇa, the Self of all, is 'magnanimous'. There is none like him or excelling him. Hence is he extremely rare. Vide BG.7.3 above.

20.0. आत्मैव सर्वः वासुदेवः इत्येवं अप्रतिपत्तौ कारणं उच्यते—

20.0. The cause of the failure to understand 'All is Vāsudeva, the Self' is stated:

कामैस्तैस्तैर्हृतज्ञानाः प्रपद्यन्तेऽन्यदेवताः ।
तं तं नियममास्थाय प्रकृत्या नियताः स्वया ॥२०॥

20. Deprived of knowledge by a variety of cravings, (people) resort to other deities; they adopt other disciplines, being constrained by their inborn nature.

20.1. कामैः इति ॥ कामैः तैः तैः पुत्रपशुस्वर्गादिविषयैः हृतज्ञानाः अपहृतविवेकविज्ञानाः प्रपद्यन्ते अन्यदेवताः प्राप्नुवन्ति वासुदेवात् आत्मनः अन्याः देवताः, तं तं नियमं देवताराधने प्रसिद्धः यः यः नियमः तं तं आस्थाय आश्रित्य प्रकृत्या स्वभावेन जन्मान्तरार्जितसंस्कारविशेषेण नियताः नियमिताः स्वया आत्मीयया ॥

20.1. 'Deprived of knowledge'—the knowledge of discrimination—by a variety of cravings for progeny, cattle, heaven etc., they resort to deities other than Vāsudeva the Self, following well-known disciplines of worship. They are constrained by their own inborn nature—by specific impressions acquired in other lives.

21.0. तेषां च कामिनाम्—

21.0. To those desire-ridden people:

यो यो यां यां तनुं भक्तः श्रद्धयार्ऽचितुमिच्छति ।
तस्य तस्याचलां श्रद्धां तामेव विदधाम्यहम् ॥२१॥

21. I give unswerving faith to each devotee who seeks to worship with faith whatever divine form (of his choice).

21.1. यो यः इति ॥ यः यः कामी यां यां देवतातनुं श्रद्धया संयुक्तः भक्तः च सन् अर्चितुं पूजयितुं इच्छति, तस्य तस्य कामिनः अचलां स्थिरां श्रद्धां ताम् एव विदधामि स्थिरीकरोमि [ययैव पूर्वं प्रवृत्तः] ॥२१॥

21.1. Whoever among the seekers of the objects of desire seeks to worship with faith the divine form of his choice, I make the faith with which he started 'unswerving'—steadfast.

22.0. स्वभावतः यः यः यां यां देवतातनुं श्रद्धया अर्चितुं इच्छति—

22.0. Whoso, as a matter of course, seeks to worship with faith a divine form.

स तया श्रद्धया युक्तस्तस्याराधनमीहते ।
लभते च ततः कामान् मयैव विहितान् हितान् ॥२२॥

22. Possessed of that faith, he desires the worship of that form. From that divinity he secures the objects of his desires; for, I Myself have ordained them.

22.1. स तया इति ॥ सः तया मद्विहितया श्रद्धया युक्तः सन् तस्याः देवतातन्वाः राधनं आराधनं ईहते चेष्टते । लभते च ततः तस्याः आराधितायाः देवतातन्वाः कामान् ईप्सितान् मया एव परमेश्वरेण सर्वज्ञेन कर्मफलविभागज्ञतया विहितान् निर्मितान्, तान् हि यस्मात् ते भगवता विहिताः कामाः तस्मात् तान् अवश्यं लभते इत्यर्थः । 'हितान्' इति पदच्छेदे हितत्वं कामानां उपचरितं कल्प्यं; न हि कामाः हिताः कस्यचित् ॥

22.1. Possessed of the faith accorded by Me, he attempts to worship that divinity. Thence—from the divinity worshipped—he wins the desired objects, fashioned by Me, the omniscient Lord, who knows the classes of the fruits of Karma. As the fruits of Karma have been ordained by Me, the devotee will assuredly gain them. If the word is taken as '*hitān*' meaning 'favourable', the favourableness of fruits has to be taken as merely figurative; for, objects of *Kāma* do no good to anyone.

23.0. यस्मात् अन्तवत्साधनव्यापाराः अविवेकिनः कामिनश्च ते, अतः—

23.0. Since desire-bound people and undiscriminating individuals operate with finite means, their operations must come to an end.

अन्तवत्तु फलं तेषां तद्भवत्यल्पमेधसाम् ।
देवान् देवयजो यान्ति मद्भक्ता यान्ति मामपि ॥२३॥

23. (So) the fruit (of Karmas) that accrues to those small-minded men must come to an end. The worship-

pers of gods proceed to the gods; My devotees come to Me.

23.1. अन्तवत् इति ॥ अन्तवत् विनाशि तु फलं तेषां तत् भवति अल्पमेधसां अल्पप्रज्ञानाम् । देवान् देवयजः यान्ति देवान् यजन्ते इति देवयजः, ते देवान् यान्ति, मद्भक्ताः यान्ति माम् अपि । एवं समाने अपि आयासे माम् एव न प्रपद्यन्ते अनन्तफलाय, अहो खलु कष्टतरं वर्तते, इत्यनुक्रोशं दर्शयति भगवान् ॥

23.1. But the fruit that they of small minds—of feeble understanding—gain must come to an end. Those who worship i.e., offer sacrifice to the gods proceed to the gods. My devotees come to Me. Thus though the exertion involved is similar in these two cases, they do not reach Me and gain an inexhaustible fruit. What a pity! The Lord thus evinces pity for the worshippers of gods.

24.0. किंनिमित्तं मां एव न प्रपद्यन्ते इति ? उच्यते—

24.0 Why do they not resort to Kṛṣṇa only? Answer:

अव्यक्तं व्यक्तिमापन्नं मन्यन्ते मामबुद्धयः ।
परं भावमजानन्तो ममाव्ययमनुत्तमम् ॥२४॥

24. They, the undiscriminating and witless ones, consider Me, the ever-present Lord, who is unmanifested or unrevealed, as become manifested or revealed now.

24.1. अव्यक्तं इति ॥ अव्यक्तं अप्रकाशं व्यक्तिं आपन्नं प्रकाशं गतं इदानीं मन्यन्ते मां नित्यप्रसिद्धं ईश्वरं अपि सन्तं अबुद्धयः अविवेकिनः परं भावं परमात्मस्वरूपं अजानन्तः अविवेकिनः मम अव्ययं व्ययरहितं अनुत्तमं निरतिशयं, मदीयं भावं अजानन्तः मन्यन्ते इत्यर्थः ॥

24.1. The unmanifest or unrevealed, now become manifest or revealed—so, they deem Me, the ever-present Lord—they, those who do not discriminate. They are ignorant of My supreme aspect as the higher Self which is immutable and unsurpassed. Not knowing this aspect of Mine they deem Me to be now manifest—this is the idea.

25.0. तदज्ञानं किंनिमित्तं इति ? उच्यते—

25.0. What is the cause of their ignorance? Answer:

नाहं प्रकाशः सर्वस्य योगमायासमावृतः ।
मूढोऽयं नाभिजानाति लोको मामजमव्ययम् ॥२५॥

25. Veiled by the delusive power of My Yoga-Maya, I do not stand revealed to all. This deluded world knows not Me, unborn and immutable.

25.1. नाहं इति ॥ न अहं प्रकाशः सर्वस्य लोकस्य, केषांचित् एव मद्भक्तानां प्रकाशः अहं इत्यभिप्रायः । योगमायासमावृतः योगः गुणानां युक्तिः घटनं, सैव माया योगमाया — अथवा, भगवतः चित्तसमाधान योगः, तत्कृता माया योगमाया —तया योगमायया समावृतः, संछन्नः इत्यर्थः । अत एव मूढः लोकः अयं न अभिजानाति मां अजं अव्ययम् ॥

25.1. I am not revealed to the whole world; only to a few devotees of Mine am I revealed—this is the idea. 'Veiled by the delusive power of Yoga-Māyā'—Yoga being the combination i.e., fabrication of Prakṛti's constituents, and this combination being Māyā. Being veiled by that power the world is deluded, so that it does not know Me, unborn and immutable.

26.0. यया योगमायया समावृतं मां लोकः नाभिजानाति, न असौ योगमाया मदीया सती मम ईश्वरस्य मायाविनः ज्ञानं प्रतिबध्नाति यथा अन्यस्यापि मायाविनः माया ज्ञानं तद्वत् । यतः एवं अतः—

26.0. The delusive power, veiled by which the world fails to know, does not impede the knowledge of the Lord himself; for, it belongs to Him. Just as a magician's delusive power does not delude him. Such being the fact,

वेदाहं समतीतानि वर्तमानानि चार्जुन ।
भविष्याणि च भूतानि मां तु वेद न कश्चन ॥२६॥

26. I know, Arjuna! the beings past, present and future; but none knows Me.

26.1. वेद इति ॥ अहं तु वेद जाने समतीतानि समतिक्रान्तानि भूतानि, तथा वर्तमानानि च अर्जुन भविष्याणि च भूतानि वेद अहम् । मां तु वेद न कश्चन मद्भक्तं मच्छरणं एकं मुक्त्वा; मत्तत्त्ववेदनाभावादेव न मां भजते ॥

26.1. But I know the beings who have passed out already; also those who exist now, Arjuna! and again, those who will come into being in future, though none knows Me except My devotee who has sought refuge in Me. They do not worship Me due to the very lack of knowledge of My truth.

27.0. केन पुनः मत्तत्त्ववेदनप्रतिबन्धेन प्रतिबद्धानि सन्ति जायमानानि सर्वभूतानि मां न विदन्ति इत्यपेक्षायां इदं आह—

27.0. "What impedes the knowledge of My truth due to whose absence beings coming into existence fail to cognise Me?" Here is the answer:

इच्छाद्वेषसमुत्थेन द्वन्द्वमोहेन भारत ।
सर्वभूतानि संमोहं सर्गे यान्ति परन्तप ॥२७॥

27. O Bhārata prince! scourge of foes! All beings in creation get confounded due to the delusion of dualities born of attachment and aversion.

27.1. इच्छा इति ॥ इच्छाद्वेषसमुत्थेन इच्छा च द्वेषश्च इच्छाद्वेषौ ताभ्यां समुत्तिष्ठतीति इच्छाद्वेषसमुत्थः तेन इच्छाद्वेषसमुत्थेन । केनेति विशेषापेक्षायां इदं आह—द्वंद्वमोहेन इति । द्वंद्वनिमित्तः मोहः द्वंद्वमोहः तेन । तौ एव इच्छाद्वेषौ शीतोष्णवत् परस्परविरुद्धौ सुखदुःखतद्धेतुविषयौ यथाकालं सर्वभूतैः संबध्यमानौ

द्वंद्वशब्देन अभिधीयेते । तत्र यदा इच्छाद्वेषौ सुखदुःखतद्धेतुसंप्राप्तया लब्धात्मकौ भवतः, तदा तौ सर्वभूतानां प्रज्ञायाः स्ववशापादनद्वारेण परमार्थात्मतत्त्वविषय-ज्ञानोत्पत्तिप्रतिबन्धकारणं मोहं जनयतः । न हि इच्छाद्वेषदोषपरवशीकृतचित्तस्य यथाभूतार्थविषयज्ञानं उत्पद्यते बहिरपि; किमु वक्तव्यं ताभ्यां आविष्टबुद्धेः संमूढस्य प्रत्यगात्मनि बहुप्रतिबन्धे ज्ञानं नोत्पद्यते इति । अतः तेन इच्छाद्वेषसमुत्थेन द्वंद्वमोहेन, भारत भरतान्वयज, सर्वभूतानि संमोहितानि सन्ति संमोहं संमूढतां सर्गे जन्मनि —उत्पत्तिकाले इत्येतत्—यान्ति गच्छन्ति हे परन्तप । मोहवशानि एव सर्व-भूतानि जायमानानि जायन्ते इत्यभिप्रायः । यतः एवं अतः तेन द्वंद्वमोहेन प्रति-बद्धप्रज्ञानानि सर्वभूतानि संमोहितानि मां आत्मभूतं न जानन्ति; अतः एव आत्म-भावेन मां न भजन्ते ॥

27.1. 'Born of attachment and aversion'—what is born? The delusion caused by dualities. These two, attachment and aversion, mutually opposed like cold and warmth, and oriented to pleasure and pain and their causes, affect, in course of time, all living beings. They are called dualities. As soon as these two come into existence due to the occurrence of pleasure and pain or their causes, they subjugate the intelligence of all beings and give rise to the delusion that impedes the dawn of knowledge of the real Self. Right knowledge of even external objects, won't rise if the mind is swayed by the flaw of attachment and aversion. Needless to say that the knowledge of the inner Self, hard to gain in any case, won't rise if one's intelligence is in the grip of delusion. So, scion of the Bharata line! due to the delusion of dualities all beings at their very birth get confounded. That beings are subject to this delusion is the idea. Therefore, with knowledge impeded by this inborn delusion, all beings get confounded and fail to know Me, their very Self. Hence they do not worship Me, their veritable Self.

28.0. के पुनः अनेन द्वंद्वमोहेन निर्मुक्ताः सन्तः त्वां विदित्वा यथाशास्त्रं आत्म-भावेन भजन्ते इत्यपेक्षितं अर्थं दर्शयितुं आह—

28.0. Who, then, are the persons, who, being free from delusion and knowing You according to the *śāstras*, worship You as their Self? The Lord sets forth as follows this logically consequent truth:

येषां त्वन्तगतं पापं जनानां पुण्यकर्मणाम् ।
ते द्वन्द्वमोहनिर्मुक्ता भजन्ते मां दृढव्रताः ॥२८॥

28. But those men who have no more sins, who act righteously and who are liberated from the delusion of dualities, worship Me with a steadfast will.

28.1. येषां इति ॥ येषां तु पुनः अन्तगतं समाप्तप्रायं क्षीणं पापं जनानां पुण्यकर्मणां पुण्यं कर्म येषां सत्त्वशुद्धिकारणं विद्यते ते पुण्यकर्माणः तेषां पुण्यकर्मणां, ते द्वंद्वमोहनिर्मुक्ताः यथोक्तेन द्वंद्वमोहेन निर्मुक्ताः भजन्ते मां परमात्मानं दृढव्रताः । "एवमेव परमार्थतत्त्वं, नान्यथा" इत्येवं सर्वपरित्यागव्रतेन निश्चितविज्ञानाः दृढव्रताः उच्यन्ते ॥

28.1. But those whose sins have practically been wiped out, whose acts are righteous and productive of mental purification, and who are liberated from the delusion of dualities—they worship Me, the Supreme Self, with a steadfast will. As their knowledge—that the truth of the supreme Reality is such and such, and not otherwise,—is unerring, they resolutely follow the path of total renunciation. So they are said to have a steadfast will.

29.0. ते किमर्थं भजन्ते इति ? उच्यते—

29.0. With what goal in view do they worship? Answer:

जरामरणमोक्षाय मामाश्रित्य यतन्ति ये ।
ते ब्रह्म तद्विदुः कृत्स्नमध्यात्मं कर्म चाखिलम् ॥२९॥

29. Resorting to Me, those who strive for release from old age and death come to know that Brahman in Its wholeness, as also the self and all the works.

29.1. जरा इति ॥ जरामरणमोक्षाय जरामरणयोः मोक्षार्थं मां परमेश्वरं आश्रित्य मत्समाहितचित्ताः सन्तः यतन्ति प्रयतन्ते ये, ते यत् ब्रह्म परं तत् विदुः

कृत्स्नं समस्तं, अध्यात्मं प्रत्यगात्मविषयं वस्तु तत् विदुः, कर्म च अखिलं समस्तं विदुः ॥

29.1. Those who strive for release from old age and death, resorting to Me, the Lord supreme i.e., with concentrated minds, come to know that Brahman in Its wholeness, the reality of the inner Self and work in its entirety.

साधिभूताधिदैवं मां साधियज्ञं च ये विदुः ।
प्रयाणकालेऽपि च मां ते विदुर्युक्तचेतसः ॥३०॥

30. Those who know Me together with My manifestation in elements, divinities and sacrifices, know Me also at the time of departure from this world, their minds being concentrated.

इति श्रीमहाभारते शतसाहस्र्यां संहितायां वैयासिक्यां भीष्मपर्वणि
श्रीमद्भगवद्गीतासूपनिषत्सु ब्रह्मविद्यायां योगशास्त्रे श्रीकृष्णार्जुनसंवादे
ज्ञानविज्ञानयोगो नाम सप्तमोऽध्यायः ॥७॥

30.1. साधि इति ॥ साधिभूताधिदैवं अधिभूतं च अधिदैवं च अधिभूताधिदैवं, सह अधिभूताधिदैवेन वर्तते इति साधिभूताधिदैवं च मां ये विदुः, साधियज्ञं च सह अधियज्ञेन साधियज्ञं ये विदुः, प्रयाणकाले मरणकाले अपि च मां ते विदुः युक्तचेतसः समाहितचित्ताः इति ॥

30.1. Amidst elements and amidst divinities I exist. Those who know Me as such and also as existent in sacrifices, know Me also at the time of 'departure', death, their minds being concentrated.

इति श्रीमत्परमहंसपरिव्राजकाचार्यगोविन्दभगवत्पूज्यपादशिष्यस्य श्रीमच्छंकरभगवतः
कृतौ श्रीभगवद्गीताभाष्ये ज्ञानविज्ञानयोगो नाम सप्तमोध्यायः ॥७॥

अष्टमोऽध्यायः

CHAPTER VIII

THE YOGA OF CONCENTRATION

0.1. 'ते ब्रह्म तद्विदु कृत्स्नम्,' [७.२९.] इत्यादिना भगवता अर्जुनस्य प्रश्नबीजानि उपदिष्टानि । अतः तत्प्रश्नार्थं अर्जुनः उवाच—

0.1. In VII.29 the Lord placed before Arjuna moot points that provoked questions. Hence Arjuna spoke raising appropriate questions:

अर्जुन उवाच :

किं तद्ब्रह्म किमध्यात्मं किं कर्म पुरुषोत्तम ।
अधिभूतं च किं प्रोक्तं अधिदैवं किमुच्यते ॥१॥

Arjuna said:

1. What is that Brahman? What is the inner self? What is work? O highest Spirit! What is said to be the elements? What is said to be the divinities?

अधियज्ञः कथं कोऽत्र देहेऽस्मिन्मधुसूदन ।
प्रयाणकाले च कथं ज्ञेयोऽसि नियतात्मभिः ॥२॥

2. Slayer of Madhu! Who, in this body, operates the sacrifices and how? At the time of departure how are You to be known by the self-controlled (Yogins)?

3.0. एषां प्रश्नानां यथाक्रमं निर्णयाय श्रीभगवान् उवाच—

3.0. In order definitively to answer these questions in their order, the blessed Lord said:

श्रीभगवानुवाच :

अक्षरं ब्रह्म परमं स्वभावोऽध्यात्ममुच्यते ।

भूतभावोद्भवकरो विसर्गः कर्मसंज्ञितः ॥३॥

The blessed Lord said:

3. The supreme Brahman is the imperishable; the inner self is Spirit as subject. Work is manifest creation, bringing beings into existence.

3.1. अक्षरं इति ॥ अक्षरं न क्षरतीति अक्षरं परमात्मा, 'एतस्य वा अक्षरस्य प्रशासने गार्गि' [बृ. उ. ३.८.९.] इति श्रुतेः । ओङ्कारस्य च 'ओमित्येकाक्षरं ब्रह्म' [८.१३.] इति परेण विशेषणात् अग्रहणम् । परमम् इति निरतिशये ब्रह्मणि अक्षरे उपपन्नतरं विशेषणम् । तस्यैव परस्य ब्रह्मणः प्रतिदेहं प्रत्यगात्मभावः स्वभावः स्वः भावः स्वभावः अध्यात्मं उच्यते । आत्मानं देहं अधिकृत्य प्रत्यगात्मतया प्रवृत्तं परमार्थब्रह्मावसानं वस्तु स्वभावः अध्यात्मं उच्यते—अध्यात्मशब्देन अभिधीयते । भूतभावोद्भवकरः भूतानां भावः भूतभावः, तस्य उद्भवः भूतभावोद्भवः तं करोति इति भूतभावोद्भवकरः, भूतवस्तूत्पत्तिकरः इत्यर्थः । विसर्गः विसर्जनं देवतोद्देशेन चरुपुरोडाशादेः द्रव्यस्य परित्यागः; स एष विसर्गलक्षणः यज्ञः कर्मसंज्ञितः कर्मशब्दितः इत्येतत् । एतस्मात् हि बीजभूतात् वृष्टयादिक्रमेण स्थावरजङ्गमानि भूतानि उद्भवन्ति ॥

3.1. What does not perish, 'the imperishable', is the Supreme Self. *Vide*: 'Gārgi! by the command of this Imperishable . . . BU.3.8.9. The syllable AUM mentioned in VIII.13 is not to be understood here as *akṣara*; for it is qualified as 'Supreme' (here). This qualification better suits Brahman, the imperishable, that is unsurpassed. The 'inner self' is the reality that in each body is the subjective spirit whose culminating aspect is the ultimate Brahman. What is called 'work' is the offering of prepared oblation directed to divinities; here it denotes creation that brings all beings into existence; for, this offering is held to be the seed whence, as rain and so forth, all beings, immobile and mobile, come into existence.

अधिभूतं क्षरो भावः पुरुषश्चाधिदैवतम् ।
अधियज्ञोऽहमेवात्र देहे देहभृतां वर ॥४॥

4. 'Elements' constitute perishable existence; the divinities are the Spirit. Thou, best of men! in the body I alone am related to sacrifices.

4.1. अधिभूतं इति ॥ अधिभूतं प्राणिजातं अधि [कृत्य] भवतीति । कोऽसौ ? क्षरः क्षरतीति क्षरः विनाशी, भावः यत्किञ्चित् जनिमत् वस्तु इत्यर्थः । पुरुषः पूर्णं अनेन सर्वम् इति, पुरि शयनात् वा पुरुषः, आदित्यान्तर्गतः हिरण्यगर्भः, सर्वप्राणिकरणानां अनुग्राहकः, सः अधिदैवतम् । अधियज्ञः सर्वयज्ञाभिमानिनी विष्वाख्या देवता, 'यज्ञो वै विष्णुः' [तै. सं. १.७.४.] इति श्रुतेः । स हि विष्णुः अहम् एव, अत्र अस्मिन् देहे यः यज्ञः तस्य अहं अधियज्ञः; यज्ञः हि देहनिर्वर्त्यत्वेन देहसमवायी इति देहाधिकरणः भवति, देहभृतां वर ॥

4.1. 'Elements' refers to what comes to be, depending on living beings. What is that? The perishable entity or whatsoever is born. The 'Puruṣa or Spirit' is that which fills all or what reclines in the city—i.e., the Hiraṇyagarbha installed in the sun who protects instruments of action and cognition. What 'relates to sacrifices' is the Deity styled Viṣṇu who claims all sacrifices as directed to Himself. *Vide*: 'Sacrifice indeed is Viṣṇu,' TS.1.7.4. And that Viṣṇu is none but Myself. I am related to the sacrifice performed by the body. Sacrifice, as such, is inseparably related to the body, existing in the body, O best of men!

अन्तकाले च मामेव स्मरन् मुक्त्वा कलेवरम् ।
यः प्रयाति स मद्भावं याति नास्त्यत्र संशयः ॥५॥

5. At the end, whoso departs giving up his body, and remembering Me alone, proceeds to My status; of this there is no doubt.

5.1. अन्तकाले इति ॥ अन्तकाले मरणकाले च माम् एव परमेश्वरं विष्णुं

स्मरन् मुक्तवा परित्यज्य कलेवरं शरीरं यः प्रयाति गच्छति, सः मद्भावं वैष्णवं तत्त्वं याति । न अस्ति न विद्यते अत्र अस्मिन् अर्थे संशयः,—याति वा न वा इति ॥

5.1. 'At the end'—at the time of death, 'remembering Me alone'—the Supreme Lord Viṣṇu alone. Whoso gives up the body thus and passes on, proceeds to the truth of Viṣṇu. In respect of this matter there is 'no doubt', i.e., as to whether he proceeds or not to that truth.

6.0. न मद्विषयः एव अयं नियमः । किं तर्हि ?—

6.0. This law has no exclusive application to Myself. On the contrary,

यं यं वाऽपि स्मरन् भावं त्यजत्यन्ते कलेबरम् ।
तं तमेवैति कौन्तेय सदा तद्भावभावितः ॥६॥

6. Remembering whatever being one gives up the body at the end, that very being one reaches, O Arjuna! ever conforming to that being.

6.1. यं इति ॥ यं यं वाऽपि यं यं भावं देवताविशेषं स्मरन् चिन्तयन् त्यजति परित्यजति अन्ते अन्तकाले प्राणवियोगकाले कलेबरं शरीरं तं तम् एव स्मृतं भावं एव एति न अन्यं कौन्तेय ! सदा सर्वदा तद्भावभावितः तस्मिन् भावः तद्भावः सः भावितः स्मर्यमाणतया अभ्यस्तः येन सः तद्भावभावितः सन् ॥

6.1. 'Remembering'—thinking of—whatever being or particular deity, one leaves the body 'at the end'—at the time of death—one reaches that very remembered being and not another, O Arjuna! For, one conforms oneself to that repeatedly remembered being.

7.0. यस्मात् एवं अन्त्या भावना देहान्तरप्राप्तौ कारणम्—

7.0. Since thus the final recollection causes the assumption of a new body,

तस्मात्सर्वेषु कालेषु मामनुस्मर युध्य च ।
मय्यर्पितमनोबुद्धिर्मामेवैष्यस्यसंशयः ॥७॥

7. Therefore, at all times, remember Me and fight. Dedicating mind and intellect to Me, rid of all doubts, you will reach Me, indeed.

7.1. तस्मात् इति ॥ तस्मात् सर्वेषु कालेषु मां अनुस्मर यथाशास्त्रम् । युध्य च युद्धं च स्वधर्मं कुरु । मयि वासुदेवे अर्पिते मनोबुद्धी यस्य तव सः त्वं मयि अर्पितमनोबुद्धिः सन् माम् एव यथास्मृतं एष्यसि आगमिष्यसि, असंशयः न संशयः अत्र विद्यते ॥

किञ्च—

7.1. Therefore at all times remember Me as the *sāstras* prescribe; and 'fight', performing your duty. With mind and intellect dedicated to Me, Vāsudeva, you will reach Me alone as recollected. There is no doubt about this. Moreover,

अभ्यासयोगयुक्तेन चेतसा नान्यगामिना ।
परमं पुरुषं दिव्यं याति पार्थानुचिन्तयन् ॥८॥

8. O Arjuna! Steadily thinking with an unswerving mind, disciplined in the Yoga of repeated practice, one proceeds to the supreme, divine Spirit.

8.1. अभ्यास इति ॥ अभ्यासयोगयुक्तेन — मयि चित्तसमर्पणविषयभूते एकस्मिन् तुल्यप्रत्ययावृत्तिलक्षणः विलक्षणप्रत्ययानन्तरितः अभ्यासः, स चासौ योगः तेन युक्तं तत्रैव व्यापृतं योगिनः चेतः, तेन चेतसा नान्यगामिना न अन्यत्र विषयान्तरे गन्तुं शीलं अस्येति नान्यगामि तेन नान्यगामिना, परमं निरतिशयं पुरुषं दिव्यं दिवि सूर्यमण्डले भवं याति गच्छति हे पार्थ ! अनुचिन्तयन् शास्त्राचार्योपदेशं अनुध्यायन् इत्येतत् ॥

8.1. 'Repeated practice' is the flow of the same ideas in regard to Me, the sole object to which the mind is directed, uninterrupted by dissimilar ideas. This flow is the Yoga. The

Yogin's mind is addressed to it, i.e., is engaged in it. With that mind seeking no other object, O Arjuna! he dwells on—contemplates—the instructions of the *śāstras* and teachers and 'proceeds'—repairs—to the supreme, divine Spirit, the Person in the sun.

9.0. किंविशिष्टं च पुरुषं याति इति ? उच्यते—

9.0. What are the attributes of the Spirit to whom the Yogin proceeds? Answer:

कविं पुराणमनुशासितारमणोरणीयांसमनुस्मरेद्यः ।
सर्वस्य धातारमचिन्त्यरूपमादित्यवर्णं तमसः परस्तात् ॥९॥

9. Whoso remembers the wise, ancient Ruler, subtler than the subtle, the Upholder of all (things), imponderable of form, resplendent like the sun beyond darkness;

9.1. कविं इति ॥ कविं क्रान्तदर्शिनं सर्वज्ञं, पुराणं चिरन्तनं, अनुशासितारं सर्वस्य जगतः प्रशासितारं, अणोः सूक्ष्मात् अपि अणीयांसं सूक्ष्मतरं अनुस्मरेत् अनुचिन्तयेत् यः कश्चित्, सर्वस्य कर्मफलजातस्य धातारं विधातारं विचित्रतया प्राणिभ्यः विभक्तारं, [विभज्य दातारं] अचिन्त्यरूपं न अस्य रूपं नियतं विद्यमानम् अपि केनचित् चिन्तयितुं शक्यते इति अचिन्त्यरूपः, तं आदित्यवर्णं आदित्यस्य इव नित्यचैतन्यप्रकाशः वर्णः यस्य तं आदित्यवर्णं तमसः परस्तात् अज्ञानलक्षणात् मोहान्धकारात् परं तं 'अनुचिन्तयन् याति' इति पूर्वेण संबन्धः ॥
किञ्च—

9.1. 'The wise'—far-sighted or omniscient. 'Ancient'—Eternal. 'Ruler'—ruler of the whole world. Subtler than the subtle. 'Whoso remembers'—recollects Him who is (also) the 'Upholder' or dispenser of the fruits of all works done by living beings, in appropriate and varying measures; whose form, though eternally existent, none indeed can 'ponder' aright; who is 'resplendent' like the sun, being luminous with the timeless light of consciousness and who is 'beyond the darkness' of nescience and delusion. Construe this with the earlier expression 'whoso remembers.' And,

प्रयाणकाले मनसाऽचलेन भक्त्या युक्तो योगबलेन चैव ।
भ्रुवोर्मध्ये प्राणमावेश्य सम्यक् स तं परं पुरुषमुपैति दिव्यम् ॥१०॥

10. 'At the hour of departure whoso with steady mind, and with devotion and the power of Yoga, sustains aright the life-force between the brows (and remembers), reaches the Spirit supreme, divine.

10.1. प्रयाण इति ॥ प्रयाणकाले मरणकाले मनसा अचलेन चलनवर्जितेन भक्त्या युक्तः भजनं भक्तिः तया युक्तः योगबलेन च एव योगस्य बलं योगबलं समाधिजसंस्कारप्रचयजनितचित्तस्थैर्यलक्षणं योगबलं तेन च युक्तः इत्यर्थः, पूर्वं हृदयपुण्डरीके वशीकृत्य चित्तं ततः ऊर्ध्वगामिन्या नाड्या भूमिजयक्रमेण भ्रुवोः मध्ये प्राणं आवेश्य स्थापयित्वा सम्यक् अप्रमत्तः सन्, सः एवं विद्वान् योगी 'कविं पुराणम्' (८.९.) इत्यादिलक्षणं तं परं [परतरं] पुरुषं उपैति प्रतिपद्यते दिव्यं द्योतनात्मकम् ॥

10.1. 'At the hour of departure'—at the time of death, 'with a steady unswerving mind, with devotion and the power of Yoga,—'the power of Yoga' means mind's steadiness born of accumulated impressions which concentration produces. First master the mind in the lotus of the heart; then, causing the life-force, *prāṇa*, to enter the space 'between the eye-brows', viz., the vertical artery, by stages, and vigilantly conquering the planes of Yogic experience, the Yogin who knows, reaches the supreme Spirit of Light.

11.0. पुनरपि वक्ष्यमाणेन उपायेन प्रतिपित्सितस्य ब्रह्मणः वेदविद्वदनादिविशेषणविशेष्यस्य अभिधानं करोति भगवान् —

11.0. Again the Lord elucidates Brahman sought to be known by the means presently to be set forth and distinguished as the sole theme of the Veda-knowers:

यदक्षरं वेदविदो वदन्ति विशन्ति यद्यतयो वीतरागाः ।
यदिच्छन्तो ब्रह्मचर्यं चरन्ति तत्ते पदं संग्रहेण प्रवक्ष्ये ॥११॥

11. That Imperishable which the Veda-knowers set forth, which ascetics, devoid of attachments, enter, and, seeking which, they live a life of continence—that goal, briefly, I shall declare to you.

11.1. यत् इति ॥ यत् अक्षरं न क्षरतीति अक्षरं अविनाशि वेदविदः वेदार्थज्ञाः वदन्ति, 'एतद्वै तदक्षरं गार्गि ब्राह्मणा अभिवदन्ति' इति श्रुतेः, सर्वविशेषनिवर्तकत्वेन अभिवदन्ति 'अस्थूलमनणु' [बृ. उ. ३.८.८.] इत्यादि । किञ्च — विशन्ति प्रविशन्ति सम्यग्दर्शनप्राप्तौ सत्यां यत् यतयः यतनशीलाः संन्यासिनः वीतरागाः वीतः विगतः रागः येभ्यः ते वीतरागाः । यत् च अक्षरं इच्छन्तः—'ज्ञातुं' इति वाक्यशेषः— ब्रह्मचर्यं गुरौ चरन्ति आचरन्ति, तत् ते पदं तत् अक्षराख्यं पदं पदनीयं ते तुभ्यं संग्रहेण संग्रह संक्षेपः तेन संक्षेपेण प्रवक्ष्ये कथयिष्यामि ॥

11.1. What does not lapse is 'the Imperishable', the indestructible; which the knowers of the contents of the Vedas declare, *Vide*: "This indeed is that Imperishable, Gārgi! which Brāhmaṇas declare" (BU.3.8.8); they declare It as free from all limitations: "Not gross, not subtle" (BU.3.8.8). And once right vision is won, the 'ascetics' or the renouncers, free from 'attachments', striving to know It 'enter' It. 'Seeking' the Imperishable i.e., to know It they observe celibacy; under the guidance of a teacher they live a life of continence. That 'goal' named the Imperishable, I shall briefly 'declare'—set forth.

12.0. 'स यो ह वै तद्भगवन् मनुष्येषु प्रायणान्तमोङ्कारमभिध्यायीत कतमं वाव स तेन लोकं जयतीति । तस्मै स होवाच एतद्वै सत्यकाम परं चापरं च ब्रह्म यदोङ्कारः' इत्युपक्रम्य 'यः पुनरेतं त्रिमात्रेणोमित्येतेनैवाक्षरेण परं पुरुषमभिध्यायीत ... स सामभिरुन्नीयते ब्रह्मलोकम्' [प्र. उ. ५.१.२.५.] इत्यादिना वचनेन 'अन्यत्र धर्मादन्यत्राधर्मात्' इति च उपक्रम्य 'सर्वे वेदा यत्पदमामनन्ति । तपांसि सर्वाणि च यद्वदन्ति । यदिच्छन्तो ब्रह्मचर्यं चरन्ति । तत्ते पदं संग्रहेण ब्रवीम्योमित्येतत्' ॥ [कठ. उ. २.१४.१५.] इत्यादिभिश्च वचनैः परस्य ब्रह्मणः वाचकरूपेण, प्रतिमावत् प्रतीकरूपेण वा, परब्रह्मप्रतिपत्तिसाधनत्वेन मन्दमध्यमबुद्धीनां विवक्षितस्य ओङ्कारस्य

उपासनं कालान्तरे मुक्तिफलं उक्तं यत्, तदेव इहापि 'कविं पुराणमनुशासितारं', 'यदक्षरं वेदविदो वदन्ति' इति च उपन्यस्तस्य परस्य ब्रह्मणः पूर्वोक्तरूपेण प्रतिपत्त्युपायभूतस्य ओङ्कारस्य कालान्तरमुक्तिफलं उपासनं योगधारणासहितं वक्तव्यं, प्रसक्तानुप्रसक्तं च यत्किञ्चित्, इत्येवमर्थः उत्तरः ग्रन्थः आरभ्यते—

12.0. 'Holy Sir! among men which world does he win who meditates on AUM as long as he lives?' To him spoke he: 'Satyakāma! AUM is both the higher and the lower Brahman' (PU 5.1.) Starting thus, the following utterances set forth the adoration of AUM. "Whoso meditates on the Supreme Spirit by means of the syllable AUM with its three elements, is led up to the world of Brahmā. (PU 5.5.)" Also KU 2.14, 15: "Apart from righteousness and unrighteousness, the goal that all Vedas proclaim, that all penances declare, seeking which they lead a life of continence—I utter that briefly for you, viz., AUM". AUM is the word that declares the supreme Brahman. Like an image or a representative symbol, it serves as a means for inquirers of slow and medium understanding to know the Supreme Brahman. Such knowledge yields liberation in the fulness of time. Here too that very meditation has been set forth in BG 8.9, 11. Meditation on AUM with the practice of Yoga that later leads to liberation has to be taught as also certain related matter. The following verses serve this purpose.

सर्वद्वाराणि संयम्य मनो हृदि निरुध्य च ।
मूर्ध्न्याधायात्मनः प्राणमास्थितो योगधारणाम् ॥१२॥

12. Controlling all gateways of the senses, confining the mind in the heart, fixing the life-breath in the crown and intent on the maintenance of Yoga;

12.1. सर्व इति ॥ सर्वद्वाराणि सर्वाणि च तानि द्वाराणि च सर्वद्वाराणि उपलब्धौ, तानि सर्वाणि संयम्य संयमनं कृत्वा मनः हृदि हृदयपुण्डरीके निरुध्य निरोधं कृत्वा निष्प्रचारं आपाद्य, तत्र वशीकृतेन मनसा हृदयात् ऊर्ध्वगामिन्या नाड्या ऊर्ध्वं आरुह्य मूर्ध्नि आधाय आत्मनः प्राणं आस्थितः प्रवृत्तः योगधारणां धारयितुम् ॥ तत्रैव च धारयन् —

12.1. 'Controlling all gateways' of cognition; 'confining the mind in the heart', the lotus of the heart, and immobilizing it there; and having mastered the mind, ascend by means of it the nerve going up from the heart. Holding the life-breath in the crown, one commences the practice of Yoga.

Holding the life-breath right there, and,

ओमित्येकाक्षरं ब्रह्म व्याहरन् मामनुस्मरन् ।
यः प्रयाति त्यजन् देहं स याति परमां गतिम् ॥१३॥

13. Uttering the monosyllable AUM representing Brahman, and remembering Me, whoso goes forth leaving the body, he proceeds to the highest goal.

13.1. ओम् इति ॥ ॐ इति एकाक्षरं ब्रह्म ब्रह्मणः अभिधानभूतं ओङ्कारं व्याहरन् उच्चारयन्, तदर्थभूतं मां ईश्वरं अनुस्मरन् अनुचिन्तयन् यः प्रयाति म्रियते सः त्यजन् परित्यजन् देहं शरीरं—'त्यजन् देहं' इति प्रयाणविशेषणार्थं, देहत्यागेन प्रयाणं आत्मनः न स्वरूपनाशेन इत्यर्थः — सः एवं त्यजन् याति गच्छति परमां प्रकृष्टां गतिम् ॥

किञ्च —

13.1. 'Uttering the monosyllabic AUM', the verbal expression of Brahman, and 'remembering Me', the Lord, its content; whoever 'goes forth' or dies, leaving the body, proceeds to the exalted goal (of *mokṣa*). The idea is that the passing forth involves only the giving up of the body and not the destruction of the Self. Moreover,

अनन्यचेताः सततं यो मां स्मरति नित्यशः ।
तस्याहं सुलभः पार्थ नित्ययुक्तस्य योगिनः ॥१४॥

14. To the single-minded Yogin in perpetual communion, who constantly remembers Me, I am easily accessible, O Arjuna!

14.1. अनन्यचेताः इति ॥ अनन्यचेताः न अन्यविषये चेतः यस्य सः अयं अनन्यचेताः योगी सततं सर्वदा यः मां परमेश्वरं स्मरति नित्यशः । 'सततं' इति नैरन्तर्यं उच्यते, 'नित्यशः इति दीर्घकालत्वं उच्यते । न षण्मासं संवत्सरं वा — किं तर्हि ? — यावज्जीवं नैरन्तर्येण यः मां स्मरति इत्यर्थः । तस्य योगिनः अहं सुलभः सुखेन लभ्यः हे पार्थ, नित्ययुक्तस्य सदा समाहितचित्तस्य योगिनः । यतः एवं, अतः अनन्यचेताः सन् मयि सदा समाहितः भवेत् ॥१४॥

14.1. 'Single-minded'—without directing the mind to any other theme. A Yogin without interruption always remembers Me, the supreme Lord. The terms 'without interruption' denote continuity, and 'constantly', length of time. Not just for six months or a year, but as long as one is alive, and 'constantly' remembering Me—this is the sense. To such a Yogin I am easily accessible as he is in perpetual communion. Such being the case, single-mindedly one must be always in communion with Me.

15.0. तव सौलभ्येन किं स्यात् इति ? उच्यते; शृणु तत् मम सौलभ्येन यत् भवति—

15.0. "What is the use of your easy accessibility?" Listen as to what it yields:

मामुपेत्य पुनर्जन्म दुःखालयमशाश्वतम् ।
नाप्नुवन्ति महात्मानः संसिद्धिं परमां गताः ॥१५॥

15. Reaching Me and winning supreme perfection, magnanimous sages no longer suffer rebirth—this ephemeral abode of all sufferings.

15.1. मां उपेत्य इति ॥ मां ईश्वरं उपेत्य मद्भावं आपद्य पुनर्जन्म पुनरुत्पत्तिं न अप्नुवन्ति न प्राप्नुवन्ति । किंविशिष्टं पुनर्जन्म न प्राप्नुवन्ति इति ? तद्विशेषणं आह — दुःखालयं दुःखानां आध्यात्मिकादीनां आलयं आश्रयं, आलीयन्ते यस्मिन् दुःखानि इति दुःखालयं जन्म । न केवलं दुःखालयं अशाश्वतं अनवस्थितस्वरूपं च । नाप्नुवन्ति ईदृशं पुनर्जन्म महात्मानः यतयः संसिद्धिं मोक्षाख्यां परमां प्रकृष्टां गताः प्राप्ताः । ये पुनः मां न प्राप्नुवन्ति ते पुनः आवर्तन्ते ॥

15.1. 'Reaching Me the Lord', having been assimilated into My being, they are not reborn. What sort of rebirth is it that they avoid? It is characterised as follows: It is 'the abode', the locus, of all sufferings due to causes, etc. Birth is the abode of sufferings which inhere in it. Besides, it is also ephemeral. No longer do they undergo this sort of rebirth—the 'magnanimous' and disciplined sages; for, they have won supreme perfection, i.e. they have been liberated. On the other hand, those who fail to reach Me are re-born.

16.0. किं पुनः त्वत्तः अन्यत् प्राप्ताः पुनः आवर्तन्ते इति ? उच्यते—

16.0. Do those who have reached goals other than You return to this earth?

आब्रह्मभुवनाल्लोकाः पुनरावर्तिनोऽर्जुन ।
मामुपेत्य तु कौन्तेय पुनर्जन्म न विद्यते ॥१६॥

16. Worlds upto and including Brahmā's are repeatedly won and lost, O Arjuna!; but, on reaching Me, there is no more rebirth.

16.1. आब्रह्मभुवनात् इति ॥ आब्रह्मभुवनात् भवन्ति अस्मिन् भूतानि इति भुवनं, ब्रह्मणो भुवनं ब्रह्मभुवनं, ब्रह्मलोकः इत्यर्थः । आब्रह्मभुवनात् सह ब्रह्मभुवनेन लोकाः सर्वे पुनरावर्तिनः पुनरावर्तस्वभावाः हे अर्जुन । मां एकं उपेत्य तु कौन्तेय पुनर्जन्म पुनरुत्पत्तिः न विद्यते ॥

16.1. That in which beings appear is a world. Brahmā's world is what pertains to him. Upto and including his world, all worlds have the feature of recurrence, O Arjuna! But on reaching Me, rebirth ceases.

17.0. ब्रह्मलोकसहिताः लोकाः कस्मात् पुनरावर्तिनः ? कालपरिच्छिन्नत्वात् । कथम् ?

17.0. Why do worlds including Brahma's recur? Because they are finite in time, How?

सहस्रयुगपर्यन्तमहर्यद्ब्रह्मणो विदुः ।
रात्रिं युगसहस्रान्तां तेऽहोरात्रविदो जनाः ॥१७॥

17. Men who know about day and night hold that a day of Brahmā consists of a thousand ages, and that night also is of a thousand ages.

17.1. सहस्र इति ॥ सहस्रयुगपर्यन्तं सहस्राणि युगानि पर्यन्तं पर्यवसानं यस्य अह्नः तत् अहः सहस्रयुगपर्यन्तं ब्रह्मणः प्रजापतेः विराजः विदुः, रात्रिं अपि युग-सहस्रान्तां अहःपरिमाणां एव । के विदुरिति ? आह—ते अहो रात्रविदः काल-संख्याविदः जनाः इत्यर्थः । यतः एवं कालपरिच्छिन्नाः ते, अतः पुनरावर्तिनः लोकाः ॥

17.1. They know that a day of Brahmā—of Prajāpati or Virāṭ extends to the limit of 1000 ages; the night too is of the same extent. 'Who knows all this' — those who know the extent of day and night, or the knowers of the measure of time. Thus, since the worlds are limited in time, they recur.

18.0. प्रजापतेः अहनि यत् भवति रात्रौ च, तत् उच्यते—

18.0. Now is stated what happens during Prajāpati's day and night:

अव्यक्ताद्व्यक्तयः सर्वाः प्रभवन्त्यहरागमे ।
रात्र्यागमे प्रलीयन्ते तत्रैवाव्यक्तसंज्ञके ॥१८॥

18. At the break of day, all individuals are born of the Unmanifest; when the night falls, they are dissolved in the same Unmanifest.

18.1. अव्यक्तात् इति ॥ अव्यक्तात् अव्यक्तं प्रजापतेः स्वापावस्था, तस्मात् अव्यक्तात् व्यक्तयः व्यज्यन्ते इति व्यक्तयः स्थावरजङ्गमलक्षणाः सर्वाः प्रजाः प्रभवन्ति अभिव्यज्यन्ते, अह्नः आगमः अहरागमः तस्मिन् अहरागमे काले ब्रह्मणः प्रबोधकाले । तथा रात्र्यागमे ब्रह्मणः स्वापकाले प्रलीयन्ते सर्वाः व्यक्तयः तत्र एव पूर्वोक्ते अव्यक्तसंज्ञके ॥

18.1. From 'the Unmanifest'—the state of Prajāpati's sleep—'individuals' or determinate beings mobile and immobile, i.e., all creatures, are 'born', become manifest. The dawn of the day is the day-break. At that time, when Brahmā wakes up, all creatures are born. Similarly, at night-fall when Brahmā sleeps, all individuals are dissolved in what was earlier called Unmanifest.

19.0. अकृताभ्यागमकृतविप्रणाशदोषपरिहारार्थं, बन्धमोक्षशास्त्रप्रवृत्तिसाफल्यप्रदर्शनार्थं, अविद्यादिक्लेशमूलकर्माशयवशाच्च अवशः भूतग्रामः भूत्वा भूत्वा प्रलीयते इत्यतः संसारे वैराग्यदर्शनार्थं च इदम् आह—

19.0. What follows serves to exclude the flaw of 'the incidence of the uneffected and the destruction of the effected'; to demonstrate the fruitfulness of action according to *śāstraic* instructions about bondage and liberation; and to evoke a sense of detachment from the empirical world in which, helplessly, hosts of beings get entangled due to Karma, impelled by afflictions like nescience, etc.

भूतग्रामः स एवायं भूत्वा भूत्वा प्रलीयते ।
रात्र्यागमेऽवशः पार्थ प्रभवत्यहरागमे ॥१९॥

19. This same host of beings, after repeated births, get dissolved, helplessly, O Arjuna! at the time of nightfall and are born at day-break.

19.1. भूतग्रामः इति ॥ भूतग्रामः स्थावरजङ्गमलक्षणः यः पूर्वस्मिन् कल्पे आसीत् स एव अयं नान्यः भूत्वा भूत्वा अहरागमे, प्रलीयते पुनः पुनः रात्र्यागमे अह्नः क्षये अवशः अस्वतन्त्रः एव, हे पार्थ, प्रभवति जायते अवशः एव अहरागमे ॥

19.1. 'This host of beings' is the multitude of mobile and immobile beings that existed in a prior age. The very same, at day-break, are obliged to come into being repeatedly, and, at nightfall, get dissolved helplessly, O Arjuna! Again at day-break they are born.

20.0. यत् उपन्यस्तं अक्षरं तस्य प्राप्त्युपायो निर्दिष्टः 'ओमित्येकाक्षरं ब्रह्म' [८.१३.] इत्यादिना । अथ इदानीं अक्षरस्यैव स्वरूपनिर्दिदिक्षया इदं उच्यते, अनेन योगमार्गेण इदं गन्तव्यं इति—.

20.0. The means of attaining the Imperishable has been indicated in 8.13 in the words 'Brahman the monosyllabic AUM', etc. Now is affirmed the following in order to determine the true nature of the Imperishable. The aim is to specify the path of Yoga by which to reach it.

परस्तस्मात्तु भावोऽन्योऽव्यक्तोऽव्यक्तात्सनातनः ।
यः स सर्वेषु भूतेषु नश्यत्सु न विनश्यति ॥२०॥

20. But beyond that Unmanifest is another eternal Unmanifest Being; It perishes not (even) when all beings perish.

20.1. परः इति ॥ परः व्यतिरिक्तः भिन्नः—कुतः ? —तस्मात् पूर्वोक्तात् । 'तु' शब्दः अक्षरस्य विवक्षितस्य अव्यक्तात् वैलक्षण्यविशेषणार्थः । भावः अक्षराख्यं परं ब्रह्म । व्यतिरिक्तत्वे सत्यपि सालक्षण्यप्रसङ्गोऽस्तीति तद्विनिवृत्त्यर्थं आह— अन्यः इति । अन्यः विलक्षणः । स च अव्यक्तः अनिन्द्रियगोचरः । 'परस्तस्मात्' इत्युक्तं; कस्मात् पुनः परः ? पूर्वोक्तात् भूतग्रामबीजभूतात् अविद्यालक्षणात् अव्यक्तात् अन्यः विलक्षणः भावः इत्यभिप्रायः । सनातनः चिरन्तनः यः सः भावः सर्वेषु भूतेषु ब्रह्मादिषु नश्यत्सु न विनश्यति ॥

20.1. 'Another'—distinct and different—from what? From what was referred to earlier. 'But' serves to stress the distinction of the eternal Being, sought to be affirmed, from the unmanifest source of matter. The eternal Being is the higher imperishable Brahman. "Though distinct, possibly. It may be similar"—to rule out this possibility the Lord speaks of 'another', meaning, 'with other characteristics'. It is Unmanifest, being beyond the range of the senses.

It is said to be 'beyond that'. Beyond what? Beyond what was earlier described as the seed state of the host of material things, called also the Unmanifest, meaning nescience. 'That

Brahman is a Being with other characteristics'—this is the idea. That eternal or everlasting Being perishes not when all others like Brahmā do perish.

अव्यक्तोऽक्षर इत्युक्तस्तमाहुः परमां गतिम् ।
यं प्राप्य न निवर्तन्ते तद्धाम परमं मम ॥२१॥

21. The Unmanifest is said to be 'the Imperishable'; they say that He is the supreme goal. My supreme abode is that, attaining which none returns.

21.1. अव्यक्तः इति ॥ योऽसौ अव्यक्तः अक्षरः इत्युक्तः तं एव अक्षरसंज्ञकं अव्यक्तं भावं आहुः परमां प्रकृष्टां गतिम् । यं परं भावं प्राप्य गत्वा न निवर्तन्ते संसाराय, तत् धाम स्थानं परमं प्रकृष्टं मम, 'विष्णोः परमं पदम्' [नृ. पू. ५.१०] इत्यर्थः ॥२१॥

21.1. That unmanifest called the Imperishable they declare to be the supreme goal. That Supreme Being beyond, reaching which they no longer return to empirical life, is My 'Supreme abode', the exalted being of Viṣṇu.

22.0. तल्लब्धेः उपायः उच्यते—

22.0. The means of winning it is laid down:

पुरुषः स परः पार्थ भक्त्या लभ्यस्त्वनन्यया ।
यस्यान्तःस्थानि भूतानि येन सर्वमिदं ततम् ॥२२॥

22. That supreme Spirit, O Arjuna! may be won by means of unswerving devotion—the Spirit in whom all beings dwell and by whom all this is pervaded.

22.1. पुरुषः इति ॥ पुरुषः पुरि शयनात् पूर्णत्वाद्वा, सः परः पार्थ, परः निरतिशयः, यस्मात् पुरुषात् न परं किञ्चित् । सः भक्त्या लभ्यस्तु ज्ञानलक्षणया अनन्यया आत्मविषयया [७. १७.] । यस्य पुरुषस्य अन्तःस्थानि मध्यस्थानि भूतानि

कार्यभूतानि; कार्यं हि कारणस्य अन्तर्वर्ति भवति । येन पुरुषेण सर्वं इदं जगत् ततं व्याप्तम् आकाशेनेव घटादि ॥

22.1. That supreme Spirit is so styled as He abides in the city of the body or as He is a plenum. He is supreme, Arjuna! being unexcelled. Nothing excels Him. He may be won through devotion which is characterized by knowledge, and which is 'unswerving'—solely directed to the Self (Vide 7.17) Within Him dwell all effected beings. Effect indeed falls within the cause. By the Spirit all this world is pervaded, just as effects like pot, etc., are by space.

23.0. प्रकृतानां योगिनां प्रणवावेशितब्रह्मबुद्धीनां कालान्तरमुक्तिभाजां ब्रह्मप्रतिपत्तये उत्तरो मार्गो वक्तव्यः इति 'यत्र काले' इत्यादि विवक्षितार्थसमर्पणार्थं उच्यते —आवृत्तिमार्गोपन्यासः इतरमार्गस्तुत्यर्थः —

23.0. The Northern Path has to be described so that, in due course, through liberation in stages, Brahman may be won by those Yogins who have set their intellect on AUM, Brahman's symbol, and to whom reference has already been made (Vide 8.13). Hence the verses from 8.23 onwards. The description of recurrence implies laudation of the other way that excludes recurrence.

यत्र काले त्वनावृत्तिमावृत्तिं चैव योगिनः ।
प्रयाता यान्ति तं कालं वक्ष्यामि भरतर्षभ ॥२३॥

23. Best of Bhārata princes! I shall declare the time departing in which, the Yogins do not return and also that, departing in which, they return.

23.1. यत्र इति ॥ यत्र काले प्रयाताः इति व्यवहितेन सम्बन्धः । यत्र यस्मिन् काले तु अनावृत्तिं अपुनर्जन्म आवृत्तिं तद्विपरीतां चैव । 'योगिनः' इति योगिनः कर्मिणश्च उच्यन्ते, कर्मिणस्तु गुणतः—'कर्मयोगेन योगिनाम्' [३.३.] इति विशेषणात्—योगिनः । यत्र काले प्रयाताः मृताः योगिनः अनावृत्तिं यान्ति, यत्र काले च प्रयाताः आवृत्तिं यान्ति, तं कालं वक्ष्यामि भरतर्षभ ॥

23.1. 'The time in which departing'—thus with the remote word '*prayātā*' have the first words to be construed. The time in which going, there is 'non-return', non-rebirth, and 'return', its opposite rebirth, happen. The term *yoginaḥ* denotes both Yogins and the agents of works. These agents, too, by virtue of quality are Yogins; for 3.3 lays it down that 'the discipline of Karma' has been prescribed for the Yogins. The time in which 'departing' or dying, the Yogins do not return and the time in which departing they return—that time I shall describe O best of Bhāratas!

24.0. तं कालं आह —

24.0. He describes the time:

अग्निर्ज्योतिरहः शुक्लः षण्मासा उत्तरायणम् ।
तत्र प्रयाता गच्छन्ति ब्रह्म ब्रह्मविदो जनाः ।।२४।।

24. The fire, light, day, the bright fortnight, the six months of the northern solar movements, departing in time marked by these, Brahman-knowers reach Brahman.

24.1. अग्निः इति ।। अग्निः कालभिमानिनी देवता । तथा — ज्योतिः अपि देवतैव कालाभिमानिनी । अथवा — अग्निज्योतिषी यथाश्रुते एव देवते । भूयसा तु निर्देशो 'यत्र काले' 'तं कालं' इति, आम्रवणवत् । तथा अहः देवता अहरभिमानिनी; शुक्लः शुक्लपक्षदेवता; षण्मासा उत्तरायणं, तत्रापि देवता एव मार्गभूता इति स्थितः अन्यत्र [ब्र. सू भाष्ये. ४.३.४.] अयं न्यायः । तत्र तस्मिन् मार्गे प्रयाताः मृताः गच्छन्ति ब्रह्म ब्रह्मविदः ब्रह्मोपासकाः ब्रह्मोपासनपराः जनाः । 'क्रमेण' इति वाक्यशेषः; न हि सद्योमुक्तिभाजां सम्यग्दर्शननिष्ठानां गतिः आगतिर्वा क्वचित् अस्ति । "न तस्य प्राणा उत्क्रामन्ति" (बृ. उ. ४.४.६.] इति श्रुतेः । ब्रह्मसंलीनप्राणाः एव ते ब्रह्ममयाः ब्रह्मभूताः एव ते ।।

24.1. The fire is the deity, presiding over time. Similarly light too is such a deity. Or fire and light are, as formulated, just deities. The expression, 'the time in which' is based on the principle of the dominance of the majority as in the expression 'a forest of mango trees'. So, too, 'day' is the deity governing day. 'Light' is the deity governing the bright fortnight. The six months of the northward course of the sun refer to the deity constituting the way of the gods. (Vide BSB. 4.3.4.) Going forth on this way, the departed Brahman-knowers, i.e., Brahman-worshippers, reach Brahman. The expression 'by stages' is understood, for movement and return are unthinkable for those who are instantly liberated and dedicated to right perception. Vide: 'His vital breaths do not depart' (BU 4.4.6.) Their breaths merge in Brahman; they are in large measure Brahman. They become Brahman, indeed.

धूमो रात्रिस्तथा कृष्णः षण्मासा दक्षिणायनम् ।
तत्र चान्द्रमसं ज्योतिर्योगी प्राप्य निवर्तते ॥२५॥

25. Smoke, night, the dark (fortnight) the six months of the sun's southern course—passing away during time marked by these, the Yogin reaches the lunar light and returns.

25.1. धूमः इति ॥ धूमः रात्रिः धूमाभिमानिनी रात्र्यभिमानिनी च देवता । तथा कृष्णः कृष्णपक्षदेवता । षण्मासा दक्षिणायनं इति च पूर्ववत् देवता एव । तत्र चंद्रमसि भवं चान्द्रमसं ज्योतिः फलं इष्टादिकारी योगी कर्मी प्राप्य भुक्त्वा तत्क्षयात् इह पुनः निवर्तते ॥

25.1. 'Smoke' and 'night' are deities presiding over these; so too is the 'dark fortnight' the deity presiding over it. The next phrase too, as in earlier cases, refers to the deity only. Departing, during periods marked by these the Yogin who has performed sacrifices, etc., experiences the fruits of his actions. When these decay, he returns from the sphere of the lunar light.

शुक्लकृष्णे गती ह्येते जगतः शाश्वते मते ।
एकया यात्यनावृत्तिमन्ययाऽऽवर्तते पुनः ॥२६॥

26. These two are indeed the light and the dark courses held to be eternal for the world. By means of the first one goes and does not return; by the other one comes back again.

26.1. शुक्ल इति ॥ शुक्लकृष्णे शुक्ला च कृष्णा च शुक्लकृष्णे, ज्ञानप्रकाशकत्वात् शुक्ला, तदभावात् कृष्णा, एते शुक्लकृष्णे हि गती—जगतः इति अधिकृतानां ज्ञानकर्मणोः, न जगतः सर्वस्य एव एते गती संभवतः—शाश्वते नित्ये, संसारस्य नित्यत्वात्, मते अभिप्रेते । तत्र एकया शुक्लया याति अनावृत्तिं, अन्यया इतरया आवर्तते पुनः भूयः ॥

26.1. The 'light and the dark'—light because it manifests knowledge, while its absence makes the other dark. These are the two courses. The expression 'for the world' refers to those who are eligible to tread the paths of knowledge and works and not to the entire world. These courses are deemed eternal; for, the empirical life is eternal. By means of the one viz. the 'light course', one achieves non-return; by means of the other, 'the dark course', one returns once more.

नैते सृती पार्थ जानन् योगी मुह्यति कश्चन ।
तस्मात्सर्वेषु कालेषु योगयुक्तो भवार्जुन ॥२७॥

27. Knowing these courses, Arjuna! no Yogin falls into delusion. Therefore, at all times apply yourself to Yoga.

27.1. नैते इति ॥ न एते यथोक्ते सृती मार्गौ पार्थ ! जानन् "संसाराय एका, अन्या मोक्षाय च" इति, योगी न मुह्यति कश्चन कश्चिदपि । तस्मात् सर्वेषु कालेषु योगयुक्तः समाहितः भव अर्जुन ॥

शृणु तस्य योगस्य माहात्म्यम् —

27.1. 'Knowing these two courses' or paths, i.e., knowing that one of them leads to the empirical state and that the other to liberation, no Yogin falls into delusion. Therefore, at all times, apply yourself to Yoga—be concentrated, O Arjuna!

Note the majesty of this Yoga:

**वेदेषु यज्ञेषु तपःसु चैव दानेषु यत्पुण्यफलं प्रदिष्टम् ।
अत्येति तत्सर्वमिदं विदित्वा योगी परं स्थानमुपैति चाद्यम् ॥२८॥**

28. The meritorious fruits (of learning) the Vedas, of sacrifices, penances and gifts—all these the Yogin transcends by knowing this, and he also reaches the supreme Primal State.

इति श्रीमहाभारते शतसाहस्र्यां संहितायां वैयासिक्यां भीष्मपर्वणि
श्रीमद्भगवद्गीतासूपनिषत्सु ब्रह्मविद्यायां योगशास्त्रे श्रीकृष्णार्जुनसंवादे
तारकब्रह्मयोगो नाम अष्टमोऽध्यायः ॥

28.1. वेदेषु सम्यगधीतेषु यज्ञेषु च साद्गुण्येन अनुष्ठितेषु तपःसु च सुतप्तेषु, दानेषु च सम्यग्दत्तेषु, एतेषु यत् पुण्यफलं प्रदिष्टं शास्त्रेण, अत्येति अतीत्य गच्छति तत् सर्वं फलजातम्, इदं विदित्वा सप्तप्रश्ननिर्णयद्वारेण उक्तं अर्थं सम्यक् अवधार्य अनुष्ठाय योगी, परं उत्कृष्टं ऐश्वरं स्थानं उपैति च प्रतिपद्यते आद्यं आदौ भवं, कारणं ब्रह्म इत्यर्थः ॥

28.1. The auspicious fruit, laid down by the *śāstra*, regarding the Vedas well-mastered, sacrifices rightly performed, penances well-undergone, and gifts duly offered—all this the Yogin, properly knowing and practising what has been stated here in the course of answering the seven questions, surpasses and reaches the primal divine status, i.e., Brahman the first cause. This is the idea.

इति श्रीमत्परमहंसपरिव्राजकाचार्यगोविन्दभगवत्पूज्यपादशिष्य —
श्रीमच्छंकरभगवतः कृतौ श्रीमद्भगवद्गीताभाष्ये धारणायोगो*
नाम अष्टमोऽध्यायः ॥८॥

*अस्याध्यायस्य महापुरुषयोग — ब्रह्माक्षरनिर्देश — अक्षरपरब्रह्मयोग — अभ्यासयोग — एवमादीनि नामान्तराणि उपलभ्यन्ते ।

नवमोऽध्यायः

CHAPTER IX

THE YOGA OF THE ROYAL SCIENCE OF THE ROYAL MYSTERY

0.1. अष्टमे नाडीद्वारेण धारणायोगः सगुणः उक्तः । तस्य च फलं अग्न्यर्चिरादिक्रमेण कालान्तरे ब्रह्मप्राप्तिलक्षणं एव अनावृत्तिरूपं निर्दिष्टम् । तत्र "अनेनैव प्रकारेण मोक्षप्राप्तिः फलं अधिगम्यते, न अन्यथा" इति तदाशङ्काव्याविवर्तयिषया श्रीभगवान् उवाच —

0.1. In the eighth chapter has been set forth the Yoga of retention with its characteristics, effected by means of the arteries. Its fruit, the eventual attainment, by stages along the path of fire, light, etc., of Brahman, whence there is no return, also has been indicated. In order to obviate the apprehension that achievement of liberation is possible only in this manner and no other, the blessed Lord said as follows:

श्रीभगवानुवाच :

इदं तु ते गुह्यतमं प्रवक्ष्याम्यनसूयवे ।
ज्ञानं विज्ञानसहितं यज्ज्ञात्वा मोक्ष्यसेऽशुभात् ॥१॥

The blessed Lord said:

1. Now I shall reveal to you, who carp not, this most recondite knowledge and its realization by mastering which you will be liberated from evil.

1.1. इदं इति ॥ इदं ब्रह्मज्ञानं, वक्ष्यमाणं, उक्तं च पूर्वेषु अध्यायेषु । तत् बुद्धौ सन्निधीकृत्य 'इदं' इत्याह । 'तु' शब्दो विशेषनिर्धारणार्थः — इदमेव तु सम्यग्ज्ञानं साक्षात् मोक्षप्राप्तिसाधनं, 'वासुदेवः सर्वमिति' [७.१९.] 'आत्मैवेदं सर्वं' [छां. उ. ७.२५.२.] 'एकमेवाद्वितीयं' [छां. उ. ६.२.१.] इत्यादिश्रुतिस्मृतिभ्यः; नान्यत्, 'अथ ते येऽन्यथाऽतो विदुः अन्यराजानः ते क्षय्यलोका भवन्ति' [छां. उ. ७.२५.२.] इत्यादिश्रुतिभ्यश्च । ते तुभ्यं गुह्यतमं गोप्यतमं प्रवक्ष्यामि कथयिष्यामि अनसूयवे असूयारहिताय । किं तत् ? ज्ञानं — किंविशिष्टं ? विज्ञानसहितं अनुभवयुक्तं, यत् ज्ञानं ज्ञात्वा प्राप्य मोक्ष्यसे अशुभात् संसारबन्धनात् ॥

1.1. 'This knowledge' of Brahman, presently to be set forth, and already expounded in previous chapters—the term 'this' is used to refer to this idea present in His mind. 'Now' serves to stress a certain distinctiveness—only this right knowledge directly leads to liberation, *Vide* the utterances in *smṛti* and *śruti:* 'That Vāsudeva is all this' (BG 7.12); 'Self is all this' (CU 7.25.2); 'One only without a second' (CU 6.2.1). No knowledge other than this will liberate. Also there are the following passages: "Now those who cognize otherwise are subject to other rulers; their worlds perish" (CU 7.25.2); 'I shall reveal to you this most recondite and hidden knowledge'; for you don't carp, are no fault-finder. What is indicated by 'this'? Knowledge and its realization or experience. Mastering it, you will be 'liberated from evil'—the bondage of empirical existence.

राजविद्या राजगुह्यं पवित्रमिदमुत्तमम् ।
प्रत्यक्षावगमं धर्म्यं सुसुखं कर्तुमव्ययम् ॥२॥

2. It is the sovereign science, the sovereign mystery, the best of purifiers. Its apprehension is immediate; it is righteous, imperishable and exceedingly easy to achieve.

2.1. राजविद्या इति ॥ राजविद्या विद्यानां राजा, दीप्त्यतिशयवत्त्वात्; दीप्यते हि इयं अतिशयेन ब्रह्मविद्या सर्वविद्यानाम्। तथा राजगुह्यं गुह्यानां राजा । पवित्रं पावनं इदं उत्तमं, सर्वेषां पावनानां शुद्धिकारणं इदं ब्रह्मज्ञानं उत्कृष्टतमम् । अनेकजन्मसहस्रसंचितं अपि धर्माधर्मादि समूलं कर्म क्षणमात्रात् एव भस्मीकरोति इत्यतः किं तस्य पावनत्वं वक्तव्यम् । किञ्च— प्रत्यक्षावगमं प्रत्यक्षेण सुखादेः इव अवगमः यस्य तत् प्रत्यक्षावगमम् । अनेकगुणवतोऽपि धर्मविरुद्धत्वं दृष्टं, न तथा आत्मज्ञानं धर्मविरोधि, किंतु धर्म्यं धर्मात् अनपेतम् । एवमपि, स्यात् दुःखसंपाद्यं इत्यत आह—सुसुखं कर्तुं, यथा रत्नविवेकविज्ञानम् । तत्र अल्पायासानां अन्येषां कर्मणां सुखसम्पाद्यानां अल्पफलत्वं, दुष्कराणां च महाफलत्वं दृष्टमिति, इदं तु सुखसम्पाद्यत्वात् फलक्षयात् व्येति इति प्राप्ते आह—अव्ययं इति । न अस्य फलतः कर्मवत् व्ययः अस्तीति अव्ययम् । अतः श्रद्धेयं आत्मज्ञानम् ॥

2.1. It is called 'the sovereign science' because it is rich in exceeding splendour. Among sciences, this science of Brahman is exceedingly resplendent. Similarly among mysteries it is 'sovereign'. This is 'the best of purifiers'; for, this Brahman-knowledge is the foremost cause of purity. Why should one elaborate the sanctifying virtue of Brahman-knowledge that burns up all works and their causes, both righteous and unrighteous, accumulated in the course of thousands of lives? Besides, its apprehension is 'immediate'—it is apprehended like pleasure, etc., immediately. Things rich in numerous merits may yet be opposed to righteousness. But this knowledge of the Self is not opposed to righteousness; it conforms to 'righteousness'. Nevertheless it may prove very hard to achieve. No, it is exceedingly 'easy to master', as is the lore of gems. It may be objected: 'Other easy activities yield but little profit, while hard jobs may yield much profit. This Self-knowledge too, being easy to acquire, may yield only ephemeral fruit and prove fleeting.' Not so, for it is 'imperishable'. Like all activity it does not wear away in respect of its fruit. Therefore Self-knowledge merits close attention.

अश्रद्दधानाः पुरुषा धर्मस्यास्य परन्तप ।
अप्राप्य मां निवर्तन्ते मृत्युसंसारवर्त्मनि ॥३॥

3. Men who have little faith in this spiritual law, O hero! return to the way of repeated deaths, failing to reach Me.

3.1. अश्रद्दधाना इति ॥ अश्रद्दधानाः श्रद्धाविरहिताः आत्मज्ञानस्य धर्मस्य अस्य स्वरूपे तत्फले च नास्तिकाः पापकारिणः, असुराणां उपनिषदं देहमात्रात्मदर्शनमेव प्रतिपन्नाः, असुतृपः पापाः पुरुषाः अश्रद्दधानाः परन्तप ! अप्राप्य मां परमेश्वरं — मत्प्राप्तौ नैव आशङ्का इति मत्प्राप्तिमार्गसाधनभेदभक्तिमात्रमपि अप्राप्य इत्यर्थः — निवर्तन्ते निश्चयेन वर्तन्ते — क्व ? — मृत्युसंसारवर्त्मनि मृत्युयुक्तः संसारः मृत्युसंसारः, तस्य वर्त्म नरकतिर्यगादिप्राप्तिमार्गः तस्मिन्नेव वर्तन्ते इत्यर्थः ॥

3.1. 'Who have little faith'—are those devoid of faith in the nature and fruit of this spiritual law of Self-knowledge. They are negationists and sinners who resort to the esoteric doctrine of *asuras*, viz., the body is the self; they are the vitalists. Failing to reach Me, the supreme Lord, they 'return' or stick to the path leading to empirical life and death, the path leading to the status of animals or to life in hell. They 'return' without gaining even devotion, the kind of spiritual practice that leads on to Me.

4.0. स्तुत्या अर्जुनं अभिमुखीकृत्य आह —

4.0. Having drawn, by means of this laudation, Arjuna's attention, the Lord declares:

मया ततमिदं सर्वं जगदव्यक्तमूर्तिना ।
मत्स्थानि सर्वभूतानि न चाहं तेष्ववस्थितः ॥४॥

4. The entire world has been pervaded by Me in My Unmanifest form. All beings dwell in Me, but I dwell not in them.

4.1. मया इति ॥ मया मम यः परो भावः तेन ततं व्याप्तं सर्वं इदं जगत् अव्यक्तमूर्तिना न व्यक्ता मूर्तिः स्वरूपं यस्य मम सः अहं अव्यक्तमूर्तिः तेन मया अव्यक्तमूर्तिना, करणागोचरस्वरूपेण इत्यर्थः । तस्मिन् मयि अव्यक्तमूर्तौ स्थितानि मत्स्थानि, सर्वभूतानि ब्रह्मादीनि स्तम्बपर्यन्तानि । न हि निरात्मकं किंचित् भूतं व्यवहाराय अवकल्पते । अतः मत्स्थानि मया आत्मना आत्मवत्त्वेन स्थितानि, अतः मयि स्थितानि इति उच्यन्ते । तेषां भूतानां अहमेव आत्मा इत्यतः तेषु स्थितः, मूर्तवत् संश्लेषाभावेन आकाशस्यापि अन्तरतमो हि अहम् । न हि असंसर्गि वस्तु क्वचित् आधेयभावेन अवस्थितं भवति ॥

4.1. 'By Me'—by that supreme form of My being all this world has been pervaded. That form of My being is Unmanifest—beyond the range of the senses of perception. This is the idea. In Me, with that Unmanifest form dwell all beings from Brahmā to a blade of grass; for no being devoid of the Self can empirically exist. Therefore, they are said to exist or have Me as their Self. That is how they are said to exist in Me. Since I alone am the Self of beings, to deluded minds I appear to dwell in them. Hence I affirm that I do not dwell in contact with them, as, unlike a concrete body, I am not held in them. Indeed I am the inmost principle even of space. No objects without contacts may have a contained existence in any receptacle.

5.0. अत एव असंसर्गित्वात् मम –

5.0. Not being in material contact with anything–

न च मत्स्थानि भूतानि पश्य मे योगमैश्वरम् ।
भूतभृन्न च भूतस्थो ममात्मा भूतभावनः ॥५॥

5. Neither do beings exist in Me—behold My sovereign Yoga! My Self brings beings into existence and sustains them, yet does not dwell in them.

5.1. न च इति ॥ न च मत्स्थानि भूतानि ब्रह्मादीनि । पश्य मे योगं युक्तिं घटनं मे मम ऐश्वरं ईश्वरस्येमं ऐश्वरं योगं, आत्मनो याथात्म्यं इत्यर्थः । तथा च श्रुतिः असंसर्गित्वात् असङ्गतां दर्शयति — 'असङ्गो न हि सज्जते' [बृ. उ. ३.९.२६.] । इदं च आश्चर्यं अन्यत् पश्य — भूतभृत्, असङ्गोऽपि सन् भूतानि बिभर्ति; न च भूतस्थः, यथोक्तेन न्यायेन दर्शितत्वात् भूतस्थत्वानुपपत्तेः । कथं तु पुनः उच्यते "असौ मम आत्मा" इति ? विभज्य देहादिसंघातं, तस्मिन् अहङ्कारं अध्यारोप्य, लोकबुद्धिं अनुसरन् व्यपदिशति 'मम आत्मा' इति, न पुनः आत्मनः आत्मा अन्यः इति लोकवत् अजानन् । तथा भूतभावनः भूतानि भावयति — उत्पादयति – वर्धयति इति वा भूतभावनः ॥

5.1. 'Beings', Brahmā, etc., do not exist in Me. Behold the manner of My creative power or of fashioning of beings by Me as the Lord, i.e. the truth of the Lord's creative process. Thus the Veda also points out the detachment of the Lord as Self, that is unassociated with all things: 'Detached, the Self cleaves not' (BU 3.9.26). And behold another marvel: though detached, My Self sustains all beings; yet it does not dwell in them, as has already been explained above. Reason shows Self to be no content. Why then is it stated 'My Self'? Analysing the conglomerate of body, senses and so forth, and super-imposing the I-sense on it, the Lord uses the expression 'My Self' as in common parlance, and not, like the deluded world, due to failure to note that Self cannot have another as *Its* Self. This Self gives rise to beings or multiplies them. Hence the expression 'brings beings into existence'.

6.0. यथोक्तेन श्लोकद्वयेन उक्त अर्थं दृष्टान्तेत उपपादयन् आह –

6.0. Illustrating and explaining the idea expressed above in the two verses the Lord declared:

यथाऽऽकाशस्थितो नित्यं वायुः सर्वत्रगो महान् ।
तथा सर्वाणि भूतानि मत्स्थानीत्युपधारय ॥६॥

6. Just as the vast (expanse of) air, eternally subsists in space while moving everywhere, even so know that all beings exist in Me.

6.1. यथा इति ॥ यथा लोके आकाशस्थितः आकाशे स्थितः नित्यं सदा वायुः सर्वत्र गच्छतीति सर्वत्रगः महान् परिमाणतः, तथा आकाशवत् सर्वगते मयि असंश्लेषेण एव स्थितानि इत्येवं उपधारय विजानीहि ॥

6.1. Just as in the world 'the air' subsists in space, and always moves everywhere—air that is vast in its dimensions—so, know that all beings exist in Me, without cleaving to Me, who am omnipresent like space.

7.0. एवं, वायुः आकाशे इव, मयि स्थितानि सर्वभूतानि स्थितिकाले; तानि —

7.0. Thus like the air in space, during the period of their existence, all beings subsist in Me.

सर्वभूतानि कौन्तेय प्रकृतिं यान्ति मामिकाम् ।
कल्पक्षये पुनस्तानि कल्पादौ विसृजाम्यहम् ॥७॥

7. All beings, Arjuna! at the end of a cycle repair to My

nature; again, at the beginning of the (next) cycle, I loose them forth.

7.1. सर्व इति ॥ सर्वभूतानि कौन्तेय प्रकृतिं त्रिगुणात्मिकां अपरां [निकृष्टां] यान्ति मामिकां मदीयां कल्पक्षये प्रलयकाले । पुनः भूयः तानि भूतानि उत्पत्तिकाले कल्पादौ विसृजामि उत्पादयामि अहम् पूर्ववत् ॥

7.1. All beings, Arjuna! repair to my lower nature, consisting of the three constituents, at the end of the cycle or the period of cosmic dissolution. Again, at the time of origination, in the beginning of the next cycle, I 'loose them forth'—i.e., originate them, as in previous cycles.

8.0. एवं अविद्यालक्षणाम् –

8.0. Thus to My Nature, nescience:

प्रकृतिं स्वामवष्टभ्य विसृजामि पुनः पुनः ।
भूतग्राममिमं कृत्स्नमवशं प्रकृतेर्वशात् ॥८॥

8. Resorting, again and again, I loose forth this entire multitude of bound beings, swayed by and dependent on that nature.

8.1. प्रकृतिं इति ॥ प्रकृतिं स्वां स्वीयां अवष्टभ्य आश्रित्य [वशीकृत्य] विसृजामि पुनः पुनः प्रकृतितो जातं भूतग्रामं भूतसमुदायं इमं वर्तमानं कृत्स्नं समस्तं अवशं अस्वतन्त्रं, अविद्यादिदोषैः परवशीकृतं, प्रकृतेः वशात् स्वभाववशात् ॥

8.1. 'Resorting to'—subduing—My Nature and depending on it, I 'loose forth' this nature-born multitude of dependent beings in their entirety. They are 'dependent' because they have been overwhelmed by flaws like nescience; for, they are swayed by their in-born tendencies.

9.0. तर्हि तस्य ते परमेश्वरस्य, भूतग्रामं इमं विषमं विदधतः, तन्निमित्ताभ्यां धर्माधर्माभ्यां संबन्धः स्यादिति ? इदं आह भगवान् –

9.0. 'If so, You, the supreme Lord, fashioning beings unequally, are subject to righteousness and its opposite, the causes of these inequalities'. In explanation, the Lord declares:

न च मां तानि कर्माणि निबध्नन्ति धनंजय ।
उदासीनवदासीनमसक्तं तेषु कर्मसु ।।९।।

9. Those actions, Arjuna! bind Me not; I am as it were, indifferent (to them all), being unattached to them.

9.1. न च इति ।। न च मां ईश्वरं तानि भूतग्रामस्य विषमसर्गनिमित्तानि कर्माणि निबध्नन्ति धनंजय । तत्र कर्मणां असंबन्धित्वे कारणं आह—उदासीनवत् आसीनं, यथा उदासीनः उपेक्षकः कश्चित् तद्वत् आसीनं, आत्मनः अविक्रियत्वात्, असक्तं फलासङ्गरहितं, अभिमानवर्जितं "अहं करोमि" इति तेषु कर्मसु । अतः अन्यस्यापि कर्तृत्वाभिमानाभावः फलासङ्गाभावश्च असम्बन्धकारणं, अन्यथा कर्मभिः बध्यते मूढः कोशकारवत् इत्यभिप्रायः ।।

9.1. 'Those actions of Mine' such as the creation of hosts of beings, 'bind me not', the Lord, O Arjuna! The reason for it is this. 'I am indifferent as it were'. As one unconcerned I subsist, for the Self is immutable; 'unattached'—not clinging to the fruits of actions. I don't have the conceit of agency in regard to those creative works. The thought, 'I do them' does not occur to Me. In the case of others, too, the cause of dissociation is the absence of the conceit of agency and the non-clinging to fruits of works. Otherwise, deluded man, like a silk-worm, will get bound by his works. This is the idea.

10.0. तत्र 'भूतग्रामं इमं विसृजामि' (९.८), 'उदासीनवत् आसीनम्' (९.९) इति च विरुद्धं उच्यते, इति तत्परिहारार्थं आह –

10.0. The statements 'I loose forth this multitude of beings', and 'I am indifferent, as it were' are contradictory. To obviate this contradiction, the Lord says:

मयाऽध्यक्षेण प्रकृतिः सूयते सचराचरम् ।
हेतुनाऽनेन कौन्तेय जगद्विपरिवर्तते ।।१०।।

10. Due to Me, the Supervisor, Nature gives birth to the world of mobile and immobile (beings). For this reason, Arjuna! it revolves in manifold ways.

10.1. मया इति ॥ मया सर्वतो दृशिमात्रस्वरूपेण अविक्रियात्मना अध्यक्षेण मया, मम माया त्रिगुणात्मिका अविद्यालक्षणा प्रकृतिः सूयते उत्पादयति सचराचरं जगत् । तथा च मन्त्रवर्णः –

एको देवः सर्वभूतेषु गूढः सर्वव्यापी सर्वभूतान्तरात्मा ।

कर्माध्यक्षः सर्वभूताधिवासः साक्षी चेता केवलो निर्गुणश्च ॥ [श्वे. उ. ६.११.] इति साक्षिमात्रेण हेतुना निमित्तेन अनेन अध्यक्षत्वेन कौन्तेय ! जगत् सचराचरं व्यक्ताव्यक्तात्मकं विपरिवर्तते सर्वावस्थासु । दृशिकर्मत्वापत्तिनिमित्ता हि जगतः सर्वा प्रवृत्तिः—'अहं इदं भोक्ष्ये,' 'पश्यामि इदम्', 'शृणोमि इदं,' 'सुखं अनुभवामि,' 'दुःखं अनुभवामि,' 'एतदर्थमिदं करिष्ये,' 'इदं ज्ञास्यामि' — इत्याद्या अवगतिनिष्ठा अवगत्यवसानैव । 'यो अस्याध्यक्षः परमे व्योमन्' [ऋ. सं. १०.१२९.७; तै. ब्रा. २.८.९.] इत्यादयश्च मन्त्राः एतमर्थं दर्शयन्ति । ततश्च एकस्य देवस्य सर्वाध्यक्ष-भूतचैतन्यमात्रस्य परमार्थतः सर्वभोगानभिसम्बन्धिनः अन्यस्य चेतनान्तरस्य अभावे भोक्तुः अन्यस्य अभावात् । किंनिमित्ता इयं सृष्टिः इत्यत्र प्रश्नप्रतिवचनेऽनुपपन्ने, 'को अद्धा वेद क इह प्रवोचत् । कुतं आजाता कुत इयं विसृष्टिः' [ऋ. सं. १०.१२९.६., तै. ब्रा. २.८.९.] इत्यादिमन्त्रवर्णेभ्यः । दर्शितं च भगवता — 'अज्ञानेनावृतं ज्ञानं तेन मुह्यन्ति जन्तवः' [५.१५.] इति ॥

एतं मां

10.1. 'Due to Me, the Supervisor', the immutable, whose essence is pure perception, My māyā, consisting of the three constituents or nescience, gives birth to the world of beings, mobile and immobile. *Vide* the *mantra* S.U. 6.11: "The one God is hidden in all beings, all-pervading, the inner Self of all beings, the supervisor of works, dwelling in all, Witness, Apprehender, Alone and beyond constituents." Due to this reason—i.e., My status as 'Supervisor'—O Arjuna! the world revolves in all its states. All activities in the world—(contents of propositions like) 'I shall enjoy this', 'I see this', 'I experience pleasure', 'I suffer pain', 'I shall do this to get at this', 'I shall cognize this' and so forth—consist of, and culminate in, knowledge only. Vedic verses demonstrate this idea: "He the Supervisor of this world in the supreme sky", (RV.10.129.7; TB.2.8.9). Thus the one Lord the Supervisor of all, who is pure consciousness, is in reality unrelated to all empirical experiences. In the absence of any other conscious being, there is no other experiencer. So it is unreasonable to ask why there is this variegated creation or offer an answer, *Vide*: "Who knows, in fact, who has ever elucidated here, why and whence this varigated creation has come into being?" RV.10.129.6, TB.2.8.9). The Lord also elucidates this: "Knowledge is shrouded in ignorance; therefore living beings are deluded" (BG.5.15).

Nevertheless, the omniscient Self of all beings, ever pure, awake and free though I am,

अवजानन्ति मां मूढा मानुषीं तनुमाश्रितम् ।।
परं भावमजानन्तो मम भूतमहेश्वरम् ।।११।।

11. Fools deride Me, who have assumed a human body; for, they are unaware of My transcendent status as the great Lord of beings.

11.1. अवजानन्ति इति ।। अवजानन्ति अवज्ञां परिभवं कुर्वन्ति मां मूढा अविवेकिनो मानुषीं मनुष्यसंबन्धिनीं तनुं देहं आश्रितं, मनुष्यदेहेन व्यवहरन्तमित्येतत् । परं प्रकृष्टं भावं परमात्मतत्त्वं आकाशकल्पं आकाशात् अपि अन्तरतमं अजानन्तो मम भूतमहेश्वरं सर्वभूतानां महान्तमीश्वरं स्वं आत्मानम् । ततश्च तस्य मम अवज्ञाभावनेनाऽऽहताः वराकास्ते ।।

कथम् ? —

11.1. 'Fools deride'—show contempt and aversion for Me, since they fail to discriminate. As I have assumed a human body, I function as a human being. They know nothing about My 'transcendent'—exalted—status, the truth of the Supreme Self that is immense like space and subtler than it. I am the great Lord of all beings, their very Self. Therefore are those unfortunate ones smitten by their attitude of contempt towards Me.

How?

मोघाशा मोघकर्माणो मोघज्ञाना विचेतसः ॥
राक्षसीमासुरीं चैव प्रकृतिं मोहिनीं श्रिताः ॥१२॥

12. Futile are their desires, futile their works, and futile their cognitions! they are mindless; (for) they have resorted to the delusive nature of monsters and demons.

12.1. मोघाशा इति ॥ मोघाशाः वृथाऽऽशाः । आशिषः येषां ते मोघाशाः । तथा मोघकर्माणः यानि च अग्निहोत्रादीनि तैः अनुष्ठीयमानानि कर्माणि तानि च, तेषां भगवत्परिभवात्, स्वात्मभूतस्य च अज्ञानात्, मोघान्येव निष्फलानि कर्माणि भवन्तीति मोघकर्माणः । तथा मोघज्ञानाः निष्फलज्ञानाः ज्ञानमपि तेषां निष्फलमेव स्यात् । विचेतसः विगतविवेकाश्च ते भवन्ति इत्यभिप्रायः । किंच ते भवन्ति राक्षसीं रक्षसां प्रकृतिं स्वभावं आसुरीं असुराणां च प्रकृतिं मोहिनीं मोहकरीं देहात्मवादिनीं श्रिताः आश्रिताः "छिन्धि, भिन्धि, पिब, खाद, परस्वम् अपहर" इत्येवंवदनशीलाः क्रूरकर्माणः भवन्तीत्यर्थः । "असुर्या नाम ते लोकाः" [ई. उ. ३.] इति श्रुतेः ॥

12.1. 'Their desires are futile' or unprofitable; so are works like the fire-sacrifice performed by them fruitless; for, they have spurned the Lord and are ignorant of their real Self, the Lord Himself. So also are their cognitions; their knowledge too is devoid of fruit. They are mindless or lacking in discrimination. This is the import. They have also resorted to the nature of monsters and demons—a nature that deludes. For, it treats the body as the Self and they habitually shout: "Cut, shatter, drink, eat, rob." Their works are ruthless. Vide: "There are the worlds called the demoniac" (IU.3).

13.0. ये पुनः श्रद्दधानाः भगवद्भक्तिलक्षणे मोक्षमार्गे प्रवृत्ताः—

13.0. On the contrary, the faithful, treading the path of deliverance marked by devotion to the Lord, are described:

महात्मानस्तु मां पार्थ दैवीं प्रकृतिमाश्रिताः ॥
भजन्त्यनन्यमनसो ज्ञात्वा भूतादिमव्ययम् ॥१३॥

13. But magnanimous persons, resorting to a nature that is divine, O Arjuna! adore Me single-mindedly, knowing Me to be the imperishable source of beings.

13.1. महात्मानः इति ॥ महात्मानः तु अक्षुद्रचित्ताः मां ईश्वरं पार्थ ! दैवीं देवानां प्रकृतिं शमदमदयाश्रद्धादिलक्षणां आश्रिताः सन्तः भजन्ति सेवन्ते अनन्यमनसः अनन्यचित्ताः ज्ञात्वा भूतादिं वियदादीनां प्राणिनां चाऽऽदिं कारणम् अव्ययम् ॥

कथम् ? —

13.1. 'But magnanimous persons' having capacious minds adore Me the Lord, Arjuna! 'resorting to a nature that is divine'—marked by restraint of mind and senses, compassion, faith, etc. They are 'single-minded'—having a mind given to nothing other than Me. They know Me to be 'the imperishable source'—the eternal cause, of things like space, etc., and of living beings. How?

सततं कीर्तयन्तो मां यतन्तश्च दृढव्रताः ॥
नमस्यन्तश्च मां भक्त्या नित्ययुक्ता उपासते ॥१४॥

14. Incessantly glorifying Me, striving with steadfast vows; prostrating; eternally united, they worship Me with devotion.

14.1. सततं इति ॥ सततं सर्वदा भगवन्तं ब्रह्मस्वरूपं मां कीर्तयन्तः यतन्तः च इन्द्रियोपसंहारशमदमदयाहिंसादिलक्षणैर्धर्मैः प्रयतन्तश्च दृढव्रताः दृढं स्थिरं अचाल्यं व्रतं येषां ते दृढव्रताः नमस्यन्तः च मां हृदयेशयं आत्मानं भक्त्या नित्ययुक्ताः सन्तः उपासते सेवन्ते ॥

14.1. 'Incessantly'—always, they glorify Me, the Lord, whose essence is Brahman; and striving—cultivating virtues like the withdrawal of sense-organs, restraint of mind and senses, compassion, non-violence, etc. Their vows are 'steadfast'—unshakable. Prostrating, they worship Me, the Lord dwelling in the heart, with devotion; they are in eternal union with Me.

15.0. ते केन प्रकारेण उपासते इति ? उच्यते —

15.0. In what all varied ways do they worship? Answer:

ज्ञानयज्ञेन चाप्यन्ये यजन्तो मामुपासते ।
एकत्वेन पृथक्त्वेन बहुधा विश्वतोमुखम् ॥१५॥

15. And others, worshipping Me with the sacrifice of knowledge, wait on Me looking up to Me as one with themselves or as different, in manifold ways—Me with face turned everywhere.

15.1. ज्ञानयज्ञेन इति ॥ ज्ञानयज्ञेन ज्ञानमेव भगवद्विषयं यज्ञः, तेन ज्ञानयज्ञेन यजन्तः पूजयन्तः मां ईश्वरं च अपि अन्ये अन्यामुपासनां परित्यज्य उपासते । तच्च ज्ञानं एकत्वेन "एकमेव परं ब्रह्म" इति परमार्थदर्शनेन यजन्तः उपासते । केचिच्च पृथक्त्वेन "आदित्यचन्द्रादिभेदेन स एव भगवान् विष्णुः अवस्थितः" इति उपासते । केचित् "बहुधा अवस्थितः स एव भगवान् सर्वतोमुखः विश्वरूपः" इति तं विश्वरूपं सर्वतोमुखं बहुधा बहुप्रकारेण उपासते ॥

15.1. 'The sacrifice of knowledge'—the knowledge whose content is 'the Lord is the sacrifice'. Some worship Me, the Lord, with *this* sacrifice, giving up all other forms of worship. That knowledge treats Me as one. 'The supreme Brahman is one only'—this metaphysically right perception is the means of their worship. Others treat Me 'as different', holding 'Lord Viṣṇu is manifest as the sun, the moon etc.', and worship. Yet others worship, in manifold ways, Me 'with face turned everywhere', holding: the same Lord exists in manifold ways; all forms are His.

16.0. यदि बहुभिः प्रकारैः उपासते, कथं त्वामेव उपासते इति ? अतः आह —

16.0. 'If they worship in many ways, why do they worship only You?' Answer:

अहं क्रतुरहं यज्ञः स्वधाऽहमहमौषधम् ।
मन्त्रोऽहमहमेवाज्यमहमग्निरहं हुतम् ॥१६॥

16. I am the elaborate Vedic rite; I am the sacrifice; I am the ancestral oblation; I am the edible herb; I am the incantation; I am the lustrated butter: I am the fire; I am the oblation.

16.1. अहं इति ॥ अहं क्रतुः, श्रौतकर्मभेदः अहमेव । अहं यज्ञः स्मार्तः । किंच स्वधा अन्नं अहं, पितृभ्यः यत् दीयते । अहं औषधं, सर्वप्राणिभिः यत् अद्यते तत् औषधशब्दशब्दितं [वाच्यं] व्रीहियवादिसाधारणम् । अथवा — 'स्वधा' इति सर्वप्राणिसाधारणं अन्नं, 'औषधं' इति व्याध्युपशमनार्थं भेषजम् । मन्त्रः अहं, येन पितृभ्यः देवताभ्यश्च हविः दीयते । अहं एव आज्यं हविश्च । अहं अग्निः, यस्मिन् हूयते हविः सः अग्निः अहम् । अहं हुतं हवनकर्म च ॥

किञ्च —

16.1. *Kratu* is a complex Vedic rite, which I am. Also am I the sacrifice enjoined by *Smṛti*. I am the offering of food made to the ancestral spirits. I am the herbs on which living beings feed, including rice, barley etc. Or, *svadhā* may denote the food of all living beings whereas *auṣadha* denotes healing herbs. I am the incantation with which offerings are made to the manes and gods. Also, I am the lustrated butter and oblation. I am the fire in which the offerings are placed, as well as the act of offering. And,

पिताऽहमस्य जगतो माता धाता पितामहः ।
वेद्यं पवित्रमोङ्कार ऋक्साम यजुरेव च ॥१७॥

17. The Father of this world am I: (its) Mother, sustainer, and grandsire; I am the holy object of knowledge; the sacred syllable AUM; Ṛk, Sāma also Yajus.

17.1. पिता इति ॥ पिता जनयिता अहं अस्य जगतः, माता जनयित्री, धाता कर्मफलस्य प्राणिभ्यः विधाता, पितामहः पितुः पिता, वेद्यं वेदितव्यं, पवित्रं पावनं, ओंकारः, ऋक्, साम, यजुः एव च ॥

किञ्च —

17.1. 'The Father'—the generator, of this world am I; its

Mother or matrix; sustainer or the regulator awarding to living beings fruits of their actions. Grandsire—father's Father, the sacred object of knowledge; AUM, Ṛk, Sāma, and Yajus. Moreover,

गतिर्भर्ता प्रभुः साक्षी निवासः शरणं सुहृत् ।
प्रभवः प्रलयः स्थानं निधानं बीजमव्ययम् ॥१८॥

18. The Goal, the Support, the Lord, the Witness, Abode, Refuge, Friend, Source, Dissolution, Existence, Treasury, and the indestructible Seed.

18.1. गतिः इति ॥ गतिः कर्मफलम्, भर्ता पोष्टा, प्रभुः स्वामी, साक्षी प्राणिनां कृताकृतस्य, निवासः यस्मिन् प्राणिनः निवसन्ति, शरणं आर्तानां — प्रपन्नानां आर्तिहरः, सुहृत् प्रत्युपकारानपेक्षः सन् उपकारी, प्रभवः उत्पत्तिः जगतः, प्रलयः प्रलीयते अस्मिन् इति, तथा स्थानं तिष्ठति अस्मिन् इति, निधानं निक्षेपः कालान्तरोपभोग्यं प्राणिनाम्, बीजं प्ररोहकारणं प्ररोहधर्मिणाम्, अव्ययं — यावत्संसारभावित्वात् अव्ययम् । न हि अबीजं किञ्चित् प्ररोहति; नित्यं च प्ररोहदर्शनात् बीजसन्ततिः न व्येति इति गम्यते ॥

किंच —

18.1. 'The 'goal' is the fruit of actions. The 'support' is He who sustains. The 'Lord' is the owner. He is the 'Witness' of both what is done and left undone. He is the 'Abode'; for, all living beings dwell in Him. He is the 'Refuge' of those who suffer—the dispeller of the sufferings of those who have sought 'Refuge. He is the 'Friend' who aids irrespective of any service in return. He is also the 'Source' or the world's origin. He is the 'Dissolution'—that in which the world is dissolved. He is 'Existence' as the world exists in Him; also the 'Treasury' of fruits which the living beings reap in future. He is the 'Seed'—the cause of sprouting of all that sprouts. It is 'indestructible' as it coexists with the world. Nothing seedless sprouts. The process of sprouting is always observed; so it follows that the chain of seeds is never terminated.

Besides,

तपाम्यहमहं वर्षं निगृह्णाम्युत्सृजामि च ।
अमृतं चैव मृत्युश्च सदसच्चाहमर्जुन ॥१९॥

19. I cause heat; I arrest and send forth rain; I am immortality and death; both being and non-being am I, O Arjuna!

19.1. तपामि इति ॥ तपामि अहं आदित्यः भूत्वा कैश्चित् रश्मिभिः उल्बणैः । अहं वर्षं कैश्चित् रश्मिभिः उत्सृजामि; उत्सृज्य पुनः । निगृह्णामि कैश्चित् रश्मिभिः अष्टभिः मासैः; पुनः उत्सृजामि प्रावृषि । अमृतं च एव देवानां, मृत्युः च मर्त्यानाम् । सत् यस्य यत् सम्बन्धितया विद्यमानं तत्, तद्विपरीतं असत् च एव अहं अर्जुन । न पुनः अत्यन्तमेव असत् भगवान्, स्वयं कार्यकारणे वा सदसती ॥

19.1. Becoming the sun, with some scorching rays I cause 'heat', and with others I 'send forth rain'. Again for eight months I 'withhold' it, sending it forth, in the rainy season, once more. I am the 'immortality' of the gods and the death of the mortals. 'Being' is what exists in relation to some, i.e., its cause; its opposite is 'non-being', which does not so exist. Both these I am—i.e., both cause and effect, O Arjuna! The Lord is never absolutely non-existent; nor is effect existent while cause is non-existent.

19.2. ये पूर्वोक्तैः निवृत्तिप्रकारैः एकत्वपृथक्त्वादिविज्ञानैः यज्ञैः मां पूजयन्तः उपासते ज्ञानविदः, ते यथाविज्ञानं माम् एव प्राप्नुवन्ति । ये पुनः अज्ञाः कामकामाः —

19.2. Those knowers who worship Me elaborately as stated earlier, 'by sacrifice' or forms of cognitions of unity, diversity, etc.—and these are forms of cessation from desire-prompted activities—do attain Me alone according to their perceptions. But regarding the ignorant, clinging to objects of desire,

त्रैविद्या मां सोमपाः पूतपापा
यज्ञैरिष्ट्वा स्वर्गतिं प्रार्थयन्ते ।
ते पुण्यमासाद्य सुरेन्द्रलोक
मश्नन्ति दिव्यान्दिवि देवभोगान् ॥२०॥

20. Conversant with the lore of the triple Vedic texts, drinkers of the Soma-juice, cleansed of sins, crave attainment of heaven after having sacrificed unto Me. They reach the meritorious world of Indra and enjoy there divine felicities.

20.1. त्रैविद्या: इति ॥ त्रैविद्या: ऋग्यजु:सामविद: मां वस्वादिदेवरूपिणं सोमपा: सोमं पिबन्तीति सोमपा:, तेनैव सोमपानेन पूतपापा: शुद्धकिल्बिषा:, यज्ञै: अग्निष्टोमादिभि: इष्ट्वा पूजयित्वा स्वर्गतिं स्वर्गगमनं, स्व: एव गति: स्वर्गति: तां, प्रार्थयन्ते । ते च पुण्यं पुण्यफलं आसाद्य संप्राप्य सुरेन्द्रलोकं शतक्रतो: स्थानं अश्नन्ति भुञ्जते दिव्यान् दिवि भवान् अप्राकृतान् देवभोगान् देवानां भोगान् ॥

20.1. 'Conversant with the lore of the 'triple Vedic texts' are those who know the Ṛg, Yajus and Sāma. They 'drink the Soma juice' and are cleansed of sins by that very drink. Thus they worship Me, who have assumed the forms of superhuman beings like Vasus etc., with sacrifices like the *agniṣṭoma* and crave 'attainment of heaven'—i.e., passage to paradise. Heaven is their goal. Attaining 'the world of Indra', the fruit of religious merit, they enjoy divine felicities—supernatural pleasures appropriate to gods.

ते तं भुक्त्वा स्वर्गलोकं विशालं क्षीणे पुण्ये मर्त्यलोकं विशन्ति ।
एवं त्रयीधर्ममनुप्रपन्ना गतागतं कामकामा लभन्ते ॥२१॥

21. Having enjoyed the vast world of heaven, their merit spent, they enter the world of mortals. Thus conforming to the law of the three Vedas and desiring objects of pleasure, they achieve movements to and from (heaven).

21.1. ते तं इति ॥ ते तं भुक्त्वा स्वर्गलोकं विशालं विस्तीर्णं क्षीणे पुण्ये मर्त्यलोकं विशन्ति आविशन्ति । एवं यथोक्तेन प्रकारेण त्रयीधर्मं केवलं वैदिकं कर्म अनुप्रपन्ना: गतागतं गतं च आगतं च गतागतं गमनागमनं कामकामा: कामान् कामयन्ते इति कामकामा: लभन्ते गतागतमेव, न तु स्वातन्त्र्यं क्वचित् लभन्ते इत्यर्थ: ॥

21.1. Having enjoyed the vast—the extensive—world of

heaven, they enter the 'world of mortals' when their 'merits are spent'. Thus, in the manner set forth, 'conforming solely to the laws of the three Vedas' and performing the Vedic rites, these seekers of desired objects gain only 'movements to and from heaven'—but not freedom anywhere. This is the idea.

22.0. ये पुनः निष्कामाः सम्यग्दर्शिनः —

22.0. But what about men of right perception who cherish no desires?

अनन्याश्चिन्तयन्तो मां ये जनाः पर्युपासते ।
तेषां नित्याभियुक्तानां योगक्षेमं वहाम्यहम् ॥२२॥

22. To men who exclusively meditate on Me and elaborately worship Me, who apply themselves incessantly (to meditation), I bring prosperity and security.

22.1. अनन्याः इति ॥ अनन्याः अपृथग्भूताः परं देवं नारायणं आत्मत्वेन गताः सन्तः चिन्तयन्तः मां ये जनाः संन्यासिनः पर्युपासते, तेषां परमार्थदर्शिनां नित्याभियुक्तानां सतताभियोगिनां योगक्षेमं, योगः अप्राप्तस्य प्रापणं, क्षेमः तद्रक्षणं, तदुभयं वहामि प्रापयामि अहम्; 'ज्ञानी त्वात्मैव मे मतम्,' 'स च मम प्रियः' [७.१८, १७.] यस्मात्, तस्मात् ते मम आत्मभूताः प्रियाश्च इति ॥

ननु अन्येषाम् अपि भक्तानां योगक्षेमं वहति एव भगवान् । सत्यं, वहति एव; किन्तु अयं विशेषः — अन्ये ये भक्ताः ते आत्मार्थं स्वयमपि योगक्षेमं ईहन्ते; अनन्यदर्शिनस्तु न आत्मार्थं योगक्षेमं ईहन्ते; न हि ते जीविते मरणे वा आत्मनः गृद्धिं कुर्वन्ति; केवलं एव भगवच्छरणाः ते; अतः भगवान् एव तेषां योगक्षेमं वहतीति ॥

22.1. 'Exclusive'—as non-different—are they who resort to 'Me', the supreme deity Nārāyaṇa as their Self; they are the renunciants who worship Me in all conceivable ways. I 'bring'—grant—to them, who are perpetually attuned to Me and who behold the metaphysical Reality, well-being or both the gift of what has been unattained and its security, because I deem the knower of the Self to be Myself, *Vide:*

"And he is dear to Me" (BG.7.17.18). Such worshippers are Myself and are dear. But does the Lord bring prosperity and security to other devotees also? Yes, He does; but there is a distinction. These other devotees seek prosperity and security by means of their own efforts also. But those who do not see themselves as different from the Lord do not seek them for themselves. They cherish no selfish cravings either in life or death. They have sought refuge in the Lord only. So the Lord Himself brings them both prosperity and security.

23.0. ननु अन्याः अपि देवताः त्वमेव चेत्, तद्भक्ताश्च त्वामेव भजन्ते । सत्यं एवम् —

23.0. 'Now if other divinities also are You yourself, their devotees are Your devotees as well.' Yes, this is true:

येऽप्यन्यदेवताभक्ता यजन्ते श्रद्धयाऽन्विताः ।
तेऽपि मामेव कौन्तेय यजन्त्यविधिपूर्वकम् ॥२३॥

23. Those also who are the devotees of other divinities, who worship them with faith, are worshipping Me only, Arjuna! but not according to Vedic injunctions.

23.1. ये इति ॥ येऽपि अन्यदेवताभक्ताः अन्यासु देवतासु भक्ताः अन्यदेवताभक्ताः सन्तः यजन्ते पूजयन्ति श्रद्धया आस्तिक्यबुद्धया अन्विताः अनुगताः, तेऽपि माम् एव कौन्तेय ! यजन्ति अविधिपूर्वकम्; अविधिः अज्ञानं, तत्पूर्वकं अज्ञानपूर्वकं यजन्ते इत्यर्थः ॥

23.1. 'Those also who are the devotees of other divinities'—of other deities—and 'who worship them with faith'—i.e., convinced of the reality of the world to come,—they also worship Me only; but 'not according to Vedic injunctions'. That is, they worship in ignorance. The idea is that they are My ignorant devotees.

24.0. कस्मात् ते अविधिपूर्वकं यजन्ते इति ? उच्यते—यस्मात्—

24.0. Why do they worship ignorantly? Answer: Because

अहं हि सर्वयज्ञानां भोक्ता च प्रभुरेव च ।
न तु मामभिजानन्ति तत्त्वेनातश्च्यवन्ति ते ।।२४।।

24. I indeed am the enjoyer and master of all sacrifices; but they do not recognise Me in truth. Therefore they lapse.

24.1. अहं इति ।। अहं हि सर्वयज्ञानां श्रौतानां स्मार्तानां च सर्वेषां यज्ञानां देवतात्मत्वेन भोक्ता च प्रभुः एव च । मत्स्वामिको हि यज्ञः, 'अधियज्ञोऽहमेवात्र' [८.४.] इति हि उक्तम् । तथा न तु मां अभिजानन्ति तत्त्वेन यथावत् । अतः च अविधिपूर्वकं इष्ट्वा यागफलात् च्यवन्ति प्रच्यवन्ते ते ।।

24.1. 'Of all sacrifices' enjoined by the Vedas and *Smṛtis*, I, as the deity to whom they are offered, am indeed the enjoyer and master. The sacrifice indeed has Me as its master: Vide BG.8.4: I also am the supervisor of sacrifices in the body'. But 'in truth they do not recognise Me'. So, having sacrificed in violation of injunctions they 'lapse'—fall off from the fruit of sacrifices.

25.0. येऽपि अन्यदेवताभक्तिमत्त्वेन अविधिपूर्वकं यजन्ते, तेषाम् अपि यागफलं अवश्यंभावि । कथम् ? —

25.0. Inevitably the fruit of sacrifices accrues even to them, who, prompted by devotion to other divinities, offer sacrifices, violating injunctions. How?

यान्ति देवव्रता देवान् पितॄन् यान्ति पितृव्रताः ।
भूतानि यान्ति भूतेज्या यान्ति मद्याजिनोऽपि माम् ।।२५।।

25. To gods repair their devotees; to the manes go those devoted to the manes. The worshippers of the elementals go to these elementals. My worshippers come to Me.

25.1. यान्ति इति ।। यान्ति गच्छन्ति देवव्रताः देवेषु व्रतं नियमः भक्तिश्च येषां ते देवव्रताः देवान् । यान्ति पितॄन् अग्निष्वात्तादीन् यान्ति पितृव्रताः श्राद्धा-

दिक्रियापराः पितृभक्ताः । भूतानि विनायकमातृगणचतुर्भगिन्यादीनि यान्ति भूतेज्याः भूतानां पूजकाः । यान्ति मद्याजिनः मद्यजनशीलाः वैष्णवाः मां एव । समाने अपि आयासे मां एव न भजन्ते अज्ञानात्; तेन ते अल्पफलभाजः भवन्ति इत्यर्थः ॥

25.1. To 'the gods' go the devotees of gods whose discipline and devotion are oriented to the gods. To the 'manes', *agniṣvātta* etc., go those devoted to the manes and engaged faithfully in obsequies. To the 'elementals', *vināyakas*, the mother spirits, the four sisters, etc., go 'the worshippers of the elementals'. My worshippers—habitual devotees of Viṣṇu—come to Me alone. Though the labour involved is the same, due to their ignorance they fail to worship Me exclusively; therefore they gain but petty results. This is the idea.

26.0. न केवलं मद्भक्तानां अनावृत्तिलक्षणं अनन्तफलम्, सुखाराधनश्च अहम् । कथम्? —

26.0. Not only do My devotees reap the eternal fruit of non-return to empirical life; but they also accomplish this easily, as My worship is easy to accomplish. How?

पत्रं पुष्पं फलं तोयं यो मे भक्त्या प्रयच्छति ।
तदहं भक्त्युपहृतमश्नामि प्रयतात्मनः ॥२६॥

26. Whoso with devotion offers Me a leaf, a flower, a fruit, or water, I enjoy what has been thus offered with devotion by that pure-hearted worshipper.

26.1. पत्रं इति ॥ पत्रं पुष्पं फलं तोयं उदकं यः मे मह्यं भक्त्या प्रयच्छति, तत् अहं पत्रादि भक्त्या उपहृतं भक्तिपूर्वकं प्रापितं भक्त्युपहृतं अश्नामि गृह्णामि प्रयतात्मनः शुद्धबुद्धेः ॥

यतः एवं अतः —

26.1. Whoso offers Me a leaf, flower, fruit or water, I enjoy, i.e., accept it as offered or given with devotion by that pure-hearted devotee, that pure-minded person.

This being the case,

यत्करोषि यदश्नासि यज्जुहोषि ददासि यत् ।
यत्तपस्यसि कौन्तेय तत्कुरुष्व मदर्पणम् ॥२७॥

27. Whatever you do, eat, sacrifice, offer as gift, perform as austerity, O Arjuna!—do all this as a dedication to Me.

27.1. यत् इति ॥ यत् करोषि स्वतः प्राप्तं, यत् अश्नासि, यत् जुहोषि हवनं निर्वर्तयसि श्रौतं स्मार्तं वा, यत् ददासि प्रयच्छसि ब्राह्मणादिभ्यः हिरण्यान्नाज्यादि, यत् तपस्यसि तपः चरसि कौन्तेय ! तत् कुरुष्व मदर्पणम् मत्समर्पणम् ॥

27.1. Whatever you do spontaneously, whatever you eat, offer as sacrifice according to Vedas and *smṛti*, whatever you give to holy men etc.,—be it gold, food, lustrated butter, etc.,—whatever penance you perform, O Arjuna! do all these as offerings to Me.

28.0. एवं कुर्वतः तव यत् भवति, तत् शृणु —

28.0. Hear what will happen to you who do thus:

शुभाशुभफलैरेवं मोक्ष्यसे कर्मबन्धनैः ।
संन्यासयोगयुक्तात्मा विमुक्तो मामुपैष्यसि ॥२८॥

28. Thus will you be released from the bonds of works with their fruits, good and evil. Liberated, with the Self integrated by the Yoga of renunciation, you will come to Me.

28.1. शुभा इति ॥ शुभाशुभफलैः शुभाशुभे इष्टानिष्टे फले येषां तानि शुभाशुभफलानि कर्माणि तैः शुभाशुभफलैः कर्मबन्धनैः कर्माणि एव बन्धनानि कर्मबन्धनानि तैः कर्मबन्धनैः एवं मदर्पणं कुर्वन् मोक्ष्यसे । सोऽयं संन्यासयोगः नाम, संन्यासश्च असौ मत्समर्पणतया, कर्मत्वात् योगश्च असौ इति; तेन संन्यासयोगेन युक्तः आत्मा अन्तःकरणं यस्य तव सः त्वं संन्यासयोगयुक्तात्मा सन् विमुक्तः कर्मबन्धनैः जीवन् एव, पतिते च अस्मिन् शरीरे मां उपैष्यसि आगमिष्यसि ॥

28.1. 'From the bonds of works with their fruits, good and evil' i.e. pleasant and unpleasant, you will be released. These very works constitute bondage. Dedicating all works to Me you will be released. This is called the Yoga of renunciation. Being a dedication to Me, it is renunciation, and being a work, it is Yoga, too. The self or the inner sense being integrated by this Yoga of renunciation, you are liberated from bonds of works even when alive; when the body drops off, you will come to Me.

29.0. रागद्वेषवान् तर्हि भगवान्, यतः भक्तान् अनुगृह्णाति, न इतरान् इति । तत् न—

29.0. 'If so, the blessed Lord is partial—He blesses the devotees only; not others'. No, not so:

समोऽहं सर्वभूतेषु न मे द्वेष्योऽस्ति न प्रियः ।
ये भजन्ति तु मां भक्त्या मयि ते तेषु चाप्यहम् ॥२९॥

29. Towards all beings I am the same: I hate none, nor hold any dear. Those who worship Me with devotion live in Me and I in them.

29.1. समः इति ॥ समः तुल्यः अहं सर्वभूतेषु । न मे द्वेष्यः अस्ति न प्रियः । अग्निवत् अहं—दूरस्थानां यथा अग्निः शीतं न अपनयति, समीपं उपसर्पतां अपनयति, तथा अहं भक्तान् अनुगृह्णामि, न इतरान् । ये भजन्ति तु मां ईश्वरं भक्त्या मयि ते—स्वभावतः एव, न मम रागनिमित्तं—वर्तन्ते । तेषु च अपि अहं स्वभावतः एव वर्ते, न इतरेषु । न एतावता तेषु द्वेषः मम ॥

29.1. 'The same'—equal, am I towards all beings: I hate none, nor hold any dear. Like fire am I. As fire does not remove cold from those remote from it, but does so from those drawing near, so do I bless devotees and not others. Those who worship Me, the Lord, with devotion dwell in Me of course, and not due to My partiality. And thus, of course I dwell in them and not in others. This implies no hatred for them.

30.0. शृणु मद्भक्तेः माहात्म्यम् —

30.0. Note the grandeur of devotion to Me:

अपि चेत्सुदुराचारो भजते मामनन्यभाक् ।
साधुरेव स मन्तव्यः सम्यग्व्यवसितो हि सः ॥३०॥

30. Despite his extremely wicked conduct, if a man worships Me exclusively he must indeed be deemed worthy; for his resolution is right.

30.1. अपि इति ॥ अपि चेत् यद्यपि सुदुराचारः सुष्ठु दुराचारः अतीव कुत्सिताचारोऽपि भजते मां अनन्यभाक् अनन्यभक्तिः सन्, साधुः एव सम्यग्वृत्तः एव स मन्तव्यः ज्ञातव्यः, सम्यक् यथावत् व्यवसितः हि सः, यस्मात् साधुनिश्चयः सः ॥

30.1. Though one's conduct has been 'extremely wicked' i.e., most reprehensible, still if one worships Me with exclusive devotion, his conduct must be reckoned worthy indeed; for his 'resolution' or determination, is appropriate.

31.0. उत्सृज्य च बाह्यां दुराचारतां अन्तःसम्यग्व्यवसायसामर्थ्यात् —

31.0. Due to his right inner resolve, rejecting his wicked external behaviour,

क्षिप्रं भवति धर्मात्मा शश्वच्छान्तिं निगच्छति ।
कौन्तेय प्रतिजानीहि न मे भक्तः प्रणश्यति ॥३१॥

31. Soon he becomes essentially righteous and attains lasting peace. Know for certain and proclaim, Arjuna! that My devotee never perishes.

31.1. क्षिप्रं इति ॥ क्षिप्रं शीघ्रं भवति धर्मात्मा धर्मचित्तः एव । शश्वत् नित्यं शान्तिं च उपशमं निगच्छति प्राप्नोति । शृणु परमार्थं — कौन्तेय ! प्रतिजानीहि

निश्चितां प्रतिज्ञां कुरु, न मे मम भक्तः मयि समर्पितान्तरात्मा मद्भक्तः न प्रणश्यति इति ॥

किञ्च —

31.1. Soon his mind becomes wholly righteous; he attains 'lasting peace' or eternal quietude. Note this supreme truth, Arjuna! Be absolutely assured and proclaim that My devotee who has dedicated his inner self to Me will never perish.

And,

मां हि पार्थ व्यपाश्रित्य येऽपि स्युः पापयोनयः ।
स्त्रियो वैश्यास्तथा शूद्रास्तेऽपि यान्ति परां गतिम् ॥३२॥

32. Seeking refuge in Me, Arjuna! those even of low birth—women, artisans and serfs—attain the supreme goal.

32.1. मां हि इति ॥ मां हि यस्मात् पार्थ व्यपाश्रित्य मां आश्रयत्वेन गृहीत्वा येऽपि स्युः भवेयुः पापयोनयः पापा योनिः येषां ते पापयोनयः पापजन्मानः — के ते इत्याह स्त्रियः वैश्याः तथा शूद्राः ते अपि यान्ति गच्छन्ति परां प्रकृष्टां गतिम् ॥

32.1. 'Seeking refuge in Me', depending on Me, even people of low or sinful birth—women, artisans, and serfs—achieve the supreme goal of life.

किं पुनर्ब्राह्मणाः पुण्या भक्ता राजर्षयस्तथा ।
अनित्यमसुखं लोकमिमं प्राप्य भजस्व माम् ॥३३॥

33. How much more certainly do so those of meritorious birth and the devout royal sages! Having come to this transient and unhappy world, worship Me.

33.1. किं पुनः इति ॥ किं पुनः ब्राह्मणाः पुण्याः पुण्ययोनयः भक्ताः राजर्षयः तथा राजानश्च ते ऋषयश्च इति राजर्षयः । यतः एवं, अतः अनित्यं क्षणभङ्गुरं

असुखं च सुखवर्जितं इमं लोकं मनुष्यलोकं प्राप्य पुरुषार्थसाधनं दुर्लभं मनुष्यत्वं लब्ध्वा भजस्व सेवस्व माम् ॥

कथम् ? —

33.1. All the more surely will those of meritorious birth and devout royal sages attain the supreme goal of life. Such being the case, having come to this 'transient' or fleeting, 'unhappy' world of men, i.e., having won the means to reach the goal of life, namely, the rare status of a human being, worship Me.

How?

मन्मना भव मद्भक्तो मद्याजी मां नमस्कुरु ।
मामेवैष्यसि युक्त्वैवमात्मानं मत्परायणः ॥३४॥

34. Set your mind on Me; be My devotee; sacrifice unto Me; pay obeisance to Me. Being wholly intent on Me, thus uniting your self, you will surely come to Me.

इति श्रीमहाभारते शतसाहस्र्यां संहितायां वैयासिक्यां भीष्मपर्वणि श्रीमद्भगवद्गीतासूपनिषत्सु ब्रह्मविद्यायां योगशास्त्रे श्रीकृष्णार्जुनसंवादे राजविद्याराजगुह्ययोगो नाम नवमोऽध्यायः ॥

34.1. मन्मना इति ॥ मयि वासुदेवे मनः यस्य तव स त्वं मन्मनाः भव । तथा मद्भक्तः भव । मद्याजी मद्यजनशीलः भव । मां एव च नमस्कुरु । मां एव ईश्वरं एष्यसि आगमिष्यसि युक्त्वा समाधाय चित्तं; एवं आत्मानं माम् — अहं हि सर्वेषां भूतानां आत्मा, परा च गतिः, परं अयनम् । तं मां एवंभूतं — 'एष्यसि' इति अतीतेन संबन्धः — मत्परायणः सन् इत्यर्थः ॥

34.1. Set your mind on Me, Vāsudeva; so too, be My devotee. Habitually sacrifice to Me; to Me alone pay obeisance. With Your mind united thus, you are sure to come to Me, the Lord. Be wholly intent on Me; for I am the Self of all beings, the goal supreme—the supreme destiny. To Me so understood you will come—thus has the construction to be made, for you are wholly intent on Me.

इति श्रीमत्परमहंसपरिव्राजकाचार्यगोविंदभगवत्पूज्यपादशिष्यश्रीमच्छंकरभगवतः कृतौ श्रीमद्भगवद्गीताभाष्ये राजविद्या-राजगुह्ययोगो नाम नवमोऽध्यायः ॥९॥

दशमोऽध्यायः

CHAPTER X

THE YOGA OF GOD'S MANIFESTED POWERS

0.1. सप्तमे अध्याये भगवतः तत्त्वं विभूतयश्च प्रकाशिताः, नवमे च । अथ इदानीं येषु येषु भावेषु चिन्त्यः भगवान्, ते ते भावाः वक्तव्याः, तत्त्वं च भगवतः वक्तव्यं उक्तमपि, दुर्विज्ञेयत्वात्, इत्यतः श्रीभगवान् उवाच —

0.1. In the seventh and ninth chapters the truth of the Lord and His powers have been revealed. Now those phenomena in which the Lord has to be contemplated, are going to be set forth as revealed. The truth of God also, in view of its abstruseness, has to be restated, though it has been already affirmed. Therefore the Lord said:

श्रीभगवानुवाच :

भूय एव महाबाहो शृणु मे परमं वचः ।
यत्तेऽहं प्रीयमाणाय वक्ष्यामि हितकाम्यया ॥१॥

1. Once more, O hero! listen to My supreme word which, seeking your good, I shall speak to you who delight in it.

1.1. भूयः इति ॥ भूयः एव भूयः पुनः महाबाहो ! शृणु मे मदीयं परमं प्रकृष्टं निरतिशयवस्तुनः प्रकाशकं वचः वाक्यं, यत् परमं ते तुभ्यं प्रीयमाणाय —मद्वचनात् प्रीयसे त्वं अतीव अमृतमिव पिबन्, ततः — वक्ष्यामि हितकाम्यया हितेच्छया ॥१॥

1.1. 'Once more'—again—O hero, mighty-armed!—listen to 'My supreme word'—an exalted utterance, which reveals the Reality that has nothing superior to it. Desirous of your good 'I shall speak that word'; for you delight much in My speech as though you are tasting ambrosia.

2.0. किमर्थं अहं वक्ष्यामि इति ? अतः आह —

2.0. 'Why should I speak?'—listen to the reply:

न मे विदुः सुरगणाः प्रभवं न महर्षयः ।
अहमादिर्हि देवानां महर्षीणां च सर्वशः ॥२॥

2. The hosts of gods know not My origin; neither do great seers; for in all respects, I am the origin of gods and the great seers.

2.1. न मे इति ॥ न मे विदुः न जानन्ति सुरगणाः ब्रह्मादयः । किं ते न विदुः ? मम प्रभवं प्रभावं प्रभुशक्त्यतिशयं, अथवा प्रभवं — प्रभवनं — उत्पत्तिम् । न अपि महर्षयः भृग्वादयः विदुः । कस्मात् ते न विदुरिति ? उच्यते — अहं आदिः कारणं हि यस्मात् देवानां महर्षीणां च सर्वशः सर्वप्रकारैः ॥
किञ्च —

2.1. 'The divine hosts know not'—what is it that they do not know? My exceedingly lordly might or 'origin'—coming into being. Nor do the 'great seers', Bhṛgu and the rest, know. Why don't they know? For, 'I am the origin'—the cause of gods and great seers in all respects.

And,

यो मामजमनादिं च वेत्ति लोकमहेश्वरम् ।
असंमूढः स मर्त्येषु सर्वपापैः प्रमुच्यते ॥३॥

3. Whoso knows Me as unborn and beginningless and as the great Lord of all the worlds is released from all sins; for he is undeluded among men.

3.1. य इति ॥ यः मां अजं अनादिं च — यस्मात् अहं आदिः देवानां महर्षीणां च, न मम अन्यः आदिः विद्यते; अतः अहं अजः अनादिश्च; अनादित्वं अजत्वे हेतुः — तं मां अजं अनादिं च यः वेत्ति विजानाति लोकमहेश्वरं लोकानां महान्तं

ईश्वरं [तुरीयं अज्ञानतत्कार्यवर्जितं] असंमूढः संमोहवर्जितः सः मर्त्येषु मनुष्येषु, सर्वपापैः सर्वैः पापैः मतिपूर्वामतिपूर्वकृतैः प्रमुच्यते प्रमोक्ष्यते ॥

3.1. 'Whoso knows Me as unborn and beginningless'—as I am the origin of the gods and the great seers, I have no origin. So I am unborn and beginningless. The reason for My being unborn is that I have no beginning. He who knows Me as such, i.e. as, the great 'Lord of the worlds—the Fourth or the Transcendent devoid of nescience and its effects—is, among mortals, undeluded; for he has no more any delusions. From all sins, consciously or unconsciously committed, he will be released.

4.0. इतश्च अहं महेश्वरः लोकानाम् —

4.0. Here is another reason why I am the great Lord of all the worlds:

बुद्धिर्ज्ञानमसंमोहः क्षमा सत्यं दमः शमः ।
सुखं दुःखं भवोऽभावो भयं चाभयमेव च ॥४॥

4. Intelligence, knowledge, non-delusion, endurance, truthfulness, sense-control, mind-control, pleasure, pain, being, non-being, fear and fearlessness;

4.1. बुद्धिः इति ॥ बुद्धिः अन्तःकरणस्य सूक्ष्माद्यर्थावबोधनसामर्थ्यं, तद्वन्तं बुद्धिमानिति हि वदन्ति । ज्ञानं आत्मादिपदार्थानां अवबोधः । असंमोहः प्रत्युत्पन्नेषु बोद्धव्येषु विवेकपूर्विका प्रवृत्तिः । क्षमा आक्रुष्टस्य ताडितस्य वा अविकृतचित्तता । सत्यं, यथादृष्टस्य यथाश्रुतस्य वा आत्मानुभवस्य परबुद्धिसङ्क्रान्तये तथैव उच्चार्यमाणा वाक् सत्यं उच्यते । दमः बाह्येन्द्रियोपशमः । शमः अन्तःकरणस्य उपशमः । सुखं आह्लादः । दुःखं [सं] तापः । भवः उद्भवः । अभावः तद्विपर्ययः । भयं च त्रासः, अभयमेव च तदभावः [तद्विपरीतम्] ॥

4.1. 'Intelligence' is the power of the inner sense to grasp ideas, which are subtle, etc. He who has it is intelligent. 'Knowledge' is cognition of entities like the self. 'Non-delusion' is discriminating action as regards things that call for understanding. 'Endurance' is mind's freedom from agitation when abused or belaboured. 'Truthfulness' consists in utterance aimed at informing another exactly of one's experience of things seen or heard. 'Sense-control' is *dama* and 'mind control' *śama*. 'Pleasure' is joy and 'pain', agony. 'Being' is birth and 'non-being' its opposite. 'Fear' is trepidation, its absence being 'fearlessness'.

अहिंसा समता तुष्टिस्तपो दानं यशोऽयशः ।
भवन्ति भावा भूतानां मत्त एव पृथग्विधाः ॥५॥

5. Non-violence, equanimity, contentment, penance, charity, renown, ill-fame—from Me alone these manifold states accrue to all beings.

5.1. अहिंसा इति । अहिंसा अपीडा प्राणिनाम् । समता समचित्तता । तुष्टिः सन्तोषः पर्याप्तबुद्धिः लाभेषु । तपः इन्द्रियसंयमपूर्वकं शरीरपीडनम् । दानं यथाशक्ति संविभागः । यशः धर्मनिमित्ता कीर्तिः । अयशः तु अधर्मनिमित्ता अकीर्तिः । भवन्ति भावाः यथोक्ताः बुद्ध्यादयः भूतानां प्राणिनां मत्तः एव ईश्वरात् पृथग्विधाः नानाविधाः स्वकर्मानुरूपेण ॥

किञ्च —

5.1. 'Non-violence' is non-infliction of injury on living beings. 'Equanimity' is mind's steadiness. 'Contentment' is the sense of adequacy as regards gains. 'Penance' is body's constraint preceded by sense-control. 'Charity' is distribution of wealth etc., according to capacity. 'Renown' is fame due to righteousness. 'Ill-fame' is disrepute due to unrighteousness. The said states intelligence etc., accrue to living beings from Me, the Lord, alone in manifold ways according to their deeds.

And,

महर्षयः सप्त पूर्वे चत्वारो मनवस्तथा ।
मद्भावा मानसा जाता येषां लोक इमाः प्रजाः ॥६॥

6. The seven great seers, the first four, and also the Manus were mind-born, endowed with My powers. These beings are their progeny.

6.1. महर्षयः इति ॥ महर्षयः सप्त भृग्वादयः, पूर्वे अतीतकालसम्बन्धिनः चत्वारः मनवः तथा सावर्णा इति प्रसिद्धाः । ते च मद्भावाः मद्गतभावनाः वैष्णवेन सामर्थ्येन उपेताः, मानसाः मनसैव उत्पादिताः मया जाताः उत्पन्नाः; येषां मनूनां महर्षीणां च सृष्टिः [जाः] लोके इमाः स्थावरजङ्गमलक्षणाः प्रजाः ॥

6.1. The 'seven great seers', Bhṛgu etc., the first four, and Manus—are all famed as belonging to by-gone ages and famed as *sāvarṇas*. Their meditations had reference to Me. They were endowed with the power of Viṣṇu. They were, all, generated mentally by Me. The creatures in this world, stationary and mobile, are the progeny of these Manus and these great seers.

एतां विभूतिं योगं च मम यो वेत्ति तत्त्वतः ।
सोऽविकम्पेन योगेन युज्यते नात्र संशयः ॥७॥

7. Whoso knows this vast power and Yoga of Mine truly, will be endowed with the steady state of integration; there is no doubt about this.

7.1. एतां इति ॥ एतां यथोक्तां विभूतिं विस्तारं योगं च युक्तिं च आत्मनः घटनं [९.५.] — अथवा, योगैश्वर्यसामर्थ्यं सर्वज्ञत्वं योगजं योगः उच्यते — मम मदीयं योगं यः वेत्ति तत्त्वतः तत्त्वेन यथावदित्येतत्, सः अविकम्पेन अप्रचलितेन योगेन सम्यग्दर्शनस्थैर्यलक्षणेन युज्यते संबध्यते । न अत्र संशयः न अस्मिन् अर्थे संशयः अस्ति ॥

7.1. This 'vast power', as indicated and 'Yoga'—i.e., My nature (Vide BG.9.5). Or, by Yoga is meant omniscience and power due to mastery of Yogic attainments. Whoso knows this Yoga of Mine truly, i.e., as it is or objectively, will come in possession of steady Yoga consisting in unshakable, right perception. There is no doubt about this.

8.0. कीदृशेन अविकम्पेन योगेन युज्यते इति ? उच्यते —

8.0. 'What kind of unshakable Yoga is it with which he is endowed'? Listen:

अहं सर्वस्य प्रभवो मत्तः सर्वं प्रवर्तते ।
इति मत्वा भजन्ते मां बुधा भावसमन्विताः ॥८॥

8. 'I am the source of all things; all things proceed from Me'—so holding with deep loyalty to truth, the wise adore Me.

8.1. अहं इति ॥ अहं परं ब्रह्म वासुदेवाख्यं सर्वस्य जगतः प्रभवः उत्पत्तिः । मत्तः एव स्थितिनाशक्रियाफलोपभोगलक्षणं विक्रियारूपं सर्वं जगत् प्रवर्तते — इति एवं मत्वा भजन्ते सेवन्ते मां बुधाः अवगतपरमार्थतत्त्वाः, भावसमन्विताः भावः — भावना — परमार्थतत्त्वाभिनिवेशः, तेन समन्विताः संयुक्ताः इत्यर्थः ॥
किञ्च —

8.1. I, the Supreme Brahman styled Vāsudeva, am 'the source' or origin of the entire world. From Me alone does the entire world—a system of changes like existence, destruction, experience of fruits of works—proceed. Holding this view, the wise who have grasped the nature of the supreme Reality adore Me with deep loyalty. Loyalty means mind's attachment to the Supreme Reality. The idea is that they adore Me with such attachment.

And,

मच्चित्ता मद्गतप्राणा बोधयन्तः परस्परम् ।
कथयन्तश्च मां नित्यं तुष्यन्ति च रमन्ति च ॥९॥

9. With minds fixed on Me, life surrendered to Me, enlightening one another, speaking (only of Me), they find contentment always and rejoice.

9.1. मच्चित्ता: इति ॥ मच्चित्ता: मयि चित्तं येषां ते मच्चित्ता:, मद्गतप्राणा: मयि [मां] गता: प्राप्ता: चक्षुरादय: प्राणा: येषां ते मद्गतप्राणा:, मयि उपसंहृतकरणा: इत्यर्थ: । अथवा — मद्गतप्राणा: मद्गतजीवना: इत्येतत् । बोधयन्त: अवगमयन्त: परस्परं अन्योन्यं, कथयन्तश्च ज्ञानबलवीर्यादिधर्मै: विशिष्टं मां, तुष्यन्ति परितोषं उपयान्ति च रमन्ति च रतिं च प्राप्नुवन्ति प्रियसंगत्या इव ॥

9.1. 'With minds fixed on Me' means mentally dwelling in Me. Their vital powers like sight, have been oriented to Me, i.e. those whose means of cognition have been given over to Me. 'Enlightening one another' and 'speaking' of Me as endowed with attributes like knowledge, strength and vigour, they find contentment and delight as though they have met with their beloved. (The second expression in the verse—*madgataprāṇāh*—may mean those whose life has been dedicated to Me).

10.0. ये यथोक्तै: प्रकारै: भजन्ते मां भक्ता: सन्त: —

10.0. These devotees who worship Me thus are further characterised:

तेषां सततयुक्तानां भजतां प्रीतिपूर्वकम् ।
ददामि बुद्धियोगं तं येन मामुपयान्ति ते ॥१०॥

10. To them who are uninterruptedly united with Me and who lovingly adore Me, I grant that intellectual union by which they draw nigh to Me.

10.1. तेषां इति ॥ तेषां सततयुक्तानां नित्याभियुक्तानां [निवृत्तसर्वबाह्यैषणानां] भजतां सेवमानानाम् । किं अर्थित्वादिना कारणेन ? नेत्याह — प्रीतिपूर्वकं प्रीति: स्नेह: तत्पूर्वकं मां भजतामित्यर्थ: । ददामि प्रयच्छामि बुद्धियोगं बुद्धि: सम्यग्दर्शनं मत्तत्त्वविषयं, तेन योग: बुद्धियोग: तं बुद्धियोगं येन बुद्धियोगेन सम्यग्दर्शनलक्षणेन मां परमेश्वरं आत्मभूतं आत्मत्वेन उपयान्ति प्रतिपद्यन्ते । के ? ते ये मच्चित्तत्वादिप्रकारै: (९) मां भजन्ते ॥

10.1. I grant to them, who are 'uninterruptedly'—perpetually—united with Me, who have renounced yearnings for all kinds of objects, who 'adore', or serve Me, not in order to gain some object or other, but moved by love or attachment—I grant them 'intellectual union'. 'Intellect' means right knowledge of the truth of the Lord. 'Union' with such knowledge is what I give them. By means of it 'they draw nigh to Me'—reach Me as their Self—Me the supreme Lord. Who do so?—those who adore Me with their minds fixed on Me, etc.

11.0. किमर्थं, कस्य वा, त्वत्प्राप्तिप्रतिबन्धहेतोः नाशकं बुद्धियोगं तेषां त्वद्भक्तानां ददासि ? इत्यपेक्षायां आह —

11.0. "Why, and for removing what obstruction on the way leading to You, do you grant intellectual union to Your devotees?" The answer is offered:

तेषामेवानुकम्पार्थमहमज्ञानजं तमः ।
नाशयाम्यात्मभावस्थो ज्ञानदीपेन भास्वता ॥११॥

11. Moved by compassion for those (devotees) and dwelling in their mental states, with the lustrous flame of knowledge, I destroy the darkness of ignorance.

11.1. तेषां इति ॥ तेषामेव कथं नु नाम श्रेयः स्यात् इति अनुकम्पार्थं दयाहेतोः अहं अज्ञानजं अविवेकतः जातं मिथ्याप्रत्ययलक्षणं मोहान्धकारं तमः नाशयामि, आत्मभावस्थः आत्मनः भावः अन्तःकरणाशयः तस्मिन्नेव स्थितः सन्, ज्ञानदीपेन विवेकप्रत्ययरूपेण भक्तिप्रसादस्नेहाभिषिक्तेन मद्भावनाभिनिवेशवातेरितेन ब्रह्मचर्यादिसाधनसंस्कारवत्प्रज्ञावर्तिना विरक्तान्तःकरणाधारेण विषयव्यावृत्तचित्तरागद्वेषाकलुषितनिवातापवरकस्थेन नित्यप्रवृत्तैकाग्र्यध्यानजनितसम्यग्दर्शनभास्वता ज्ञानदीपेनेत्यर्थः ॥

11.1. "How can I promote their well-being?"—thinking thus 'compassionately' due to benevolence, I destroy the 'darkness of delusion born of ignorance' or non-discrimination. This delusion consists of wrong cognitions. Dwelling in their 'mental states' or within their inner-sense, I destroy nescience with the 'flame of knowledge'—i.e., discriminating cognitions. This flame is fed on the oil of clear devotion and enlivened by the breeze of intense love of contemplation on Me. Its wick is the intellect strengthened by impressions of strivings to cultivate celibacy, etc. It is ensconced in the sense of detachment where the gusts of attachment and aversions do not blow as the mind has withdrawn from the sphere of objects and has the 'lustre' of right perception born of ceaseless one-pointed meditation.

12.0. यथोक्तां भगवतः विभूतिं योगं च श्रुत्वा अर्जुनः उवाच —

12.0. Listening to the statement of the Lord's power and Yoga,

अर्जुन उवाच :
परं ब्रह्म परं धाम पवित्रं परमं भवान् ।
पुरुषं शाश्वतं दिव्यमादिदेवमजं विभुम् ॥१२॥

Arjuna said:
12. You are the supreme Brahman, the supreme abode, the supreme sanctification; You are also the everlasting divine Spirit, the primordial God, unborn and all-pervading;

12.1. परं इति ॥ परं ब्रह्म [परमात्मा] परं धाम परं तेजः, पवित्रं पावनं परमं प्रकृष्टं भवान् । पुरुषं शाश्वतं नित्यं दिव्यं दिवि भवं आदिदेवं सर्वदेवानां आदौ भवं आदिदेवं अजं विभुं विभवनशीलम् ॥
ईदृशम् —

12.1. The 'supreme Brahman' is the supreme Self; the 'supreme abode' is the 'supreme effulgence'. The 'supreme sanctification' is the highest purifying power of the Lord. The 'everlasting Spirit' is the eternal divine—the heavenly 'primordial God' who was before all gods, unborn and all-pervading.

आहुस्त्वामृषयः सर्वे देवर्षिर्नारदस्तथा ।
असितो देवलो व्यासः स्वयं चैव ब्रवीषि मे ॥१३॥

13. Thus have all seers hailed You; likewise, too, the heavenly seer Nārada, Asita, Devala and Vyāsa, and to me You yourself declare the same.

13.1. आहुः इति ॥ आहुः कथयन्ति त्वां ऋषयः वसिष्ठादयः सर्वे देवर्षिः नारदः तथा, असितः देवलः अपि एवमेवाह, व्यासः च, स्वयं चैव त्वं च ब्रवीषि मे ॥

13.1. All seers, Vasiṣṭha, etc., have hailed You thus. The heavenly seer Nārada, Asita, Devala and Vyāsa say so; and the same You yourself affirm.

सर्वमेतदृतं मन्ये यन्मां वदसि केशव ।
न हि ते भगवन् व्यक्तिं विदुर्देवा न दानवाः ॥१४॥

14. Kṛṣṇa! All this that you tell me I deem true. Neither the gods nor the demons know, O blessed-Lord! Your manifestation.

14.1. सर्वं इति ॥ सर्वमेतत् यथोक्तं ऋषिभिः त्वया च, एतत् ऋतं सत्यमेव मन्ये, यत् मां प्रति वदसि भाषसे हे केशव । न हि ते तव भगवन् ! व्यक्तिं प्रभवं विदुः देवाः, न दानवाः ॥

14.1. All that has been stated by You and the seers, I deem true, indeed. Neither the gods nor the demons know, O blessed Lord! Your 'manifestation' or origin.

15.0. यतः त्वं देवादीनां आदिः, अतः —

15.0. Because you are the source of gods, etc; therefore,

स्वयमेवात्मनाऽऽत्मानं वेत्थ त्वं पुरुषोत्तम ।
भूतभावन भूतेश देवदेव जगत्पते ॥१५॥

15. Supreme Spirit! the cause of all beings! the Lord of all beings! God of gods! the world's Lord! Only You Yourself know the Self, by Yourself.

15.1. स्वयम् इति ॥ स्वयमेव आत्मना आत्मानं वेत्थ जानासि त्वं निरतिशयज्ञानैश्वर्यबलादिशक्तिमन्तं ईश्वरं पुरुषोत्तम । भूतानि भावयतीति भूतभावन । भूतेश ! भूतानां ईश । हे देवदेव जगत्पते ॥

15.1. Only Yourself, through self, know the Self—You with unexcelled knowledge, lordliness, strength, vigour and so forth know the Self, the Lord, O Supreme Spirit! He is the cause of all beings. As He brings them all into being, He is their Lord, the God of gods and the Lord of the world.

वक्तुमर्हस्यशेषेण दिव्या ह्यात्मविभूतयः ।
याभिर्विभूतिभिर्लोकानिमांस्त्वं व्याप्य तिष्ठसि ॥१६॥

16. You ought indeed to recount, in their entirety, Your powers divine, by means of which You abide, pervading all these worlds.

16.1. वक्तुं इति ॥ वक्तुं कथयितुं अर्हसि अशेषेण, दिव्याः हि आत्मविभूतयः, आत्मनो विभूतयो याः ताः वक्तुं अर्हसि । याभिः विभूतिभिः आत्मनो माहात्म्यविस्तरैः इमान् लोकान् त्वं व्याप्य तिष्ठसि ॥

16.1. You ought to set them forth wholly—Your divine powers. Those far-reaching powers of Yours, You ought to recount, by means of which, in expansive grandeur, You pervade and abide in these worlds.

कथं विद्यामहं योगिंस्त्वां सदा परिचिन्तयन् ।
केषु केषु च भावेषु चिन्त्योऽसि भगवन्मया ॥१७॥

17. O Yogin! How shall I, ever contemplating, know

You? O blessed Lord! In what all objects am I to meditate on You?

17.1. कथं इति ॥ कथं विद्यां विजानीयां अहं हे योगिन् ! त्वां सदा परिचिन्तयन् । केषु केषु च भावेषु वस्तुषु चिन्त्यः असि ध्येयः असि भगवन् ! मया ॥

17.1. O Yogin! Always contemplating, how shall I know You? In what all objects am I to meditate on You? O blessed Lord!

विस्तरेणात्मनो योगं विभूतिं च जनार्दन ।
भूयः कथय तृप्तिर्हि शृण्वतो नास्ति मेऽमृतम् ॥१८॥

18. O Janārdana! Once more recount at length Your Yoga and powers; for I am not sated as I listen to this ambrosial (account).

18.1. विस्तरेण इति ॥ विस्तरेण आत्मनो योगं योगैश्वर्यशक्तिविशेषं विभूतिं च विस्तरं ध्येयपदार्थानां हे जनार्दन — अर्दतेः गतिकर्मणः रूपम् — असुराणां देवप्रतिपक्षभूतानां जनानां नरकादिगमयितृत्वात् जनार्दन, अभ्युदयनिःश्रेयसपुरुषार्थप्रयोजनं सर्वैः जनैः याच्यते इति वा । भूयः पूर्वं उक्तमपि कथय; तृप्तिः परितोषः हि यस्मात् नास्ति मे मम शृण्वतः त्वन्मुखनिःसृतवाक्यामृतम् ॥

18.1. Your 'Yoga'—the unique power of Yogic lordliness—and 'power'—the scope of objects worthy of meditation—O Kṛṣṇa! set forth at length once more, though, earlier You did set them forth. 'Janārdana' is derived from the root *ard* meaning 'to send', since the Lord sends the demons, the adversaries of the gods, to hell, etc., or, from the root meaning 'to beg of', since all people pray to Him for the human goods of prosperity and salvation. I have had no sense of full satisfaction as I listen to the ambrosial utterances flowing from your lips.

श्रीभगवानुवाच :

हन्त ते कथयिष्यामि दिव्या ह्यात्मविभूतयः ।
प्राधान्यतः कुरुश्रेष्ठ नास्त्यन्तो विस्तरस्य मे ॥१९॥

The blessed Lord said:

19. Well, the more prominent of those divine powers of Mine I shall enumerate for you, chief Kuru Prince!; for there is no end to a detailed account of them all.

19.1. हन्त इति ॥ हन्त इदानीं ते तव दिव्याः दिवि भवाः आत्मविभूतयः आत्मनः मम विभूतयः याः ताः कथयिष्यामि इत्येतत् । प्राधान्यतः यत्र यत्र प्रधाना या या विभूतिः तां तां प्रधानां प्राधान्यतः कथयिष्यामि अहं कुरुश्रेष्ठ । अशेषतस्तु वर्षशतेनापि न शक्या वक्तुं, यतः नास्ति अन्तः विस्तरस्य मे मम विभूतीनां इत्यर्थः ॥

19.1. Well, now, I shall enumerate for you those 'divine'—heaven-born powers of Mine. With reference to their 'prominence'—whatsoever prominent powers are there I shall enumerate, Kuru Prince! In their entirety, even in a hundred years, they cannot be enumerated; for, there is no end to the extent of My powers. This is the idea.

20.0. तत्र प्रथममेव तावत् शृणु —

20.0. Now in the first place, listen:

अहमात्मा गुडाकेश सर्वभूताशयस्थितः ।
अहमादिश्च मध्यं च भूतानामन्त एव च ॥२०॥

20. Master of sleep (Arjuna!) I am the Self resident in the inner sense of all beings; also, I am the beginning, the middle and the end of all beings.

20.1. अहं इति ॥ अहं आत्मा प्रत्यगात्मा गुडाकेश — गुडाका निद्रा, तस्याः ईशः गुडाकेशः, जितनिद्रः इत्यर्थः; घनकेशः इति वा — सर्वभूताशयस्थितः सर्वेषां भूतानां आशये अन्तर्हृदि स्थितः अहमात्मा प्रत्यगात्मा नित्यं ध्येयः । तदशक्तेन च उत्तरेषु भावेषु चिन्त्यः अहम्; यस्मात् अहं एव आदिः भूतानां कारणं, तथा मध्यं च स्थितिः, अन्तः प्रलयश्च ॥

20.1. I am the Self—the Subject, O master of sleep! *Guḍākā* is sleep; its lord is he who has vanquished sleep. Or the term may mean thick-tressed. As 'resident in all beings'—as residing in the hearts of all beings, I, the Self, the Subject, am to be meditated on, always. One not competent to do it may meditate on Me as dwelling in objects to be set forth below; for, I alone am the beginning, the cause, of beings; so too their 'middle', the state of existence, and their 'end' or dissolution.

21.0. एवं च ध्येयः अहम् —

21.0. I may also be meditated on as follows:

आदित्यानामहं विष्णुर्ज्योतिषां रविरंशुमान् ।
मरीचिर्मरुतामस्मि नक्षत्राणामहं शशी ॥२१॥

21. I am Viṣṇu among the Ādityas. Of the luminaries I am the radiant sun. Of the gods, I am Marīci; among stars I am the moon.

21.1. आदित्यानां इति ॥ आदित्यानां द्वादशानां विष्णुः नाम आदित्यः अहं, ज्योतिषां रविः प्रकाशयितॄणां अंशुमान् रश्मिमान् । मरीचिः नाम मरुतां मरुद्देवताभेदानां अस्मि । नक्षत्राणां अहं शशी चंद्रमाः ॥

21.1. Of the twelve 'Ādityas' I am Viṣṇu, Aditi's son. Of the 'luminaries' that illumine, I am the radiant sun. I am Marīci among the storm 'gods', and among the 'stars' I am the moon.

वेदानां सामवेदोऽस्मि देवानामस्मि वासवः ।
इन्द्रियाणां मनश्चास्मि भूतानामस्मि चेतना ॥२२॥

22. Among the Vedas I am the Sāma Veda. Of the gods I am Indra. Among the senses, I am the mind, and of beings, I am intelligence.

22.1. वेदानां इति ॥ वेदानां मध्ये सामवेदः अस्मि । देवानां रुद्रादित्यादीनां

वासवः इन्द्रः अस्मि । इद्रियाणां एकादशानां चक्षुरादीनां मनश्च अस्मि संकल्पविकल्पात्मकं मनश्चास्मि । भूतानां अस्मि चेतना कार्यकरणसङ्घाते नित्याभिव्यक्ता बुद्धिवृत्तिः चेतना ॥

22.1. Among the 'Vedas', I am the Sāma Veda. Of the 'gods', Rudras, Adityas etc., I am Indra. Among the eleven 'senses', like the sense of sight, etc., I am the mind that is essentially imagination and construction. Of 'beings' I am 'intelligence'—the mental modification ever manifest in the conglomerate of body and senses.

रुद्राणां शङ्करश्चास्मि वित्तेशो यक्षरक्षसाम् ।
वसूनां पावकश्चास्मि मेरुः शिखरिणामहम् ॥२३॥

23. And I am Śaṁkara among the Rudras. Of Yakṣas and demons I am Kubera the Lord of wealth. Of Vasus, I am the purifying fire and among the mountains I am Meru.

23.1. रुद्राणां इति ॥ रुद्राणां एकादशानां शङ्करश्च अस्मि । वित्तेशः कुबेरः यक्षरक्षसां यक्षाणां रक्षसां च । वसूनां अष्टानां पावकश्च अस्मि अग्निः । मेरुः शिखरिणां शिखरवतां अहम् ॥

23.1. Among the eleven 'Rudras' I am Śaṁkara. Among 'Yakṣas' and demons I am Kubera, the lord of wealth. Of the 'eight Vasus', I am the purifying fire, and among the 'mountains' I am the Meru.

पुरोधसां च मुख्यं मां विद्धि पार्थ बृहस्पतिम् ।
सेनानीनामहं स्कन्दः सरसामस्मि सागरः ॥२४॥

24. Arjuna! Know Me to be Bṛhaspati, the chief among the priests. Among the war-lords I am Skanda and among lakes, I am the sea.

24.1. पुरोधसां इति ॥ पुरोधसां च राजपुरोहितानां च मुख्यं प्रधानं मां विद्धि जानीहि हे पार्थ ! बृहस्पतिम् । स हि इन्द्रस्येति मुख्यः स्यात् पुरोधसाम् । सेनानीनां सेनापतीनां अहं स्कन्दः देवसेनापतिः । सरसां यानि देवखातानि सरांसि तेषां सरसां सागरः अस्मि भवामि ॥

24.1. Among the 'priests of rulers', know I am the chief, Bṛhaspati. Indeed he is the chief of Indra's priests. Among the 'war-lords', I am Skanda, the leader of the armies of gods. Among the 'natural lakes', I am the sea.

महर्षीणां भृगुरहं गिरामस्म्येकमक्षरम् ।
यज्ञानां जपयज्ञोऽस्मि स्थावरणां हिमालयः ॥२५॥

25. I am Bhṛgu among the great seers; the mono-syllable among utterances; the sacrifice of muttered prayers among sacrifices and the Himālayas among immobile objects.

25.1. महर्षीणां इति ॥ महर्षीणां भृगुः अहम् । गिरां वाचां पदलक्षणानां एकं अक्षरं ओङ्कारः अस्मि । यज्ञानां जपयज्ञः अस्मि, स्थावराणां स्थितिमतां हिमालयः ॥

25.1. Among great seers I am 'Bhṛgu'; among 'verbal utterances' I am the mono-syllable AUM. Among 'sacrifices' I am that of the muttered prayer (Japa). Among immobile objects I am the Himālayas.

अश्वत्थः सर्ववृक्षाणां देवर्षीणां च नारदः ।
गन्धर्वाणां चित्ररथः सिद्धानां कपिलो मुनिः ॥२६॥

26. Among trees I am the holy fig; among divine seers, Nārada; among divine minstrels, I am Citraratha; and among perfected sages I am the sage, Kapila.

26.1. अश्वत्थः इति ॥ अश्वत्थः सर्ववृक्षणां, देवर्षीणां च नारदः, देवाः एव सन्तः ऋषित्वं प्राप्ताः मन्त्रदर्शित्वात्ते देवर्षयः, तेषां नारदः अस्मि । गन्धर्वाणां

चित्ररथः नाम गन्धर्वः अस्मि । सिद्धानां जन्मनैव धर्मज्ञानवैराग्यैश्वर्यातिशयं प्राप्तानां कपिलो मुनिः ॥

26.1. Among 'trees' I am the holy fig and among the 'divine sages' Nārada. Though celestial by birth, some gods (like Nārada), too, attain the status of seers, being the seers of hymns. So they are 'divine seers'. Among them I am Nārada. Among the 'divine minstrels', I am the one named Citraratha. I am Kapila among 'the perfected'—i.e., those who have attained, from the very birth, a high degree of virtues, knowledge, detachment and lordship.

उच्चैःश्रवसमश्वानां विद्धि माममृतोद्भवम् ।
ऐरावतं गजेन्द्राणां नराणां च नराधिपम् ॥२७॥

27. Among horses, know Me to be Uccaiḥśravāḥ born of ambrosia; among lordly elephants, Airāvata; and among human beings, their ruler.

27.1. उच्चैः इति ॥ उच्चैःश्रवसं अश्वानां उच्चैश्रवाः नाम अश्वराजः तं मां विद्धि विजानीहि अमृतोद्भवम् अमृतनिमित्तमथनोद्भवम् । ऐरावतं इरावत्याः अपत्यं गजेन्द्राणां हस्तीश्वराणां, तं "मां विद्धि" इति अनुवर्तते । नराणां च मनुष्याणां च नराधिपं राजानं मां विद्धि जानीहि ॥

27.1. Among the 'horses' know Me to be their king named Uccaiḥśravāḥ who was born of the sea when it was churned for ambrosia; 'Airāvata', the offspring of Irāvatī, among lordly elephants. 'Know Me to be'—this expression is to be understood as having reference to every attribute. And among 'human beings' know Me to be their ruler.

आयुधानामहं वज्रं धेनूनामस्मि कामधुक् ।
प्रजनश्चास्मि कन्दर्पः सर्पाणामस्मि वासुकिः ॥२८॥

28. I am (Indra's) thunderbolt among weapons; the

wish-granting cow among cows; I am the begetter, Kandarpa; among serpents I am Vāsuki.

28.1. आयुधानां इति ॥ आयुधानां अहं वज्रं दधीच्यस्थिसम्भवम् । धेनूनां दोग्ध्रीणां अस्मि कामधुक् वसिष्ठस्य सर्वकामानां दोग्ध्री, सामान्या वा कामधुक् । प्रजनः प्रजनयिता अस्मि कन्दर्पः कामः । सर्पाणां सर्पभेदानां अस्मि वासुकिः सर्पराजः ॥

28.1. Among the weapons I am the 'thunderbolt' forged from the bone of Dadhīci. Among the cows I am the 'wish-granting cow' of Vasiṣṭha, yielding objects of all desires, or, a 'wish-granting cow' in general. I am Kandarpa the god of love, 'the begetter' of off-spring. Among 'serpents', a class of reptiles, I am Vāsuki their king.

अनन्तश्चास्मि नागानां वरुणो यादसामहम् ।
पितॄणामर्यमा चास्मि यमः संयमतामहम् ॥२९॥

29. And among the nāga-snakes, I am Ananta their king. Of the creatures in water, I am Varuṇa; among the manes, I am Aryama. Among the subduers, I am Yama.

29.1. अनन्त इति ॥ अनंतश्च अस्मि नागानां नागविशेषाणां नागराजः । वरुणो यादसां अहं अब्देवतानां राजा अहम् । पितॄणां अर्यमा नाम पितृराजः च अस्मि । यमः संयमतां संयमनं कुर्वतां अहम् ॥

29.1. Among the Nāgas' or snakes (with human heads) I am Ananta their king. Of the 'creatures in water', I am Varuṇa, the king of the water spirits. Of 'the manes', I am Aryamā the king of the ancestral spirits. Of 'those who subdue', I am Yama.

प्रह्लादश्चास्मि दैत्यानां कालः कलयतामहम् ।
मृगाणां च मृगेन्द्रोऽहं वैनतेयश्च पक्षिणाम् ॥३०॥

30. Among the demons, I am Prahlāda; among reckoners, I am Time. Of beasts, I am the lion, their king. Of the birds, I am Garuḍa, the son of Vinatā.

30.1. प्रह्लादः इति ॥ प्रह्लादो नाम च अस्मि दैत्यानां दितिवंश्यानाम् । कालः कलयतां कलनं गणनं कुर्वतां अहम् । मृगाणां च मृगेन्द्रः सिंहो व्याघ्रो वा अहम्। वैनतेयश्च गरुत्मान् विनतासुतः पक्षिणां पतत्रिणाम् ॥

30.1. Among 'those born of Diti', I am he who is called Prahlāda. Among 'those who reckon', I am Time. Of 'beasts', I am their king, lion or tiger. Of the 'birds', I am Garuḍa, the son of Vinatā.

पवनः पवतामस्मि रामः शस्त्रभृतामहम् ।
झषाणां मकरश्चास्मि स्रोतसामस्मि जाह्नवी ॥३१॥

31. Among purifiers, I am the wind; among the bearers of weapons, I am Rāma. Among aquatic creatures I am the shark, and among rivers, I am the Ganges.

31.1. पवन इति ॥ पवनः वायुः पवतां पावयितॄणां अस्मि । रामः शस्त्रभृतां अहम् शस्त्राणां धारयितॄणां दाशरथिः राम अहम् । झषाणां मत्स्यादीनां मकरः नाम जातिविशेषः अहम् । स्रोतसां स्रवन्तीनां अस्मि जाह्नवी गङ्गा ॥

31.1. Among the 'purifiers', I am the wind. Among 'those who bear weapons' I am Dasaratha's son. Among 'fishes, and other aquatic animals', I am the shark. Among 'the rivers', I am the Ganges.

सर्गाणामादिरन्तश्च मध्यं चैवाहमर्जुन ।
अध्यात्मविद्या विद्यानां वादः प्रवदतामहम् ॥३२॥

32. Of creations, I am the beginning, the end and the middle, O Arjuna! Among the sciences, I am the science of the Self. Of those who discuss, I am the dialectic.

32.1. सर्गाणां इति ॥ सर्गाणां सृष्टीनां आदिः अन्तश्च मध्यं. चैव अहं उत्पत्तिस्थितिलयाः अहं अर्जुन । भूतानां जीवाधिष्ठितानामेव आदिः अन्तश्च इत्याद्युक्तं उपक्रमे (२०); इह तु सर्वस्यैव सर्गमात्रस्य इति विशेषः । अध्यात्मविद्या विद्यानां मोक्षार्थत्वात् प्रधानं अस्मि । वादः अर्थनिर्णयहेतुत्वात् प्रवदतां प्रधानं अतः सः अहं अस्मि । प्रवक्तृद्वारेण वदनभेदानामेव वादजल्पवितण्डानां इह ग्रहणं 'प्रवदतां' इति ॥

32.1. 'O Arjuna! I am the beginning, the middle and the end of creations—i.e., the origin, existence and dissolution of contingent beings. Earlier, in verse 20, the reference was to the origin and end of living beings; here the reference is to creation as a whole. Of the 'sciences', the science of the Self, promoting liberation is pre-eminent—I am *that*. Being the cause of determination of facts, discussion is pre-eminent as regards 'those who discuss'; so I am that sort of discussion or dialectic. The phrase, 'of those who discuss', refers to varieties of discussion like dispute, prattle and wrangling.

अक्षराणामकारोऽस्मि द्वन्द्वः सामासिकस्य च ।
अहमेवाक्षयः कालो धाताऽहं विश्वतोमुखः ॥३३॥

33. Among letters I am 'a'; among the compounds I am the Dvandva (the additive); I alone am Time imperishable; I am the dispenser, facing all directions.

33.1. अक्षराणां इति ॥ अक्षराणां वर्णानां अकारो वर्णः अस्मि । द्वन्द्वः समासः अस्मि सामासिकस्य च समाससमूहस्य । किञ्च — अहमेव अक्षयः अक्षीणः कालः प्रसिद्धः क्षणाद्याख्यः, अथवा परमेश्वरो वा कालस्यापि कालः अस्मि। धाता अहं कर्मफलस्य विधाता सर्वजगतः विश्वतोमुखः सर्वतोमुखः ॥

33.1. 'Among the letters' I am 'a'; I am the compound *Dvandva* among 'the grammatical compounds'. And I alone am 'Time imperishable', well-known as moments, etc. Or, I am Śiva, the Lord Supreme, being the destroyer of Yama himself. I am 'the multifaced dispenser' of the fruits of works of the entire world.

मृत्युः सर्वहरश्चाहमुद्भवश्च भविष्यताम् ।
कीर्तिः श्रीर्वाक्च नारीणां स्मृतिर्मेधा धृतिः क्षमा ॥३४॥

34. I am Death, carrying all away. Of things yet to be, I am the origin. Of women, I am the fame, glory, speech, memory, intelligence, endurance and patience.

34.1. मृत्युः इति ॥ मृत्युः द्विविधः, धनादिहरः प्राणहरश्च । तत्र यः प्राणहरः, स सर्वहरः उच्यते; सः अहम् इत्यर्थः । अथवा, परः ईश्वरः प्रलये सर्वहरणात् सर्वहरः, सः अहम् । उद्भवः उत्कर्षः अभ्युदयः तत्प्राप्तिहेतुः च अहम् — केषां ? — भविष्यतां भाविकल्याणानां, उत्कर्षप्राप्तियोग्यानां इत्यर्थः । कीर्तिः, श्रीः, वाक् च नारीणां स्मृतिः, मेधा, धृतिः, क्षमा — इत्येताः उत्तमाः स्त्रीणां अहं अस्मि, यासां आभासमात्रसम्बन्धेनापि लोकः कृतार्थम् आत्मानं मन्यते ॥

34.1. Death is twofold; the first is the destruction of wealth, etc., and the second that of life. The second is described as 'carrying all away'. I am *that.* Or the supreme Lord is said to 'carry all away' in the state of dissolution. I am He. 'The origin' is the rise of prosperity—I am the cause of achieving it. Of what all things? Of all forms of 'future prosperity' which deserve enhancement. Of women, fame, glory, speech, memory, intelligence, endurance, patience at their best—I am these. Contact with a mere semblance of any of these excellences fills people with a sense of fulfilment.

बृहत्साम तथा साम्नां गायत्री छन्दसामहम् ।
मासानां मार्गशीर्षोऽहमृतूनां कुसुमाकरः ॥३५॥

35. Among the Sāman-chants I am the Bṛhat; among the Vedic metres I am the Gāyatrī; among the months, I am the Mārgaśīrṣa, and among the seasons, I am spring, the abode of flowers.

35.1. बृहत्साम इति ॥ बृहत्साम तथा साम्नां प्रधानं अस्मि । गायत्री छन्दसां

अहं, गायत्र्यादिच्छन्दोविशिष्टानां ऋचां गायत्री ऋक् अहं अस्मि इत्यर्थः । मासानां मार्गशीर्षः अहं, ऋतूनां कुसुमाकरः वसन्तः ॥

35.1. Similarly I am the *Bṛhat-sāman*, chief among the Sāman-melodies. Among metres I am the *Gāyatrī*, i.e. among the verses composed in Vedic-metres, I am the Gāyatrī-verse. Among the months I am the Mārgaśīrṣa and among the seasons, spring when flowers abound.

द्यूतं छलयतामस्मि तेजस्तेजस्विनामहम् ।
जयोऽस्मि व्यवसायोऽस्मि सत्त्वं सत्त्ववतामहम् ॥३६॥

36. Of the tricksters I am the game of dice; of the vigorous I am the vigour; I am victory, I am resolution; of the virtuous I am the virtue.

36.1. द्यूतं इति ॥ द्यूतं अक्षदेवनादिलक्षणं छलयतां छलस्य कर्तॄणां अस्मि । तेजस्विनां तेजः अहम् । जयः अस्मि जेतॄणां, व्यवसायः अस्मि व्यवसायिनां, सत्त्वं सत्त्ववतां सात्त्विकानां अहम् ॥

36.1. Of the tricksters who cheat, I am the game of dice, etc. I am the vigour of the vigorous. Of conquerors, I am the victory. Of men of resolution, I am the resolve. Of men of virtue, I am the virtue.

वृष्णीनां वासुदेवोऽस्मि पाण्डवानां धनञ्जयः ।
मुनीनामप्यहं व्यासः कवीनामुशना कविः ॥३७॥

37. Among the members of the Vṛṣṇi-clan, I am Vāsudeva; among the Pāṇḍavas, I am Arjuna. Among the contemplative sages, I am Vyāsa; among the seers I am the seer, Uśanāḥ.

37.1. वृष्णीनां इति ॥ वृष्णीनां यादवानां वासुदेवः अस्मि अयमेव अहं त्वत्सखा ।

पाण्डवानां धनञ्जयः त्वमेव । मुनीनां मननशीलानां सर्वपदार्थज्ञानिनां अपि अहं व्यासः, कवीनां क्रान्तदर्शिनां उशना कविः अस्मि ॥

37.1. Among the Yādavas, I am Vāsudeva—I who am your companion. Among the Pāṇḍavas, you yourself am I. Among professional thinkers who know about all objects, I am Vyāsa. Among the farsighted men of vision, I aṃ Uśanāḥ, the seer (the sage Śukra).

दण्डो दमयतामस्मि नीतिरस्मि जिगीषताम् ।
मौनं चैवास्मि गुह्यानां ज्ञानं ज्ञानवतामहम् ॥३८॥

38. Of those who chastise, I am the rod; of those who seek victory, I am the tactics. Of secrets, I am the silence, and of the learned, I am the knowledge.

38.1. दण्डः इति ॥ दण्डः दमयतां दमयितॄणां अस्मि अदान्तानां दमनकारणम् । नीतिः अस्मि जिगीषतां जेतुमिच्छताम् । मौनं चैव अस्मि गुह्यानां गोप्यानाम् । ज्ञानं ज्ञानवतां अहम् ॥

38.1. I am the rod of the chastisers who subdue the turbulent. I am the tactics of those who seek victory. I am the silence of the 'secrets' and the knowledge of the learned.

यच्चापि सर्वभूतानां बीजं तदहमर्जुन ।
न तदस्ति विना यत्स्यान्मया भूतं चराचरम् ॥३९॥

39. And that which is the seed of all beings, I am, Arjuna! That which is without Me, mobile or stationary, exists not.

39.1. यच्चापि इति ॥ यत् च अपि, सर्वभूतानां बीजं प्ररोहकारणं, तत् अहं अर्जुन । प्रकरणोपसंहारार्थं विभूतिसंक्षेपं आह — न तत् अस्ति भूतं चराचरं चरं अचरं वा मया विना यत् स्यात् भवेत् । मया अप्रकृष्टं परित्यक्तं निरात्मकं शून्यं हि तत् स्यात् । अतः मदात्मकं सर्वं इत्यर्थः ॥

39.1. I am that which is the seed of all beings which causes them to multiply, O Arjuna! In order to conclude the topic in hand, the Lord summarises His powers. There is nothing moving or unmoving, that exists without Me. What is not uplifted by Me or is abandoned by Me will be without a Self—indeed, null and void. Therefore all have Me as their Self—this is the idea.

नान्तोऽस्ति मम दिव्यानां विभूतीनां परन्तप ।
एष तूद्देशतः प्रोक्तो विभूतेर्विस्तरो मया ॥४०॥

40. Scourge of foes! There is no limit to My divine powers. What has been stated by Me is only illustrative of the extent of that puissance.

40.1. नान्तः इति ॥ न अन्तः अस्ति मम दिव्यानां विभूतीनां विस्तराणां परन्तप । न हि ईश्वरस्य सर्वात्मनः दिव्यानां विभूतीनां इयत्ता शक्या वक्तुं ज्ञातुं वा केनचित् । एष तु उद्देशतः एकदेशेन प्रोक्तः विभूतेः विस्तरः मया ॥

40.1. To the extent of My divine power there is no end. Indeed, none may either know or express the measure of the divine powers of God, the Self of all. However, what has been offered here only illustrates the extent of My powers.

यद्यद्विभूतिमत्सत्त्वं श्रीमदूर्जितमेव वा ।
तत्तदेवावगच्छ त्वं मम तेजोंशसंभवम् ॥४१॥

41. Whatever being has power, glory, or energy, know (each of them) to be born of a part of My splendour.

41.1. यद्यत् इति ॥ यद्यत् लोके विभूतिमत् विभूतियुक्तं सत्त्वं वस्तु श्रीमत् ऊर्जितमेव वा श्रीः लक्ष्मीः तया सहितं, उत्साहोपेतं वा, तत्तदेव अवगच्छ त्वं जानीहि मम ईश्वरस्य तेजोंशसंभवं तेजसः अंशः एकदेशः संभवः यस्य तत् तेजोंशसंभवं इति अवगच्छ त्वम् ।

41.1. 'Whatever being or thing in the world has power, glory or energy', i.e., is potent, know each such being to be derived from a fragment of My lordly splendour.

अथवा बहुनैतेन किं ज्ञातेन तवार्जुन ।
विष्टभ्याहमिदं कृत्स्नमेकांशेन स्थितो जगत् ॥४२॥

42. Or, Arjuna! Wherefore should you know so much of all these? Encompassing this entire world by a fragment of My power, do I abide, eternally.

इति श्रीमहाभारते शतसाहस्र्यां संहितायां वैयासिक्यां भीष्मपर्वणि
श्रीमद्भगवद्गीतासूपनिषत्सु ब्रह्मविद्यायां योगशास्त्रे श्रीकृष्णार्जुनसंवादे
विभूतियोगो नाम दशमोऽध्यायः ॥

42.1. अथवा इति ॥ अथवा बहुना एतेन एवमादिना किं ज्ञातेन तव अर्जुन ! स्यात् सावशेषेण । अशेषतः त्वं उच्यमानं अर्थं शृणु — विष्टभ्य विशेषतः स्तम्भनं [दृढं] कृत्वा इदं कृत्स्नं जगत् एकांशेन एकावयवेन एकपादेन — सर्वभूतस्वरूपेण इत्येतत्; तथा च मन्त्रवर्णः 'पादोऽस्य विश्वा भूतानि' [तै — आ. ३०.१२; ऋ. सं. १०.९०.३] इति — स्थितः अहं इति ॥

42.1. Or, why should you know much of all these with so much left unsaid? The expression is bound to be incomplete. Listen to this comprehensive summing up. Steadying the whole world with but a part—a quarter—that has assumed the form of all that exists, do I abide for ever. Vide: 'All beings form but a quarter of Him' (Ṛ.V.10.90.3; TA.30.12).

इति श्रीमत्परमहंसपरिव्राजकाचार्यगोविंदभगवत्पूज्यपादशिष्यश्रीमच्छंकरभगवतः
कृतौ श्रीमद्भगवद्गीताभाष्ये विभूतियोगो नाम दशमोऽध्यायः ॥१०॥

एकादशोऽध्यायः
CHAPTER XI
THE YOGA OF THE VISION OF THE COSMIC FORM

0.1. भगवतो विभूतय उक्ताः । तत्र च 'विष्टभ्याहमिदं कृत्स्नमेकांशेन स्थितो जगत्' (१०.४२.) इति भगवता अभिहितं श्रुत्वा यत् जगदात्मरूपं आद्यं ऐश्वरं तत् साक्षात्कर्तुं इच्छन् अर्जुनः उवाच —

0.1. The powers of the Lord have been enumerated. Hearing His affirmation (10.42) "encompassing the entire world with a fragment of My Self, do I abide," and desiring to behold directly that primordial and divine cosmic form,

अर्जुन उवाच :

मदनुग्रहाय परमं गुह्यमध्यात्मसंज्ञितम् ।
यत्त्वयोक्तं वचस्तेन मोहोऽयं विगतो मम ॥१॥

Arjuna said:

1. By the words You have spoken, supreme, occult and spiritual, in order to bless me, this delusion of mine has gone.

1.1. मत् इति ॥ मदनुग्रहाय ममानुग्रहार्थं परमं निरतिशयं गुह्यं गोप्यं अध्यात्मसंज्ञितं आत्मानात्मविवेकविषयं यत् त्वया उक्तं वचः वाक्यं, तेन ते वचसा मोहः अयं विगतो, मम अविवेकबुद्धिः अपगता इत्यर्थः ॥

किञ्च —

1.1. 'In order to bless me' i.e., for conferring a blessing on me, You gave utterance to what is 'the supreme' or unexcelled, 'the occult' or the mysterious, and 'the spiritual' or pertaining to the distinction between the Self and the non-Self. By that utterance this delusion of mine has gone—my perplexity has vanished. This is the idea.

And,

भवाप्ययौ हि भूतानां श्रुतौ विस्तरशो मया ।
त्वत्तः कमलपत्राक्ष माहात्म्यमपि चाव्ययम् ॥२॥

2. About the birth and dissolution of beings I have heard from You at length, O Lotus-eyed! as also about your immutable grandeur.

2.1. भव इति ॥ भवः [उद्भवः]—उत्पत्तिः; अप्ययः प्रलयो तौ भवाप्ययौ हि भूतानां श्रुतौ विस्तरशः न संक्षेपतः मया त्वत्तः त्वत्सकाशात् कमलपत्राक्ष! कमलस्य पत्रं कमलपत्रं तद्वत् अक्षिणी यस्य तव स त्वं कमलपत्राक्षः, हे कमलपत्राक्ष महात्मनः भावः माहात्म्यमपि च अव्ययं अक्षयं, 'श्रुतं' इति अनुवर्तते ॥

2.1. 'The birth'—the coming into being or origin of beings; 'dissolution' is their passing away. Those too I have heard 'at length', not too briefly, from You, O Lotus-eyed! The Lotus-eyed is one having eyes resembling lotus petals. Your magnanimity is Your grandeur, which is immutable. 'About this too, I have heard'—it is to be understood here also from the first half of the verse.

एवमेतद्यथाऽऽत्थ त्वमात्मानं परमेश्वर ।
द्रष्टुमिच्छामि ते रूपमैश्वरं पुरुषोत्तम ॥३॥

3. Supreme Lord! Highest Spirit! It is even as You have described Yourself. Yet I would like to see this lordly form of Yours.

3.1. एवं इति ॥ एवमेतत् नान्यथा यथा येन प्रकारेण आत्थ कथयसि त्वं आत्मानं परमेश्वर। तथापि द्रष्टुं इच्छामि ते तव ज्ञानैश्वर्यबलशक्तिवीर्यतेजोभिः संपन्नं ऐश्वरं वैष्णव रूपं पुरुषोत्तम॥

3.1. 'Thus it is', not otherwise. The way You have set forth, Supreme Lord! about Your Self, I wish to see,—Your all-pervading form characterized by knowledge, power, strength, vigour, heroism and glory.

मन्यसे यदि तच्छक्यं मया द्रष्टुमिति प्रभो ।
योगेश्वर ततो मे त्वं दर्शयात्मानमव्ययम् ।।४।।

4. If You think, Lord, that I may see it, then, Master of Yogas! reveal to me that immutable Self of Yours.

4.1. मन्यसे इति ।। मन्यसे चिन्तयसि यदि मया अर्जुनेन तत् शक्यं द्रष्टुं इति प्रभो ! स्वामिन् ! योगेश्वर ! योगिनो योगाः, तेषां ईश्वरः योगेश्वरः, हे योगेश्वर । यस्मात् अहं अतीव अर्थी द्रष्टुं, ततः तस्मात् मे मदर्थं दर्शय त्वं आत्मानं अव्ययम् ।।

4.1. If You think, Lord, that I, Arjuna, may see it, master-Yogin! reveal to me Your immutable Self for my sake (*Yogeśvara* means Master of Yogins, as Yoga, in the term *Yogeśvara*, means Yogins). I desire to see it very much.

5.0. एवं चोदितः अर्जुनेन श्रीभगवान् उवाच —

5.0. Thus urged by Arjuna,

श्रीभगवानुवाच :

पश्य मे पार्थ रूपाणि शतशोऽथ सहस्रशः ।
नानाविधानि दिव्यानि नानावर्णाकृतीनि च ।।५।।

The blessed Lord said:

5. Behold then, Arjuna! hundreds of My forms, nay, thousands, varied, divine, variously coloured and shaped.

5.1. पश्य इति ।। पश्य मे पार्थ ! रूपाणि शतशः अथ सहस्रशः, अनेकशः इत्यर्थः । तानि च नानाविधानि अनेकप्रकाराणि, दिवि भवानि दिव्यानि अप्रा-

कृतानि, नानावर्णाकृतीनि च नाना विलक्षणाः नीलपीतादिप्रकाराः वर्णाः तथा आकृतयश्च अवयवसंस्थानविशेषाः येषां रूपाणां तानि नानावर्णाकृतीनि च ॥

5.1. Behold Arjuna! then 'hundreds, nay, thousands', of My forms i.e., in their multiplicity. They are of 'various kinds', 'divine' or shaped in heaven, i.e., they are not of Prakṛiti or Matter, and 'varied in colour'—blue, yellow, etc.,—and shaped in many ways.

पश्यादित्यान् वसून् रुद्रानश्विनौ मरुतस्तथा ।
बहून्यदृष्टपूर्वाणि पश्याश्चर्याणि भारत ॥६॥

6. Behold Ādityas, Vasus, Rudras, the two Aśvins and forms hiterto unseen.

6.1. पश्य इति ॥ पश्य आदित्यान् द्वादश, वसून् अष्टौ, रुद्रान् एकादश, अश्विनौ द्वौ, मरुतः सप्त सप्तगणाः ये तान् । तथा च बहूनि अन्यान्यपि अदृष्टपूर्वाणि मनुष्यलोके त्वया, त्वत्तः अन्येन वा केनचित्, पश्य आश्चर्याणि अद्भुतानि भारत ॥

न केवलं एतावदेव —

6.1. Behold the twelve 'Ādityas', the eight 'Vasus', the eleven 'Rudras', the two 'Aśvins' and the seven groups of 'Maruts'. Also behold many marvels hitherto unseen by you in the world of human beings or by any one else, O Bhārata prince!

Nay, more,

इहैकस्थं जगत्कृत्स्नं पश्याद्य सचराचरम् ।
मम देहे गुडाकेश यच्चान्यद्द्रष्टुमिच्छसि ॥७॥

7. Here now behold the entire world with beings, moving and unmoving, extant in 'one abode', in My body, O subduer of lethargy! and also other things you fain would see.

7.1. इह इति ॥ इह एकस्थं एकस्मिन्नेव स्थितं जगत् कृत्स्नं समस्तं पश्य अद्य इदानी सचराचरं सह चरेण अचरेण च वर्तते मम देहे गुडाकेश । यच्च अन्यत् जयपराजयादि, यत् शङ्कसे, 'यद्वा जयेम यदि वा नो जयेयुः' [२.६.] इति यत् अवोचः, तदपि द्रष्टुं यदि इच्छसि ॥

किन्तु—

7.1. Now behold 'here', situated just in one place i.e., in My body, 'the entire', the whole, world, together with 'the beings that move and those that move not', O subduer of lethargy! (i.e., Arjuna) And the 'other things' i.e., victory, defeat, etc., about which you entertain doubt. You asked: 'Shall we win or shall we be defeated?' (2.6); that, too, You can see if you seek to see.

But,

न तु मां शक्यसे द्रष्टुमनेनैव स्वचक्षुषा ।
दिव्यं ददामि ते चक्षुः पश्य मे योगमैश्वरम् ॥८॥

8. You, however, cannot see Me with just this eye of yours. I shall give you a divine eye; behold My sovereign Yoga.

8.1. न तु इति ॥ न तु मां विश्वरूपधरं शक्यसे द्रष्टुं अनेनैव प्राकृतेन स्वचक्षुषा स्वकीयेन चक्षुषा । येन तु शक्यसे द्रष्टुं, दिव्येन, तत् दिव्यं ददामि ते तुभ्यं चक्षुः । तेन पश्य मे योगं ऐश्वरं ईश्वरस्य मम ऐश्वरं योगं योगशक्त्यतिशयं इत्यर्थः ॥

8.1. But you cannot see Me in My cosmic form with just this normal eye of yours. But an eye with which you may see, a 'divine eye', I shall give you. With that see My Yoga that is sovereign, i.e., whose power is supreme. This is the sense.

सञ्जय उवाच :

एवमुक्त्वा ततो राजन् महायोगेश्वरो हरिः ।
दर्शयामास पार्थाय परमं रूपमैश्वरम् ॥९॥

Sañjaya said:

9. Then, thus speaking, O King! Hari, the great master of Yogas, revealed to Arjuna a transcendent and sovereign form.

9.1. एवं इति ॥ एवं यथोक्तेन प्रकारेण उक्त्वा, ततः अनन्तरं राजन् ! धृतराष्ट्र ! महांश्च असौ योगेश्वरश्च महायोगेश्वरः हरिः नारायणः दर्शयामास दर्शितवान् पार्थाय पृथासुताय परमं रूपं विश्वरूपं ऐश्वरम् ॥

9.1. Having spoken thus, as stated, O king Dhṛtarāṣṭra! Hari, 'the great master of Yogas', or Nārāyaṇa, revealed to Arjuna His transcendent and cosmic form.

अनेकवक्त्रनयनमनेकाद्भुतदर्शनम् ।
अनेकदिव्याभरणं दिव्यानेकोद्यतायुधम् ॥१०॥

10. With many a mouth and many an eye, with many marvellous aspects, with many a divine ornament, with many weapons, uplifted;

10.1. अनेक इति ॥ अनेकवक्त्रनयनं अनेकानि वक्त्राणि नयनानि च यस्मिन् रूपे तत् अनेकवक्त्रनयनं, अनेकाद्भुतदर्शनं अनेकानि अद्भुतानि विस्मापकानि दर्शनानि यस्मिन् तत् अनेकाद्भुतदर्शनं रूपं, तथा अनेकदिव्याभरणं अनेकानि दिव्यानि आभरणानि यस्मिन् तत् अनेकदिव्याभरणं, तथा दिव्यानेकोद्यतायुधं दिव्यानि अनेकानि अस्यादीनि उद्यतानि आयुधानि यस्मिन् तत् दिव्यानेकोद्यतायुधं, 'दर्शयामास' इति पूर्वेण सम्बन्धः ॥
किंच —

10.1. A form with many mouths and eyes, with many aspects, rousing a sense of wonder, with many divine ornaments and, similarly, with many divine and uplifted weapons like swords, etc. Construe all this with 'He revealed . . .' in verse 9 above.

And,

दिव्यमाल्याम्बरधरं दिव्यगन्धानुलेपनम् ।
सर्वाश्चर्यमयं देवमनन्तं विश्वतोमुखम् ॥११॥

11. Wearing divine garlands and vestments, smeared with divine scents, full of marvels, an infinite God with faces turned everywhere.

11.1. दिव्य इति ॥ दिव्यमाल्याम्बरधरं दिव्यानि माल्यानि पुष्पाणि अम्बराणि वस्त्राणि च ध्रियन्ते येन ईश्वरेण तं दिव्यमाल्याम्बरधरं, दिव्यगन्धानुलेपनम् दिव्यं गन्धानुलेपनं यस्य तत् दिव्यगन्धानुलेपनं, सर्वाश्चर्यमयं सर्वाश्चर्यप्रायं देवं अनन्तं न अस्य अन्तः अस्ति इति अनन्तः तं अनन्तं, विश्वतोमुखं सर्वतोमुखं — सर्वभूतात्मभूतत्वात्, 'तं दर्शयामास'। 'अर्जुनः ददर्श' इति वा अध्याह्रियते ॥

11.1. He revealed Himself 'wearing divine garlands', flowers and robes, and having 'a smear of divine scents' and a glory infinite, endless and wondrous, and facing all beings, as their Self. Or, here the expression 'Arjuna beheld' may be added.

12.0. या पुनः भगवतः विश्वरूपस्य भाः, तस्याः उपमा उच्यते —

12.0. As regards the splendour of the blessed Lord in His cosmic form an analogue is offered:

दिवि सूर्यसहस्रस्य भवेद्युगपदुत्थिता ।
यदि भाः सदृशी सा स्याद्भासस्तस्य महात्मनः ॥१२॥

12. If in the firmament the simultaneous splendour of a thousand suns were to explode, it will have a semblance to that of that mighty Being.

12.1. दिवि इति ॥ दिवि अन्तरिक्षे तृतीयस्यां वा दिवि सूर्याणां सहस्रं सूर्यसहस्रं तस्य युगपदुत्थितस्य सूर्यसहस्रस्य या युगपदुत्थिता भाः, सा यदि, सदृशी स्यात् तस्य महात्मनः विश्वरूपस्यैव भासः । यदि वा न स्यात् ततोऽपि विश्वरूपस्यैव भाः अतिरिच्यते इत्यभिप्रायः ॥

किञ्च —

12.1. 'In the firmament', i.e., in the sky or in the third sphere of heaven where there is the simultaneous splendour of a thousand suns risen all together—it would be similar to the blazing light of that mighty Being in His cosmic form. Or maybe it is not similar; as the light of that Being will surpass it. This is the idea.

And,

तत्रैकस्थं जगत्कृत्स्नं प्रविभक्तमनेकधा ।
अपश्यद्देवदेवस्य शरीरे पाण्डवस्तदा ॥१३॥

13. Then the Pāṇḍava prince beheld the entire world residing in the body of that God of gods, variegated in manifold ways.

13.1. तत्र इति ॥ तत्र तस्मिन् विश्वरूपे एकस्मिन् स्थितं एकस्थं जगत् कृत्स्नं प्रविभक्तं अनेकधा देवपितृमनुष्यादिभेदैः अपश्यत् दृष्टवान् देवदेवस्य हरेः शरीरे पाण्डवः अर्जुनः तदा ॥

13.1. There, in that single being with cosmic form—in the body of Hari, the God of gods—the Paṇḍava prince Arjuna beheld 'the entire world, variegated in endless ways', as gods, manes, humans, etc.

ततः स विस्मयाविष्टो हृष्टरोमा धनञ्जयः ।
प्रणम्य शिरसा देवं कृताञ्जलिरभाषत ॥१४॥

14. Then filled with amazement and with hairs standing on end, Arjuna spoke to the Lord, his head bent and hands folded.

14.1. ततः इति ॥ ततः तं दृष्ट्वा सः विस्मयेन आविष्टः विस्मयाविष्टः हृष्टानि रोमाणि यस्य सः अयं हृष्टरोमा च अभवत् धनञ्जयः । प्रणम्य प्रकर्षेण नमनं कृत्वा प्रह्वीभूतः सन् शिरसा देवं विश्वरूपधरं कृताञ्जलिः नमस्कारार्थं संपुटीकृतहस्तः सन् अभाषत उक्तवान् ॥

14.1. 'Then', on beholding Him, Arjuna was filled with amazement; his hairs stood on end. 'Head bent', i.e., very humbly, and 'hands folded' to pay obeisance, he spoke to the Lord in His cosmic form.

15.0. कथं ? यत् त्वया दर्शितं विश्वरूपं, तत् अहं पश्यामीति स्वानुभवं आविष्कुर्वन् अर्जुनः उवाच—

15.0. How? Affirming his own experience in the words such as 'I see Your cosmic form as revealed by You' etc.

अर्जुन उवाच :

पश्यामि देवांस्तव देव देहे सर्वांस्तथा भूतविशेषसङ्घान् ।
ब्रह्माणमीशं कमलासनस्थमृषींश्च सर्वानुरगांश्च दिव्यान् ॥१५॥

Arjuna said:

15. Lord! in Your body I see all gods, as also groups of contingent beings—the mighty Brahmā seated in the lotus, all the seers, and all the celestial serpents.

15.1. पश्यामि इति ॥ पश्यामि उपलभे हे देव ! तव देहे देवान् सर्वान्, तथा भूतविशेषसङ्घान् भूतविशेषाणां स्थावरजङ्गमानां नानासंस्थानविशेषाणां सङ्घाः भूतविशेषसङ्घाः तान्, किञ्च—ब्रह्माणं चतुर्मुखं ईशं ईशितारं प्रजानां कमलासनस्थं पृथिवीपद्ममध्ये मेरुकर्णिकासनस्थं इत्यर्थः, ऋषींश्च वसिष्ठादीन् सर्वान्, उरगांश्च वासुकिप्रभृतीन् दिव्यान् दिवि भवान् ॥

15.1. I 'see', cognize, O Lord! in Your body all the gods; also groups of particular beings, moving and unmoving, in varied shapes; the 'four-faced Brahmā seated on the lotus-throne', the Lord of the creatures who resides on Meru, the pericarp of the earth-lotus. Also all the 'seers', Vasiṣṭha and the rest, and the 'celestial serpents', Vāsuki and the rest.

अनेकबाहूदरवक्त्रनेत्रं पश्यामि त्वा सर्वतोऽनन्तरूपम् ।
नान्तं न मध्यं न पुनस्तवादिं पश्यामि विश्वेश्वर विश्वरूप ॥१६॥

16. I behold You with many hands, bellies, faces and eyes, with a form infinite in all directions. No end, middle or beginning for You I see, Lord of the Universe!

16.1. अनेक इति ॥ अनेकबाहूदरवक्त्रनेत्रं अनेके बाहवः उदराणि वक्त्राणि नेत्राणि च यस्य तव सः त्वं अनेकबाहूदरवक्त्रनेत्रः तं अनेकबाहूदरवक्त्रनेत्रम् । पश्यामि त्वा त्वां सर्वतः सर्वत्र अनन्तरूपं अनन्तानि रूपाणि अस्य इति अनन्तरूपः तं अनन्तरूपम् । न अन्तं, अन्तः अवसानं, न मध्यं, मध्यं नाम द्वयोः कोटचोः अन्तरं, न पुनः तव आदिं — न तव देवस्य अन्तं पश्यामि, न मध्यं पश्यामि, न पुनः आदिं पश्यामि हे विश्वेश्वर ! हे विश्वरूप ॥

किञ्च —

16.1. I see You having numerous hands, bellies, faces and eyes, everywhere possessing infinite forms. No end, no middle, i.e. the space between two extreme points, and, again no beginning for You, Lord! do I see. I see neither end, middle nor beginning, O Lord of the universe! Omni-formed Being!

And,

किरीटिनं गदिनं चक्रिणं च
तेजोराशिं सर्वतोदीप्तिमन्तम् ।
पश्यामि त्वां दुर्निरीक्ष्यं समन्ताद्-
दीप्तानलार्कद्युतिमप्रमेयम् ॥१७॥

17. I see you (adorned) with diadem, mace, and discus; a massed splendour, blazing in all directions—dazzling all around with the light of blazing fire and sun, immeasurable.

17.1. किरीटिनं इति ॥ किरीटिनं किरीटं नाम शिरोभूषणविशेषः तत् यस्य अस्ति सः किरीटी तं किरीटिनम्, तथा गदिनं गदा अस्य विद्यते इति गदी तं गदिनम्, तथा चक्रिणं चक्रं अस्य अस्तीति चक्री तं चक्रिणं च, तेजोराशिं तेजः-पुञ्जं, सर्वतोदीप्तिमन्तं सर्वतो दीप्तिः अस्य अस्तीति सर्वतोदीप्तिमान्, तं सर्व-तोदीप्तिमन्तं पश्यामि त्वां दुर्निरीक्ष्यं दुःखेन निरीक्ष्यः दुर्निरीक्ष्यः तं दुर्निरीक्ष्यं समन्तात् समन्ततः, दीप्तानलार्कद्युतिं अनलश्च अर्कश्च अनलार्कौ दीप्तौ अनलार्कौ

दीप्तानलार्कौ तयोः दीप्तानलार्कयोः द्युतिरिव द्युतिः तेजः यस्य तव स त्वं दीप्तानलार्कद्युतिः तं दीप्तानलार्कद्युतिं, अप्रमेयं न प्रमेयं अशक्यपरिच्छेदं इत्येतत् ॥

17.1. 'Diadem' is a head-ornament; one having it is the 'diademed'; similarly, one having a mace and having a discus; 'a mass of splendour blazing in all direction'—I see You have all these and on all sides You are dazzling; (so You are) hard to behold. Again, I see You have a light like that of a 'blazing fire' and of 'the sun' 'immeasurable', undeterminable.

18.0. इत एव ते योगशक्तिदर्शनात् अनुमिनोमि —

18.0. In view of the power of Your Yoga, I infer:

त्वमक्षरं परमं वेदितव्यं त्वमस्य विश्वस्य परं निधानम् ।
त्वमव्ययः शाश्वतधर्मगोप्ता सनातनस्त्वं पुरुषो मतो मे ॥१८॥

18. You are the supreme Imperishable, worthy to be known; You are the ultimate ground of the universe. You, the immutable, are the guardian of eternal righteousness; I deem You to be the everlasting Spirit.

18.1. त्वं इति ॥ त्वं अक्षरं न क्षरतीति अक्षरं परमं ब्रह्म वेदितव्यं ज्ञातव्यं मुमुक्षुभिः । त्वं अस्य विश्वस्य समस्तस्य जगतः परं प्रकृष्टं निधानं निधीयते अस्मिन्निति निधानं, परः आश्रयः इत्यर्थः । किञ्च — त्वं अव्ययः न तव व्ययो विद्यते इति अव्ययः, शाश्वतधर्मगोप्ता शश्वद्भवः शाश्वतः नित्यः धर्मः तस्य गोप्ता शाश्वतधर्मगोप्ता । सनातनः चिरन्तनः त्वं पुरुषः परमः मतः अभिप्रेतः मे मम ॥
किञ्च —

18.1. What does not perish is 'the Imperishable', the supreme Brahman; who, for the seekers after liberation, is fit to know. Of this entire universe, You are 'the ultimate', or the exalted 'ground,'—the receptacle in which it rests, i.e., its final support. Besides, You, the immutable, who wither not, are the guardian of eternal righteousness. I deem You the Supreme Spirit, to be the everlasting One.

And,

अनादिमध्यान्तमनन्तवीर्य-
मनन्तबाहुं शशिसूर्यनेत्रम् ।
पश्यामि त्वां दीप्तहुताशवक्त्रं
स्वतेजसा विश्वमिदं तपन्तम् ॥१९॥

19. I see You, who have no beginning, middle and end, endowed with inexhaustible energy, and numberless arms, with the sun and moon for Your eyes, the blazing fire for face, burning the universe with Your radiance.

19.1. अनादि इति ॥ अनादिमध्यान्तं आदिश्च मध्यं च अन्तश्च न विद्यते यस्य सः अयं अनादिमध्यान्तः तं त्वां अनादिमध्यान्तं, अनन्तवीर्यं न तव वीर्यस्य अन्तः अस्ति इति अनन्तवीर्यः तं अनन्तवीर्यं, तथा अनन्तबाहुं अनन्ताः बाहवः यस्य तव सः त्वं अनन्तबाहुः तं त्वां अनन्तबाहुं, शशिसूर्यनेत्रं शशिसूर्यौ नेत्रे यस्य तव सः त्वं शशिसूर्यनेत्रः तं त्वां शशिसूर्यनेत्रं तं चन्द्रादित्यनयनं पश्यामि त्वां दीप्तहुताशवक्त्र दीप्तश्च असौ हुताशश्च सः वक्त्रं यस्य तव सः त्वं दीप्तहुताशवक्त्रः तं त्वां दीप्तहुताशवक्त्रं, स्वतेजसा विश्वं इदं समस्तं तपन्तं सन्तापयन्तम् ॥

19.1. You have neither beginning, middle nor end; Your energy is endless and arms numberless. The sun and the moon are Your eyes. I see You thus, whose face is a blazing fire causing this universe to burn with Your radiance.

द्यावापृथिव्योरिदमन्तरं हि व्याप्तं त्वयैकेन दिशश्च सर्वाः ।
दृष्ट्वाऽद्भुतं रूपमिदं तवोग्रं लोकत्रयं प्रव्यथितं महात्मन् ॥२०॥

20. Indeed this space between the firmament and the earth has been pervaded solely by You, as also all points of space. Beholding this marvellous, menacing form of Yours, magnanimous Being! the three worlds are overwhelmed.

20.1. द्यावा इति ॥ द्यावापृथिव्योः इदं अन्तरं हि अन्तरिक्षं व्याप्तं त्वया विश्वरूपधरेण एकेन, दिशश्च सर्वाः व्याप्ताः । दृष्ट्वा उपलभ्य अद्भुतं विस्मापकं

रूपं इदं तव उग्रं क्रूरं लोकत्रयं लोकानां त्रयं प्रव्यथितं भीतं प्रचलितं वा हे महात्मन् अक्षुद्रस्वभाव ॥

20.1. 'This space between the firmament and the earth'—the atmosphere and beyond—has been pervaded by You alone, O Bearer of the cosmic form! So also, all the points of the compass. 'Beholding', perceiving, this 'marvellous', amazing, form of Yours that 'menaces' or terrifies, these three worlds are smitten with fear or are shaken, O 'magnanimous' i.e., mighty Being!

21.0. अथ अधुना पुरा 'यद्वा जयेम यदि वा नो जयेयुः' [२.६.] इति अर्जुनस्य यः संशयः आसीत्, तन्निर्णयाय पाण्डवविजयं ऐकान्तिकं दर्शयामि इति प्रवृत्तः भगवान्, तं पश्यन् आह —
किञ्च —

21.0. Now, in order to resolve Arjuna's earlier doubt, 'whether we shall conquer or they will conquer us' (BG.2.61), the Lord wishes to reveal the decisive victory of the Pāṇḍavas. Seeing Him thus engaged, Arjuna says:

अमी हि त्वां सुरसंघा विशन्ति
केचिद्भीताः प्राञ्जलयो गृणन्ति ।
स्वस्तीत्युक्त्वा मर्हर्षिसिद्धसंघाः
स्तुवन्ति त्वां स्तुतिभिः पुष्कलाभिः ॥२१॥

21. Verily these hosts of gods enter into You; some frightened and with folded hands extol. Groups of eminent seers and perfected souls, exclaiming 'Let there be prosperity' extol You with hymns rich in contents.

21.1. अमी इति ॥ अमी हि युध्यमानाः ये योद्धारः त्वा त्वां सुरसङ्घाः ये अत्र भूभारावताराय अवतीर्णाः वस्वादिदेवसङ्घाः मनुष्यसंस्थानाः ते त्वां विशन्ति प्रविशन्तः दृश्यन्ते । तत्र केचित् भीताः प्राञ्जलयः सन्तो गृणन्ति स्तुवन्ति त्वां

अन्ये पलायनेऽपि अशक्ताः सन्तः । युद्धे प्रत्युपस्थिते उत्पातादिनिमित्तानि उपलक्ष्य स्वस्ति अस्तु जगतः इति उक्त्वा महर्षिसिद्धसङ्घाः महर्षीणां सिद्धानां च सङ्घाः स्तुवन्ति त्वां स्तुतिभिः पुष्कलाभिः संपूर्णाभिः ॥

किञ्चान्यत् —

21.1. Vasus and other celestials, who have taken human form and are now fighting in order to lessen the earth's burden, enter into You—they are seen to do so. Among them are some 'frightened' ones, who, with 'folded hands, extol', being powerless even to flee. When the battle is about to begin, noting evil omens, 'hosts of great seers and perfected souls' extol You, saying, "May the world prosper", and chanting hymns 'rich in content'—complete in all respects.

Besides,

रुद्रादित्या वसवो ये च साध्या विश्वेऽश्विनौ मरुतश्चोष्मपाश्च ।
गन्धर्वयक्षासुरसिद्धसंघा वीक्षन्ते त्वां विस्मिताश्चैव सर्वे ॥२२॥

22. Rudras, Ādityas, Vasus, lesser perfected souls, Viśvēdevas, the two Aśvins, Maruts, the ancestral spirits, hosts of celestial minstrels, Yakṣas, demons, and perfected souls gaze at You; and they are all amazed.

22.1. रुद्रादित्याः इति ॥ रुद्रादित्या वसवो ये च साध्याः रुद्रादयः गणाः विश्वे देवाः, अश्विनौ च देवौ, मरुतश्च, ऊष्मपाश्च पितरः, गन्धर्वयक्षासुरसिद्धसङ्घाः — गन्धर्वाः हाहाहूहूप्रभृतयः, यक्षाः कुबेरप्रभृतयः, असुराः विरोचनप्रभृतयः, सिद्धाः कपिलादयः — तेषां सङ्घाः गन्धर्वयक्षासुरसिद्धसङ्घाः — ते वीक्षन्ते पश्यन्ति त्वां विस्मिताः विस्मयं आपन्नाः सन्तः ते एव सर्वे ॥

यस्मात् —

22.1. 'Rudras, Ādityas, Vasus, and lesser perfected souls'—of these, Rudras, etc., are ogre groups; the Viśvedevas, and the two Aśvins are deities. Then there are the Maruts and the ancestral spirits. The celestial minstrels are Hāhā, Hūhū, etc., Yakṣas are Kubera and so forth; demons, Virocana, etc.

'The perfected souls' refer to Kapila and others like him. The hosts of all these gaze at You and are amazed.

For,

रूपं महत्ते बहुवक्त्रनेत्रं महाबाहो बहुबाहूरुपादम् ।
बहूदरं बहुदंष्ट्राकरालं दृष्ट्वा लोकाः प्रव्यथितास्तथाऽहम् ॥२३॥

23. Seeing Your immense form with its many mouths and eyes, Mighty-armed! Your many arms, thighs, and feet, and bellies, terrifying because of many tusks, the worlds are consternated; so am I.

23.1. रूपं इति ॥ रूपं महत् अतिप्रमाणं ते तव बहुवक्त्रनेत्रं बहूनि वक्त्राणि मुखानि नेत्राणि चक्षूंषि च यस्मिन् रूपे तत् रूपं बहुवक्त्रनेत्रं, हे महाबाहो ! बहुबाहूरुपादं बहवो बाहवः ऊरवः पादाश्च यस्मिन् रूपे तत् बहुबाहूरुपादं, किञ्च — बहूदरं बहूनि उदराणि यस्मिन्निति तत् बहूदरं, बहुदंष्ट्राकरालं बह्वीभिः दंष्ट्राभिः करालं विकृतं तत् बहुदंष्ट्राकरालं — दृष्ट्वा रूपं ईदृशं लोकाः लौकिकाः प्राणिनः प्रव्यथिताः प्रचलिताः भयेन; तथा अहं अपि ॥

तत्रेदं कारणम् —

23.1. Your form exceeding all measure, with its many mouths and eyes, O Mighty-armed! with its many hands, thighs and feet seeing it the world's living beings are 'consternated'—shaken with terror; so am I.

Here is the reason for it:

नभःस्पृशं दीप्तमनेकवर्णं
व्यात्ताननं दीप्तविशालनेत्रम् ।
दृष्ट्वा हि त्वां प्रव्यथितान्तरात्मा
धृतिं न विन्दामि शमं च विष्णो ॥२४॥

24. On seeing You touching the sky, blazing, many-hued, with open mouths and eyes distended and flaming, my inner self is deeply troubled, O Viṣṇu!;

I have neither courage nor inner calm.

24.1. नभःस्पृशं इति ॥ नभःस्पृशं द्युस्पर्शं इत्यर्थः, दीप्तं प्रज्वलितं, अनेकवर्णं अनेके वर्णाः भयङ्कराः नानासंस्थानाः यस्मिन् त्वयि तं त्वां अनेकवर्णं, व्यात्ताननं व्यात्तानि विवृतानि आननानि मुखानि यस्मिन् त्वयि तं त्वा व्यात्ताननम्, दीप्त-विशालनेत्रं दीप्तानि प्रज्वलितानि विशालानि विस्तीर्णानि नेत्राणि यस्मिन् त्वयि तं त्वां दीप्तविशालनेत्रं दृष्ट्वा हि त्वां प्रव्यथितान्तरात्मा प्रव्यथितः अन्तरात्मा मनः यस्य मम सः अहं प्रव्यथितान्तरात्मा सन् धृतिं धैर्यं न विन्दामि न लभे शमं च उपशमं मनस्तुष्टिं, हे विष्णो ॥

कस्मात् ? —

24.1. 'Touching the sky'—the firmament; 'blazing'—flaming; 'with many terrifying hues' or dispositions; 'mouths wide-open, eyes flaming and distended—seeing You thus, my inner self or mind is deeply troubled. I can find no courage; nor have I inner calm, i.e., peace of mind, O Viṣṇu.

Why?

दंष्ट्राकरालानि च ते मुखानि दृष्ट्वैव कालानलसन्निभानि ।
दिशो न जाने न लभे च शर्म प्रसीद देवेश जगन्निवास ॥२५॥

25. On just seeing Your mouths terrifying due to tusks, glowing like the all-consuming fire of Time, I can't find my bearings; I can't find peace. Be gracious, God of gods! abode of worlds!

25.1. दंष्ट्राकरालानि इति ॥ दंष्ट्राकरालानि दंष्ट्राभिः करालानि विकृतानि ते तव मुखानि दृष्ट्वैव उपलभ्य कालानलसन्निभानि प्रलयकाले लोकानां दाहकः अग्निः कालानलः तत्सदृशानि कालानलसन्निभानि मुखानि दृष्ट्वा इति एतत्, दिशः पूर्वापरविवेकेन न जाने दिङ्मूढो जातः अस्मि । अतः न लभे न उपलभे च शर्म सुखम् । अतः प्रसीद प्रसन्नो भव हे देवेश ! जगन्निवास ॥

25.1. On just seeing Your mouths 'terrifying due to tusks', distorted and 'glowing like the all-consuming fire of Time' at the dissolution of world, I fail to know the distinction between directions like east and west, i.e., I have lost my bearings.

Therefore, I can't get peace of mind. So, God of gods! Abode of worlds! Be gracious.

26.0. येभ्यः मम पराजयशङ्का या [प्रागेव] आसीत् सा च अपगता । यतः —

26.0. All those children of Dhṛtarāṣṭra, at whose hands I had a fear of defeat—a fear that has now gone.

अमी च त्वां धृतराष्ट्रस्य पुत्राः सर्वे सहैवावनिपालसंघैः ।
भीष्मो द्रोणः सूतपुत्रस्तथाऽसौ सहास्मदीयैरपि योधमुख्यैः ॥२६॥

26. All those children of Dhṛtarāṣṭra together with the hosts of earth's rulers, Bhīṣma, Droṇa, and the charioteer's son, as also the leading warriors on our side (rush into Your mouths);

26.1. अमी इति ॥ अमी च त्वां धृतराष्ट्रस्य पुत्राः दुर्योधनप्रभृतयः — 'त्वरमाणाः त्वां विशन्ति' (२७) इति व्यवहितेन सम्बन्धः — सर्वे सहैव सहिताः अवनिपालसङ्घैः अवनिं पृथ्वीं पालयन्तीति अवनिपालाः तेषां सङ्घैः, किञ्च — भीष्मः, द्रोणः, सूतपुत्रः कर्णः तथा असौ, सह अस्मदीयैरपि धृष्टद्युम्नप्रभृतिभिः योधमुख्यैः योधानां प्रधानैः सह ॥

किञ्च —

26.1. 'Those children of Dhṛtarāṣṭra', Duryodhana and the rest—construe this with the phrase 'rush into your mouths', remotely placed in verse 27. All of them with the hosts of earth's rulers and also Bhīṣma, Droṇa and Karṇa, as well as the leading warriors on our side, Dhṛṣṭadyumna, etc.

वक्त्राणि ते त्वरमाणा विशन्ति दंष्ट्राकरालानि भयानकानि ।
केचिद्विलग्ना दशनान्तरेषु संदृश्यन्ते चूर्णितैरुत्तमाङ्गैः ॥२७॥

27. Rush into Your awesome mouths, terrifying due to their tusks. Sticking between the teeth are observed some, with their heads crushed.

27.1. वक्त्राणि इति ॥ वक्त्राणि मुखानि ते तव त्वरमाणाः त्वरायुक्ताः सन्तः विशन्ति — किंविशिष्टानि मुखानि ? — दंष्ट्राकरालानि भयानकानि भयङ्कराणि । किञ्च — केचित् मुखानि प्रविष्टानां मध्ये विलग्नाः दशनान्तरेषु दन्तान्तरेषु मांसम् इव भक्षितं संदृश्यन्ते उपलभ्यन्ते चूर्णितैः चूर्णीकृतैः उत्तमाङ्गैः शिरोभिः ॥

27.1. Rushing they enter into Your mouths, awesome due to the terrifying tusks in them. Also, among those who have thus entered are found some sticking between the teeth, like remnants of eaten flesh, their heads crushed to powder.

28.0. कथं प्रविशन्ति मुखानि इति ? आह —

28.0. Like what do they enter the mouths? Answer:

यथा नदीनां बहवोऽम्बुवेगाः समुद्रमेवाभिमुखा द्रवन्ति ।
तथा तवामी नरलोकवीरा विशन्ति वक्त्राण्यभिविज्वलन्ति ॥२८॥

28. As the multitudinous streams of rivers rush towards the sea alone, so these heroes among men enter your blazing mouths.

28.1. यथा इति ॥ यथा नदीनां स्रवन्तीनां बहवः अनेके अम्बूनां वेगाः अम्बुवेगाः त्वराविशेषाः समुद्रमेव अभिमुखाः प्रतिमुखाः द्रवन्ति प्रविशन्ति, तथा तद्वत् तव अमी भीष्मादयः नरलोकवीराः मनुष्यलोके शूराः विशन्ति वक्त्राणि अभिविज्वलन्ति प्रकाशमानानि ॥

28.1. As the many torrents of rivers rushing exclusively towards the sea enter it, so these human heroes, Bhīṣma and the rest, enter Your 'blazing' or luminous mouths.

29.0. ते किमर्थं प्रविशन्ति कथं च इति ? आह —

29.0. Why and how do they enter?

यथा प्रदीप्तं ज्वलनं पतङ्गा विशन्ति नाशाय समृद्धवेगाः ।
तथैव नाशाय विशन्ति लोकास्तवापि वक्त्राणि समृद्धवेगाः ॥२९॥

29. Just as moths, with accelerated speed, enter a blazing fire for self-destruction, just so, to perish, people too enter Your mouths with accelerated speed.

29.1. यथा इति ।। यथा प्रदीप्तं ज्वलनं अग्निं पतङ्गाः पक्षिणः विशन्ति नाशाय विनाशाय, समृद्धवेगाः समृद्धः उद्भूतः वेगः गतिः येषां ते समृद्धवेगाः, तथैव नाशाय विशन्ति लोकाः प्राणिनः तवापि वक्त्राणि समृद्धवेगाः ।।
त्वं पुनः —

29.1. Just as winged insects enter a blazing fire for destruction with enhanced speed, just so, to perish, 'people', i.e., living beings, enter Your mouths with enhanced speed.

And You,

**लेलिह्यसे ग्रसमानः समन्ताल्लोकान् समग्रान् वदनैर्ज्वलद्भिः ।
तेजोभिरापूर्य जगत् समग्रं भासस्तवोग्राः प्रतपन्ति विष्णो ।।३०।।**

30. Repeatedly lick, swallowing on all sides, with blazing mouths entire worlds (of living beings). O Viṣṇu, filling the entire universe with luminous energy, Your dreadful radiations scorch.

30.1. लेलिह्यसे इति ।। लेलिह्यसे आस्वादयसि ग्रसमानः अन्तःप्रवेशयन् समन्तात् समन्ततः लोकान् समग्रान् समस्तान् वदनैः वक्त्रैः ज्वलद्भिः दीप्यमानैः तेजोभिः आपूर्य संव्याप्य जगत् समग्रं सह अग्रेण समस्तं इत्येतत् । किञ्च — भासः दीप्तयः तव उग्राः क्रूराः प्रतपन्ति संतापं कुर्वन्ति, हे विष्णो व्यापनशील ।।

30.1. You 'repeatedly lick', enjoy, 'swallowing', gobbling up, on all sides, all living beings with mouths 'blazing'—glowing and 'filling', pervading, the entire world with luminous energy. Also Your dreadful radiations or flames, scorch, O Viṣṇu, all-pervading Spirit!

31.0. यत एवं उग्रस्वभावः, अतः —

31.0. Being so menacing in Your attitude, please,

आख्याहि मे को भवानुग्ररूपो नमोऽस्तु ते देववर प्रसीद ।
विज्ञातुमिच्छामि भवन्तमाद्यं न हि प्रजानामि तव प्रवृत्तिम् ॥३१॥

31. Tell me who You are with Your awesome form. Salutation to You, Chief of the gods! be gracious. I wish to know You, the primordial Being; for I understand not (the nature of) Your activity.

31.1. आख्याहि इति ॥ आख्याहि कथय—मे मह्यं कः भवान् एवं उग्ररूपः क्रूराकारः । नमः अस्तु ते तुभ्यं, हे देववर देवानां प्रधान, प्रसीद प्रसादं कुरु। विज्ञातुं विशेषेण ज्ञातुं इच्छामि भवन्तं आद्यं आदौ भवं आद्यं; न हि यस्मात् प्रजानामि तव त्वदीयां प्रवृत्तिं चेष्टाम् ॥

31.1. Tell me who You are with Your 'awesome form'—form dreadful to behold. Salutation to You, O Chief of gods! the Leader of the gods! Be gracious. I 'wish to know', to understand, specially You as primordial Being; for I do not understand 'Your activity'—Your doings.

श्रीभगवानुवाच :
कालोऽस्मि लोकक्षयकृत्प्रवृद्धो
लोकान्समाहर्तुमिह प्रवृत्तः ।
ऋतेऽपि त्वा न भविष्यन्ति सर्वे
येऽवस्थिताः प्रत्यनीकेषु योधाः ॥३२॥

The Blessed Lord said:
32. Dominant Time am I, wreaking the dissolution of the world. Here I am active, gathering the worlds unto Me. Even without you, these warriors marshalled in these opposing forces will cease to be.

32.1. कालः इति ॥ कालः अस्मि लोकक्षयकृत् लोकानां क्षयं करोतीति लोकक्षयकृत् प्रवृद्धः (प्र)वृद्धिं गतः । यदर्थं प्रवृद्धः तत् शृणु—लोकान् समाहर्तुं संहर्तुं इह अस्मिन् काले प्रवृत्तः । ऋतेऽपि विनापि त्वा त्वां न भविष्यन्ति भीष्म-

द्रोणकर्णप्रभृतयः सर्वे, येभ्यः तव आशङ्का, ये अवस्थिताः प्रत्यनीकेषु अनीकमनीकं प्रति प्रत्यनीकेषु प्रतिपक्षभूतेषु अनीकेषु योधाः योद्धारः ॥

यस्मात् एवम् —

32.1. As 'dominant Time', I am wreaking the dissolution of the worlds. Hear why I am active in destroying the worlds now. Even without You, all these warriors will cease to be—Bhīṣma, Droṇa, Karṇa, etc., who rouse your fear and are marshalled in these opposing ranks.

Such being the case,

तस्मात्त्वमुत्तिष्ठ यशो लभस्व जित्वा शत्रून्भुङ्क्ष्व राज्यं समृद्धम् ।
मयैवैते निहताः पूर्वमेव निमित्तमात्रं भव सव्यसाचिन् ॥३३॥

33. Stand up therefore; win renown, conquering your foes. Enjoy this opulent kingdom. Already have these been slain by Me, skilful bow-man! be but an occasion (for the end of your foes).

33.1. तस्मात् इति ॥ तस्मात् त्वं उत्तिष्ठ "भीष्मद्रोणप्रभृतयः अतिरथाः (अवस्थिताः), अजेयाः देवैरपि, अर्जुनेन जिताः" इति यशः लभस्व; केवलं पुण्यैः हि तत् प्राप्यते । जित्वा शत्रून् दुर्योधनप्रभृतीन् भुङ्क्ष्व राज्यं समृद्धं असपत्नं अकण्टकम् । मया एव एते निहताः निश्चयेन हताः प्राणैः वियोजिताः पूर्वमेव । निमित्तमात्रं भव त्वं हे सव्यसाचिन्! —सव्येन वामेनापि हस्तेन शराणां क्षेपात् सव्यसाची इति उच्यते अर्जुनः ॥

33.1. Therefore stand up; win renown due to the fact that you, Arjuna, have vanquished heroes, Bhīṣma, Droṇa, etc., whom even gods can't beat. Through religious merit alone may such renown be achieved. Conquering foes like Duryodhana and the rest, enjoy this kingdom, unopposed by adversaries. By Me, indeed, have all these been 'slain'—despatched already. Be but an occasion, skilfull bowman! Arjuna is so styled (*savyasācin*), as he shoots arrows even with his left hand.

द्रोणं च भीष्मं च जयद्रथं च
कर्णं तथाऽन्यानपि योधवीरान् ।
मया हतांस्त्वं जहि मा व्यथिष्ठा
युध्यस्व जेतासि रणे सपत्नान् ॥३४॥

34. Kill Droṇa, Bhīṣma, Jayadratha, Karṇa and similarly other heroic warriors too, slain by Me; don't worry. Fight, you will conquer in war.

34.1. द्रोणं इति ॥ द्रोणं च—येषु येषु योधेषु अर्जुनस्य आशङ्का तांस्तान् व्यपदिशति भगवान्, मया हतानिति । तत्र द्रोणभीष्मयोः तावत् प्रसिद्धं आशङ्का-कारणम् । द्रोणः धनुर्वेदाचार्यः दिव्यास्त्रसंपन्नः, आत्मनश्च विशेषतः गुरुः गरिष्ठः । भीष्मश्च स्वच्छन्दमृत्युः दिव्यास्त्रसम्पन्नश्च परशुरामेण द्वन्द्वयुद्धं अगमत्, न च पराजितः । तथा जयद्रथः, यस्य पिता तपः चरति "मम पुत्रस्य शिरः भूमौ निपातयिष्यति यः, तस्यापि शिरः पतिष्यति" इति । कर्णोऽपि वासवदत्तया शक्त्या त्वमोघया सम्पन्नः सूर्यपुत्रः कानीनः यतः, अतः तं नाम्नैव निर्दिशति । मया हतान् त्वं जहि निमित्तमात्रेण । मा व्यथिष्ठाः, तेभ्यः भयं मा कार्षीः । युध्यस्व जेतासि दुर्योधनप्रभृतीन् रणे युद्धे सपत्नान् शत्रून् ॥

34.1. Those warriors who have roused Arjuna's fear the Lord singles out as already slain by Him. It is well-known why Droṇa and Bhīṣma caused fear. Droṇa is the master of the science of archery and of supernatural weapons; he is the highly honoured teacher of Arjuna himself. With his power to withstand death till he himself chooses to die, Bhīṣma too is a master of supernatural arms who was not vanquished even by Paraśurāma with whom he fought a duel. Similarly Jayadratha was formidable because his father had embarked on penance to cause his son's slayer's head to fall. Being the son of the sun-god and the virgin, Karṇa, too, equipped with the unfailing dart gifted by Indra, is just mentioned. These, slain by Me, just despatch, you being but the occasion of their death. Have no fear on their account. Fight; you will conquer your foes, Duryodhana and the rest, in this battle.

सञ्जय उवाच :

एतच्छ्रुत्वा वचनं केशवस्य कृताञ्जलिर्वेपमानः किरीटी ।
नमस्कृत्वा भूय एवाह कृष्णं सगद्गदं भीतभीतः प्रणम्य ॥३५॥

Sañjaya said:

35. Listening to Kṛṣṇa's words, trembling, with folded hands, Arjuna saluted Kṛṣṇa; falling prostrate and quite nervous, he spoke to Him falteringly as follows:

35.1. एतच्छ्रुत्वा इति ॥ एतत् श्रुत्वा वचनं केशवस्य पूर्वोक्तं, कृताञ्जलिः सन् वेपमानः कम्पमानः किरीटी नमस्कृत्वा, भूयः पुनः एव आह उक्तवान् कृष्णं सगद्गदं भयाविष्टस्य दुःखाभिघातात्, स्नेहाविष्टस्य च हर्षोद्भवात्, अश्रुपूर्णनेत्रत्वे सति श्लेष्मणा कण्ठावरोधः; तेन वाचः अपाटवं मन्दशब्दत्वं यत् स गद्गदः तेन सह वर्तत इति । "सगद्गदं वचनं आह" इति वचनक्रियाविशेषणं एतत् । भीतभीतः पुनः पुनः भयाविष्टचेताः सन् प्रणम्य प्रह्वः भूत्वा, 'आह' इति व्यवहितेन सम्बन्धः ॥

35.1. Arjuna spoke 'falteringly'; for, he was in the grip of fear and also influenced by his love for Kṛṣṇa. Being tearful, phlegm choked his throat. So his words were indistinct and low in pitch. 'Falteringly' qualifies Arjuna's speech or act of speaking. Repeatedly seized by fear, he bowed low and spoke. So construe the remotely placed words of the text.

35.2. अत्र अवसरे सञ्जयवचनं साभिप्रायम् । कथं ? द्रोणादिषु अर्जुनेन निहतेषु अजेयेषु चतुर्षु, निराश्रयः दुर्योधनः निहतः एव इति मत्वा धृतराष्ट्रः जयं प्रति निराशः सन् सन्धिं करिष्यति, ततः शान्तिः उभयेषां भविष्यति इति । तदपि न अश्रौषीत् धृतराष्ट्रः, भवितव्यवशात् ॥

36.0. At this juncture Sañjaya's words were motivated. How? Once the unconquerable four, Droṇa etc., are slain by Arjuna, Duryodhana is as good as slain. Thus thinking, Dhṛtarāṣṭra will cease to hope for victory and will ask for truce. Thence will follow peace between the two forces. But, being a victim of fate's decree, Dhṛtarāṣṭra did not pay any heed.

अर्जुन उवाच :

स्थाने हृषीकेश तव प्रकीर्त्या जगत्प्रहृष्यत्यनुरज्यते च ।
रक्षांसि भीतानि दिशो द्रवन्ति सर्वे नमस्यन्ति च सिद्धसंघाः ॥३६॥

Arjuna said:

36. Indeed it is proper, Kṛṣṇa! that the whole world in extolling You, should rejoice and be gratified. The demons flee frightened, away into space, and all groups of perfected souls do reverence.

36.1. स्थाने इति ॥ स्थाने युक्तम् । किं तत् ? तव प्रकीर्त्या त्वन्माहात्म्य-कीर्तनेन श्रुतेन, हे हृषीकेश ! यत् जगत् प्रहृष्यति प्रहर्षं उपैति, तत् स्थाने युक्तं इत्यर्थः । अथवा — विषयविशेषणं स्थाने इति । युक्तः हर्षादिविषयः भगवान्, यतः ईश्वरः सर्वात्मा सर्वभूतसुहृच्च इति । तथा अनुरज्यते अनुरागं च उपैति; तच्च विषये इति व्याख्येयम् । किञ्च — रक्षांसि भीतानि भयाविष्टानि दिशः द्रवन्ति गच्छन्ति; तच्च स्थाने विषये । सर्वे नमस्यन्ति नमस्कारं कुर्वन्ति च सिद्धसङ्घाः सिद्धानां समुदायाः कपिलादीनां; तच्च स्थाने ॥

36.1. 'It is proper'—what? That in extolling Your grandeur the worlds should rejoice. Or, the term 'proper' may be taken as qualifying the object of praise, namely, the Lord. It is proper that the Lord is the occasion for rejoicing; for He is the Self of all, the friend of all living beings. So rightly is the world also gratified. This too is a right explanation. Moreover, the frightened demons flee away into space. This too is proper; groups of all perfected souls, Kapila, etc., are doing reverence. This again is proper.

37.0. भगवतः हर्षादिविषयत्वे हेतुं दर्शयति —

37.0. Here is given the reason why the Lord should occasion rejoicing:

कस्माच्च ते न नमेरन्महात्मन् गरीयसे ब्रह्मणोऽप्यादिकर्त्रे ।
अनन्त देवेश जगन्निवास त्वमक्षरं सदसत्परं यत् ॥३७॥

37. Great Being! Why shouldn't they salute You, the pre-eminent, primal creator of even Brahmā? Infinite, Lord of gods, the world's abode, You are the imperishable, at once being and non-being, and also what is beyond both.

37.1. कस्मात् इति ॥ कस्मात् च हेतोः ते तुभ्यं न नमेरन् न नमस्कुर्युः हे महात्मन्! गरीयसे गुरुतराय — यतः ब्रह्मणः हिरण्यगर्भस्य अपि आदिकर्ता कारणं अतः तस्मात् — आदिकर्त्रे कथं एते न नमस्कुर्युः? अतः हर्षादीनां नमस्कारस्य च स्थानं त्वं अर्हः विषयः इत्यर्थः। हे अनन्त! देवेश! हे जगन्निवास! त्वं अक्षरं तत् परं, यत् वेदान्तेषु श्रूयते। किं तत्? सदसत् इति। सत् विद्यमानं, असत् च यत्र नास्ति इति बुद्धिः। ते उपाधि — [उपधान —] भूते सदसती यस्य अक्षरस्य, यद् द्वारेण सदसती इति उपचर्यते। परमार्थतस्तु सदसतोः परं तत् अक्षरं, यत् अक्षरं वेदविदः वदन्ति। तत् त्वमेव, न अन्यत् इति अभिप्रायः॥

पुनरपि स्तौति —

37.1. Why should they not bow down to You, great Being! who are greater than they all? You are the primal creator of Brahmā even—of the Hiraṇyagarbha. So, why should they not salute You? Therefore, You are the right occasion for feelings like delight, and the fit object of salutation. O infinite One! The Lord of gods! The abode of the worlds! You are the transcendent Imperishable that the Vedāntas set forth. What is that? Being and non-being. Being is the existent and the non-being, what engenders the idea of non-existence. These are the adjuncts of the Imperishable due to which arises the empirical usage of the expressions, being and non-being. In truth, however, the Imperishable which the knowers of the Vedas declare is beyond being and non-being. You alone are that and none else.

Again, Arjuna extols:

त्वमादिदेवः पुरुषः पुराणः त्वमस्य विश्वस्य परं निधानम्।
वेत्ताऽसि वेद्यं च परं च धाम त्वया ततं विश्वमनन्तरूप ॥३८॥

38. You are the primal Lord, the ancient Spirit, the

supreme Abode of this universe. You are the knower, the object to be known, the transcendent abode, O Being of infinite forms! The universe has been pervaded by You.

38.1. त्वं इति ॥ त्वं आदिदेवः, जगतः स्रष्टृत्वात् । पुरुषः पुरि शयनात् पुराणः चिरन्तनः त्वं एव अस्य विश्वस्य परं प्रकृष्टं निधानं निधीयते अस्मिन् जगत् सर्वं महाप्रलयादौ इति । किञ्च — वेत्ता असि, वेदिता असि सर्वस्य एव वेद्यजातस्य । यत् च वेद्यं वेदनार्हं तच्चासि, परं च धाम परमं पदं वैष्णवम् । त्वया ततं व्याप्तं विश्वं समस्तं, हे अनन्तरूप ! अन्तः न विद्यते तव रूपाणाम् ॥

किञ्च —

38.1. 'You are the 'primal Lord', being the Creator of the universe; 'Spirit or Purusha' dwelling in the city of the body; 'ancient'—everlasting. Of this universe You alone are the supreme or exalted Abode, that in which, at the time of the great dissolution, etc., the universe is resolved. Moreover, You are 'the knower' of all that there is to know. Besides whatsoever is 'fit to be known' is You, as also the transcendent status of Viṣṇu. The entire universe has been pervaded by You, O Being of infinite forms. Of your forms there is no end.

And,

वायुर्यमोऽग्निर्वरुणः शशाङ्कः प्रजापतिस्त्वं प्रपितामहश्च ।
नमो नमस्तेऽस्तु सहस्रकृत्वः पुनश्च भूयोऽपि नमो नमस्ते ॥३९॥

39. The wind, the god of death, the fire, Varuṇa the god of waters, the moon, the lord of creatures, and the grand sire—You are. To You salutations, salutations a thousand times; again, repeatedly, salutations to You.

39.1. वायुः इति ॥ वायुः त्वं, यमः च, अग्निः, वरुणः अपांपतिः, शशाङ्कः चन्द्रमाः, प्रजापतिः त्वं कश्यपादिः, प्रपितामहश्च पितामहस्यापि पिता प्रपितामहः, ब्रह्मणोऽपि पिता इत्यर्थः । नमो नमः ते तुभ्यं अस्तु सहस्रकृत्वः । पुनश्च भूयः अपि नमो नमः ते । बहुशो नमस्कारक्रियाभ्यासावृत्तिगणनं कृत्वसुचा उच्यते । 'पुनश्च' 'भूयोऽपि' इति श्रद्धाभक्त्यतिशयात् अपरितोषं आत्मनः दर्शयति ॥

तथा —

39.1. You are the wind-god and the god of death, the fire-god, Varuṇa the god of waters, the moon, the progenitor (of creatures), like Kaśyapa, and the father even of creation's author. That You are the father even of Brahmā is the sense. Salutations to You a thousand times; again, repeatedly, salutations to You. The repeated acts of salutation are expressed by the suffix *kṛtvasuc*. The use of expressions like 'and again', 'once more', shows the sense of inadequacy felt by the speaker because of his reverence, love and sense of wonder.

Similarly,

नमः पुरस्तादथ पृष्ठतस्ते नमोऽस्तु ते सर्वत एव सर्व ।
अनन्तवीर्यामितविक्रमस्त्वं सर्वं समाप्नोषि ततोऽसि सर्वः ॥४०॥

40. Salutations in front of You and behind You; salutations be on all sides of You, the all. Your power is infinite and Your energy unmeasured. You achieve all and so You are the all.

40.1. नमः इति । नमः पुरस्तात् पूर्वस्यां दिशि तुभ्यं, अथ पृष्ठतः ते पृष्ठतः अपि च ते नमः अस्तु, ते सर्वतः एव सर्वासु दिक्षु सर्वत्र स्थिताय हे सर्व । अनन्तवीर्यामितविक्रमः अनन्तं वीर्यं अस्य, अमितः विक्रमः अस्य । वीर्यं सामर्थ्यं, विक्रमः पराक्रमः । वीर्यवानपि कश्चित् शत्रुवधादिविषये न पराक्रमते, मन्दपराक्रमः वा । त्वं तु अनन्तवीर्यः अमितविक्रमश्च इति अनन्तवीर्यामितविक्रमः । सर्वं समस्तं जगत् समाप्नोषि सम्यक् एकेन आत्मना व्याप्नोषि यतः, ततः तस्मात् असि भवसि सर्वः त्वं, त्वया विनाभूतं न किञ्चित् अस्ति इति अभिप्रायः ॥

40.1. 'In front', may also mean in the east, salutations to You; also behind You let salutations be. 'On all sides'—in all points of the compass, salutations 'to you', the resident in all places, to You who are 'all'. Your powers are infinite and energy unmeasured. 'Power' means ability, and 'energy', heroic action. Even a powerful being may fail to exercise it to exterminate foes; or may prove to be sluggish. But Your power is infinite and energy unmeasured.Therefore You are styled as such in the text. Since You alone pervade the entire universe,

You are 'the all'. The idea is that there is nothing divorced from You.

41.0. यतः अहं त्वन्माहात्म्यापरिज्ञानात् अपराद्धः, अतः —

41.0. Inasmuch as I have erred, unaware of your majesty, therefore,

सखेति मत्वा प्रसभं यदुक्तम् हे कृष्ण हे यादव हे सखेति ।
अजानता महिमानं तवेदं मया प्रमादात्प्रणयेन वाऽपि ॥४१॥
यच्चावहासार्थमसत्कृतोऽसि विहारशय्यासनभोजनेषु ।
एकोऽथवाऽप्यच्युत तत्समक्षं तत्क्षामये त्वामहमप्रमेयम् ॥४२॥

41.-42. Taking you for a comrade, I have addressed you as Kṛṣṇa, cowherd, friend. Unaware of this majesty of Yours and out of affection or thoughtlessness I have treated you unceremoniously, in privacy or in public, while resting, sitting, dining or playing games. I beg You, the Immeasurable, to forgive all this.

41.1. सखा इति ॥ सखा समानवयाः इति मत्वा ज्ञात्वा विपरीतबुद्धया प्रसभं अभिभूय प्रसह्य यत् उक्तं हे कृष्ण ! हे यादव ! हे सखेति च अजानता अज्ञानिना मूढेन — किं अजानता इति ? आह — महिमानं माहात्म्यं तव इदं ईश्वरस्य विश्वरुपम् । "तव इदं महिमानं अजानता" इति वैयधिकरण्येन सम्बन्धः । 'तवेमं' इति पाठो यदि अस्ति, तदा सामानाधिकरण्यमेव । मया प्रमादात् विक्षिप्तचित्ततया, प्रणयेन वाऽपि, प्रणयो नाम स्नेहनिमित्तः विस्रम्भः, तेनापि कारणेन यत् उक्तवान् अस्मि ॥

41.1. 'Deeming You comrade'—of the same age as myself—due to ignorance, I spoke hastily addressing You Kṛṣṇa, scion of Yadus and comrade. Ignorance of what? of this majesty of Yours—this universal form of the Lord. The expressions *idam* and *mahimānam* in the text are non-appostional. If the reading *imam* is available, they become appositional. My speech was hasty due to carelessness or affection. 'Affection' means the sense of confidence born of love.

42.1. यच्च इति ॥ यच्च अवहासार्थं परिहासप्रयोजनाय असत्कृतः परिभूतः असि भवसि त्वं — क्व ? — विहारशय्यासनभोजनेषु, विहरणं विहारः पादव्यायामः, शयनं शय्या, आसनं आस्थायिका, भोजनं अदनं, इति एतेषु विहारशय्यासनभोजनेषु, एकः परोक्षः सन् असत्कृतः असि परिभूतः असि; अथवाऽपि हे अच्युत ! तत् समक्षं — तच्छब्दः क्रियाविशेषणार्थः — प्रत्यक्षं वा असत्कृतः असि तत् सर्वं अपराधजातं क्षामये क्षमां कारये त्वां अहं अप्रमेयं प्रमाणातीतम् ॥

यतः त्वम् —

42.1. In jest I treated You with lack of respect—i.e., with scorn. 'Where?' in sport, etc. 'Sport' refers to walking for exercise; 'rest on a bedstead; 'sitting' on chairs, etc.; 'dining'—in all these activities and places I scorned You in Your absence or presence, O Unlapsing one! All these offences I beg You to pardon, You the Infinite—beyond all determination.

Because,

पिताऽसि लोकस्य चराचरस्य त्वमस्य पूज्यश्च गुरुर्गरीयान् ।
न त्वत्समोऽस्त्यभ्यधिकः कुतोऽन्यो लोकत्रयेऽप्यप्रतिमप्रभाव ॥४३॥

43. You are the father of the world of beings, moving and unmoving; You are worthy of its worship, being its pre-eminent Teacher. There is none equal to You. How can there be one greater in all the three worlds? O You of matchless might!

43.1. पिता इति ॥ पिता असि जनयिता असि लोकस्य प्राणिजातस्य चराचरस्य स्थावरजङ्गमस्य । न केवलं त्वं अस्य जगतः पिता, पूज्यश्च पूजार्हः, यतः गुरुः गरीयान् गुरुतरः । कस्मात् गुरुतरः त्वं इति ? आह — न त्वत्समः त्वत्तुल्यः अन्यः अस्ति । न हि ईश्वरद्वयं संभवति अनेकेश्वरत्वे व्यवहारानुपपत्तेः । त्वत्सम एव तावत् अन्यः न संभवति; कुतः एव अन्यः अभ्यधिकः स्यात् लोकत्रयेऽपि सर्वस्मिन् ? अप्रतिमप्रभाव ! प्रतिमीयते यया सा प्रतिमा, न विद्यते प्रतिमा यस्य तव प्रभावस्य सः त्वं अप्रतिमप्रभावः हे अप्रतिमप्रभाव ! निरतिशयप्रभाव ! इत्यर्थः ॥

यत एवम् —

43.1. Of this world, of all beings moving and unmoving, You are the 'father', the generator. Not only are You the father of this world, but also worthy of worship; for You are the pre-eminent teacher. In what way are You that? 'None is equal to You'.

Of course it is impossible that there should be two Gods. Empirical activities will become impossible in case there are more than one God. None else can be even equal to You, not to speak of any one being greater in all the three worlds, O You, of 'matchless might!' An analogue is what is similar. Your might has no analogue. Hence are You of 'matchless might'—of unsurpassed power. This is the import.

Such being the case,

तस्मात्प्रणम्य प्रणिधाय कायं प्रसादये त्वामहमीशमीड्यम् ।
पितेव पुत्रस्य सखेव सख्युः प्रियः प्रियायार्हसि देव सोढुम् ॥४४॥

44. Therefore, saluting and prostrating my body, I crave Your grace, adorable and mighty Being! Lord! You should bear with me, as father does with his son, a comrade with comrade, a lover with the beloved.

44.1. तस्मात् इति ॥ तस्मात् प्रणम्य नमस्कृत्य, प्रणिधाय प्रकर्षेण नीचैः धृत्वा कायं शरीरं, प्रसादये प्रसादं कारये त्वां अहं ईशं ईशितारं, ईड्यं स्तुत्यम् । त्वं पुनः पुत्रस्य अपराधं पिता यथा क्षमते सर्वं, सखा इव च सख्युः अपराधं, यथा वा प्रियः प्रियायाः अपराधं क्षमते, एवं अर्हसि हे देव सोढुं प्रसहितुं, क्षन्तुं इत्यर्थः ॥

44.1. Therefore having saluted, keeping my body very low in the act of prostration, I crave Your grace, mighty Lord worthy of adoration. And You, O divine Being, ought to forgive my transgressions even as a father forgives a son's transgression, a comrade a comrade's, and a lover the beloved's.

अदृष्टपूर्वं हृषितोऽस्मि दृष्ट्वा भयेन च प्रव्यथितं मनो मे ।
तदेव मे दर्शय देव रूपं प्रसीद देवेश जगन्निवास ॥४५॥

45. Seeing what hitherto has been unseen, I am thrilled

and my mind is smitten with fear, Lord! Reveal that familiar form; be gracious, God of gods! Abode of the worlds!

45.1. अदृष्टपूर्वं इति ॥ अदृष्टपूर्वं न कदाचिदपि दृष्टपूर्वं इदं विश्वरूपं तव मया अन्यैर्वा, तत् अहं दृष्ट्वा हृषितः अस्मि । भयेन च प्रव्यथितं मनः मे । अतः तदेव मे मम दर्शय हे देव रूपं यत् मत्सखम् । प्रसीद देवेश ! जगन्निवास, जगतो निवासो जगन्निवासः, हे जगन्निवास ॥

45.1. 'Seeing what has never been seen before', i.e., Your cosmic form, either by men or by others, I am thrilled. Also, fear smites my mind. Therefore, resume the familiar form You display as my friend. Be gracious, God of gods! Abode of the worlds!

किरीटिनं गदिनं चक्रहस्तमिच्छामि त्वां द्रष्टुमहं तथैव ।
तेनैव रूपेण चतुर्भुजेन सहस्रबाहो भव विश्वमूर्ते ॥४६॥

46. (Your form) with the diadem, mace, and discus in hand, I wish to see in the way I am used to, O thousand-armed Being with the cosmic form! Assume that form with the four arms.

46.1. किरीटिनं इति ॥ किरीटिनं किरीटवन्तं, तथा गदिनं गदावन्तं, चक्रहस्तं इच्छामि त्वां प्रार्थये त्वां द्रष्टुं अहं तथैव, पूर्ववत् इत्यर्थः । यतः एवं, तस्मात् तेनैव रूपेण वसुदेवपुत्ररूपेण चतुर्भुजेन, सहस्रबाहो — वार्तमानिकेन विश्वरूपेण, भव विश्वमूर्ते; उपसंहृत्य विश्वरूपं, तेनैव रूपेण भव इत्यर्थः ॥

46.1. 'I wish'—pray—to see You as before with the diadem, mace, and discus in hand'. Such being the case, O thousand-armed! withdrawing the cosmic form, resume Your four-armed form as the son of Vasudeva.

47.0. अर्जुनं भीतं उपलभ्य, उपसंहृत्य विश्वरूपं, प्रियवचनेन आश्वासयन् श्रीभगवान् उवाच —

47.0. Knowing that Arjuna is fear-struck, the blessed Lord withdrew His cosmic form and spoke affectionate words consolingly:

श्रीभगवानुवाच :

मया प्रसन्नेन तवार्जुनेदं रूपं परं दर्शितमात्मयोगात् ।
तेजोमयं विश्वमनन्तमाद्यं यन्मे त्वदन्येन न दृष्टपूर्वम् ॥४७॥

The blessed Lord said:

47. By the power of My Yoga, O Arjuna! in a gracious mood, I have revealed to you this supreme form of Mine, effulgent, cosmic, infinite and primal, which none but you ever beheld before.

47.1. मया इति ॥ मया प्रसन्नेन, प्रसादः नाम त्वयि अनुग्रहबुद्धिः, तद्वता प्रसन्नेन मया तव हे अर्जुन ! इदं परं रूपं विश्वरूपं दर्शितं आत्मयोगात् आत्मनः ऐश्वर्यस्य सामर्थ्यात् । तेजोमयं तेजःप्रायं विश्वं समस्तं अनन्तं अन्तरहितं आदौ भवं आद्यं यत् रूपं मे मम त्वदन्येन त्वत्तः अन्येन केनचित् न दृष्टपूर्वम् ॥

47.1. 'Grace' means the mood of benevolence towards you; in that mood this supreme cosmic form has been revealed to you by the power—the competence—of My Yoga. 'Effulgent'—made of brilliant power. 'Cosmic'—universal. 'Infinite'—endless. 'Primal'—what was in the beginning. This form of Mine, none other than you ever saw before.

48.0. आत्मनः मम रूपदर्शनेन कृतार्थः एव त्वं संवृत्तः इति तत् स्तौति —

48.0. You have gained life's goal having seen this form of Mine, universal Self. The vision is now extolled:

न वेदयज्ञाध्ययनैर्न दानैर्न च क्रियाभिर्न तपोभिरुग्रैः ।
एवंरूपः शक्य अहं नृलोके द्रष्टुं त्वदन्येन कुरुप्रवीर ॥४८॥

48. By means neither of the Vedas, sacrifices, studies,

nor of the making of gifts, neither by ritual acts nor by severe austerities can I, in this form, be seen in this world of men by anyone other than you, O hero of the Kurus!

48.1. न वेद इति ॥ न वेदयज्ञाध्ययनैः चतुर्णामपि वेदानां अध्ययनैः यथावत् यज्ञाध्ययनैश्च — वेदाध्ययनैरेव यज्ञाध्ययनस्य सिद्धत्वात् पृथक् यज्ञाध्ययनग्रहणं यज्ञविज्ञानोपलक्षणार्थं — तथा न दानैः तुलापुरुषादिभिः, न च क्रियाभिः अग्निहोत्रादिभिः श्रौतादिभिः, न अपि तपोभिः उग्रैः चान्द्रायणादिभिः घोरैः, एवंरूपः यथादर्शितं विश्वरूपं यस्य सः अहं एवंरूपः न शक्यः अहं नृलोके मनुष्यलोके द्रष्टुं त्वदन्येन त्वत्तः अन्येन कुरुप्रवीर ॥

48.1. By means of studying all the four Vedas and by the correct performance of sacrifices and by studies and the making of gifts of gold equal to the weight of the givers, etc; by means of ritual acts like the fire-sacrifice enjoined by the Vedas and Codes; and by means of severe penances like the *Cāndrāyaṇa*, I can't be seen in this cosmic form (as you have seen) in this world by men, by any other than you. The study of the Vedas includes that of sacrifices.

मा ते व्यथा मा च विमूढभावो
दृष्ट्वा रूपं घोरमीदृङ्ममेदम् ।
व्यपेतभीः प्रीतमनाः पुनस्त्वं
तदेव मे रूपमिदं प्रपश्य ॥४९॥

49. Don't be fear-stricken and confused due to the vision of this awesome form of Mine which you have had. Rid of fear and glad at heart, behold again that (familiar) form of Mine.

49.1. मा ते व्यथा इति ॥ मा ते व्यथा, मा भूत् ते भयम्, मा च विमूढभावः विमूढचित्तता, दृष्ट्वा उपलभ्य रूपं घोरं ईदृक् यथादर्शितं मम इदम् । व्यपेतभीः विगतभीः विगतभयः, प्रीतमनाः च सन् पुनः भूयः त्वं तदेव चतुर्भुजं रूपं शङ्खचक्रगदाधरं तव इष्टं रूपं इदं प्रपश्य ॥

49.1. Have no fear and confusion in mind, on account of having seen My awesome form revealed to you. With fear gone and a gladdened mind, behold again that four-armed form of Mine which is dear to you—the form marked by the conch, discus, and mace.

सञ्जय उवाच :

इत्यर्जुनं वासुदेवस्तथोक्त्वा स्वकं रूपं दर्शयामास भूयः ।
आश्वासयामास च भीतमेनं भूत्वा पुनः सौम्यवपुर्महात्मा ॥५०॥

Samjaya said:

50. Having thus spoken to Arjuna, Vāsudeva once more revealed His familiar form; assuming His gentle form, once more, the mighty Being consoled Arjuna in his terror.

50.1. इत्यर्जुनं इति ॥ इति एवं अर्जुनं वासुदेवः तथाभूतं वचनं उक्त्वा, स्वकं वसुदेवस्य गृहे जातं रूपं दर्शयामास दर्शितवान् भूयः पुनः । आश्वासयामास च आश्वासितवान् भीतं एनं, भूत्वा पुनः सौम्यवपुः प्रसन्नदेहः महात्मा ॥

50.1. Thus speaking to Arjuna, Vāsudeva revealed that form of His with which He was born in Vasudeva's home. And He, the mighty Being, consoled Arjuna in his terror, having once again assumed a gentle human form.

अर्जुन उवाच :

दृष्ट्वेदं मानुषं रूपं तव सौम्यं जनार्दन ।
इदानीमस्मि संवृत्तः सचेताः प्रकृतिं गतः ॥५१॥

Arjuna said:

51. O Kṛṣṇa! Seeing this, Your gentle human form, now I have regained my equanimity; I have been restored to my proper nature.

51.1. दृष्ट्वेदं इति ॥ दृष्ट्वा इदं मानुषं रूपं मत्सखं प्रसन्नं तव सौम्यं जनार्दन !

इदानीं अधुना अस्मि संवृत्तः सञ्जातः — किं ? — सचेताः प्रसन्नचित्तः प्रकृतिं स्वभावं गतः च अस्मि ॥

51.1. Seeing this gentle friendly form of Yours, Kṛṣṇa! now I have won back my equanimity and regained my normal nature.

श्रीभगवानुवाच :

सुदुर्दर्शमिदं रूपं दृष्टवानसि यन्मम ।
देवा अप्यस्य रूपस्य नित्यं दर्शनकाङ्क्षिणः ॥५२॥

The blessed Lord said:

52. That form of Mine, extremely hard to behold, which you have seen—that form even the gods perpetually crave to see.

52.1. सुदुर्दर्शं इति ॥ सुदुर्दर्शं सुष्ठु दुःखेन दर्शनं अस्य इति सुदुर्दर्शं इदं रूपं दृष्टवान् असि यत् मम, देवाः अपि अस्य मम रूपस्य नित्यं सर्वदा दर्शनकाङ्क्षिणः, दर्शनेप्सवोऽपि न त्वमिव दृष्टवन्तः, न द्रक्ष्यन्ति च इति अभिप्रायः ॥
कस्मात् ? —

52.1. That form, whose vision is extremely hard to obtain, and which you have seen—that form of Mine even gods crave to see. Though desirous, they have not, unlike you, seen it; nor will they see it. This is the idea.

Why?

नाहं वेदैर्न तपसा न दानेन न चेज्यया ।
शक्य एवंविधो द्रष्टुं दृष्टवानसि मां यथा ॥५३॥

53. Not by the Vedas nor by penance, nor by gifts nor by sacrifice may I be seen, thus, as you have.

53.1. नाहं इति ॥ न अहं वेदैः ऋग्यजुःसामाथर्ववेदैः चतुर्भिः अपि न तपसा उग्रेण चांद्रायणादिना, न दानेन गोभूहिरण्यादिना, न च इज्यया यज्ञेन पूजया वा

शक्यः एवंविधः यथादर्शितप्रकारः द्रष्टुं, दृष्टवान् असि मां यथा त्वम् ॥

53.1. Not by the 'four Vedas' Ṛg, Yajus, Sāma and Atharva or by hard penance, *cāndrāyaṇa*, etc; nor by the gift of cows, land, gold and the like, nor by sacrifice—sacrificial worship, may I be seen 'thus'—in the way you have seen Me revealed.

54.0. कथं पुनः शक्यः इति ? उच्यते—

54.0. How then is it possible?

भक्त्या त्वनन्यया शक्यो ह्यहमेवंविधोऽर्जुन ।
ज्ञातुं द्रष्टुं च तत्त्वेन प्रवेष्टुं च परन्तप ॥५४॥

54. But by undivided devotion may I be known, truthfully seen, and entered, Arjuna! scourge of foes!; for, My nature is such.

54.1. भक्त्या इति ॥ भक्त्या तु—किंविशिष्टया इति ? आह—अनन्यया अपृथग्भूतया—भगवतः अन्यत्र पृथक् न कदाचिदपि (या) भवति (सा तु अनन्या भक्तिः) । सर्वैः अपि करणैः वासुदेवादन्यत् न उपलभ्यते यया, सा अनन्या भक्तिः, तया अनन्यया भक्त्या शक्यः अहं एवंविधः विश्वरूपप्रकारः हे अर्जुन ! ज्ञातुं शास्त्रतः—न केवलं ज्ञातुं शास्त्रतः—द्रष्टुं च साक्षात्कर्तुं तत्त्वेन तत्त्वतः, प्रवेष्टुं च मोक्षं च गन्तुं, परन्तप ॥

54.1. 'By devotion'—of what kind? 'undivided', i.e., not directed to aught else than the Lord, at any time. When by all means of cognition nothing but Vāsudeva is known, there results undivided devotion. By that means I may be known according to the *śāstras* in this manner as endowed with the cosmic form. Not only may I be known according to the *śāstras* but also seen truthfully and 'entered'—be liberated, O scourge of foes!

55.0. अधुना सर्वस्य गीताशास्त्रस्य सारभूतः अर्थः निश्रेयसार्थः अनुष्ठेयत्वेन समुच्चित्य उच्यते—

55.0. Now is stated the essential import of the entire science of the Gītā aimed at liberation and summarised for practice:

मत्कर्मकृन्मत्परमो मद्भक्तः सङ्गवर्जितः ।
निर्वैरः सर्वभूतेषु यः स मामेति पाण्डव ॥५५॥

55. Whoso does My works, makes Me his supreme goal, becomes My devotee, rid of all attachments, is free from malice towards all beings, will come to Me, O Pāṇḍava Prince!

इति श्रीमहाभारते शतसाहस्र्यां संहितायां वैयासिक्यां भीष्मपर्वणि
श्रीमद्भगवद्गीतासूपनिषत्सु ब्रह्मविद्यायां योगशास्त्रे श्रीकृष्णार्जुनसंवादे
विश्वरूपदर्शनं नामैकादशोऽध्यायः ॥

55 1. मत्कर्म इति ॥ मत्कर्मकृत् मदर्थं कर्म मत्कर्म, तत् करोतीति मत्कर्मकृत् । मत्परमः — करोति भृत्यः स्वामिकर्म, न तु आत्मनः परमा प्रेत्य गन्तव्या गतिरिति स्वामिनं प्रतिपद्यते; अयं तु मत्कर्मकृत् मामेव परमां गतिं प्रतिपद्यते इति मत्परमः, अहं परमः परा गतिः यस्य सः अयं मत्परमः । तथा मद्भक्तः मामेव सर्वप्रकारैः सर्वात्मना सर्वोत्साहेन च भजते इति मद्भक्तः । सङ्गवर्जितः धन-पुत्रमित्रकलत्रबन्धुवर्गेषु सङ्गवर्जितः सङ्गः प्रीतिः — स्नेहः — तद्वर्जितः । निर्वैरः निर्गतवैरः सर्वभूतेषु शत्रुभावरहितः आत्मनः अत्यन्तापकारप्रवृत्तेष्वपि । यः ईदृशः मद्भक्तः सः मां एति, अहमेव तस्य परा गतिः, न अन्या गतिः काचित् भवति । अयं तव उपदेशः इष्टः मया उपदिष्टः हे पाण्डव ! इति ॥

55.1. Work for My sake is 'My work'; whoso performs it. A servant does his master's work but does not reach him as his supreme goal to be attained after death. Here not only he does My work but he also comes to Me as his supreme goal; for, I am his supreme goal. Similarly, he is My devotee, as he worships Me in all possible ways, with all his heart—with total enthusiasm. He is free from all 'attachment' to wealth, progeny, friends, wife and relations. 'Attachment' is due to pleasure or affection—he is devoid of it. Free from 'malice 'towards all beings'—free from all feelings of enmity even towards those who have wronged most. He who answers to this description comes to Me, I being his supreme goal. He has no other goal. This is My counsel for you, Arjuna!

इति श्रीमत्परमहंसपरिव्राजकाचार्यगोविंदभगवत्पूज्यपादशिष्यश्रीमच्छंकरभगवतः
कृतौ श्रीमद्भगवद्गीताभाष्ये विश्वरूपदर्शनं योगो नामैकादशोऽध्यायः ॥११॥

द्वादशोऽध्यायः

CHAPTER XII

YOGA OF DEVOTION

0.1. द्वितीयाध्यायप्रभृतिषु विभूत्यन्तेषु अध्यायेषु (१०) परमात्मनः ब्रह्मणः अक्षरस्य विध्वस्तसर्वोपाधिविशेषस्य उपासनं उक्तं; सर्वयोगैश्वर्यसर्वज्ञानशक्तिमत्सत्त्वोपाधेः ईश्वरस्य तव च उपासनं तत्र तत्र उक्तम् । विश्वरूपाध्याये (११) तु ऐश्वरं आद्यं समस्तजगदात्मरूपं विश्वरूपं त्वदीयं दर्शितं उपासनार्थमेव त्वया । तच्च दर्शयित्वा उक्तवानसि 'मत्कर्मकृत्' (११.५५.) इत्यादि । अतः अहं अनयोः उभयोः पक्षयोः विशिष्टतरबुभुत्सया त्वां पृच्छामि इति अर्जुन उवाच—

0.1. In the chapters from the second to the tenth which deals with the divine powers, has been set forth the worship of Brahman the supreme Self, the Imperishable devoid of adjuncts. In certain contexts, worship addressed to You, God with the adjuncts of Yogic powers and marked by the Sāttvic power of omniscience has also been discussed. In chapter 11, entitled the Cosmic Form, has been revealed, for the purpose of this very worship, Your cosmic form, primordial and lordly, the very Self of the entire world. After revealing it, You said, "Whoso performs My works, etc." (II.55). Therefore, desiring to know which of these two approaches is superior, I, Arjuna, ask You:

अर्जुन उवाच :

एवं सततयुक्ता ये भक्तास्त्वां पर्युपासते ।
ये चाप्यक्षरमव्यक्तं तेषां के योगवित्तमाः ॥१॥

Arjuna said:

1. Of those devotees, who, ever integrated, worship

You thus elaborately, and those who worship the Unmanifest, the Imperishable,—who among them know Yoga best?

1.1. एवं इति ॥ 'एवं' इति अतीतानन्तरश्लोकेन उक्तं अर्थं परामृशति 'मत्कर्मकृत्' (११.५५.) इत्यादिना । एवं सततयुक्ताः नैरन्तर्येण भगवत्कर्मादौ यथोक्ते अर्थे समाहिताः सन्तः प्रवृत्ताः इत्यर्थः । ये भक्ताः अनन्यशरणाः सन्तः त्वां यथादर्शितं विश्वरूपं पर्युपासते ध्यायन्ति । ये च अन्ये अपि त्यक्तसर्वैषणाः संन्यस्तसर्वकर्माणः यथाविशेषितं ब्रह्म अक्षरं, निरस्तसर्वोपाधित्वात् अव्यक्तं अकरणगोचरं—यत् हि लोके करणगोचरं तत् व्यक्तं उच्यते, अञ्जेः धातोः तत्कर्मकत्वात्; इदं तु अक्षरं तद्विपरीतं—शिष्टैश्च उच्यमानैः विशेषणैः विशिष्टम्, तत् ये चापि पर्युपासते—तेषां उभयेषां मध्ये के योगवित्तमाः, के अतिशयेन योगविदः ? इत्यर्थः ॥

1.1. 'Thus' refers to the ideas set forth in the immediately preceding verse (11.55). 'Thus ever integrated' are those who unintermittently apply themselves to God's works—works for God's sake, etc., as already explained. There are on the one hand those devotees, whose sole refuge is Yourself and who meditate on You in Your cosmic form. And there are, on the other, those who have renounced all cravings and all works, and worship the imperishable Brahman described earlier—Brahman who is unmanifest, being adjunctless and beyond the range of the senses. What falls within the range of the senses is said to be manifest. The root *añj* refers to the act of manifestation. This Imperishable is other than the manifest and, further, is distinguished by the adjectives set forth in this context. Of these two groups of devotees, who is it that understands Yoga better? This is the import.

2.0. ये तु अक्षरोपासकाः सम्यग्दर्शिनः निवृत्तैषणाः, ते तावत् तिष्ठन्तु; तान् प्रति यत् वक्तव्यं तत् उपरिष्टात् वक्ष्यामः (श्लोके १३–२०) ये तु इतरे—

2.0. Let us leave alone for the moment the worshippers of the Imperishable whose perceptions are valid and who are free from all cravings. What may be said about them will be stated later (verses 12–20). As regards the others—

श्रीभगवानुवाच :

मय्यावेश्य मनो ये मां नित्ययुक्ता उपासते ।
श्रद्धया परयोपेतास्ते मे युक्ततमा मताः ॥२॥

The Blessed Lord said:

2. Setting their minds on Me, ever integrated, those who worship Me with absolute faith, I deem the best integrated.

2.1. मयि इति ॥ मयि विश्वरूपे परमेश्वरे आवेश्य समाधाय मनः ये भक्ताः सन्तः मां सर्वयोगेश्वराणां अधीश्वरं सर्वज्ञं विमुक्तरागादिक्लेशतिनिरदृष्टिं, नित्ययुक्ताः अतीतानन्तराध्यायान्ते उक्तश्लोकार्थन्यायेन सततयुक्ताः सन्तः उपासते श्रद्धया परया प्रकृष्टया उपेताः ये, ते मे मम युक्ततमाः मताः अभिप्रेताः युक्ततमाः इति। नैरन्तर्येण हि ते मच्चित्ततया अहोरात्रं अतिवाहयन्ति (अहोरात्रं अतिमात्रं मां ध्यायन्ति), अतः युक्तं तान् प्रति युक्ततमाः इति वक्तुम् ॥

2.1. The best integrated are those devotees who 'setting'—concentrating—their minds on Me, worship Me, the supreme Lord with the cosmic form, the supreme Master of all those who have mastered Yoga, the Omniscient lifted above all perceptions due to afflictions like attachment and so forth. This is My view, for, they are always integrated in the sense of the last verse in Chapter 11. Their faith is 'absolute'—pre-eminent. They spend their days and nights fixing their mind on Me without a break. So it is poper to describe them as the best integrated.

3.0. किं इतरे युक्ततमाः न भवन्ति ? न; किंतु तान् प्रति यत् वक्तव्यं तत् शृणु —

3.0. Are not the others best integrated as well? Not that they are not. But listen to what may be remarked in regard to them:

ये त्वक्षरमनिर्देश्यमव्यक्तं पर्युपासते ।
सर्वत्रगमचिन्त्यं च कूटस्थमचलं ध्रुवम् ॥३॥

3. But those who elaborately worship the Imperishable, the Ineffable, the Unmanifest, the Omnipresent, the Imponderable, the Immutable, the Immobile, the Unwavering;

3.1. ये तु इति ।। ये तु अक्षरं अनिर्देश्यं अव्यक्तत्वात् अशब्दगोचरं इति न निर्देष्टु शक्यते, अतः अनिर्देश्यं, अव्यक्तं न केनापि प्रमाणेन व्यज्यते इति अव्यक्तं पर्युपासते परि समन्तात् उपासते । उपासनं नाम यथाशास्त्रं उपास्यस्य अर्थस्य विषयीकरणेन सामीप्यं उपगम्य तैलधारावत् समानप्रत्ययप्रवाहेण दीर्घकालं यत् आसनं, तत् उपासनं आचक्षते । अक्षरस्य विशेषणं आह उपास्यस्य—सर्वत्रगं व्योमवत् व्यापि अचिन्त्यं च—यत् हि करणगोचरं तत् मनसाऽपि चिन्त्यं, तद्विपरीतत्वात् अचिन्त्यं अक्षरं कूटस्थं, दृश्यमानगुणकं अन्तर्दोषं वस्तु कूटम् । 'कूटरूपकं,' 'कूटसाक्ष्यं' इत्यादौ कूटशब्दः प्रसिद्धः लोके । तथा च अविद्याद्यनेकसंसारबीजं अन्तर्दोषवत् मायाऽव्याकृताद्यनेकशब्दवाच्यतया 'मायां तु प्रकृतिं विद्यात् मायिनं तु महेश्वरम्' (श्वे. उ. ४.१०.), 'मम माया दुरत्यया' (७.१४) इत्यादौ प्रसिद्धं यत् तत् कूटं, तस्मिन् कूटे स्थितं कूटस्थं तदध्यक्षतया । अथवा—राशिरिव स्थितं कूटस्थम् । अत एव अचलम् । यस्मात् अचलं, तस्मात् ध्रुवं, नित्यं इत्यर्थः ।।

3.1. 'But those who worship the Imperishable, the Ineffable'; being unmanifest, It is beyond the range of words and is not capable of being described. It is 'Unmanifest', as It is not revealed by any means of cognition. Those who 'elaborately worship' means—worship in all possible ways. 'Worship' means a prolonged state characterised by the flow of an identical idea, like a flow of oil, after the mind takes up a theme as its object (of meditation) in conformity with the '*Sāstraic* prescriptions. Another adjective of the Imperishable is offered—the Omnipresent like space spread everywhere. The 'Imponderable': what is within the range of the senses is, also, an object of thought, its opposite is the Imponderable. 'The Immutable' (*kūṭastha*): what is attractive outside and defective inside is *kūṭa*, as borne out by expressions like, "having a false form", "false evidence", etc. these illustrate the well-known sense of the term *kūṭa*. Similarly what is variously named *māyā*, *avyakta*, etc., and what has, within it, numerous seeds of empirical life like nescience and so forth is also *kūṭa*. Vide the scriptural texts (ŚU.4.10; BG.7.14) bear out this sense. What is present in *kūṭa* as its presiding Power is the Immutable. Or, it is what stands as a mass (*kūṭa*). Hence It is the Immobile. Being Immobile, It is the Unwavering, i.e. Eternal.

संनियम्येन्द्रियग्रामं सर्वत्र समबुद्धयः ।
ते प्राप्नुवन्ति मामेव सर्वभूतहिते रताः ॥४॥

4. Controlling all sense organs fully, with the cognition of sameness at all times, devoted to the welfare of all beings, they attain Me, indeed.

4.1. संनियम्य इति ॥ संनियम्य सम्यक् नियम्य उपसंहृत्य इन्द्रियग्रामं इन्द्रियसमुदायं, सर्वत्र सर्वस्मिन् काले समबुद्धयः समा तुल्या बुद्धिः येषां इष्टानिष्टप्राप्तौ ते समबुद्धयः । ते ये एवंविधाः ते प्राप्नुवन्ति माम् एव सर्वभूतहिते रताः । न तु तेषां वक्तव्यं किंचित् "मां ते प्राप्नुवन्ति" इति, 'ज्ञानी त्वात्मैव मे मतं' (७.१८) इति हि उक्तम् । न हि भगवत्स्वरूपाणां सतां युक्ततमत्वं, अयुक्ततमत्वं वा वाच्यम् ॥
किन्तु —

4.1. 'Controlling fully' i.e. withdrawing all sense-organs, and at all times, with 'the cognition of sameness', in pleasures and pains alike, the sages attain Me, indeed; they are devoted to the welfare of all beings. However, no remark about them is called for. It has already been stated (7.18) that the knower is verily My Self. Remarks about their level of integration are inappropriate; for they are entirely one with the Lord.
But,

क्लेशोऽधिकतरस्तेषामव्यक्तासक्तचेतसाम् ।
अव्यक्ता हि गतिर्दुःखं देहवद्भिरवाप्यते ॥५॥

5. Their toil is harder, their minds being set on the Unmanifest; embodied beings find it hard to tread the path of the Unmanifest.

5.1. क्लेशः इति ॥ क्लेशः अधिकतरः—यद्यपि मत्कर्मादिपराणां अधिकः एव

क्लेशः, अधिकतरस्तु अक्षरात्मनां परमात्मदर्शिनां देहाभिमानपरित्यागनिमित्तः– अव्यक्तासक्तचेतसां अव्यक्ते आसक्तं चेतः येषां ते अव्यक्तासक्तचेतसः तेषां अव्यक्तामक्तचेतसाम् । अव्यक्ता हि यस्मात् (या) गतिः अक्षरात्मिका दुःखं (सा) देहवद्भिः देहाभिमानवद्भिः अवाप्यते, अतः क्लेशः अधिकतरः ।

5.1. 'Their toil is harder'. Though the toil of those who do My work and so forth is great, greater is the toil of those whose Self is the Imperishable, i.e., those who behold only the Self; for, they have had to renounce conceit in the body. Their mind is attached to the Unmanifest. So their toil is harder. The goal (*gati*) whose essence is the Imperishable, being Unmanifest, is attained painfully by the embodied who have conceit in the body.

6.0. अक्षरोपासकानां यत् वर्तनं तत् उपरिष्टात् (श्लोकेषु १२.१३-२०) वक्ष्यामः ॥

6.0. The life and works of the worshippers of the Imperishable will be set forth later (in verses 13–20).

ये तु सर्वाणि कर्माणि मयि संन्यस्य मत्पराः ।
अनन्येनैव योगेन मां ध्यायन्त उपासते ॥६॥

6. Those, however, who surrender all works to Me, making Me their supreme (goal) and worship Me, meditating on Me in a state of undivided union;

6.1. ये तु इति ॥ ये तु सर्वाणि कर्माणि मयि ईश्वरे संन्यस्य मत्पराः अहं परः येषां ते मत्पराः सन्तः अनन्येन एव अविद्यमानं अन्यत् आलम्बनं विश्वरूपं देवं ध्यायन्तः चिन्तयन्तः उपासते ॥

तेषां किम् ? —

6.1. Those who surrender all works to Me, the Lord, regarding Me as their supreme goal, meditating on Me, or thinking about Me in a state of undivided union, or concentration, without having any object of thought other than the

Lord with the cosmic form, and worship Me—what happens to them?

तेषामहं समुद्धर्ता मृत्युसंसारसागरात् ।
भवामि न चिरात्पार्थ मय्यावेशितचेतसाम् ॥७॥

7. Of them (all) who have set their thoughts on Me, I shall soon be the deliverer from the sea of empirical life leading to death, O Arjuna!

7.1. तेषां इति ॥ तेषां मदुपासनैकपराणां अहं ईश्वरः समुद्धर्ता—कुतः इति ? आह—मृत्युसंसारसागरात् मृत्युयुक्तः संसारः मृत्युसंसारः, स एव सागर इव सागरः, दुस्तरत्वात्, तस्मात् मृत्युसंसारसागरात् अहं तेषां समुद्धर्ता भवामि न चिरात्—किं तर्हि ?—क्षिप्रमेव हे पार्थ ! मयि आवेशितचेतसां मयि विश्वरूपे आवेशितं समाहितं चेतः येषां ते मय्यावेशितचेतसः तेषाम् ॥

यतः एवं, तस्मात्—

7.1. I, the Lord, shall deliver them who are solely engaged in worshipping Me. Deliver from what?—the sea of 'empirical life leading to death'. Being hard to cross, it is called a sea. Thence shall I deliver them. Not after a long time, but 'soon', indeed O Arjuna! for they have concentrated their thoughts on Me in My cosmic form.

This being the case, therefore,

मय्येव मन आधत्स्व मयि बुद्धिं निवेशय ।
निवसिष्यसि मय्येव अत ऊर्ध्वं न संशयः ॥८॥

8. Fix your mind on Me alone; let your understanding be absorbed in Me; henceforth, doubtless, in Me alone will you dwell.

8.1. मय्येव इति ॥ मयि एव विश्वरूपे ईश्वरे मनः सङ्कल्पविकल्पात्मकं समाधत्स्व स्थापय । मयि एव अध्यवसायं कुर्वतीं बुद्धिं च आधत्स्व निवेशय । ततः ते किं स्यात् इति ? शृणु—निवसिष्यसि निवत्स्यसि निश्चयेन मदात्मना मयि वासं करिष्यसि एव अतः शरीरपातात् ऊर्ध्वम् । न संशयः, संशयः अत्र न कर्तव्यः ॥

8.1. 'On Me alone'—i.e., the Lord in the cosmic form; fix your mind with its characteristics of doubt and imagination on that form. Let your 'understanding'—whose function is to decide—'get absorbed in Me'. 'What will all this mean to you?' Listen: Surely you will dwell as one with Me and in Me, 'henceforth'—after the body's fall. Have no doubts on this issue.

अथ चित्तं समाधातुं न शक्नोषि मयि स्थिरम् ।
अभ्यासयोगेन ततो मामिच्छाप्तुं धनञ्जय ॥९॥

9. If you are unable to concentrate your mind steadfastly on Me, seek, Arjuna! to reach out to Me through the Yoga of repeated efforts.

9.1. अथ इति ॥ अथ एवं यथा अवोचं तथा मयि चित्तं समाधातुं स्थापयितुं स्थिरं अचलं न शक्नोषि चेत्, ततः पश्चात् अभ्यासयोगेन, चित्तस्य एकस्मिन् आलम्बने सर्वतः समाहृत्य पुनःपुनः स्थापनं अभ्यासः, तत्पूर्वकः योगः समाधानलक्षणः तेन अभ्यासयोगेन मां विश्वरूपं इच्छ प्रार्थयस्व आप्तुं हे धनञ्जय ! ॥

9.1. In the manner described, if you are unable to concentrate your mind steadfastly on Me, then through the Yoga of 'repeated efforts'—repeated efforts consist in fixing the mind, after withdrawing it from all else, on a single object, and Yoga means the concentration resulting from such efforts—'seek to reach out to Me' in My cosmic form.

अभ्यासेऽप्यसमर्थोऽसि मत्कर्मपरमो भव ।
मदर्थमपि कर्माणि कुर्वन् सिद्धिमवाप्स्यसि ॥१०॥

10. If you cannot make even these repeated efforts, devote yourself wholly to My works. Even by doing works for My sake you will achieve perfection.

10.1. अभ्यासे इति ॥ अभ्यासे अपि असमर्थः असि अशक्तः असि, तर्हि मत्क-

र्मपरमः भव, मदर्थं कर्म मत्कर्म, तत्परमः मत्कर्मपरमः, मत्कर्मप्रधानः इत्यर्थः । अभ्यासेन विना मदर्थम् अपि कर्माणि केवलं कुर्वन् सिद्धिं सत्त्वशुद्धियोगज्ञानप्राप्तिद्वारेण अवाप्स्यसि ॥

10.1. If you cannot even make repeated efforts, are too weak to do so, devote yourself wholly to My works. Work for My sake is 'My work'. Devote yourself to that, let the doing of such work become the main thing for you. This is the idea. In the absence of repeated efforts, even by the doing of My works you will achieve perfection through mental purification and attainment of the knowledge of Yoga.

अथैतदप्यशक्तोऽसि कर्तुं मद्योगमाश्रितः ।
सर्वकर्मफलत्यागं ततः कुरु यतात्मवान् ॥११॥

11. Now if, resorting to union with Me, you are unable to do even this, then, with self-control, renounce the fruits of all works.

11.1. अथैतद् इति ॥ अथ पुनः एतत् अपि यत् उक्तं मत्कर्मपरमत्वं तत् कर्तुं अशक्तः असि, मद्योगं आश्रितः, मयि क्रियमाणानि कर्माणि संन्यस्य यत् करणं तेषां अनुष्ठानं सः मद्योगः, तं आश्रितः सन्—सर्वकर्मफलत्यागं सर्वेषां कर्मणां फलसंन्यासं सर्वकर्मफलत्यागं ततः अनन्तरं कुरु यतात्मवान् संयतचित्तः सन् इत्यर्थः ॥

11.1. Again if what has been stated—devotion to the doing of My works—is beyond your ability, then, resorting to union with Me, and endowed with self-control, renounce the fruits of all works. 'Union with Me' means performing works with a sense of surrender to Me. 'Self-control' means a disciplined mind.

12.0. इदानीं सर्वकर्मफलत्यागं स्तौति —

12.0. Now is lauded the renunciation of the fruits of all works:

श्रेयो हि ज्ञानमभ्यासाज्ज्ञानाद्ध्यानं विशिष्यते ।
ध्यानात्कर्मफलत्यागस्त्यागाच्छान्तिरनन्तरम् ॥१२॥

12. Knowledge is superior to repeated efforts; superior to knowledge is meditation. Renunciation of the fruits of works is superior to meditation. Of this renunciation is peace born, immediately.

12.1. श्रेयः इति ॥ श्रेयः हि प्रशस्यतरं ज्ञानं—कस्मात् ?—(अ) विवेकपूर्वकात् अभ्यासात् तस्मात् अपि ज्ञानात् ज्ञानपूर्वकं ध्यानं विशिष्यते । ज्ञानवतः ध्यानात् अपि कर्मफलत्यागः, 'विशिष्यते' इति अनुषज्यते । एवं कर्मफलत्यागात् पूर्वोक्त-विशेषणवतः (११) शान्तिः उपशमः सहेतुकस्य संसारस्य अनन्तरं एव स्यात्, न तु कालान्तरं अपेक्षते ॥

12.1. 'Superior' or more praiseworthy is knowledge—than what? Than repeated efforts without discrimination. Better than knowledge is meditation guided by knowledge. It is understood that superior to the meditation of the man of knowledge is the 'renunciation of the fruits of works'. Thus is peace born of the renunciation of the fruits of works, qualified as stated in verse 11. Then takes place the quiescence of empirical life and its cause; it is not postponed to a later hour.

12.2. अज्ञस्य कर्मणि प्रवृत्तस्य पूर्वोपदिष्टोपायानुष्ठानाशक्तौ सर्वकर्मणां फलत्यागः श्रेयस्साधनं इति उपदिष्टं, न प्रथममेव। अतश्च 'श्रेयो हि ज्ञानं' इत्याद्युत्तरोत्तर-विशिष्टत्वोपदेशेन सर्वकर्मफलत्यागः स्तूयते, सम्पन्नसाधनानुष्ठानाशक्तौ अनुष्ठे-यत्वेन श्रुतत्वात्। केन धर्मेण स्तुतित्वं ? 'यदा सर्वे प्रमुच्यन्ते' [कठ. उ. ६.१४.] इति सर्वकामप्रहाणात् अमृतत्वं उक्तं; तत् प्रसिद्धं (बृ. उ. ४. ४. ६.) । कामाश्च सर्वे श्रौतस्मार्तकर्मणां फलानि। तत्त्यागे च विदुषः ध्याननिष्ठस्य अनन्तरा एव शान्तिः । इति सर्वकामत्यागसामान्यं अज्ञकर्मफलत्यागस्य अपि अस्ति इति तत्सा-मान्यात् सर्वकर्मफलत्यागस्तुतिः इयं प्ररोचनार्था । यथा अगस्त्येन ब्राह्मणेन समुद्रः पीतः इति इदानीन्तनाः अपि ब्राह्मणाः ब्राह्मणत्वसामान्यात् स्तूयन्ते । एवं कर्म-फलत्यागात् कर्मयोगस्य श्रेयस्साधनत्वं अभिहितम् ॥

12.2. The renunciation of the fruits of works has been prescribed as the means to spiritual well-being in respect of the ignorant man engaged in works who is unable to undertake the spiritual discipline set forth above; it was not commended right at the start. And so this renunciation is extolled as a step in which the series of means set forth in the words 'Knowledge is superior', etc., culminates (12.12). It is prescribed as fit for one who cannot take up the richer complex of means. On the basis of which attribute is this passage a commendation of renunciation of the fruits of works? According to KU.6.14 'When all desires are rejected. . . .' immortality is held to result from the renunciation of all desires. BU.4.4.6 has also proclaimed this truth. Objects of desires are the fruits of works enjoined by '*sruti* and *smṛti*. On renouncing them, the knower, established in meditation, indeed wins immediate peace. This general feature of renunciation of all desires is shared by the ignorant man's rencunciation of fruits also. Hence this praise of the renunciation of the fruits of all works is meant to create a zest for it. For example the statement that the Brahmana Agastya drank up the sea extols the modern Brahmana, too, Brahminhood being the common factor. Similarly owing to the renunciation of fruits, it is declared that Karma Yoga promotes spiritual well-being.

13.0. अत्र च आत्मेश्वरभेदं आश्रित्य विश्वरूपे ईश्वरे चेतःसमाधानलक्षणः योगः उक्तः, ईश्वरार्थं कर्मानुष्ठानादि च । 'अथैतदप्यशक्तोऽसि' (१२.११) इति अज्ञानकार्यसूचनात् न अभेददर्शिनः अक्षरोपासकस्य कर्मयोगः उपपद्यते इति दर्शयति। तथा कर्मयोगिनः अक्षरोपासनानुपपत्तिं दर्शयति भगवान् 'ते प्राप्नुवन्ति मामेव' (१२.४) इति अक्षरोपासकानां कैवल्यप्राप्तौ स्वातन्त्र्यं उक्त्वा, इतरेषां पारतन्त्र्यात् ईश्वराधीनतां दर्शितवान् 'तेषामहं समुद्धर्ता' (१२.७) इति । यदि हि ईश्वरस्य आत्मभूताः ते मताः अभेददर्शित्वात्, अक्षरस्वरूपाः एव ते इति समुद्धरणकर्मविषयवचनं तान् प्रति अपेशलं स्यात् ।

यस्माच्च अर्जुनस्य अत्यन्तम् एव हितैषी भगवान् तस्य सम्यग्दर्शनानन्वितं कर्मयोगं भेददृष्टिमन्तम् एव उपदिशति । न च आत्मानं ईश्वरं प्रमाणतः बुद्ध्वा कस्यचित् गुणभावं जिगमिषति कश्चित्, विरोधात् । तस्मात् अक्षरोपासकानां सम्यग्दर्शननिष्ठानां संन्यासिनां त्यक्तसर्वैषणानां 'अद्वेष्टा सर्वभूतानां' इत्यादिधर्मपूगं साक्षात् अमृतत्वकारणं वक्ष्यामि इति प्रवर्तते—

13.0. Here, assuming the distinction between self and God, Yoga, or the concentration of mind on the all-pervasive God, has been praised: also has been praised the performance of works etc., for the sake of God. In 12.11 it is suggested that the worshipper of the Imperishable, who perceives no difference, cannot reasonably perform Karma Yoga, as this is an offspring of nescience. Similarly the Lord shows the impropriety of a Karma-yogin betaking himself to the worship of the Imperishable. The verse 12.4 (they reach Me alone) states that the worshippers of the Imperishable freely attain 'Aloneness' while 12.7 (I am their deliverer) shows the dependence of others on the Lord. If the worshippers of the Imperishable have been assimilated to the Lord—have become His very Self since they see no difference whatsoever—it will be improper to suggest that they are the objects of an act of deliverance.

Also because the Lord, very much concerned with Arjuna's well-being, instructs him only in Karma Yoga, that is unrelated to right perception but is entrenched in the perception of difference. None who has, through the right means of perception, known the Lord as his very Self, seeks to subordinate himself to any one else or thing. That will be self-contradictory. Therefore the Lord begins to set forth the group of characteristics (verses 13ff) which directly immortalizes the worshippers of the Imperishable who have secured right perception and who have renounced all desires.

अद्वेष्टा सर्वभूतानां मैत्रः करुण एव च ।
निर्ममो निरहङ्कारः समदुःखसुखः क्षमी ।।१३।।

13. He hates no beings, is friendly and compassionate; he is rid of all sense of possession and of egoism; he is the same in pleasure and pain and is long-suffering.

13.1. अद्वेष्टा इति ।। अद्वेष्टा सर्वभूतानां सर्वेषां भूतानां न द्वेष्टा, आत्मनः दुःखहेतुमपि न किञ्चित् द्वेष्टि, सर्वाणि भूतानि आत्मत्वेन पश्यति । मैत्रः—मित्रभावः मैत्री, मित्रतया वर्तते इति—मैत्रः । करुणः एव च, करुणा कृपा दुःखितेषु दया, तद्वान् करुणः, सर्वभूताभयप्रदः, संन्यासी इत्यर्थः । निर्ममः ममप्रत्ययवर्जितः । निरहङ्कारः निर्गताहंप्रत्ययः । समदुःखसुखः, समे दुःखसुखे द्वेषरागयोः अप्रवर्तके यस्य

सः समदुःखसुखः । क्षमी क्षमावान् आक्रुष्टः अभिहतो वा अविक्रियः एव आस्ते ॥

13.1. 'He hates no beings', not even what causes pain to him; for he sees all beings as his Self. 'Friendly'—he maintains friendliness, or the attitude of a friend, to all. 'Compassionate'—compassion is kindness to those who suffer. He who has compassion extends freedom from fear to all living beings; he is the world-renouncing mendicant. He is 'rid of all sense of possession and egoism'. He looks upon pain and pleasure with detachment. He is not moved to act by pain and pleasure. He is long-suffering, i.e., reacts without emotion even when abused and smitten.

सन्तुष्टः सततं योगी यतात्मा दृढनिश्चयः ।
मय्यर्पितमनोबुद्धिर्यो मद्भक्तः स मे प्रियः ॥१४॥

14. He is happy without a break, integrated, self-disciplined and of steadfast resolve; He is My devotee who has steeped his mind and intellect in Me; he is dear to Me.

14.1. सन्तुष्टः इति ॥ सन्तुष्टः सततं नित्यं, देहस्थितिकारणस्य लाभे अलाभे च उत्पन्नालंप्रत्ययः । तथा गुणवल्लाभे विपर्यये च सन्तुष्टः । सततं योगी समाहितचित्तः । यतात्मा संयतस्वभावः । दृढनिश्चयः, दृढः स्थिरः निश्चयः अध्यवसायः यस्य आत्मतत्त्वविषये सः दृढनिश्चयः । मय्यर्पितमनोबुद्धिः सङ्कल्पविकल्पात्मकं मनः, अध्यवसायलक्षणा बुद्धिः, ते मयि एव अर्पिते स्थापिते यस्य संन्यासिनः स मय्यर्पितमनोबुद्धिः । यः ईदृशः मद्भक्तः सः मे प्रियः । 'प्रियो हि ज्ञानिनोऽत्यर्थमहं स च मम प्रियः' (७.१७) इति सप्तमे अध्याये सूचितं तत् इह प्रपञ्चयते ॥

14.1. 'He is happy without a break' i.e., always; both when he gains and when he fails to gain sustenance for the maintenance of his body, he has sense of sufficiency. So too is he happy both when he gets goods things and when he fails to do so. He is 'integrated' without a break, his mind being concentrated. He has a 'disciplined mind'—a disciplined nature. His mind and intellect are steeped in Me. Essentially the mind imagines and doubts; the intellect is the organ of decision. The reference here is to the renouncer who has fixed both his mind and intellect on Me alone. My devotee who answers to this description is dear to Me. What was hinted at in 7.17 is elaborated here.

यस्मान्नोद्विजते लोको लोकान्नोद्विजते च यः ।
हर्षामर्षभयोद्वेगैर्मुक्तो यः स च मे प्रियः ॥१५॥

15. From him the world does not shrink, nor does he shrink from the world. He is free from elation, intolerance, fear and agitation. He is dear to Me.

15.1. यस्मात् इति ॥ यस्मात् संन्यासिनः न उद्विजते न उद्वेगं गच्छति न संतप्यते, न संक्षुभ्यति लोकः, तथा लोकात् न उद्विजते च यः, हर्षामर्षभयोद्वेगैः, हर्षश्च अमर्षश्च भयं च उद्वेगश्च तैः हर्षामर्षभयोद्वेगैः मुक्तः—हर्षः प्रियलाभे अन्तः-करणस्य उत्कर्षः रोमाञ्चनाश्रुपातादिलिङ्गः, अमर्षः असहिष्णुता, भयं त्रासः, उद्वेगः उद्विग्नता, तैः मुक्तः यः सः च मे प्रियः ॥

15.1. From that renouncer 'the world does not shrink'—the world is not agitated by him; 'nor does he shrink from the world'. He is free from the feelings of elation, intolerance, fear and agitation. Elation is the mind's upsurge when anything pleasurable is won; it is marked by horripilation, tears, etc. Intolerance is impatience. Fear is the emotion due to alarm. Agitation is the state of the antagonised mind. He is devoid of all these and is dear to Me.

अनपेक्षः शुचिर्दक्ष उदासीनो गतव्यथः ।
सर्वारम्भपरित्यागी यो मद्भक्तः स मे प्रियः ॥१६॥

16. Dear to Me is My devotee who craves not, is pure, an adept, indifferent, unworried and who shuns all undertakings.

16.1. अनपेक्ष: इति ॥ अनपेक्ष: देहेन्द्रियविषयसम्बन्धादिषु अपेक्षा यस्य नास्ति न: अनपेक्ष: नि:स्पृह: । शुचि:, बाह्येन आभ्यन्तरेण च शौचेन सम्पन्न: । दक्ष:, प्रत्युत्पन्नेषु कार्येषु सद्य: यथावत् प्रतिपत्तुं समर्थ: । उदासीन: न कस्यचित् मित्रादे: पक्षं भजते य: स: उदासीन:—यति: । गतव्यथ: गतभय: । सर्वारम्भपरित्यागी, आरभ्यन्ते इति आरम्भा: इहामुत्रफलभोगार्थानि कामहेतूनि कर्माणि सर्वारम्भा:, तान् परित्यक्तुं शीलं अस्य इति सर्वारम्भपरित्यागी य: मद्भक्त: स: मे प्रिय: ॥

किञ्च—

16.1. He 'craves nothing' of what concerns the body, senses and objects—he cherishes no desires. He is 'pure', having cleanliness both external and internal. 'An adept' is he who is competent to grasp factually and at once all kinds of developments. He is 'indifferent', for he takes no sides with friends, etc. He is 'unworried' or fearless. He 'shuns all undertakings'. Undertakings are activities aimed at pleasures here and hereafter and prompted by cravings. My devotee habitually renounces them all and is dear to Me.

Besides,

यो न हृष्यति न द्वेष्टि न शोचति न काङ्क्षति ।
शुभाशुभपरित्यागी भक्तिमान् य: स मे प्रिय: ॥१७॥

17. He is not elated, does not hate or grieve or desire. He has given up both good and evil—such a devotee is dear to Me.

17.1. यो न इति ॥ य: न हृष्यति इष्टप्राप्तौ, न द्वेष्टि अनिष्टप्राप्तौ, न शोचति प्रियवियोगे, न च अप्राप्तं काङ्क्षति, शुभाशुभे कर्मणी परित्यक्तुं शीलं अस्य इति शुभाशुभपरित्यागी भक्तिमान् य: स: मे प्रिय: ॥

17.1. He is not 'elated' when good falls to his lot; he does not 'hate' when evil befalls. He 'grieves not' when the pleasant is lost and does not desire what has not been gained. Habitually he gives up both good and evil acts. (i.e. abandons the egoistic sense of doing good or evil.) Such a devotee is dear to Me.

समः शत्रौ च मित्रे च तथा मानापमानयोः ।
शीतोष्णसुखदुःखेषु समः सङ्गविवर्जितः ॥१८॥

18. He is the same towards friend and foe as also in honour and dishonour; the same in cold and warmth, pleasure and pain; for, he is detached.

18.1. समः इति ॥ समः शत्रौ च मित्रे च, तथा मानापमानयोः पूजापरिभवयोः, शीतोष्णसुखदुःखेषु समः, सर्वत्र सङ्गविवर्जितः ॥
किञ्च—

18.1. Towards 'friend and foe' the same, as also 'in honour and dishonour' or adoration and scorn. He is the same in cold and warmth, and scorns pleasure and pain' ; for he is detached in all circumstances.

तुल्यनिन्दास्तुतिर्मौनी सन्तुष्टो येन केनचित् ।
अनिकेतः स्थिरमतिर्भक्तिमान्मे प्रियो नरः ॥१९॥

19. He treats alike contempt and praise; is silent, content with whatever accrues; he is homeless and steadfast—such a devotee is dear to Me.

19.1. तुल्य इति ॥ तुल्यनिन्दास्तुतिः निन्दा च स्तुतिश्च निन्दास्तुती ते तुल्ये यस्य सः तुल्यनिन्दास्तुतिः । मौनी मौनवान् संयतवाक् । सन्तुष्टः येन केनचित् शरीरस्थितिहेतुमात्रेण; तथा च उक्तम्—

येन केनचिदाच्छन्नो येन केनचिदाशितः ।
यत्र क्वचन शायी स्यात्तं देवा ब्राह्मणं विदुः ॥

—[शान्तिपर्व. २४५. १२.] इति । किञ्च—अनिकेतः निकेतः आश्रयः निवासः नियतः न विद्यते यस्य सः अनिकेतः, 'नागारे' इत्यादिस्मृत्यन्तरात् । स्थिरमतिः स्थिरा परमार्थवस्तुविषया यस्य मतिः सः स्थिरमतिः । भक्तिमान् मे प्रियः नरः ॥

19.1. He treats 'contempt and praise' in the same way; he is 'silent', having controlled his speech. He is content with watever means is available to him to maintain physical existence. Thus has it been declared: "Clad somehow and fed somehow; resting anywhere—such a one the gods reckon a veritable Brāhmaṇa (M.Bha. 12.245.12)

Besides, he is homeless—having no fixed abode to dwell. 'He is a liberated soul who has no attachment to a room, water, clothing, sacred tanks, houses, seats and even food.' (quoted by Ānandagiri). His understanding about the Real is firm. Such a devotee is dear to Me.

20.0. 'अद्वेष्टा सर्वभूतानां' [१२.१३.] इत्यादिना अक्षरोपासकानां निवृत्तसर्वैषणानां संन्यासिनां परमार्थज्ञाननिष्ठानां धर्मजातं प्रक्रान्तं उपसंहरति—

20.0. The Lord concludes the list of characteristics, begun in verse 12.13, of the worshippers of the Imperishable, the renouncers who have shed all desires and are consecrated to the knowledge of the Real:

ये तु धर्म्यामृतमिदं यथोक्तं पर्युपासते ।
श्रद्दधाना मत्परमा भक्तास्तेऽतीव मे प्रियाः ॥२०॥

20. Those devotees who nurture, indeed, those immortal virtues set forth above, with faith, deeming Me the supreme Being, are exceedingly dear to Me.

इति श्रीमहाभारते शतसाहस्त्र्यां संहितायां वैयासिक्यां
भीष्मपर्वणि श्रीमद्भगवद्गीतासूपनिषत्सु ब्रह्मविद्यायां
योगशास्त्रे श्रीकृष्णार्जुनसंवादे भक्तियोगो
नाम द्वादशोऽध्यायः ॥

20.1. ये तु इति ॥ ये तु संन्यासिनः धर्म्यामृतं धर्मादनपेतं धर्म्यं च तत् अमृतं च तत्, अमृतत्वहेतुत्वात्, इदं यथोक्तं 'अद्वेष्टा सर्वभूतानां' इत्यादिना पर्युपासते अनुतिष्ठन्ति श्रद्दधानाः सन्तः मत्परमाः यथोक्ताः अहं अक्षरात्मा परमः निरतिशया गतिः येषां ते मत्परमाः, मद्भक्ताः च उत्तमां परमार्थज्ञानलक्षणां भक्तिं आस्थि-(श्रि)ताः ते अतीव मे प्रियाः । 'प्रियो हि ज्ञानिनोऽत्यर्थम्' [७.१७.] इति यत् सूचितं तत् व्याख्याय इह उपसंहृतं 'भक्तास्तेऽतीव मे प्रियाः' इति । यस्मात् धर्म्यामृतं इदं यथोक्तं अनुतिष्ठन् भगवतः विष्णोः परमेश्वरस्य अतीव प्रियः भवति,

तस्मात् इदं धर्म्यामृतं मुमुक्षुणा यत्नतः अनुष्ठेयं, विष्णोः प्रियं परं धाम जिगमिषुणा — इति वाक्यार्थः ।।

20.1. Those renouncers who 'nurture'—live upto—'the immortal virtues' or immortalizing virtues as set forth above—i.e., the righteous monks, 'with a faith that deems Me as the supreme Being', are exceedingly dear to Me. I, the imperishable Self, am their final or unsurpassed goal; they have resorted to the devotion distinguished by the knowledge of the Real. In the words 'those devotees are exceedingly dear to Me' has been concluded, after due explication, the principle laid down in 7.17 ('I am indeed extremely dear to the knower'). As one becomes dear to the Lord Viṣṇu, God Supreme, by practising the immortal virtues recounted here, the seeker after liberation who would attain to the beloved abode of Viṣṇu should practise them. This is the sense of the entire context.

इति श्रीमत्परमहंसपरिव्राजकाचार्यगोविंदभगवत्पूज्यपादशिष्य-
श्रीमच्छंकरभगवतः कृतौ श्रीभगवद्गीताभाष्ये भक्ति-
योगो नाम द्वादशोऽध्यायः ।।१२।।

त्रयोदशोऽध्यायः

CHAPTER XIII

THE YOGA OF THE FIELD AND THE FIELD-KNOWER

0.1. सप्तमे अध्याये द्वे प्रकृती सूचिते ईश्वरस्य त्रिगुणात्मिका अष्टधा भिन्ना अपरा संसारहेतुत्वात्, परा च अन्या जीवभूता क्षेत्रज्ञलक्षणा ईश्वरात्मिका; याभ्यां प्रकृतिभ्यां ईश्वरः जगदुत्पत्तिस्थितिलयहेतुत्वं प्रतिपद्यते । तत्र क्षेत्रक्षेत्रज्ञलक्षण-प्रकृतिद्वयनिरूपणद्वारेण तद्वतः ईश्वरस्य तत्त्वनिर्धारणाय क्षेत्राध्यायः आरभ्यते । अतीतानन्तराध्याये च 'अद्वेष्टा सर्वभूतानां' [१२.१३.] इत्यादिना यावत् अध्यायपरिसमाप्तिः तावत् तत्त्वज्ञानिनां संन्यासिनां निष्ठा यथा ते वर्तन्ते इत्येतत् उक्तम् । केन पुनः ते तत्त्वज्ञानेन युक्ताः यथोक्तधर्माचरणात् भगवतः प्रियाः भवन्ति ?—इति एवमर्थः च अयं अध्यायः आरभ्यते । प्रकृतिः च त्रिगुणात्मिका सर्वकार्य-करणविषयाकारेण परिणता पुरुषस्य भोगापवर्गार्थकर्तव्यतया देहेन्द्रियाद्याकारेण संहन्यते । सोऽयं संघातः इदं शरीरम् । तत् एतत् श्रीभगवान् उवाच—

0.1. In chapter VII two *prakṛtis*, natures, of God have been mentioned. The first, an inferior one, consists of the three constituents and is eight-fold; it is the cause of the empirical life. The second is a superior one, living and cognizant of the field, whose essence is God. By means of these two natures, God is the cause of the origination, sustentation and dissolution of the world. The present chapter on the field is begun to determine the truth about God by means of a study of the two powers, viz., the field and the field-knower, since God is the owner of these two powers. In chapter XII immediately preceding the present chapter, in verses 13–20, was set forth the discipline of the renouncers who know the Truth. Of what kind is the knowledge of that Truth, whose possession together with the practice of the characteristics mentioned, makes one dear to the Lord? Chapter XIII is begun also in order to answer this question. The power consisting of the three constituents is transformed into all kinds of effects, instruments, and objects. Thus it assumes the form of the human body, sense-organs etc., in order to promote man's empirical life and liberation. The human body is this conglomerate. The blessed Lord sets this forth:

श्रीभगवानुवाच :

इदं शरीरं कौन्तेय क्षेत्रमित्यभिधीयते ।
एतद्यो वेत्ति तं प्राहुः क्षेत्रज्ञ इति तद्विदः ॥१॥

1. O son of Kuntī! this body is called the field; him who knows this field, its knowers designate as the field-knower.

1.1. इदं इति ॥ 'इदं' इति सर्वनाम्ना उक्तं विशिनष्टि 'शरीरं' इति । हे कौन्तेय ! क्षतत्राणात् क्षयात्, क्षरणात्, क्षेत्रवत् वा अस्मिन् कर्मफलनिष्पत्तेः क्षेत्रं इति—'इति' शब्दः एवंशब्दपदार्थकः—क्षेत्रं इति एवं अभिधीयते कथ्यते । एतत् शरीरं क्षेत्रं यः वेत्ति विजानाति, आपादतलमस्तकं ज्ञानेन विषयीकरोति, स्वाभाविकेन औपदेशिकेन वा वेदनेन विषयीकरोति विभागशः तं वेदितारं प्राहुः कथयन्ति 'क्षेत्रज्ञः' इति—'इति' शब्दः एवंशब्दपदार्थकः एव पूर्ववत्—क्षेत्रज्ञः इति एवम् आहुः । के ? तद्विदः तौ क्षेत्रक्षेत्रज्ञौ ये विदन्ति विजानन्ति ते तद्विदः ॥

1.1. What is denoted by the pronoun 'this' is specified as the body, O son of Kuntī! It is called 'the field' as it protects from injury; or, as it perishes or disintegrates; or as it gives rise to fruits of works just as a field does. '*Iti*' in the text means 'thus'. Him who knows this field—this body 'from the foot to the head'—makes it an object of knowledge, either spontaneous or acquired, they describe as the knower of the field. Here too '*Iti*' means '*thus*'. Who are they? The knowers thereof—i.e., of the field and of the field-knower.

2.0. एवं क्षेत्रक्षेत्रज्ञौ उक्तौ । किं एतावन्मात्रेण ज्ञानेन ज्ञातव्यौ इति ? न इति उच्यते—

2.0. Thus have been mentioned the field and its knower. Is it all that is to be known? The answer is 'no':

क्षेत्रज्ञं चापि मां विद्धि सर्वक्षेत्रेषु भारत ।
क्षेत्रक्षेत्रज्ञयोर्ज्ञानं यत्तज्ज्ञानं मतं मम ॥२॥

2. Know Me, O Bhārata prince! as the field-knower also, present in all fields. I deem real knowledge to be the knowledge of the field and of the field-knower.

2.1. क्षेत्रज्ञं इति ॥ क्षेत्रज्ञं यथोक्तलक्षणं च अपि मां परमेश्वरं असंसारिणं विद्धि जानीहि । सर्वक्षेत्रेषु यः क्षेत्रज्ञः ब्रह्मादिस्तम्बपर्यन्तानेकक्षेत्रोपाधिप्रविभक्तः तं निरस्तसर्वोपाधिभेदं सदसदादिशब्दप्रत्ययागोचरं विद्धि इति अभिप्रायः । हे भारत ! यस्मात् क्षेत्रक्षेत्रज्ञेश्वरयाथात्म्यव्यतिरेकेण न ज्ञानगोचरं अन्यत् अवशिष्टं अस्ति, तस्मात् क्षेत्रक्षेत्रज्ञयोः ज्ञेयभूतयोः यत् ज्ञानं, क्षेत्रक्षेत्रज्ञौ येन ज्ञानेन विषयीक्रियेते, तत् ज्ञानं सम्यक् ज्ञानं इति मतं अभिप्रायः मम ईश्वरस्य विष्णोः ॥

2.1. Know Me, the supreme Lord, who is not subject to transmigration, also to be the field-knower as stated above. The idea is that the field-knower, present in and variegated by these countless fields beginning from Brahmā and extending down to clumps, is devoid of all differences derived from the adjuncts and is beyond the range of expressions like being and non-being. Since there is nothing to be known other than the truth of the fields, field-knowers and God, My view—the view of Lord Viṣṇu—is that the content of right knowledge is fields and field-knowers.

2.2. ननु सर्वक्षेत्रेषु एकः एव ईश्वरः, न अन्यः तद्व्यतिरिक्तः भोक्ता विद्यते चेत्, ततः ईश्वरस्य संसारित्वं प्राप्तं; ईश्वरव्यतिरेकेण वा संसारिणः अन्यस्य अभावात् ससाराभावप्रसङ्गः । तत् च उभयं अनिष्टं, बन्धमोक्षतद्धेतुशास्त्रानर्थक्यप्रसङ्गात्, प्रत्यक्षादिप्रमाणविरोधाच्च—प्रत्यक्षेण तावत् सुखदुःखतद्धेतुलक्षणः संसारः उपलभ्यते; जगद्वैचित्र्योपलब्धेः च धर्माधर्मनिमित्तः संसारः अनुमीयते । सर्वं एतत् अनुपपन्नं आत्मेश्वरैकत्वे ।

2.2. *Objection:* Now, if in all fields there is present but the one Lord—none other than He—as the experiencer or subject of knowledge, He becomes an empirical agent or transmigrator. Or, the sphere of empirical life would cease to exist as there are no empirical agents other than the Lord. Both these contingencies are unwelcome since they entail the futility of the *śāstras* that teach the doctrines of bondage, liberation and their causes, and since they run counter to the evidence of perception and so forth. Perception reveals the sphere of empirical life marked by pleasures, pains and their causes. The sphere may also be inferred as the consequence of virtue and vice; for the world's variety stares one in the face. All this becomes inconsistent if man's self and God are one.

2.3. नः, ज्ञानाज्ञानयोः अन्यत्वेन उपपत्तेः– 'दूरमेते विपरीते विषूची अविद्या या च विद्येति ज्ञाता' [कठ. उ. २. ४.] । तथाच तयोः विद्याऽविद्ययोः फलभेदोऽपि विरुद्धः निर्दिष्टः 'श्रेयश्च प्रेयश्च' [कठ. २.२.] इति—विद्याविषयः श्रेयः, प्रेयस्तु अविद्याकार्यं इति । तथा च व्यासः– 'द्वाविमावथ पन्थानौ' [शांतिप. २४०.६.] इत्यादि, 'इमौ द्वावेव पन्थानौ' [१] इत्यादि च । इह च द्वे निष्ठे उक्ते । अविद्या च कार्येण सह हातव्या इति श्रुतिस्मृतिन्यायेभ्यः अवगम्यते । श्रुतयः तावत्—'इह चेदवेदीदथ सत्यमस्ति न चेदिहावेदीन्महती विनष्टिः' [के. उ. २.५.], 'तमेवं विद्वानमृत इह भवति । नान्यः पन्था विद्यतेऽयनाय' [पुरुषसूक्ते. तै. आ. ३.१२; श्वे. उ. ३.८.], 'विद्वान्न बिभेति कुतश्चन' [तै. उ. २.४.] । अविदुषः तु–'अथ तस्य भयं भवति' [तै. उ. २.७.], 'अविद्यायामन्तरे वर्तमानाः' [कठ. उ. २.५.], 'ब्रह्म वेद ब्रह्मैव भवति' [मुं. उ. ३.२.९.], 'अन्योऽसावन्योऽहमस्मीति न स वेद यथा पशुरेवं स देवानां' [बृ. उ. १.४.१०.] । आत्मवित् यः 'स इदं सर्वं भवति' [बृ. उ. १.४.१०.], 'यदा चर्मवत्' [श्वे. उ. ६.२०.] इत्याद्याः सहस्रशः । स्मृतयः च—'अज्ञानेनावृतं ज्ञानं तेन मुह्यन्ति जन्तवः' [५.१५.], 'इहैव तैर्जितः सर्गो येषां साम्ये स्थितं मनः' [५. १९.] 'समं पश्यन् हि सर्वत्र' [१३.२८.] इत्याद्याः ।

2.3. *Reply:* Not so; for, it is proper to distinguish between knowledge and ignorance. Vide K.U.2.4: "The two known as ignorance and knowledge are in sharp contrast to each other; they point in opposite directions." Accordingly, the difference between the opposed fruits of knowledge and ignorance has been noted as "the good and the pleasant" (K.U.2.2.). The good is the sphere of knowledge; the pleasant is the effect of ignorance. Vyāsa confirms this: "Now these two paths", etc. M.Bhā.12.240.6. Also, "These two alone are the paths." And, here in BG, the two disciplines have been set forth. From the *Śruti*, *Smṛti* and reasoning it may be known that ignorance with its effects must be rejected. Here are the *Sruti* texts: "If one knows it here, the Truth is affirmed; if one fails to know, great is the loss", K.U.2.5; "Knowing Him thus one becomes immortal here; there is no other path that leads to progress", Puruṣasūkta: Tait.Ar:3.12; ŚU.3.8; "The knower is afraid of nothing", T.U.2.4. In contrast, "For the ignorant, there is fear", T.U.2.7; "Living within the sphere of ignorance", K.U.2.5; "Whoso knows Brahman becomes this very Brahman", MU.3.2.9; "He does not know (who deems) he is one, I am another; he is like a beast of the gods", BU.1.4.10; "He who is a Self-knower, he becomes all this", Ibid; "When like a hide" . . . . ŚU.6.20 and many other *Śruti* texts in their thousands. So also passages in the *Smṛti*: "Knowledge is shrouded in ignorance; therefore living beings are confounded", BG.5.15. "This order of creation has been vanquished by them whose mind is fixed in equality", BG.5.19; "Seeing the same Brahman everywhere", BG.13.28, etc.

2.4. न्यायतः च—
सर्पान् कुशाग्राणि तथोदपानं ज्ञात्वा मनुष्याः परिवर्जयन्ति ।
अज्ञानतस्तत्र पतन्ति केचिज्ज्ञाने फलं पश्य यथा विशिष्टम् ॥ [शांतिप. २०१.१६.]
तथा च—देहादिषु आत्मबुद्धिः अविद्वान् रागद्वेषादिप्रयुक्तः धर्माधर्मानुष्ठानकृत् 'जायते म्रियते च' इति अवगम्यते; देहादिव्यतिरिक्तात्मदर्शिनः रागद्वेषादिप्रहाणात् तदपेक्षधर्माधर्मप्रवृत्त्युपशमात् मुच्यन्ते—इति न केनचित् प्रत्याख्यातुं शक्यं न्यायतः । तत्र एवं सति, क्षेत्रज्ञस्य ईश्वरस्य एव सतः अविद्याकृतोपाधिभेदतः संसारित्वम् इव भवति, यथा देहाद्यात्मत्वं आत्मनः । सर्वजन्तूनां हि प्रसिद्धः देहादिषु अनात्मसु आत्मभावः निश्चितः अविद्याकृतः, यथा स्थाणौ पुरुषनिश्चयः । न च एतावता पुरुषधर्मः स्थाणोः भवति, स्थाणुधर्मः वा पुरुषस्य । तथा न चैतन्यधर्मः देहस्य, देहधर्मः वा चेतनस्य । एवं सुखदुःखमोहात्मकत्वादिः आत्मनः न युक्तः, अविद्याकृतत्वाविशेषात् जरामृत्युवत् ।

2.4. This also accords with reasoning. "Recognising the nature of snakes, blades of *kuśa*-grass and reservoirs of water, men avoid them; due to ignorance a few fall victims. Note this destination of knowledge as regards its fruits", Ma.Bhā. 12.201.16. The fact is that the ignorant, mistaking the body and so forth for the Self and impelled by attachment, aversion, etc., and conforming to righteousness and its opposite undergo birth and death; but those who see that the Self is other than the body and the like, eschew attachment, aversion and so on, as well as the activities issuing from them; they are liberated. None may reasonably repudiate this account. Such being the case, the field-knower who metaphysically is God Himself, due to differences of the adjuncts of nescience becomes, as it were, the transmigrator, even as the Self (Atman) is identified with the body and so on. It is well known that all living beings unhesitatingly treat non-self like body as the self due to ignorance, just as a stump is mistaken unhesitatingly for a man. In this process, of course, human characteristics don't get lodged in the stump or vice versa. Similarly the characteristics of the Spirit do not attach themselves to the body nor do those of the body to the Spirit. Therefore it is not proper to predicate of the Self pleasure, pain, delusion, etc., for these two are exactly like old age and death, products of nescience.

2.5. न, अतुल्यत्वात्; इति चेत्—स्थाणुपुरुषौ ज्ञेयौ एव सन्तौ ज्ञात्रा अन्योन्यस्मिन् अध्यस्तौ अविद्यया; देहात्मनोः तु ज्ञेयज्ञात्रोः एव इतरेतराध्यासः, इति न समः दृष्टान्तः। अतः देहधर्मः ज्ञेयोऽपि ज्ञातुः आत्मनः भवति इति चेत्—

2.5. *Objection:* "No, the two cases are not parallel. The stump and the man are wholly objects and are mutually superimposed due to ignorance by the subject (who superimposes). But in the case of the body and the Self the former is object and the latter subject, and yet they get mutually superimposed. Thus the two cases are not parallel. So, the attributes of the body, though falling within the sphere of objects of knowledge, may be predicated of the knowing subject."

2.6. न, अचैतन्यादिप्रसङ्गात्। यदि हि ज्ञेयस्य देहादेः क्षेत्रस्य धर्माः सुखदुःखमोहेच्छाद्वेषादयः ज्ञातुः आत्मनः भवन्ति, तदा "ज्ञेयस्य क्षेत्रस्य धर्माः केचित् आत्मनः भवन्ति अविद्याध्यारोपिताः, जरामरणादयः तु न भवन्ति" इति विशेषहेतुः वक्तव्यः। "न भवन्ति" इति अस्ति अनुमानं—अविद्याध्यारोपितत्वात् जरामरणा-

दिवत् इति, हेयत्वात्, उपादेयत्वात् च इत्यादि । तत्र एवं सति, कर्तृत्वभोक्तृत्वलक्षणः संसारः ज्ञेयस्थः ज्ञातरि अविद्यया अध्यारोपितः इति, न तेन ज्ञातुः किञ्चित् दुष्यति, यथा बालैः अध्यारोपितेन आकाशस्य तलमलिनत्वादिना ॥

एवं च सति, सर्वक्षेत्रेषु अपि सतः भगवतः क्षेत्रज्ञस्य ईश्वरस्य संसारित्वगन्धमात्रं अपि न आशङ्क्यम् । न हि क्वचिदपि लोके अविद्याध्यस्तेन धर्मेण कस्यचित् उपकारः अपकारः वा दृष्टः ॥

2.6. "Not so, for, then will arise, through mutual superimposition, the contingency that the Self will turn out to be inert, etc. If the subjective self can acquire the attributes of cognised objects such as the body, etc., that constitute the field—attributes like pleasure, pain, delusion, desire, aversion, and so forth—, a special reason must be furnished for the fact that only certain attributes of the field come to be associated with the self due to nescience-prompted superimposition, while others like old age and death do not. That they do not may be inferred; for, those attributes are superimposed only through ignorance and (not) others like old age, as these are to be rejected".

In these circumstances, transmigratory life, marked by agency, experiences pleasant or painful, etc., pertains only to the known object. It is superimposed on the cognizer due to nescience. Still, the cognizer cannot be adversely affected in any way by superimposition just as the sky is not through superimposition on it of impurities, etc., by the ignorant. Therefore one cannot even remotely ascribe a transmigratory status to the divine Being who is also the field-knower, present alike in all kinds of fields or embodiments. In actual life no advantage or disadvantage accrues to an entity by means of a feature ignorantly superimposed on it.

2.7. यत्तु उक्तं "न समः दृष्टान्तः इति," तत् असत् । कथं ?—अविद्याऽध्यासमात्रं हि दृष्टान्तदार्ष्टान्तिकयोः साधर्म्यं विवक्षितम् । तत् न व्यभिचरति । यत्तु "ज्ञातरि व्यभिचरति" इति मन्यसे, तस्य अपि अनैकान्तिकत्वं दर्शितं जरादिभिः ॥

अविद्यावत्त्वात् क्षेत्रज्ञस्य संसारित्वं इति चेत्—

न; अविद्यायाः तामसत्वात् । तामसः हि प्रत्ययः—आवरणात्मकत्वात् अविद्या विपरीतग्राहकः, संशयोपस्थापकः वा, अग्रहणात्मकः वा; विवेकप्रकाशभावे तदभावात्,

तामसे च आवरणात्मके तिमिरादिदोषे सति अग्रहणादेः अविद्यात्रयस्य उपलब्धेः ॥

2.7. To elucidate it further: The above remark that the cases are not parallel is improper. Why? The intended parallelism is confined to the fact that in both the examples and the exemplified, an act of superimposition due to nescience is involved. This remains valid. Your contention that it is invalid as regards the cognizer has been shown to be inconclusive by referring to characteristics like old age and the like. It may be contended that due to the nescience, the field-knower must transmigrate. Our reply is 'no', for, nescience is *tāmasic*. Indeed nescience is a *tāmasic* notion; for, basically it is what obscures. It gives rise to misapprehension, doubt, or non-apprehension. It does not exist where there is the light of discrimination. Only where there are flaws due to *tamas* whose essence is obscuration, there operates the three-fold nescience such as non-apprehension, etc.

2.8. अत्र आह—एवं तर्हि ज्ञातृधर्मः अविद्या ?

न; करणे चक्षुषि तैमिरिकत्वादिदोषोपलब्धेः । यत् तु मन्यसे ज्ञातृधर्मः अविद्या, तदेव च अविद्याधर्मवत्त्वं क्षेत्रज्ञस्य संसारित्वं; तत्र यदुक्तं "ईश्वरः एव क्षेत्रज्ञः, न संसारी" इत्येतत् अयुक्तम् इति—तत् न; यथा करणे चक्षुषि विपरीतग्राहकादिदोषस्य दर्शनात् । न विपरीतादिग्रहणं तन्निमित्तं वा तैमिरिकत्वादिदोषः ग्रहीतुः, चक्षुषः संस्कारेण तिमिरे अपनीते ग्रहीतुः अदर्शनात् न ग्रहीतुः अधर्मः यथा, तथा सर्वत्र एव अग्रहणविपरीतसंशयप्रत्ययाः तन्निमित्ताः करणस्य एव कस्यचित् भवितुं अर्हन्ति, न ज्ञातुः क्षेत्रज्ञस्य । संवेद्यत्वाच्च तेषां प्रदीपप्रकाशवत् न ज्ञातृधर्मत्वं —संवेद्यत्वात् एव स्वात्मव्यतिरिक्तसंवेद्यत्वं; सर्वकरणवियोगे च कैवल्ये सर्ववादिभिः अविद्यादिदोषवत्त्वानभ्युपगमात् । आत्मनः यदि क्षेत्रज्ञस्य अग्न्युष्णवत् स्वः धर्मः, ततः न कदाचित् अपि तेन वियोगः स्यात् । अविक्रियस्य च व्योमवत् सर्वगतस्य अमूर्तस्य आत्मनः केनचित् संयोगवियोगानुपपत्तेः, सिद्धं क्षेत्रज्ञस्य नित्यम् एव ईश्वरत्वं; 'अनादित्वान्निर्गुणत्वात्' [१३.३१.] इति ईश्वरवचनाच्च ॥

2.8. In this context it may be held that nescience is an attribute of the cognizer. It is not right. Flaws like blindness pertain to the eye, the cognizer's instrument of cognition and not to the cognizer as the objector maintains; so it cannot constitute the cognizer's transmigratory life. So God alone is the *kshetrajña* and not the transmigrating Jiva. Your contention that this is illogical is not correct. The defect leading to misapprehension, etc., exists in the eye, the instrument of cognition, and not in the cognizer. When the eye is cured by right treatment, the cognizer's vision ceases to be defective. Similarly non-apprehension, etc., are due to the defects of instruments of perception and not of the field-knower who perceives. Besides, being objects of knowledge, these defects cannot pertain to the perceiver in the way that light pertains to the lamp. Being knowable, these defects have to be cognised by a principle other than themselves; for, all disputants agree that in the state of freedom or *mukti*, where instruments of cognition no longer exist, the perceiver has no flaws like nescience, etc. If any attributes pertained to the Self who is also the field-knower, as, for instance, heat does to the fire, it would never be free from it. And it is unreasonable to hold that the Self, incorporeal, immutable and all-pervading like space, has contact with, or disjunction from, aught else. Hence it is established that the field-knower is the eternal Lord. Vide also Kṛṣṇa's words (13.31) "Being beginningless and beyond the constituents. . ."

2.9. ननु एवं सति संसारसंसारित्वाभावे शास्त्रानर्थक्यादिदोषः स्यात् इति चेत्—न; सर्वैः अभ्युपगतत्वात् सर्वैः हि आत्मवादिभिः अभ्युपगतः दोषः न एकेन परिहर्तव्यः भवति । कथं अभ्युपगतः इति? —मुक्तात्मनां हि संसारसंसारित्व-व्यवहाराभावः सर्वैः एव आत्मवादिभिः इष्यते । न च तेषां शास्त्रानर्थक्यादिदोष-प्राप्तिः अभ्युपगता । तथा नः, क्षेत्रज्ञानां ईश्वरैकत्वे सति, शास्त्रानर्थक्यं भवतु; अविद्याविषये च अर्थवत्त्वम्—यथा द्वैतवादिनां सर्वेषां बन्धावस्थायाम् एव शास्त्रा-द्यर्थवत्त्वं, न मुक्तावस्थायां, एवम् ॥

ननु आत्मनः बन्धमुक्तावस्थे परमार्थतः एव वस्तुभूते [मते] द्वैतवादिनां सर्वेषाम् । अतः हेयोपादेयतत्साधनसद्भावे शास्त्राद्यर्थवत्त्वं स्यात् । अद्वैतिनां पुनः, द्वैतस्या परमार्थत्वात्, अविद्याकृतत्वात् बन्धावस्थायाश्च आत्मनः अपरमार्थत्वे निर्विषयत्वात् शास्त्राद्यानर्थक्यं इति चेत्—

2.9. *Objection:* "But in these circumstances drawbacks like the futility of the *śāstras* will follow." *Reply:* "No, for this position is common to all disputants. All who uphold the doctrine of the Self are obliged to maintain this position of alleged error. Why then should one of these disputants, i.e. the Advaitin, bother to remedy it?" *Objection:* "How is it common to all disputants?" *Reply:* "All who uphold the doctrine of the Self grant that the liberated selves go beyond the sphere of distinctions like the states of transmigration and of transmigrator. For this reason, they have not been held to reduce the *śāstras* to futility, etc. Similarly the Advaitin grants that his position entails the futility of the *śāstras* in the state of liberation, since the *Jiva* has realised he is one with God. However the *sāstras* continue to be relevant in the sphere of nescience, of course. All dualistic schools, similarly, hold that the *śāstras* are relevant only in the state of bondage, and not in the state of liberation also." *Objection:* "But for the dualists of all schools the states of bondage and liberation are real in the most ultimate sense. Therefore, as there are good, evil, and their respective means, the *śāstras* become significant. On the contrary, for the Advaitins duality is unreal. The state of bondage being a product of nescience will have no reference to anything real. The self or *Jīva.* also is unreal; hence the futility of *śāstras* is inevitable."

2.10. न; आत्मनः अवस्थाभेदवत्त्वानुपपत्तेः । यदि तावत् आत्मनः बन्धमुक्तावस्थे युगपत् स्यातां, क्रमेण वा? युगपत् तावत् विरोधात् न सम्भवतः स्थितिगती इव एकस्मिन् । क्रमभावित्वे च, निर्निमित्तत्वं, सनिमित्तत्वं वा? निर्निमित्तत्वे अनिर्मोक्षप्रसङ्गः । स [अन्य—] निमित्तत्वे च, स्वतः अभावात्, अपरमार्थत्वप्रसङ्गः । तथा च सति अभ्युपगमहानिः । किञ्च—बन्धमुक्तावस्थयोः पौर्वापर्यानिरूपणायां बन्धावस्था पूर्वं प्रकल्प्या, अनादिमती अन्तवती च; तच्च प्रमाणविरुद्धम् । तथा मोक्षावस्था सादिमती अनन्ता च प्रमाणविरुद्धा एव अभ्युपगम्यते । न च अवस्थावतः अवस्थान्तरं गच्छतः नित्यत्वं उपपादयितुं शक्यम् । अथ अनित्यत्वदोषपरिहाराय बन्धमुक्तावस्थाभेदः न परिकल्प्यते, अतः द्वैतिनामपि शास्त्रानर्थक्यादिदोषः अपरिहार्यः एव; इति समानत्वात् न अद्वैतवादिना परिहर्तव्यः दोषः ॥

2.10. *Reply:* We disagree; for it is not reasonable to ascribe to the Self different states. These states may be predicated of the Self as existing either simultaneously or in sequence. Their simultaneous existence is impossible as they are mutually contradictory like rest and movement in the same object. As for their existence in sequence, are they caused or uncaused? If uncaused, there arises the contingency of non-liberation. If caused, not being natural to It, liberation ceases to be supremely real. Thus you are obliged to abandon a doctrine already accepted by you. Moreover, in regard to the order of the states of bondage and liberation, the state of bondage has to be thought of as prior, beginningless, and terminable. This runs counter to all means of proof—a state of liberation with a beginning but without an end! The eternity of an entity with states and mutability cannot be rationally maintained. To escape from defects like impermanence, if the distinction between the states of bondage and liberation is not upheld, the futility of *śāstras*, etc., becomes unavoidable for the dualists also. Thus, being common, the defect in question need not be remedied by the non-dualists alone.

2.11. न च शास्त्रानर्थक्यं, यथाप्रसिद्धाविद्वत्पुरुषविषयत्वात् शास्त्रस्य । अविदुषां हि फलहेत्वोः अनात्मनोः आत्मदर्शनम्; न विदुषां, विदुषां हि फलहेतुभ्यां आत्मन अन्यत्वदर्शने सति तयोः अहमिति आत्मदर्शनानुपपत्तेः । न हि अत्यन्तमूढः उन्मत्तादिः अपि जलाग्न्योः छायाप्रकाशयोः वा एकात्मतां पश्यति; किमुत विवेकी ! तस्मात् न विधिप्रतिषेधशास्त्रं तावत्, फलहेतुभ्यां आत्मनः अन्यत्वदर्शिनः भवति । न हि "देवदत्त ! त्वं इदं कुरु" इति कस्मिश्चित् कर्मणि नियुक्ते विष्णुमित्रः "अहं नियुक्तः" इति तत्रस्थः नियोगं शृण्वन्नपि प्रतिपद्यते । नियोगविषयविवेकाग्रहणात् तु उपपद्यते प्रतिपत्तिः, तथा फलहेत्वोः अपि ॥

2.11. In fact the defect of the *śāstras*' futility is non-existent; for the *śāstras* will remain applicable to the well-known category of the ignorant. Indeed it is the ignorant who mistake for selves 'the 'fruit and its cause' (the sense of agency and of enjoyership), which are non-selves; the enlightened never do so. Perceiving the otherness of the Self from 'the fruit and its cause', it is inconsistent for the enlightened to mistake the latter for the real Self. Even the densest minds—for example mad men—do not identify water with fire or shade with light. How then can a man of discernment do it? Therefore, the *śāstras*, enjoining and forbidding appropriate lines of work are not relevant to one who perceives the Self as other than 'the fruit and its cause'. Indeed, when the order to act in the words, "Devadatta! do this", goes out, Viṣṇudatta, present at the spot and listening, does not take it to refer to himself! But a mistaken understanding of this kind is in order, provided there is a failure to distinguish between him who is enjoined and another who is not so enjoined. The same holds true of 'the fruit and its cause'.

2.12. ननु प्राक्तसम्बन्धापेक्षया युक्ताः एव प्रतिपत्तिः शास्त्रार्थविषया—फलहेतुभ्यां अन्यात्मविषयदर्शनेऽपि मति—इष्टफलहेतौ प्रवर्तितः अस्मि, अनिष्टफलहेतोश्च निवर्तितः अस्मीति; यथा पितृपुत्रादीनां इतरेतरात्मान्यत्वदर्शने सत्यपि अन्योन्यनियोगप्रतिषेधार्थप्रतिपत्तिः [बृ. उ. १.५.१७.] ॥

न; व्यतिरिक्तात्मदर्शनप्रतिपत्तेः प्राक् एव फलहेत्वोः आत्माभिमानस्य सिद्धत्वात् । प्रतिपन्ननियोगप्रतिषेधार्थो हि फलहेतुभ्यां आत्मनः अन्यत्वं प्रतिपद्यते न पूर्वम् [ब्र. सू. ३.४.२६-२७] । तस्मात् विधिप्रतिषेधशास्त्रं अविद्वद्विषयं इति सिद्धम् ॥

ननु 'स्वर्गकामो यजेत' [आप. श्रौ. सू. १०.२.१.], 'न कलञ्जं भक्षयेत्' [?] इत्यादौ आत्मव्यतिरेकदर्शिनां अप्रवृत्तौ, केवलदेहाद्यात्मदृष्टीनां च, अतः कर्तुः अभावात् शास्त्रानर्थक्यम् इति चेत्—

न; यथाप्रसिद्धितः एव प्रवृत्तिनिवृत्त्युपपत्तेः । ईश्वरक्षेत्रज्ञैकत्वदर्शी ब्रह्मवित् तावत् न प्रवर्तते । तथा नैरात्म्यवादी अपि "नास्ति परलोकः" इति न प्रवर्तते । यथाप्रसिद्धितस्तु विधिप्रतिषेधशास्त्रश्रवणान्यथाऽनुपपत्त्या अनुमितात्मास्तित्वः आत्मविशेषानभिज्ञः कर्मफलसञ्जाततृष्णः श्रद्धधानतया च प्रवर्तते इति सर्वेषां नः प्रत्यक्षम् । अतः न शास्त्रानर्थक्यम् ॥

2.12. *Objection:* "But even where there is a perception of the otherness of the Self from 'the fruit and its cause', legitimate is the understanding of the *śāstras*' directions to act for securing well-being and to desist from action for avoiding disagreeable results in respect of the agent. This is similar to the case where a father and his son, knowing themselves as separate from each other, still assume as relevant to themselves injunctions and prohibitions addressed to them separately." *Reply:* No; because only before the dawn of the perception of the Self's otherness, the conceit of the Self regarding 'the fruit and its cause' will operate. Only he who has already grasped the sense of the injunctions and prohibitions perceives the otherness of the Self (cf. B.S.3.4.26, 27). Therefore it is established that the *śāstra*, which enjoins and prohibits, addresses itself to the ignorant." *Objection:* "But for those who perceive the otherness of the Self injunctions and prohibitions such as 'The seeker after heaven shall sacrifice' (Ap.ŚS 10.2.1), 'Don't consume poisoned food', etc., will not hold good. Similarly it will not hold good also for those who identify the self with the body. Thus the *śāstras* will remain futile for lack of appropriate agents to act in conformity with them." *Reply:* "No; for appropriate action and inaction will follow the course of established practice. He who perceives the identity of God and the field-knower, i.e., the knower of Brahman, of course won't act. So also he who maintains that there is no Self at all and no future world, will not act according to the *śāstras*. But in accordance with established practice, one who infers from the *Śrutis* the existence of the Self and the need for the injunctions and prohibitions, and who, at the same time, has no intimate knowledge of the Self and yearns for the fruits of works, will initiate works through faith in the *śāstras*. This fact is clear to all. Therefore, there does not arise the contingency of the futility of the *śāstra*."

2.13. विवेकिनां अप्रवृत्तिदर्शनात् तदनुगामिनां अप्रवृत्तौ शास्त्रानर्थक्यं इति चेत्—

न; कस्यचित् एव विवेकोपपत्तेः । अनेकेषु हि प्राणिषु कश्चित् एव विवेकी स्यात्, यथैव इदानीम् । न च विवेकिनं अनुवर्तन्ते मूढाः; रागादिदोषतन्त्रत्वात् प्रवृत्तेः, अभिचरणादौ च प्रवृत्तिदर्शनात्, स्वाभाव्याच्च प्रवृत्तेः— 'स्वभावस्तु प्रवर्तते' [५.१४.] इति हि उक्तम् ॥

तस्मात् अविद्यामात्रं संसारः यथादृष्टविषयः एव । न क्षेत्रज्ञस्य केवलस्य अविद्या तत्कार्यं च । न च मिथ्याज्ञानं परमार्थवस्तु दूषयितुं समर्थम् । न हि ऊषरदेशं स्नेहेन पङ्कीकर्तुं शक्नोति मरीच्युदकम् । तथा अविद्या क्षेत्रज्ञस्य न किञ्चित् कर्तुं शक्नोति । अतः उक्तं इदं 'क्षेत्रज्ञं चापि मां विद्धि,' (२), 'अज्ञानेनावृतं ज्ञानं' [५.१५.] इति च ॥

2.13. *Objection:* "But those who discriminate between the real Self and the unreal world refrain from *śāstraic* activites;

their followers, imitating them, will also refrain. Thus will result the futility of the *Śastra*". *Reply:* "No; such discrimination is very rare. Among numerous beings, rare is he who discriminates, as the case is at present. Deluded human beings, in fact, do not conform to the ways of one who discriminates. For, activity is governed by flaws like attachment. This is borne out by people's indulgence in activities like sorcery. And, at the same time, activity is spontaneous. Indeed it has been declared: 'But one's own nature acts,' (BG.5.14)."

Therefore the transmigratory sphere, *saṁsāra*, is but nescience as experience substantiates. The field-knower, in himself, has neither nescience nor its effects. Nor is false knowledge competent to infect ultimate Reality. The water of the mirage can't possibly wet the desert or make it miry. Even so is nescience incompetent to affect the field-knower. Hence the declaration: 'Also know Me, as the field-knower' (BG. 13.2), and, 'Knowledge has been shrouded in ignorance' (BG.5.15).

2.14. अथ किं इदं संसारिणाम् इव "अहं एवं" "ममैवेदं" इति पण्डितानाम् अपि ?

शृणु; इदं तत् पाण्डित्यं, यत् क्षेत्रे एव आत्मदर्शनम् । यदि पुनः क्षेत्रज्ञं अविक्रियं पश्येयुः, ततः न भोगं कर्म वाऽऽकाङ्क्षेयुः "मम स्यात्" इति । विक्रिया एव हि भोगकर्मणी । अथ एवं सति, फलार्थित्वात् अविद्वान् प्रवर्तते । विदुषः पुनः अविक्रियात्मदर्शिनः फलार्थित्वाभावात् प्रवृत्त्यनुपपत्तौ कार्यकरणसङ्घातव्यापारोपरमे निवृत्तिः उपचर्यते ॥

इदं च अन्यत् पाण्डित्यं केषांचित् अस्तु—क्षेत्रज्ञः ईश्वर एव । क्षेत्रं च अन्यत् क्षेत्रज्ञस्य एव विषयः । अहं तु संसारी सुखी दुःखी च । संसारोपरमश्च मम कर्तव्यः क्षेत्रक्षेत्रज्ञविज्ञानेन, ध्यानेन च ईश्वरं क्षेत्रज्ञं साक्षात्कृत्वा तत्स्वरूपावस्थानेनेति । यश्च एवं बुध्यते, यश्च बोधयति, नासौ क्षेत्रज्ञः इति ॥

एवं मन्वानः यः सः पण्डितापसदः, संसारमोक्षयोः शास्त्रस्य च अर्थवत्त्वं करोमीति; आत्महा (च;) स्वयं मूढः अन्यांश्च व्यामोहयति शास्त्रार्थसम्प्रदायरहितत्वात्, श्रुतहानिं अश्रुतकल्पनां च कुर्वन् । तस्मात्, असम्प्रदायवित् सर्वशास्त्रविदपि मूर्खवदेव उपेक्षणीयः ॥

2.14. *Objection:* "But among the learned as much as among the transmigrating *jīvas* prevails a notion whose content is the judgement: 'I am so and so; this is mine only.' Why is this notion?" *Reply:* "Listen. Their 'learning' consists in seeing the Self exclusively in the field (body)! Had they perceived the immutable field-knower, they would not have hankered after worldly experience and activity seeking to make it their own. Experience and activity are nothing but mutation. This being the case, hankering after the fruits of action, the ignorant man acts. On the other hand, with the knower who perceives the immutable Self and who is free from hankerings after fruits of actions, activity is inconsistent. When his body and organs cease to operate, he is figuratively said to withdraw from the sphere of activities."

There is yet another type of learning. They affirm: "The field-knower is God alone. The field is entirely different from Him, and is the object of His perception. But as for me, I am a transmigrator, happy or unhappy. My duty is to withdraw from the sphere of transmigration by means of an experiential knowledge of the field and the field-knower by means of realising the field-knower through meditation and getting assimilated to Him." He who knows thus and teaches thus, is not a real field-knower. He who thinks thus is the meanest type of a scholar who egoistically assigns a novel sense to the states of bondage and liberation and to the *śāstra.*; he also is a self-destroyer. Himself deluded, he confounds others; for he has had not the discipline of right traditions of scriptural knowledge. He is guilty of rejecting what is taught and dogmatically constructing something novel. Hence, one who is thus ignorant of right traditions, even though versed in all *śāstras*, deserves to be rejected as an ignoramus.

2.15. यत्तूक्तम् "ईश्वरस्य क्षेत्रज्ञैकत्वे संसारित्वं प्राप्नोति; क्षेत्रज्ञानां च ईश्वरैकत्वे संसारिणः अभावात् संसाराभावप्रसङ्गः" इति—एतौ दोषौ प्रत्युक्तौ "विद्याऽविद्ययोः वैलक्षण्याभ्युपगमात्" इति । कथम् ? —अविद्यापरिकल्पितदोषेण तद्विषयं वस्तु पारमार्थिकं न दुष्यतीति । तथा च दृष्टान्तः दर्शितः—मरीच्यम्भसा ऊषरदेशः न पङ्कीक्रियते इति । संसारिणः अभावात् संसाराभावप्रसङ्गदोषोऽपि संसारसंसारिणोः अविद्याकल्पितत्वोपपत्त्या प्रत्युक्तः ।

ननु अविद्यावत्त्वम् एव क्षेत्रज्ञस्य संसारित्वदोषः । तत्कृतं च सुखित्वदुःखित्वादि प्रत्यक्षं उपलभ्यते इति चेत्—

न; ज्ञेयस्य क्षेत्रधर्मत्वात्, ज्ञातुः क्षेत्रज्ञस्य तत्कृतदोषानुपपत्तेः । यावत् किञ्चित् क्षेत्रज्ञस्य दोषजातं अविद्यमानं आसञ्जयसि, तस्य ज्ञेयत्वोपपत्तेः क्षेत्रधर्मत्वम् एव, न क्षेत्रज्ञधर्मत्वम् । न च तेन क्षेत्रज्ञः दुष्यति, ज्ञेयेन ज्ञातुः संसर्गानुपपत्तेः । यदि हि संसर्गः स्यात्, ज्ञेयत्वम् एव नोपपद्येत । यदि आत्मनः धर्मः अविद्यावत्त्वं दुःखित्वादि च, कथं भोः प्रत्यक्षं उपलभ्यते, कथं वा क्षेत्रज्ञधर्मः ? "ज्ञेयं च तत् सर्वं क्षेत्रं, ज्ञातैव क्षेत्रज्ञः" इति अवधारिते, "अविद्यादुःखित्वादेः क्षेत्रज्ञविशेषणत्वं क्षेत्रज्ञधर्मत्वं, तस्य च प्रत्यक्षोपलभ्यत्वं" इति विरुद्धं उच्यते अविद्यामात्रावष्टम्भात् केवलम् ॥

2.15. The two objections raised above, viz., (1) due to identity with the field-knower, God becomes transmigratory and (ii) there ceases to be a transmigratory state as there is none to transmigrate, the field-knower being one with God,—these have been rejected when we distinguished knowledge from ignorance. How? It was pointed out that by a flaw superimposed due to ignorance, its object, viz., the ultimate Reality, is not vitiated. And an analogy was offered to illustrate this—how a desert is not made miry by the waters of a mirage. The contingency of the disappearance of transmigratory life in the absence of a real transmigrator was set aside on the ground that both transmigrator and transmigratory life may very well be there as products of nescience.

Objection: "But the field-knower's taint of being a transmigrator is just this subjection to nescience; its consequences—pleasure and pain and so forth—are directly perceived."

Reply: "No; for, whatever is known pertains to the field; the field-knower cannot reasonably be affected by the flaws of the field. Whatever non-existent flaws are ascribed to the field-knower are, properly, cognised objects and, as such, are attributes of the field and not those of the field-knower. How then can the field-knower be stained by them? The known cannot reasonably be related to the knower. If the relation were there, they would not have been known at all. If nescience, pain and pleasure were the Self's attributes, how could they be directly perceived and still be deemed the field-knower's attributes? Once it is established that what is known constitutes the field, and that the field-knower is only the knower, it would be contradictory to state that nescience, pain, etc., are adjectival to the field-knower and are, yet, directly perceived. A statement like that has only nescience as its support."

2.16. अत्र आह—सा अविद्या कस्य ? इति।
यस्य दृश्यते तस्य एव।
कस्य दृश्यते इति ?

अत्र उच्यते—"अविद्या कस्य दृश्यते ?" इति प्रश्नः निरर्थकः । कथं ?— दृश्यते चेत् अविद्या, तद्वन्तमपि पश्यसि । न च तद्वति उपलभ्यमाने "सा कस्य ?" इति प्रश्नः युक्तः । न हि गोमति उपलभ्यमाने "गावः कस्य ?" इति प्रश्नः अर्थवान् भवति ॥

ननु विषमः दृष्टान्तः—गवां तद्वतश्च प्रत्यक्षत्वात् तत्सम्बन्धोऽपि प्रत्यक्षः इतिः प्रश्नः निरर्थकः । न तथा अविद्या तद्वांश्च प्रत्यक्षौ, यतः प्रश्नः निरर्थकः स्यात् ॥

अप्रत्यक्षेण अविद्यावता अविद्यासम्बन्धे ज्ञाते, किं तव स्यात् ?

अविद्यायाः अनर्थहेतुत्वात् परिहर्तव्या स्यात् ।

यस्य अविद्या, सः तां परिहरिष्यति ।

ननु ममैव अविद्या।

जानासि तर्हि अविद्यां तद्वन्तं च आत्मानम् ।

जानामि, न तु प्रत्यक्षेण ।

अनुमानेन चेत् जानासि, कथं सम्बन्धग्रहणम् ? न हि तव ज्ञातुः ज्ञेयभूतया अविद्यया तत्काले सम्बन्धः ग्रहीतुं शक्यते, अविद्यायाः विषयत्वेन एव (अविद्याविषयीत्वेन एव) ज्ञातुः उपयुक्तत्वात् । न च ज्ञातुः अविद्यायाश्च सम्बन्धस्य यः ग्रहीता, ज्ञानं च अन्यत् तद्विषयं सम्भवति, अनवस्थाप्राप्तेः । यदि ज्ञात्राऽपि ज्ञेयसम्बन्धः ज्ञायेत, अन्यः ज्ञाता कल्प्यः स्यात् तस्यापि अन्यः, तस्यापि अन्यः इति अनवस्था अपरिहार्या । यदि पुनः अविद्या ज्ञेया, अन्यद्वा ज्ञेयं, ज्ञेयमेव । तथा ज्ञाताऽपि ज्ञातैव, न ज्ञेयं भवति । यदा च एवं अविद्यादुःखित्वाद्यैः न ज्ञातुः क्षेत्रज्ञस्य किञ्चित् दुष्यति ॥

2.16. *Objection:* One may ask here: whose is this nescience?
Reply: His, by whom it is seen.
Objection: Who sees it?
Reply: Senseless is the question, whose is nescience? How? If nescience is perceived by you, him also you perceive who has it. And, perceiving him, the question who has it, is senseless, just as the question whose are the cows is senseless after perceiving the owner of the cows.

Objection: This analogy is inappropriate. Both the cows and their owner, being directly visible, the relation between the two also is visible. So the question whose are the cows is senseless. But nescience and its owner being imperceptible, the question whose is nescience, is not senseless.

Reply: How does the knowledge of the relation of nescience with its imperceptible owner profit you?

Objection: Being the cause of mishaps, nescience has to be eschewed.

Reply: "He who is affected by it will eschew it."

Objection: "Now, that nescience is mine."

Reply: "So you know nescience and its owner, the self."

Objection: "Yes, I know but not directly."

Reply: "If you know inferentially, how is the relation grasped? Indeed, it is impossible for you, the knower, to cognise your relation with nescience also at the same time; for, nescience, the object of the cogniser's cognition, fully engages him. He who is the cogniser of the relation between the cogniser and nescience cannot have an independent cognition of that relation alone. That will unavoidably result in an infinite regress. If the relation of nescience is knowable to the knower, he has to be conceived as a different knower. This latter too with reference to the second knower and so on. Thus regress becomes unavoidable. If, however, nescience or aught else is knowable, it must remain as knowable alone. This being the case, the field-knower, or the cogniser, is not adversely affected in any way by nescience, pain, etc."

2.17. ननु अयमेव दोषः, यत् दोषवत्क्षेत्रविज्ञातृत्वम्, इति चेत्—न, विज्ञानस्वरूपस्य एव अविक्रियस्य एव विज्ञातृत्वोपचारात्; यथा उष्णतामात्रेण अग्नेः तप्तिक्रियोपचारः तद्वत् । यथा च अत्र भगवता क्रियाकारकफलात्मत्वाभावः आत्मनि स्वतः एव दर्शितः—अविद्याध्यारोपितः एव क्रियाकारकादिः आत्मनि उपचर्यते; तथा तत्र तत्र 'य एनं वेत्ति हन्तारं' (२.१९.), 'प्रकृतेः क्रियमाणानि गुणैः कर्माणि सर्वशः (३.२७.), 'नादत्ते कस्यचित्पापं' (५.१५.) इत्यादिप्रकरणेषु दर्शितः—तथैव च व्याख्यातं अस्माभिः । उत्तरेषु च प्रकरणेषु दर्शयिष्यामः ॥

हन्त ! तर्हि आत्मनि क्रियाकारकफलात्मतायाः स्वतः अभावे, अविद्यया च अध्यारोपितत्वे, "कर्माणि अविद्वत्कर्तव्यान्येव, न विदुषां" इति प्राप्तम् ॥

सत्यं एवं प्राप्तं, एतदेव च 'न हि देहभृता शक्यं' (१८.११) इत्यत्र दर्श-

यिष्यामः । सर्वशास्त्रार्थोपसंहारप्रकरणे च 'समासेनैव कौन्तेय ! निष्ठा ज्ञानस्य या परा' (१८.५०) इत्यत्र विशेषतः दर्शयिष्यामः । अलं इह बहुप्रपञ्चेन, इति उपसंह्रियते ॥

2.17. *Objection:* "But there is this defect—that the field-knower cognises the defective field." *Reply:* "No, this cogniser-ship is only figuratively ascribed to the immutable essence of cognition, as the action of burning is only a figurative ascription to the fire that is nothing but a state of burning. Or, it is again, just as in contexts like 2.19, 3.27 and 5.15, where the Lord has demonstrated the absence in the Self of activity, its accessories and fruits, these being only superimposed on the Self due to nescience; they are only figuratively imputed to It. So has all this been explicated by us. In future contexts also it shall be similarly demonstrated." *Objection:* "Well then, if the Self is naturally devoid of activities, accessories and fruits and these are but super-imposed on It due to nescience, it follows that the agents of activities are the ignorant only and not the wise."

Reply: "Indeed it is so and we shall demonstrate it in our comment on 18.11. In particular we shall demonstrate it in our comment on 18.50. To avoid prolixity this topic is concluded here."

3.0. 'इदं शरीरं [१] इत्यादिश्लोकोपदिष्टस्य क्षेत्राध्यायार्थस्य संग्रहश्लोकः अयं उपन्यस्यते 'तत्क्षेत्रं यच्च' [३] इत्यादि, व्याचिख्यासितस्य हि अर्थस्य संग्रहोपन्यासः न्याय्यः इति—

3.0. The contents of the chapter on the Field set forth in 13.1 is summarised in verse 13.3, since it is but proper to put in a nut-shell the contents sought to be elucidated:-

तत्क्षेत्रं यच्च यादृक्च यद्विकारि यतश्च यत् ।
स च यो यत्प्रभावश्च तत्समासेन मे शृणु ॥३॥

3. Listen to Me as I briefly set forth what that field is,

what it is like, how it is transformed and the cause of such transformation; also what the field-knower is and His powers are.

3.1. तत् इति ॥ यत् निर्दिष्टं 'इदं शरीरं' इति तत् तच्छब्देन परामृशति । यच्च इदं निर्दिष्टं क्षेत्रं, तत् यादृक् यादृशं स्वकीयैः धर्मैः । 'च—' शब्दः समुच्चयार्थः । यद्विकारि यः विकारः यस्य तत् यद्विकारि, यतः यस्मात् च यत्, 'कार्यं उत्पद्यते' इति वाक्यशेषः । सः च यः क्षेत्रज्ञः निर्दिष्टः सः यत्प्रभावः ये प्रभावाः उपाधिकृताः शक्तयः यस्य सः यत्प्रभावः च । तत् क्षेत्रक्षेत्रज्ञयोः याथात्म्यं यथाविशेषितं समासेन संक्षेपेण मे मम वाक्यतः शृणु, श्रुत्वा अवधारय इत्यर्थः ॥

3.1. The word *tat*, 'that, refers to what was denoted by the expression 'this body'. What this field thus referred to is like as regards its attributes—listen to it now. *Ca*, 'and', adds up the mentioned items. What its transformations are and which effects derive from which causes, and the powers of the field-knower (are going to be noted). These powers are derived from the adjuncts. Hear from My brief utterance the truth about the field and the field-knower thus qualified, and hearing, know about it for certain. This is the sense.

4.0. तत् क्षेत्रक्षेत्रज्ञयाथात्म्यं विवक्षितं स्तौति श्रोतृबुद्धिप्ररोचनार्थम्—

4.0. The truth of the field and the field-knower sought to be set forth, the Lord lauds in order to stimulate the listener's intelligence:

ऋषिभिर्बहुधा गीतं छन्दोभिर्विविधैः पृथक् ।
ब्रह्मसूत्रपदैश्चैव हेतुमद्भिर्विनिश्चितैः ॥४॥

4. It has been sung variously by seers in varied hymns; as also stated in the reasoned and definitive words of the Brahmasūtras.

4.1. ऋषिभिः इति ॥ ऋषिभिः वसिष्ठादिभिः बहुधा बहुप्रकारं गीतं कथितम् । छन्दोभिः छन्दांसि ऋगादीनि तैः छन्दोभिः विविधैः नानाभावैः नानाप्रकारैः पृथक्

विवेकतः गीतम् । किञ्च—ब्रह्मसूत्रपदैः च एव, ब्रह्मणः सूचकानि वाक्यानि ब्रह्म-सूत्राणि, तैः पद्यते गम्यंते ज्ञायते ब्रह्म इति तानि पदानि उच्यन्ते, तैः एव च क्षेत्रक्षेज्ञयोः याथात्म्यं 'गीतं' इति अनुवर्तते । 'आत्मेयेवोपासीत' (बृ. उ. १.४.७.) इत्येवमादिभिः ब्रह्मसूत्रपदैः आत्मा ज्ञायते, हेतुमद्भिः युक्तियुक्तैः विनिश्चितैः निःस-शयरूपैः निश्चितप्रत्ययोत्पादकैः इत्यर्थः ॥

4.1. By seers like Vasiṣṭha, in various ways, it has been sung. The hymns are those of the Ṛg Veda, etc. By means of these varied Vedic hymns it has been sung distinctively. Besides, in the words of the *Brahmasūtras* has it been stated. The *Brahmasūtras* are statements pointing to Brahman. Being the means to know, i.e. to attain, Brahman, they are called *padaiḥ*, steps, by which Brahman is reached or known. It follows that by means of them also the truths of the field and of the field-knower have been stated. "One should worship with the thought that He is just one's Self" (BU.1.4.7). By means of words constituting Brahman-utterances like these, the Self is known. These words are reasoned and definitive—are free from doubts and generative of veridical knowledge.

5.0. स्तुत्या अभिमुखीभूताय अर्जुनाय आह भगवान्—

5.0. To Arjuna whose attention has been secured the Lord says:

महाभूतान्यहंकारो बुद्धिरव्यक्तमेव च ।
इन्द्रियाणि दशैकं च पञ्च चेन्द्रियगोचराः ॥५॥

5. The great elements, the ego, the intellect and the unmanifest too, the ten senses and one and the five objects of the senses;

5.1. महाभूतानि इति ॥ महाभूतानि महान्ति च तानि भूतानि, सर्वविका-रव्यापकत्वात् । भूतानि च सूक्ष्माणि (न स्थूलानि) । स्थूलानि तु इन्द्रियगोचर-शब्देन अभिधायिष्यन्ते । अहङ्कारः महाभूतकारणं अहंप्रत्ययलक्षणः । अहङ्कारकारणं बुद्धिः अध्यवसायलक्षणा । तत्कारणं अव्यक्तम् एव च, न व्यक्तं अव्यक्तं अव्याकृतं

ईश्वरशक्तिः 'मम माया दुरत्यया' [७.१४.] इयुक्तम् । एवशब्दः प्रकृत्यवधारणार्थः —एतावती एव अष्टधा भिन्ना प्रकृतिः । 'च' शब्दः भेदसमुच्चयार्थः । इन्द्रियाणि दश—श्रोत्रादीनि पञ्च बुद्ध्युत्पादकत्वात् बुद्धीन्द्रियाणि, वाक्पाण्यादीनि पञ्च कर्मनिर्वर्तकत्वात् कर्मेन्द्रियाणि; तानि दश; एकं च—किं तत् ?—मनः एकादशं सङ्कल्पाद्यात्मकम् । पञ्च च इन्द्रियगोचराः शब्दादयः विषयाः । तानि एतानि साङ्ख्याः चतुर्विंशतितत्त्वानि आचक्षते ॥

5.1. The elements are 'great' or pervasive. They pervade all transformations of *Prakṛti*. The elements in this expression are subtle. The gross ones will be referred to as sense-objects. The ego is the cause of the great elements and it is marked by the I-sense. The cause of the ego is the intellect whose characteristic is determination. Its cause is the unmanifest or what is not manifest, i.e., the unevolved, the state of *Prakṛti* that is devoid of modification or God's power, denoted in 7.14 by the expression, 'My *māyā* is hard to cross over'. The word *eva* (too) serves to delimit *Prakṛti*. So far only is the realm of the eight-fold *Prakṛti*. And (*ca*) adds up the different items. The ten senses are the ear, etc. Those that generate the five-fold cognition are called the cognitive senses. The five such as tongue, hand and so forth are the organs of action since they serve to accomplish actions. These add up to ten. There is 'one' more, namely, the mind as the eleventh. This eleventh has, as its essence, conception, etc. Then follow the five objects of the senses such as sound etc. The Sāṃkhyas designate all these together as the twentyfour principles.

6.0. अथ इदानीं आत्मगुणाः इति यान् आचक्षते वैशेषिकाः, ते अपि क्षेत्रधर्माः एव, न तु क्षेत्रज्ञस्य इति आह भगवान्—

6.0. Now the Lord says that what the Vaiśeṣikas call the qualities of the self also are the attributes of the field only and not those of the field-knower:

इच्छा द्वेषः सुखं दुःखं संघातश्चेतना धृतिः ।
एतत्क्षेत्रं समासेन सविकारमुदाहृतम् ॥६॥

6. Desire, antipathy, pleasure, pain, the group, awareness, sustentation—these, briefly, are said to be the field and its transformations.

6.1. इच्छा इति ॥ इच्छा—यज्जातीयं सुखात्मकं अर्थं उपलब्धवान् पूर्वं, पुनः तज्जातीयं समुपलभमानः तं अर्थं समादातुं इच्छति सुखहेतुरिति; सा इयं इच्छा अन्तःकरणस्य धर्मः, ज्ञेयत्वात् क्षेत्रम् । तथा द्वेषः—यज्जातीयं अर्थं दुःखहेतुत्वेन अनुभूतवान्, पुनः तज्जातीयं अर्थं उपलभमानः तं द्वेष्टि; सोऽयं द्वेषः ज्ञेयत्वात् क्षेत्रमेव । तथा सुखं—अनुकूलं प्रसन्नसत्त्वात्मकं, ज्ञेयत्वात् क्षेत्रमेव । दुःखं—प्रतिकूलात्मकं; ज्ञेयत्वात् तदपि क्षेत्रम् । सङ्घातः देहेन्द्रियाणां संहतिः । तस्मिन् अभिव्यक्तान्तःकरणवृत्तिः, तप्ते लोहपिण्डे अग्निः इव, आत्मचैतन्याभासरसविद्धा चेतना; सा च क्षेत्रं, ज्ञेयत्वात् । धृतिः यया अवसादं प्राप्तानि देहेन्द्रियाणि ध्रियन्ते; सा च ज्ञेयत्वात् क्षेत्रम् । सर्वान्तःकरणधर्मोपलक्षणार्थं इच्छादिग्रहणम् । यत् उक्तं तत् उपसंहरति—एतत् क्षेत्रं समासेन सविकारं सह विकारेण महदादिना उदाहृतं उक्तम् ॥

6.1. Here 'desire' is taken as an attribute of the inner sense. Due to it one seeks to acquire, once more, the object that yielded pleasure earlier. Being an object of knowledge, it is part of the field. So too 'antipathy'. The kind of thing which was once experienced as a source of pain is hated when it is met with again. This is 'antipathy'; it too is part of the field, being an object of knowledge. Similarly 'pleasure' or that which is agreeable and essentially, *sattva*, is also field only for the same reason. What is antagonistic, i.e., pain too is field, being knowable. 'The 'group' refers to the body and the senses. 'Awareness' is a modification of the inner sense manifested within the 'group'. Like fire manifest in heated metal, the 'group' is pervaded by the quintessence of Self's intelligence as 'awareness'. That, too, being a knowable is field. 'Sustentation', by which are upheld the depleted body and the senses, also, being a knowable, is field. Desire, etc., are cited here to connote all the attributes of the inner sense. What was stated is concluded in the words: 'briefly thus has been set forth the field together with its transformations like the universal mind'.

7.0. यस्य क्षेत्रभेदजातस्य संहतिः 'इदं शरीरं क्षेत्रं' (१) इति उक्तं, तत् क्षेत्रं व्याख्यातं महाभूतादिभेदभिन्नं धृत्यन्तम् (५–६) क्षेत्रज्ञः वक्ष्यमाणविशेषणः—यस्य सप्रभावस्य क्षेत्रज्ञस्य परिज्ञानात् अमृतत्वं भवति, तं 'ज्ञेयं यत्तत्प्रवक्ष्यामि' [१३.१२.] इत्यादिना सविशेषणं स्वयमेव वक्ष्यति भगवान् । अधुना तु तज्ज्ञान-साधनगणं [–गुणं] अमानित्वादिलक्षणं—यस्मिन् सति तज्ज्ञेयविज्ञाने योग्यः अधिकृतः भवति, यत्परः संन्यासी ज्ञाननिष्ठः उच्यते, तं अमानित्वादिगणं, ज्ञान-साधनत्वात् ज्ञानशब्दवाच्यं, विदधाति भगवान्—

7.0. Already has been set forth in 13.1–6 the field, namely, the group of transformations comprising the gross elements, etc., and other attributes upto sustentation. 13.5,6. The field-knower's characteristics will now be set forth. The Lord Himself in 13.12 will elucidate the field-knower and his characteristics. The knowledge of the field-knower and his potency yields immortality. But now are enumerated the traits, non-egoism, etc., which, as means to knowledge, is styled knowledge, by possessing which one becomes eligible for grasping the knowable and due to intentness on which the renouncer is said to be dedicated to knowledge.

अमानित्वमदम्भित्वमहिंसा क्षान्तिरार्जवम् ।
आचार्योपासनं शौचं स्थैर्यमात्मविनिग्रहः ॥७॥

7. Humility, unostentatiousness, non-violence, endurance, simplicity, service to the teacher, purity, persistence, self-control;

7.1. अमानित्वं इति ॥ अमानित्वं—मानिनः भावः मानित्वं आत्मनः श्लाघनं, तदभावः अमानित्वम् । अदम्भित्वं—स्वधर्मप्रकटीकरणं दम्भित्वं, तदभावः अदम्भित्वम् । अहिंसा—अहिंसनं प्राणिनां अपीडनम् । क्षान्तिः परापराधप्राप्तौ अविक्रिया । आर्जवं—ऋजुभावः अवक्रत्वम् । आचार्योपासनं—मोक्षसाधनोपदेष्टुः आचार्यस्य शुश्रूषादिप्रयोगेण सेवनम् । शौचं कायमलानां मृज्जलाभ्यां प्रक्षालनं; अन्तश्च मनसः प्रतिपक्षभावनया रागादिमलानां अपनयनं शौचम् । स्थैर्यं—स्थिरभावः मोक्षमार्गे एव कृतव्यवसायित्वम् [—ताध्यवसायत्वम्] । आत्मविनिग्रहः—आत्मनः

अपकारकतया आत्मशब्दवाच्यस्य कार्यकरणसङ्घातस्य विनिग्रहः स्वभावेन सर्वतः प्रवृत्तस्य सन्मार्गे एव निरोधः आत्मविनिग्रहः ॥

किञ्च—

7.1. Pride is the state of a conceited person who is boastful; its absence is 'humility'. Showing off one's righteousness is ostentation, whose negation is unostentatiousness. 'Non-violence' consists in not harming living beings. 'Endurance' is the non-agitation of mind even when subjected to wrong. 'Simplicity' is straight-forwardness, absence of crookedness. 'Service to the teacher' consists in waiting on him who instructs as regards the means to salvation. 'Purity' results from the washing away of body's defilements with earth and water externally, and internally, from the removal of defilement like attachment by cultivating their opposites. 'Persistence' is firmness, the exclusive pursuit of the way leading to salvation. 'Self-control' is the discipline imposed on the body and the senses when they function against our real interest and the confinement of their activities to righteous paths.

Moreover,

इन्द्रियार्थेषु वैराग्यमनहङ्कार एव च ।
जन्ममृत्युजराव्याधिदुःखदोषानुदर्शनम् ॥८॥

8. Aversion to sense-objects, as well as absence of egoism; the perception of evils in birth, death, old age, diseases and pains;

8.1. इन्द्रियार्थेषु इति ॥ इन्द्रियार्थेषु शब्दादिषु दृष्टादृष्टेषु विषयभोगेषु विरागभावो वैराग्यं, अनहङ्कारः अहङ्काराभावः एव च जन्ममृत्युजराव्याधिदुःखदोषानुदर्शनं —जन्म च मृत्युश्च जरा च व्याधयश्च दुःखानि च तेषु जन्मादिदुःखान्तेषु प्रत्येकं दोषानुदर्शनम् । जन्मनि गर्भवासयोनिद्वारनिःसरणं दोषः, तस्य अनुदर्शनं आलोचनम् । तथा मृत्यौ दोषानुदर्शनम् । तथा जरायां प्रज्ञाशक्तितेजोनिरोधदोषानुदर्शनं, परिभूतता चेति । तथा व्याधिषु शिरोरोगादिषु दोषानुदर्शनम् । तथा दुःखेषु अध्यात्माधिभूताधिदैवनिमित्तेषु । अथवा—दुःखान्येव दोषः दुःखदोषः तस्य जन्मादिषु पूर्ववत् अनुदर्शनं—दुःखं जन्म, दुःखं मृत्युः, दुःखं जरा, दुःखं व्याधयः । दुःख-

निमित्तत्वात् जन्मादयः दुःखानि, न पुनः स्वरूपेणैव दुःखं इति । एवं जन्मादिषु दुःखदोषानुदर्शनात् देहेन्द्रियादिविषयभोगेषु वैराग्यं उपजायते । ततः प्रत्यगात्मनि प्रवृत्तिः करणानां आत्मदर्शनाय । एवं ज्ञानहेतुत्वात् ज्ञानं उच्यते जन्मादिदुःखदोषानुदर्शनम् ॥

किञ्च—

8.1. 'Aversion to sense objects' like sounds and so forth, including direct and indirect objective experiences, as also the 'absence of egoism'. 'Perception of evils' in each of the following: birth, death, old age, diseases, pains. The evil in birth consists in confinement to the womb and the exit therefrom. Its perception means reflection on the evil thereof. Similarly perception of evil in regard to death, old age, viz., the decline of intellectual power and enfeeblement of energy—their overthrow. So too the perception of evil in diseases like affliction of head, and in bodily pains due to alien beings, elemental and supernatural. Or, the evil in question is this very pain. Birth is pain, and so too death, old age and disease. All these are pains, because these occasion pain. They are not so in themselves. Due to such perception of evils arises aversion to them all—body, senses, objects and objective experiences. Thus takes place a movement of senses in the direction of the inner Self in order to perceive that Self. As engendering knowledge the perception of evils itself is styled knowledge.

Further,

असक्तिरनभिष्वङ्गः पुत्रदारगृहादिषु ।
नित्यं च समचित्तत्वमिष्टानिष्टोपपत्तिषु ॥९॥

9. Non-clinging, lack of excessive love for children, wife, home, etc., unfailing equanimity in circumstances pleasant and unpleasant;

9.1. असक्तिः इति ॥ असक्तिः—सक्तिः सङ्गनिमित्तेषु विषयेषु प्रीतिमात्रं, तदभावः असक्तिः । अनभिष्वङ्गः अभिष्वङ्गाभावः । अभिष्वङ्गो नाम सक्तिविशेष एव अनन्यात्मभावनालक्षणः, यथा अन्यस्मिन् सुखिनि दुःखिनि वा "अहमेव सुखी,

अहमेव दुःखी च," जीवति मृते वा "अहमेव जीवामि मरिष्यामि च" इति । क्व इति ? आह—पुत्रदारगृहादिषु पुत्रेषु दारेषु गृहेषु—'आदि'ग्रहणात् अन्येष्वपि अत्यन्तेष्टेषु दासवर्गादिषु । तच्च उभयं ज्ञानार्थत्वात् ज्ञानं उच्यते । नित्यं च समचित्तत्वं तुल्यचित्तता—क्व ? —इष्टानिष्टोपपत्तिषु इष्टानां अनिष्टानां च उपपत्तयः संप्राप्तयः तासु इष्टानिष्टोपपत्तिषु नित्यमेव तुल्यचित्तता । इष्टोपपत्तिषु न हृष्यति, न कुप्यति च अनिष्टोपपत्तिषु । तच्च एतत् नित्यं समचित्तत्वं ज्ञानम् ॥ किञ्च—

9.1. Clinging is feeling pleasure in objects that attract; its absence is 'non-clinging'. 'Lack of excessive love'—excessive love is indeed a form of pleasure that treats what occasions it as identical with oneself. For example, when another is glad or sad, the feeling 'I am glad or sad', or when another is alive or dead, the feeling 'I am alive or shall die'. In regard to what? To children, wives, homes, etc. Etc. refers to others like dependants who are also causes of it. Both these, non-clinging and lack of excessive love, are called knowledge as they promote it. And 'unfailing equanimity' or sameness of mind when good or evil happens. One is not elated when good befalls nor gets angry when evil betides. This 'unwavering equanimity' is knowledge.

And,

मयि चानन्ययोगेन भक्तिरव्यभिचारिणी ।
विविक्तदेशसेवित्वमरतिर्जनसंसदि ॥१०॥

10. Unwavering devotion to Me without attachment to aught else; resort to solitary spots and aversion to human crowds;

10.1. मयि इति ॥ मयि च ईश्वरे अनन्ययोगेन—अपृथक्समाधिना "न अन्यो भगवतो वासुदेवात् परः अस्ति, अतः स एव नः गतिः" इत्येवं निश्चिता अव्यभिचारिणी बुद्धिः अनन्ययोगः, तेन भजनं भक्तिः न व्यभिचरणशीला अव्यभिचारिणी । सा च ज्ञानम् । विविक्तदेशसेवित्वं, विविक्तः स्वभावत संस्कारेण वा अशुच्यादिभिः सर्पचोरव्याघ्रभयादिभिश्च रहितः, अरण्यनदीपुलिनदेवगृहादिः विविक्तो देशः, तं सेवितुं शीलं अस्य इति विविक्तदेशसेवी, तस्य भावः विविक्तदेशसेवित्वम् ।

विविक्ते हि देशे चित्तं प्रसीदति यतः, ततः आत्मादिभावना विविक्ते संजायते। अतः विविक्तदेशसेवित्वं ज्ञानं उच्यते। अरतिः अरमणं जनसंसदि, जनानां प्राकृतानां संस्कारशून्यानां अविनीतानां संसत् समवायः जनसंसत्; न संस्कारवतां विनीतानां संसत्, तस्याः ज्ञानोपकारित्वात्। अतः प्राकृतजनसंसदि अरतिः ज्ञानार्थत्वात् ज्ञानम्॥

किञ्च—

10.1. Devotion to Me, the Lord, 'without attachment to aught else' i.e. with unfailing concentration. The conviction that 'there is none other than the Lord Vāsudeva; so He alone is our refuge' is devotion with non-attachment to aught else. Devotion inspired by conviction that wavers not, is 'unwavering devotion'. This devotion is knowledge. 'Solitary' in the expression 'resort to solitary spots' refers to spots like forests, river banks, temples, etc., naturally free from or rendered free from unwelcome intruders like serpents, thieves, tigers and so forth. He who habitually dwells in such spots is referred to. In such a spot the mind is peaceful and the thought of the Self, etc., is generated. Hence habitual resort to such spots is styled knowledge. Aversion to crowds of people who are unregenerate, unrefined, uncultured is what is mentioned in the text, and not the groups of cultured disciplined men; these latter promote knowledge. Hence aversion to uncultured crowds, which promotes knowledge, is called knowledge. And,

अध्यात्मज्ञाननित्यत्वं तत्त्वज्ञानार्थदर्शनम्।
एतज्ज्ञानमिति प्रोक्तमज्ञानं यदतोऽन्यथा॥११॥

11. Unfailing cultivation of spiritual knowledge, perception of the content of philosophical knowledge—all this is said to be knowledge. What is other than this is ignorance.

11.1. अध्यात्म इति॥ अध्यात्मज्ञाननित्यत्वं आत्मादिविषयं ज्ञानं अध्यात्मज्ञानं, तस्मिन् नित्यभावः नित्यत्वम्। अमानित्वादीनां (७) ज्ञानसाधनानां भावनापरिपाकनिमित्तं तत्त्वज्ञानं, तस्य अर्थः मोक्षः संसारोपरमः; तस्य आलोचनं तत्त्व-

ज्ञानार्थदर्शनं ; तत्त्वज्ञानफलालोचने हि तत्साधनानुष्ठाने प्रवृत्तिः स्यादिति । एतत् अमानित्वादितत्त्वज्ञानार्थदर्शनान्तं उक्तं ज्ञानं इति प्रोक्तं, ज्ञानार्थत्वात् । अज्ञानं यत् अतः एतस्मात् यथोक्तात् अन्यथा विपर्ययेण—मानित्वं, दम्भित्वं, हिंसा, अक्षान्तिः, अनार्जवं इत्यादि अज्ञानं विज्ञेयं परिहरणाय, संसारप्रवृत्तिकारणत्वात् इति ॥

11.1. 'Unfailing cultivation of spiritual knowledge': Spiritual knowledge is that of the Self, etc; constancy in cultivating it. What is born of mature meditation on the means of knowledge such as humility, etc., (13.7 ff) is philosophical knowledge. Its content is liberation or the cessation of empirical life. Meditation on it is the 'perception of the content of philosophical knowledge'. Indeed, only when there is such meditation may one cultivate the means thereof. The group of components from 'humility' upto the 'perception of the content' is said to be knowledge since it promotes knowledge. Ignorance is what is other than this group and opposed to it, viz., conceit, vanity, violence, impatience, crookedness, etc. Know these to constitute ignorance in order to avoid them; for these set empirical life in motion.

12.0. यथोक्तेन ज्ञानेन ज्ञातव्यं किम् ? इत्याकाङ्क्षायां आह—'ज्ञेयं यत्तत्' इत्यादि (१२) ।

ननु यमाः नियमाश्च अमानित्वादयः । न तैः ज्ञेयं ज्ञायते । न हि अमानित्वादि कस्यचित् वस्तुनः परिच्छेदकं दृष्टम् । सर्वत्रैव च, यद्विषयं ज्ञानं, तदेव तस्य ज्ञेयस्य परिच्छेदकं दृश्यते । न हि अन्यविषयेण ज्ञानेन अन्यत् उपलभ्यते, यथा घटविषयेण ज्ञानेन अग्निः ।

नैष दोषः, ज्ञाननिमित्तत्वात् ज्ञानं उच्यते इति हि अवोचाम; ज्ञानसहकारिकारणत्वाच्च ॥

12.0. The question what is to be known by the knowledge stated above is answered in verses 13.12 ff. *Objection:* "Are not 'humility', etc. (cf. 7 to 11), restraints and observances? By means of them what ought to be known cannot be known. Indeed, humility and so forth do not precisely determine any object. It is universally understood that knowledge alone determines its objective content. Knowledge of one object does not lead to the apprehension of what is different from it.

By the knowledge of a pot, fire is not grasped." *Reply:* "This is no flaw. We have already pointed out that humility, etc., are called knowledge because they lead to knowledge and also because they cooperate with the direct cause of knowledge".

ज्ञेयं यत्तत्प्रवक्ष्यामि यज्ज्ञात्वाऽमृतमश्नुते ।
अनादिमत्परं ब्रह्म न सत्तन्नासदुच्यते ॥१२॥

12. I shall (now) set forth the knowable by grasping which one attains immortality—the supreme Brahman without a beginning. It is said to be neither existent nor non-existent.

12.1. ज्ञेयं इति ॥ ज्ञेयं ज्ञातव्यं तत् यत् प्रवक्ष्यामि प्रकर्षेण यथावत् वक्ष्यामि । किंफलं तत् इति प्ररोचनेन श्रोतुः अभिमुखीकरणाय आह—यत् ज्ञेयं ज्ञात्वा अमृतं अमृतत्वं अश्नुते, न पुनः म्रियते इत्यर्थः । अनादिमत् आदिः अस्य अस्तीति आदिमत् न आदिमत् अनादिमत्—किं तत् ?—परं निरतिशयं ब्रह्म 'ज्ञेयं' इति प्रकृतम् ॥

12.1. The knowable is what ought to be known. I shall set it forth truthfully and clearly. To rouse the attention of the listener, the fruit of such knowledge is indicated. The knowable is that by grasping which one attains immortality; there is no more death for the knower of it. That which has no origin is the supreme, is Brahman, the theme of this discussion.

12.2. अत्र केचित् 'अनादिमत्परं' इति पदं छिन्दन्ति, बहुव्रीहिणा उक्ते अर्थे मतुपः आनर्थक्यं अनिष्टं स्यात् इति । अर्थविशेषं च दर्शयन्ति—अहं वासुदेवाख्या परा शक्तिः यस्य तत् मत्परं इति ॥

सत्यं एवं अपुनरुक्तं स्यात्, अर्थः चेत् सम्भवति । न तु अर्थः सम्भवति, ब्रह्मणः सर्वविशेषप्रतिषेधेन एव विजिज्ञापयिषितत्वात् 'न सत्तन्नासदुच्यते' इति । विशिष्ट-शक्तिमत्त्वप्रदर्शनं, विशेषप्रतिषेधश्च, इति विप्रतिषिद्धम् । तस्मात् मतुपः बहुव्रीहिणा समानार्थत्वेऽपि प्रयोगः श्लोकपूरणार्थः ॥

12.2. In this context some explain the expression 'without a beginning, the supreme' otherwise, breaking up the compound into *anādi* and *matparam*, 'treating of Me as the supreme'. They argue that when the sense is expressed by an adjectival compound or *bahuvrīhi*, the possessive suffix that follows is uncalled for. The sense yielded, according to them is: I, Vāsudeva, am Its (Brahman's) pre-eminent Power. True, redundancy may be avoided were the sense admissible; but the latter is not the case. What is sought to be taught is Brahman by repudiating qualifications of all kinds. Vide: "It is neither the existent nor the non-existent." This pointing to a special power owned by It and the repudiation of all determinations are incompatible. Therefore, the possessive suffix and the adjectival compound yield the same sense; they are employed in the interest of metre.

12.3. अमृतत्वफलं ज्ञेयं मया उच्यते इति प्ररोचनेन अभिमुखीकृत्य आह—न सत् तत् ज्ञेयं उच्यते, न अपि असत् तत् उच्यते ।

ननु महता (परिकरबन्धेन) कण्ठरवेण उद्धुष्य 'ज्ञेयं प्रवक्ष्यामि' इति, अननुरूपं उक्तं 'न सत्तन्नासदुच्यते' इति ।

न अनुरूपम् एव उक्तम् । कथम्? —सर्वासु हि उपनिषत्सु ज्ञेयं ब्रह्म 'नेति नेति' (बृ. उ. २.३.६.), 'अस्थूलमनणु' (बृ. उ. ३.८.८.) इत्यादिविशेषप्रतिषेधेन एव निर्दिश्यते "न इदं तत्" इति, वाचः अगोचरत्वात् ॥

ननु न तत् अस्ति, यत् वस्तु 'अस्ति' शब्देन न उच्यते । अथ 'अस्ति' शब्देन न उच्यते, नास्ति तत् ज्ञेयम् । विप्रतिषिद्धं च—"ज्ञेयं तत्", "अस्ति शब्देन नोच्यते" इति च ।

न तावन्नास्ति, नास्तिबुद्ध्यविषयत्वात् ॥

ननु सर्वाः बुद्धयः अस्तिनास्तिबुद्ध्यनुगताः एव । तत्र एवं सति ज्ञेयम् अपि अस्तिबुद्ध्यनुगतप्रत्ययविषयं वा स्यात्, नास्तिबुद्ध्यनुगतप्रत्ययविषयं वा स्यात् ।

न, अतीन्द्रियत्वेन उभयबुद्ध्यनुगतप्रत्ययाविषयत्वात् । यत् हि इन्द्रियगम्यं वस्तु घटादिकं, तत् अस्तिबुद्ध्यनुगतप्रत्ययविषयं स्यात्, नास्ति बुद्ध्यनुगतप्रत्ययविषयं वा स्यात् । इदं तु ज्ञेयं अतीन्द्रियत्वेन शब्दैकप्रमाणगम्यत्वात् न घटादिवत् उभयबुद्ध्यनुगतप्रत्ययविषयं, इत्यतः 'न सत्तन्नासत्' इति उच्यते ॥

यत्तु उक्तं विरुद्धं उच्यते, 'ज्ञेयं तत्' 'न सत्तन्नासदुच्यते' इति—न विरुद्धं, 'अन्यदेव तद्विदितादथो अविदितादधि' (के. उ. १.३.) इति श्रुतेः ॥

श्रुतिः अपि विरुद्धार्था इति चेत्—यथा यज्ञाय शालां आरभ्य 'यद्यमुष्मिँल्लोकेऽस्ति वा न वेति' (तै सं. ६.१.१.) इत्येवमिति चेत् —

न; विदिताविदितान्यत्वश्रुतेः अवश्यविज्ञेयार्थप्रतिपादनपरत्वात् । 'यद्यमुष्मिन्' इत्यादि तु विधिशेषः अर्थवादः ।

12.3. "The knowable, the fruit of whose knowledge is immortality, is going to be stated by Me"—with these stimulating words attention was aroused; then it is said:- The knowable is neither the existent nor the non-existent. *Objection:* "After the loud proclamation, 'I shall set forth the knowable', what is stated, namely, that it is neither the existent nor the non-existent, is inconsistent". *Reply:* "No, what is stated is quite consistent. How? In all the Upaniṣads the knowable or Brahman has been expounded in terms that repudiate all determinations. Vide; 'not this'; 'not this' (BU.2.3.6); 'not gross, not subtle' (BU.3.8.8). The reason is that Brahman transcends all verbal expressions". *Objection:* "Surely what is not denoted by the expression 'it is' does not exist. If it is not so expressed, it is to be known as non-existent. It is self-contradictory to assert that something is knowable and yet is not denoted by the expression 'it is'." *Reply:* "It is not non-existent, of course; for it is not the content of a cognition of non-existence." *Objection:* "All cognitions, surely, must conform to the concept of existence or of non-existence. Therefore the knowable also must conform either to the concept of existence or to that of non-existence." *Reply:* "No, being supersensible, It transcends both these concepts. Sensible objects like a pot indeed conform either to the concept of existence or to that of non-existence. But the knowable in question, being supersensible, may be cognized exclusively by means of revelation. Unlike pot, etc., It cannot conform to the concept of existence or non-existence. Hence It is said to be neither existent nor non-existent. As for the remark that the two statements, 'It is a knowable', and that 'It is neither existent nor non-existent', are contradictory, we observe that they are not; vide *Śruti* Ke U.1.3—'It is other than the known and also beyond the unknown.' If, however, you maintain that this *Śruti* also is self-contradictory—as is the statement in TS.6.1.1, 'whether in that world it is or it is not' (i.e. whether the rituals yield any fruit at all), the reply is: not so; for the Kena passage advances a truth that ought to be known, whereas the TS passage is merely glorificatory in character, an *arthavāda*."

12.4. उपपत्तेश्च सदसदादिशब्दैः ब्रह्म नोच्यते इति । सर्वो हि शब्दः अर्थ-प्रकाशनाय प्रत्युक्तः, श्रूयमाणश्च श्रोतृभिः, जातिक्रियागुणसम्बन्धद्वारेण संकेत-ग्रहणसव्यपेक्षः अर्थं प्रत्याययति; न अन्यथा, अदृष्टत्वात् । तत् यथा—'गौः' 'अश्वः' इति वा जातितः, 'पचति' 'पठति' इति वा क्रियातः, 'शुक्लः' 'कृष्णः' इति वा गुणतः, 'धनी' 'गोमान्' इति वा सम्बन्धतः । न तु ब्रह्म जातिमत्, अतः न सदादि-शब्दवाच्यम् । नापि गुणवत्—येन गुणशब्देन उच्येत—निर्गुणत्वात् । नापि क्रिया-शब्दवाच्यं, निष्क्रियत्वात् 'निष्कलं निष्क्रियं शान्तं' (श्वे. उ. ६.१९.) इति श्रुतेः । न च सम्बन्धी, एकत्वात् । अद्वयत्वात्, अविषयत्वात्, आत्मत्वाच्च न केनचित् शब्देन उच्यते इति युक्तम्; 'यतो वाचो निवर्तन्ते' (तै. उ. २.९.१.) इत्यादिश्रुतिभिश्च ॥

12.4. Reason supports the view that Brahman cannot be expressed in terms like existence and non-existence. All words used in a discourse are meant to convey sense to the listeners by means of their link with notions of class, acts, attributes and relations. There is no other means to convey sense except this conventional link. For example, terms like cow and horse convey sense through their link with genera; terms like 'cooks' and 'reads' *via* activities; 'white' and 'black' *via* qualities; 'wealthy' and 'cow-owning' *via* relation. On the other hand, Brahman has no genus; so It cannot be denoted by words like *sat*; nor has It attributes. Again It cannot be expressed by verbs as It is actionless. Vide ŚU.6.19—'Partless, actionless, quiescent.' It is unrelated, for It is one only. Being non-dual, non-objective, and spiritual, it is appropriate that all words should fail to describe It. Hence such *Śruti* as 'Whence words recoil'' (TU.2.9.9).

13.0. सच्छब्दप्रत्ययाविषयत्वात् असत्त्वाशङ्कायां ज्ञेयस्य सर्वप्राणिकरणोपाधि-द्वारेण तदस्तित्वं प्रतिपादयन् तदाशङ्कानिवृत्त्यर्थं आह—

13.0. Being beyond the range of the word *sat* or existent, there arises the doubt that the Knowable is non-existent. To remove this doubt Its existence is affirmed as borne out by the sense-organs, the adjuncts of all living beings:

सर्वतःपाणिपादं तत् सर्वतोऽक्षिशिरोमुखम् ।
सर्वतःश्रुतिमल्लोके सर्वमावृत्य तिष्ठति ॥१३॥

13. On all sides It has hands and feet; on all sides, eyes, heads, and mouths. It has ears on all sides here in this world; It stands encompassing all things.

13.1. सर्वत: इति ॥ सर्वत: पाणिपादं सर्वत: पाणय: पादाश्च अस्य इति सर्वत:-पाणिपादं तत् ज्ञेयम् । सर्वप्राणिकरणोपाधिभि: क्षेत्रज्ञस्य अस्तित्वं विभाव्यते । क्षेत्रज्ञश्च क्षेत्रोपाधित: उच्यते । क्षेत्रं च पाणिपादादिभि: अनेकधा भिन्नम् । क्षेत्रोपाधिभेदकृतं च विशेषजातं मिथ्या एव क्षेत्रज्ञस्य, इति तदपनयनेन ज्ञेयत्वं उक्तं 'न सत्तन्नासदुच्यते' इति । उपाधिकृतं मिथ्यारूपम् अपि अस्तित्वाधिगमाय ज्ञेयधर्मवत् परिकल्प्य उच्यते 'सर्वत:पाणिपादं' इत्यादि । तथा हि सम्प्रदायविदां वचनं —'अध्यारोपापवादाभ्यां निष्प्रपञ्चं प्रपञ्चयते ।' इति । सर्वत्र सर्वदेहावयवत्वेन गम्यमाना: पाणिपादादय: ज्ञेयशक्तिसद्भावनिमित्तस्वकार्या: इति ज्ञेयसद्भावे लिङ्गानि ''ज्ञेयस्य'' इति उपचारत: उच्यन्ते । तथा व्याख्येयं अन्यत् । सर्वत:पाणिपादं तत् ज्ञेयं सर्वतोऽक्षिशिरोमुखं, सर्वत: अक्षीणि शिरांसि मुखानि च यस्य तत् सर्वतोऽक्षिशिरोमुखम्; सर्वत:श्रुतिमत् श्रुति: श्रवणेन्द्रियम्, तत् यस्य तत् श्रुतिमत् लोके प्राणिनिकाये; सर्वं आवृत्य सर्वं व्याप्य तिष्ठति स्थितिं लभते ॥

13.1. The Knowable has 'hand and feet' on all sides. The existence of the field-knower is apprehended by the sense-organs, the adjuncts, of all living beings. It is designated field-knower due to Its adjunct, the field. The field is variously pluralised due to hands, feet, etc. The multiplicity of the particulars due to the plurality of the adjuncts like the bodies, is unreal regarding the field-knower. Therefore, Its status as the Knowable was affirmed through the abolition of the unreal in the words: 'It is said to be neither existent nor non-existent'. Even the unreal form due to adjuncts, as it leads to the knowledge of Its reality, is posited as if it were an attribute of the Knowable in the affirmation 'on all sides It has hands and feet' and so forth. Vide the assertion of traditional scholars: "The acosmic (*Niṣprapañca*) is objectified through the process of superimposition and sublation." 'Hands and feet', cognised universally as parts of bodies and each operating in its own way, due to the potency of the Knowable inherent in them, are the signs of the existence of the Knowable. They are ascribed to the Knowable but figuratively. The rest of the attributes may also be explicated similarly. That Knowable has hands and feet on all sides; also eyes, heads and mouths; It has ears in the whole sphere of living beings. 'Encompassing'—pervading—all, It affirms Its existence.

14.0. उपाधिभूतपाणिपादादीन्द्रियाध्यारोपणात् ज्ञेयस्य तद्वत्ताशङ्का मा भूत् इत्येवमर्थः श्लोकारम्भः—

14.0. The doubt may arise that the knowable has in fact organs like hands and feet. To ward off this doubt and show that they are only adjuncts due to superimposition, the next verse is set forth:

सर्वेन्द्रियगुणाभासं सर्वेन्द्रियविवर्जितम् ।
असक्तं सर्वभृच्चैव निर्गुणं गुणभोक्तृ च ॥१४॥

14. Apparently possessing all sense-organs and their properties, but in truth devoid of them all: unattached and veritably sustaining all; beyond all constituents and yet experiencing them;

14.1. सर्वेन्द्रिय इति ॥ सर्वेन्द्रियगुणाभासं सर्वाणि च तानि इन्द्रियाणि श्रोत्रादीनि बुद्धीन्द्रियकर्मेन्द्रियाख्यानि, अन्तःकरणे च बुद्धिमनसी—ज्ञेयोपाधित्वस्य तुल्यत्वात्—सर्वेन्द्रियग्रहणेन गृह्यन्ते । अपि च, अन्तःकरणोपाधिद्वारेण एव श्रोत्रादीनाम् अपि उपाधित्वं इत्यतः अन्तःकरणबहिष्करणोपाधिभूतैः सर्वेन्द्रियगुणैः अध्यवसायसङ्कल्पश्रवणवचनादिभिः अवभासते इति सर्वेन्द्रियगुणाभासं, सर्वेन्द्रियव्यापारैः व्यापृतम् इव तत् ज्ञेयं इत्यर्थः; 'ध्यायतीव लेलायतीव' [बृ. उ. ४. ३. ७.] इति श्रुतेः । कस्मात् पुनः कारणात् न व्यापृतम् एव इति गृह्यते इति ? अतः आह—सर्वेन्द्रियविवर्जितं सर्वकरणरहितम् इत्यर्थः । अतः न करणव्यापारैः व्यापृतं तत् ज्ञेयम् । यस्तु अयं मन्त्रः—'अपाणिपादो जवनो ग्रहीता पश्यत्यचक्षुः स शृणोत्यकर्णः' [श्वे. उ. ३. १९.] इत्यादिः सः सर्वेन्द्रियोपाधिगुणानुगुण्यभजनशक्तिमत् तत् ज्ञेयं इत्येवं प्रदर्शनार्थः; न तु साक्षादेव जवनादिक्रियावत्त्वप्रदर्शनार्थः । 'अन्धो मणिमविन्दत्' [तै. आ. १. १.] इत्यादिमन्त्रार्थवत् तस्य मन्त्रस्य अर्थः । यस्मात् सर्वकरणवर्जितं तत् ज्ञेयं, तस्मात् असक्तं सर्वसंश्लेषवर्जितम् । यद्यपि एवं, तथापि सर्वभृत् च एव । सदास्पदं हि सर्वं, सर्वत्र सद्बुद्ध्यनुगमात् । न हि मृगतृष्णिकादयः अपि निरास्पदाः भवन्ति । अतः सर्वभृत् सर्वं बिभर्ति इति । स्यात् इदं च अन्यत् ज्ञेयस्य सत्त्वा-

धिगमद्वारम्—निर्गुणं सत्त्वरजस्तमांसि गुणाः तैः वर्जितं तत् ज्ञेयं, तथापि गुणभोक्तृ च गुणानां सत्त्वरजस्तमसां शब्दादिद्वारेण सुखदुःखमोहाकारपरिणतानां भोक्तृ च उपलब्धृ च तत् ज्ञेयं इत्यर्थः ॥

किञ्च—

14.1. 'All sense-organs' are ear, etc., (both cognitive and conative); the inner organ consists of intellect and mind. All these, constituting the adjuncts of the Knowable, are to be understood by the expression '*sarvendriya*'. Moreover, the senses become the adjuncts of the knowable only through the mediation of the inner sense. Therefore, through these adjuncts, constituted of the powers of all sense-organs, internal and external, such as determination, imagination, audition, articulation, etc., the Knowable appears. It apparently operates by means of all sense-organs. Vide: "It meditates, as it were, moves about, as it were" (BU.4.3.7). Why not then take it that in truth It operates? It is devoid of all sense-organs, i.e., It owns nothing like instruments at all. Therefore know that the knowable does not operate by means of the senses. Vide ŚU 3.19: "Devoid of hands and feet, He is quick, a grasper. Eyeless, He sees; earless, He hears." This conveys the idea that the Knowable is endowed with the power of conforming to the characteristics of all adjuncts—i.e., all sense-organs—and not that It directly performs functions like movements, etc. The sense of this *mantra* is like that of T.A.1.11. "The blind man won a gem." Since the Knowable is devoid of all sense-organs, It is 'unattached'—free from all kinds of contacts. Nevertheless It sustains all; for, all things are rooted in the Existent, and the idea of existence pervades all things. Even phenomena like mirages are not ungrounded. Hence the knowable sustains all. There is an additional factor leading to the apprehension of the existence of the Knowable. It is beyond the range of the three constituents, *sattva* etc. At the same time It experiences them all via the perception of their transformations like pleasure, pain and delusion.

And,

बहिरन्तश्च भूतानामचरं चरमेव च ।
सूक्ष्मत्वात्तदविज्ञेयं दूरस्थं चान्तिके च तत् ॥१५॥

15. It is both outside and inside beings; it is what moves not and what moves. Being subtle, It is hard to know; It is far off as well as near.

15.1. बहिः इति ॥ बहिः त्वक्पर्यन्तं देहं आत्मत्वेन अविद्याकल्पितं अपेक्ष्य तम् एव अवधिं कृत्वा बहिः उच्यते । तथा प्रत्यगात्मानं अपेक्ष्य देहम् एव अवधिं कृत्वा अन्तः उच्यते । 'बहिरन्तश्च' इत्युक्ते मध्ये अभावे प्राप्ते इदं उच्यते—अचरं चरम् एव च, यत् चराचरं देहाभासम् अपि, तत् एव ज्ञेयं, यथा रज्जुसर्पाभासः । यदि अचरं चरम् एव च स्यात् व्यवहारविषयं सर्वं ज्ञेयं, किमर्थं "इदं" इति सर्वैः न विज्ञेयं इति ? उच्यते—सत्यं सर्वाभासं; तथापि व्योमवत् सूक्ष्मम् । अतः सूक्ष्मत्वात् स्वेन रूपेण तत् ज्ञेयम् अपि अविज्ञेयं अविदुषाम् । विदुषां तु—'आत्मैवेदं सर्वम्' [बृ. उ. २.४.६.], 'ब्रह्मैवेदं सर्वम्' (बृ. उ. २.५.१.) इत्यादिप्रमाणतः नित्यं विज्ञातम् । अविज्ञाततया दूरस्थं वर्षसहस्रकोटयाऽपि अविदुषां अप्राप्यत्वात् । अन्तिके च तत्, आत्मत्वात् विदुषाम् ॥

किंच—

15.1. With reference to the body including the skin, that is mistaken for the Self due to nescience, the term 'outside' is used. Similarly in relation to the inner self, regarding this very body as a limit, the term 'inside' is also used. These terms suggest a vacuum in between. Hence the terms 'what moves not and what moves.' The physical appearance, resembling the illusory rope-snake, is also that very Knowable. If both what moves not and what moves—all empirical phenomena—are that Knowable, why are they not grasped as such by all? The answer is: True, It alone appears as everything; still like the sky It is subtle. Being subtle, though Knowable in Itself, to the ignorant It is unknowable. To the enlightened, however, It is eternally known. Vide: "Self alone is all this." (BU.2.4.6); "Brahman alone is all this," (BU.2.5.1) etc. As unknown It is far away, beyond the reach of the ignorant even for millions of years. To the wise, being their very Self, It is near.

Also,

अविभक्तं च भूतेषु विभक्तमिव च स्थितम् ।
भूतभर्तृ च तज्ज्ञेयं ग्रसिष्णु प्रभविष्णु च ॥१६॥

16. In all It abides undivided; yet It seems divided; the knowable is the sustainer of being, their consumer, and generator, too.

16.1. अविभक्तं इति ॥ अविभक्तं च प्रतिदेहं व्योमवत् तत् एकम् । भूतेषु सर्वप्राणिषु विभक्तम् इव च स्थितं, देहेषु एव विभाव्यमानत्वात् । भूतभर्तृ च भूतानि बिभर्ति इति तत् ज्ञेयं भूतभर्तृ च स्थितिकाले । प्रलयकाले च ग्रसिष्णु ग्रसनशीलम् । उत्पत्तिकाले प्रभविष्णु च प्रभवनशीलं, यथा रज्ज्वादिः सर्पादेः मिथ्याकल्पितस्य ॥१

16.1. In each body It is undivided and one like space. In all living beings It abides, but, as it were, divided; for, only in bodies It appears. That knowable is what sustains beings during their existence; in dissolution It consumes them, and at the time of manifestation, It originates them illusorily, as do ropes, etc., the rope-snake and so forth.

17.0. किंच—सर्वत्र विद्यमानम् अपि सत् न उपलभ्यते चेत्, ज्ञेयं तमः तर्हि ? न । किं तर्हि ?

17.0. And if it is not apprehended though universally present, is that Knowable any better than darkness? No, on the contrary,

ज्योतिषामपि तज्ज्योतिस्तमसः परमुच्यते ।
ज्ञानं ज्ञेयं ज्ञानगम्यं हृदि सर्वस्य विष्ठितम् ॥१७॥

17. It is the Light of all lights; It is said to be beyond darkness. The knowable is knowledge, accessible through knowledge, and entrenched in the hearts of all.

17.1. ज्योतिषां इति ॥ ज्योतिषां आदित्यादीनां अपि तत् ज्ञेयं ज्योतिः ।

आत्मचैतन्यज्योतिषा इद्धानि हि आदित्यादीनि ज्योतीषि दीप्यन्ते, 'येन सूर्यस्तपति तेजसेद्धः' [तै. ब्रा. ३.१२.९.], 'तस्य भासा सर्वमिदं विभाति' [श्वे. उ. ६.१४.] इत्यादिमन्त्रेभ्यः; स्मृतेश्च इहैव—'यदादित्यगतं तेजः' [१५.१२.] इत्यादेः तमसः अज्ञानात् परं असंस्पृष्टं उच्यते । ज्ञानादेः दुःखसम्पादनबुद्ध्या प्राप्तावसादस्य उत्तम्भनार्थं आह—ज्ञानं अमानित्वादि [१३.७–११.]; ज्ञेयं 'ज्ञेयं यत् तत् प्रवक्ष्यामि' [१३.१२–१७.] इत्यादिना उक्तं; ज्ञानगम्यं, ज्ञेयम् एव ज्ञातं सत् ज्ञानफलम् इति ज्ञानगम्यं उच्यते; ज्ञायमानं तु तत् ज्ञेयम् । तत् एतत् त्रयमपि हृदि बुद्धौ सर्वस्य प्राणिजातस्य विष्ठितं विशेषेण स्थितम् । तत्रैव हि एतत् त्रय विभाव्यते ॥

17.1. That knowable is the Light of all lights such as the sun. These latter shine only when they are kindled by the spiritual fire of the Self. Vide the following *mantras*: 'Kindled by which splendour the sun burns (TB.3.12.9). All this shines by Its light (ŚU.6.14).' Also there is *smṛti* in our text: 'That splendour present in the sun' (BG.15.12). It is said to be beyond the darkness of ignorance, i.e., untouched by it. In order to encourage Arjuna who was dejected at the thought that knowledge, etc., are hard to win, the Lord says: Knowledge (13.7–11), the knowable (13.12–10) and what is accessible to knowledge (the knowable as known)—all these three are entrenched in the hearts of all. The heart is the intellect; these three factors are rightly distinguished only in the intellect.

18.0. यथोक्तार्थोपसंहारार्थः अयं श्लोकः आरभ्यते—

18.0. The following verse concludes the topic on hand:

इति क्षेत्रं तथा ज्ञानं ज्ञेयं चोक्तं समासतः ।
मद्भक्त एतद्विज्ञाय मद्भावायोपपद्यते ॥१८॥

18. Thus have the field, knowledge, and the knowable been briefly set forth. Knowing this, My devotee becomes fit for assimilation to Me.

18.1. इति क्षेत्रं इति ॥ इति एवं क्षेत्रं महाभूतादि धृत्यन्तं [१३.५–६], तथा ज्ञानं अमानित्वादि तत्त्वज्ञानार्थदर्शनपर्यन्तं [१३.७–११], ज्ञेयं च 'ज्ञेयं यत् तत्'

[१३.१२] इत्यादि 'तमसः परमुच्यते' [१३.१७] इत्येवमन्तं, उक्तं समासतः संक्षेपतः । एतावान् हि सर्वः वेदार्थः गीतार्थश्च उपसंहृत्य उक्तः । अस्मिन् सम्यग्दर्शने कः अधिक्रियते इति ? उच्यते—मद्भक्तः मयि परमेश्वरे सर्वज्ञे परमगुरौ वासुदेवे समर्पितसर्वात्मभावः यत् पश्यति शृणोति स्पृशति वा "सर्वमेव भगवान् वासुदेवः" इत्येवंग्रहाविष्टबुद्धिः मद्भक्तः सः एतत् यथोक्तं सम्यग्दर्शनं विज्ञाय, मद्भावाय मम भावः परमात्मभावः तस्मै मद्भावाय उपपद्यते—घटते, मोक्षं गच्छति ॥

18.1. Thus have the field (13.5–6), knowledge (13.7–11) and the knowable (13.12–17) been briefly set forth. So far the entire contents of both the Vedas and the Gītā have been briefly stated. Who is fit to grasp this right perception? "My devotee—he who has surrendered his self in its totality to Me, the supreme Lord, the omniscient and supreme Teacher, Vāsudeva; he who has the intellectual conviction that whatever is seen, heard, or touched is the blessed Lord Vāsudeva. Winning the perception thus set forth, My devotee becomes fit to be assimilated to My status, the status of the supreme Self; he attains liberation.

19.0. तत्र सप्तमे अध्याये ईश्वरस्य द्वे प्रकृती उपन्यस्ते परापरे क्षेत्रक्षेत्रज्ञलक्षणे; 'एतद्योनीनि भूतानि' [७.६.] इति च उक्तम् । क्षेत्रक्षेत्रज्ञप्रकृतिद्वययोनित्वं कथं भूतानां इति ? अयं अर्थः अधुना उच्यते —

19.0. In chapter VII, two *prakṛtis* or powers of God were formulated, a superior and an inferior one, constituting the field and the field-knower. Further, it was affirmed that all beings are born of them. (7.6) The question how all beings are born of these two powers—the field and the field-knower—is answered below:

प्रकृतिं पुरुषं चैव विद्ध्यनादी उभावपि ।
विकारांश्च गुणांश्चैव विद्धि प्रकृतिसम्भवान् ॥१९॥

19. Know both Prakrti and Puruṣa—Power and Spirit—

to be beginningless; also know that transformations and the constituents are born of Prakṛti.

19.1. प्रकृतिं इति ॥ प्रकृतिं पुरुषं च एव ईश्वरस्य प्रकृती, तौ प्रकृतिपुरुषौ उभौ अपि अनादी विद्धि, न विद्यते आदिः ययोः तौ अनादी । नित्येश्वरत्वात् ईश्वरस्य तत्प्रकृत्योः अपि युक्तं नित्यत्वेन भवितुम् । प्रकृतिद्वयवत्त्वम् एव हि ईश्वरस्य ईश्वरत्वं, याभ्यां प्रकृतिभ्यां ईश्वरः जगदुत्पत्तिस्थितिप्रलयहेतुः । ते द्वे अनादी सत्यौ संसारस्य कारणम् ॥

19.1. Know that both *prakṛti* and *puruṣa* are God's powers and that they are without beginning. Since God is eternal, His powers should also be without beginning. The godhood of God consists in His having these powers by means of which He originates, sustains and dissolves the world. These beginningless powers cause the world.

19.2. "न आदी अनादी" इति तत्पुरुषसमासं केचित् वर्णयन्ति । तेन हि किल (केवलेश्व०) ईश्वरस्य कारणत्वं सिध्यति । यदि पुनः प्रकृतिपुरुषौ एव नित्यौ स्यातां, तत्कृतम् एव जगत्, न ईश्वरस्य जगतः कर्तृत्वं इति ॥

तत् असत्; प्राक् प्रकृतिपुरुषयोः उत्पत्तेः ईशितव्याभावात् ईश्वरस्य अनीश्वरत्वप्रसङ्गात्, संसारस्य निर्निमित्तत्वे अनिर्मोक्षप्रसंगात्, शास्त्रानर्थक्यप्रसङ्गात्, बन्धमोक्षाभावप्रसङ्गात् च । नित्यत्वे पुनः ईश्वरप्रकृत्योः सर्वं एतत् उपपन्नं भवेत् । कथम् ?

विकारान् च गुणान् च वक्ष्यमाणान् विकारान् बुद्ध्यादिदेहेन्द्रियान्तान् गुणान् च सुखदुःखमोहप्रत्ययाकारपरिणतान् वक्ष्यमाणान् विद्धि जानीहि प्रकृतिसम्भवान्, प्रकृतिः ईश्वरस्य विकारकारणशक्तिः त्रिगुणात्मिका माया, सा सम्भवः येषां विकाराणां गुणानां च तान् विकारान् गुणान् च विद्धि जानीहि प्रकृतिसम्भवान् प्रकृतिपरिणामान् ॥

19.2. Some construe the compound *anādī* as a *tatpuruṣa*, meaning without beginnings. They hold that thus only can God be posited as the cause of the world. "If *prakṛti* and *puruṣa*, in themselves, are without beginning, and the world, their product, God won't be the maker of the world." This argument is not sound; for, before these two, Power and Spirit, arise, God won't be God, as there won't be anything of which He is the Lord;

thus He won't be God at all. Thus also arises the contingency of non-liberation, since transmigratory life becomes uncaused. The *śāstras* thus become futile and finally there would be neither bondage nor liberation. On the other hand, when both God and His power are held to be eternal, all this will become consistent. How? 'Transformations and constitutents' to be recounted presently; intellect, etc., up to body and sense-organs; apprehensions of pleasure, pain and delusion which are the transformations of *guṇas*—know these to be born of *prakṛti*. *Prakṛti* is God's causal power to produce transformations; it is *māyā* whose essence is the three constituents. This power gives rise to the transformations and *guṇas*. These latter are born of the transformations of *prakṛti*.

20.0. के पुनः ते विकाराः गुणाः च प्रकृतिसम्भवाः इति ? आह—

20.0. Now, what are these *Prakṛti*-born transformations and constituents? Answer:

कार्यकरणकर्तृत्वे हेतुः प्रकृतिरुच्यते ।
पुरुषः सुखदुःखानां भोक्तृत्वे हेतुरुच्यते ॥२०॥

20. Prakṛti is said to be the cause that accomplishes the effects and the instruments (in the form of the body and the senses); Puruṣa (spirit) is said to be the cause of the experience of pleasures and pains.

20.1. कार्य इति ॥ कार्यकरणकर्तृत्वे—कार्यं शरीरं, करणानि तत्स्थानि त्रयोदश । देहारंभकाणि भूतानि, पञ्च विषयाश्च प्रकृतिसम्भवाः विकाराः पूर्वोक्ताः इह कार्यग्रहणेन गृह्यन्ते । गुणाश्च प्रकृतिसम्भवाः सुखदुःखमोहात्मकाः करणाश्रयत्वात् करणग्रहणेन गृह्यन्ते । तेषां कार्यकरणानां कर्तृत्वं उत्पादकत्वं यत् तत् कार्यकरणकर्तृत्वं, तस्मिन् कार्यकरणकर्तृत्वे हेतुः कारणं आरम्भकत्वेन प्रकृतिः उच्यते । एवं कार्यकरणकर्तृत्वेन संसारस्य कारणं प्रकृतिः । 'कार्यकारणकर्तृत्वे' इत्यस्मिन्नपि पाठे—कार्यं, यत् यस्य परिणामः तत् तस्य कार्यं विकारः, विकारि कारणं, तयोः विकारविकारिणोः कार्यकारणयोः कर्तृत्वे—इति तानि एव कार्यकारणानि उच्यन्ते । अथवा—षोडश विकाराः कार्यं, सप्त प्रकृतिविकृतयः कारणं, तेषां कर्तृत्वे हेतुः

प्रकृतिः उच्यते, आरम्भकत्वेन एव । पुरुषश्च संसारस्य कारणं यथा स्यात् तत् उच्यते—पुरुषः जीवः क्षेत्रज्ञः भोक्ता इति पर्यायः, सुखदुःखानां भोग्यानां भोक्तृत्वे उपलब्धृत्वे हेतुः उच्यते ॥

20.1. The 'effect' is the body; the 'instruments' are the thirteen senses lodged in the body. The five elements forming the body, the five objects, in fact all the *Prakṛti*-born transformations mentioned earlier, are here referred in their toality as 'effect'.' The *Prakṛti*-born constituents, which are essentially of the nature of pleasure, pain and delusion, are mentioned as the 'instruments', as these are grounded in the senses. To produce 'effects' and 'instruments' is what is meant by being their cause. *Prakṛti* is said to be the 'cause' that produces them. Thus by producing effects and instruments, *Prakṛti* is the cause of transmigratory life. If the reading is, "being the cause of effects and causes", 'effect' will be the transformation of that which is its cause. What is transformed is the cause. As the maker of these two—effect and cause—the very same *Prakṛti* is set forth as cause. Or, the sixteen transformations (consisting of the ten senses, the five sense objects and the mind) are the effects; the seven transformations of *prakṛti* (like *Mahattatva*, *Ahankara* and the five sense objects) are the causes. *Prakṛti* is said to be the cause, being the maker of them all. How the *Puruṣa* or Spirit is the cause of transmigratory life, is being explained. The *Puruṣa*, the *Jīva*, the field-knower, the experiencer—all these are synonymous. He is said to be the cause of experiencing or of knowing objects, i.e. pleasure and pain.

20.2. कथं पुनः अनेन कार्यकरणकर्तृत्वेन सुखदुःखभोक्तृत्वेन च प्रकृतिपुरुषयोः संसारकारणत्वं उच्यते इति ?

अत्र उच्यते—कार्यकरणसुखदुःखरूपेण हेतुफलात्मना प्रकृतेः परिणामाभावे, पुरुषस्य च चेतनस्य असति तदुपलब्धृत्वे, कुतः संसारः स्यात् ? यदा पुनः कार्यकरण-सुखदुःखस्वरूपेण हेतुफलात्मना परिणतया प्रकृत्या भोग्यया पुरुषस्य तद्विपरीतस्य भोक्तृत्वेन अविद्यारूपः संयोगः स्यात्, तदा संसारः स्यात् इति । अतः यत् प्रकृतिपुरुषयोः कार्यकरणकर्तृत्वेन सुखदुःखभोक्तृत्वेन च संसारकारणत्वं उक्तं, तत् युक्तं उक्तम् ॥

कः पुनः अयं संसारः नाम ?
सुखदुःखसंभोगः संसारः। पुरुषस्य सुखदुःखानां संभोक्तृत्वं संसारित्वं इति ॥

20.2. How can Spirit and Power (*puruṣa* and *prakṛti*) be said to cause transmigratory life by experiencing pleasures and pains and by accomplishing 'effects and instruments'? It is explained as follows:- If *prakṛti* is not transformed as effects and instruments or body, sense-organs, pleasure and pain, and if Spirit does not cognize them, how can there be transmigratory life? But when there is the nescience-born contact of the subject or experiencer (*Puruṣa*) with the opposite factor, namely the object or *Prakṛti* which transforms into various experienceable effects,—then transmigratory life may ensue. Hence it is reasonable to affirm that *prakṛti* and *puruṣa* accomplish effects and instruments on the one hand, and the experience of pleasures and pains, on the other. Thus they become causes of transmigratory life. Now, what exactly is this transmigratory life? It is the experience of pleasure and pain. Spirit's status as transmigrator consists in his experience of pleasures and pains.

21.0. यत् पुरुषस्य सुखदुःखानां भोक्तृत्वं इति संसारित्वं उक्तं, तस्य तत् किंनिमित्तं इति ? उच्यते—

21.0. Why does *Puruṣa* experience pleasures and pains and suffer transmigration?

पुरुषः प्रकृतिस्थो हि भुङ्क्ते प्रकृतिजान् गुणान् ।
कारणं गुणसङ्गोऽस्य सदसद्योनिजन्मसु ॥२१॥

21. Puruṣa lodged in Prakṛti experiences the constituents born of Prakṛti. The cause of his birth in wombs, good and evil, is his clinging to these constituents.

21.1. पुरुषः इति ॥ पुरुषः भोक्ता प्रकृतिस्थः प्रकृतौ अविद्यालक्षणायां कार्यकरणरूपेण परिणतायां स्थितः प्रकृतिस्थः—प्रकृतिं आत्मत्वेन गतः इत्येतत्—हि

यस्मात् तस्मात् भुङ्क्ते—उपलभते इत्यर्थः—प्रकृतिजान् प्रकृतितः जातान् सुख-दुःखमोहाकाराभिव्यक्तान् गुणान् "सुखी, दुःखी, मूढः, पण्डितः अहं" इत्येवम् । सत्याम् अपि अविद्यायां सुखदुःखमोहेषु गुणेषु भुज्यमानेषु यः सङ्गः आत्मभावः, सः प्रधानं कारणं अस्य पुरुषस्य जन्मनः 'स यथाकामो भवति तत्क्रतुर्भवति' [बृ. उ. ४.४.५.] इत्यादिश्रुतेः । तदेतत् आह—कारणं हेतुः गुणसङ्गः गुणेषु सङ्गः अस्य पुरुषस्य भोक्तुः सदसद्योनिजन्मसु, सच्च असच्च सदसती, तयोः योनयः सदसद्योनयः, तासु सदसद्योनिषु जन्मानि सदसद्योनिजन्मानि, तेषु सदसद्योनिजन्मसु विषयभूतेषु कारणं गुणसङ्गः । अथवा—सदसद्योनिजन्मसु अस्य संसारस्य कारणं गुणसङ्गः, इति संसारपदं अध्याहार्यम् । सद्योनयः देवादियोनयः । असद्योनयः पश्वादियोनयः । सामर्थ्यात् सदसद्योनयः मनुष्ययोनयोऽपि अविरुद्धाः द्रष्टव्याः ॥

21.1. *Puruṣa*, the experiencer lodged in *prakṛti*, which is nescience and which is transformed into effects and instruments, experiences or cognises the constituents; for, he mistakes *prakṛti* for his very self. The constituents manifest themselves as pleasure, pain and delusion. He thinks, "I am happy, miserable, deluded or learned." In this context of nescience, the main cause of the Spirit's birth or embodiment is attachment or conceit of being the self regarding the constituents experienced as pleasure, pain and delusions. Vide: "According to his desires he wills (BU.4.4.5)." The idea is expressed in the words—'the cause of his birth in wombs, good and evil, is the clinging to constituents.' Or, stressing on empirical life, it may be interpreted that the cause of empirical life resulting in births in wombs, good and evil, is the clinging to the constituents. 'Good wombs' means birth as Devas or Celestials; 'evil wombs' means birth as beasts, etc. 'Partly good and partly evil wombs' may point to human births too.

21.2. एतत् उक्तं भवति—प्रकृतिस्थत्वाख्या अविद्या, गुणेषु च सङ्गः कामः, संसारस्य कारणमिति । तच्च परिवर्जनाय उच्यते । अस्य च निवृत्तिकारणं—ज्ञानवैराग्ये ससंन्यासे—गीताशास्त्रे प्रसिद्धम् । तच्च ज्ञानं पुरस्तात् उपन्यस्तं क्षेत्रक्षेत्रज्ञविषयम् 'यत् ज्ञात्वाऽमृतमश्नुते' [१३.१२.] इति । उक्तं च अन्यापोहेन अतद्धर्माध्यारोपेण च [१३.१३.] ॥

21.2. The gist of it is as follows: The cause of empirical life is nescience meaning lodgement in *Prakṛti* and the clinging to the constituents or desire. This is mentioned so that it may be shunned. What dispels it is knowledge and dispassion together with renunciation. This truth has been proclaimed in the Gītā's system of thought. The relevant knowledge has already been set forth (13.12) as referring to the field and the field-knower—knowledge through which immortality is won. It has been set forth through passages that first reject all entities other than that Truth, and next by passages superimposing on It attributes not Its own.

22.0. तस्यैव पुनः साक्षात् निर्देशः क्रियते—

22.0. Again He, the Spirit, is directly described:

उपद्रष्टाऽनुमन्ता च भर्ता भोक्ता महेश्वरः ।
परमात्मेति चाप्युक्तो देहेऽस्मिन् पुरुषः परः ॥२२॥

22. Close Observer, Giver of sanction, Sustainer, Experiencer, the pre-eminent Lord, supreme Self—thus is styled the supreme Spirit in (the human) body.

22.1. उपद्रष्टा इति ॥ उपद्रष्टा समीपस्थः सन् द्रष्टा स्वयं अव्यापृतः । यथा ऋत्विग्यजमानेषु यज्ञकर्मव्यापृतेषु तटस्थः अन्यः अव्यापृतः यज्ञविद्याकुशलः ऋत्विग्यजमानव्यापारगुणदोषाणां ईक्षिता, तद्वत् च कार्यकरणव्यापारेषु अव्यापृतः अन्यः तद्विलक्षणः तेषां कार्यकरणानां सव्यापाराणां सामीप्येन द्रष्टा उपद्रष्टा । अथवा—देहचक्षुर्मनोबुद्ध्यात्मानः द्रष्टारः; तेषां बाह्यः द्रष्टा देहः, ततः आरभ्य अन्तरतमश्च प्रत्यक् समीपे आत्मा द्रष्टा, यतः परः अन्तरतमः नास्ति द्रष्टा; सः अतिशयसामीप्येन द्रष्टृत्वात् उपद्रष्टा स्यात् । यज्ञोपद्रष्टृवत् वा सर्वविषयीकरणात् उपद्रष्टा । अनुमन्ता च—अनुमोदनं अनुमननं, कुर्वत्सु तत्क्रियासु परितोषः, तत्कर्ता अनुमन्ता च । अथवा, अनुमन्ता—कार्यकरणप्रवृत्तिषु स्वयं अप्रवृत्तोऽपि प्रवृत्तः इव तदनुकूलः विभाव्यते, तेन अनुमन्ता । अथवा—प्रवृत्तान् स्वव्यापारेषु तत्साक्षिभूतः कदाचिदपि न निवारयति इति अनुमन्ता । भर्ता—भरणं नाम देहेन्द्रियमनोबुद्धीनां संहतानां चैतन्यात्मपारार्थ्येन निमित्तभूतेन चैतन्याभासानां यत् स्वरूपधारणं तत् चैतन्यात्मकृतम् एव इति भर्ता आत्मा उच्यते । भोक्ता—अग्न्युष्णवत् नित्यचैतन्यस्वरूपेण बुद्धेः सुखदुःखमोहात्मकाः प्रत्ययाः सर्वविषयविषयाः चैतन्यात्मग्रस्ताः इव जायमानाः विभक्ताः विभाव्यन्ते इति भोक्ता आत्मा उच्यते । महेश्वरः—सर्वात्मत्वात् स्वतन्त्रत्वाच्च महांश्च असौ ईश्वरश्च इति महेश्वरः । परमात्मा—

देहादीनां बुद्ध्यन्तानां, प्रत्यगात्मत्वेन परिकल्पितानां अविद्यया, परमः उपद्रष्टृत्वादिलक्षणः आत्मा इति परमात्मा । सः अतः "परमात्मा" इत्यनेन शब्देन च अपि उक्तः कथितः श्रुतौ । क्व असौ ?—अस्मिन् देहे पुरुषः परः अव्यक्तात्, "उत्तमः पुरुषस्त्वन्यः परमात्मेत्युदाहृतः" [१५.१७.] इति यः वक्ष्यमाणः ॥

22.1. 'Close Observer'—one who, though inactive, still observes, standing by. Just as, while the officiating priests and the sacrificer busy themselves with sacrificial activities, another, an expert in the science of sacrifice, observes their merits or flaws, without participating in them, He observes them all, being close to them. Or, the observers are the body, the eye, mind, intellect and self, the body being the outermost. Proceeding inwards therefrom, the innermost observer is the Self, none else being closer or more inward. Thus this most inward observer is styled 'close Observer'. Or, like the observer in the sacrificial ceremony, He observes all objects. Also He accords sanction or approval to those who perform and to their actions. Hence He is their approver. Or, though He does not participate in the activities of the body and its instruments, He seems to do so, promoting them all. Hence He is the 'Sanctioner'. Or, never thwarting those who act, but witnessing them all—He is the 'sanctioner'. 'Sustainer'—sustentation is the maintenance of the apparently intelligent forms of body, senses, mind and intellect held together to subserve the Spirit. It is accomplished by the intelligent Self; so He is called the 'Sustainer'. The Self is styled 'Experiencer', because due to It, the mental states like pleasures, pains, and delusions, which refer to objective forms, get intelligised as it were at the source itself and are apprehended distinctively. As He is the Self of all and independent, He is at once pre-eminent and Lord. He is supreme and the close observer of entities like the body, etc., which are mistaken, due to nescience, for the Self. In scriptures He is also styled the supreme Self. 'Who?'—the supreme Spirit dwelling in the body; He is beyond the Unmanifest. In chapter 15, verse 17, He will be described as the supreme Spirit, the Other, the supreme Self.

23.0. 'क्षेत्रज्ञं चापि मां विद्धि' [१३.२.] इति उपन्यस्तः, व्याख्याय उपसंहृतश्च, तं एतं यथोक्तलक्षणं आत्मानम्—

23.0. In 13.2 the Self was introduced in the words, 'Know Me also as the field-knower' and, later, fully explicated. This Self thus set forth,

य एवं वेत्ति पुरुषं प्रकृतिं च गुणैः सह ।
सर्वथा वर्तमानोऽपि न स भूयोऽभिजायते ॥२३॥

23. Whoso knows thus the Spirit and His power together with the constituents, is no more born, no matter how he fares (in the world).

23.1. य एवं इति ॥ यः एवं यथोक्तेन प्रकारेण वेत्ति पुरुषं साक्षात् आत्मभावेन "अयं अहं अस्मि" इति, प्रकृतिं च यथोक्तां अविद्यालक्षणां गुणैः स्वविकारैः सह निवर्तितां अभावं आपादितां विद्यया, सर्वथा सर्वप्रकारेण वर्तमानः अपि न सः भूयः पुनः पतिते अस्मिन् विद्वच्छरीरे देहान्तराय न अभिजायते न उत्पद्यते, देहान्तरं न गृह्णाति इत्यर्थः । अपि शब्दात् किमु वक्तव्यं स्ववृत्तस्थः न जायते ?— इति अभिप्रायः ॥

23.1. Whoso knows, as has been set forth, the Spirit directly as Self—as 'here am I'—and also the power or *Prakṛti* as nescience, together with the constituents that are its own modifications is no more born, is no more embodied after the fall of the knower's body. *Api* ('though', 'no matter how') implies that for one who does not deviate from his proper being, the question of re-embodiment does not arise at all.

23.2. ननु—यद्यपि ज्ञानोत्पत्त्यनन्तरं पुनर्जन्माभाव उक्तः, तथाऽपि प्राक् ज्ञानोत्पत्तेः कृतानां कर्मणां, उत्तरकालभाविनां च, यानि च अतिक्रान्तानेक जन्मकृतानि तेषां च, फलं अदत्त्वा नाशः न युक्तः इति, स्युः त्रीणि जन्मानि, कृतविप्रणाशो हि न युक्तः इति, यथा फले प्रवृत्तानां आरब्धजन्मनां कर्मणाम् न च कर्मणां विशेषः अवगम्यते । तस्मात् त्रिप्रकाराणि अपि कर्माणि त्रीणि जन्मानि आरभेरन्; संहतानि वा सर्वाणि एकं जन्म आरभेरन् । अन्यथा कृतविप्रणाशे सर्वत्र अनाश्वा-

सप्रसङ्गः, शास्त्रानर्थक्यं च स्यात् । इत्यतः इदं अयुक्तं उक्तं 'न सः भूयोऽभि-जायते इति ॥

न; 'क्षीयन्ते चास्य कर्माणि' [मु. उ. २.२.८.], 'ब्रह्म वेद ब्रह्मैव भवति' [मुं. उ. ३.२.९.], 'तस्य तावदेव चिरं' [छां. उ. ६.१४.२.], 'इषीकातूलवत् सर्वाणि कर्माणि प्रदूयन्ते' [छां. उ. ५.२४.३. अर्थतः अनुवादः] इत्यादिश्रुतिशतेभ्यः उक्तः विदुषः सर्वकर्मदाहः । इहापि च उक्तः 'यथैधांसि' [४.३७.] इत्यादिना सर्वकर्मदाहः वक्ष्यति च [१८.६६.] उपपत्तेश्च—अविद्याकामक्लेशबीजनिमित्तानि हि कर्माणि जन्मान्तराङ्कुरं आरभन्ते; इहापि च "साहङ्काराभिसन्धीनि कर्माणि फलारम्भकाणि, न इतराणि" इति तत्र तत्र भगवता उक्तम् ।

बीजान्यग्न्युपदग्धानि न रोहन्ति यथा पुनः ।
ज्ञानदग्धैस्तथा क्लेशैर्नात्मा सम्पद्यते पुनः ॥ [वनप. २००.११०.] इति च ॥

[मुं. उ. ३.२.९.], 'तस्य तावदेव चिरं' [छां. उ. ६.१४.२.], 'इषीकातूलवत् सर्वाणि

23.2. *Objection:* As regards the absence of rebirth after the dawn of knowledge, it may be argued that even for the knower three births are inevitable; for, it is not reasonable to hold that actions done before the dawn of knowledge, actions done after it, and actions done in the many past lives will all perish without producing their appropriate results. The principle involved is that nothing done can be blotted out. The case is similar to those actions which have produced the current life and have started to yield their results. In this respect no distinction may be drawn among actions. Therefore, the three kinds of actions adverted to must generate three births, or, jointly, they may produce one birth. Otherwise, due to the violation of the principle of imperishability of accomplished actions, faith in law will suffer and the *śāstraic* mandates may prove futile. Hence it is unreasonable to hold that he is born no more.

Reply: No; that all actions of the knower are wholly consumed has been inclucated in hundreds of passages in the *śruti*. Vide: 'and his actions perish' MU.2.2.8; 'whoso knows Brahman becomes Brahman' (Ibid.3.2.9); 'he waits only till' (CU.6.14.2); 'all actions are consumed like a reed' (CU.5.24.3). In BG, too, it has been affirmed that all actions are burned up like fuel (4.37), and the same will be reaffirmed in 18.66. Besides, reason supports this view. Only those actions that are caused by the seeds of nescience—desires, afflictions—

generate the sprout of a new birth. On several occasions the Lord has declared in the Gītā that only egoistic and desire-prompted actions originate fruits and not others. Vide: 'Just as seeds consumed in fire do not germinate, afflictions consumed in the fire of knowledge no longer lead to the self's embodiment'. (Vanaparva 200.110).

23.3. अस्तु तावत् ज्ञानोत्पत्तेः उत्तरकालकृतानां कर्मणां ज्ञानेन दाहः, ज्ञान-सहभावित्वात् । न तु इह जन्मनि ज्ञानोत्पत्तेः प्राक् कृतानां कर्मणां अतीतानेकजन्मकृतानां च दाहः युक्तः ॥

न; 'सर्वकर्माणि' (४.३७) इति विशेषणात् ।

ज्ञानोत्तरकालभाविनाम् एव सर्वकर्मणां इति चेत्—

न; सङ्कोचे कारणानुपपत्तेः ।

यत्तु उक्तं "यथा वर्तमानजन्मारम्भकाणि कर्माणि न क्षीयन्ते फलदानाय प्रवृत्तानि एव सत्यपि ज्ञाने, तथा अनारब्धफलानामपि कर्मणां क्षयः न युक्तः"—इति तत् असत् । कथं?—तेषां मुक्तेषुवत् प्रवृत्तफलत्वात् । यथा पूर्वं लक्ष्यवेधाय मुक्तः इषुः धनुषः लक्ष्यवेधोत्तरकालमपि आरब्धवेगक्षयात् पतनेन एव निवर्तते, एवं शरीरारम्भकं कर्म शरीरस्थितिप्रयोजने निवृत्ते अपि, आ संस्कारवेगक्षयात् पूर्ववत् प्रवर्तते एव । यथा सः एव इषुः प्रवृत्तिनिमित्तानारब्धवेगस्तु अमुक्तः धनुषि प्रयुक्तोऽपि उपसंह्रियते, तथा अनारब्धफलानि कर्माणि स्वाश्रयस्थानि एव तत्त्वज्ञानेन निर्बीजीक्रियन्ते इति, पतिते अस्मिन् विद्वच्छरीरे 'न स भूयोऽभिजायते' इति, युक्तम् एव उक्तम् इति सिद्धम् ॥

23.3. *Objection:* "Let us grant that actions done after the dawn of knowledge are consumed in the fire of knowledge since they are accompanied by knowledge; but those done before that dawn in this life and in the numerous by-gone lives ought not to perish." *Reply:* "No; vide BG.4.37: 'All actions (are consumed)'", *Objection:* "But the expression may refer only to all actions done after the dawn of knowledge." *Reply:* "No; there is no reason to narrow the scope of the operation of knowledge. Unsound is the argument that as the actions leading to the present embodiment do not perish despite knowledge, so too should not perish those actions which have not started yielding their fruits. How? The former are like discharged arrows; they have already started their operations. As an arrow shot at the target will keep moving even after hitting the target till its momentum is exhaused, so also though the purpose of the body has been accomplished, still the actions that have originated the present body will keep operating till the object of embodiment is realised, and their momentum is exhausted. An undischarged arrow, though set on the bow-string, may well be withheld. Similarly actions not yet operative may be rendered barren by the power of knowledge. So it is reasonable to hold that when the body of the knower falls 'he will not be born again'."

24.0. अत्र आत्मदर्शने बहवः उपायविकल्पाः इमे ध्यानादयः उच्यन्ते—

24.0. Several alternative paths to Self-realisation like meditation are enumerated now:

ध्यानेनात्मनि पश्यन्ति केचिदात्मानमात्मना ।
अन्ये सांख्येन योगेन कर्मयोगेन चापरे ॥२४॥

24. Some perceive the Self, in and by the self, by means of meditation; others by the Yoga of Sāṁkhya, and yet others by means of Karmayoga.

24.1. ध्यानेन इति ॥ ध्यानेन—ध्यानं नाम शब्दादिभ्यो विषयेभ्यः श्रोत्रादीनि करणानि मनसि उपसंहृत्य, मनश्च प्रत्यक्चेतयितरि, एकाग्रतया यत् चिन्तनं, तत् ध्यानम्; तथा, ध्यायतीव बकः, "ध्यायतीव पृथिवी . . . ध्यायन्तीव पर्वताः" [छां. उ. ७. ६. १.] इति उपमोपादानात् तैलधारावत् सन्ततः अविच्छिन्नप्रत्ययः ध्यानं, तेन ध्यानेन आत्मनि बुद्धौ पश्यन्ति आत्मानं प्रत्यक्चेतनं आत्मना स्वेनैव प्रत्यक्चेतनेन ध्यानसंस्कृतेन अन्तःकरणेन केचित् योगिनः । अन्ये सांख्येन योगेन—सांख्यं नाम "इमे सत्त्वरजस्तमांसि गुणाः मया दृश्याः अहं तेभ्यः अन्यः तद्व्यापारसाक्षिभूतः नित्यः गुणविलक्षणः आत्मा" इति चिन्तनं; एषः सांख्यः योगः, तेन 'पश्यन्ति आत्मानं आत्मना' इति वर्तते । कर्मयोगेन—कर्मैव योगः, ईश्वरार्पणबुद्ध्या अनुष्ठीयमानं घटनरूपं योगार्थत्वात् योगः उच्यते गुणतः; तेन सत्त्वशुद्धिज्ञानोत्पत्तिद्वारेण च अपरे ॥

24.1. 'By means of meditation': meditation is one-pointed thought after withdrawing into the mind sense-organs like the ear from their respective objects like sounds and fixing the mind on the inner self. Hence the following usages: The stork meditates as it were; the earth meditates as it were: the mountains meditate, as it were (CU.7.6.1). From these analogies it follows that meditation is incessant thought in an unbroken stream like a current of oil. By means of it, in the self, i.e. in the intellect, some Yogins perceive the self through the instrumentality of the inner organ, purified by meditation. 'Others by means of the Yoga of Sāṁkhya': Here Sāṁkhya means analytic thought in the following way: These are the constituents, *sattva*, *rajas* and *tamas*, the Self is their opposite, being the wintess of their operations. This thought is a Yoga by which they see 'the Self by the self', the last phrase being understood. 'Karmayoga': here Karma itself is the Yoga, it being performed as an offering to God. It is done for securing Yoga; hence it is styled Yoga, qualitatively. By it, through mind's purity and the resulting knowledge, yet others perceive the Self.

अन्ये त्वेवमजानन्तः श्रुत्वाऽन्येभ्य उपासते ।
तेऽपि चातितरन्त्येव मृत्युं श्रुतिपरायणाः ॥२५॥

25. Some, however, not knowing thus, hear from others about the Self and worship; they also, intent on hearing, overcome death indeed.

25.1. अन्ये तु इति ॥ अन्ये तु एतेषु विकल्पेषु अन्यतमेन अपि एवं यथोक्तं आत्मानं अजानन्तः अन्येभ्यः आचार्येभ्यः श्रुत्वा "इदं एवं चिन्तयत" इति उक्ताः उपासते श्रद्धधानाः सन्तः चिन्तयन्ति । तेऽपि च अतितरन्ति एव अतिक्रामन्ति एव मृत्युम्—मृत्युयुक्तं संसारं इत्येतत्—श्रुतिपरायणाः श्रुतिः श्रवणं परं अयनं गमनं मोक्षमार्गप्रवृत्तौ परं साधनं येषां ते श्रुतिपरायणाः, केवलपरोपदेशप्रमाणाः स्वयं विवेकरहिताः इत्यभिप्रायः । किमु वक्तव्यं प्रमाणं प्रति स्वतन्त्राः विवेकिनः मृत्युं अतिक्रामन्ति ? इति ॥

25.1. However, not knowing the Self described in any of the ways mentioned above, and taking instructions from 'others' or teachers, others (other aspirants) think about It thus, i.e. worship or meditate with reverence. They also overcome 'death' or transmigratory life whose end is death. They are 'intent on hearing'—have 'hearing' as their sole form of endeavour on the road to liberation. They seek right cognition through the instruction of their teachers. The point is that they do not themselves discriminate. Of course, those who do discriminate and independently pursue right cognition, do overcome death.

26.0. 'क्षेत्रज्ञं चापि मां विद्धि' [१३.२] इति क्षेत्रज्ञेश्वरैकत्वविषयं ज्ञानं मोक्षसाधनं 'यत् ज्ञात्वाऽमृतमश्नुते' [१३.१२] इत्युक्तम्, तत् कस्मात् हेतोरिति? तद्धेतुप्रदर्शनार्थं श्लोकः आरभ्यते । यस्मात् —

26.0. In 13.2 it was stated that the means to liberation is the knowledge of the identity of the field-knower and God. Why is it so? The next verse states the reason:-

यावत्संजायते किंचित्सत्त्वं स्थावरजङ्गमम् ।
क्षेत्रक्षेत्रज्ञसंयोगात्तद्विद्धि भरतर्षभ ॥२६॥

26. Whatever being is born, either unmoving or moving, know it to be due to the union of the field and the field-knower, best of Bharatas!

26.1. यावत् इति ॥ यावत् यत् किंचित् संजायते समुत्पद्यते सत्त्वं वस्तु—किं अविशेषेण इति? न इत्याह—स्थावरजङ्गमं स्थावरं जङ्गमं च, क्षेत्रक्षेत्रज्ञसंयोगात् तत् जायते इत्येवं विद्धि जानीहि हे भरतर्षभ ॥

कः पुनः अयं क्षेत्रक्षेत्रज्ञयोः संयोगः अभिप्रेतः? न तावत् रज्ज्वा इव घटस्य अवयवसंश्लेषद्वारकः सम्बन्धविशेषः संयोगः क्षेत्रेण क्षेत्रज्ञस्य संभवति, आकाशवत् निरवयवत्वात् । नापि समवायलक्षणः तन्तुपटयोरिव क्षेत्रक्षेत्रज्ञयोः इतरेतरकार्यकारणभावानभ्युपगमात् इति ।

उच्यते—क्षेत्रक्षेत्रज्ञयोः विषयविषयिणोः भिन्नस्वभावयोः इतरेतरतद्धर्माध्यासलक्षणः संयोगः क्षेत्रक्षेत्रज्ञस्वरूपविवेकाभावनिबन्धनः, रज्जुशुक्तिकादीनां तद्विवेकज्ञानाभावात् अध्यारोपितसर्परजतादिसंयोगवत् । सः अयं अध्यासस्वरूपः क्षेत्रक्षेत्रज्ञयोः संयोगः मिथ्याज्ञानलक्षणः । यथाशास्त्रं क्षेत्रक्षेत्रज्ञलक्षणभेदपरिज्ञानपूर्वकं प्राक्

दर्शितरूपात् क्षेत्रात्, मुञ्जादिव इषीकां, यथोक्तलक्षणं क्षेत्रज्ञं प्रविभज्य 'न सत्तन्नासदुच्यते' [१३.१२.] इत्यनेन निरस्तसर्वोपाधिविशेषं ज्ञेयं ब्रह्मस्वरूपेण यः पश्यति, क्षेत्रं च मायानिर्मितहस्ति [-हर्म्यादिवत्] स्वप्नदृष्टवस्तु [-वत्] गन्धर्वनगरादिवत् "असदेव सदिव अवभासते" इति एवं निश्चितविज्ञानः यः, तस्य यथोक्तसम्यग्दर्शनविरोधात् अपगच्छति मिथ्याज्ञानम् । तस्य जन्महेतोः अपगमात् 'य एवं वेत्ति पुरुषं प्रकृतिं च गुणैः सह' [१३.२३.] इत्यनेन "विद्वान् भूयः न अभिजायते" इति यत् उक्तं तत् उपपन्नं उक्तम् ॥

26.1. Whatever particularised being is born, unmoving or moving, know that it does so due to the union of the field-knower and the field, best of Bharata princes! *Objection:* "What is meant by this union? Surely a relation like that of a cord and a pot through contact of parts cannot happen in this case; for the knower is partless like space. Nor can it be a case of inherence since the field and its knower are not related as cause and effect." *Reply:* The answer is that the union in question is a case of superimposition of the two and their attributes due to the absence of discriminative knowledge of the field and the field-knower—the object and the subject—that are essentially different. This union resembles that of the rope, nacre, etc., on the one hand and, on the other, the snake, silver, etc., superimposed on them due to lack of discriminative knowledge of the ground and what is superimposed on it. This union that is a form of superimposition is essentially nescience that will perish in the case of him who discriminates between the field-knower and the field. Being opposed to right perception, this nescience will vanish when, in the light of BG. 13.12[1] and other *śāstraic* assertions, one perceives the Knowable as Brahman devoid of all attributes and discriminates It as different from 'the field', just as its pith is grasped as different from the reed[2]. Then he sees the field as he does magical elephants and mansions or objects in a dream or cities in the sky—as non-existent. When the cause of birth disappears, the statement in 13.23[3], that the

1 "It is neither existent nor non-existent"

2 Cf. "Him one should draw out from one's body like an arrow-shaft from a reed . . ." KU.6.17.

3 "Whoso knows . . . is no more born". BG. 13.23.

knower is born no more is proved to be reasonable.

27.0. 'न स भूयोऽभिजायते' [१३.२३.] इति सम्यग्दर्शनफलं अविद्यादि-ससारबीजनिवृत्तिद्वारेण जन्माभावः उक्तः । जन्मकारणं च अविद्यानिमित्तकः क्षेत्र-क्षेत्रज्ञसंयोगः उक्तः, [यतः] अतः तस्याः अविद्यायाः निवर्तकं सम्यग्दर्शनं उक्तम् अपि पुनः शब्दान्तरेण उच्यते—

27.0. The fruit of right perception, viz., the absence of birth owing to the abolition of the seed of transmigratory life, i.e., nescience, has been stated in 13.23. Also has been set forth the cause of birth, the union between the field and field-knower. Once more, in fresh words, is here pin-pointed the right knowledge that abolishes nescience:

समं सर्वेषु भूतेषु तिष्ठन्तं परमेश्वरम् ।
विनश्यत्स्वविनश्यन्तं यः पश्यति स पश्यति ॥२७॥

27. He alone perceives who sees Him, the supreme Lord, dwelling alike in all beings and not perishing, when they perish.

27.1. समं इति ॥ समं निर्विशेषं तिष्ठन्तं स्थितिं कुर्वन्तं—क्व ? —सर्वेषु समस्तेषु भूतेषु ब्रह्मादिस्थावरान्तेषु प्राणिषु—कं ? परमेश्वरं देहेन्द्रियमनोबुद्ध्यव्यक्तात्मनः अपेक्ष्य [परमश्च असौ ईश्वरश्च ईशनशीलश्च इति] परमेश्वरः, तं सर्वेषु भूतेषु समं तिष्ठन्तम् । तानि विशिनष्टि 'विनश्यत्सु' इति, तं च परमेश्वरं 'अविनश्यन्तं' इति, भूतानां परमेश्वरस्य च अत्यन्तवैलक्षण्यप्रदर्शनार्थम् । कथं ? सर्वेषां हि भावविकाराणां जनिलक्षणः भावविकारो मूलम्, जन्मोत्तरकालभाविनः अन्ये सर्वे भावविकाराः विनाशान्ताः; विनाशात् परः न कश्चित् अस्ति भावविकारः, भावाभावात् । सति हि धर्मिणि धर्माः भवन्ति । अतः अन्त्यभावविकाराभावानुवादेन तत्पूर्वभाविनः सर्वे भावविकाराः प्रतिषिद्धाः भवन्ति सह तत्कार्यैः । तस्मात् सर्वभूतैः वैलक्षण्यं अत्यन्तम् एव परमेश्वरस्य सिद्धं, निर्विशेषत्वं, एकत्वं च । यः एवं यथोक्तं परमेश्वरं पश्यति, सः पश्यति ॥

27.1. 'Alike'—without distinction of any kind. 'Dwelling' where? In all beings—all living beings, extending from Brahmā to things stationary. Whom?—the supreme Lord in relation to body, senses, mind, intellect, the unmanifest and the individual self. He who rules is the supreme and the Lord. He dwells alike in all beings who are characterised as 'perishing'. He is distinguished as 'not perishing' to stress the total difference between these beings and the supreme Lord. Whence this difference? The root of all transformations to which beings are subject is birth; other transformations follow it. The last transformation is destruction; nothing remains after it to suffer further transformations. Attributes presuppose substance. Therefore, by affirming the absence of the last transformation, all prior transformations and their consequences have been repudiated. Thus follow the total otherness of the supreme Lord as against all contingent beings, the absence in Him of all adjuncts and His unity. He only sees, who perceives the supreme Lord as set forth above.

27.2. ननु सर्वोऽपि लोकः पश्यति, किं विशेषणेन ? इति ।
सत्यं पश्यति; किन्तु विपरीतं पश्यति । अतः विशिनष्टि—स एव पश्यतीति । यथा तिमिरदृष्टिः अनेकं चन्द्रं पश्यति, तं अपेक्ष्य एकचन्द्रदर्शी विशिष्यते—स एव पश्यतीति; तथा इहापि एकं अविभक्तं यथोक्तं आत्मानं यः पश्यति, सः विभक्तानेकात्मविपरीतदर्शिभ्यः विशिष्यते—स एव पश्यतीति । इतरे पश्यन्तोऽपि न पश्यन्ति, विपरीतदर्शित्वात् अनेकचन्द्रदर्शिवत् इत्यर्थः ॥

27.2. *Objection:* "All people in the world do see, don't they? Why this qualification then?" *Reply:* "True, they see but contrarily. Hence the perceiver is rightly qualified. For example, a man of defective vision sees many moons; in relation to him the man who sees but one moon is qualified as one who alone sees. Similar is the present case. In respect of those who see many disparate selves, he who perceives the single undivided Self has been qualified. Others do not see, since their seeing is erroneous, as of the man who sees many moons."

28.0. यथोक्तस्य सम्यग्दर्शनस्य फलवचनेन स्तुतिः कर्तव्या, इति श्लोकः आरभ्यते—

28.0. To praise right perception as described above with reference to its consequences, the following verse is set forth:

समं पश्यन् हि सर्वत्र समवस्थितमीश्वरम् ।
न हिनस्त्यात्मनाऽऽत्मानं ततो याति परां गतिम् ॥२८॥

28. For, beholding alike the Lord dwelling everywhere, one injures not the Self by the self; thus one reaches the highest goal.

28.1. समं इति ॥ समं पश्यन् उपलभमानः हि यस्मात् सर्वत्र सर्वभूतेषु समवस्थितं तुल्यतया अवस्थितं ईश्वरं, अतीतानन्तरश्लोकोक्तलक्षणं इत्यर्थः । समं पश्यन् किं ?—न हिनस्ति हिंसां न करोति आत्मना स्वेनैव स्वं आत्मानम् । ततः तदहिंसनात् याति परां प्रकृष्टां गतिं मोक्षाख्याम् ।

ननु नैव कश्चित् प्राणी स्वयं स्वं आत्मानं हिनस्ति, । कथं उच्यते अप्राप्तं 'न हिनस्ति' इति ? यथा 'न पृथिव्यां नान्तरिक्षे न दिव्यग्निश्चेतव्यः' [तै. सं. ५.२.७.१.] इत्यादि ॥

नैष दोषः अज्ञानां आत्मतिरस्करणोपपत्तेः । सर्वो हि अज्ञः अत्यन्तप्रसिद्धं साक्षात् अपरोक्षं आत्मानं तिरस्कृत्य अनात्मानं आत्मत्वेन परिगृह्य, तमपि धर्माधर्मौ कृत्वा उपात्तं आत्मानं हत्वा अन्यं आत्मानं उपादत्ते नवं, तं चैवं हत्वा अन्यं, एवं तमपि हत्वा अन्यं, इत्येवं उपात्तम् उपात्तं आत्मानं हन्ति, इति आत्महा सर्वः अज्ञः । यस्तु परमार्थात्मा, असावपि सर्वदा अविद्यया हतः इव, विद्यमानफलाभावात्, इति सर्वे आत्महनः एव अविद्वांसः । यस्तु इतरः यथोक्तात्मदर्शी, सः उभयथाऽपि आत्मना आत्मानं न हिनस्ति न हन्ति । ततः याति परां गतिं, यथोक्तं फलं तस्य भवति इत्यर्थः ॥

28.1. 'For beholding alike' i.e. cognizing, 'everywhere', in all beings, the Lord dwelling equally—the Lord deseribed in verse 27. What does that beholder do? He injures not the Self by the self. 'Thus,—by this abstention from injuring—he reaches the 'highest goal' called liberation. *Objection*: "Surely no man injures himself. Why then is this imposible contingency mentioned at all? This resembles the statement in the Tait. Saṁhitā (5.2.7.1.) 'neither on earth nor in the sky nor in the firmament should a fire be built up'." *Reply:* "This is no flaw; for the ignorant may very well repudiate the Self. Indeed all ignorant people repudiate this most explicit and immediate Self, resort to the non-self as the Self proper, go on repeatedly choosing and rejecting selves, and act righteously and unrighteously. Thus the Self gets hurt. Thus all ignorant people are Self-destroyers. As regards the metaphysical Self, even that always gets hurt, as it were. So the non-knowers of the Self are Self-destroyers; they do not reap the real fruit of that Self." Opposed to these, the perceiver of the real Self, as explained above, does not injure the Self by the self in any way—does not destroy It. Thus he reaches the highest goal; the fruit of spiritual life accrues to him. This is the idea.

29.0. "सर्वभूतस्थं ईश्वरं समं पश्यन् न हिनस्ति आत्मना आत्मानं" इति उक्तम् । तत् अनुपपन्नं स्वगुणकर्मवैलक्षण्यभेदभिन्नेषु आत्मसु, इत्येतत् आशङ्क्य आह—

29.0. It was affirmed that 'seeing alike the Lord dwelling in all beings, one does not injure the Self by the self'. Some characterise this as unreasonable regarding the selves, which are inherently different in themselves due to their varying 'qualities and actions'. In reply it is stated as follows:-

प्रकृत्यैव च कर्माणि क्रियमाणानि सर्वशः ।
यः पश्यति तथाऽऽत्मानमकर्तारं स पश्यति ॥२९॥

29. He alone sees who, on all sides, sees actions solely performed by Prakṛti and sees, also, the Self as a non-agent.

29.1. प्रकृत्या इति ॥ प्रकृत्या—प्रकृतिः भगवतः माया त्रिगुणात्मिका, 'मायां तु प्रकृतिं विद्यात्' [श्वे. उ. ४.१०.] इति मन्त्रवर्णात्, तया प्रकृत्या एव च—न अन्येन—महदादिकार्यकरणाकारपरिणतया कर्माणि वाङ्मनःकायारभ्याणि क्रियमाणानि निर्वर्त्यमानानि सर्वशः सर्वप्रकारैः यः पश्यति उपलभते, तथा आत्मानं क्षेत्रज्ञं अकर्तारं सर्वोपाधिविवर्जितं, सः पश्यति, सः परमार्थदर्शी इत्यभिप्रायः निर्गुणस्य अकर्तुः निर्विशेषस्य आकाशस्य इव भेदे प्रमाणानुपपत्तिः इत्यर्थः ॥

29.1. *Prakṛti* with the three constituents is the *māyā* of the Lord; for ŚU.4.10 teaches: "Know *māyā* to be *prakṛti*." By that *prakṛti*, solely, that has transformed itself into effects and instruments such as *mahat*, etc., are the activities of speech, mind and body performed, 'on all sides'—in all manner of ways. He who sees this and, also, that the Self or the field-knower devoid of adjuncts is a non-agent, alone sees the supreme truth. This is the idea. An entity devoid of attributes, like space, is a non-agent; it cannot be proved to have differences.

30.0. पुनरपि तदेव सम्यग्दर्शनं शब्दान्तरेण प्रपञ्च्यते—

30.0. Once more the theme of right perception is explicated in yet other words:

यदा भूतपृथग्भावमेकस्थमनुपश्यति ।
तत एव च विस्तारं ब्रह्म संपद्यते तदा ॥३०॥

30. When one sees the multiplicity of beings as abiding in the One and plurality as proceeding from that One alone, he becomes Brahman.

30.1. यदा इति ॥ यदा यस्मिन् काले भूतपृथग्भावं भूतानां पृथग्भावं पृथक्त्वं एकस्मिन् आत्मनि स्थितं एकस्थं, अनुपश्यति शास्त्राचार्योपदेशं अनु आत्मानं प्रत्यक्षत्वेन पश्यति "आत्मैव इदं सर्वं" [बृ. उ. २.४.६.] इति, तत एव च तस्मादेव च विस्तारं उत्पत्तिं विकासं "आत्मतः प्राण आत्मत आशा आत्मतः स्मर आत्मत आकाश आत्मतस्तेज आत्मत आप आत्मत आविर्भावतिरोभावावात्मतोऽन्नं" [छां. उ. ७.२६.१.] इत्येवमादिप्रकारैः विस्तारं यदा पश्यति, ब्रह्म संपद्यते ब्रह्मैव भवति तदा तस्मिन् काले इत्यर्थः ॥

30.1. He who directly perceives, according to the instructions of the *śāstras* and teachers, 'the multiplicity of beings as abiding in the one Self'—perceives 'that all this is Self alone' (BU.2.4.8)—and as proceeding from that very Self, becomes, at that very time, Brahman. This is the idea.

31.0. एकस्य आत्मनः सर्वदेहात्मत्वे तद्दोषसम्बन्धे प्राप्ते इदं उच्यते—

31.0. As Self's contact with the flaws of the bodies, of which It is the self, is a possibility, the following statement is made:

अनादित्वान्निर्गुणत्वात् परमात्माऽयमव्ययः ।
शरीरस्थोऽपि कौन्तेय न करोति न लिप्यते ॥३१॥

31. Due to His beginninglessness and freedom from attributes this imperishable and supreme Self, though dwelling in bodies, neither acts nor gets stained.

31.1. अनादित्वात् इति ॥ अनादित्वात्—अनादेः भावः अनादित्वं, आदिः कारणं, तत् यस्य नास्ति तत् अनादि । यद्धि आदिमत् तत् स्वेन आत्मना व्येति; अयं तु अनादित्वात् निरवयवः इति कृत्वा न व्येति । तथा निर्गुणत्वात् । सगुणः हि गुणव्ययात् व्येति; अयं तु निर्गुणत्वात् न व्येति; इति परमात्मा अयं अव्ययः, न अस्य व्ययः विद्यते इति अव्ययः । यतः एवं, अतः शरीरस्थः अपि, शरीरेषु आत्मनः उपलब्धिः भवतीति शरीरस्थः उच्यते; तथापि न करोति कर्म । तद-करणादेव तत्फलेन न लिप्यते । यो हि कर्ता, सः कर्मफलेन लिप्यते । अयं तु अकर्ता, अतः न फलेन लिप्यते इत्यर्थः ॥

कः पुनः देहेषु करोति लिप्यते च ? यदि तावत् अन्यः परमात्मनः देही करोति लिप्यते च, ततः इदं अनुपपन्नं उक्तं क्षेत्रज्ञेश्वरैकत्वं 'क्षेत्रज्ञं चापि मां विद्धि' [१३.२.] इत्यादि । अथ नास्ति ईश्वरात् अन्यः देही, कः करोति लिप्यते च ?—इति वाच्यं; परो वा नास्ति इति । सर्वथा दुर्विज्ञेयं दुर्वाच्यं च इति भगवत्प्रोक्तं औपनिषदं दर्शनं परित्यक्तं वैशेषिकैः, सांख्यार्हतबौद्धैश्च ॥

31.1. 'Beginninglessness' is the state of what is devoid of 'beginning' or cause. What has no cause is beginningless, of course. What has cause undergoes essential change. This Self, being uncaused, is impartite; so It does not change. Similarly, being 'attributeless', too, It does not change. What has attributes changes through the erosion of these attributes. Thus the supreme Self is imperishable. He does not diminish. This being the case, though abiding in all bodies—for the Self is known in them all—, He does no work, and is not stained by their fruits. "Who then is the agent in these bodies?; who gets stained? If some embodied being other than the supreme Self works and gets stained, then the identity of the Lord and the field-knower laid down in 13.2 becomes untenable. If, however, there is no embodied being other than the Lord, who works and gets stained?" Being hard to grasp and state, this Upanisadic philosophy proclaimed by the Lord has been rejected by the Vaiśeṣika and Sāṁkhya philosophers as well as by the Jainas and the Buddhists.

31.2. तत्र अयं परिहारो भगवता स्वेनैव उक्तः—'स्वभावस्तु प्रवर्तते' [५.१४.] इति। अविद्यामात्रस्वभावो हि करोति लिप्यते च इति व्यवहारो भवति, न तु परमार्थतः एव तस्मिन् (—र्थत एकस्मिन्) परमात्मनि तत् अस्ति। अत एव, एतस्मिन् परमार्थसांख्यदर्शने स्थितानां ज्ञाननिष्ठानां परमहंसपरिव्राजकानां तिरस्कृताविद्याव्यवहाराणां कर्माधिकारो नास्ति इति तत्र तत्र दर्शितं भगवता ॥

31.2. The Lord Himself has offered an answer in the words: "The nature of things, however, operates" (B.G.5.14). The empirical expression "some one acts and gets stained" is no more than an expression of nescience; in truth such acting and getting stained does not exist in the supreme Self. Precisely for this reason the Lord has stated in several contexts that the renouncers of the order of Paramahaṃsas, who are established in the philosophy of the sages and have risen above all empirical activities, are not called upon to do any work.

32.0. किमिव न करोति न लिप्यते इति ? अत्र दृष्टान्तमाह—

32.0. Whom does He resemble in not working and not getting stained? An analogy is offered.

यथा सर्वगतं सौक्ष्म्यादाकाशं नोपलिप्यते ।
सर्वत्रावस्थितो देहे तथाऽऽत्मा नोपलिप्यते ॥३२॥

32. Just as all-pervading space, due to its subtlety, is not stained, so is the Self, present in the body everywhere, not stained.

32.1. यथा इति ॥ यथा सर्वगतं सर्वव्यापि अपि सत् सौक्ष्म्यात् सूक्ष्मभावात् आकाशं खं न उपलिप्यते न सम्बध्यते, सर्वत्र अवस्थितः देहे तथा आत्मा न उपलिप्यते ॥

किंच—

32.1. Just as space, though all-pervading—i.e., present in all places—, due to its subtlety is not stained, or does not get related to anything, so, though present everywhere in the body, the Self is unstained. Also,

यथा प्रकाशयत्येकः कृत्स्नं लोकमिमं रविः ।
क्षेत्रं क्षेत्री तथा कृत्स्नं प्रकाशयति भारत ॥३३॥

33. Just as the one sun illumines this entire world, so, Arjuna! the Owner of the field illumines the entire field.

33.1. यथा इति ॥ यथा प्रकाशयति अवभासयति एकः कृत्स्नं लोकं इमं रविः सविता आदित्यः, तथा तद्वत् अव्यक्तमहाभूतादि धृत्यन्तं क्षेत्रं एकः सन् प्रकाशयति —कः ? —क्षेत्री परमात्मा इत्यर्थः, भारत ! । रविदृष्टान्तः अत्र आत्मनः उभयार्थोऽपि भवति—रविवत् सर्वक्षेत्रेषु एकः एव आत्मा, अलेपकश्च इति ॥

33.1. Just as the single sun lights up this entire world, so the entire field from the 'great elements' (*mahābhūta*) etc., upto 'sustentation', *dhṛti*—(vide 13.5–6), He lights up. Who? The Owner of the field, the supreme Self, O Arjuna! The analogy of the sun serves two purposes: (1) like the sun the Self is one only in all bodies; (2) He is unstained.

34.0. समस्ताध्यायार्थोपसंहारार्थः अयं श्लोकः—

34.0. The following verse concludes the theme of this whole chapter:

क्षेत्रक्षेत्रज्ञयोरेवमन्तरं ज्ञानचक्षुषा ।
भूतप्रकृतिमोक्षं च ये विदुर्यान्ति ते परम् ॥३४॥

34. Thus those who see, with the eye of wisdom, the difference between the field and the field-knower and the way of release from Prakṛti, the cause of materiality, repair to the supreme goal.

इति श्रीमहाभारते शतसाहस्र्यां संहितायां वैयासिक्यां भीष्मपर्वणि श्रीमद्भगवद्-
गीतासूपनिषत्सु ब्रह्मविद्यायां योगशास्त्रे श्रीकृष्णार्जुनसंवादे
प्रकृतिपुरुषविवेकयोगो नाम त्रयोदशोऽध्यायः ॥

34.1. क्षेत्रक्षेत्रज्ञयोः इति ॥ क्षेत्रक्षेत्रज्ञयोः यथाव्याख्याततयोः एवं यथादर्शितप्रकारेण अन्तरं इतरेतरवैलक्षण्यविशेषं ज्ञानचक्षुषा शास्त्राचार्यप्रसादोपदेशजनितं आत्मप्रत्ययिकं ज्ञानं चक्षुः, तेन ज्ञानचक्षुषा, भूतप्रकृतिमोक्षं च, भूतानां प्रकृतिः अविद्यालक्षणा अव्यक्ताख्या, तस्याः भूतप्रकृतेः मोक्षणं अभावगमनं च ये विदुः विजानन्ति, यान्ति गच्छन्ति ते परं परमार्थतत्त्वं ब्रह्म, न पुनः देहं आददते इत्यर्थः ॥

34.1. Of the two, the field and the field-knower, as already elucidated, whoso with the eye of wisdom born of the *śāstras*, the grace of teachers, and one's own experience, directly perceive the distinction as also the 'release'—the extermination of *prakṛti* or nescience—repair to the supreme goal, the Truth of the supreme Self or Brahman. No more is there embodiment for them.

इति श्रीमत्परमहंसपरिव्राजकाचार्यगोविंदभगवत्पूज्यपादशिष्य-
श्रीमच्छंकरभगवतः कृतौ श्रीमद्भगवद्गीताभाष्ये क्षेत्र-
क्षेत्रज्ञयोगो नाम त्रयोदशोऽध्यायः ॥१३॥

A NOTE ON THE COMMENTARY ON 13.2

In the commentary on B.G. 13.2. Saṁkara discusses and refutes the objections that may be brought up against his doctrine of identity between God and Jīva, the field-knower (Ksetrajña); for he takes the assertion '*kṣetrajñam cāpi māṁ viddhi*' as pivotal to his metaphysics and ethics. Note that God i.e. Kṛṣṇa, is also the Absolute, or *nirguṇa brahman*. He establishes the metaphysical identity of the contents of the three terms *nirguṇa brahman*, *saguṇa brahman*, and *Jīva*. Is the Supreme God, *Parameśvara*, then a transmigrator also? *Jīva* has body as his empirical *upādhi* or adjunct; in truth, God has no *upādhi* at all and, so, terms like *sat* and *asat* can't be applied to Him. Valid knowledge has no content other than *satyam*, *jñānam* and *ānanda*.

Does not this position imply that God is subject to transmigration? Also, since there is no real transmigrator, won't empirical life get abolished? Both these are unwelcome contingencies, because, in this case, *śāstras*, scriptures, will turn out to be futile. These *śāstras* teach bondage, release and their causes. Other means of valid cognition also point to the facts of empirical life, based on *dharma* and *adharma*.

Śaṁkara's answer points out that the Advaitic theory of nescience and saving knowledge takes care of all the above objections. On these themes consult Mahabharata etc., quoted in the *bhāsya* text on BGB 13.2. Sufferings fall to the lot of the ignorant only; the knowers, the wise, do not suffer, but get liberated, instead. Ignorance leads to superimposition which consists in the ascription of qualities, good and bad, to the ground of superimposition, which in fact is devoid of them. But ascribed traits never get lodged in their ground; e.g. the rope does not become snaky. Similarly, Brahman does not become transmigratory. Evils of ignorance and the advantages of knowledge are detailed in the *bhāsya* text at this stage.

What has been stated has the support of reasoning. In the

light of reasoning, it is seen that superimposition is the source of *saṁsāra* and that the pure Spirit remains wholly unaffected. When the Self, the pure Spirit, is seen as other than body etc., all motives for action disappear and liberation ensues. Thus the transmigrator is the Spirit on which the psycho-physical organism has been superimposed, or the Spirit having body etc., as *upādhis*. But superimposition can never materialise Spirit or spiritualise matter.

The objection that only objects and their attributes get mutually superimposed is not valid. It has already been noted that nescience is the cause of superimposition and that no real transference of objects and attributes happens. Factors of transmigratory life like agency, pain, pleasure etc., pertain to objects (vide 2. para 6). Their transference, by superimposition to the field-knower leaves the latter intact. Thus the Spirit (or God, the field-knower, the Self) does not and cannot transmigrate.

Whose is nescience, the cause of superimpositon? It does not belong to the cognizer just as flaws like short sight pertain only to the instruments of perception (the eye, etc.,) and not to the percepient. If nescience did belong to the cogniser, liberation would have proved inaccessible, just as coolness is out of question for fire, as its very nature is heat.

This situation ought not to revive the fear that *śāstras* may prove futile. All disputants hold that at some state (e.g. in liberation) the *śāstras* become irrelevant. The non-Advaitins make bondage and liberation products, thus impermanent and illogical. Bondage without a beginning ought not to cease, and liberation with a beginning might not be eternal. Advaita holds that the *śāstras* will continue to be relevant to the ignorant many, though not to the wise few.

Pretensions to knowledge would do no good. Each embodied Self is not exclusively identified with the Supreme Spirit. The claimants to knowledge falsify themselves through cravings or *eṣaṇāḥ* and matching activities. Activity is impossible for the full-fledged knower, only *nivṛtti*, cessation from activity, and renunciation are open to him. Beware of the meanest among scholars, the *paṇḍitāpasadas*, who maintain the following propositions: The field-knower is indeed God. He perceives the field as different from Himself. But 'I', the empirical self, transmigrate and suffer. My duty is to wind up *saṁsāra* through knowledge of the field and field-knower, and through meditation to realise God and get assimilated to Him. This type of 'scholar' advances novel interpretations based on delusions. His worst offence is his total alienation from sound Vedantic traditions. Shun him.

Para 16. faces the vital question—whose is nescience? It is, of course, his who feels he is ignorant. To perceive ignorance implies the perception of the victim of ignorance also. "But nescience and its owners are imperceptible". The knowledge that one is ignorant is not indirect or merely inferred. At any given instant the object of perception or ignorance fully engages the percipient. He cannot be, and is not, distracted by any other object of perception, such as the victim of ignorance. To introduce a relation between ignorance and its victim (or owner) entails infinite regress (vide 2. para 16). Cognizership of ignorance is only figurative; it is a product of superimposition only. Activities and the factors involved in them are constructions of the nescient mind. For further light study BGB 18.11 and 18.50.

चतुर्दशोऽध्यायः

CHAPTER XIV

THE YOGA OF THE THREE CONSTITUENTS

0.1. सर्वं उत्पद्यमानं क्षेत्रक्षेत्रज्ञसंयोगात् उत्पद्यते इति उक्तम् । तत् कथमिति ? तत्प्रदर्शनार्थं 'परं भूयः' इत्यादिः अध्यायः आरभ्यते । अथवा–"ईश्वरपरतन्त्रयोः क्षेत्रक्षेत्रज्ञयोः जगत्कारणत्वं, न तु सांख्यानामिव स्वतन्त्रयोः" इत्येवमर्थं; प्रकृतिस्थत्वं गुणेषु च सङ्गः संसारकारणं इत्युक्तम् [१३.२१.]। कस्मिन् गुणे कथं सङ्गः ? के वा गुणाः ? कथं वा ते बध्नन्ति ? गुणेभ्यश्च मोक्षणं कथं स्यात् ? मुक्तस्य च लक्षणं वक्तव्यं, इत्येवमर्थं च भगवान् उवाच—

0.1. It has been declared that every being takes birth due to the union of the field and the field-knower. How does it happen? In order to demonstrate it, is begun the chapter opening with the words "Again the supreme, etc." Or it is to show that the cause of the world is the field and the field-knower depending on God, and not, as the Sāṁkhyas aver, as independent entities. Further, it was stated that the cause of empirical life is man's involvement in *prakṛti* and attachment to its constituents (BG.13.21). How does this attachment happen and to what constituents? Which are the constituents? How do they bind? How is one released therefrom? How is the liberated individual defined? With all this in view the Lord spoke as follows:

श्रीभगवानुवाच :

परं भूयः प्रवक्ष्यामि ज्ञानानां ज्ञानमुत्तमम् ।
यज्ज्ञात्वा मुनयः सर्वे परां सिद्धिमितो गताः ॥१॥

The Blessed Lord said:

1. Again I shall elucidate that highest and best knowledge among all forms of knowledge, by mastering which all silent sages have attained supreme perfection beyond this (empirical sphere).

1.1. परं भूयः इति ॥ परं–'ज्ञानं' इति व्यवहितेन सम्बन्धः–भूयः पुनः पूर्वेषु सर्वेषु अध्यायेषु असकृत् उक्तम् अपि, प्रवक्ष्यामि । तच्च परं परवस्तुविषयत्वात् । किं तत्? —ज्ञानं सर्वेषां ज्ञानानां उत्तमं, उत्तमफलत्वात् । 'ज्ञानानां' इति न अमानित्वादीनाम् [१३.७-१०.]; किं तर्हि? —यज्ञादिज्ञेयवस्तुविषयाणां इति । तानि न मोक्षाय, इदं तु मोक्षाय इति परोत्तमशब्दाभ्यां स्तौति श्रोतृबुद्धिरुच्युत्पादनार्थम् । यत् ज्ञात्वा यत् ज्ञानं ज्ञात्वा प्राप्य संन्यासिनः मननशीलाः सर्वे परां सिद्धिं मोक्षाख्यां इतः अस्मात् देहबन्धनात् ऊर्ध्वं गताः प्राप्ताः ॥

1.1. 'The highest' is related to the term 'knowledge' that occurs after many other words. 'Again'—indicates that it has been repeatedly mentioned in all previous chapters; but still, I shall elucidate it. It is 'the highest' knowledge, because its content is the highest reality. What is it? This 'knowledge' is called the best among all (forms) of knowledge, because its fruit is the best. The forms of knowledge do not refer to the virtues enumerated in BG.13.7–10, but to the knowledge of sacrifices and other knowables. These do not lead to liberation; but the highest knowledge does. So it is extolled by means of the adjectives, 'the highest and best', in order to excite the listener's interest. By mastering it, all contemplative renouncers achieve 'supreme perfection' named liberation, beyond and above the bondage of embodiment.

2.0. अस्याश्च सिद्धेः ऐकान्तिकत्वं उच्यते—

2.0. The certitude of this perfection is affirmed:-

इदं ज्ञानमुपाश्रित्य मम साधर्म्यमागताः ।
सर्गेऽपि नोपजायन्ते प्रलये न व्यथन्ति च ॥२॥

2. Resorting to this knowledge, they have achieved My own nature; they are not born at the time of the manifestation (of the world); nor are they distressed at the time of its dissolution.

2.1. इदं इति ॥ इदं ज्ञानं यथोक्तं उपाश्रित्य–ज्ञानसाधनं अनुष्ठाय इत्येतत्—मम परमेश्वरस्य साधर्म्यं मत्स्वरूपतां आगताः प्राप्ताः इत्यर्थः । न तु समानधर्मता

साधर्म्यं, क्षेत्रज्ञेश्वरयोः भेदानभ्युपगमात् गीताशास्त्रे । फलवादश्च अयं स्तुत्यर्थं उच्यते । सर्गेऽपि सृष्टिकालेऽपि न उपजायन्ते न उत्पद्यन्ते । प्रलये ब्रह्मणोऽपि विनाशकाले न व्यथन्ति च व्यथां न आपद्यन्ते, न च्यवन्ति इत्यर्थः ॥

2.1. 'Resorting to this knowledge' as set forth, i.e., having taken the steps leading to this knowledge, they have achieved 'the same nature as Mine' or identity with Myself—identity with the supreme Lord. This is the idea. It is not a matter of being similar to Me; for, in the science of the Gītā, difference between the field-knower and God is not recognised. The following declaration about the final end of this knowledge is meant to be eulogistic: 'Even at the time of manifestation of the world they are not born', nor 'at the time of dissolution', when even Brahmā perishes, 'are they distressed'. That is, they do not lapse from the state of release.

3.0. क्षेत्रक्षेत्रज्ञसंयोगः ईदृशः भूतकारणं इत्याह—

3.0. It is next explained in what manner the union of the field and the field-knower causes the generation of all beings:

मम योनिर्महद्ब्रह्म तस्मिन् गर्भं दधाम्यहम् ।
सम्भवः सर्वभूतानां ततो भवति भारत ॥३॥

3. My womb is Brahman, the Mahat; I cast the seed therein. Thence, O scion of the Bharatas! are born all beings.

3.1. मम इति ॥ मम स्वभूता मदीया माया त्रिगुणात्मिका प्रकृतिः योनिः सर्वभूतानां कारणम् । सर्वकार्येभ्यः महत्त्वात् कारणत्वात् बृंहणत्वाच्च [भरणाच्च] स्वविकाराणां, महत् ब्रह्म इति योनिः एव विशिष्यते । तस्मिन् महति ब्रह्मणि योनौ गर्भं हिरण्यगर्भजन्मनः बीजं, सर्वभूतजन्मकारणं बीजं, दधामि निक्षिपामि क्षेत्रक्षेत्रज्ञप्रकृतिद्वयशक्तिमान् ईश्वरः अहं—अविद्याकामकर्मोपाधिस्वरूपानुविधायिनं क्षेत्रज्ञं क्षेत्रेण संयोजयामि इत्यर्थः । सम्भवः समुत्पत्तिः सर्वभूतानां हिरण्यगर्भोत्पत्ति-द्वारेण ततः तस्मात् गर्भनिधानात् भवंति हे भारत! ॥

3.1. My Māyā—the Māyā that belongs to Me. It consists

of the three constituents. It is My Prakṛti, the womb or cause of all beings. "My womb" (Prakṛti) is described as *mahat-brahma*, because it is vast in relation to all its effects, and because it is their cause and controller. In this great Brahman I cast the seed of Hiraṇyagarbha's birth—the seed of the birth of all beings. I cast it as the Lord with My two-fold power of the field and the field-knower. The idea is that I bring about the union of the field with the field-knower who is associated with the adjuncts of nescience, desires and actions. The birth of all beings *via* the origination of Hiraṇyagarbha proceeds from this casting of the seed by Me, O Arjuna!

सर्वयोनिषु कौन्तेय मूर्तयः सम्भवन्ति याः ।
तासां ब्रह्म महद्योनिरहं बीजप्रदः पिता ॥४॥

4. Son of Kuntī! Whatever forms spring up from all kinds of wombs, their womb is this great Brahman, and I am the father, the supplier of the seed.

4.1. सर्वयोनिषु इति ॥ देवपितृमनुष्यपशुमृगादिषु सर्वयोनिषु कौन्तेय ! मूर्तयः देहसंस्थानलक्षणाः मूर्छिताङ्गावयवाः मूर्तयः सम्भवन्ति याः, तासां मूर्तीनां ब्रह्म महत् सर्वावस्थं योनिः कारणं, अहं ईश्वरः बीजप्रदः पिता गर्भाधानस्य कर्ता पिता ॥

4.1. In all wombs, i.e., among the gods, manes, men, animals and beasts whatever organized forms spring up, of them all this great Brahman (Prakṛti) with all its states is the womb or cause, and I, the Lord, am the seed-supplying father, the impregnator.

5.0. के गुणाः ? कथं बध्नन्तीति ? उच्यते—

5.0. Which are the constituents? How do they bind? Answer:

सत्त्वं रजस्तम इति गुणाः प्रकृतिसम्भवाः ।
निबध्नन्ति महाबाहो देहे देहिनमव्ययम् ॥५॥

5. Sattva, Rajas, and Tamas, the Prakṛti-born constituents, bind the embodied and immutable (Spirit), O mighty-armed!

5.1. सत्त्वं इति ॥ सत्त्वं रजः तमः इति एवंनामानः । 'गुणाः' इति पारिभाषिकः शब्दः, न रूपादिवत् द्रव्याश्रिताः गुणाः । न च गुणगुणिनोः अन्यत्वं अत्र विवक्षितम् । तस्मात् गुणाः इव नित्यपरतन्त्राः क्षेत्रज्ञं प्रति, अविद्यात्मकत्वात् क्षेत्रज्ञं निबध्नन्तीव । तं आस्पदीकृत्य आत्मानं प्रतिलभन्ते इति 'निबध्नन्ति' इति उच्यते । ते च प्रकृतिसम्भवाः भगवन्मायासम्भवाः निबध्नन्ति इव हे महाबाहो, महान्तौ समर्थतरौ आजानुप्रलम्बौ बाहू यस्य सः महाबाहुः, हे महाबाहो ! देहे शरीरे देहिनं देहवन्तं अव्ययं—अव्ययत्वं च उक्तं 'अनादित्वात्' [१३.३१.] इत्यादिश्लोकेन ॥

ननु "देही न लिप्यते" [१३.३१.] इत्युक्तम् । तत्, कथं इह निबध्नन्ति, इति अन्यथा उच्यते ?

परिहृतं अस्माभिः इवशब्देन 'निबध्नन्ति इव' इति ॥

5.1. The constituents (Guṇas) are named '*sattva*, *rajas*, and *tamas*.' The word constituents, *guṇāḥ*, is technical; it does not denote qualities like colour, etc., inhering in substances. Nor is any distinction intended between the constituents and what is constituted by them. Like qualities they are eternally dependent, being related to the field-knower. Being essentially nescience, they bind the field-knower, as it were. Resorting to Him, these constituents posit themselves and so they are said to bind. Born of *prakṛti*—i.e., of the *māyā* of the Lord—, they bind, as it were, the imperishable embodied Spirit. 'Mighty-armed!'—Thou whose powerful arms extend to the knees. Spirit's imperishability has been elucidated in the verse 13.31, where it was stated that the embodied Spirit is not stained. *Objection:* Why then is it said, discordantly in the present verse, that 'they bind Him'! *Reply:* This objection has been met by the expression, 'they bind, as it were'.

6.0. तत्र सत्त्वादीनां सत्त्वस्य एव तावत् लक्षणं उच्यते—

6.0. Among these constituents *sattva* is being defined:

तत्र सत्त्वं निर्मलत्वात् प्रकाशकमनामयम् ।
सुखसङ्गेन बध्नाति ज्ञानसङ्गेन चानघ ॥६॥

6. Among them Sattva being stainless, illumines and heals, sinless prince! It binds with the clinging to pleasure and to knowledge.

6.1. तत्र सत्त्वं इति ॥ निर्मलत्वात् स्फटिकमणिरिव प्रकाशकं अनामयं निरुपद्रवं सत्त्वं तत् बध्नाति । कथं? —सुखसङ्गेन "सुखी अहं" इति विषयभूतस्य सुखस्य विषयिणि आत्मनि संश्लेषापादनं मृषैव सुखे सञ्जनम् । सैषा अविद्या । न हि विषयधर्मः विषयिणः भवति । इच्छादि च धृत्यन्तं क्षेत्रस्यैव विषयस्य धर्मः इति उक्तं भगवता [१३.६.] । अतः अविद्ययैव स्वकीयधर्मभूतया विषयविषय्यविवेकलक्षणया अस्वात्मभूते सुखे सञ्जयति इव, आसक्तमिव करोति, असङ्गं सक्तमिव करोति, असुखिनं सुखिनमिव । तथा ज्ञानसङ्गेन च—ज्ञानमिति सुखसाहचर्यात् क्षेत्रस्यैव विषयस्य अन्तःकरणस्य धर्मः, न आत्मनः; आत्मधर्मत्वे सङ्गानुपपत्तेः बन्धानुपपत्तेश्च । सुखे इव ज्ञानादौ सङ्गः मन्तव्यः । अनघ ! अव्यसन ! ॥

6.1. 'Being stainless' like a crystal, *sattva* is luminous and pleasant. It binds—how? With the clinging to pleasure. In the experience of pleasure, the object, pleasure, induces in the experiencing self a futile clinging to that pleasure. This is nescience; for, the characteristic of an object cannot pertain to the subject. Qualities like 'desire (vide 13.6) upto sustentation' pertain to the object as the Lord has already affirmed. Therefore through its attribute, nescience, which consists in the non-discrimination between the object and the subject, *sattva* engenders in the self a clinging to the pleasure that is alien to it. *Sattva* makes the self attached, as it were—the self that is, in fact, detached and free of objective pleasure, is made gay as it were. Similarly, it generates in the self 'clinging to knowledge'. This knowledge, mentioned together with pleasure, is an attribute of the inner sense and therefore objective; it is not an attribute of the Self. Were it so, clinging to it would be irrational, just as bondage is irrational. The clinging to knowledge must be understood in the same way as clinging to pleasure. 'Sinless' means free from addiction to vice.

रजो रागात्मकं विद्धि तृष्णाऽऽसङ्गसमुद्भवम् ।
तन्निबध्नाति कौन्तेय कर्मसङ्गेन देहिनम् ॥७॥

7. Know that Rajas is essentially attachment; it is the source of craving and passion. O Son of Kuntī! It binds the embodied Spirit with attachment to works.

7.1. रजः इति ॥ रजः रागात्मकं—रञ्जनात् रागः गैरिकादिवद्रागात्मकं विद्धि जानीहि । तृष्णाऽऽसङ्गसमुद्भवं तृष्णा अप्राप्ताभिलाषः, आसङ्गः प्राप्ते विषये मनसः प्रीतिलक्षणः संश्लेषः, तृष्णाऽऽसङ्गयोः समुद्भवं तृष्णाऽऽसङ्गसमुद्भवम् । तत् रजः निबध्नाति कौन्तेय! कर्मसङ्गेन, दृष्टादृष्टार्थेषु कर्मसु सञ्जनं तत्परता कर्मसङ्गः, तेन निबध्नाति रजः देहिनम् ॥

7.1. Know that *rajas* is essentially attachment. What stains is *rāga*, i.e. attachment, just as ochre, etc., do. It is the source of craving and passion. Craving is the desire for what, as yet, is unattained, while passion is mind's fondness for an object already secured. Son of Kuntī! This *rajas* binds the 'embodied Spirit with attachment to works' aimed at goals, seen and unseen.

तमस्त्वज्ञानजं विद्धि मोहनं सर्वदेहिनाम् ।
प्रमादालस्यनिद्राभिस्तन्निबध्नाति भारत ॥८॥

8. Know Tamas to spring from nescience; it deludes all embodied beings, O Bhārata prince! It binds with error, indolence, and sleepiness.

8.1. तम इति ॥ तमः तृतीयः गुणः अज्ञानजं अज्ञानात् जातं अज्ञानजं विद्धि, मोहनं मोहकरं अविवेककरं सर्वदेहिनां सर्वेषां देहवताम् । प्रमादालस्यनिद्राभिः प्रमादश्च आलस्यं च निद्रा च प्रमादालस्यनिद्राः ताभिः प्रमादालस्यनिद्राभिः तत् तमः निबध्नाति भारत! ॥

8.1. *Tamas* is the third constituent. Know that it springs from nescience. It deludes all embodied beings causing non-discrimination. With error, indolence and sleepiness, *tamas* binds, O Arjuna!

9.0. पुनः गुणानां व्यापारः संक्षेपतः उच्यते—

9.0. Again is briefly set forth the operation of each of these constituents:

सत्त्वं सुखे सञ्जयति रजः कर्मणि भारत ।
ज्ञानमावृत्य तु तमः प्रमादे सञ्जयत्युत ॥९॥

9. Sattva causes clinging to pleasure; Rajas to works, while Tamas, shrouding knowledge, causes clinging to error.

9.1. सत्त्वं इति ॥ सत्त्वं सुखे सञ्जयति संश्लेषयति, रजः कर्मणि हे भारत! 'सञ्जयति' इति अनुवर्तते । ज्ञानं सत्त्वकृतं विवेकं आवृत्य आच्छाद्य तु तमः स्वेन आवरणात्मना प्रमादे सञ्जयति उत प्रमादः प्राप्तकर्तव्याकरणम् ॥

9.1. 'O Arjuna! *Sattva* causes clinging to pleasure, and *rajas* to works'. 'Causes clinging' must be understood here. And shrouding knowledge or discrimination arising from *sattva*, *tamas* with its essentially enveloping operation makes one cling to error. 'Error' is the failure to perform one's proper duty.

10.0. उक्तं कार्यं कदा कुर्वन्ति गुणाः इति? उच्यते—

10.0. When do the constituents operate in the way mentioned above?

रजस्तमश्चाभिभूय सत्त्वं भवति भारत ।
रजः सत्त्वं तमश्चैव तमः सत्त्वं रजस्तथा ॥१०॥

10. Subjugating Rajas and Tamas, Sattva comes into being, O Arjuna! Subjugating Sattva and Tamas, does

Rajas do so; and similarly, subjugating Sattva and Rajas, Tamas comes into being.

10.1. रजस्तमः इति ॥ रजः तमः च उभौ अपि अभिभूय सत्त्वं भवति उद्भवति वर्धते यदा, तदा लब्धात्मकं सत्त्वं स्वकार्यं ज्ञानसुखादि आरभते, हे भारत। तथा रजो गुणः सत्त्वं तमश्च एव उभौ अपि अभिभूय वर्धते यदा, तदा कर्म तृष्णादि स्वकार्यं आरभते । तथा एव तमआख्यः गुणः सत्त्वं रजश्च उभौ अपि अभिभूय वर्धते यदा, तदा ज्ञानावरणादि स्वकार्यं आरभते ॥

10.1. Subjugating both *rajas* and *tamas*, *sattva* comes into being—i.e. becomes dominant. Positing itself thus, it produces its effects, knowledge, pleasure, etc. Similarly subjugating *sattva* and *tamas*, *rajas* dominates and produces its effects—work, craving, etc. Likewise when *tamas* becomes dominant over *sattva* and *rajas*, it produces its effects, viz., the shrouding of knowledge and so forth.

11.0. यदा यः गुणः उद्भूतः भवति, तदा तस्य किं लिङ्गं इति ? उच्यते—

11.0. What are the marks of the domination of each of these constituents? Answer:-

सर्वद्वारेषु देहेऽस्मिन् प्रकाश उपजायते ।
ज्ञानं यदा तदा विद्याद्विवृद्धं सत्त्वमित्युत ॥११॥

11. When the light of knowledge shines at all the openings of the senses in this body, one may know that Sattva is dominant.

11.1. सर्वद्वारेषु इति ॥ सर्वद्वारेषु—आत्मनः उपलब्धिद्वाराणि श्रोत्रादीनि सर्वाणि करणानि, तेषु सर्वेषु द्वारेषु अन्तःकरणस्य बुद्धेः वृत्तिः प्रकाशः देहे अस्मिन् प्रकाशशब्दवाच्यः सर्वद्वारेषु उपजायते । तदेव ज्ञानम् । यदा एवं प्रकाशः ज्ञानाख्यः उपजायते, तदा ज्ञानप्रकाशेन लिङ्गेन विद्यात् विवृद्धं उद्भूतं सत्त्वं इति उत अपि ॥

11.1. The expression 'the openings' refers to the gate-ways

of cognition—the ear, etc., forming the sense-organs. The 'light' referred to here is the modification of the inner organ, the intellect. When it shines out at all the openings of the body, it is knowledge. When the light of knowledge shines thus, taking it as a mark, one may know that the *sattva* is predominant.

12.0. रजसः उद्भूतस्य इदं चिह्नम्—

12.0. The mark of the predominance of *rajas* is as follows:

लोभः प्रवृत्तिरारम्भः कर्मणामशमः स्पृहा ।
रजस्येतानि जायन्ते विवृद्धे भरतर्षभ ॥१२॥

12. Greed, activity, commencement of works, disquiet, desire—these appear when Rajas predominates, O thou, the best of the Bharatas!

12.1. लोभः इति ॥ लोभः परद्रव्यादित्सा, प्रवृत्तिः प्रवर्तनं सामान्यचेष्टा, आरम्भः—कस्य ? —कर्मणां, अशमः अनुपशमः—हर्षरागादिप्रवृत्तिः, स्पृहा सर्वसामान्यवस्तुविषया तृष्णा—रजसि गुणे विवृद्धे एतानि लिङ्गानि जायन्ते हे भरतर्षभ ! ॥

12.1. 'Greed' is the desire to grasp others' possessions; 'activity' is effort in general, 'Commencement' is starting of works. 'Disquiet' consists in the effort induced by pleasure, attachment, etc; 'desire' is directed to all kinds of ordinary objects. These mental states become evident when *rajas* predominates.

अप्रकाशोऽप्रवृत्तिश्च प्रमादो मोह एव च ।
तमस्येतानि जायन्ते विवृद्धे कुरुनन्दन ॥१३॥

13. Gloom, inaction, error and delusion, too, O thou scion of Kurus! come into being when Tamas increases.

13.1. अप्रकाशः इति ॥ अप्रकाशः अविवेकः, अत्यन्तं अप्रवृत्तिश्च प्रवृत्त्यभावः तत्कार्यं, प्रमादः मोहः एव च [तत्कार्ये,] अविवेकः मूढता इत्यर्थः । तमसि गुणे विवृद्धे एतानि लिङ्गानि जायन्ते, हे कुरुनन्दन ! ॥

13.1. 'Gloom' is lack of discrimination; extreme 'inaction' is its effect. 'Error' and 'delusion' too are its effects. Lack of discrimination is 'delusion'. When the constituent *tamas* increases, these signs become evident, O Arjuna!

14.0. मरणद्वारेण अपि यत् फलं प्राप्यते, तदपि सङ्गरागहेतुकं सर्वं गौणम् एव इति दर्शयन् आह—

14.0. Even the consequence after death is due to attachment and clinging alone: it is derived from the constituents. This is now shown:-

यदा सत्त्वे प्रवृद्धे तु प्रलयं याति देहभृत् ।
तदोत्तमविदां लोकानमलान् प्रतिपद्यते ॥१४॥

14. Passing away when the Sattva dominates, the embodied self attains the unstained worlds pertaining to the best knowers.

14.1. यदा इति ॥ यदा सत्त्वे प्रवृद्धे तु उद्भूते तु प्रलयं मरणं याति प्रतिपद्यते देहभृत् आत्मा, तदा उत्तमविदाम्—महदादितत्त्वविदां इत्येतत्—लोकान् अमलान् मलरहितान् प्रतिपद्यते प्राप्नोति इत्येतत् ॥

14.1. If a man dies when *sattva* 'dominates' or has full play, he attains the 'unstained worlds' of the best of knowers or the *Sāṁkyas*, those who know the evolutes like the *mahat*.

रजसि प्रलयं गत्वा कर्मसङ्गिषु जायते ।
तथा प्रलीनस्तमसि मूढयोनिषु जायते ॥१५॥

15. Dying when Rajas is dominant one is born among

those addicted to works. Likewise, dying in Tamas one is born amidst the deluded.

15.1. रजसि इति ॥ रजसि गुणे प्रवृद्धे तु प्रलयं मरणं गत्वा प्राप्य कर्मसङ्गिषु कर्मासक्तियुक्तेषु मनुष्येषु जायते । तथा तद्वदेव प्रलीनः मृतः तमसि प्रवृद्धे मूढयोनिषु पश्वादियोनिषु जायते ॥

15.1. Dying in a state of 'dominant *rajas*', one is born among men 'addicted to works'. Likewise dying in a state of dominant *tamas*, one is born in the wombs of animals and so forth.

16.0. अतीतश्लोकार्थस्य एव संक्षेपः उच्यते—

16.0. The gist of the ideas expressed in the foregoing verses is set forth:-

कर्मणः सुकृतस्याहुः सात्त्विकं निर्मलं फलम् ।
रजसस्तु फलं दुःखमज्ञानं तमसः फलम् ॥१६॥

16. They say that stainless and Sāttvic fruit proceeds from meritorious works; but of Rajas the fruit is pain; and of Tamas the fruit is ignorance.

16.1. कर्मणः इति ॥ कर्मणः सुकृतस्य—सात्त्विकस्य इत्यर्थः—आहुः शिष्टाः सात्त्विकं एव निर्मलं फलं इति । रजसस्तु फलं दुःखं—राजसस्य कर्मणः इत्यर्थः, कर्माधिकारात्—फलं अपि दुःखं एव, कारणानुरूप्यात् राजसमेव । तथा अज्ञानं तमसः तामसस्य कर्मणः अधर्मस्य फलं पूर्ववत् ॥

किंच गुणेभ्यः भवति—?

16.1. Of 'meritorious work', i.e. of *sāttvic* work, the virtuous maintain, the fruit is *sāttvic* and stainless, exclusively. But of *rajas* or *rājasic* work 'the fruit is mere pain'. We talk of *rājasic* work as the present is the context of works. Due to conformity with the cause, the fruit also is *rājasic*. Likewise, 'ignorance' is the fruit of *tāmasic* work, i.e. of unrighteous work.

What else emanates from the constituents?

सत्त्वात्संजायते ज्ञानं रजसो लोभ एव च ।
प्रमादमोहौ तमसो भवतोऽज्ञानमेव च ॥१७॥

17. Of Sattva is born knowledge; and of Rajas, greed. Error, delusion and ignorance are born of Tamas.

17.1. सत्त्वात् इति ॥ सत्त्वात् लब्धात्मकात् सञ्जायते समुत्पद्यते ज्ञानं, रजसः लोभः एव च, प्रमादमोहौ प्रमादश्च मोहश्च प्रमादमोहौ उभौ तमसः गुणात् भवतः, अज्ञानम् एव च भवति ॥

किंच—

17.1. Of dominating *sattva* 'knowledge 'is born'—it springs up from *sattva*. 'Greed' is born of *rajas*. 'Error, delusion, and also ignorance' result from the constituent *tamas*.

And,

ऊर्ध्वं गच्छन्ति सत्त्वस्था मध्ये तिष्ठन्ति राजसाः ।
जघन्यगुणवृत्तस्था अधो गच्छन्ति तामसाः ॥१८॥

18. Those confirmed in Sattva go up; the Rājasic abide in the middle zone, while the Tāmasic folk, abiding in the ways of the lowest constituent, go down.

18.1. ऊर्ध्वं इति ॥ ऊर्ध्वं गच्छन्ति देवलोकादिषु उत्पद्यन्ते सत्त्वस्थाः सत्त्वगुणवृत्तस्थाः । मध्ये तिष्ठन्ति मनुष्येषु उत्पद्यन्ते राजसाः । जघन्यगुणवृत्तस्थाः जघन्यश्च असौ गुणश्च जघन्यगुणः तमः, तस्य वृत्तं निद्राऽऽलस्यादि, तस्मिन् स्थिताः जघन्यगुणवृत्तस्थाः मूढाः अधः गच्छन्ति पश्वादियोनिषु उत्पद्यन्ते—(के ?)—तामसाः ॥

18.1. 'To go up' means to be born in the worlds of gods (Devas), etc. Those who are confirmed in *sattva*—who live as men of *sattva* should—do so. *Rājasic* natures are born among human beings. Abiding in the ways of the lowest constituent, *tamas*—those whose life is marked by sleep, indolence, etc., who are deluded, 'go down'. They are born in animal wombs. Who do so? The *tāmasic* folk.

19.0. ''पुरुषस्य प्रकृतिस्थत्वरूपेण मिथ्याज्ञानेन युक्तस्य भोग्येषु गुणेषु सुखदुःख-मोहात्मकेषु 'सुखी दुःखी मूढः अहं अस्मि' इत्येवंरूपः यः सङ्गः सः कारणं पुरुषस्य सदसद्योनिजन्मप्राप्तिलक्षणस्य संसारस्य'' इति समासेन पूर्वाध्याये यत् उक्तं, तत् इह 'सत्त्वं रजस्तम इति गुणाः प्रकृतिसम्भवाः' [१४.५.] इति आरभ्य गुणस्वरूपं, गुणवृत्तं, स्ववृत्तेन च गुणानां बन्धकत्वं, गुणवृत्तनिबद्धस्य च पुरुषस्य या गतिः, इत्येतत् सर्वं मिथ्याज्ञानमूलं बन्धकारणं विस्तरेण उक्त्वा, अधुना सम्यग्दर्शनात् मोक्षः वक्तव्यः इत्यतः आह भगवान्—

19.0. In the preceding chapter it was briefly stated that the cause of man's empirical life, marked by births in good and evil wombs, is attachment, which consists in the experience 'I am happy, I am unhappy, I am deluded' with reference to the constituents whose essence is pleasure, pain and delusion, respectively. These experiences accrue to a man subject to nescience by being caught in the clutches of the constituents. Such a man is apt to think that he is involved in *prakṛti*. In this chapter, that brief statement is expanded into the verses from the fifth onwards in which are set forth the nature of the constituents, their operations, bondage and the destiny of the bound man. Now is the time to explain the nature of deliverance through right knowledge. Therefore the Lord says:

नान्यं गुणेभ्यः कर्तारं यदा द्रष्टाऽनुपश्यति ।
गुणेभ्यश्च परं वेत्ति मद्भावं सोऽधिगच्छति ॥१९॥

19. When the percipient sees no agent other than the constituents and knows My status beyond them, he attains My status.

19.1. नान्यं इति ॥ न अन्यं कार्यकरणविषयाकारपरिणतेभ्यः गुणेभ्यः कर्तारं अन्यं यदा द्रष्टा विद्वान् सन् न अनुपश्यति—गुणाः एव सर्वावस्थाः सर्वकर्मणां कर्तारः इत्येवं पश्यति, गुणेभ्यः च परं गुणव्यापारसाक्षिभूतं वेत्ति, मद्भावं मम भावं वासुदेवत्वं ''वासुदेवः सर्वम्'' [७.१९.] इत्येवं पश्यन् सन् सः द्रष्टा अधिगच्छति ॥

19.1. When the 'percipient', i.e., the enlightened man,

sees 'no agent other than the constituents' that have transformed themselves into body, organs and objects of perception—sees that only the constituents in their varied states are the agents in all works, and sees, also, what is beyond these constituents, viz., the witness of their operations—, then he attains My status as Vāsudeva; for, he sees that everything is Vāsudeva (vide BG.7.19).

20.0. कथं सः अधिगच्छति इति ? उच्यते—

20.0. How does he attain that status? Listen:

गुणानेतानतीत्य त्रीन् देही देहसमुद्भवान् ।
जन्ममृत्युजरादुःखैर्विमुक्तोऽमृतमश्नुते ॥२०॥

20. Transcending these three constituents whence the body has sprung up, the embodied self is liberated from birth, death, old age and pains and attains immortality.

20.1. गुणान् इति ॥ गुणान् एतान् यथोक्तान् अतीत्य जीवन्नेव अतिक्रम्य मायोपाधिभूतान् त्रीन् देही देहसमुद्भवान् देहोत्पत्तिबीजभूतान् जन्ममृत्युजरादुःखैः जन्म च मृत्युश्च जरा च दुःखानि च जन्ममृत्युजरादुःखानि तैः जीवन्नेव विमुक्तः सन् विद्वान् अमृतं अश्नुते, एवं मद्भावं अधिगच्छति इत्यर्थः ॥

20.1. Transcending, while alive, these three constituents, these adjuncts of *māyā*, the seeds whence the body has sprung up, the embodied self, in this very life, is released from birth, death, old age and pains. Thus the enlightened sage attains immortality, My status.

21.0. जीवन्नेव गुणान् अतीत्य अमृतं अश्नुते इति प्रश्नबीजं प्रतिलभ्य, अर्जुनः उवाच—

21.0. Noting a point that provokes a question in that statement, Arjuna asked:

अर्जुन उवाच :

कैर्लिङ्गैस्त्रीन् गुणानेतानतीतो भवति प्रभो ।
किमाचारः कथं चैतांस्त्रीन् गुणानतिवर्तते ॥२१॥

Arjuna said:

21. By what signs is he distinguished who has transcended the three constituents? O Lord! How does he behave? How does he get beyond the constituents?

21.1. कैर्लिंगैः इति ॥ कैः लिङ्गैः चिह्नैः त्रीन् गुणान् एतान् व्याख्यातान् अतीतः अतिक्रान्तः भवति प्रभो! किमाचारः कः अस्य आचारः इति किमाचारः कथं केन च प्रकारेण एतान् त्रीन् गुणान् अतिवर्तते अतीत्य वर्तते ॥

21.1. By what 'signs' or marks is 'he distinguished who has transcended the constituents', the nature of which has been described already? How does he 'behave'? How does he live after going beyond the three constituents?

22.0. गुणातीतस्य लक्षणं गुणातीतत्वोपायं च अर्जुनेन पृष्टः अस्मिन् श्लोके प्रश्नद्वयार्थं प्रतिवचनं भगवान् उवाच—यत् तावत् "कैः लिङ्गैः युक्तो गुणातीतो भवति" इति, तत् शृणु—

22.0. Arjuna wanted a definition of the sage who has passed beyond the constituents and also asked how the sage passed beyond them. The Lord replies in this verse:

श्रीभगवानुवाच :

प्रकाशं च प्रवृत्तिं च मोहमेव च पाण्डव ।
न द्वेष्टि संप्रवृत्तानि न निवृत्तानि काङ्क्षति ॥२२॥

The blessed Lord said:

22. Pāṇḍava prince! That sage neither hates light, action and delusion when these spring up, nor seeks them when these disappear.

22.1. प्रकाशं इति ॥ प्रकाशं च सत्त्वकार्यं, प्रवृत्तिं च रजःकार्यं, मोहम् एव च तमःकार्यं, इत्येतानि न द्वेष्टि सम्प्रवृत्तानि सम्यग्विषयभावेन उद्भूतानि—"मम तामसः प्रत्ययः जातः, तेन अहं मूढः; तथा राजसी प्रवृत्तिः मम उत्पन्ना दुःखात्मिका, तेन अहं रजसा प्रवर्तितः प्रचलितः स्वरूपात्; कष्टं मम वर्तते यः अयं मत्स्वरूपावस्थानात् भ्रंशः; तथा सात्त्विकः गुणः प्रकाशात्मा मां विवेकित्वं आपादयन् सुखेन च सञ्जयन् बध्नाति" इति तानि द्वेष्टि असम्यग्दर्शित्वेन । तत् एवं गुणातीतः न द्वेष्टि सम्प्रवृत्तानि । यथा च सात्त्विकादिपुरुषः सत्त्वादिकार्याणि आत्मानं प्रति प्रकाश्य निवृत्तानि काङ्क्षति, न तथा गुणातीतः निवृत्तानि काङ्क्षति इत्यर्थः । एतत् न परप्रत्यक्षं लिङ्गम् । किं तर्हि?—स्वात्मप्रत्यक्षत्वात् आत्मविषयम् एव एतत् लक्षणम् । न हि स्वात्मविषयं द्वेषं आकाङ्क्षां वा परः पश्यति ॥

22.1. Light is the effect of *sattva*; action, of *rajas*; and delusion, of *tamas*. The sage does not hate these when they spring up: "A *tāmasic* mental state has arisen, so am I deluded; a *rājasic* action, essentially painful, has sprung up which drags me down from my real nature. This slip from my real nature as Self is tragic. Likewise an essentially luminous *sāttvic* state, inducing discrimination and promoting pleasure has arisen." Only he whose vision is defective hates these states; not so the sage who has transcended the constituents. Unlike the *sāttvic*, the *rājasic* and the *tāmasic* man who desires these states when they lapse, the sage does not desire them when they disappear. This is the idea. The sage's attitude to these states is not obvious to the outsider; rather, being evident only to the Self, the sage alone may perceive his inner marks. An outsider, of course, cannot discern the inwardly felt aversion and attachment.

23.0. अथ इदानीं "गुणातीतः किमाचारः?" इति प्रश्नस्य प्रतिवचनं आह—

23.0. Now is given the reply to the question how the transcendent sage behaves:

उदासीनवदासीनो गुणैर्यो न विचाल्यते ।
गुणा वर्तन्त इत्येव योऽवतिष्ठति नेङ्गते ॥२३॥

23. Seated as if indifferent, he is not disturbed by the

constituents: he stirs not but remains steadfast, holding that constituents alone prevail.

23.1. उदासीनवत् इति ॥ उदासीनवत् यथा उदासीनः न कस्यचित् पक्षं भजते, तथा अयं गुणातीतत्वोपायमार्गे अवस्थितः आसीनः आत्मवित् गुणैः यः संन्यासी न विचाल्यते विवेकदर्शनावस्थातः । तदेतत् स्फुटीकरोति—गुणाः कार्यकरण-विषयाकारपरिणताः अन्योन्यस्मिन् वर्तन्ते इति यः अवतिष्ठति—छन्दोभङ्गभयात् परस्मैपदप्रयोगः—'यः अनुतिष्ठति' इति वा पाठान्तरं—न इङ्गते न चलति, स्वरूपावस्थः एव भवति इत्यर्थः ॥

किंच—

23.1. 'As if indifferent'—as an indifferent man does not take sides, so too is the transcendent sage who is seated or set on the path leading beyond the constituents. He is the knower of the Self, he is the renouncer. He is not disturbed from his discriminating vision by the constituents. This fact is clarified: He stirs not who is established in the knowledge that the constituents are transformed into the body, senses, and objects, and that they conjointly exist. He abides as pure Self. To maintain the metre intact the active voice is used instead of—*avatiṣṭhate*, the middle voice. Or, the reading may be taken as *anutiṣṭhati*.

And,

समदुःखसुखः स्वस्थः समलोष्टाश्मकाञ्चनः ।
तुल्यप्रियाप्रियो धीरस्तुल्यनिन्दात्मसंस्तुतिः ॥२४॥

24. Pain and pleasure are one to him who abides in his Self. He treats alike clod, stone, and gold. To the wise, the pleasant and the unpleasant are alike; so too censure and praise.

24.1. समदुःख इति ॥ समदुःखसुखः समे दुःखसुखे यस्य सः समदुःखसुखः, स्वस्थः स्वे आत्मनि स्थितः प्रसन्नः, समलोष्टाश्मकाञ्चनः, लोष्टं च अश्मा च कांचनं च लोष्टाश्मकाञ्चनानि समानि यस्य सः समलोष्टाश्मकाञ्चनः तुल्यप्रियाप्रियः प्रियं च अप्रियं च प्रियाप्रिये तुल्ये समे यस्य सः अयं तुल्यप्रियाप्रियः, धीरः धीमान्,

तुल्यनिन्दात्मसंस्तुतिः निन्दा च आत्मसंस्तुतिश्च निन्दात्मसंस्तुती, तुल्ये निन्दात्मसंस्तुती यस्य यतेः सः तुल्यनिन्दात्मसंस्तुतिः ॥

किंच–

24.1. To this sage pain and pleasure are equal. He abides in his Self calmly, undisturbed by such experiences. A clod, stone and gold are the same to him. So also the pleasant and the unpleasant, blame and praise. And,

मानापमानयोस्तुल्यस्तुल्यो मित्रारिपक्षयोः ।
सर्वारम्भपरित्यागी गुणातीतः स उच्यते ॥२५॥

25. He is equal in honour and disgrace; equal towards friend and foe. He does not initiate any action. Such a one is styled the transcendent sage.

25.1. मान इति ॥ मानापमानयोः तुल्यः समः निर्विकारः तुल्यः मित्रारिपक्षयोः— यद्यपि उदासीनाः भवन्ति केचित् स्वाभिप्रायेण, तथापि पराभिप्रायेग मित्रारिपक्षयोः इव भवन्ति इति । अयं तु तुल्यः मित्रारिपक्षयोः इत्याह । सर्वारम्भपरित्यागी— दृष्टादृष्टार्थानि कर्माणि आरभ्यन्ते इति आरम्भाः, सर्वान् आरम्भान् परित्यक्तुं शीलं अस्य इति सर्वारम्भपरित्यागी, देहधारणमात्रनिमित्तव्यतिरेकेण सर्वकर्मपरित्यागी इत्यर्थः । गुणातीतः सः उच्यते ॥

25.1. 'Honour and disgrace' are the same to him; he is serene. He is the same towards 'friends and foes'. Though some may consider themselves disinterested, others may view them as partial, friendly or inimical. But this transcendent sage is 'the same to friends and foes', says the Lord. Actions are works undertaken to promote purposes, seen or unseen. The nature of the sage is such that 'he does not initiate any action' i.e., renounces all actions except what is meant to support life in the body. Such a one is called the transcendent sage.

26.0. 'उदासीनवत्' इत्यादि 'गुणातीतः स उच्यते' [२३–२५] इत्येतदन्तं उक्तं

यावत् यत्नसाध्यं तावत् संन्यासिनः अनुष्ठेयं गुणातीतत्वसाधनं मुमुक्षोः, स्थिरीभूतं तु स्वसंवेद्यं सत् गुणातीतस्य यतेः लक्षणं भवति इति । अधुना "कथं च त्रीन् गुणान् अतिवर्तते ?" इत्यस्य प्रश्नस्य प्रतिवचनं आह—

26.0. The characteristics set forth in the verses 14.23-25 demand effort to achieve. The renouncer, the seeker after liberation, has to cultivate them, they being the means leading to the state of transcendence. Once secured, these characteristics become directly discernible in the transcendent sage as his unique marks. Now is given the reply to the question how one is to transcend the three constituents.

मां च योऽव्यभिचारेण भक्तियोगेन सेवते ।
स गुणान् समतीत्यैतान् ब्रह्मभूयाय कल्पते ॥२६॥

26. He who, with the unwavering Yoga of devotion, serves Me, transcends these constituents and becomes fit for the status of Brahman.

26.1. मां इति ॥ मां च ईश्वरं नारायणं सर्वभूतहृदयाश्रितं यः यतिः कर्मी वा अव्यभिचारेण न कदाचित् यः व्यभिचरति भक्तियोगेन—भजनं भक्तिः, सैव योगः—तेन [विवेकविज्ञानात्मकेन] भक्तियोगेन–[स हि भक्तियोगः भगवदनुग्रहप्रसादजः भवति]–सेवते, सः गुणान् समतीत्य एतान् यथोक्तान् ब्रह्मभूयाय, भवनं भूयः, ब्रह्मभूयाय ब्रह्मभवनाय मोक्षाय कल्पते समर्थः भवति इत्यर्थः ॥

26.1. And he, the renouncer or worker who serves, with the Yoga of love, of undeviating devotion, Me, Lord Nārāyaṇa dwelling in the hearts of all beings, transcends the constituents. Love here means devotion, and the Yoga of love has, as essence, discriminative knowledge resulting from divine grace. Such a sage becomes fit, i.e. competent, for winning liberation. *Brahmabhūya* means status as Brahman.

27.0. कुत एतदिति ? उच्यते—

27.0. What is the rationale of this?

ब्रह्मणो हि प्रतिष्ठाऽहममृतस्याव्ययस्य च ।
शाश्वतस्य च धर्मस्य सुखस्यैकान्तिकस्य च ॥२७॥

27. Indeed I am the ground of Brahman, immortal and immutable, as also of eternal righteousness and unfailing bliss.

इति श्रीमहाभारते शतसाहस्र्यां संहितायां वैयासिक्यां
भीष्मपर्वणि श्रीमद्भगवद्गीतासूपनिषत्सु ब्रह्मविद्यायां
योगशास्त्रे श्रीकृष्णार्जुनसंवादे गुणत्रयविभागयोगो
नाम चतुर्दशोऽध्यायः ॥

27.1. ब्रह्मणः इति ॥ ब्रह्मणः परमात्मनः हि यस्मात् प्रतिष्ठा अहं प्रतितिष्ठति अस्मिन् इति प्रतिष्ठा अहं प्रत्यगात्मा । कीदृग्भूतस्य ब्रह्मणः ?— अमृतस्य अविनाशिनः, अव्ययस्य अविकारिणः, शाश्वतस्य च नित्यस्य, धर्मस्य धर्मज्ञानस्य ज्ञानयोगधर्मप्राप्यस्य सुखस्य आनन्दरूपस्य ऐकान्तिकस्य अव्यभिचारिणः अमृतादिस्वभावस्य परमानन्दरूपस्य परमात्मनः प्रत्यगात्मा प्रतिष्ठा, सम्यग्ज्ञानेन परमात्मतया निश्चीयते । तत् एतत् 'ब्रह्म भूयाय कल्पते' (२६) इति उक्तम् । यया च ईश्वरशक्त्या भक्तानुग्रहादिप्रयोजनाय ब्रह्म प्रतितिष्ठते प्रवर्तते, सा शक्तिः ब्रह्मैव अहं शक्तिशक्तिमतोः अनन्यत्वात् इत्यभिप्रायः ।

27.1. For, I, the inner Self, am the ground in which dwells Brahman, the Supreme Self. What is the nature of this Brahman? It is the immortal and immutable sustainer of eternal righteousness, i.e. of knowledge, of righteousness and of unfailing bliss, attainable through the Yoga of knowledge and righteousness. The inner Self is the ground of the Supreme Self whose essence is immortality, etc., and the highest bliss. This inner Self is ascertained to be the Supreme Self through right knowledge. This truth has already been affirmed in 14.26, "becomes fit for the status of Brahman." That power of God by means of which Brahman functions to promote well-being, etc., of the devotees is the same as Brahman or Myself; for power and its possessor are one. This is the idea.

27.2. अथवा—ब्रह्मशब्दवाच्यत्वात् सविकल्पकं ब्रह्म । तस्य ब्रह्मणः निर्विकल्पकः अहमेव नान्यः प्रतिष्ठा आश्रयः । तथा—किंविशिष्टस्य ? अमृतस्य अमरणधर्मस्य अव्ययस्य च व्ययरहितस्य । किञ्च—शाश्वतस्य च नित्यस्य, धर्मस्य ज्ञाननिष्ठालक्षणस्य सुखस्य तज्जनितस्य ऐकान्तिकस्य एकान्तनियतस्य च, 'प्रतिष्ठा अहं' इति अनुवर्तते ॥

27.2. Or, 'Brahman' here refers to Brahman with attributes as It is the denotation of the term Brahman. Of this Brahman, I, who am beyond all attributes, alone am the ground, and none else. The qualifications of Brahman with attributes are—'immortal and immutable'. I am also the ground of 'eternal righteousness and of unfailing bliss' which are marked by steadfastness in the knowledge generating unfailing bliss. 'I am the ground'—this expression is implied in this context.

इति श्रीमत्परमहंसपरिव्राजकाचार्यगोविदभगवत्पूज्यपादशिष्य-
श्रीमच्छंकरभगवतः कृतौ श्रीमद्भगवद्गीताभाष्ये गुणत्रय-
विभागयोगो नाम चतुर्दशोऽध्यायः ॥१४॥

पञ्चदशोऽध्यायः

CHAPTER XV

THE YOGA OF THE SUPREME SPIRIT

0.1. यस्मात् मदधीनं कर्मिणां कर्मफलं, ज्ञानिनां च ज्ञानफलं, अतः भक्तियोगेन मां ये सेवन्ते ते मम प्रसादात् ज्ञानप्राप्तिक्रमेण गुणातीताः मोक्षं गच्छन्ति । किमु वक्तव्यं आत्मनः तत्त्वमेव सम्यक् विजानन्तः इति । अतः भगवान् अर्जुनेन अपृष्टोऽपि आत्मनः तत्त्वं विवक्षुः उवाच 'ऊर्ध्वमूलं' इत्यादिना । तत्र तावत् वृक्षरूपककल्पनया वैराग्यहेतोः संसारस्वरूपं वर्णयति—विरक्तस्य हि संसारात् भगवत्तत्त्वज्ञाने अधिकारः; न अन्यस्येति ॥

0.1. Since I control the fruits of works of those who do them and the fruits of the knower's knowledge, those who devote themselves to Me, conforming to the Yoga of devotion, achieve liberation after they transcend the constituents of Prakṛti through knowledge won by My grace. Where is the need, then, to speak of those who have mastered the truth of the Self? Therefore, the Lord, though unasked by Arjuna, seeking to set forth the truth about Himself, uttered the following verses of this chapter. In the first place, to generate detachment, He describes, employing the metaphor of the tree, the nature of empirical life; for only one detached from empirical life is competent to grasp the truth about the Lord; none else.

श्रीभगवानुवाच :

ऊर्ध्वमूलमधःशाखमश्वत्थं प्राहुरव्ययम् ।
छन्दांसि यस्य पर्णानि यस्तं वेद स वेदवित् ॥१॥

The blessed Lord said:

1. They speak of the eternal fig tree whose roots are above and branches below. Its leaves are the Vedic hymns. He who knows it knows the Vedas.

1.1. ऊर्ध्वमूलं—इति ॥ ऊर्ध्वमूलं कालतः सूक्ष्मत्वात्, कारणत्वात् नित्यत्वात् महत्त्वाच्च उच्यते ऊर्ध्वमिति ब्रह्म अव्यक्तं मायाशक्तिमत्, तत् मूलं अस्येति सोऽयं संसारवृक्षः ऊर्ध्वमूलः । श्रुतेश्च—'ऊर्ध्वमूलोऽवाक्शाखः एषोऽश्वत्थः सनातनः' [कठ. उ. ६. १.] इति, पुराणे च—

अव्यक्तमूलप्रभवस्तस्यैवानुग्रहोच्छ्रितः ।
बुद्धिस्कन्धमयश्चैव इन्द्रियान्तरकोटरः ॥
महाभूतविशाखश्च विषयैः पत्रवांस्तथा ।
धर्माधर्मसुपुष्पश्च सुखदुःखफलोदयः ॥
आजीव्यः सर्वभूतानां ब्रह्मवृक्षः सनातनः ।
एतद्ब्रह्मवनं चैव ब्रह्मवृक्षस्य तस्य तत् ॥
एतच्छित्त्वा च भित्त्वा च ज्ञानेन परमासिना ।
ततश्चात्मरतिं प्राप्य तस्मान्नावर्तते पुनः ।
[अश्वमे. पर्व. ३५.२०–२२; ४७. १२–१५.]

1.1. Being subtler than time and being the cause, eternal and great, Brahman the unmanifest, who is endowed with the power of Māyā, is said to be 'above'. That Brahman is the root of this tree of transmigrating life. *Sruti* affirms the same. 'With root above and branches below' this fig tree is eternal, (*KU.* 3.2.1). In the *Purāṇas* it is affirmed: "The eternal tree Brahman has sprung from the unmanifest root; it rises high due to His blessing; it consists largely of the branches of the intellect, the hollows of the sense-organs, the varied twigs of material elements. Its leaves are sense-objects. Its glorious flowers are righteousness and unrighteousness. Fruits borne by this tree are pleasures and pains. On it depend all beings. This is also the forest of Brahman, consisting of that Brahman-tree. Having cut it and split it with the supreme sword of knowledge, and gaining the bliss of Self, none returns therefrom, (*Aśva.parvaṇ*, 35.20–22; 47.12–15, etc.).

1.2. इत्यादि । तं ऊर्ध्वमूलं संसारं मायामयं वृक्षं आहुः । महदहङ्कारतन्मात्रादयः शाखाः इव अस्य अधः भवन्तीति सोऽयं अधःशाखः, तं अधःशाखम् । न श्वोऽपि स्थाता इति अश्वत्थः तं क्षणप्रध्वंसिनं अश्वत्थं प्राहुः कथयन्ति । अव्ययं—संसारमायायाः अनादिकालप्रवृत्तत्वात् सोऽयं संसारवृक्षः अव्ययः—अनाद्यनन्तदेहादिसन्तानाश्रयः हि सुप्रसिद्धः—तं अव्ययम् । तस्यैव संसारवृक्षस्य इदं अन्यत् विशेषणम्—छन्दांसि यस्य पर्णानि छन्दांसि छादनात् ऋग्यजुःसामलक्षणानि यस्य

संसारवृक्षस्य पर्णानीव पर्णानि । यथा वृक्षस्य परिरक्षणार्थानि पर्णानि, तथा वेदाः संसारवृक्षपरिरक्षणार्थाः, धर्माधर्मतद्धेतुफलप्रदर्शनार्थत्वात् । यथाव्याख्यातं संसारवृक्षं समूलं यः तं वेद सः वेदवित्, वेदार्थवित् इत्यर्थः । न हि समूलात् संसारवृक्षात् अस्मात् ज्ञेयः अन्यः अणुमात्रोऽपि अवशिष्टः अस्ति इत्यतः सर्वज्ञः सर्ववेदार्थविदिति समूलसंसारवृक्षज्ञानं स्तौति ॥

1.2. They say that this tree of transmigratory life with its root above is a riddle. 'Its branches are below', consisting of the *mahat* (the principle of the intellect), egoism, the rudimentary elements and so forth. This tree does not last till the next day even; hence it is called *aśvattha*. Every moment it perishes, they (sages) declare. It is eternal as well, since the riddle of transmigratory life has been there from beginningless time. It is well-known as the ground of a beginningless and ceaseless stream of body, etc. Here is an additional attribute of this tree—'its leaves are the Vedic hymns'. The term *chandas* means the Vedic hymns that cover this tree of *saṁsāra*, which is meant to manifest righteousness, unrighteousness, their causes and their effects. He who knows this tree as explained is 'the knower of the Vedas', i.e., one who knows the sense of the Vedas. Indeed there is nothing else left, not even an iota, to be known other than this tree of *saṁsāra* and its root. Hence the knower of all Vedas is omniscient. This declaration eulogizes the knowledge of the tree of *saṁsāra* and its cause.

2.0. तस्य एतस्य संसारवृक्षस्य अपरा अवयवकल्पना उच्यते—

2.0. Another way of picturing the parts of this tree is offered:

अधश्चोर्ध्वं प्रसृतास्तस्य शाखा गुणप्रवृद्धा विषयप्रवालाः ।
अधश्च मूलान्यनुसन्ततानि कर्मानुबन्धीनि मनुष्यलोके ॥२॥

2. Both below and above spread its branches flourishing because of the constituents; sense-objects are its shoots. Below in the world of men extend its roots that link up actions.

2.1. अधश्च इति ॥ अधः मनुष्यादिभ्यः यावत् स्थावरं, अतः ऊर्ध्वञ्च यावत् ब्रह्मणः विश्वसृजः धाम इत्येतदन्तं यथाकर्म यथाश्रुतं ज्ञानकर्मफलानि, तस्य वृक्षस्य शाखा इव शाखाः प्रसृताः प्रगताः, गुणप्रवृद्धाः गुणैः सत्त्वरजस्तमोभिः प्रवृद्धाः स्थूलीकृताः उपादानभूतैः, विषयप्रवालाः विषयाः शब्दादयः प्रवालाः इव देहादि-कर्मफलेभ्य शाखादिभ्यः अङ्कुरीभवन्तीव, तेन विषयप्रवालाः शाखाः । संसारवृक्षस्य परममूलं उपादानकारणं पूर्वं उक्तम् । अथ इदानीं कर्मफलजनितरागद्वेषादिवासनाः मूलानीव धर्माधर्मप्रवृत्तिकारणानि अवान्तरभावीनि तानि अधश्च–देवाद्यपेक्षया–मूलानि अनुसन्ततानि अनुप्रविष्टानि कर्मानुबन्धीनि कर्म धर्माधर्मलक्षणं अनुबन्धः पश्चाद्भावि, येषां उद्भूतिं अनु उद्भवति, तानि कर्मानुबन्धीनि मनुष्यलोके विशेषतः । अत्र हि मनुष्याणां कर्माधिकारः प्रसिद्धः

2.1. 'Below' is the sphere of living beings from men to stationary objects like trees, and 'above'—up to the sphere of the creator Brahmā—extends the region of the fruits of knowledge and work conforming to works and the teachings of *śruti*. 'The branches of this tree', like those of any tree, 'extend' : 'They flourish fed by the constituents', *sattva*, etc., their material causes. 'Sense-objects', sounds and so forth, are 'the shoots'; for, like shoots, they grow from the branches, viz., the fruits of the actions of body, speech, mind. So the branches of this tree are said to have sense-objects as their shoots. The ultimate root, the material cause of this tree of *saṁsāra*, has already been mentioned. Now are pointed out the intermediate roots or causes, namely, impressions left in the mind by the fruits of actions, viz., attachment, aversion etc., those impressions being the causes of other actions, righteous and unrighteous. These extend below the ranges of beings like the roots. They conform to other righteous and unrighteous acts and engender consequences of a like nature. Appearance of beings in the human sphere, especially, is a result of these acts. It is well-known that human beings are here to do works continuing from prior works.

3.0. यस्तु अयं वर्णितः संसारवृक्षः—

3.0. Of this tree of transmigratory life as described;

न रूपमस्येह तथोपलभ्यते नान्तो न चादिर्न च सम्प्रतिष्ठा ।
अश्वत्थमेनं सुविरूढमूलम् असङ्गशस्त्रेण दृढेन छित्त्वा ।।३।।

3. The form here is not known as such; it has no end and no beginning, and no foundation. With the strong weapon of detachment, having split this fig tree with its well-nourished roots;

3.1. न रूपं इति ॥ न रूपं अस्य इह यथा उपवर्णितं तथा नैव उपलभ्यते, स्वप्नमरीच्युदकमायागन्धर्वनगरसमत्वात्; दृष्टनष्टस्वरूपो हि स इति । अत एव न अन्तः न पर्यन्तः, निष्ठा, परिसमाप्तिः वा विद्यते । तथा न च आदिः, "इतः आरभ्य अयं प्रवृत्तः" इति न केनचित् अवगम्यते । न च सम्प्रतिष्ठा स्थितिः मध्यं अस्य केनचित् उपलभ्यते । अश्वत्थं एनं यथोक्तं सुविरूढमूलं सुष्ठु विरूढानि विरोहं गतानि सुदृढानि मूलानि यस्य तं एनं सुविरूढमूलं, असङ्गशस्त्रेण असङ्गः पुत्रवित्तलोकैषणाभ्यः व्युत्थानं, तेन असङ्गशस्त्रेण दृढेन परमात्माभिमुख्यनिश्चयदृढीकृतेन पुनः पुनः विवेकाभ्यासाश्मनिशितेन छित्त्वा संसारवृक्षं सबीजं उद्धृत्य ॥

3.1. Its form as described is not known for certain here at all; for it is like a dream, water of the mirage or a city in the sky. It is fugitive. Therefore, it has no end, fixity or conclusion. Similarly it has no beginning. None knows it as having a firm existence or middle state. Having split or eradicated this fig tree with its stout roots by means of 'the strong weapon of detachment', consisting in the absence of desire for children, wealth, renown, and fame; then seek that Status. The 'strength of the weapon' is derived from the sure orientation of mind towards the supreme Self. It has to be sharpened by repeatedly rubbing it on the whetstone of discriminative knowledge.

ततः पदं तत्परिमार्गितव्यं यस्मिन् गता न निवर्तन्ति भूयः ।
तमेव चाद्यं पुरुषं प्रपद्ये यतः प्रवृत्तिः प्रसृता पुराणी ।।४।।

4. Then that Status has to be laboriously sought after reaching which there is no return. It should be sought

(feeling), 'I take refuge in the Primeval Spirit whence has emanated this ancient process' (of creation, etc.)

4.1. ततः इति ॥ ततः पश्चात् यत् पदं वैष्णवं तत् परिमार्गितव्यं, परिमार्गणं अन्वेषणं, ज्ञातव्यमित्यर्थः । यस्मिन् पदे गताः प्रविष्टाः न निवर्तन्ति न आवर्तन्ते भूयः पुनः संसाराय । कथं परिमार्गितव्यमिति ? आह—तमेव च यः पदशब्देन उक्तः आद्यं आदौ भवं आद्यं पुरुषं प्रपद्ये इत्येवं परिमार्गितव्यं, तच्छरणतया इत्यर्थः । कः असौ पुरुषः इति ? उच्यते—यतः यस्मात् पुरुषात् संसारमायावृक्षप्रवृत्तिः प्रसृता निःसृता, ऐन्द्रजालिकादिव माया, पुराणी चिरन्तनी ॥

4.1. Then that all pervading 'Status' must be laboriously sought. This seeking is a search for knowledge—the Status has to be known. Once it is attained there is no more return from it to this transmigratory life. How is it to be sought? Seek for it in that 'Primeval Spirit', termed 'Status'. 'I take refuge'—with such an attitude one surrenders oneself to that Spirit and seeks refuge. Who is this Spirit? 'That from which has emanated the ancient and everlasting process' of the growth of the tree of transmigratory life as a magical show from a wizard.

5.0. कथंभूताः तत् पदं गच्छन्तीति ? उच्यते—

5.0. Equipped with what virtues do they attain to that Status? Answer:

निर्मानमोहा जितसंगदोषा अध्यात्मनित्या विनिवृत्तकामाः ।
द्वन्द्वैर्विमुक्ताः सुखदुःखसंज्ञैः गच्छन्त्यमूढाः पदमव्ययं तत् ॥५॥

5. Devoid of egoism and delusion, overcoming the flaws of attachment, firm in spirituality, free from lusts, released from dualities called pleasures and pains, the undeluded (sages) repair to that imperishable 'Status'.

5.1. निर्मानमोहाः इति ॥ निर्मानमोहाः मानश्च मोहश्च मानमोहौ, तौ निर्गतौ

येभ्यः ते निर्मानमोहाः मानमोहवर्जिताः जितसङ्गदोषाः सङ्ग एव दोषः सङ्गदोषः, जितः सङ्गदोषो यैः ते जितसङ्गदोषाः । अध्यात्मनित्याः परमात्मस्वरूपालोचने नित्याः तत्पराः । विनिवृत्तकामाः विशेषतो निर्लेपेन निवृत्ताः कामाः येषां ते विनिवृत्तकामाः यतयः संन्यासिनः द्वन्द्वैः प्रियाप्रियादिभिः विमुक्ताः सुखदुःखसंज्ञैः परित्यक्ताः गच्छन्ति अमूढाः मोहवर्जिताः पदं अव्ययं तत् यथोक्तम् ॥

5.1. 'Devoid of egoism and delusion' are they from whom these qualities have departed, and thus are free from both. Attachment is the flaw they have overcome. They are intent on the contemplation of the Essence—the Supreme Self. Without leaving a trace, passions have left them. Such ascetics, renouncers, are released from dualities like the pleasant and the painful. 'Undeluded', they repair to the imperishable 'status' already described.

6.0. तदेव पदं पुनः विशिष्यते—

6.0. That very 'status' is further distinguished:

न तद्भासयते सूर्यो न शशाङ्को न पावकः ।
यद्गत्वा न निवर्तन्ते तद्धाम परमं मम ॥६॥

6. The sun does not illumine it; neither does the moon nor does the fire. That is My abode supreme, after reaching which none falls back.

6.1. न तत् इति ॥ तत् धाम इति व्यवहितेन धाम्ना सम्बध्यते—तत् धाम तेजोरूपं पदं न भासयते सूर्यः आदित्यः सर्वावभासनशक्तिमत्त्वेऽपि सति । तथा न शशाङ्कः चन्द्रः, न पावकः न अग्निरपि । यत् धाम वैष्णवं पदं गत्वा प्राप्य न निवर्तन्ते, यच्च सूर्यादिः न भासयते तत् धाम पदं परमं विष्णोः मम पदम्, यत् गत्वा न निवर्तन्ते इत्युक्तम् ॥

6.1. 'That abode'—these sundered terms must be associated with each other. 'That abode' is a mass of splendour. 'The sun does not illumine it', though the sun is potent to illumine all things. Similarly, also 'the moon and the fire'.

That all-pervasive 'status' after reaching which none falls back and which the sun and the rest cannot illumine is 'My supreme Abode'—the abode of Viṣṇu.

7.0. ननु सर्वा हि गतिः आगत्यन्ता, 'संयोगाः विप्रयोगान्ताः' [स्त्रीपर्व २.३; मोक्षपर्व. २७.३१; ३३०.२०; वा. रा. अयो. १०५.१६. इत्यादौ] इति प्रसिद्धम् । कथं उच्यते "तत् धाम गतानां नास्ति निवृत्तिः" इति ? शृणु तत्र कारणम्—

7.0. "Now, all movement entails an eventual return. 'Unions end in severance' (MBhā. Rā). Why then is it affirmed that those who repair to that Abode do not return?" Listen to the reason:

ममैवांशो जीवलोके जीवभूतः सनातनः ।
मनःषष्ठानीन्द्रियाणि प्रकृतिस्थानि कर्षति ॥७॥

7. An eternal part of Myself alone has become the Jīva in the world of living beings. It pulls the senses together with mind as the sixth that are set in Prakṛti.

7.1. मम इति ॥ मम एव परमात्मनः नारायणस्य, अंशः भागः अवयवः एकदेशः इति अनर्थान्तरं, जीवलोके जीवानां लोके संसारे जीवभूतः कर्ता भोक्ता इति प्रसिद्धः सनातनः चिरन्तनः; यथा जलसूर्यकः सूर्यांशः जलनिमित्तापाये सूर्यमेव गत्वा न निवर्तते—तेनैव आत्मना गच्छति, एवमेव; यथा वा घटाद्युपाधिपरिच्छिन्नः घटाद्याकाशः आकाशांशः सन् घटादिनिमित्तापाये आकाशं प्राप्य न निवर्तते इत्येवम् । अतः उपपन्नं उक्तं 'यद्गत्वा न निवर्तन्ते' [१५.६] इति ॥

7.1. Of Me the Supreme Self, Nārāyaṇa, 'a part', a limb, has become a Jīva in the world of living beings. The Jīva is well-known as the eternal agent and experiencer. As the sun reflected in water is a part of the sun that goes back to the sun and does not come back when the water, the medium of reflection, is no longer there; or as the pot-ether, etc. determined by the pot and so forth, is a part of ether and ceases to exist when the conditions of such determination cease to exist, but go back to ether and do not fall back from it, so the *jīvas* too become one with Me, once they attain Me. Thus the declaration—'after reaching which none falls back'—in 15.6 is all right.

7.2. ननु निरवयवस्य परमात्मनः कुतः अवयवः एकदेशः अंशः इति ? सावयवत्वे च विनाशप्रसङ्गः अवयवविभागात् ।

नैष दोषः, अविद्याकृतोपाधिपरिच्छिन्नः एकदेशः अंश इव कल्पितो यतः । दर्शितश्च अयं अर्थः क्षेत्राध्याये [१३.] विस्तरशः ॥

7.2. *Objection:* "But the supreme Spirit is impartite. How can He have a limb, part or portion? In case He has parts they may get separated and He may perish." *Reply:* "This danger is not there; for the portion or part is only imagined as such due to limitations imposed by nescience. This idea has already been elaborated in chapter 13.

7.3. स च जीवः मदंशत्वेन कल्पितः कथं संसरति उत्क्रामति च इति ? उच्यते—मनःषष्ठानि इन्द्रियाणि श्रोत्रादीनि प्रकृतिस्थानि स्वस्थाने कर्णशष्कुल्यादौ प्रकृतौ स्थितानि कर्षति आकर्षति ॥

कस्मिन् काले ? —

7.3. How does the Jīva, (the living being), postulated as My part, transmigrate leaving the body? 'The Jīva pulls the sense-organs, namely, ear and so forth, with the mind as the sixth'—all firm-set in *prakṛti*, their proper abodes being the auricle and so forth.

At what time?

शरीरं यदवाप्नोति यच्चाप्युत्क्रामतीश्वरः ।
गृहीत्वैतानि संयाति वायुर्गन्धानिवाशयात् ॥८॥

8. When the potent Jīva gains a fresh body and moves out of it, it takes these (the sense organs), just as air does the scents from their abodes.

8.1. शरीरं इति ॥ यत् च अपि यदा चापि उत्क्रामति ईश्वरः देहादिसङ्घात-

स्वामी जीवः, तदा 'कर्षति' इति श्लोकस्य द्वितीयपादः अर्थवशात् प्राथम्येन सम्बध्यते। यदा च पूर्वस्मात् शरीरात् शरीरान्तरं अवाप्नोति तदा गृहीत्वा एतानि मनःषष्ठानि इन्द्रियाणि संयाति सम्यक् याति गच्छति—किमिव इति? आह—वायुः पवनः गन्धान् इव आशयात् पुष्पादेः ॥

कानि पुनः तानि इति? —

8.1. And when the potent *Jīva*, the master of the psycho-physical organism, moves out of it, he takes these sense-organs. The second line of the previous verse must be syntactically connected as the first term of verse 8. From the previous body when the *Jīva* reaches out to a fresh one, 'taking the sense organs, with the mind as the sixth', he moves forth. Like what?—'like the air, taking scents from their abodes'—flowers, etc.

Which sense organs are referred to?

श्रोत्रं चक्षुः स्पर्शनं च रसनं घ्राणमेव च ।
अधिष्ठाय मनश्चायं विषयानुपसेवते ॥९॥

9. The ear, the eye, the skin, the tongue and the nose as well as the mind—resorting to these, the Jīva experiences objects.

9.1. श्रोत्रं इति ॥ श्रोत्रं चक्षुः स्पर्शनं च त्वगिन्द्रियं रसनं जिह्वा घ्राणम् एव च, मनः च षष्ठं प्रत्येकं इन्द्रियेण सह, अधिष्ठाय देहस्थः विषयान् शब्दादीन् उपसेवते ॥

एवं देहगतं देहात्—

9.1. Dwelling in the body and 'resorting to the five sense-organs', ear etc., the mind being the sixth, the Jīva experiences objects.

The dweller in the body while leaving it,

उत्क्रामन्तं स्थितं वापि भुञ्जानं वा गुणान्वितम् ।
विमूढा नानुपश्यन्ति पश्यन्ति ज्ञानचक्षुषः ॥१०॥

10. The deluded do not perceive him, going out or staying or experiencing through association with the Gunas. Only those who have wisdom's eye perceive him.

10.1. उत्क्रामन्तं इति ॥ उत्क्रामन्तं देहं पूर्वोपात्तं परित्यजन्तं स्थितं वाऽपि देहे तिष्ठन्तं भुञ्जानं वा शब्दादींश्च उपलभमानं गुणान्वितं सुखदुःखमोहाख्यैः गुणैः अन्वितं अनुगतं संयुक्तमित्यर्थः । एवंभूतमपि एनं अत्यन्तदर्शनगोचरप्राप्तं विमूढाः दृष्टादृष्टविषयभोगबलाकृष्टचेतस्तया अनेकधा मूढाः न अनुपश्यन्ति— अहो ! कष्टं वर्तते इति अनुक्रोशति च भगवान् । ये तु पुनः प्रमाणजनितज्ञानचक्षुषः ते एनं पश्यन्ति ज्ञानचक्षुषः, विविक्तदृष्टयः इत्यर्थः ॥
केचित्तु—

10.1. As the *Jīva* gives up a body previously tenanted, or when it dwells there experiencing objects like sounds and so forth, it is in contact with constituents whose essences are pleasure, pain and delusion. It is fit to be perceived vividly, yet the deluded fools fail to perceive it; for, their minds, in the grip of varied objective experiences, are distracted. The Lord expresses His pity for their sad plight. In contrast, those who have the eye of valid knowledge, yielded by the right means of knowledge, are clear-eyed and do see the *Jīva*.

But some

यतन्तो योगिनश्चैनं पश्यन्त्यात्मन्यवस्थितम् ।
यतन्तोऽप्यकृतात्मानो नैनं पश्यन्त्यचेतसः ॥११॥

11. Those who persevere, endued with Yoga, see the Jīva dwelling in the inner self; but they of unpurified minds, not having mastered the inner self, fail to see despite perseverance.

11.1. यतन्तः इति ॥ यतन्तः प्रयत्नं कुर्वन्तः योगिनः च समाहितचित्ताः एनं प्रकृतं आत्मानं पश्यन्ति "अयं अहं अस्मि" इति उपलभन्ते आत्मनि स्वस्यां बुद्धौ अवस्थितम् । यतन्तोऽपि शास्त्रादिप्रमाणैः, अकृतात्मानः असंस्कृतात्मानः तपसा इन्द्रियजयेन च, दुश्चरितात् अनुपरताः, अशान्तदर्पाः, प्रयत्नं कुर्वन्तोऽपि न एनं पश्यन्ति अचेतसः अविवेकिनः ॥

11.1. 'Persevering'—striving hard. Such Yogins with concentrated minds see the *Jīva*, knowing, 'here I am, the self'. The content of their knowledge takes the form, 'here I am'. This perception occurs in the inner self, the intellect. Though 'striving hard', employing the means of knowledge, there are others who, 'not having mastered the inner sense', or purified it by means of penance such as sense-control, not having abstained from the wicked ways of life, and not having abolished vanity—do not see the Self (the *Jīva*). They are the mindless or undiscriminating.

12.0. यत् पदं सर्वस्य अवभासकमपि अग्न्यादित्यादिकं ज्योतिः न अवभासयते, यत् प्राप्ताश्च मुमुक्षवः पुनः संसाराभिमुखाः न निवर्तन्ते, यस्य च पदस्य उपाधिभेदं अनु विधीयमानाः जीवाः—घटकाशादयः इव आकाशस्य—अंशाः, तस्य पदस्य सर्वात्मत्वं सर्वव्यवहारास्पदत्वं च विवक्षुः चतुर्भिः श्लोकैः विभूतिसंक्षेपमाह भगवान्—

12.0. That Status which, while illuminating all, itself needs no illumination by the light of fire, sun, etc., after attaining which seekers after liberation no more return to transmigratory life, in accordance with whose varying adjuncts living beings are fashioned as Its parts just as the pot-ether, etc., are fashioned according to the adjuncts of the ether enclosed—that Status is set forth in four verses as the Self of all things and the ground of all empirical activities. Also, these verses summarise the powers of the Status in question. The blessed Lord said:

यदादित्यगतं तेजो जगद्भासयतेऽखिलम् ।
यच्चन्द्रमसि यच्चाग्नौ तत्तेजो विद्धि मामकम् ॥१२॥

12. The luminous energy of the sun illuminating the entire world, the same that is in the moon and fire—know that radiance to be Mine.

12.1. यदादित्य इति ॥ यत् आदित्यगतं आदित्याश्रयं—किं तत्? —तेजः दीप्तिः प्रकाशः जगत् भासयते प्रकाशयति अखिलं समस्तं; यत् चन्द्रमसि शशभृति

तेजः अवभासकं वर्तते, यत् च अग्नौ हुतवहे. तत् तेजः विद्धि विजानीहि मामकं मदीयं मम विष्णोः तत् ज्योतिः ॥

अथवा—यत् आदित्यगतं तेजः चैतन्यात्मकं ज्योतिः, यत् चन्द्रमसि, यच्च अग्नौ वर्तते तत् तेजः विद्धि मामकं मदीयं विष्णोः तत् ज्योतिः ।

ननु स्थावरेषु जङ्गमेषु च तत् समानं चैतन्यात्मकं ज्योतिः । तत्र कथं इदं विशेषणं 'यदादित्यगतम्' इत्यादि ?

नैष दोषः; सत्त्वाधिक्यात् आविस्तरत्वोपपत्तेः । आदित्यादिषु हि सत्त्वं अत्यन्तप्रकाशं अत्यन्तभास्वरं, अतः तत्रैव आविस्तरं ज्योतिः इति तत् विशिष्यते, न तु तत्रैव तत् अधिकं इति । यथा हि लोके, तुल्येऽपि मुखसंस्थाने, न काष्ठकुड्यादौ मुखं आविर्भवति, आदर्शादौ तु स्वच्छे स्वच्छतरे च तारतम्येन आविर्भवति, तद्वत् ॥

किंच—

12.1. That luminous energy, the splendour, the light of the sun which illumines the entire world, the same as that which exists in the moon and the fire,—know that to be Mine who am Viṣṇu. Or, the luminous conscious light in the sun as also in the moon and fire—know that to be Mine, i.e., of Viṣṇu. *Objection:* "Now, both in objects unmoving and moving is equally present the light of consciousness; then why qualify it as what is present in the sun, etc?" *Reply:* "This is no flaw; for, due to the excess of the luminous power it is reasonable to hold that there are differing degrees of its manifestation. In the sun and so forth, *sattva* with its excess of light is extremely resplendent; so light is more manifest there. Therefore, the sun, the moon, etc., have been selected to qualify that light, and it is not suggested that it is confined to them. This case is similar to the reflection of one's face that vividly shines forth in mirrors of varying degrees of clarity and not in opaque materials like wood and stone.

And,

गामाविश्य च भूतानि धारयाम्यहमोजसा ।
पुष्णामि चौषधीः सर्वाः सोमो भूत्वा रसात्मकः ॥१३॥

13. Entering into the earth, with prowess I sustain all

beings; becoming the moon with its essence of sap, I foster all plants and herbs.

13.1. गां इति ॥ गां पृथिवीं आविश्य प्रविश्य धारयामि भूतानि जगत् अहं ओजसा बलेन; यत् बलं कामरागविवर्जितं ऐश्वरं रूपं जगद्विधारणाय पृथिव्यां आविष्टं, येन पृथिवी गुर्वी न अधः पतति, न विदीर्यते च । तथा च मन्त्रवर्णः—'येन द्यौरुग्रा पृथिवी च दृढा' [तै. सं. ४.१.८.] इति, 'स दाधार पृथिवीम्' [तै. सं. ४.१.८.] इत्यादिश्च । अतः गामाविश्य च भूतानि चराचराणि धारयामि इति युक्तमुक्तम् । किंच—पृथिव्यां जाताः ओषधीः सर्वाः व्रीहियवाद्याः पुष्णामि पुष्टिमतीः रसस्वादुमतीः च करोमि सोमः भूत्वा रसात्मकः सोमः सन् रसात्मकः रसस्वभावः । सर्वरसानां आकरः सोमः । स हि सर्वरसात्मकः सर्वाः ओषधीः स्वात्मरसान् अनुप्रवेशयन् पुष्णाति ॥

किंच—

13.1. 'Entering into the earth' I sustain all beings—i.e. the whole world—with My prowess, free from cravings and attachments. The reference is to the divine form present in the earth for its sustenance. Due to it the earth does not collapse and splinter. Hence the affirmation in the TS: 'By which the firmament and the mighty earth are held steadfast, (4.1.8); 'He upheld the earth' (Ibid). Hence also has it been declared aright. 'I sustain the beings, moving and unmoving, having entered the earth.' Moreover, plants and herbs—i.e., barley and so forth—I sustain, becoming the sapful moon; I make them juicy and sweet. The moon is the abode of all essences; it instils their respective saps in all plants and herbs. Thus I foster them.

Besides,

अहं वैश्वानरो भूत्वा प्राणिनां देहमाश्रितः ।
प्राणापानसमायुक्तः पचाम्यन्नं चतुर्विधम् ॥१४॥

14. Becoming the fire (of hunger) and dwelling in the bodies of living beings, together with the inbreath and the outbreath, I digest the four-fold food.

14.1. अहं इति ॥ अहं एव वैश्वानरः उदरस्थः अग्निः भूत्वा—'अयमग्नि-

वैश्वानरो योऽयमन्तः पुरुषे येनेदमन्नं पच्यते' [बृ. उ. ५.९.१.] इत्यादिश्रुतेः— वैश्वानरः सन् प्राणिनां प्राणवतां देहं आश्रितः प्रविष्टः प्राणापानसमायुक्तः प्राणापानाभ्यां समायुक्तः संयुक्तः पचामि पक्तिं करोमि अन्नं अशनं चतुर्विधं चतुष्प्रकारं— भोज्यं, भक्ष्यं, चोष्यं, लेह्यं च। "भोक्ता वैश्वानरः अग्निः, अग्नेः भोज्यं अन्नं सोमः तदेतत् उभयं अग्नीषोमौ सर्वम्" इति पश्यतः अन्नदोषलेपः न भवति ॥

किंच—

14.1. Becoming the fire in the stomach, the Vaiśvānara, and dwelling in the bodies of living beings, conjointly with the inbreath and the outbreath, I digest the four kinds of food. Vide: "This fire is Vaiśvānara who is inside man and by whom food is digested" (BU.5.9.1). The four kinds of food are: what is masticated, swallowed, licked and sucked. He who perceives that the eater is Vaiśvānara fire and what it consumes, its food, is Soma,—those two, the fire and Soma, constituting all that exists—is never affected by the defects of food.

And,

सर्वस्य चाहं हृदि संनिविष्टो मत्तः स्मृतिर्ज्ञानमपोहनं च।
वेदैश्च सर्वैरहमेव वेद्यो वेदान्तकृद्वेदविदेव चाहम् ॥१५॥

15. I dwell in the heart of all; from Me spring memory, knowledge, and forgetfulness. By means of all the Vedas, I alone am to be known. I am the maker of the Vedānta as well as the knower of the Vedas.

15.1. सर्वस्य इति ॥ सर्वस्य च प्राणिजातस्य अहं आत्मा सन् हृदि बुद्धौ संनिविष्टः। अतः मत्तः आत्मनः सर्वप्राणिनां स्मृतिः ज्ञानं तदपोहनं अपगमनं च; येषां यथा पुण्यकर्मिणां पुण्यकर्मानुरोधेन ज्ञानस्मृती भवतः, तथा पापकर्मिणां पापकर्मानुरूपेण स्मृतिज्ञानयोः अपोहनं च अपायनं अपगमनं च। वेदैः च सर्वैः अहम् एव परमात्मा वेद्यः वेदितव्यः। वेदान्तकृत् वेदान्तार्थसम्प्रदायकृत् इत्यर्थः, वेदवित् वेदार्थवित् एव च अहम् ॥

15.1. Being the Self, I dwell in the heart—in the intellect—of all living beings. Therefore, due to Me, the Self, take place their memory, knowledge, and the disappearance of these two.

In the case of meritorious beings, according to their acts of merit, knowledge and memory happen; in the case of the wicked, according to their evil deeds, there occurs the disappearance, the slipping away of these two. By means of all the Vedas, I, the supreme Self, alone am to be known. I am the Maker of the Vedāntas—He who establishes the tradition of Vedāntic teachings, and the knower of the contents of the Vedas, too.

16.0. भगवतः ईश्वरस्य नारायणाख्यस्य विभूतिसंक्षेपः उक्तः विशिष्टोपाधिकृतः 'यदादित्यगतं तेजः' [१५.१२.] इत्यादिना । अथ अधुना तस्यैव क्षराक्षरोपाधिप्रविभक्ततया निरुपाधिकस्य केवलस्य तत्त्व-(स्वरूप-) निर्दिधारयिषया उत्तरे श्लोकाः आरभ्यन्ते । तत्र सर्वमेव अतीतानागताध्यायार्थजातं त्रिधा राशीकृत्य आह—

16.0. In the verses of 15.12, etc. has been offered a summary of the powers of God Nārāyaṇa, the Lord, due to His excellent adjuncts. To determine the principle of the pure unqualified nature of the same Lord, who has also been distinguished by His perishable and imperishable adjuncts, the subsequent verses are offered. Collecting in three groups the contents of all the previous and the following chapters, the Lord says:

द्वाविमौ पुरुषौ लोके क्षरश्चाक्षर एव च ।
क्षरः सर्वाणि भूतानि कूटस्थोऽक्षर उच्यते ॥१६॥

16. In the world are these two Persons, the perishable and the imperishable. The perishable consists of all beings, the imperishable is the immovable.

16.1. द्वाविमौ इति ॥ द्वौ इमौ पृथग्राशीकृतौ पुरुषौ इति उच्येते लोके संसारे—क्षरश्च क्षरतीति क्षरः विनाशी इति एको राशिः; अपरः पुरुषः अक्षरः तद्विपरीतः, भगवतः मायाशक्तिः, क्षराख्यस्य पुरुषस्य उत्पत्तिबीजं अनेकसंसारिजन्तुकामकर्मादिसंस्काराश्रयः, अक्षरः पुरुषः उच्यते । कौ तौ पुरुषौ इति ? आह स्वयमेव भगवान्—क्षरः सर्वाणि भूतानि, समस्तं विकारजातं इत्यर्थः । कूटस्थः कूटः राशिरिव स्थितः । अथवा—कूटः माया, वञ्चना, जिह्मता, कुटिलता इति पर्यायाः ।

अनेकमायावञ्चनादिप्रकारेण स्थितः कूटस्थः, संसारबीजानन्त्यात् न क्षरति इति अक्षरः उच्यते ॥

16.1. In the world of transmigratory life there are 'two Persons'—grouped as two: 'the perishable' consisting of all that perishes or wears away is the first group. The second is 'the imperishable Person' opposed to the first, the Lord's power of *māyā*, the seed whence the first group springs up, on which depend the cravings, acts and impressions of the numerous beings that transmigrate. The Lord Himself points out which these two persons are: the 'perishable person' consists of all beings, the entire body of transformations. 'The immovable', the stable group, resembles a heap—*kūṭa*. Or *kūṭa* is *māyā*, deception, tortuousness, crookedness of will—all these being synonymous. It is what stands forth as the manifold *māyā* of deception; for, the seeds of transmigratory life are 'inexhaustible'. So it is styled 'imperishable'.

17.0. आभ्यां क्षराक्षराभ्यां अन्यः विलक्षणः क्षराक्षरोपाधिद्वयदोषेण अस्पृष्टः नित्यशुद्धबुद्धमुक्तस्वभावः—

17.0. Other than these two, the perishable and the imperishable, untouched by the taints of these two groups of adjuncts, and eternally pure, awake, and free is the Supreme Spirit.

उत्तमः पुरुषस्त्वन्यः परमात्मेत्युदाहृतः ।
यो लोकत्रयमाविश्य बिभर्त्यव्यय ईश्वरः ॥१७॥

17. Distinct from these is the Supreme Spirit known as the Supernal Self. Having entered the three worlds, the mighty Lord upholds them.

17.1. उत्तमः इति ॥ उत्तमः उत्कृष्टतमः पुरुषस्तु अन्यः अत्यन्तविलक्षणः आभ्यां परमात्मा इति—परमश्च असौ देहाद्यविद्याकृतात्मभ्यः, आत्मा च सर्वभूतानां प्रत्यक्चेतनः, इत्यतः परमात्मा इति—उदाहृतः उक्तः वेदान्तेषु । स एव विशिष्यते

—यः लोकत्रयं भूर्भुवःस्वराख्यं स्वकीयया चैतन्यबलशक्त्या आविश्य प्रविश्य बिभर्ति स्वरूपसद्भावमात्रेण बिभर्ति धारयति, अव्ययः न अस्य व्ययः विद्यते इति अव्ययः —कः ?— ईश्वरः सर्वज्ञः नारायणाख्यः ईशनशीलः ॥

17.1. The 'Supreme Spirit', on the other hand, is 'the other', altogether different from the first two. It is beyond these two persons—body, etc., postulated through nescience. It is also the Self, the inner Self, of all beings. It is called the 'Supreme Self' in the Upaniṣads, dealing with the quintessence of the Vedas. Again He is characterized as the one who upholds, by His presence, the three worlds—the earth, the middle region and the heavens—by virtue of His spiritual potency and strength. He is immutable, for He knows no diminution. Who is He?—the omniscient Lord, called Nārāyaṇa who rules, as a matter of course.

18.0. यथाव्याख्यातस्य ईश्वरस्य "पुरुषोत्तमः" इत्येतत् नाम प्रसिद्धम् । तस्य नामनिर्वचनप्रसिद्ध्या अर्थवत्त्वं नाम्नो दर्शयन् "निरतिशयः अहं ईश्वरः" इति आत्मानं दर्शयति भगवान्—

18.0. The celebrated name of the Lord as explained above is the 'Supreme Spirit' (Puruṣottama). Etymologizing the name to reveal its denotative power, the Lord presents Himself as the unsurpassed Sovereign:

यस्मात् क्षरमतीतोऽहमक्षरादपि चोत्तमः ।
अतोऽस्मि लोके वेदे च प्रथितः पुरुषोत्तमः ॥१८॥

18. Since I surpass the perishable and am exalted above the imperishable, both in common speech and in the Vedas, I am celebrated as the Supreme Spirit.

18.1. यस्मात् इति ॥ यस्मात् क्षरं अतीतः अहं संसारमायावृक्षं अश्वत्थाख्यं अतिक्रान्तः अहं अक्षरादपि संसारमायावृक्षबीजभूतादपि च उत्तमः उत्कृष्टतमः ऊर्ध्वतमो वा, अतः ताभ्यां क्षराक्षराभ्यां उत्तमत्वात् अस्मि भवामि लोके वेदे च प्रथितः प्रख्यातः । पुरुषोत्तमः इत्येवं मां (भक्त-) जनाः विदुः । कवयः काव्यादिषु

च इदं नाम निबध्नन्ति पुरुषोत्तम इत्यनेनाभिधानेनाभिगृणन्ति ॥

18.1. Since I surpass the 'perishable—the magic fig tree of transmigratory life—and exceed even the 'imperishable', the seed of this tree, I am 'the supreme', the highest. Being above these two, the perishable and the imperishable, 'I am celebrated in common speech and the Vedas'. The devotees call Me the Supreme Spirit. The poets employ this name in their poems and so forth, extolling Me.

19.0. अथ इदानीं यथानिरुक्तं आत्मानं यो वेद, तस्य इदं फलं उच्यते—

19.0. Now is stated the reward of one knowing the Self as described above:

यो मामेवमसंमूढो जानाति पुरुषोत्तमम् ।
स सर्वविद्भजति मां सर्वभावेन भारत ॥१९॥

19. He who, undeluded, knows Me thus as the Supreme Spirit is all-knowing; he adores Me, O Bhārata prince! in all possible moods.

19.1. यः इति ॥ यः मां ईश्वरं यथोक्तविशेषणं एवं यथोक्तेन प्रकारेण असंमूढः संमोहवर्जितः सन् जानाति "अयं अहं अस्मि" इति पुरुषोत्तमं, सः सर्ववित्—सर्वात्मना सर्वं वेत्तीति सर्वज्ञः—(सर्वभूतस्थं) भजति मां सर्वभावेन सर्वात्म (चित्त-) तया हे भारत ॥

19.1. He who, 'undeluded'—shorn of all delusions—knows Me with the attributes already set forth, knows the Supreme Spirit as 'He is I'; he is the all-knower. He knows all as the Self of all. He is omniscient. He adores Me as dwelling in all, as the Self of all, O Bhārata prince!

20.0. अस्मिन् अध्याये भगवत्तत्त्वज्ञानं मोक्षफलं उक्त्वा अथ इदानीं तत् स्तौति—

20.0. Elucidating the knowledge of the truth of the Lord, this chapter now extols it:

इति गुह्यतमं शास्त्रमिदमुक्तं मयाऽनघ ।
एतद्बुद्ध्वा बुद्धिमान् स्यात्कृतकृत्यश्च भारत ॥२०॥

20. Thus has been set forth by Me this most occult Śāstra, O sinless Bhārata prince! Knowing this, one becomes wise; he will have done all his duties.

इति श्रीमहाभारते शतसाहस्त्र्यां संहितायां वैयासिक्यां
भीष्मपर्वणि श्रीमद्भगवद्गीतासूपनिषत्सु ब्रह्मविद्यायां
योगशास्त्रे श्रीकृष्णार्जुनसंवादे पुरुषोत्तमयोगो
नाम पञ्चदशोऽध्यायः ॥

20.1. इति इति ॥ इति एतत् गुह्यतमं गोप्यतमं, अत्यन्तरहस्यं इत्येतत् । किं तत् ? शास्त्रम् । यद्यपि गीताख्यं समस्तं "शास्त्रं" उच्यते; तथा अयमेव अध्यायः इह "शास्त्रं" इति उच्यते स्तुत्यर्थं, प्रकरणात् । सर्वो हि गीताशास्त्रार्थः अस्मिन् अध्याये समासेन उक्तः न केवलं गीताशास्त्रार्थ एव, किन्तु सर्वश्च वेदार्थः इह परिसमाप्तः । 'यस्तं वेद स वेदवित्' [१५.१.] 'वेदैश्च सर्वैरहमेव वेद्यः' [१५.१५.] इति च उक्तम् । इदं उक्तं कथितं मया हे अनघ ! अपाप ! । एतत् शास्त्रं यथा-दर्शितार्थं बुद्ध्वा बुद्धिमान् स्यात् भवेत्—न अन्यथा—कृतकृत्यश्च भारत ! कृतं कृत्यं कर्तव्यं येन सः कृतकृत्यः, विशिष्टजन्मप्रसूतेन ब्राह्मणेन यत् कर्तव्यं तत् सर्वं भगवत्तत्त्वे विदिते कृतं भवेत् इत्यर्थः; न च अन्यथा कर्तव्यं परिसमाप्यते कस्यचित् इत्यभिप्रायः । 'सर्वं कर्माखिलं पार्थ ! ज्ञाने परिसमाप्यते' [४.३३.] इति च उक्तम् ।

एतद्धि जन्मसामग्र्यं (साफल्यं) ब्राह्मणस्य विशेषतः ।
प्राप्यैतत्कृतकृत्यो हि द्विजो भवति नान्यथा ॥ [मनुस्मृ. १२.९३.] इति च मानवं वचनम् । यतः एतत् परमार्थतत्त्वं मत्तः श्रुतवान् असि, अतः कृतार्थः त्वं भारत ! इति ॥

20.1. Thus this 'most occult, most hidden, *śāstra*' has been set forth. Though the entire Gītā is held to be a *śāstra* this chapter by itself is here styled *śāstra* by way of eulogy. This is clear from the context, because the import of the entire Gītā has been briefly set forth here. Not only the import of the Gītā but also the entire import of the Veda has been given here in summary. Whoso knows it, is the knower of the Vedas (15.1); I am to be known by means of all the Vedas (15.15). This has been set forth by Me. Knowing this *śāstra* with its import as explained 'one becomes wise'; not otherwise. Such a knower 'will also have performed all his duties'—i.e., he will have discharged his duties. What is to be done by a Brāhmaṇa with his high birth gets done, once the truth of the Lord is known. By no other means is any one's duty fully discharged. (Vide BG.4.33 and Manu 12.93.) "In this consists the fruitfulness of human life, especially in the case of a Brāhmaṇa. Acquiring this, the twice-born fully discharges his duty. There is no other way". Since you have received from Me this transcendental Truth, you, O Bhārata prince! have realized life's purpose.

इति श्रीमत्परमहंसपरिव्राजकाचार्यगोविंदभगवत्पूज्यपादशिष्य-
श्रीमच्छंकरभगवतः कृतौ श्रीमद्भगवद्गीताभाष्ये
पुरुषोत्तमयोगो नाम पञ्चदशोऽध्यायः ॥१५॥

षोडशोऽध्यायः

CHAPTER XVI

THE YOGA OF DIVISION OF ATTRIBUTES, DIVINE AND DEMONIAC

0.1. दैवी आसुरी राक्षसी च इति प्राणिनां प्रकृतयः नवमे अध्याये सूचिताः। तासां विस्तरेण प्रदर्शनाय 'अभयं सत्त्वसंशुद्धिः' इत्यादिः अध्यायः आरभ्यते। तत्र संसारमोक्षाय दैवी प्रकृतिः, निबन्धाय आसुरी राक्षसी च इति दैव्याः आदानाय प्रदर्शनं क्रियते, इतरयोः परिवर्जनाय च।

0.1. In the ninth chapter a reference was made to the division of the nature of living beings into the divine and the demoniac. The present chapter beginning with the verse "Fearlessness, mental purity and so forth. . ." is begun to elucidate them in detail. The divine nature promotes release from transmigratory life; the demoniac and the monstrous nature binds; the divine has to be cultivated while the demoniac and the monstrous are to be shunned.

श्रीभगवानुवाच :

अभयं सत्त्वसंशुद्धिर्ज्ञानयोगव्यवस्थितिः।
दानं दमश्च यज्ञश्च स्वाध्यायस्तप आर्जवम् ॥१॥

The blessed Lord said:

1. Fearlessness, mental purity, persistence in the practice of knowledge, charity, sense-control, sacrifice, study of scripture, penance, uprightness;

1.1. अभयं इति ॥ अभयं अभीरुता। सत्त्वसंशुद्धिः सत्त्वस्य अन्तःकरणस्य संशुद्धिः संव्यवहारेषु परवञ्चनामायाऽनृतादिपरिवर्जनं, शुद्धसत्त्वभावेन व्यवहारः इत्यर्थः। ज्ञानयोगव्यवस्थितिः—ज्ञानं शास्त्रतः आचार्यतश्च आत्मादिपदार्थानां अवगमः, अवगतानां इन्द्रियाद्युपसंहारेण एकाग्रतया स्वात्मसंवेद्यतापादनं योगः, तयोः ज्ञानयोगयोः व्यवस्थितिः व्यवस्थानं तन्निष्ठता। एषा प्रधाना दैवी सात्त्विकी

सम्पत् । यत्र येषां अधिकृतानां या प्रकृतिः सम्भवति, सात्त्विकी सा उच्यते । दानं यथाशक्ति संविभागः अन्नादीनाम् । दमश्च बाह्यकरणानां उपशमः—अन्तःकरणस्य उपशमं शान्तिं वक्ष्यति (१६.२–३.), यज्ञश्च श्रौतः अग्निहोत्रादिः, स्मार्तश्च देवयज्ञादिः स्वाध्यायः ऋग्वेदाद्यध्ययनं अदृष्टार्थम् । तपः वक्ष्यमाणं शारीरादि आर्जवं ऋजुत्वं सर्वदा ॥

किंच—

1.1. 'Fearlessness', is the negation of cowardice. Mental purity is the untainted state of the inner sense, the eschewing of deceit, wiles, falsity, etc., in behaviour, i.e. candour in dealings. 'Persistence in the practice of knowledge': knowledge here means understanding of entities like the self, gathered from the *śāstra* and the teacher—the one-pointed and vivid realization of these truths preceded by Yogic introversion. Devotion to all these is meant here. This is the most important among divine attributes. *Sāttvic* nature manifests itself when eligible persons address themselves to their vocations. 'Charity' is the sharing of food, etc., according to one's resources. 'Sense-control' refers to the disciplining of external senses; that of the inner sense will be referred to later (i.e., in 16.2.3). 'Sacrifice' refers to the performance of rites enjoined by *śruti* and *smṛti*, *agnihotra* and so forth and the worship of celestial beings, respectively. 'The study of scriptures' means the study of the Vedas, Ṛg, etc., to secure a supernatural end. 'Penance' points to the disciplining of the body, etc. 'Uprightness' consists in candour at all times. And,

अहिंसा सत्यमक्रोधस्त्यागः शान्तिरपैशुनम् ।
दया भूतेष्वलोलुप्त्वं मार्दवं ह्रीरचापलम् ॥२॥

2. Non-violence, truthfulness, freedom from wrath, renunciation, tranquillity, absence of envy, kindness to living beings, uncovetousness, gentleness, modesty, dignity;

2.1. अहिंसा इति ॥ अहिंसा अहिंसनं प्राणिनां पीडावर्जनम् । सत्यं अप्रियानृ-

तर्वजितं यथाभूतार्थवचनम् । अक्रोधः परैः आक्रुष्टस्य अभिहतस्य वा प्राप्तस्य क्रोधस्य उपशमनम् । त्यागः संन्यासः—पूर्वं दानस्य उक्तत्वात् । शान्तिः अन्तः-करणस्य उपशमः । अपैशुनं अपिशुनता; परस्मै पररन्ध्रप्रकटीकरणं पैशुनं, तदभावः अपैशुनम् । दया कृपा भूतेषु दुःखितेषु । अलोलुप्त्वं इन्द्रियाणां विषयसंन्निधौ अविक्रिया । मार्दवं मृदुता अक्रौर्यम् । ह्रीः लज्जा । अचापलं असति प्रयोजने वाक्पाणिपादादीनां अव्यापारयितृत्वम् ॥

किंच—

2.1. 'Non-violence' consists in non-injury to living beings. 'Truthfulness' is served by giving expression to facts avoiding falsehood and shock to the listener. 'Freedom from wrath' denotes suppression of anger when abused or hit by others. By 'renunciation' is meant *tyāga*, not charity that has already been mentioned. 'Tranquillity' is inner peace. 'Absence of envy' marks him who won't expose others' weaknesses to their adversaries. 'Kindness' is pity towards the suffering. 'Uncovetousness' consists in freedom from agitation of the senses, when exposed to their objects. 'Gentleness' points to softness, absence of anger. 'Modesty' is a sense of shame. 'Dignity' is the absence of vain activity of tongue, hand, feet, etc.

Moreover,

तेजः क्षमा धृतिः शौचमद्रोहो नातिमानिता ।
भवन्ति सम्पदं दैवीमभिजातस्य भारत ॥३॥

3. Splendour, patience, vigour, cleanliness, benevolence, non-haughtiness—these pertain to one inheriting divine attributes.

3.1. तेजः इति ॥ तेजः प्रागल्भ्यं, न त्वगता दीप्तिः । क्षमा आक्रुष्टस्य ताडितस्य वा अन्तर्विक्रियाऽनुत्पत्तिः—उत्पन्नायां विक्रियायां उपशमनं अक्रोधः इति अवोचाम । इत्थं क्षमायाः अक्रोधस्य च विशेषः । धृतिः देहेन्द्रियेषु अवसादं प्राप्तेषु तस्य प्रतिषेधकः अन्तःकरणवृत्तिविशेषः, येन उत्तम्भितानि करणानि देहश्च न अवसीदन्ति । शौचं द्विविधं, मृज्जलकृतं बाह्यं, आभ्यन्तरं च मनोबुद्ध्योः नैर्मल्यं मायारागादिकालुष्याभावः; एवं द्विविधं शौचम् । अद्रोहः परजिघांसाऽभावः अहिंसनम् । नातिमानिता अत्यर्थं मानः अतिमानः, सः यस्य विद्यते सः अतिमानी,

तद्भावः अतिमानिता, तदभावः नातिमानिता—आत्मनः पूज्यताऽतिशयभावनाऽभाव इत्यर्थः । भवन्ति अभयादीनि एतदन्तानि सम्पदं अभिजातस्य—किंविशिष्टां संपदम् ? —दैवीं, देवानां या सम्पत् तां अभिलक्ष्य जातस्य देवविभूत्यर्हस्य भाविकल्याणस्य इत्यर्थः, हे भारत ! ॥

3.1. 'Splendour' is executive ability, not the lustre of the skin. 'Patience' is the absence of mind's agitation when abused or beaten; the quelling of such agitation when roused is freedom from anger as noted above (16.2). Thus patience may be distinguished from 'freedom from anger'. 'Vigour' is mind's energy that pushes aside the weakness of the body and the senses, and maintains them unenfeebled. 'Cleanliness' is of two kinds—the external, induced by earth and water, and the internal, the purity of mind and intellect or the negation of flaws like guile, craving, etc. 'Benevolence' is the negation of the will to injure; it is non-violence. 'Non-haughtiness' negates excessive pride; it is the absence of the notion that one is more respectable than all others. Excellences like fearlessness pertain to him who has inherited the wealth of divine attributes and who is destined to reap future good fortune. This is the sense.

4.0. अथ इदानीं आसुरी सम्पत् उच्यते—

4.0. Now is stated what the demoniac attributes are:

दम्भो दर्पोऽतिमानश्च क्रोधः पारुष्यमेव च ।
अज्ञानं चाभिजातस्य पार्थ सम्पदमासुरीम् ॥४॥

4. Hypocrisy, arrogance, excessive vanity, anger, harshness and ignorance, Arjuna! are his who has inherited demoniac attributes.

4.1. दम्भः इति ॥ दम्भः धर्मध्वजित्वम् । दर्पः विद्याधनस्वजनादिनिमित्तः उत्सेकः । अतिमानः पूर्वोक्तः । क्रोधश्च, पारुष्यमेव च परुषवचनं—यथा काणं "चक्षुष्मान्", विरूपं "रूपवान्", हीनाभिजनं "उत्तमाभिजनः" इत्यादि । अज्ञानं च अविवेकज्ञानं कर्तव्याकर्तव्यादिविषयमिथ्याप्रत्ययः । अभिजातस्य पार्थ ! —किं अभि-

जातस्येति ? आह—संपदं आसुरीं असुराणां सम्पत् आसुरी तां अभिजातस्य इत्यर्थः ॥

4.1. 'Hypocrisy' is ostentatious religiosity. 'Arrogance' is elation due to knowledge, wealth, strength of relations, etc. 'Excessive vanity' or *nātimānitā*, has been explained under verse 3 above. 'Harshness' is blunt speech like references to a one-eyed man as a man with bright eyes, to a plain man as handsome, to one of low birth as high-born, etc. 'Ignorance' is non-discriminative cognition, erroneous notions regarding duties and other actions. These are his who has inherited demoniac attributes.

5.0. अनयोः सम्पदोः कार्यं उच्यते—

5.0. The effects of these two types of attributes are pointed out:

दैवी सम्पद्विमोक्षाय निबन्धायासुरी मता ।
मा शुचः सम्पदं दैवीमभिजातोऽसि पाण्डव ॥५॥

5. The divine attributes conduce to liberation; the demoniac attributes, to bondage. Pāṇḍava prince! grieve not; you have inherited divine attributes.

5.1. दैवी इति ॥ दैवी सम्पत् या, सा विमोक्षाय संसारबन्धनात् । निबन्धाय नियतः बन्धः निबन्धः तदर्थं आसुरी सम्पत् मता अभिप्रेता । तथा राक्षसी च । तत्र एवं उक्ते सति अर्जुनस्य अन्तर्गतं भावं "किं अहं आसुरीसम्पद्युक्तः ? किं वा दैवीसम्पद्युक्तः ?" इत्येवं आलोचनारूपं आलक्ष्य आह भगवान्—मा शुचः शोकं मा कार्षीः, सम्पदं दैवीं अभिजातः असि अभिलक्ष्य जातोऽसि, भाविकल्याणः त्वं असि इत्यर्थः, हे पाण्डव ! ॥

5.1. The host of divine attributes conduce to liberation from transmigratory life; and the demoniac ones to sure bondage. This is the doctrine. So too do the monstrous (*rākṣasī*) attributes. Noting that on hearing this Arjuna must be wondering whether his attributes are the divine or the demoniac, the Lord remarks: Don't grieve, you have inherited divine attributes. Good fortune is in store for you, O Pāṇḍava!

द्वौ भूतसर्गौ लोकेऽस्मिन् दैव आसुर एव च ।
दैवो विस्तरशः प्रोक्त आसुरं पार्थ मे शृणु ॥६॥

6. Two orders of beings have been created in this world—the divine and the demoniac. The divine has been set forth in detail; listen, Arjuna! to a statement of the demoniac.

6.1. द्वौ इति ॥ द्वौ द्विसङ्खचाकौ भूतसर्गौ भूतानां मनुष्याणां सर्गौ सृष्टी भूतसर्गौ—सृज्येते इति सर्गौ, भूतान्येव सृज्यमानानि दैवासुरसम्पद्द्वययुक्तानि इति द्वौ भूतसर्गौ इति उच्यते, 'द्वया ह वै प्राजापत्या देवाश्चासुराश्च' [बृ. उ. १.३.१.] इति श्रुतेः—लोके अस्मिन्, संसारे इत्यर्थः; सर्वेषां द्वैविध्योपपत्तेः । कौ तौ भूतसर्गौ इति ? उच्यते—प्रकृतावेव दैवः आसुरः एव च । उक्तयोरेव पुनः अनुवादप्रयोजनं आह—दैवः भूतसर्गः 'अभयं सत्त्वसंशुद्धिः' [१६.१.] इत्यादिना विस्तरशः विस्तार-प्रकारैः प्रोक्तः कथितः, न तु आसुरः विस्तरशः इति । अतः तत्परिवर्जनार्थं आसुरं पार्थ ! मे मम वचनात् उच्यमानं विस्तरशः शृणु अवधारय ॥

6.1. Two orders of beings, i.e., of human beings, have been created. Beings created with the divine and demoniac attributes are called the orders of creation. Vide BU 1.3.1—"Two sets of Prajāpati's progeny—gods and demons." They are here in this empirical world. All things may reasonably be put in two groups. Relevant to the context are the divine and the demoniac. Of these the first, the divine order, has been detailed in verses 16.1, etc. Not so the second, the demoniac. Therefore to facilitate its eschewal, listen to a detailed enumeration of it.

7.0. आ अध्यायपरिसमाप्तेः आसुरी सम्पत् प्राणिविशेषणत्वेन प्रदर्श्यते, प्रत्यक्षीकरणेन च शक्यते तस्याः परिवर्जनं कर्तुमिति—

7.0. Till the end of this chapter the demoniac attributes are set forth as qualifying living beings; they are vividly pictured so that they may be eschewed.

प्रवृत्तिं च निवृत्तिं च जना न विदुरासुराः ।
न शौचं नापि चाचारो न सत्यं तेषु विद्यते ॥७॥

7. Demoniac men don't distinguish between action and inaction; they are not clean. They have no observances, no truth.

7.1. प्रवृत्तिं इति ॥ प्रवृत्तिं च प्रवर्तनं, यस्मिन् पुरुषार्थसाधने कर्तव्ये प्रवृत्तिः तां, निवृत्तिं च एतद्विपरीतां, यस्मात् अनर्थहेतोः निवर्तितव्यं सा निवृत्तिः तां तां च, जनाः आसुराः न विदुः न जानन्ति । न केवलं प्रवृतिनिवृत्ती एव ते न विदुः—न शौचं नापि च आचारः न सत्यं तेषु विद्यते—अशौचाः अनाचाराः, मायाविनः, अनृतवादिनो हि आसुराः ॥

किंच—

7.1. 'Action' is effort to cultivate the means to reach human values. 'Inaction' is its opposite, a turning away from the means to disvalues. The demoniac folk know nothing of these. Not only of these two are they ignorant; they don't know cleanliness, right observances or truth. They are indeed unclean, ill-conducted, deceptive and untruthful.

Moreover,

असत्यमप्रतिष्ठं ते जगदाहुरनीश्वरम् ।
अपरस्परसम्भूतं किमन्यत्कामहैतुकम् ॥८॥

8. They declare that this world is untrue, ungrounded, and Godless, and is born of mutual union; it is nothing but lust-born.

8.1. असत्यं इति ॥ असत्यं यथा वयं अनृतप्रायाः तथा इदं जगत् सर्वं असत्यं, अप्रतिष्ठं च—न अस्य धर्माधर्मौ प्रतिष्ठा, अतः अप्रतिष्ठं च—इति ते आसुराः जनाः जगत् आहुः अनीश्वरम्—न च धर्माधर्मसव्यपेक्षकः अस्य शासिता ईश्वरः विद्यते इति अतः अनीश्वरं जगत् आहुः । किंच—अपरस्परसम्भूतं कामप्रयुक्तयोः स्त्रीपुरुषयोः अन्योन्यसंयोगात् जगत् सर्वं सम्भूतम् । किं अन्यत् कामहैतुकं—

कामहेतुः एव कामहैतुकम्; किं अन्यत् जगतः कारणं? न किञ्चित् अदृष्टं धर्माधर्मादि कारणान्तरं विद्यते जगतः। "काम एव प्राणिनां कारणं" इति लोकायतिकदृष्टिः इयम्॥

8.1. Just as we are, for the most part, false, so this entire world is untrue'; it has no ground. For, righteousness and unrighteousness are not its foundation. Such is the declaration of the demoniac folk. It is 'Godless'. There is no God to take into account righteousness and unrighteousness. There is none to rule the world—hence it is 'Godless'. Besides, the whole world is born of sexual relation between man and woman. It is lust-born. What other cause has it? No transcendent cause like righteousness and unrighteousness prevails. This is the materialist philosophy of lust alone being the source of living beings.

एतां दृष्टिमवष्टभ्य नष्टात्मानोऽल्पबुद्धयः।
प्रभवन्त्युग्रकर्माणः क्षयाय जगतोऽहिताः॥९॥

9. Depending on this view, having lost their souls, and equipped with puny intellects, these enemies exert themselves fiercely to destroy the world.

9.1. एतां इति॥ एतां दृष्टिं अवष्टभ्य आश्रित्य नष्टात्मानः नष्टस्वभावाः विभ्रष्टपरलोकसाधनाः अल्पबुद्धयः विषयविषया अल्पैव बुद्धिः येषां ते अल्पबुद्धयः प्रभवन्ति उद्भवन्ति उग्रकर्माणः क्रूरकर्माणः हिंसात्मकाः। क्षयाय जगतः—'प्रभवन्ति' इति सम्बन्धः। जगतः अहिताः शत्रवः इत्यर्थः॥
ते च—

9.1. Relying on this philosophy, having lost their proper nature, falling away from practices leading to the next world, their puny intellects oriented to objects, they sally forth, fiercely violent, and work to destroy the world; they are the enemies of the world.

And they,

काममाश्रित्य दुष्पूरं दम्भमानमदान्विताः ।
मोहाद्गृहीत्वाऽसद्ग्राहान् प्रवर्तन्तेऽशुचिव्रताः ॥१०॥

10. Resorting to lust insatiable, with hypocrisy, vanity, and euphoria, deludedly clinging to dogmas, they work with unclean resolve.

10.1. कामं इति ॥ कामं इच्छाविशेषं आश्रित्य अवष्टभ्य दुष्पूरं अशक्यपूरणं दम्भमानमदान्विताः दम्भश्च मानश्च मदश्च दम्भमानमदाः तैः अन्विताः दम्भमानमदान्विताः मोहात् अविवेकतः गृहीत्वा उपादाय असद्ग्राहान् अशुभनिश्चयान् प्रवर्तन्ते लोके अशुचिव्रताः अशुचीनि व्रतानि येषां ते अशुचिव्रताः ॥

किंच—

10.1. 'Resorting to lust', a particular craving hard to satisfy, with hyprocrisy, etc., 'deludedly' or through lack of discrimination, 'holding false dogmas', they strive in this world with unclean resolves'. Besides,

चिन्तामपरिमेयां च प्रलयान्तामुपाश्रिताः ।
कामोपभोगपरमा एतावदिति निश्चिताः ॥११॥

11. Depending on endless speculation till their dissolution, intent on the enjoyment of objects of desire, sure 'that much' alone is true;

11.1. चिन्तां इति ॥ चिन्तां अपरिमेयां च, न परिमातुं शक्यते यस्याः चिन्तायाः इयत्ता, सा अपरिमेया, तां अपरिमेयां प्रलयान्तां मरणान्तां उपाश्रिताः, सदा चिन्तापराः इत्यर्थः । कामोपभोगपरमाः, काम्यन्ते इति कामाः विषयाः शब्दादयः, तदुपभोगपरमाः 'अयमेव परमः पुरुषार्थो यः कामोपभोगः' इत्येवं निश्चितात्मानः, एतावत् इति निश्चिताः ॥

11.1. Resorting to 'speculation' that may not be measured—that is illimitable—till the moment of death, i.e., ever speculating; 'intent on the enjoyment of sense-objects' like sounds, etc.; assuring themselves that this enjoyment is the supreme goal of life, that this is the truth;

आशापाशशतैर्बद्धाः कामक्रोधपरायणाः ।
ईहन्ते कामभोगार्थमन्यायेनार्थसंचयान् ॥१२॥

12. Bound by a hundred cords of hopes, given up to lust and wrath, they seek unjustly heaps of wealth to enjoy the objects of their lusts.

12.1. आशापाश इति ॥ आशापाशशतैः आशा एव पाशाः तच्छतैः आशापाशशतैः बद्धाः नियन्त्रिताः सन्तः सर्वतः आकृष्यमाणाः, कामक्रोधपरायणाः कामक्रोधौ परं अयनं आश्रयः येषां ते कामक्रोधपरायणाः, ईहन्ते चेष्टन्ते कामभोगार्थं कामभोगप्रयोजनाय न धर्मार्थं अन्यायेन परस्वापहरणादिना इत्यर्थः—किं ? —अर्थसञ्चयान् अर्थप्रचयान् ॥

ईदृशश्च तेषां अभिप्रायः—

12.1. The very hopes are the 'cords'; bound by hundreds of them and pulled in all directions are they whose main props are 'lust and wrath'. To indulge in these two they strive, and not to promote righteousness. 'Unjustly' i.e., by seizing others' property, etc., they accumulate wealth.

Their idea is as follows:

इदमद्य मया लब्धमिदं प्राप्स्ये मनोरथम् ।
इदमस्तीदमपि मे भविष्यति पुनर्धनम् ॥१३॥

13. Today I have won this; I shall fulfil that hope soon. Now this is; this wealth, again, shall be mine.

13.1. इदं इति ॥ इदं द्रव्यं अद्य इदानीं मया लब्धम् । इदं च अन्यत् प्राप्स्ये मनोरथं मनस्तुष्टिकरम् । इदं च अस्ति इदम् अपि मे भविष्यति आगामिनि संवत्सरे पुनः धनं, तेन अहं धनी विख्यातः भविष्यामि इति ॥

13.1. This wealth I have gained now; I shall fulfil that hope to gratify my mind. This is in my possession, and this wealth, too, shall be mine next year. That will make me wealthy and famous.

असौ मया हतः शत्रुर्हनिष्ये चापरानपि ।
ईश्वरोऽहमहं भोगी सिद्धोऽहं बलवान् सुखी ॥१४॥

14. That foe I have slain; other foes, too, I shall slay. I am the mighty lord, the enjoyer. I am all right, strong and happy.

14.1. असौ मया इति ॥ असौ देवदत्तनामा मया हतः दुर्जयः शत्रुः । हनिष्ये च अपरान् अन्यान् वराकान् अपि । किं एते करिष्यन्ति तपस्विनः ? सर्वथाऽपि नास्ति मत्तुल्यः । कथम् ?—ईश्वरः अहं, अहं भोगी । सर्वप्रकारेण च सिद्धः अहं सम्पन्नः पुत्रैः नप्तृभिः, न केवलं मानुषः, बलवान् सुखी च अहमेव ॥

14.1. That formidable foe, say Devadatta, has been slain by me; other petty foes I shall slay. What can these puny fellows do? In no wise can any one equal me. How? I am the 'mighty lord, I the enjoyer'. In every way, I am all right—as regards children, grand-children etc. No ordinary man am I. I am very strong and happy. (Other men are but burdens for the earth).

आढ्योऽभिजनवानस्मि कोऽन्योऽस्ति सदृशो मया ।
यक्ष्ये दास्यामि मोदिष्य इत्यज्ञानविमोहिताः ॥१५॥

15. I am wealthy, high born; who is there equal to me? I sacrifice, give gifts, and make merry—so, deluded by ignorance, they deem.

15.1. आढ्य: इति ॥ आढ्यः धनेन, अभिजनवान् सप्तपुरुषं श्रोत्रियत्वादिसम्पन्नः—तेनापि न मम तुल्यः अस्ति कश्चित् । कः अन्यः अस्ति सदृशः तुल्यः मया ? किं च—यक्ष्ये यागेनापि अन्यान् अभिभविष्यामि, दास्यामि नटादिभ्यः,

मोदिष्ये हर्षं च अतिशयं प्राप्स्यामि, इति एवं अज्ञानविमोहिताः अज्ञानेन विमोहिताः विविधं अविवेकभावं आपन्नाः ॥

15.1. By virtue of riches I am 'wealthy'; 'high-born', having been born in a family of noted Vedic scholars all through seven generations. For this reason none equals me. Who is there equal to me? Besides, by sacrifices, too, I shall surpass others. I shall give gifts to actors, etc. I shall make merry to the utmost. Thus are they ignorantly deluded, having lost all powers of discrimination.

अनेकचित्तविभ्रान्ता मोहजालसमावृताः ।
प्रसक्ताः कामभोगेषु पतन्ति नरकेऽशुचौ ॥१६॥

16. Distracted by myriad fancies, caught in a net of delusion, chasing lustful enjoyments, they fall into unclean hell.

16.1. अनेक इति ॥ अनेकचित्तविभ्रान्ताः उक्तप्रकारैः अनेकैः चित्तैः विविधं भ्रान्ताः अनेकचित्तविभ्रान्ताः; मोहजालसमावृताः मोहः अविवेक अज्ञानं, तदेव जालमिव आवरणात्मकत्वात्, तेन समावृताः । प्रसक्ताः कामभोगेषु तत्रैव निषण्णाः सन्तः तेन उपचितकल्मषाः पतन्ति नरके अशुचौ वैतरण्यादौ ॥

16.1. Distracted by 'numerous fancies', as stated above; shrouded by 'delusion' or non-discrimination, which, since it covers, is a veritable net; addicted to 'lustful enjoyments' whereby, multiplying sins, they fall into an 'unclean hell' such as the Vaitaraṇī.

आत्मसम्भाविताः स्तब्धा धनमानमदान्विताः ।
यजन्ते नामयज्ञैस्ते दम्भेनाविधिपूर्वकम् ॥१७॥

17. Self-exalted, stubborn, rich, conceited and arrogant, they hypocritically offer nominal worship, defying sacred rules.

17.1. आत्म इति ॥ आत्मसम्भाविताः सर्वगुणविशिष्टतया आत्मनैव सम्भाविताः आत्मसम्भाविताः, न साधुभिः । स्तब्धाः अप्रणतात्मानः । धनमानमदान्विताः धननिमित्तः मानः मदश्च, ताभ्यां धनमानमदाभ्यां अन्विताः । यजन्ते नामयज्ञैः नाममात्रैः यज्ञैः ते दम्भेन धर्मध्वजितया अविधिपूर्वकं विधिविहिताङ्गेतिकर्तव्यतारहितम् ॥

17.1. They 'exalt themselves' claiming to possess all excellences; but no good men would praise them. 'Stubborn', not meek; being 'rich', they are 'conceited and arrogant'. Their sacrifices are 'nominal' only and 'hypocritical', meant to show off their religiosity. They neglect the accessories prescribed by 'scriptural rules'.

अहङ्कारं बलं दर्पं कामं क्रोधं च संश्रिताः ।
मामात्मपरदेहेषु प्रद्विषन्तोऽभ्यसूयकाः ॥१८॥

18. Relying on egoism, power, pride, lust and wrath, spurning Me in themselves and others; they are malicious.

18.1. अहंकारं इति ॥ अहङ्कारं अहङ्करणं अहङ्कारः—विद्यमानैः अविद्यमानैश्च गुणैः आत्मनि अध्यारोपितैः विशिष्टमात्मानं "अहं" इति मन्यते सः अहङ्कारः अविद्याख्यः कष्टतमः, सर्वदोषाणां मूलं सर्वानर्थप्रवृत्तीनां च, तथा बलं पराभिभवनिमित्तं कामरागान्वितम् । दर्पं—दर्पो नाम यस्य उद्भवे धर्मं अतिक्रामतीति सः अयं अन्तःकरणाश्रयः दोषविशेषः । कामं स्त्र्यादिविषयम् । क्रोधं अनिष्टविषयम् —एतान् अन्यान् च महतः दोषान् संश्रिताः । किं च—ते मां ईश्वरं आत्मपरदेहेषु स्वदेहे परदेहेषु च तद् बुद्धिकर्मसाक्षिभूतं मां प्रद्विषन्तः, मच्छासनातिवर्तित्वं प्रद्वेषः, तं कुर्वन्तः अभ्यसूयकाः सन्मार्गस्थानां गुणेषु असहमानाः ॥

18.1. They exalt themselves 'egoistically' in regard to qualities real or fancied, which they have imputed to themselves. This 'egoism' or nescience is their worst flaw, the root of all failings as well as of sinful activities. 'Power' is conjoined to greed and leads to the overthrow of others. 'Pride' is that fault of the mind that leads to the disregard of righteousness. 'Lust' has reference to women, etc. 'Wrath' refers to what is disliked.

These traits and other gross faults they resort to. And they spurn Me, the Witness of thoughts and acts in their own bodies as well as in those of others. To spurn is to defy My ordinances. They are malicious, as is evident from their comments on the virtues of the righteous.

तानहं द्विषतः क्रूरान् संसारेषु नराधमान् ।
क्षिपाम्यजस्रमशुभानासुरीष्वेव योनिषु ॥१९॥

19. Those who hate and are wrathful, who are the vilest among men in this transmigratory life, and who are impious—I perpetually fling into demoniac wombs.

19.1. तानहं इति ॥ तान् अहं सन्मार्गप्रतिपक्षभूतान् साधुद्वेषिणः द्विषतः च मां क्रूरान् संसारेषु एव अनेकनरकसंसारमार्गेषु नराधमान् अधर्मदोषवत्त्वात् क्षिपामि प्रक्षिपामि अजस्रं सन्ततं अशुभान् अशुभकर्मकारिणः आसुरीष्वेव क्रूरकर्मप्रायासु व्याघ्रसिंहादि योनिषु—'क्षिपामि' इत्यनेन सम्बन्धः ॥

19.1. Those who are the adversaries of the righteous; who are 'wrathful' and who 'hate' the virtuous; who are the lowest among men, living worldly lives leading to hells—them I fling perpetually into 'demoniac wombs'. They are impious as they do evil works. These 'demoniac wombs' are the wombs of violent beasts like tigers and lions.

आसुरीं योनिमापन्ना मूढा जन्मनि जन्मनि ।
मामप्राप्यैव कौन्तेय ततो यान्त्यधमां गतिम् ॥२०॥

20. Born in a demoniac womb, deluded in repeated births, never reaching Me, Arjuna! they proceed, therefore, to an ignoble state.

20.1. आसुरीं इति ॥ आसुरीं योनिं आपन्नाः प्रतिपन्नाः, मूढाः अविवेकिनः जन्मनि जन्मनि प्रतिजन्म तमोबहुलास्वेव योनिषु जायमानाः अधो गच्छन्तः मूढाः मां ईश्वरं अप्राप्य अनासाद्य एव, हे कौन्तेय ! ततः तस्मादपि यान्ति अधमां गतिं

निकृष्टतमां गतिम् । 'मां अप्राप्यैव' इति—न मत्प्राप्तौ काचिदपि आशङ्का अस्ति, अतः—मच्छिष्टसाधुमार्गप्राप्ति अप्राप्य इत्यर्थः ॥

20.1. Born in a 'demoniac womb', the deluded—those lacking discrimination—, being born every time in wombs predominantly darksome, downwards they plunge, failing to reach Me, the Lord, O Arjuna! Thence they proceed to the very nadir. 'Failing to reach Me' suggests that, had they reached Me, of course there would have been no more worry. But without taking to the right way taught by Me they suffer. This is the sense intended.

21.0. सर्वस्याः आसुर्याः सम्पदः संक्षेपः अयं उच्यते, यस्मिन् त्रिविधे सर्वः आसुरीसंपद्भेदः अनन्तोऽपि अन्तर्भवति । यत्परिहारेण परिहृतश्च भवति, यत् मूलं सर्वस्य अनर्थस्य तत् एतत् उच्यते—

21.0. Here is a summary of all the conceivable demoniac attributes; in this threefold evil the endless demoniac attributes are entailed. They could all be avoided by avoiding the three evils to be presently mentioned, these constituting the very root of all misfortunes.

त्रिविधं नरकस्येदं द्वारं नाशनमात्मनः ।
कामः क्रोधस्तथा लोभस्तस्मादेतत्त्रयं त्यजेत् ॥२१॥

21. Threefold is the gate of hell, destructive of self—lust, wrath and, likewise, greed. Therefore one should reject them.

21.1. त्रिविधं इति ॥ त्रिविधं त्रिप्रकारं नरकस्य प्राप्तौ इदं द्वारं नाशनं आत्मनः, यत् द्वारं प्रविशन्नेव नश्यति आत्मा; कस्मैचित् पुरुषार्थाय योग्यो न भवति इत्येतत् उच्यते 'द्वारं नाशनम् आत्मनः' इति । किं तत्?—कामः क्रोधः तथा लोभः । तस्मात् एतत् त्रयं त्यजेत् । यतः एतत् द्वारं नाशनं आत्मनः, तस्मात् कामादित्रयं एतत् त्यजेत् ॥

त्यागस्तुतिरियम्—

21.1. 'Gateway leading to hell' is of three kinds; each is destructive of self. As soon as one enters it, the self perishes, becomes unfit for achieving any human goal whatsoever. Such is the force of the expression 'destructive of self'. What is this 'three-fold gate'? 'Lust, wrath and, likewise, greed'. Therefore must one reject those three, lust and so forth.

Here is a laudation of such rejection:

एतैर्विमुक्तः कौन्तेय तमोद्वारैस्त्रिभिर्नरः ।
आचरत्यात्मनः श्रेयस्ततो याति परां गतिम् ॥२२॥

22. Released from these three doors of darkness, Arjuna! man attends to what promotes his good; thus he proceeds to the supreme goal.

22.1. एतैः इति ॥ एतैः विमुक्तः कौन्तेय! तमोद्वारैः तमसः नरकस्य दुःखमोहात्मकस्य द्वाराणि कामादयः तैः एतैः त्रिभिः विमुक्तः नरः आचरति अनुतिष्ठति—किं? आत्मनः श्रेयः । यत्प्रतिबद्धः पूर्वं न आचचार, तदपगमात् आचरति । ततः तदाचरणात् याति परां गतिं, मोक्षमपि इति ॥

22.1. Released from them, 'the doors of hell' whose essence is suffering and delusion, man does—what? He does what 'promotes his good'. Blocked by them before, he could not do so; now that they are no more there, he can. Doing what promotes his good, he proceeds to the supreme goal, even emancipation.

23.0. सर्वस्य एतस्य आसुरीसंपत्परिवर्जनस्य श्रेयआचरणस्य च शास्त्रं कारणम् । शास्त्रप्रमाणात् उभयं शक्यं कर्तुं, न अन्यथा । अतः—

23.0. The cause that brings about rejection of demoniac attributes and promotes action leading to the good is the *śāstra*. Due to the authority of the *śāstra* both may be accomplished. There is no other way. So,

यः शास्त्रविधिमुत्सृज्य वर्तते कामकारतः ।
न स सिद्धिमवाप्नोति न सुखं न परां गतिम् ॥२३॥

23. Rejecting the prescription of the Śāstra and living a desire-ridden life, one does not achieve fulfilment, happiness, or the supreme goal.

23.1. यः इति ॥ यः शास्त्रविधिं शास्त्रं वेदः तस्य विधिं कर्तव्याकर्तव्यज्ञान-कारणं विधिप्रतिषेधाख्यं उत्सृज्य त्यक्त्वा वर्तते कामकारतः कामप्रयुक्तः सन्, न सः सिद्धिं पुरुषार्थयोग्यतां अवाप्नोति, न अपि अस्मिन् लोके सुखं, न अपि परां प्रकृष्टां गतिं स्वर्गं मोक्षं वा ॥

23.1. The '*śātra*' is the Veda. Rejecting its positive and negative ordinances regarding the ought and the ought not, he who lives according to the promptings of lust, does not achieve fulfilment or fitness for the goals of life; nor happiness in the world, nor, of course, the supreme goal—heaven or emancipation.

तस्माच्छास्त्रं प्रमाणं ते कार्याकार्यव्यवस्थितौ ।
ज्ञात्वा शास्त्रविधानोक्तं कर्म कर्तुमिहार्हसि ॥२४॥

24. Therefore the Śāstra shall be your guide as regards what should or should not be done. Knowing the work prescribed by the Śāstra, you ought to perform it here.

इति श्रीमहाभारते शतसाहस्र्यां संहितायां वैयासिक्यां भीष्मपर्वणि
श्रीमद्भगवद्गीतासूपनिषत्सु ब्रह्मविद्यायां योगशास्त्रे श्रीकृष्णार्जुन-
संवादे दैवासुरसंपद्विभागयोगो नाम षोडशोऽध्यायः ॥

24.1. तस्मात् इति ॥ तस्मात् शास्त्रं प्रमाणं ज्ञानसाधनं ते तव कार्याकार्य-व्यवस्थितौ कर्तव्याकर्तव्यव्यवस्थायाम् । अतः ज्ञात्वा बुद्ध्वा शास्त्रविधानोक्तं विधिः विधानं, शास्त्रमेव विधानं शास्त्रविधानं, "कुर्यात्, न कुर्यात्" इत्येवंलक्षणं, तेन उक्तं स्वकर्म यत् तत् कर्तुं इह अर्हसि—'इह' इति कर्माधिकारभूमिप्रदर्शनार्थं इति ॥

24.1. Therefore *śāstra* shall be your guide or means of acquiring valid knowledge about 'oughts' and 'ought-nots'. Knowing *śāstraic* prescriptions—the commands and the prohibitions of the *śāstras*—do your work. 'Here' reveals the field of duties to those called upon to perform them.

इति श्रीमत्परमहंसपरिव्राजकाचार्यगोविंदभगवत्पूज्यपादशिष्यश्रीमच्छंकर-
भगवतः कृतौ श्रीमद्भगवद्गीताभाष्ये दैवासुरसंपद्विभागयोगो
नाम षोडशोऽध्यायः ॥१६॥

सप्तदशोऽध्यायः

CHAPTER XVII

THE YOGA OF THREEFOLD FAITH

0.1. 'तस्माच्छास्त्रं प्रमाणं ते' इति भगवद्वाक्यात् लब्धप्रश्नबीजः अर्जुनः उवाच—

0.1. Seizing from the Lord's expression, "*Śāstra* shall be your guide"—a point that prompts a query,

अर्जुन उवाच :

ये शास्त्रविधिमुत्सृज्य यजन्ते श्रद्धयाऽन्विताः ।
तेषां निष्ठा तु का कृष्ण सत्त्वमाहो रजस्तमः ॥१॥

Arjuna said:

1. What, O Kṛṣṇa! is the status of those who sacrifice with faith while ignoring śāstraic injunction? Is it Sāttvic, Rājasic or Tāmasic?

1.1. ये इति ॥ ये केचित् अविशेषिताः शास्त्रविधिं शास्त्रविधानं श्रुतिस्मृतिशास्त्रचोदनां उत्सृज्य परित्यज्य यजन्ते देवादीन् पूजयन्ति श्रद्धया अन्विताः श्रद्धया आस्तिक्यबुद्ध्या अन्विताः संयुक्ताः सन्तः—श्रुतिलक्षणं स्मृतिलक्षणं वा कंचित् शास्त्रविधिं अपश्यन्तः वृद्धव्यवहारदर्शनादेव श्रद्दधानतया ये देवादीन् पूजयन्ति ते इह 'ये शास्त्रविधिमुत्सृज्य यजन्ते श्रद्धयाऽन्विताः' इत्येवं गृह्यन्ते । ये पुनः कंचित् शास्त्रविधिं उपलभमाना एव तं उत्सृज्य अयथाविधि देवादीन् पूजयन्ति ते इह "ये शास्त्रविधिमुत्सृज्य यजन्ते" इति न परिगृह्यन्ते । कस्मात् ? —श्रद्धया अन्वितत्वविशेषणात् । देवादिपूजाविधिपरं किंचित् शास्त्रं पश्यन्त एव तत् उत्सृज्य अश्रद्दधानतया तद्विहितायां देवादिपूजायां श्रद्धया अन्विताः प्रवर्तन्ते इति न शक्यं कल्पयितुं यस्मात्, तस्मात् पूर्वोक्ता एव "ये शास्त्रविधिमुत्सृज्य यजन्ते श्रद्धयाऽन्विताः' इत्यत्र गृह्यन्ते । तेषां एवंभूतानां निष्ठा तु अवस्थानं का कृष्ण ! —सत्त्वं आहो रजः तमः; किं सत्त्वं निष्ठा अवस्थानं, आहोस्वित् रजः, अथवा तमः इति ? । एतत् उक्तं भवति—या तेषां देवादिविषया पूजा, सा किं सात्त्विकी आहोस्वित् राजसी, उत तामसी इति ? ॥

1.1. The discussion is general about whosoever ignores

śāstraic injunctions, i.e. prescriptions of *śruti* and *smṛti*, and yet offers sacrifice—worships gods, etc.,—faithfully conforming to current traditions. The people meant are those who are unaware of injunctions in *śruti* and *smṛti* and yet, due to faith in the practices of their elders, worship deities; and not those who, despite their awareness of scriptural injunctions, choose to ignore them and worship deities in their own way. Why? Because of the qualification 'with faith'. It is impossible to assume that persons with faith can address themselves to worship while ignoring scriptural injuctions in regard to the method of such worship. What is the status of these worshippers with faith, O Kṛṣṇa! what is their 'status', *sāttvic*, *rājasic* or *tāmasic*?

2.0. सामान्यविषयोऽयं प्रश्नः न अप्रविभज्य प्रतिवचनं अर्हतीति श्रीभगवान् उवाच—

2.0. To what category does their worship belong?

श्रीभगवानुवाच :

त्रिविधा भवति श्रद्धा देहिनां सा स्वभावजा ।
सात्त्विकी राजसी चैव तामसी चेति तां शृणु ॥२॥

2. Three-fold is the faith of embodied beings according to their by-gone impressions; it may be Sāttvic, Rājasic or Tāmasic. Listen to the following classification.

2.1. त्रिविधा इति ॥ त्रिविधा त्रिप्रकारा भवति श्रद्धा—यस्यां निष्ठायां त्वं पृच्छसि—देहिनां शरीरिणां सा स्वभावजा—जन्मान्तरकृतधर्मादिसंस्कारः मरणकाले अभिव्यक्तः "स्वभावः" उच्यते, ततो जाता स्वभावजा । सात्त्विकी सत्त्वनिर्वृत्ता देवपूजादिविषया । राजसी रजोनिर्वृत्ता यक्षरक्षःपूजादिविषया । तामसी तमोनिर्वृत्ता प्रेतपिशाचादिपूजादिविषया । एवं त्रिविधां तां उच्यमानां श्रद्धां शृणु अवधारय ॥

2.1. Faith is 'threefold'—of three kinds—regarding the discipline pertaining to which you have raised this question. It is inherent in human beings. 'Impressions' are the resultants of acts, righteous, etc., done in previous lives. It becomes manifest at the time of death. Faith is what is born of these resultants.

Sāttvic is the faith fashioned by *sattva* and devoted to the worship of gods and so forth. *Rājasic* is the faith fashioned by *rajas*, its object being the worship of superhuman beings—*yakṣas*, *monsters*, etc. *Tāmasic* faith is fashioned by *tamas* and directed to the worship of ancestral spirits, ghosts, etc. Threefold thus is the faith which is being elucidated; pay heed.

3.0. सा इयं त्रिविधा भवति—

3.0. This faith is three-fold:

सत्त्वानुरूपा सर्वस्य श्रद्धा भवति भारत ।
श्रद्धामयोऽयं पुरुषो यो यच्छ्रद्धः स एव सः ॥३॥

3. In the case of all men faith conforms, Arjuna! to their inner sense. Predominantly, man consists of his faith; he is what his faith makes of him.

3.1. सत्त्वानुरूपा इति ॥ सत्त्वानुरूपा विशिष्टसंस्कारोपेतान्तःकरणानुरूपा सर्वस्य प्राणिजातस्य श्रद्धा भवति भारत! । यदि एवं ततः किं स्यादिति ? उच्यते— श्रद्धामयः श्रद्धाप्रायः अयं पुरुषः संसारी जीवः । कथं ? —यः यच्छ्रद्धः, या श्रद्धा यस्य जीवस्य सः यच्छ्रद्धः सः एव तच्छ्रद्धानुरूप एव सः जीवः ॥

3.1. The faith in all living beings, O Arjuna! is shaped by the mind according to the specialised impressions it is endowed with. So what? Hear: Man here, in this transmigratory life, is largely determined by his faith. How? The nature of his faith shapes him according to itself.

4.0. ततश्च कार्येण लिङ्गेन देवादिपूजया सत्त्वादिनिष्ठा अनुमेया इत्याह—

4.0. Therefore based on the effect of the worship he offers to gods, etc., may be inferred his devotion to *sattva* and the rest:

यजन्ते सात्त्विका देवान् यक्षरक्षांसि राजसाः ।
प्रेतान् भूतगणांश्चान्ये यजन्ते तामसा जनाः ॥४॥

4. Those of Sāttvic faith offer sacrifice to the gods; those of Rājasic faith to supernatural beings and monsters. Others, the men of Tāmasic faith, offer sacrifice to ancestral spirits and hosts of ghosts.

4.1. यजन्ते इति ।। यजन्ते पूजयन्ति सात्त्विकाः सत्त्वनिष्ठाः देवान्, यक्षरक्षांसि राजसाः, प्रेतान् भूतगणांश्च सप्तमातृकादींश्च अन्ये यजन्ते तामसाः जनाः ।।

4.1. Those of *sāttvic* temperament, i.e., those established in *sattva*, offer sacrifice to deities. The *rājasic* ones do so to supernatural beings and monsters. Others, the people of *tāmasic* temperament, sacrifice to ancestral spirits, hosts of ghosts, the seven mothers, etc.

5.0. एवं कार्यतः निर्णीतः सत्त्वादिनिष्ठाः शास्त्रविध्युत्सर्गे । तत्र कश्चिदेव सहस्रेषु देवपूजादिपरः सत्त्वनिष्ठः भवति, बाहुल्येन तु रजोनिष्ठाः तमोनिष्ठाश्चैव प्राणिनः भवन्ति ।। कथम् ? —

5.0. The adherence to *sattva*, etc., has been determined with regard to these effects by *śāstraic* prescriptions. But only rarely, say one among thousands, do people address themselves to worship of deities, taking their guidance from *sattva*; the vast majority of beings are attracted to *rajas* and *tamas*. How?

अशास्त्रविहितं घोरं तप्यन्ते ये तपो जनाः ।
दम्भाहङ्कारसंयुक्ताः कामरागबलान्विताः ।।५।।

5. Full of force of lust and greed, and moved by hypocrisy and egoism, those who do terrific penance, unordained by the śāstras.

5.1. अशास्त्र इति ।। अशास्त्रविहितं न शास्त्रविहितं घोरं पीडाकरं प्राणिनां आत्मनश्च तपः तप्यन्ते निर्वर्तयन्ति ये जनाः ते च दम्भाहङ्कारसंयुक्ताः, दम्भश्च अहङ्कारश्च दम्भाहङ्कारौ, ताभ्यां संयुक्ताः दम्भाहङ्कारसंयुक्ताः, कामरागबलान्विताः कामश्च रागश्च कामरागौ, तत्कृतं बलं कामरागबलं, तेन अन्विताः, कामरागबलान्विताः; कामरागबलैः वा अन्विताः ।।

5.1. 'Unordained by the *śāstras*'—not moved by their injuctions—and 'terrific' or painful to living beings as well as to themselves, is the penance done by the people who are impelled by hypocrisy and egoism. They are supported by 'the force of lust and greed'. This may also mean that they are full of lust, greed and force.

कर्शयन्तः शरीरस्थं भूतग्राममचेतसः ।
मां चैवान्तःशरीरस्थं तान् विद्धयासुरनिश्चयान् ॥६॥

6. Such senseless fools enfeebling the organs of the body, and persecuting also Me dwelling within the body, know them to be demoniacally resolved.

6.1. कर्शयन्तः इति ॥ कर्शयन्तः कृशीकुर्वन्तः शरीरस्थं भूतग्रामं करणसमुदायं अचेतसः अविवेकिनः मां च एव तत्कर्मबुद्धिसाक्षिभूतं अन्तःशरीरस्थं नारायणं कर्शयन्तः—मदनुशासनाकरणमेव मत्कर्शनं—तान् विद्धि आसुरनिश्चयान्, आसुरः निश्चयः येषां ते आसुरनिश्चयाः तान् परिहरणार्थं विद्धि इति उपदेशः ॥

6.1. Such undiscriminating persons who enfeeble the sense-organs of the body and also Me, Nārāyaṇa, the witness of their activities and those of the intellect, by failing to carry out My commands,—know them to have demoniac resolves. Know them in order to shun them.

7.0. आहाराणां च रस्यस्निग्धादिवर्गत्रयरूपेण भिन्नानां यथाक्रमं सात्त्विकराजसतामसपुरुषप्रियत्वप्रदर्शनं इह क्रियते—रस्यस्निग्धादिषु आहारविशेषेषु आत्मनः प्रीत्यतिरेकेण लिङ्गेन सात्त्विकत्वं राजसत्वं च बुद्ध्वा रजस्तमोलिङ्गानां आहाराणां परिवर्जनार्थं सत्त्वलिङ्गानां च उपादानार्थम् । तथा यज्ञादीनामपि सत्त्वादिगुणभेदेन त्रिविधत्वप्रतिपादनं इह "राजसतामसान् बुद्ध्वा कथं नु नाम परित्यजेत्, सात्त्विकानेव अनुतिष्ठेत्" इत्येवमर्थम् । आह—

7.0. Three kinds of food are discriminated here, each distinguished by characteristics like relishability, oiliness, etc. They pertain respectively to the three groups, *sāttvic* and so forth, being pleasant to people who are *sāttvic*, etc. From the fondness one has for these kinds of food one may know oneself to be *sāttvic* and so forth. The *sāttvic* food may be sought after and the others rejected. The same is the case with the division of sacrifice, etc., also. In the three groups the *sāttvic* types are to be chosen and the others shunned.

आहारस्त्वपि सर्वस्य त्रिविधो भवति प्रियः ।
यज्ञस्तपस्तथा दानं तेषां भेदमिमं शृणु ॥७॥

7. Similarly three kinds of food prove dear, as also do sacrifice, penance and charity. Listen to their distincitions.

7.1. आहारः इति ॥ आहारः तु अपि सर्वस्य भोक्तुः प्राणिनः त्रिविधः भवति प्रियः इष्टः, तथा यज्ञः, तथा तपः, तथा दानम् । तेषां आहारादीनां भेदं इमं वक्ष्यमाणं शृणु ॥

7.1. And three kinds of food are dear to all who eat—to all living beings. So too are sacrifice, penance and charity. Listen to their distinctions presently to be set forth.

आयुःसत्त्वबलारोग्यसुखप्रीतिविवर्धनाः ।
रस्याः स्निग्धाः स्थिरा हृद्या आहाराः सात्त्विकप्रियाः ॥८॥

8. Foods promoting longevity, strength of mind, power, health, comfort and pleasure, which are delectable, oily, firm and appetising, appeal to men of Sāttvic temperament.

8.1. आयुः इति ॥ आयुश्च सत्त्वं च बलं च आरोग्यं च सुखं च प्रीतिश्च आयुःसत्त्वबलारोग्यसुखप्रीतयः तासां आयुःसत्त्वादीनां विवर्धनाः आयुस्सत्त्वबलारोग्यसुखप्रीतिविवर्धनाः, ते च रस्याः रसोपेताः स्निग्धाः स्नेहवन्तः, स्थिराः चिरकालस्थायिनः देहे, हृद्याः हृदयप्रियाः आहाराः सात्त्विकप्रियाः सात्त्विकस्य इष्टाः ॥

8.1. The foods which promote the complex of longevity,

mental strength, power, health, comfort and pleasure, which prove delectable, and which are oily, firm and appetising, attract people of *sāttvic* temperament.

कट्वम्ललवणात्युष्णतीक्ष्णरूक्षविदाहिनः ।
आहारा राजसस्येष्टा दुःखशोकामयप्रदाः ॥९॥

9. The foods which please the Rājasic temperaments are excessively bitter, sour, saltish, hot, pungent, harsh, burning; they cause pain, suffering and ill-health.

9.1. कटु इति ॥ कट्वम्ललवणात्युष्णतीक्ष्णरूक्षविदाहिनः—इत्यत्र अतिशब्दः कट्वादिषु सर्वत्र योज्यः, 'अतिकटुः', 'अतितीक्ष्णः' इत्येवं—कटुश्च अम्लश्च लवणश्च अत्युष्णश्च तीक्ष्णश्च रूक्षश्च विदाही च ते आहाराः राजसस्य इष्टाः, दुःखशोकामयप्रदाः दुःखं च शोकं च आमयं च प्रयच्छन्तीति दुःखशोकामयप्रदाः ॥

9.1. The term *ati* meaning 'excessively', must be taken to qualify each of the terms bitter, sour, etc., thus signifying excessively bitter, etc. These kinds of foods, pleasing to the *rājasic* temperament, cause or yield pain, suffering and ill-health.

यातयामं गतरसं पूति पर्युषितं च यत् ।
उच्छिष्टमपि चामेध्यं भोजनं तामसप्रियम् ॥१०॥

10. The food dear to the Tāmasic temperament is ill-cooked, tasteless, smelling, decayed, refuse and impure.

10.1. यातयामं इति ॥ यातयामं मन्दपक्वं, निर्वीर्यस्य गतरसशब्देन उक्तत्वात् । गतरसं रसवियुक्तम्, पूति दुर्गन्धि, पर्युषितं च पक्वं सत् रात्र्यन्तरितं च यत्, उच्छिष्टम् अपि भुक्तशिष्टं उच्छिष्टं, अमेध्यं अयज्ञार्हं, भोजनं ईदृशं तामसप्रियम् ॥

10.1. The food pleasing to the *tāmasic* mind is inadquately cooked, and is 'tasteless', *gatarasa*, lacking in sustaining power. What is unpalatable fails to sustain. It is tasteless. The smelling food, cooked and kept throughout the night, and what is left over after eating, 'impure'—unfit for use in worship—such is the food that pleases the *tāmasic* temperament.

11.0. अथ इदानीं यज्ञः त्रिविधः उच्यते—

11.0. Now is set forth the threefold sacrifice:

अफलाकाङ्क्षिभिर्यज्ञो विधिदृष्टो य इज्यते ।
यष्टव्यमेवेति मनः समाधाय स सात्त्विकः ॥११॥

11. Sāttvic is the sacrifice offered without desire for its fruit and according to scriptural prescriptions with the unshakable thought, 'The sacrifice has to be offered.'

11.1. अफल इति ॥ अफलाकाङ्क्षिभिः अफलार्थिभिः यज्ञः विधिदृष्टः शास्त्रचोदनादृष्टः यः यज्ञः इज्यते निर्वर्त्यते यष्टव्यम् एव इति यज्ञस्वरूपनिर्वर्तनमेव कार्यं इति मनः समाधाय, "न अनेन पुरुषार्थो मम कर्तव्यः" इत्येवं निश्चित्य, 'सः सात्त्विकः यज्ञः उच्यते ॥

11.1. A sacrifice is called *sāttvic* when it is laid down by *śāstraic* prescriptions and offered by those who seek no rewards, with the unshakable thought that 'the sacrificial ceremony has to be performed though I have no end of my own to secure through this'.

अभिसन्धाय तु फलं दम्भार्थमपि चैव यत् ।
इज्यते भरतश्रेष्ठ तं यज्ञं विद्धि राजसम् ॥१२॥

12. But know, best of Bhārata princes! that sacrifice to be Rājasic which is hypocritically offered with desire for its fruit.

12.1. अभिसंधाय इति ॥ अभिसन्धाय तु उद्दिश्य फलं दम्भार्थम् अपि च एव यत् इज्यते भरतश्रेष्ठ ! तं यज्ञं विद्धि राजसम् ॥

12.1. If a sacrifice is offered with an eye on its reward and hypocritically, know, best of Bhāratas, that sacrifice to be *Rājasic*.

विधिहीनमसृष्टान्नं मन्त्रहीनमदक्षिणम् ।
श्रद्धाविरहितं यज्ञं तामसं परिचक्षते ॥१३॥

13. They say that sacrifice is Tāmasic, which is not scripturally enjoined, in which no food is offered, which is done without sacred chants and the giving of priestly fees and is uninspired by faith.

13.1. विधिहीनं इति ॥ विधिहीनं यथाचोदितविपरीतं, असृष्टान्नं ब्राह्मणेभ्यः न सृष्टं न दत्तं अन्नं यस्मिन् यज्ञे सः असृष्टान्नः; तं असृष्टान्नं, मन्त्रहीनं स्वरतः वर्णतः वा वियुक्तं मन्त्रहीनम्, अदक्षिणं उक्तदक्षिणारहितं, श्रद्धाविरहितं यज्ञं तामसं परिचक्षते तमोनिर्वृत्तं कथयन्ति ॥

13.1. 'Not scripturally enjoined' means in opposition to what has been enjoined. 'In which no food is offered' refers to the feeding of holy men, the poor, etc. 'Without sacred chants' refers to chants defective as regards accents and consonantal sounds. 'The priestly fees' refers to the prescribed fees for priests officiating in the sacrifice. Also the sacrifice that is not inspired by faith—sacrifice such as this, they say, is effected by *tamas*.

14.0. अथ इदानीं तपः त्रिविधं उच्यते—

14.0. Now is described the threefold penance:

देवद्विजगुरुप्राज्ञपूजनं शौचमार्जवम् ।
ब्रह्मचर्यमहिंसा च शारीरं तप उच्यते ॥१४॥

14. Reverence to the Devas, the twice-born, the preceptors, and wise scholars, cleanliness, guilelessness, continence, and non-violence—these constitute the penance of the body.

14.1. देव इति ।। देवाश्च द्विजाश्च गुरवश्च प्राज्ञाश्च देवद्विजगुरुप्राज्ञाः, तेषां पूजनं देवद्विजगुरुप्राज्ञपूजनं, शौचं, आर्जवं ऋजुत्वं, ब्रह्मचर्यं अहिंसा च शरीरनिर्वर्त्यं शारीरं शरीरप्रधानैः सर्वैरेव—कार्यकरणैः कर्त्रादिभिः साध्यं शारीरं तपः उच्यते—'पञ्चैते तस्य हेतवः' [१८.१५.] इति हि वक्ष्यति ॥

14.1. 'Reverence shown to the group of Devas, the twice-born, the preceptors, and wise scholars'—this constitutes the first factor. Then follow cleanliness, guilelessness or simplicity, continence and non-violence. These, together, constitute bodily penance, because the body, the psycho-physical organism including agents, etc., is dominant in its achievement. Vide 18.15 which declares 'these five are the causal factors in regard to it'.

अनुद्वेगकरं वाक्यं सत्यं प्रियहितं च यत् ।
स्वाध्यायाभ्यसनं चैव वाङ्मयं तप उच्यते ॥१५॥

15. An utterance that does not offend, is truthful, pleasing, good, and the habitual reading of scriptures constitute verbal penance.

15.1. अनुद्वेग इति ।। अनुद्वेगकरं प्राणिनां अदुःखकरं वाक्यं सत्यं प्रियहितं च यत्—प्रियहिते दृष्टादृष्टार्थे । अनुद्वेगकरत्वादिभिः धर्मैः वाक्यं विशेष्यते । विशेषणधर्मसमुच्चयार्थः चशब्दः । परप्रत्ययार्थं प्रयुक्तस्य वाक्यस्य सत्यप्रियहितानुद्वेगकरत्वानां अन्यतमेन द्वाभ्यां त्रिभिर्वा हीनता स्याद्यदि, न तत् वाङ्मयं तपः । तथा सत्यवाक्यस्य इतरेषां अन्यतमेन द्वाभ्यां त्रिभिर्वा विहीनतायां न वाङ्मयतपस्त्वम् । तथा प्रियवाक्यस्यापि इतरेषां अन्यतमेन द्वाभ्यां त्रिभिर्वा विहीनस्य न वाङ्मयतपस्त्वम् । तथा हितवाक्यस्यापि इतरेषां अन्यतमेन द्वाभ्यां त्रिभिर्वा विहीनस्य न वाङ्मयतपस्त्वम् । किं पुनः तत् तपः ? —यत् सत्यं वाक्यं अनुद्वेगकरं प्रियं हितं च तत् तपः वाङ्मयं, यथा "शान्तो भव वत्स !, स्वाध्यायं योगं च

अनुतिष्ठ, तथा ते श्रेयो भविष्यति'' इति । स्वाध्यायाभ्यसनं च एव यथाविधि वाङ्मयं तपः उच्यते ॥

15.1. Words that do not pain living beings, truthful, pleasing and good. The last epithets refer to results, visible and invisible. 'Words' are qualified by attributes such as inoffensiveness. 'And' links together all such attributes. If words uttered to evoke belief in the listeners are lacking in one or more of these attributes, they won't constitute verbal penance. To achieve verbal penance, all tnose attributes must be present in the utterances. What then is such penance? An utterance truthful, etc., "Child! be quiet, do your prescribed scriptural reading or pursue Yogic practice. Thus will prosperity accrue to you". This scriptural reading according to injunctions is also verbal penance.

मनःप्रसादः सौम्यत्वं मौनमात्मविनिग्रहः ।
भावसंशुद्धिरित्येतत्तपो मानसमुच्यते ॥१६॥

16. Mental calmness, gentleness, silence, self-control, extreme emotional purity—these constitute penance of the mind.

16.1. मनः इति ॥ मनः प्रसादः मनसः प्रशान्तिः, स्वच्छतापादनं प्रसादः । सौम्यत्वं—यत् सौमनस्यं आहुः—मुखादिप्रसादादिकार्योन्नेया अन्तःकरणस्य वृत्तिः । मौनं—वाक्संयमोऽपि मनःसंयमपूर्वको भवति इति कार्येण कारणं उच्यते मनःसंयमो मौनमिति । आत्मविनिग्रहः—मनोनिरोधः सर्वतः सामान्यरूपः आत्मविनिग्रहः, वाग्विषयस्यैव मनसः संयमः मौनं, इति विशेषः । भावसंशुद्धिः—परैः व्यवहारकाले अमायावित्वं भावसंशुद्धिः । इत्येतत् तपः मानसं उच्यते ॥

16.1. 'Mental calmness' is its profound quietude. 'Calmness' refers to the reduction of the mind to extreme purity. Gentleness is otherwise styled 'goodwill'. It is the mental state inferred from its effects like the composure of face, etc. 'Silence', restraint of speech achieved through mind's restraint; again it is a reference to the cause from its effect. 'Self-control' is the control of the mind, in general, whereas 'silence' is mind-control as regards activities of speech alone. 'Extreme emotional purity' consists in candour, freedom from hypocrisy, in dealing with others. All these make up the penance of the mind.

17.0. यथोक्तं कायिकं वाचिकं मानसं च तपः तप्तं नरैः सत्त्वादिगुणभेदेन कथं त्रिविधं भवतीति ? उच्यते—

17.0. What form does the threefold penance, physical, verbal, and mental, take when people who are *sāttvic* etc., address themselves to it? Listen:

श्रद्धया परया तप्तं तपस्तत्त्रिविधं नरैः ।
अफलाकाङ्क्षिभिर्युक्तैः सात्त्विकं परिचक्षते ॥१७॥

17. They say that this threefold penance, practised with supreme faith, by integrated men free from desire for reward is Sāttvic.

17.1. श्रद्धया इति ॥ श्रद्धया आस्तिक्यबुद्ध्या परया प्रकृष्टया तप्तं अनुष्ठितं तपः तत् प्रकृतं त्रिविधं त्रिप्रकारं त्र्यधिष्ठानं नरैः अनुष्ठातृभिः अफलाकाङ्क्षिभिः फलाकाङ्क्षारहितैः युक्तैः समाहितैः—यत् ईदृशं तपः तत् सात्त्विकं सत्त्वनिर्वृत्तं परिचक्षते कथयन्ति शिष्टाः ॥

17.1. 'Faith' is intellectual assent to traditional wisdom. When the threefold penance is performed with total faith by integrated men, devoid of desire for rewards, that is styled as *sāttvic* by savants.

सत्कारमानपूजार्थं तपो दम्भेन चैव यत् ।
क्रियते तदिह प्रोक्तं राजसं चलमध्रुवम् ॥१८॥

18. Penance performed hypocritically to win respect,

honour, and reverence is classed here as Rājasic; it is fickle and uncertain.

18.1. सत्कार इति ।। सत्कारः साधुकारः "साधुः अयं तपस्वी ब्राह्मणः" इत्येवमर्थं, मानः माननं प्रत्युत्थानाभिवादनादिः तदर्थं, पूजा पादप्रक्षालनार्चनाशयितृत्वादि तदर्थं च तपः सत्कारमानपूजार्थं, दम्भेन च एव यत् क्रियते तपः तत् इह प्रोक्तं कथितं राजसं चलं कादाचित्कफलत्वेन अध्रुवम् ।।

18.1. 'Respect' is gratulation expressed as follows: 'This is indeed an ascetic, holy man'. 'Honour' is active expression like getting up to receive and paying of obeisance. 'Reverence' consists in washing the feet, offering flowers, and feeding. To win all this, penance is done by some hypocritically—and it is called as *Rājasic* here, its fruit being occasional and uncertain.

मूढग्राहेणात्मनो यत्पीडया क्रियते तपः ।
परस्योत्सादनार्थं वा तत्तामसमुदाहृतम् ।।१९।।

19. Penance that is performed obstinately or that which tortures the self and aims at injuring others is Tāmasic.

19.1. मूढ इति ।। मूढग्राहेण अविवेकनिश्चयेन आत्मनः पीडया यत् क्रियते तपः परस्य उत्सादनार्थं विनाशार्थं वा तत् तामसं तपः उदाहृतम् ।।

19.1. 'Obstinately' with firmness due to lack of discrimination. It tortures the self or is aimed at injuring others, i.e., for destroying others. Such sacrifice is said to be *tāmasic*.

20.0. इदानीं दानत्रैविध्यं उच्यते—

20.0. Now is three-fold charity described:

दातव्यमिति यद्दानं दीयतेऽनुपकारिणे ।
देशे काले च पात्रे च तद्दानं सात्त्विकं स्मृतम् ।।२०।।

20. A Sāttvic gift is one made at the right place and time

with the thought 'It is good to make a gift', to a deserving recipient, who cannot make a return for it.

20.1. दातव्यं इति ॥ दातव्यमिति एवं मनः कृत्वा यत् दानं दीयते अनुपकारिणे प्रत्युपकारासमर्थाय, समर्थाय अपि निरपेक्षं दीयते, देशे पुण्ये कुरुक्षेत्रादौ, काले संक्रान्त्यादौ पात्रे च षडङ्गविद्वेदपारगे इत्यादौ, तत् दानं सात्त्विकं स्मृतम् ॥

20.1. '*Sāttvic* charity' is one offered to a person who is unable to make a return for it or to one to whom, though competent to make a return, the gift has been offered without such consideration. 'At the right place' means in places like Kurukṣetra, etc., and 'right time' the junction of months and the like. It is offered to the 'right recipient'—a Vedic scholar, a master of the Vedas with all their six limbs.

यत्तु प्रत्युपकारार्थं फलमुद्दिश्य वा पुनः ।
दीयते च परिक्लिष्टं तद्दानं राजसं स्मृतम् ॥२१॥

21. It is said to be rājasic when offered unwillingly, with expectation of a gift in return, or with an eye to some advantage.

21.1. यत्तु इति ॥ यत्तु दानं प्रत्युपकारार्थं, काले तु अयं मां प्रत्युपकरिष्यतीत्येवमर्थं, फलं वा, अस्य दानस्य मे भविष्यति अदृष्टं इति, तत् उद्दिश्य पुनः दीयते च परिक्लिष्टं खेदसंयुक्तं, तत् दानं राजसं स्मृतम् ॥

21.1. 'A gift with expectation of a return' is made with the hope that in due course the recipient will do a good turn to the giver of the gift; or hoping that his gift will produce a favourable unseen result. The gift made regretfully, to the accompaniment of such thinking, is held to be *rājasic*.

अदेशकाले यद्दानमपात्रेभ्यश्च दीयते ।
असत्कृतमवज्ञातं तत्तामसमुदाहृतम् ॥२२॥

22. A Tāmasic gift is what is improperly and insultingly offered at the wrong place and time, to undeserving recipients.

22.1. अदेश इति ॥ अदेशकाले अदेशे अपुण्यदेशे म्लेच्छाशुच्यादिसंकीर्णे, अकाले पुण्यहेतुत्वेन अप्रख्याते संक्रान्त्यादिविशेषरहिते, अपात्रेभ्यः च मूर्खतस्करादिभ्यः, देशादिसंपत्तौ वा असत्कृतं प्रियवचनपादप्रक्षालनपूजादिरहितं अवज्ञातं पात्रपरिभवयुक्तं च यत् दानं, तत् तामसं उदाहृतम् ॥

22.1. 'The wrong place' is an unrighteous spot inhabited by barbarous, unclean people. 'The wrong time' is a period not known to favour accumulation of religious merit such as the period of transition of the sun from month to month. 'The underserving recipients' are fools, robbers, etc. Even if the place and time favour gift-giving it may be unaccompained by pleasant speech, washing of feet, obeisance, etc., and may be made insultingly. This sort of gift-giving is *tāmasic*.

23.0. यज्ञदानतपःप्रभृतीनां साद्गुण्यकरणाय अयं उपदेशः उच्यते—

23.0. To enrich sacrifice, gifts, penance, etc., with excellences, the following counsel is offered:

ॐ तत्सदिति निर्देशो ब्रह्मणस्त्रिविधः स्मृतः ।
ब्राह्मणास्तेन वेदाश्च यज्ञाश्च विहिताः पुरा ॥२३॥

23. It is held that reference to Brahman is three-fold as AUM, Tat and Sat. Thus of yore were fashioned Brāhmaṇas, Vedas and sacrifices.

23.1. ॐ इति ॥ ॐ तत् सत् इति एवं निर्देशः निर्दिश्यते अनेनेति निर्देशः त्रिविधः नामनिर्देशः ब्रह्मणः स्मृतः चिन्तितः वेदान्तेषु ब्रह्मविद्भिः । ब्राह्मणाः तेन निर्देशेन त्रिविधेन वेदाश्च यज्ञाश्च विहिताः निर्मिताः पुरा पूर्वं—इति निर्देशस्तुत्यर्थं उच्यते ॥

23.1. 'AUM, *tat*, *sat*' traditionally constitute the three-fold designation of Brahman in the Vedāntas, according to the knowers of Brahman. In this three-fold manner were set up Brāhmaṇas, Vedas and sacrifices. 'Of yore' is added to extol the designations.

तस्मादोमित्युदाहृत्य यज्ञदानतपःक्रियाः ।
प्रवर्तन्ते विधानोक्ताः सततं ब्रह्मवादिनाम् ॥२४॥

24. Therefore, always, those who maintain the doctrine of Brahman, commence ordained rites like sacrifices, gift-giving and penance, after uttering the syllable AUM.

24.1. तस्मात् इति ॥ तस्मात् 'ॐ' इति उदाहृत्य उच्चार्य यज्ञदानतपःक्रियाः यज्ञादिस्वरूपाः क्रियाः प्रवर्तन्ते विधानोक्ताः शास्त्रचोदिताः सततं सर्वदा ब्रह्मवादिनां ब्रह्मवदनशीलानाम् ॥

24.1. So after uttering *aum* the acts of sacrifice, etc., scripturally prescribed start. This is the unbroken practice of all who maintain the doctrine of Brahman.

तदित्यनभिसन्धाय फलं यज्ञतपः क्रियाः ।
दानक्रियाश्च विविधाः क्रियन्ते मोक्षकाङ्क्षिभिः ॥२५॥

25. Various rites of sacrifice, gift-giving and penance are begun after uttering the term Tat by the seekers after liberation without thought of rewards.

25.1. तत् इति ॥ 'तत्' इति अनभिसन्धाय—'तत्' इति ब्रह्माभिधानं उच्चार्य, अनभिसन्धाय च यज्ञादिकर्मणः फलं, यज्ञतपःक्रियाः यज्ञक्रियाश्च तपःक्रियाश्च यज्ञतपःक्रियाः दानक्रियाः च विविधाः क्षेत्रहिरण्यप्रदानादिलक्षणाः क्रियन्ते निर्वर्त्यन्ते मोक्षकाङ्क्षिभिः मोक्षार्थिभिः मुमुक्षुभिः ॥

25.1. After uttering the word *tat* denoting Brahman and not desiring the fruits of works, sacrificial actions, penance, and various kinds of gift-giving including plots of ground and gold are performed by seekers after liberation.

26.0. ॐ तच्छब्दयोः विनियोगः उक्तः । अथ इदानीं सच्छब्दस्य विनियोगः कथ्यते—

26.0. The practical use of *aum* and *tat* has been stated; now follows that of the term *sat*:

सद्भावे साधुभावे च सदित्येतत्प्रयुज्यते ।
प्रशस्ते कर्मणि तथा सच्छब्दः पार्थ युज्यते ॥२६॥

26. The word Sat is used to denote existence and righteousness; also, Arjuna! it is used to denote a noble deed.

26.1. सद्भावे इति ॥ सद्भावे असतः सद्भावे, यथा अविद्यमानस्य पुत्रस्य जन्मनि, तथा साधुभावे च असद्वृत्तस्य असाधोः सद्वृत्तता साधुभावः तस्मिन् साधुभावे च 'सत्' इत्येतत् अभिधानं ब्रह्मणः प्रयुज्यते अभिधीयते । प्रशस्ते कर्मणि विवाहादौ च तथा सच्छब्दः पार्थ ! युज्यते प्रयुज्यते इत्येतत् ॥

26.1. The existence of something yet to be, like the birth of a non-existent son as well as the righteousness of one hitherto wicked, is denoted by the word *sat*, the designation of Brahman. It is also used, Arjuna! with reference to noble acts like marriage.

यज्ञे तपसि दाने च स्थितिः सदिति चोच्यते ।
कर्म चैव तदर्थीयं सदित्येवाभिधीयते ॥२७॥

27. Also does Sat denote devotion to sacrifice, penance and gift-giving; so, too, the work promoting all these is styled Sat.

27.1. यज्ञे इति ॥ यज्ञे यज्ञकर्मणि या स्थितिः, तपसि च या स्थितिः, दाने च या स्थितिः, सा 'सत्' इति च उच्यते विद्वद्भिः । कर्म च एव तदर्थीयं यज्ञ-

दानतपोऽर्थीयं—अथवा यस्य अभिधानत्रयं प्रकृतं तदर्थीयं ईश्वरार्थीयं इत्येतत्, 'सत्' इत्येव अभिधीयते ॥

तत् एतत् यज्ञदानतपआदि कर्म असात्त्विकं विगुणमपि श्रद्धापूर्वकं ब्रह्मणः अभिधानत्रयप्रयोगेण सगुणं सात्त्विकं संपादितं भवति ॥

27.1. Devotion to the act of sacrifice, penance, and gift-giving is also styled *sat* by scholars. So too work promoting these, or work dedicated to God, whose three designations constitute the present context, is again designated *sat*. The idea is that *non-sāttvic*, unmeritorious acts of sacrifice, penance, gift-giving, etc., become meritorious and *sāttvic* when they are preceded by the faithful utterence of these designations of Brahman.

28.0. तत्र च सर्वत्र श्रद्धाप्रधानतया सर्वं संपाद्यते यस्मात्, तस्मात्—

28.0. Since in these activities everything may be secured by the predominant virtue of faith,

अश्रद्धया हुतं दत्तं तपस्तप्तं कृतं च यत् ।
असदित्युच्यते पार्थ न च तत्प्रेत्य नो इह ॥२८॥

28. What is sacrificed, given as gift, performed as penance, or done, without faith is said, O Arjuna! to be Non-sat; it is effective neither here nor hereafter.

इति श्रीमहाभारते शतसाहस्र्यां संहितायां वैयासिक्यां भीष्मपर्वणि
श्रीमद्भगवद्गीतासूपनिषत्सु ब्रह्मविद्यायां योगशास्त्रे श्रीकृष्णार्जुनसंवादे
श्रद्धात्रयविभागयोगो नाम सप्तदशोऽध्यायः ॥

28.1. अश्रद्धया इति ॥ अश्रद्धया हुतं हवनं कृतं, अश्रद्धया दत्तं च ब्राह्मणेभ्यः, अश्रद्धया तपः तप्तं अनुष्ठितं, तथा अश्रद्धया एव कृतं च यत् स्तुतिनमस्कारादि, तत् सर्वं 'असत्' इति उच्यते—मत्प्राप्तिसाधनमार्गबाह्यत्वात्—पार्थ ! न च तत् बहुलायासम् अपि प्रेत्य फलाय, नोऽपि इहार्थं, साधुभिः निन्दितत्वात् इति ॥

28.1. Whatever is offered as oblation, given as gift to holy ones, etc., performed as penance or work accomplished—work of laudation, prostration, etc.,—all these if done without faith, are termed *asat*; for they fall outside the way leading to Me, O Arjuna! Though these may entail much labour, they prove futile after death as well as here; they have earned the censure of the righteous.

इति श्रीमत्परमहंसपरिव्राजकाचार्यगोविंदभगवत्पूज्यपादशिष्य श्रीमच्छंकर-
भगवतः कृतौ श्रीमद्भगवद्गीताभाष्ये श्रद्धात्रयविभागयोगो नाम
सप्तदशोऽध्यायः ॥१७॥

अष्टादशोऽध्यायः

CHAPTER XVIII

THE YOGA OF LIBERATION AND RENUNCIATION

0.1. सर्वस्यैव गीताशास्त्रस्य अर्थः अस्मिन् अध्याये उपसंहृत्य सर्वश्च वेदार्थः वक्तव्यः इत्येवमर्थः अयं अध्यायः आरभ्यते । सर्वेषु हि अतीतेषु अध्यायेषु उक्तः अर्थः अस्मिन् अध्याये अवगम्यते । अर्जुनस्तु संन्यासत्यागशब्दार्थयोः एव विशेषं बुभुत्सुः उवाच—

0.1. In order to conclude here the contents of the entire science of the Gītā as well as those of the Vedas, is begun the present chapter. The ideas expressed in all the previous chapters may be grasped from this chapter alone. But Arjuna seeks to know the distinction between renunciation and relinquishment (*tyāga*) ; so he said:

अर्जुन उवाच :

संन्यासस्य महाबाहो तत्त्वमिच्छामि वेदितुम् ।
त्यागस्य च हृषीकेश पृथक् केशिनिषूदन ॥१॥

Arjuna said:

1. Mighty armed! Lord of the senses! slayer of Kesin! I should like to know the distinction between the truth of renunciation and that of relinquishment.

1.1. संन्यासस्य इति ॥ संन्यासस्य—संन्यासशब्दार्थस्य इत्येतत्—हे महाबाहो! तत्त्वं तस्य भावः तत्त्वं, याथात्म्यम् इत्येतत्, इच्छामि वेदितुं ज्ञातुं; त्यागस्य च त्यागशब्दार्थस्य इत्येतत्, हृषीकेश! पृथक् इतरेतरविभागतः, केशिनिषूदन! केशिनामा हयच्छद्मा कश्चित् असुरः, तं निषूदितवान् भगवान् वासुदेवः, तेन तन्नाम्ना सम्बोध्यते अर्जुनेन ॥

1.1. O mighty armed! I desire to know the truth of renunciation, or the content of the term *sannyāsa*, as also that of the term *tyāga* or relinquishment. I desire to know their distinction. Keśin was a demon disguised as a horse; the Lord Vāsudeva slew him; so He is addressed as the slayer of Keśin.

2.0. संन्यासत्यागशब्दौ तत्र तत्र निर्दिष्टौ, न निर्लुठितार्थौ, पूर्वेषु अध्यायेषु। अतः अर्जुनाय पृष्टवते तन्निर्णयाय भगवान् उवाच —

2.0. The terms renunciation and relinquishment have been employed in a number of passages in the previous chapters, but their meanings have not been clearly explicated. Hence the Lord answered Arjuna who queried, in order to give him a decision in this matter.

श्रीभगवानुवाच :

काम्यानां कर्मणां न्यासं संन्यासं कवयो विदुः ।
सर्वकर्मफलत्यागं प्राहुस्त्यागं विचक्षणाः ॥२॥

The blessed Lord said:

2. Sages know renunciation to be the rejection of works prompted by desire for their fruits. Experts declare relinquishment to be the giving up of the fruits of all works.

2.1. काम्यानां इति ॥ काम्यानां अश्वमेधादीनां कर्मणां न्यासं परित्यागं संन्यासं संन्यासशब्दार्थं, अनुष्ठेयत्वेन प्राप्तस्य अननुष्ठानं, कवयः पण्डिताः केचित् विदुः विजानन्ति । नित्यनैमित्तिकानां अनुष्ठीयमानानां सर्वकर्मणां आत्मसम्बन्धितया प्राप्तस्य फलस्य परित्यागः सर्वकर्मफलत्यागः तं प्राहुः कथयन्ति त्यागं त्यागशब्दार्थं विचक्षणाः पण्डिताः । यदि काम्यकर्मपरित्यागः फलपरित्यागः वा अर्थः वक्तव्यः, सर्वथा परित्यागमात्रं संन्यासत्यागशब्दयोः एकः अर्थः स्यात्, न घटपटशब्दौ इव जात्यन्तरभूतार्थौ ॥

2.1. Works prompted by desire for their fruits may be exemplified by sacrifices like the Aśvamedha. The sense of the term renunciation is 'the relinquishment' of such works. Some sages know that when an occasion for doing such work arises, in their non-performance consists renunciation. Experts (however) with special knowledge declare the relinquishment of the fruits of obligatory and occasional works, when they accrue, to be *tyāga*. It is not a question of relinquishing desire-prompted works or the fruits of work in general. Were it so, no clear-cut difference would emerge between renunciation and relinquishment such as, for example, there exists between a pot and a cloth.

2.2. ननु नित्यनैमित्तिकानां कर्मणां फलमेव नास्ति इति आहुः । कथं उच्यते तेषां फलत्यागः, यथा वन्ध्यायाः पुत्रत्यागः ?

2.2. *Objection:* "Now the *pūrva mīmāṁsā* maintains that obligatory and occasional works have no fruits of their own at all. How, then, can one talk of relinquishing their fruits? It will be like a barren woman abandoning her son."

2.3. नैषः दोषः, नित्यानाम् अपि कर्मणां भगवता फलवत्त्वस्य इष्टत्वात् । वक्ष्यति हि भगवान् 'अनिष्टमिष्टं मिश्रं च' [१८.१२.] इति,' 'न तु संन्यासिनां' [१८.१२.] इति च । संन्यासिनामेव हि केवलं कर्मफलासम्बन्धं दर्शयन् असंन्यासिनां नित्यकर्मफलप्राप्तिं 'भवत्यत्यागिनां प्रेत्य' [१८.१२.] इति दर्शयति ॥

Reply: "No; the Lord holds that even obligatory works yield fruits; vide B.G.18.12; only, these fruits do not accrue to the renunciants (ibid.). Thus, according to Him, the fruits of such works accrue to the non-renunciants."

त्याज्यं दोषवदित्येके कर्म प्राहुर्मनीषिणः ।
यज्ञदानतपःकर्म न त्याज्यमिति चापरे ॥ ३॥

3. Some intellectuals maintain that faulty work must be relinquished; others, that the work of sacrifice, gift-giving, and penance ought not to be relinquished (at all).

3.1. त्याज्यं इति ॥ त्याज्यं त्यक्तव्यं दोषवत् दोषः अस्य अस्तीति दोषवत्—किं तत् ? —कर्म, बन्धहेतुत्वात् सर्वम् एव । अथवा—दोषः यथा रागादिः त्यज्यते,

तथा त्याज्यं इति एके कर्म प्राहुः मनीषिणः पण्डिताः साङ्ख्यादिदृष्टिं आश्रिताः, अधिकृतानां कर्मिणाम् अपि इति । तत्रैव यज्ञदानतपःकर्म न त्याज्यं इति च अपरे ॥

3.1. Work that is faulty must be relinquished; for, all such work binds. *Doṣavat* means having faults or faulty. Or, just as faults like attachment are relinquished, so should work, as such, be relinquished. This is the view of some wise men who adopt the philosophic view of the Sāṁkhyas. This should apply even to those who are called upon to work. Others however exclude the works of sacrifice, gift-giving and penance from what has to be relinquished.

3.2. कर्मिणः एव अधिकृताः, तान् अपेक्ष्य एते विकल्पाः, न तु ज्ञाननिष्ठान् व्युत्थायिनः संन्यासिनः अपेक्ष्य । 'ज्ञानयोगेन सांख्यानां निष्ठा मया पुरा प्रोक्ता' [३.३.] इति कर्माधिकारात् अपोद्धृताः ये, न तान् प्रति चिन्ता ॥

ननु 'कर्मयोगेन योगिनां' [३.३.] इति अधिकृताः पूर्वं विभक्तनिष्ठाः अपि इह सर्वशास्त्रार्थोपसंहारप्रकरणे यथा विचार्यन्ते, तथा सांख्या अपि ज्ञाननिष्ठाः विचार्यन्तां इति ।

न, तेषां मोहदुःखनिमित्तत्यागानुपपत्तेः । न कायक्लेशनिमित्तं दुःखं साङ्ख्याः आत्मनि पश्यन्ति, इच्छादीनां क्षेत्रधर्मत्वेन एव दर्शितत्वात् । अतः ते न कायक्लेश-दुःखभयात् कर्म परित्यजन्ति । नापि ते कर्माणि आत्मनि पश्यन्ति, येन नियतं कर्म मोहात् परित्यजेयुः । गुणानां कर्म 'नैव किंचित् करोमि' [५.८.] इति हि ते संन्यस्यन्ति । 'सर्वकर्माणि मनसा संन्यस्य' [५.१३.] इत्यादिभिः तत्त्वविदः संन्यासप्रकारः उक्तः । तस्मात् ये अन्ये अधिकृताः कर्मणि अनात्मविदः, येषां च मोहनिमित्तः त्यागः सम्भवति कायक्लेशभयाच्च, ते एव तामसाः त्यागिनः राजसाश्च इति निन्द्यन्ते, कर्मिणां अनात्मज्ञानां कर्मफलत्यागस्तुत्यर्थम्; 'सर्वारम्भपरित्यागी' ...'मौनी सन्तुष्टो येन केनचित् । अनिकेतः स्थिरमतिः' [१२.१६–१९] इति गुणातीतलक्षणे च परमार्थसंन्यासिनः विशेषितत्वात् । वक्ष्यति च 'निष्ठा ज्ञानस्य या परा' [१८.५०.] इति । तस्मात् ज्ञाननिष्ठाः संन्यासिनः न इह विवक्षिताः । कर्मफलत्यागः एव सात्विकत्वेन गुणेन तामसत्वाद्यपेक्षया संन्यासः उच्यते, न मुख्यः सर्वकर्मसंन्यासः ॥

3.2. These alternatives apply only to activists, *karmiṇaḥ*, and not to those who pursue the path of knowledge, who have gone out of the sphere of works. The discussion under way does not apply to those who have transcended the sphere of activities according to the statement in 3.3: I have declared of yore the discipline of knowledge for the Sāṁkhyas. *Objection:* "Just as in this concluding section of the Gītā activists are discussed, though their sphere also was demarcated in 3.3., why not deem that the Sāṁkhyas, the pursuers of knowledge, also are proposed to be discussed here?" *Reply* "No; because it does not stand to reason that they would any longer be called upon to relinquish the cause of delusion and sorrow; for, the Sāṁkhyas don't perceive in the Self sorrow occasioned by the troubles of the flesh. Desire, etc, have already been shown to be attributes of the field (cf. Chapter XIII). Hence the question of their relinquishing works for fear of sorrow arising from the frailties of the body does not arise. Neither do they behold works in the Self. Hence they cannot relinquish obligatory work, which is entailed by delusion. They renounce the works of the *guṇas*, convinced, 'Never do I perform any work whatsoever' (vide B.G.5.8). The way of renunciation of works by the knower of Truth has been set forth in 5.13. Therefore, the relinquishers of works censured here are the non-knowers of the Self. In 12.16-19 have been set forth the marks of the full-fledged renouncers in the context describing the transcenders of the *guṇas*. Another reference to them will be made later in XVIII-50. Therefore in the present context, the renouncers whose discipline is knowledge, are not referred to. Hence the relinquishing of the fruits of works is described as *sāttvic* renunciation, qualitatively, in relation to the *rājasic* and *tāmasic* relinquishment. The unqualified total renunciation is not the current theme."

3.3. सर्वकर्मसंन्यासासम्भवे च 'न हि देहभृता' [१८.११.] इति हेतुवचनात् मुख्यः एव इति चेत्—

न, हेतुवचनस्य स्तुत्यर्थत्वात् । यथा 'त्यागाच्छान्तिरनन्तरं' [१२.१२.] इति कर्मफलत्यागस्तुतिः एव, यथोक्तानेकपक्षानुष्ठानाशक्तिमन्तं अर्जुनं अज्ञं प्रति विधानात्; तथा इदमपि 'न हि देहभृता शक्यं' [१८.११.] इति कर्मफलत्यागस्तुत्यर्थं; न 'सर्वकर्माणि मनसा संन्यस्य नैव कुर्वन्न कारयन्नास्ते' [५.१३.] इत्यस्य पक्षस्य अपवादः केनचित् दर्शयितुं शक्यः । तस्मात् कर्मणि अधिकृतान् प्रत्येव एषः संन्यासत्यागविकल्पः । ये तु परमार्थदर्शिनः साङ्ख्याः, तेषां ज्ञाननिष्ठायाम् एव सर्वकर्मसंन्यासलक्षणायां अधिकारः, न अन्यत्र, इति न ते विकल्पार्हाः । तच्च उपपादितं

अस्माभिः 'वेदाविनाशिनं' [२.२१.] इत्यस्मिन् प्रदेशे, तृतीयादौ च ॥
तत्र एतेषु विकल्पभेदेषु—

3.3. *Objection:* "The theme here ought to be total renunciation; for, a reason has been advanced to explain why such renunciation is impracticable. Vide 18.11: It is not possible for an embodied being. . . etc." *Reply:* No, the reason advanced is meant only to extol. Just as in 12.12, the proposition, 'from relinquishment follows immediate peace', only extols the giving up of the fruits of works in view of the fact that it has been propounded to nescient Arjuna, who is in no position to act upon the numerous alternatives set forth there, here, too, 18.11 extols the giving up of the fruits of works. None indeed can point out a negation of the position stated in 5.13.'. . . neither doing nor causing to do.' Therefore, the alternatives stated as between renunciation and relinquishment in the present context are addressed exclusively to those directed to perform work. Those wedded to knowledge, the Sāṁkhyas, who have realised the supreme Reality, are called upon to devote themselves to the discipline of knowledge marked by total renunciation of all works, and not to aught else. There are no alternatives before them. In the context of 2.21, we have elucidated it as well as in the prelude to Chapter III.

As for these alternatives:-

निश्चयं शृणु मे तत्र त्यागे भरतसत्तम।
त्यागो हि पुरुषव्याघ्र त्रिविधः संप्रकीर्तितः ॥४॥

4. With reference to this theme, best of Bhāratas! listen to my decision. O hero! relinquishment has been celebrated as being threefold.

4.1. निश्चयं इति ॥ निश्चयं शृणु अवधारय मे मम वचनात् तत्र त्यागे त्यागसंन्यासविकल्पे यथादर्शिते भरतसत्तम ! भरतानां साधुतम । त्यागः हि—त्यागसंन्यासशब्दवाच्यः हि यः अर्थः स एकः एवेति अभिप्रेत्य आह 'त्यागो हि' इति—पुरुषव्याघ्र ! त्रिविधः त्रिप्रकारः तामसादिकारैः संप्रकीर्तितः शास्त्रेषु सम्यक्

कथितः । यस्मात् तामसादिभेदेन त्यागसंन्यासशब्दवाच्यः अर्थः अधिकृतस्य कर्मिणः अनात्मज्ञस्य त्रिविधः सम्भवति, न परमार्थदर्शिनः, इत्ययमर्थः दुर्ज्ञानः तस्मात् अत्र तत्त्वं न अन्यः वक्तुं समर्थः । तस्मात् निश्चयं परमार्थशास्त्रार्थविषयं अध्यवसायं ऐश्वरं मे मत्तः शृणु ॥

4.1. Grasp My decision as I state it in regard to this distinction between relinquishment and renunciation, you, best of Bhārata princes! In this context it is affirmed that the contents of both these expressions are identical. Threefold—*tāmasic*, etc.— is this 'giving up', according to the scriptural texts. As far as the non-self-knower is concerned, 'the giving up' or relinquishment, is three-fold such as the *tāmasic*, *rājasic* and *sāttvic*. It is irrelevent to the self-knower. The subtle truth of this matter, being hard to comprehend, none else than the Lord can pronounce a decision. Therefore, in regard to this scriptural truth bearing on the metaphysical reality, listen to My decisive view as I set it forth.

5.0. कः पुनः असौ निश्चयः ? इति आह—

5.0. What is this decisive view?

यज्ञदानतपःकर्म न त्याज्यं कार्यमेव तत् ।
यज्ञो दानं तपश्चैव पावनानि मनीषिणाम् ॥५॥

5. The work of sacrifice, gift-giving, and penance should not be relinquished; it must necessarily be accomplished; for, sacrifice, gift-giving, and penance purify wise men.

5.1. यज्ञ इति ॥ यज्ञः दानं तपः इत्येतत् त्रिविधं कर्म न त्याज्यं न त्यक्तव्यं, कार्यं करणीयं एव तत् । कस्मात् ? यज्ञः दानं तपः च एव पावनानि विशुद्धिकराणि मनीषिणां फलानभिसन्धीनां इत्येतत् ॥

5.1. The three-fold work of sacrifice, gift-giving and penance should not be relinquished, but accomplished. Why? They purify the wise—bestow purity on those who expect no rewards.

एतान्यपि तु कर्माणि सङ्गं त्यक्त्वा फलानि च ।
कर्तव्यानीति मे पार्थ निश्चितं मतमुत्तमम् ॥६॥

6. But even these works, Arjuna! must be done without attachment to them and to their fruits: this is My firm and most valid decision.

6.1. एतान्यपि इति ॥ एतानि अपि तु कर्माणि यज्ञदानतपांसि पावनानि उक्तानि सङ्गं आसक्तिं तेषु त्यक्त्वा फलानि च तेषां परित्यज्य कर्तव्यानि इति अनुष्ठेयानि इति मे मम निश्चितं मतं उत्तमम् ॥

'निश्चयं शृणु मे तत्र' [१८.४.] इति प्रतिज्ञाय, पावनत्वं च हेतुं उक्त्वा, 'एतान्यपि कर्माणि कर्तव्यानि' इत्येतत् 'निश्चितं मतमुत्तमं' इति प्रतिज्ञातार्थोपसंहारः एव, न अपूर्वार्थं वचनं 'एतान्यपि' इति, प्रकृतसन्निकृष्टार्थत्वोपपत्तेः । सासङ्गस्य फलार्थिनः बन्धहेतवः एतानि अपि कर्माणि मुमुक्षोः कर्तव्यानि इति अपिशब्दस्य अर्थः । न तु अन्यानि कर्माणि अपेक्ष्य 'एतान्यपि' हति उच्यते ॥

6.1. But even these purifying works must be done after giving up attachment to them and their fruits. This is My firm and most valid view. This is no novel affirmation, but only the concluding statement of a position earlier propounded in 18.4 as the decision going to be offered. The reason for it is the purifying power of these works. The words, 'even these' ought to link up with what is immediately relevant. *Api*, means that even such works, which bind when their agents have attachment and desire for their fruits, have to be performed without attachment by the agent who seeks liberation; It does not imply that there are some types of work to be performed.

6.2. अन्ये तु वर्णयन्ति—नित्यानां कर्मणां फलाभावात् 'सङ्गं त्यक्त्वा फलानि च' इति न उपपद्यते । अतः 'एतान्यपि' इति यानि काम्यानि कर्माणि नित्येभ्यः अन्यानि, एतानि अपि कर्तव्यानि, किमुत यज्ञदानतपांसि नित्यानि इति ॥

तत् असत्, नित्यानाम् अपि कर्मणां इह फलवत्त्वस्य उपपादितत्वात्, 'यज्ञो दानं तपश्चैव पावनानि' इत्यादिना वचनेन । नित्यानि अपि कर्माणि बन्धहेतुत्वाशङ्कया

जिहासोः मुमुक्षोः कुतः काम्येषु प्रसङ्गः ? 'दूरेण ह्यवरं कर्म' [२.४९.] इति च निन्दितत्वात्, 'यज्ञार्थात् कर्मणोऽन्यत्र' [३.९.] इति च काम्यकर्मणां बन्धहेतुत्वस्य निश्चितत्वात्, 'त्रैगुण्यविषया वेदाः' [२.४५], 'त्रैविद्या मां सोमपाः' [९.२०.] 'क्षीणे पुण्ये मर्त्यलोकं विशन्ति' [९.२१.] इति च, दूरव्यवहितत्वात्, च न काम्येषु 'एतान्यपि' इति व्यपदेशः ॥

6.2. Others however explain it as follows: "Obligatory works bear no fruits at all. So reference to giving up attachment to them and their fruits makes no sense. Hence 'even these' must mean occasional works that are other than obligatory works. If occasional works have to be done, obviously 'sacrifice, gift giving, etc.', must be performed, too." This explanation is unsound; for we have already explained how even obligatory works do bear fruits. The proof is the affirmation that 'sacrifices, etc., purify'. The seeker after liberation would fain give up even obligatory works lest they bind; how then can he do occasional works? 'Work' has been censured in 2.49. That occasional works bind has already been established in 3.9. Vide also passages like 2.45, 9.20, and 9.21. "Even these" cannot include occasional works, for the present context is far removed from the cited passages discussing desire-prompted works.

7.0. तस्मात् अज्ञस्य अधिकृतस्य मुमुक्षोः—

7.0. Therefore, for one who is nescient and called upon to work,

नियतस्य तु संन्यासः कर्मणो नोपपद्यते।
मोहात्तस्य परित्यागस्तामसः परिकीर्तितः ॥७॥

7. It is unreasonable to renounce obligatory work. Its renunciation due to delusion is well-known to be Tāmasic.

7.1. नियतस्य इति ॥ नियतस्य तु नित्यस्य संन्यासः परित्यागः कर्मणः न उपपद्यते, अज्ञस्य पावनत्वस्य इष्टत्वात् । मोहात् अज्ञानात् तस्य नियतस्य परित्यागः

—नियतं च अवश्यं कर्तव्यं, त्यज्यते च, इति विप्रतिषिद्धं; अतः मोहनिमित्तः परित्यागः —तामसः परिकीर्तितः मोहश्च तमः इति ॥

किं च—

7.1. The renunciation of obligatory works, which should always be done, is not reasonable; for, the nescient agent would seek purification. Its relinquishment can be due only to delusion. That the obligatory work which must inevitably be done, is sought to be given up is a contradiction in terms. So its relinquishment is traced to delusion. Therefore it is *tāmasic* also: delusion is darkness.

Moreover,

दुःखमित्येव यत्कर्म कायक्लेशभयात्त्यजेत् ।
स कृत्वा राजसं त्यागं नैव त्यागफलं लभेत् ॥८॥

8. Due to bodily fatigue, if work is given up as troublesome, such relinquishment is Rājasic; the fruit of such relinquishment won't accrue to the agent.

8.1. दुःखं इति ॥ दुःखं इति एव यत् कर्म कायक्लेशभयात् शरीरदुःखभयात् त्यजेत् परित्यजेत्, सः कृत्वा राजसं रजोनिर्वर्त्यं त्यागं न एव त्यागफलं ज्ञानपूर्वकस्य सर्वकर्मत्यागस्य फलं मोक्षाख्यं न लभेत् नैव लभेत ॥

8.1. Fearing bodily fatigue—bodily sufferings—as troublesome if one gives up work, that act is *rājasic* relinquishment—a result of *rajas*; one doing so won't reap the fruit of relinquishment that is preceded by knowledge, implying the surrender of all works as such. The fruit in question is liberation.

9.0. कः पुनः सात्त्विकः त्यागः इति ? आह—

9.0. What then is *sāttvic* relinquishment? Answer:

कार्यमित्येव यत्कर्म नियतं क्रियतेऽर्जुन ।
सङ्गं त्यक्त्वा फलं चैव स त्यागः सात्त्विको मतः ॥९॥

9. Holding that work is to be done without break, O Arjuna, and giving up both attachment and fruit, the relinquishment (entailed) is deemed Sāttvic.

9.1. कार्यं इति ॥ कार्यं कर्तव्यं इति एव यत् कर्म नियतं नित्यं क्रियते निर्वर्त्यते हे अर्जुन ! सङ्गं त्यक्त्वा फलं च एव । एतत्—नित्यानां कर्माणां फलवत्त्वे भगवद्वचनं प्रमाणं अवोचाम । अथ वा—यद्यपि फलं न श्रूयते नित्यस्य कर्मणः, तथाऽपि नित्यं कर्म कृतं आत्मसंस्कारं प्रत्यवायपरिहारं वा फलं करोति आत्मनः इति कल्पयति एव अज्ञः । तत्र ताम् अपि कल्पनां निवारयति 'फलं त्यक्त्वा' इत्यनेन । अतः साधु उक्तं 'सङ्गं त्यक्त्वा फलं च' इति । सः त्यागः नित्यकर्मसु सङ्गफलपरित्यागः सात्त्विकः सत्त्वनिर्वृत्तः मतः अभिप्रे(म)तः ॥

9.1. Suppose duty is performed without break, O Arjuna! giving up attachment and fruit. We have already stated that the Lord's affirmation is proof of the fruitfulness of obligatory works. Or, though *śruti* does not state that obligatory works yield fruits, nescient man imagines that their performance stores up right impressions or serves to ward off the sin of omission. Even such an imagination has to be shunned according to this text. Hence "giving up both. . . ." is in place. This relinquishment of attachment and of fruit is *sāttvic*, i.e. is effected by the constituent *sattva*.

9.2. ननु कर्मपरित्यागः त्रिविधः संन्यासः इति च प्रकृतः । तत्र तामसः । राजसश्च उक्तः त्यागः । कथं इह सङ्गफलत्यागः तृतीयत्वेन उच्यते ? यथा त्रयः ब्राह्मणाः आगताः, तत्र षडङ्गविदौ द्वौ, क्षत्रियः तृतीयः इति, तद्वत् ॥

नैष दोषः, त्यागसामान्येन स्तुत्यर्थत्वात् । अस्ति हि कर्मसंन्यासस्य फलाभिसन्धित्यागस्य च त्यागत्वसामान्यम् । तत्र राजसतामसत्वेन कर्मत्यागनिन्दया कर्मफलाभिसन्धित्यागः सात्त्विकत्वेन स्तूयते 'स त्यागः सात्त्विको मतः' इति ॥

9.2. *Objection*: The matter under discussion is the threefold renunciation and the relinquishment (of work). Their *tāmasic* and *rājasic* varieties have been set forth. But how can this verse talk about the renunciation of fruit and attachment as the third variety? It is like the statement that three Brahmins have arrived, two being versed in the 'six vedic limbs', and the third being a *kṣatriya*. *Reply*: This may be thus explained.

The relevant theme may be taken to be the praise of relinquishment in general. Both in renunciation of works and in that of the desire for fruits is present the common characteristic of relinquishment. Condemning relinquishment of work as *rājasic* one extols as *sāttvic* relinquishment of attachment to fruits.

10.0. यस्तु अधिकृतः सङ्गं त्यक्त्वा फलाभिसन्धिं च नित्यं कर्म करोति, तस्य फलरागादिना अकलुषीक्रियमाणं अन्तःकरणं नित्यैश्च कर्मभिः संस्क्रियमाणं विशुध्यति। तत् विशुद्धं प्रसन्नं आत्मालोचनक्षमं भवति। तस्य एव नित्यकर्मानुष्ठानेन विशुद्धान्तःकरणस्य आत्मज्ञानाभिमुखस्य क्रमेण यथा तन्निष्ठा स्यात् तत् वक्तव्यम् इति आह—

10.0. The mind of an eligible man who does obligatory work without attachment to work and its fruit is not agitated; it gets purified. Thus purified and clarified, it becomes fit to ponder over the Self. Here is explained how it gradually becomes devoted to the knowledge of the Self, now that it has already been purified through the performance of obligatory works and oriented to Self-knowledge.

न द्वेष्टयकुशलं कर्म कुशले नानुषज्जते।
त्यागी सत्त्वसमाविष्टो मेधावी छिन्नसंशयः ॥१०॥

10. The renouncer, well established in Sattva, intelligent and rid of doubts, neither hates unmeritorious work nor clings to meritorious work.

10.1. न द्वेष्टि इति ॥ न द्वेष्टि अकुशलं अशोभनं काम्यं कर्म, शरीरारम्भद्वारेण संसारकारणं, 'किं अनेन ?' इत्येवम्। कुशले शोभने नित्ये कर्मणि "सत्त्वशुद्धिज्ञानोत्पत्तितन्निष्ठाहेतुत्वेन मोक्षकारणं इदं" इत्येवं न अनुषज्जते, अनुषङ्गं प्रीतिं न करोति इत्येतत्। कः पुनः असौ ? त्यागी, पूर्वोक्तेन सङ्गफलत्यागेन तद्वान् त्यागी, यः कर्मणि सङ्गं त्यक्त्वा तत्फलं च नित्यकर्मानुष्ठायी सः त्यागी। कदा पुनः असौ अकुशलं कर्म न द्वेष्टि, कुशले च न अनुषज्जते इति ? उच्यते—सत्त्वसमाविष्टः यदा सत्त्वेन आत्मानात्मविवेकविज्ञानहेतुना समाविष्टः संव्याप्तः, संयुक्तः इत्येतत्। अत एव च मेधावी मेधया आत्मज्ञानलक्षणया प्रज्ञया संयुक्तः तद्वान् मेधावी। मेधावित्वात् एव छिन्नसंशयः छिन्नः अविद्याकृतः संशयः यस्य "आत्म-

स्वरूपावस्थानम् एव परं निःश्रेयससाधनं, न अन्यत् किंचित्" इत्येवं निश्चयेन छिन्नसंशयः ॥

यः अधिकृतः पुरुषः पूर्वोक्तेन प्रकारेण कर्मयोगानुष्ठानेन क्रमेण संस्कृतात्मा सन् जन्मादिविक्रियारहितत्वेन निष्क्रियं आत्मानं आत्मत्वेन संबुद्धः, सः सर्वकर्माणि मनसा संन्यस्य नैव कुर्वन् न कारयन् आसीनः नैष्कर्म्यलक्षणां ज्ञाननिष्ठां अश्नुते इत्येतत् । पूर्वोक्तस्य कर्मयोगस्य प्रयोजनं अनेनैव श्लोकेन उक्तम् ॥

10.1. The renouncer does not hate unmeritorious—unattractive and desire-prompted—work which causes transmigratory life by entailing embodiment. 'Does not hate' means 'does not seek to avoid' such work. 'Does not cling to' means does not take pleasure in meritorious obligatory work that emancipates through the generation of devotion to knowledge preceded by mental purity. Who is the person concerned? The renouncer, who has given up attachment and fruits of works, and who performs obligatory works. In what circumstances does he do so? When he is pervaded by *sattva* that generates the discrimination between the Self and the non-Self. He is 'Intelligent' who has such knowledge, which dispels all doubts. He is convinced that the means to the summum bonum is nothing but Self-abidance. The competent man thus gradually purifies himself by means of Karma Yoga. He realises his stirless Self, free from all mutabilities like birth, etc. Having renounced all works mentally he dwells neither doing nor causing to do. This is devotion to knowledge which entails 'absolute worklessness'. This verse teaches the purpose served by Karma Yoga.

11.0. यः पुनः अधिकृतः सन् देहात्माभिमानित्वेन देहभृत् अज्ञः अबाधितात्मकर्तृत्वाविज्ञानतया "अहं कर्ता" इति निश्चितबुद्धिः, तस्य अशेषकर्मपरित्यागस्य अशक्यत्वात् कर्मफलत्यागेन चोदितकर्मानुष्ठाने एव अधिकारः, न तत्त्यागे इति एतं अर्थं दर्शयितुं आह—

11.0. What about that type of competent man who has the conceit of self in regard to his body, who bears the burden of his body? He is nescient and has not discarded the view that his Self is a doer—he is obviously wedded to the notion "I am the agent". Of course he cannot renounce all works. He is competent only to do the scripturally ordained works, while giving up the fruits of works. He cannot relinquish them. This idea is expressed as follows:

न हि देहभृता शक्यं त्यक्तुं कर्माण्यशेषतः।
यस्तु कर्मफलत्यागी स त्यागीत्यभिधीयते ॥११॥

11. Embodied man cannot indeed totally renounce works; but he who relinquishes the fruits of works is said to be the relinquisher.

11.1. न हि इति ॥ न हि यस्मात् देहभृता—देहं बिभर्ति इति देहभृत्—देहात्माभिमानवान् देहभृत् उच्यते, न हि विवेकी; स हि 'वेदाविनाशिनं' [२.२१.] इत्यादिना कर्तृत्वाधिकारात् निर्वर्तितः। अतः तेन देहभृता अज्ञेन न शक्यं त्यक्तुं संन्यसितुं कर्माणि अशेषतः निःशेषेण। तस्मात् यः तु अज्ञः अधिकृतः नित्यानि कर्माणि कुर्वन् कर्मफलत्यागी कर्मफलाभिसन्धिमात्रसंन्यासी सः त्यागी इति अभिधीयते कर्मी अपि सन् इति—स्तुत्यभिप्रायेण। तस्मात् परमार्थदर्शि[-त्वे-]ना एव अदेहभृता देहात्मभावरहितेन अशेषकर्मसंन्यासः शक्यते कर्तुम् ॥

11.1. The embodied man is the man who bears the body. Since he has conceit in respect of his body, he is styled 'the body-bearer'. Indeed, he has little discrimination. The discriminator has been taken out of the ranks of the doers of works. The non-discriminator cannot renounce or give up works in their totality. Hence the nescient individual, whose sphere is that of works, does obligatory works; but at the same time, discards their fruits. In spite of his doing works, he is called a relinquisher as he has given up the fruits of his works. The intention is to commend the giving up of the fruits of works. It follows that the percipient of the supreme Reality alone bears no body, i.e. does not mistake the body for the Self, and can possibly renounce works in their totality.

12.0. किं पुनः तत् प्रयोजनं, यत् सर्वकर्मसंन्यासात् स्यात् इति उच्यते—

12.0. What purpose is realised through total renunciation?

अनिष्टमिष्टं मिश्रं च त्रिविधं कर्मणः फलम्।
भवत्यत्यागिनां प्रेत्य न तु संन्यासिनां क्वचित् ॥१२॥

12. The fruit of work is three-fold—disagreeable, agreeable, and mixed. It accrues to the non-relinquishers after their death, but never to the renouncers.

12.1. अनिष्टं इति ॥ अनिष्टं नरकतिर्यगादिलक्षणं, इष्टं देवादिलक्षणं, मिश्रं इष्टानिष्टसंयुक्तं मनुष्यलक्षणं च, तत् त्रिविधं त्रिप्रकारं कर्मणः धर्माधर्मलक्षणस्य फलं बाह्यानेककारकव्यापारनिष्पन्नं सत् अविद्याकृतं इन्द्रजालमायोपमं महामोहकरं प्रत्यगात्मोपसर्पि इव—फल्गुतया लयं अदर्शनं गच्छति इति फलनिर्वचनं—तत् एतत् एवंलक्षणं फलं भवति अत्यागिनां अज्ञानां कर्मिणां अपरमार्थसंन्यासिनां प्रेत्य शरीरपातात् ऊर्ध्वम् । न तु संन्यासिनां परमार्थसंन्यासिनां परमहंसपरिव्राजकानां केवलज्ञाननिष्ठानां क्वचित् । न हि केवलसम्यग्दर्शननिष्ठा अविद्यादिसंसारबीजं न उन्मूलयति कदाचित् इत्यर्थः । अतः परमार्थदर्शिनः एव अशेषकर्मसंन्यासित्वं सम्भवति, अविद्याऽध्यारोपितत्वात् आत्मनि क्रियाकारकफलानाम्; न तु अज्ञस्य अधिष्ठानादीनि क्रियाकर्तृकारकाणि आत्मत्वेन पश्यतः अशेषकर्मसंन्यासः सम्भवति ॥

12.1. 'The disagreeable' refers to fruits like hell, life as sub-human creatures etc.; 'the agreeable' is life as gods, etc; 'the mixed' includes both the elements as in life as man. These are the fruits of works which are righteous or unrighteous. They are produced by the operations of several external factors. Of course they are of the stuff of nescience resembling magical shows. They cause delusion and apparently affect the inner self. The term *phala* points to something that gets liquidated and disappears, being petty. These fruits accrue after death to the nescient, unrelinquishing agents of works who are other than genuine renouncers; but never to genuine renouncers who are exclusively devoted to the discipline of knowledge. This devotion never indeed fails to destroy the seeds of transmigratory life. Therefore total renunciation is possible only for the realizers of the Supreme Reality. Actions, its accessories, and fruits have been super-imposed on the Self through ignorance. Total renunciation is thus not possible for the ignorant who indentify the factors set forth in 18.13, as constitutents of the Self.

13.0. तत् एतत् उत्तरैः श्लोकैः दर्शयति—

13.0. This truth is elucidated in the next few verses:

पञ्चैतानि महाबाहो कारणानि निबोध मे ।
सांख्ये कृतान्ते प्रोक्तानि सिद्धये सर्वकर्मणाम् ॥१३॥

13. Mighty-armed! know from Me the five causes, set forth in the Sāṃkhya system, as promoting the accomplishment of all works.

13.1. पञ्च इति ॥ पञ्च एतानि वक्ष्यमाणानि हे महाबाहो ! कारणानि निर्वर्तकानि । निबोध मे इति उत्तरत्र चेतःसमाधानार्थं, वस्तुवैषम्यप्रदर्शनार्थं च । तानि च कारणानि ज्ञातव्यतया स्तौति—सांख्ये, ज्ञातव्याः पदार्थाः संख्यायन्ते यस्मिन् शास्त्रे तत् सांख्यं वेदान्तः, कृतान्ते इति तस्यैव विशेषणम्—कृतं इति कर्म उच्यते, तस्य अन्तः परिसमाप्तिः यत्र सः कृतान्तः, कर्मान्तः इत्येतत् । 'यावानर्थ उदपाने' [२.४६.], 'सर्वं कर्माखिलं पार्थ ज्ञाने परिसमाप्यते' [४.३३.] इति आत्मज्ञाने संजाते सर्वकर्मणां निवृत्तिं दर्शयति । अतः तस्मिन् आत्मज्ञानार्थे सांख्ये कृतान्ते वेदान्ते प्रोक्तानि कथितानि सिद्धये निष्पत्त्यर्थं सर्वकर्मणाम् ॥

13.1. The five causes accomplishing works are presently to be set forth. 'Know from Me'—this expression is used to draw attention and direct it to that heterogeneity. They are now extolled. Sāṃkhya is the science of Vedānta wherein are enumerated the principles to be known. *Kṛtānta* qualifies it; *kṛta* is work, and the science which elucidates its end is the Vedānta. BG.2.46 and 4.33 refer to the Self-knowledge that terminates all works. Thus in the science of Vedānta are stated the causes which promote the accomplishment of all works.

14.0. कानि तानि इति ? उच्यते—

14.0. Which are the causes in question? Answer:

अधिष्ठानं तथा कर्ता करणं च पृथग्विधम् ।
विविधाश्च पृथक्चेष्टा दैवं चैवात्र पञ्चमम् ॥१४॥

14. (There are) the ground, the agent, various instruments, and manifold movement together with the supernatural as the fifth among them.

14.1. अधिष्ठानं इति ॥ अधिष्ठानं इच्छाद्वेषसुखज्ञानादीनां अभिव्यक्तिः आश्रयः अधिष्ठानं शरीरं, तथा कर्ता उपाधिलक्षणः भोक्ता, करणं च श्रोत्रादि शब्दाद्युपलब्धये पृथग्विधं नानाप्रकारं तत् द्वादशसंख्यं, विविधाः च पृथक्चेष्टाः वायवीयाः प्राणापानाद्याः, दैवं च एव दैवम् एव च अत्र एतेषु चतुर्षु पञ्चमं पञ्चानां पूरणं आदित्यादि चक्षुराद्यनुग्राहकम् ॥

14.1. 'The ground' is the body in which are manifested attachment, aversion, etc. (vide BG 13.6). The agent is the delimited self who is also the reaper of the fruits of works. The instruments are the sense-organs, twelve in number—ear, etc. which apprehend objects like sound. 'Manifold movement' refers to the movements of 'the vital airs'—the in-breath, out-breath, etc. The supernatural element is the fifth in this list; it is the solar deity, etc., superintending and guiding the function of the sense organs such as the eye.

शरीरवाङ्मनोभिर्यत्कर्म प्रारभते नरः।
न्याय्यं वा विपरीतं वा पञ्चैते तस्य हेतवः॥१५॥

15. These five are the five causes of whatever work, right or wrong, that a man initiates with his body, speech and mind.

15.1. शरीर इति ॥ शरीरवाङ्मनोभिः यत् कर्म त्रिभिः एतैः प्रारभते निर्वर्तयति नरः, न्याय्यं वा धर्म्यं शास्त्रीयं, विपरीतं वा अशास्त्रीयम् अधर्म्यं यच्च अपि निमिषितचेष्टितादि जीवनहेतुः तत् अपि पूर्वकृतधर्माधर्मयोः एव कार्यम् इति न्याय्यविपरीतयोः एव ग्रहणेन गृहीतं, पञ्च एते यथोक्ताः तस्य सर्वस्य एव कर्मणः हेतवः कारणानि ॥

15.1. Whatever work a man does with the three (instruments)—i.e., body, speech, and mind—, whether right or wrong—i.e., in accordance with or opposed to the *śāstras*, righteous or unrighteous—, the causes are as stated above. Even the involuntary movements of the body entailed by living are determined by right and wrong done earlier. Hence the expression 'right or wrong' include *dharma* and *adharma*, merit and demerit. The five factors as stated above are the causes of all work.

15.2. ननु एतानि अधिष्ठानादीनि सर्वकर्मणां निर्वर्तकानि । कथं उच्यते 'शरीरवाङ्मनोभिः यत् कर्म प्रारभते' इति ?

नैष दोषः; विधिप्रतिषेधलक्षणं सर्वं कर्म शरीरादित्रयप्रधानं; तदङ्गतया दर्शनश्रवणादि च जीवनलक्षणं त्रिधा एव राशीकृतं उच्यते शरीरादिभिः आरभ्यते इति । फलकालेऽपि तत्प्रधानैः साधनैः भुज्यते इति पञ्चानाम् एव हेतुत्वं न विरुध्यते इति ॥

15.2. *Objection:* "Now works as such are accomplished by the five causes. Why then specify saying work done by means of body, speech and mind?" *Reply:* "This is no flaw. All works, commended or forbidden, are dominated by one of these three. Seeing, hearing etc. are parts of these works and grouped into three with reference to body, etc. At the time of reaping their consequences they are experienced mainly through these three means. Hence the causality ascribed to the five factors is not inconsistent."

तत्रैवं सति कर्तारमात्मानं केवलं तु यः ।
पश्यत्यकृतबुद्धित्वान्न स पश्यति दुर्मतिः ॥१६॥

16. This being the case, whoever beholds, due to lack of disciplined reason, the pure Self as agent, sees not at all; his is misunderstanding.

16.1. तत्र इति ॥ तत्र इति प्रकृतेन सम्बध्यते—एवं सति एवं यथोक्तैः पञ्चभिः हेतुभिः निर्वर्त्ये सति कर्मणि । 'तत्रैवं सति' इति दुर्मतित्वस्य हेतुत्वेन सम्बध्यते । तत्र एतेषु आत्मानन्यत्वेन अविद्यया परिकल्पितैः क्रियमाणस्य कर्मणः 'अहमेव कर्ता' इति कर्तारं आत्मानं केवलं शुद्धं तु यः पश्यति अविद्वान्—कस्मात् ? —वेदान्ताचार्योपदेशन्यायैः अकृतबुद्धित्वात् असंस्कृतबुद्धित्वात्—योऽपि देहादिव्य-

तिरिक्तात्मवादी आत्मानम् एव केवलं कर्तारं पश्यति, असौ अपि अकृतबुद्धिः– अतः अकृतबुद्धित्वात् न सः पश्यति आत्मनः तत्त्वं कर्मणः वा इत्यर्थः । अतः दुर्मतिः, कुत्सिता विपरीता दुष्टा अजस्रं जननमरणप्रतिपत्तिहेतुभूता मतिः अस्य इति दुर्मतिः । सः पश्यन् अपि न पश्यति, यथा तैमिरिकः अनेकं चन्द्रं, यथा वा अभ्रेषु धावत्सु चन्द्रं धावन्तं, यथा वा वाहने उपविष्टः अन्येषु धावत्सु आत्मानं धावन्तम् ॥

16.1. 'This' refers to the present context 'This being the case' means—since work can be done only with the cooperation of the five causal factors. The cause of misunderstanding is set forth in this expression—'this being the case'. As work is done cooperatively by the five factors deemed to be other than the Self, the ignoramus who looks upon the pure Self as the agent, due to nescience, fails to grasp the truth about the Self or about the works. This mis-perception results from the fact that his intellect has not been trained in the teachings of the Vedānta or of competent teachers or in the processes of reasoning. Even he who holds that the Self is other than the body, etc., is wrong if he deems the Self alone to be the doer of works; he has only misunderstanding. His 'understanding' merits censure, as it leads to ceaseless births and deaths. 'Seeing' he fails to see, just as a man of defective vision sees many moons or a speeding moon when only the clouds stir. A man seated in a palanquin deems himself moving when people carrying the palanquin alone are moving.

17.0. कः पुनः सुमतिः यः सम्यक् पश्यति इति ? उच्यते—

17.0. Whose understanding then is right? who sees aright? listen:

यस्य नाहंकृतो भावो बुद्धिर्यस्य न लिप्यते।
हत्वाऽपि स इमाँल्लोकान्न हन्ति न निबध्यते ॥१७॥

17. He whose attitude is unegoistic, whose understanding is untainted, even after slaying all living beings, neither slays, nor is bound.

17.1. यस्य इति ॥ यस्य शास्त्राचार्योपदेशन्यायसंस्कृतात्मनः न भवति अहंकृतः "अहं कर्ता" इत्येवंलक्षणः भावः भावना प्रत्ययः—एते एव पञ्च अधिष्ठानादयः अविद्यया आत्मनि कल्पिताः सर्वकर्मणां कर्तारः, न अहं, अहं तु तद्व्यापाराणां साक्षिभूतः 'अप्राणो ह्यमनाः शुभ्रो ह्यक्षरात्परतः परः' [मु. उ. २.१.२.] केवलः अविक्रियः इत्येवं पश्यति इति एतत्—बुद्धिः अन्तःकरणं यस्य आत्मनः उपाधिभूता न लिप्यते न अनुशयिनी भवति—"इदं अहं अकार्षं, तेन अहं नरकं गमिष्यामि" इत्येवं यस्य बुद्धिः न लिप्यते—सः सुमतिः, सः पश्यति । हत्वा अपि सः इमान् लोकान्, सर्वान् इमान् प्राणिनः इत्यर्थः, न हन्ति हननक्रियां न करोति, न निबध्यते नापि तत्कार्येण अधर्मफलेन सम्बध्यते ॥

17.1. He has the right understanding, he sees aright, who does not deem himself the doer of works. His self has been purified by the teachings of the *śāstras* and his teacher and by the processes of reasoning. The five factors (BG 18.14) superimposed due to nescience on the Self are the doers of all work and not 'I'. 'I' am only the witness of their operations, Vide MU 2.1.2: "Without vital breaths, indeed mindless, luminous, beyond the Imperishable, the Supreme, I am the Alone, the Immutable." He knows all this. His intellect—the inner sense—is untainted; it does not cling to thoughts such as 'I did this, so I shall fall into hell.' His thoughts are auspicious. He sees aright. Even after slaying all these living beings, he is no killer and is not bound—he is not related to its fruits, the fruits of unrighteousness".

17.2. ननु हत्वाऽपि न हन्ति इति विप्रतिषिद्धं उच्यते यद्यपि स्तुतिः ? नैष दोषः, लौकिकपारमार्थिकदृष्टयपेक्षया तदुपपत्तेः । देहाद्यात्मबुद्ध्या 'हन्ता अहं' इति लौकिकीं दृष्टिं आश्रित्य 'हत्वाऽपि' इति आह; यथार्दर्शितां पारमार्थिकीं दृष्टिं आश्रित्य 'न हन्ति न निबध्यते' इति—एतत् उभयं उपपद्यते एव ॥ ननु अधिष्ठानादिभिः संभूय करोति एव आत्मा, 'कर्तारमात्मानं केवलं तु' [१८.१६.] इति 'केवल' शब्दप्रयोगात् ।

नैषः दोषः, आत्मनः अविक्रियस्वभावत्वे अधिष्ठानादिभिः संहतत्वानुपपत्तेः । विक्रियावतः हि अन्यैः संहननं सम्भवति, संहत्य वा कर्तृत्वं स्यात् । न तु अविक्रियस्य आत्मनः केनचित् संहननं अस्ति इति न संभूय कर्तृत्वं उपपद्यते । अतः केवलत्वं आत्मनः स्वाभाविकम् इति केवलशब्दः अनुवादमात्रम् । अविक्रियत्वं च आत्मनः श्रुतिस्मृतिन्यायप्रसिद्धम् । "अविकार्योऽयमुच्यते" [२.२५.], "गुणैरेव कर्माणि क्रियन्ते" [३.२७.], 'शरीरस्थोऽपि न करोति' [१३.३१.] इत्यादि

असकृत् उपपादितं गीतासु एव तावत् । श्रुतिषु च 'ध्यायतीव लेलायतीव' [बृ. उ. ४.३.७.] इत्येवमाद्यासु । न्यायतश्च—निरवयवं, अपरतन्त्रं, अविक्रियं आत्मतत्त्वं इति राजमार्गः । विक्रियावत्त्वाभ्युपगमेऽपि आत्मनः स्वकीया एव विक्रिया स्वस्य भवितुं अर्हति, न अधिष्ठानादीनां कर्माणि आत्मकर्तृकाणि स्युः । न हि परस्य कर्म परेण अकृतं आगन्तुं अर्हति । यत्तु अविद्यया गमितं, न तत् तस्य; यथा रजतत्वं न शुक्तिकायाः; यथा वा तलमलिनत्वं बालैः गमितं अविद्यया न आकाशस्य तथा अधिष्ठानादिविक्रियाऽपि तेषाम् एव, न आत्मनः । तस्मात् युक्तं उक्तम् "अहंकृतत्वबुद्धिलेपाभावात् विद्वान् न हन्ति न निबध्यते" इति ।

17.2. *Objection:* Though meant as commendatory only, this statement that though he slays he slays not is paradoxical. *Reply:* "This is no flaw; for it may be explained with reference to the distinction between the empirical and metaphysical view-points. 'Having slain' refers to the empirical view-point according to which body, etc., constitute the self. 'He slays not' refers to the metaphysical view-point, as has already been elucidated." *Objection:* "Surely the self together with the ground' (i.e. body etc.), does the work; for 18.16 objects only to the view that the mere self works." *Reply*: "Granting the immortality of the Self, It cannot combine with the ground (i.e. body etc). Combination with other factors is possible only if an entity is susceptible to modification; then only may It have joint doership. The immortal Self cannot combine with aught else and acquire a joint doership. Aloneness, then, is inherent in the Self. Mereness or aloneness is not predicative; it points to the nature of the subject, Self. Its immutability is celebrated in *śruti* and *smṛti* and supported by reason. cf.BG.2.15, 3.27; 13.21. Also BU.4.3.7, etc. Reasoning is as follows: The Self is impartite, independent, and immutable. Even if Self mutates, only Its own changes may occur in It. Some one's acts cannot accrue to another who has not performed them. What is ascribed through nescience cannot belong to It. Note that silverness does not belong to the nacre; the murkiness of the ground cannot belong to the sky to which the ignorant attribute it. Similarly, the mutations of the ground, etc., belong only to them and not to the Self. Therefore, the observation, 'being unegoistic and of untainted understanding, the knower neither slays nor gets bound,' is in order."

17.3. 'नायं हन्ति न हन्यते' इति प्रतिज्ञाय 'न जायते' इत्यादिहेतुवचनेन अविक्रियत्वं आत्मनः उक्त्वा, 'वेदाविनाशिनं' [२.१९,२०,२१.] इति विदुषः कर्माधिकारनिवृत्तिं शास्त्रादौ संक्षेपतः उक्त्वा, मध्ये प्रसारितां, तत्र तत्र प्रसङ्गं कृत्वा इह उपसंहरति शास्त्रार्थपिण्डीकरणाय "विद्वान् न हन्ति न निबध्यते" इति।

एवं च सति देहभृत्त्वाभिमानानुपपत्तौ अविद्याकृताशेषकर्मसंन्यासोपपत्तेः संन्यासिनां अनिष्टादि त्रिविधं कर्मणः फलं (१८.१२.) न भवति इति उपपन्नं; तद्विपर्ययात् च इतरेषां भवति इति एतत् च अपरिहार्यं इति एषः गीताशास्त्रार्थः उपसंहृतः। स एषः सर्ववेदार्थसारः निपुणमतिभिः पण्डितैः विचार्य प्रतिपत्तव्यः इति तत्र तत्र प्रकरणविभागेन दर्शितः अस्माभिः शास्त्रन्यायानुसारेण ॥

17.3. Having affirmed, 'he neither slays nor gets bound', and set forth the reason for it in the words, 'he is not born, etc.,' which elucidate the Self's immortality, at the beginning of the Gītā (2.19-21), and having shown also the reason for the knower's withdrawal from the sphere of activities—the Lord concludes the Gītā's ideas on this topic in 18.17. These ideas have also been mentioned in various passages throughout the course of the Gītā. In these circumstances it stands to reason that the three-fold fruit of works does not accrue to the renouncers who have no conceit in the body-mind complex, and have therefore given up all works. On the contrary to the non-renouncers the three-fold fruit inevitably does accrue. Thus also is concluded the theme of BG. With penetrating discrimination the scholars must ponder on the essence of this Vedic wisdom and master it. This view has been set forth by us in several contexts analytically, in harmony with the *śāstra* and reason.

18.0. अथ इदानीं कर्मणां प्रवर्तकं उच्यते—

18.0. Now is stated the factor that impels all works:

ज्ञानं ज्ञेयं परिज्ञाता त्रिविधा कर्मचोदना।
करणं कर्म कर्तेति त्रिविधः कर्मसंग्रहः ॥१८॥

18. Knowledge, the knowable and knower—is the three-fold mandate to work. The instrument, work and agent constitute the three-fold summary of work.

18.1. ज्ञानं इति ॥ ज्ञानं ज्ञायते अनेन इति सर्वविषयं अविशेषेण उच्यते, तथा ज्ञेयं ज्ञातव्यं, तदपि सामान्येन एव सर्वं उच्यते; तथा परिज्ञाता उपाधिलक्षणः अविद्याकल्पितः भोक्ता—इति एतत् त्रयं अविशेषेण सर्वकर्मणां प्रवर्तिका त्रिविधा त्रिप्रकारा कर्मचोदना । ज्ञानादीनां हि त्रयाणां सन्निपाते हानोपादानादिप्रयोजनः सर्वकर्मारम्भः स्यात् । ततः पञ्चभिः अधिष्ठानादिभिः आरब्धं वाङ्मनःकायाश्रय-भेदेन त्रिधा राशीभूतं त्रिषु करणादिषु संगृह्यते इति एतत् उच्यते—करणं क्रियते अनेन इति बाह्यं श्रोत्रादि, अन्तःस्थं बुद्ध्यादि, कर्म ईप्सिततमं कर्तुः क्रियया व्याप्यमानम्, कर्ता करणानां व्यापारयिता उपाधिलक्षणः, इति त्रिविधः त्रिप्रकारः कर्मसंग्रहः—संगृह्यते अस्मिन् इति संग्रहः, कर्मणः संग्रहः कर्मसंग्रहः—कर्म एषु हि त्रिषु समवैति, तेन अयं त्रिविधः कर्मसंग्रहः ॥

18.1. Knowledge in general is meant here; the distinctions among particular cognitions are ignored. Such is the case with the knowable and the knower. The knower is bound up with adjuncts due to nescience—the experiencer in general. These three in their generality constitute the three-fold mandate to do work; for, only when these three converge, a beginning to work, directed to acquisition, rejection, etc., can happen. Then are noted three groups of work-factors. The instrument, that by which the work is done, is external sense-organs like the ear, and internal ones like the intellect. Work is what is most intently sought after and pervaded by activity. Agent is the wielder of instruments and his mark is adjuncts like mind and body. Indeed work inheres in these three factors.

19.0. अथ इदानीं क्रियाकारकफलानां सर्वेषां गुणात्मकत्वात् सत्त्वरजस्तमो-गुणभेदतः त्रिविधः भेदः वक्तव्यः इति आरभ्यते—

19.0. Now is set forth the three-fold distinction among these factors based on the constituents of nature like *sattva*, etc. For, work, instrument and fruit of work are, essentially, these constituents.

ज्ञानं कर्म च कर्ता च त्रिधैव गुणभेदतः ।
प्रोच्यते गुणसंख्याने यथावच्छृणु तान्यपि ।।१९।।

19. Knowledge, work, and doer are just three-fold with reference to the constituents as elucidated in the light of these constituents; listen to a factual statement of these also.

19.1. ज्ञानं इति ।। ज्ञानं कर्म च—कर्म क्रिया, न कारकं पारिभाषिकं ईप्सिततमं कर्म—कर्ता च निर्वर्तकः क्रियाणां त्रिधा एव—अवधारणं गुणव्यतिरिक्तजात्यन्तराभावप्रदर्शनार्थं—गुणभेदतः सत्त्वादिभेदेन इत्यर्थः । प्रोच्यते कथ्यते गुणसंख्याने कापिले शास्त्रे—तदपि गुणसंख्यानशास्त्रं गुणभोक्तृविषये प्रमाणम् एव । परमार्थब्रह्मैकत्वविषये यद्यपि विरुध्यते, तथाऽपि ते हि कापिलाः गुणगौणव्यापारनिरूपणे अभियुक्ताः इति तच्छात्रम् अपि वक्ष्यमाणार्थस्तुत्यर्थत्वेन उपादीयते इति न विरोधः । यथावत् यथान्यायं, यथाशास्त्रं शृणु तानि अपि ज्ञानादीनि तद्भेदजातानि गुणभेदकृतानि शृणु, वक्ष्यमाणे अर्थे मनःसमाधिं कुरु इत्यर्थः ।।

19.1. Knowledge, work—work means activity and not the technical part of speech defined (in 18.18) as what is most sought after—,and the doer, or he who accomplishes activity—thus has work a three-fold division. 'Just three-fold'—rules out all generality apart from the constituents. This is based on the three-fold constituents, *sattva*, *rajas* and *tamas*. "As elucidated in the light . . . ." refers to the system of Kapila. This *śāstra* is a valid source of knowledge about the constituents and the *jivas* who experience. Though it contradicts in respect of the non-duality of the metaphysical Real or Brahman, the followers of Kapila are adepts as regards constituents and their operations. Hence their system is cited as worthy of commendation. Listen to their account, keeping reasoning in view. The distinctions drawn are based upon the differences among the constituents; pay heed.

20.0. ज्ञानस्य तु तावत् त्रिविधत्वं उच्यते—

20.0. The three-foldness of knowledge is affirmed:

सर्वभूतेषु येनैकं भावमव्ययमीक्षते।
अविभक्तं विभक्तेषु तज्ज्ञानं विद्धि सात्त्विकम् ॥२०॥

20. Know that knowledge to be Sāttvic by which one sees in all beings a single immutable existence though these beings themselves are divided.

20.1. सर्वभूतेषु इति ॥ सर्वभूतेषु अव्यक्तादिस्थावरान्तेषु भूतेषु येन ज्ञानेन एकं भावं वस्तु—भावशब्दः वस्तुवाची, एकं आत्मवस्तु इत्यर्थः—अव्ययं, न व्येति स्वात्मना स्वधर्मेण वा, कूटस्थं इत्यर्थः, ईक्षते पश्यति येन ज्ञानेन, तं च भावं अविभक्तं प्रतिदेहं, विभक्तेषु देहभेदेषु न विभक्तं तत् आत्मवस्तु, व्योमवत् निरन्तरम् इत्यर्थः, तत् ज्ञानं साक्षात् सम्यग्दर्शनं अद्वैतात्मविषयं सात्त्विकं विद्धि इति ॥

20.1. In all beings from the unmanifest to stationary things, the knowledge by which is seen a single existence—the reality or the immutable Self—is *sāttvic*. This reality does not mutate either by itself or through the mutation of its attributes; it is undivided in each of the divided bodies. This undivided Self is like the sky. The knowledge of this non-dual Self is immediate and veridical and it is held to be *sāttvic*.

21.0. यानि द्वैतदर्शनानि तानि असम्यग्भूतानि राजसानि तामसानि च इति न साक्षात् संसारोच्छित्तये भवन्ति—

21.0. Perceptions of dualities are non-veridical—they are *rājasic* or *tāmasic;* they don't directly terminate the life of transmigration:

पृथक्त्वेन तु यज्ज्ञानं नानाभावान् पृथग्विधान्।
वेत्ति सर्वेषु भूतेषु तज्ज्ञानं विद्धि राजसम् ॥२१॥

21. But know as Rajasic the knowledge by which one knows all beings as existents of various kinds.

21.1. पृथक्त्वेन इति ॥ पृथक्त्वेन तु भेदेन प्रतिशरीरं अन्यत्वेन यत् ज्ञानं नाना-भावान् भिन्नान् आत्मनः पृथग्विधान् पृथक्प्रकारान् भिन्नलक्षणान् इत्यर्थः, वेत्ति विजानाति यत् ज्ञानं सर्वेषु भूतेषु—ज्ञानस्य कर्तृत्वासम्भवात् येन ज्ञानेन वेत्ति इत्यर्थः—तत् ज्ञानं विद्धि राजसं रजोगुणनिर्वृत्तम् ॥

21.1. Know as *rājasic* or as fashioned by *rajas*, the knowledge by which, one knows varied beings as different in different bodies. Of course, knowledge does not know, but by means of it one knows:

यत्तु कृत्स्नवदेकस्मिन् कार्ये सक्तमहैतुकम् ।
अतत्त्वार्थवदल्पं च तत्तामसमुदाहृतम् ॥२२॥

22. That is said to be Tāmasic knowledge, which unreasonably sticks to an object as if it were a whole, and whose content is unveridical and petty.

22.1. यत्तु इति ॥ यत् तु ज्ञानं कृत्स्नवत् समस्तवत् सर्वविषयम् इव एकस्मिन् कार्ये देहे बहिर्वा प्रतिमादौ सक्तं "एतावानेव आत्मा ईश्वरः वा, न अतः परं अस्ति" इति, यथा नग्नक्षप [-श्रम-] णकादीनां शरीरान्तर्वर्ती देहपरिमाणः जीवः, ईश्वरः वा पाषाणदार्वादिमात्रम्, इत्येवं एकस्मिन् कार्ये सक्तं अहैतुकं हेतुवर्जितं निर्युक्तिकं, अतत्त्वार्थवत् अयथाभूतार्थवत् यथाभूतः अर्थः तत्त्वार्थः, सः अस्य ज्ञेयभूतः अस्ति इति तत्त्वार्थवत्, न तत्त्वार्थवत् अतत्त्वार्थवत्—अहैतुकत्वात् एव अल्पं च, अल्प-विषयत्वात् अल्पफलत्वात् वा । तत् तामसं उदाहृतम् । तामसानां हि प्राणिनां अविवेकिनां ईदृशं ज्ञानं दृश्यते ॥

22.1. But the knowledge that identifies the whole with the body or with something extended like an image, holding the Self or God to be only so much and nothing more exists— is *tamasic*. Witness the naked Jains who hold that the Self or *jiva* is of the size of the body it inhabits. God is only the image, stone or wood, and no more. There is no reasoning to support such views. They are false and petty, relating to a finite object. Its fruit, too, is petty. Such knowledge is said to be *tāmasic*. Only *tāmasic* beings, lacking in discrimination, entertain such knowledge.

23.0. अथ इदानीं कर्मणः त्रैविध्यं उच्यते—

23.0. Now is stated how work is threefold:

नियतं सङ्गरहितमरागद्वेषतः कृतम् ।
अफलप्रेप्सुना कर्म यत्तत्सात्त्विकमुच्यते ॥२३॥

23. Sāttvic is said to be the work that is obligatory, done without attachment, passion or aversion, by one who seeks not its fruit.

23.1. नियतं इति ॥ नियतं नित्यं सङ्गरहितं आसक्तिवर्जितं अरागद्वेषतः कृतं रागप्रयुक्तेन द्वेषप्रयुक्तेन च कृतं रागद्वेषतः कृतं, तद्विपरीतं अरागद्वेषतः कृतं, अफलप्रेप्सुना फलं प्रेप्सति इति फलप्रेप्सुः फलतृष्णः तद्विपरीतेन अफलप्रेप्सुना कर्त्रा कृतं कर्म यत् तत् सात्त्विकं उच्यते ॥

23.1. Obligatory work done without attachment, passion or aversion by one who does not desire to secure its fruit—who does not hanker after its fruit—is said to be *sāttvic*.

यत्तु कामेप्सुना कर्म साहङ्कारेण वा पुनः ।
क्रियते बहुलायासं तद्राजसमुदाहृतम् ॥२४॥

24. The work done with passion for a desired fruit by an egoistic agent, which entails much labour, is said to be Rājasic.

24.1. यत्तु इति ॥ यत्, तु कामेप्सुना कर्मफलप्रेप्सुना इत्यर्थः, कर्म साहङ्कारेण इति न तत्त्वज्ञानापेक्षया—किं तर्हि?—लौकिकश्रोत्रियनिरहङ्कारापेक्षया । यः हि परमार्थनिरहङ्कारः आत्मवित्, न तस्य कामेप्सुत्वबहुलायासकर्तृत्वप्राप्तिः आस्ति । सात्त्विकस्य अपि कर्मणः अनात्मवित् साहङ्कारः कर्ता, किमुत राजसतामसयोः । लोके अनात्मवित् अपि श्रोत्रियः निरहङ्कारः उच्यते 'निरहङ्कारः अयं ब्राह्मणः' इति तस्मात् तदपेक्षया एव 'साहङ्कारेण वा' इति उक्तम् । पुनःशब्दः पादपूरणार्थः । क्रियते बहुलायासं कर्म (कर्त्रा) महता आयासेन निर्वर्त्यते, तत् कर्म राजसं उदाहृतम् ॥

24.1. *Rājasic* is the work done by one who seeks its fruit, who is egoistic, who is devoid of even the prevalent knowledge of truth: i.e. who is more than ordinarily egoistic. The reference is not to one who is rid of the principle of egoism; for such an agent will be a knower of the Self with whom can never be associated passion for a desired fruit, etc. The agent even of *sāttvic* work is egoistic, not to speak of *rājasic* and *tāmasic* works. A Vedic scholar, though not a knower of the Self, is widely deemed unegoistic of whom one says: 'This Brāhmaṇa is unegoistic'. Compared with him the agent of *rājasic* work is said to be egoistic. The term *punaḥ* in the verse only completes the first half of the verse. This *rājasic* work is done with much labour by its agent.

अनुबन्धं क्षयं हिंसामनपेक्ष्य च पौरुषम् ।
मोहादारभ्यते कर्म यत्तत्तामसमुच्यते ॥२५॥

25. The work undertaken due to delusion and without regard for consequences, loss, violence involved, and competence is said to be Tāmasic.

25.1. अनुबन्धं इति ॥ अनुबन्धं पश्चाद्भावि यत् वस्तु सः अनुबन्धः उच्यते तं च अनुबन्धं, क्षयं यस्मिन् कर्मणि क्रियमाणे शक्तिक्षयः अर्थक्षयः वा स्यात् तं क्षयं, हिंसां प्राणिबाधां (-पीडां) च, अनपेक्ष्य च पौरुषं पुरुषकारं 'शक्नोमि इदं कर्म समापयितुं' इत्येवं आत्मसामर्थ्यम्, इति एतानि अनुबन्धादीनि अनपेक्ष्य पौरुषान्तानि मोहात् अविवेकतः आरभ्यते कर्म यत् तत् तामसं तमोनिर्वृत्तं उच्यते ॥

25.1. Consequence is what follows the work. Loss is that which the work causes—loss of power or wealth. Violence is injury to life. Competence is confidence in one's ability to accomplish the work. Work undertaken without regard for these factors, through delusion or lack of discrimination, is *tāmasic*—is done due to *tamas*.

26.0. इदानीं कर्तृभेदः उच्यते—

26.0. Now are set forth the different kinds of agents:

मुक्तसङ्गोऽनहंवादी धृत्युत्साहसमन्वितः ।
सिद्ध्यसिद्ध्योर्निर्विकारः कर्ता सात्त्विक उच्यते ॥२६॥

26. Sāttvic is the agent devoid of attachment, unegoistic, rich in resolution and zeal, and changeless in success and failure.

26.1. मुक्त इति ॥ मुक्तसङ्गः मुक्तः परित्यक्तः सङ्गः येन सः मुक्तसङ्गः, अनहंवादी न अहंवदनशीलः, धृत्युत्साहसमन्वितः धृतिः धारणं, उत्साहः उद्यमः, ताभ्यां समन्वितः संयुक्तः धृत्युत्साहसमन्वितः सिद्ध्यसिद्ध्योः क्रियमाणस्य कर्मणः फलसिद्धौ असिद्धौ च सिद्ध्यसिद्ध्योः निर्विकारः—केवलं शास्त्रप्रमाणेन प्रयुक्तः न फलरागादिना यः सः निर्विकारः उच्यते । एवम्भूतः कर्ता यः सः सात्त्विकः उच्यते ॥

26.1. He who has given up attachment, is not pushing himself to the fore, rich in endurance and application, immutable in success and failure, i.e. who has been impelled by the *śāstraic* mandate and not greed for work's fruit, is said to be *sāttvic*.

रागी कर्मफलप्रेप्सुर्लुब्धो हिंसात्मकोऽशुचिः ।
हर्षशोकान्वितः कर्ता राजसः परिकीर्तितः ॥२७॥

27. The agent who is attached, seeks the fruit of works, is greedy, violent, unclean, glad and sad—is known as Rājasic.

27.1. रागी इति ॥ रागी रागः अस्य अस्तीति रागी, कर्मफलप्रेप्सुः कर्मफलार्थी इत्यर्थः, लुब्धः परद्रव्येषु संजाततृष्णः, तीर्थादौ स्वद्रव्यापरित्यागी वा, हिंसात्मकः परपीडाकरस्वभावः, अशुचिः बाह्याभ्यन्तरशौचवर्जितः, हर्षशोकान्वितः इष्टप्राप्तौ हर्षः, अनिष्टप्राप्तौ इष्टवियोगे च शोकः, ताभ्यां हर्षशोकाभ्यां अन्वितः संयुक्तः, तस्यैव च कर्मणः सम्पत्तिविपत्तिभ्यां हर्षशोकौ स्यातां, ताभ्यां संयुक्तः यः कर्ता सः राजसः परिकीर्तितः ॥

27.1. He who has attachment is 'the attached', i.e. one who seeks the fruit of his works; the 'greedy' is the one who is eager to seize the wealth of others or who won't give away his own wealth as charity in sacred places. The 'violent' is one hurting others; the 'unclean', one lacking in internal and external cleanliness; the 'glad', one of pleasant experiences, and the 'sad', one without pleasant experiences. Or, when one's work prospers he may be glad, and sad when it is ruined. An agent like this is known as *rājasic*.

अयुक्तः प्राकृतः स्तब्धः शठो नैष्कृतिकोऽलसः ।
विषादी दीर्घसूत्री च कर्ता तामस उच्यते ॥२८॥

28. Unintegrated, uncultured, stiff, deceitful, malicious, indolent, downcast and procrastinating is the Tāmasic agent.

28.1. अयुक्त इति ॥ अयुक्तः न युक्तः असमाहितः; प्राकृतः अत्यन्तासंस्कृतबुद्धिः बालसमः; स्तब्धः दण्डवत् न नमति कस्मैचित्; शठः मायावी शक्तिगूहनकारी; नैष्कृतिकः परविभेदनपरः (परवृत्तिच्छेदनपरः); अलसः अप्रवृत्तिशीलः कर्तव्येषु अपि, विषादी विषादवान् सर्वदा अवसन्नस्वभावः; दीर्घसूत्री च कर्तव्यानां दीर्घप्रसारणः, सर्वदा मन्दस्वभावः, यत् अद्य श्वः वा कर्तव्यं तत् मासेन अपि न करोति; यश्च एवम्भूतः सः कर्ता तामसः उच्यते ॥

28.1. 'Unintegrated', or unconcentrated; 'uncultured', extremely unregenerate intellectually and childish; 'stiff' or like a stick, unbending before any one; 'deceitful' or tricky, hiding one's strength; 'malicious' or undermining others or ruining others' livelihood; 'indolent' neglecting even one's own duties; 'ever despondent' always pessimistic in outlook; 'ever tardy', one who delays taking up an urgent work even after a month—this sort of agent is held to be *tāmasic*.

बुद्धेर्भेदं धृतेश्चैव गुणतस्त्रिविधं शृणु ।
प्रोच्यमानमशेषेण पृथक्त्वेन धनंजय ॥२९॥

29. Also listen, O Arjuna, to the three-fold variety of

intellect and of resolve with reference to the constituents, as it is elucidated distinctively and fully.

29.1. बुद्धेर्भेदं इति ॥ बुद्धेः भेदं धृतेः च एव भेदं गुणतः सत्त्वादिगुणतः त्रिविधं शृणु—इति सूत्रोपन्यासः । प्रोच्यमानं कथ्यमानं अशेषेण निरवशेषतः यथावत् पृथक्त्वेन विवेकतः धनंजय ! —दिग्विजये मानुषं दैवं च प्रभूतं धनं जितवान्, तेन असौ धनंजयः अर्जुनः ॥

29.1. Listen to the distinctions of intellect and resolve, each three-fold, with reference to the constituents. This is an aphoristic statement indicating the gist of what follows. 'Distinctively' i.e. analytically elucidated without any loose ends. Arjuna is styled Dhanaṁjaya because he collected, during his victorious expeditions, immense wealth—both human and divine.

प्रवृत्तिं च निवृत्तिं च कार्याकार्ये भयाभये ।
बन्धं मोक्षं च या वेत्ति बुद्धिः सा पार्थ सात्त्विकी ॥३०॥

30. That intellect is Sāttvic, Arjuna! which knows action and inaction, duty and non-duty, fear and fearlessness, bondage and liberation.

30.1. प्रवृत्तिं च इति ॥ प्रवृत्तिं च प्रवृत्तिः प्रवर्तनं बन्धहेतुः कर्ममार्गः शास्त्रविहितविषयः, निवृत्तिं च निवृत्तिः मोक्षहेतुः संन्यासमार्गः—बन्धमोक्षसनानवाक्यत्वात् प्रवृत्तिनिवृत्ती कर्मसंन्यासमार्गौ इति अवगम्यते—कार्याकार्ये विहितप्रतिषिद्धे लौकिके वैदिके वा शास्त्रबुद्धेः कर्तव्याकर्तव्ये करणाकरणे इत्येतत्—कस्य ?—देशकालाद्यपेक्षया दृष्टादृष्टार्थानां कर्मणाम् । भयाभये बिभेति अस्मात् इति भयं चोरव्याघ्रादि, न भयं अभयं, भयं अभयं च भयाभये, दृष्टादृष्टविषययोः भयाभययोः कारणे इत्यर्थः । बन्धं सहेतुकं मोक्षं च सहेतुकं या वेत्ति विजानाति बुद्धिः सा पार्थ ! सात्त्विकी । तत्र ज्ञानं बुद्धेः वृत्तिः; बुद्धिस्तु वृत्तिमती । धृतिः अपि वृत्तिविशेषः एव बुद्धेः ॥

30.1. 'Action' is movement leading to bondage—the way of works enjoined by the *śāstras*. 'Inaction' is its opposite leading to liberation—the way of renunciation. As these two terms occur in the same sentence, where also occur the terms bondage and liberation, we take them to mean the paths of works and of renunciation. 'Duty and non-duty' are works enjoined and prohibited by the *śāstras* and related to the Vedic and secular spheres. Such works have results visible or invisible. 'Fear and fearlessness' refer to their causes like thieves, tigers, etc. The reference is to the causes of fears in relation to visible and invisible goals. The *sāttvic* intellect knows (about) 'bondage and liberation' with their causes. Knowledge is a modification of the intellect to which it pertains. 'Resolve' too is only a particular modification of the intellect.

यया धर्ममधर्मं च कार्यं चाकार्यमेव च ।
अयथावत्प्रजानाति बुद्धिः सा पार्थ राजसी ॥३१॥

31. Rājasic is the intellect, O Arjuna! by which one understands erroneously righteousness and unrighteousness, duty and non-duty.

31.1. यया इति ॥ यया धर्मं शास्त्रचोदितं, अधर्मं च प्रतिषिद्धं, कार्यं च अकार्यम् एव च पूर्वोक्ते एव कार्याकार्ये [१८.३०.], अयथावत् न यथावत् सर्वतः निर्णयेन न प्रजानाति, बुद्धिः सा पार्थ ! राजसी ॥

31.1. 'Righteousness' is (action) enjoined by the *śāstras* while 'unrighteousness' is what is forbidden by them. 'Duty and non-duty' have already been explained in 18.30. Erroneously, i.e. not after exhaustive examination and decision. The intellect doing this is *rājasic*.

अधर्मं धर्ममिति या मन्यते तमसाऽऽवृता ।
सर्वार्थान् विपरीतांश्च बुद्धिः सा पार्थ तामसी ॥३२॥

32. Tāmasic, Arjuna! is the intellect shrouded in Tamas (ignorance) which mistakes unrighteousness for righteousness and knows all kinds of things contrarily.

32.1. अधर्मं इति ॥ अधर्मं प्रतिषिद्धं धर्मं विहितं इति या मन्यते जानाति तमसा आवृता सती, सर्वार्थान् सर्वान् एव ज्ञेयपदार्थान् विपरीतान् च विपरीतान् एव विजानाति, बुद्धिः सा पार्थ! तामसी ॥

32.1. The 'intellect shrouded in ignorance' that deems unrighteousness i.e., what is prohibited by the *sāstras*, to be 'righteousness' and knows all knowables 'contrarily' is *tāmasic*.

धृत्या यया धारयते मनःप्राणेन्द्रियक्रियाः ।
योगेनाव्यभिचारिण्या धृतिः सा पार्थ सात्त्विकी ॥३३॥

33. The unfaltering resolve is Sāttvic, Arjuna! by which, through concentration, one maintains the functions of mind, vital breaths and the senses.

33.1. धृत्या इति ॥ धृत्या यया—अव्यभिचारिण्या इति व्यवहितेन सम्बन्धः—धारयते—किं ?—मनःप्राणेन्द्रियक्रियाः मनश्च प्राणाश्च इन्द्रियाणि च मनःप्राणेन्द्रियाणि, तेषां क्रियाः चेष्टाः, ताः उच्छास्त्रमार्गप्रवृत्तेः धारयते धारयति—धृत्या हि धार्यमाणाः उच्छास्त्रमार्गविषयाः न भवन्ति—योगेन समाधिना, अव्यभिचारिण्या—नित्यसमाध्यनुगतया इत्यर्थः । एतत् उक्तं भवति—अव्यभिचारिण्या धृत्या मनःप्राणेन्द्रियक्रियाः धार्यमाणाः योगेन धारयति इति । या एवंलक्षणा धृतिः सा पार्थ ! सात्त्विकी ॥

33.1. The remote expression 'unfaltering' should be related to 'resolve' or *dhṛti.* One 'maintains'—what? The functions the mind, vital breaths and the senses, preventing them from taking a path opposed to the *śāstras*. Thus are they made to conform to *śāstraic* ways. This is done through 'concentration' or *samādhi*. 'Unfalteringness' consists in accordance with unbroken concentration. The sense is that the functions of the mind and so forth, maintained through unfaltering resolve, are in fact maintained through concentration. This kind of resolve is *sāttvic.*

यया तु धर्मकामार्थान् धृत्या धारयतेऽर्जुन ।
प्रसङ्गेन फलाकाङ्क्षी धृतिः सा पार्थ राजसी ॥३४॥

34. But the resolve, Arjuna! by which one upholds righteousness, sexual attachment and wealth while occasionally desiring fruits of works, is Rājasic.

34.1. यया इति ॥ यया तु धर्मकामार्थान् धर्मश्च कामश्च अर्थश्च धर्मकामार्थाः तान् धर्मकामार्थान् धृत्या यया धारयते मनसि नित्यम् एव कर्तव्यरूपान् अवधारयति हे अर्जुन ! प्रसङ्गेन यस्य यस्य धर्मादेः धारणप्रसङ्गः तेन तेन प्रसङ्गेन फलाकाङ्क्षी च भवति यः पुरुषः, तस्य धृतिः या सा पार्थ ! राजसी ।

34.1. But the resolve by which one upholds 'righteousness' (Dharmaḥ), sexual desire (Kāmaḥ) and wealth (Arthaḥ), treating them as eternal oughts to be accomplished, and seeking their fruits as occasions arise is *rājasic*, O Arjuna.

यया स्वप्नं भयं शोकं विषादं मदमेव च ।
न विमुञ्चति दुर्मेधा धृतिः सा पार्थ तामसी ॥३५॥*

35. Tāmasic is the resolve, Arjuna! by which a mean-minded man clings to sleep, fear, grief, dejection and indulgence.

35.1. यया इति ॥ यया स्वप्नं निद्रां, भयं त्रासं, शोकं, विषादं [अवसादं] विषण्णतां, मदं विषयसेवां आत्मनः बहुमेन्यमानः मत्तः इव मदं एव च मनसि नित्यम् एव कर्तव्यरूपतया कुर्वन् न विमुञ्चति धारयति एव दुर्मेधाः कुत्सितमेधाः पुरुषः यः, तस्य धृतिः या सा पार्थ ! तामसी [मता] ॥

35.1. The resolve by which a 'mean-minded man' does not give up but 'clings to sleep, fear, grief, dejection and indulgence in objective pleasures', like one intoxicated—doing all this as a compulsory duty—is deemed to be *tāmasic*, O Arjuna!

36.0. गुणभेदेन क्रियाणां कारकाणां च त्रिविधः भेदः उक्तः । अथ इदानीं फलस्य सुखस्य त्रिविधः उच्यते—

*सा तामसी मता—इति पाठः ।

36.0. The three-foldness of works and their accessories with references to the constituents has been set forth; now is stated that of fruits and pleasure.

सुखं त्विदानीं त्रिविधं शृणु मे भरतर्षभ।
अभ्यासाद्रमते यत्र दुःखान्तं च निगच्छति॥३६॥

36. Now listen, best of Bhāratas! to (the elucidation of) threefold pleasure. That in which, through practice, one delights, reaching the end of pains;

36.1. सुखं इति ॥ सुखं तु इदानीं त्रिविधं शृणु—समाधानं कुरु इत्येतत्—मे मम भरतर्षभ ! अभ्यासात् परिचयात् आवृत्तेः रमते रतिं प्रतिपद्यते यत्र यस्मिन् सुखानुभवे दुःखान्तं च दुःखावसानं दुःखोपशमं च निगच्छति निश्चयेन प्राप्नोति ॥

36.1. Now listen to 'three-fold pleasure'—focus your mind on it, as I state it. That experience of pleasure in which, 'through practice', or repetition, one delights and surely 'reaches the end of pain';

यत्तदग्रे विषमिव परिणामेऽमृतोपमम्।
तत्सुखं सात्त्विकं प्रोक्तमात्मबुद्धिप्रसादजम्॥३७॥

37. Which, in the beginning, is like poison, but, at the end, is like ambrosia—that is declared to be Sāttvic pleasure, born of the clarity of one's intellect:

37.1. यत् इति ॥ यत् तत् सुखं अग्रे पूर्वं प्रथमसन्निपाते ज्ञानवैराग्यध्यान-समाध्यारम्भे अत्यन्तायासपूर्वकत्वात् विषम् इव दुःखात्मकं भवति, परिणामे ज्ञानवैराग्यादिपरिपाकजं सुखं अमृतोपमं, तत् सुखं सात्त्विकं प्रोक्तं विद्वद्भिः, आत्मनः बुद्धिः आत्मबुद्धिः प्रसादः नैर्मल्यं सलिलस्य इव स्वच्छता, ततः जातं आत्मबुद्धि-प्रसादजम् । आत्मविषया वा आत्मावलम्बना वा बुद्धिः आत्मबुद्धिः, तत्प्रसाद-प्रकर्षात् वा । जातम् इत्येतत् । तस्मात् सात्त्विकं तत् ॥

37.1. The pleasure which in the 'beginning'—at the first

contact, or at the start of knowledge, dëtachment, meditation and concentration—, is 'like poison' or painful due to the arduousness involved; which at the end, is 'ambrosial', being born of the maturity of knowledge, etc.—this pleasure is declared to be *sāttvic* by the wise. It emanates from the 'clarity of one's intellect'—its purity resembles the purity of water. Knowledge whose content is, or depends on, the Self may alternatively be understood by the term *ātmabuddhi*. Of its intensity is this pleasure born. Hence it is *sāttvic*.

विषयेन्द्रियसंयोगाद्यत्तदग्रेऽमृतोपमम् ।
परिणामे विषमिव तत् सुखं राजसं स्मृतम् ।।३८।।

38. It is held that Rājasic is the pleasure that in the beginning, due to contact between objects and senses, is ambrosial but is like poison, at the end.

38.1. विषय इति ।। विषयेन्द्रियसंयोगात् जायते यत् सुखं तत् सुखं अग्रे प्रथमक्षणे अमृतोपमं अमृतसमं, परिणामे विषम् इव, बलवीर्यरूपप्रज्ञामेधाधनोत्साहहानिहेतुत्वात् अधर्मतज्जनितनरकादिहेतुत्वाच्च परिणामे तदुपभोगपरिणामान्ते विषम् एव, तत् सुखं राजसं स्मृतम् ।।

38.1. The pleasure born of 'contact between objects and senses', which, 'in the beginning'—at the first moment— is 'ambrosial', but is 'like poison' at the end of its experience leading to decline of power, vigour, beauty, intelligence, understanding, wealth and zeal, and (besides) is the source of unrighteousness and hell—this pleasure is held to be *rājasic*.

यदग्रे चानुबन्धे च सुखं मोहनमात्मनः ।
निद्राऽऽलस्यप्रमादोत्थं तत्तामसमुदाहृतम् ।।३९।।

39. Tāmsic is said to be the pleasure that, both in the beginning and in its consequences, deludes the self and springs from sleep, sloth and error.

39.1. यदग्रे इति ॥ यत् अग्रे च अनुबन्धे च अवसानोत्तरकाले च सुखं मोहनं मोहकरं आत्मनः निद्राऽऽलस्यप्रमादोत्थं निद्रा च आलस्यं च प्रमादश्च तेभ्यः समुत्तिष्ठति इति निद्राऽऽलस्यप्रमादोत्थं, तत् तामसं उदाहृतम् ॥

39.1. The pleasure which, in its 'beginning and consequences', its end and sequel, 'deludes the self and arises from sleep, sloth and error' is said to be *tāmasic*.

40.0. अथ इदानीं प्रकरणोपसंहारार्थः श्लोकः आरभ्यते—

40.0. The following verse now concludes the current theme:-

न तदस्ति पृथिव्यां वा दिवि देवेषु वा पुनः ।
सत्त्वं प्रकृतिजैर्मुक्तं यदेभिः स्यात् त्रिभिर्गुणैः ॥४०॥

40. In this world, in heaven or again, among gods, no being is found that is free from these three constituents of Prakṛti,

40.1. न तत् इति ॥ न तत् अस्ति तत् नास्ति पृथिव्यां वा मनुष्यादिषु सत्त्वं प्राणिजातं, अन्यत् वा अप्राणि, दिवि देवेषु वा पुनः सत्त्वं, प्रकृतिजैः प्रकृतितः जातैः एभिः त्रिभिः गुणैः सत्त्वादिभिः मुक्तं परित्यक्तं यत् स्यात् भवेत्—'न तत् अस्ति' इति पूर्वेण सम्बन्धः ॥

40.1. There are no living beings on 'earth' i.e., among men, etc., or anything material in 'heaven or among gods' or a being 'free from'—devoid of—these three-fold constituents of *prakṛti*—*sattva* and so forth.

41.0. सर्वः संसारः क्रियाकारकफललक्षणः सत्त्वरजस्तमोगुणात्मकः अविद्यापरिकल्पितः समूलः अनर्थः उक्तः, वृक्षरूपकल्पनया च 'ऊर्ध्वमूलं' [१५.१.] इत्यादिना, "तं च असङ्गशस्त्रेण दृढेन छित्त्वा ततः पदं तत् परिमार्गितव्यं" [१५.३, ४.] इति च उक्तम् । तत्र च सर्वस्य त्रिगुणात्मकत्वात् संसारकारणनिवृत्त्यनुपपत्तौ प्राप्तायां, यथा तन्निवृत्तिः स्यात् तथा वक्तव्यं, सर्वश्च गीताशास्त्रार्थः उपसंहर्तव्यः, एतावान् एव च सर्ववेदस्मृत्यर्थः पुरुषार्थं इच्छद्भिः अनुष्ठेयः इत्येवमर्थं 'ब्राह्मणक्षत्रियविशां' इत्यादिः आरभ्यते—

41.0. The entire empirical world consisting of actions, their accessories and fruits, all of which are transformations of the three constituents and postulated by nescience, has been set forth together with its cause; this world is a disvalue. In the metaphor of the tree with 'the roots up' (15.1) 'after cutting which with the sharp weapon of detachment,' 'that Status has to be sought' (15.3,4)—the same has been stated. Since all this is substantially one with the three constituents, the cause of empirical life may be regarded as unabolishable. Thus arises the need to indicate a way to abolish it. Also, the contents of the science of the *Gītā* have to be concluded—the contents embracing the totality of those of the Vedas and Smṛtis which have to be put into practice by those who aim at the goals of human life. Therefore is commenced the next theme beginning with 18.41.

ब्राह्मणक्षत्रियविशां शूद्राणां च परन्तप ।
कर्माणि प्रविभक्तानि स्वभावप्रभवैर्गुणैः ॥४१॥

41. Scourge of foes! The works of Brāhmaṇas, Kṣatriyas and Vaiśyas, as also those of the Sudras have been allotted according to the constituents of their nature.

41.1. ब्राह्मण इति ॥ ब्राह्मणाश्च क्षत्रियाश्च विशश्च ब्राह्मणक्षत्रियविशः, तेषां ब्राह्मणक्षत्रियविशां शूद्राणां च—शूद्राणां असमासकरणं एकजातित्वे सति वेदानधिकारात्—हे परन्तप! कर्माणि प्रविभक्तानि इतरेतरविभागेन व्यवस्थापितानि—केन ? स्वभावप्रभवैः गुणैः, स्वभावः ईश्वरस्य प्रकृतिः त्रिगुणात्मिका माया, सा प्रभवः येषां गुणानां ते स्वभावप्रभवाः, तैः शमादीनि कर्माणि प्रविभक्तानि ब्राह्मणादीनाम् ॥

41.1. Of Brāhmaṇas, Kṣatriyas and Vaiśyas as well as of the Śūdras the works have been allotted—separately assigned—according to the constituents (The term Sūdra has been dropped from the compound because, though the Śūdras belong to the same genus, they are not entitled to learn the Vedas). Nature is God's *prakṛti*, *māyā* consisting of the three constituents. Of this *māyā* are the constituents born, with reference to which have the works, restraint and so forth, of the four classes been assigned.

41.2. अथवा ब्राह्मणस्वभावस्य सत्त्वगुणः प्रभवः कारणं, तथा क्षत्रियस्वभावस्य सत्त्वोपसर्जनं रजः प्रभवः, वैश्यस्वभावस्य तमउपसर्जनं रजः प्रभवः, शूद्रस्वभावस्य रजउपसर्जनं तमः प्रभवः, प्रशान्त्यैश्वर्येहामूढतास्वभावदर्शनात् चतुर्णाम् ॥

41.2. Alternatively, it may be explained that *sattva* is the cause of the nature of the Brāhmaṇas. *Rajas* subordinating *sattva* is the cause of Kṣatriya nature, while *rajas*, subordinating *tamas*, is the cause of Vaiśya nature. The cause of the Śūdra nature is *tamas* subordinating *rajas*. Serenity, power, covetousness and delusion are observed as natural to each of these four classes.

41.3. अथवा—जन्मान्तरकृतसंस्कारः प्राणिनां वर्तमानजन्मनि स्वकार्याभिमुखत्वेन अभिव्यक्तः स्वभावः, सः प्रभवः येषां गुणानां ते स्वभावप्रभवाः गुणाः—गुणप्रादुर्भावस्य निष्कारणत्वानुपपत्तेः । "स्वभावः कारणं" इति च कारणविशेषोपादानम् । एवं स्वभावप्रभवैः प्रकृतिप्रभवैः सत्त्वरजस्तमोभिः गुणैः स्वकार्यानुरूपेण शमादीनि कर्माणि प्रविभक्तानि ॥

41.3. Or, again, impressions accumulated in lives and manifested in the current lives leading to their respective fruits constitute the 'nature' mentioned in this verse. Of this nature are born the constituents. The manifestation of a constituent cannot be without a cause. 'One's nature is the cause' (vide 18.40)—this dictum makes it necessary to state the causes (of all phenomena). Thus according to these three constituents born of *prakṛti*, restraint, etc., have been ascribed to their natural causes (present in the classes, Brāhmaṇas, etc).

41.4. ननु शास्त्रप्रविभक्तानि शास्त्रेण विहितानि ब्राह्मणादीनां शमादीनि कर्माणि; कथं उच्यते सत्त्वादिगुणप्रविभक्तानि इति ?
नैषः दोषः; शास्त्रेण अपि ब्राह्मणादीनां सत्त्वादिगुणविशेषापेक्षया एव शमादीनि कर्माणि प्रविभक्तानि, न गुणानपेक्षया, इति शास्त्रप्रविभक्तानि अपि कर्माणि गुणप्रविभक्तानि इति उच्यते ॥

41.4. "But are not restraint, etc., works assigned to Brāhmaṇas and so forth, enjoined by the *śāstras*? Why is it declared that they have been allotted according to the constituents?" This is no flaw; for, even *śāstras* allot restraint etc., to the classes not without due regard for *sattva* and so forth. Hence no logical flaw is entailed in the expression 'according to the constituents'.

42.0. कानि पुनः तानि कर्माणि इति ? उच्यते—

42.0. Now, what are the works in question?

शमो दमस्तपः शौचं क्षान्तिरार्जवमेव च ।
ज्ञानं विज्ञानमास्तिक्यं ब्रह्मकर्म स्वभावजम् ।।४२।।

42. Restraint (of mind), restraint of senses, penance, cleanliness, endurance, guilelessness, knowledge, realization, faith in the scriptures—these constitute the work of Brāhmaṇas.

42.1. शमः इति ।। शमः दमः च यथाव्याख्यातार्थौ [१६.१,२.] तपः यथोक्त शारीरादि [१७.१४-१६.], शौचं व्याख्यातम् [१६.३.], क्षान्तिः क्षमा, आर्जवं ऋजुता एव च ज्ञानं विज्ञानं, आस्तिक्यं आस्तिकभावः श्रद्दधानता आगमार्थेषु, ब्रह्मकर्म ब्राह्मणजातेः कर्म स्वभावजं—यत् उक्तं 'स्वभावप्रभवैः गुणैः प्रविभक्तानि' [४१] इति तदेव उक्तं 'स्वभावजं' इति ।।

42.1. The words *śama* and *dama* have been explained (16.12); so too *tapas*, physical, etc. (17.14-16); also *śauca* (16.3). 'Endurance' is patience; 'guilelessness' is straightforwardness. 'Knowledge', 'realization'; 'faith in the scriptures' or belief in the contents in the scriptural lore—these make up the work of the Brāhmaṇas derived from their nature referred to earlier (18.41).

शौर्यं तेजो धृतिर्दाक्ष्यं युद्धे चाप्यपलायनम् ।
दानमीश्वरभावश्च क्षात्रं कर्म स्वभावजम् ।।४३।।

43. Courage, power, resolution, skill, non-flight from battle, generosity, and might constitute the work of the Kṣatriyas derived from their nature.

43.1. शौर्यं इति ॥ शौर्यं शूरस्य भावः, तेजः प्रागल्भ्यं, धृतिः धारणं, सर्वावस्थासु अनवसादः भवति यया धृत्या उत्तम्भितस्य, दाक्ष्यं दक्षस्य भावः, सहसा प्रत्युत्पन्नेषु कार्येषु अव्यामोहेन प्रवृत्तिः, युद्धे च अपि अपलायनं अपराङ्मुखीभावः शत्रुभ्यः, दानं देयद्रव्येषु मुक्तहस्तता, ईश्वरभावः च, ईश्वरस्य भावः, प्रभुशक्तिप्रकटीकरणं ईशितव्यान् प्रति, क्षात्रं कर्म क्षत्रियजातेः विहितं कर्म क्षात्रं कर्म स्वभावजम् ॥

43.1. 'Courage' is what marks the brave; 'power' is ability; 'resolution' is the will, supported by which one does not suffer from dejection in any condition of life; 'skill' is resourcefulness in action in crises; 'non-flight from battle' means facing the foe; 'generosity' is free distribution of wealth; 'might' is the lordliness, the display of strength, towards dependents. These constitute the work of the Kṣatriya class, enjoined on them and derived from their nature.

कृषिगौरक्ष्यवाणिज्यं वैश्यकर्म स्वभावजम् ।
परिचर्यात्मकं कर्म शूद्रस्यापि स्वभावजम् ॥४४॥

44. Agriculture, rearing of cattle, and trade are the works of the Vaiśyas born of their nature. The work of the Śūdras born of Śūdra-nature is menial service in essence.

44.1. कृषि इति ॥ कृषिगौरक्ष्यवाणिज्यं कृषिश्च गौरक्ष्यं च वाणिज्यं च कृषिगौरक्ष्यवाणिज्यं—कृषिः भूमेः विलेखनं, गौरक्ष्यं गाः रक्षतीति गोरक्षः तस्य भावो गौरक्ष्यं पशुपाल्यं इत्यर्थः, वाणिज्यं वणिक्कर्म क्रयविक्रयादिलक्षणं—वैश्यकर्म वैश्यजातेः कर्म वैश्यकर्म स्वभावजम् । परिचर्यात्मकं शुश्रूषास्वभावं कर्म शूद्रस्य अपि स्वभावजम् ॥

44.1. 'Agriculture' refers to the ploughing of the land, etc.; herding of farm-animals; purchase and selling of goods— all these make up the work of the Vaiśyas. Personal service is the work that pertains to the Śūdras; it is derived from their nature.

45.0. एतेषां ज्ञातिविहितानां कर्मणां सम्यगनुष्ठितानां स्वर्गप्राप्तिः फलं स्वभावतः, 'वर्णा आश्रमाश्च स्वकर्मनिष्ठाः प्रेत्य कर्मफलम् अनुभूय ततः शेषेण विशिष्टदेशजातिकुलधर्मायुःश्रुतवृत्तवित्तसुखमेधसः जन्म प्रतिपद्यन्ते' [गौ. ध. सू. ११. २९.] इत्यादिस्मृतिभ्यः; पुराणे च वर्णिनां आश्रमिणां च लोकफलभेदविशेषस्मरणात् । कारणान्तरात् तु इदं वक्ष्यमाणं फलम्—

45.0. Of these works, allotted class-wise, the natural fruit is the attainment of heaven. Vide G.D.S.11.29. Classes and stations, devoted to their respective works experience their fruits after death; then by virtue of the residuum they take birth in particular places, classes, families, with (allotment of) merits, life-periods, knowledge, character, wealth, joys and intelligence. In the *Purāṇas* too statements have been made about the distinctive spheres and fruits of the different classes and stations. The fruit presently to be stated however has other causes.

स्वे स्वे कर्मण्यभिरतः संसिद्धिं लभते नरः ।
स्वकर्मनिरतः सिद्धिं यथा विन्दति तच्छृणु ॥४५॥

45. Man achieves perfection through devotion to his allotted work. Listen how one wins perfection through such devotion.

45.1. स्वे स्वे इति ॥ स्वे स्वे यथोक्तलक्षणभेदे कर्मणि अभिरतः तत्परः संसिद्धिं स्वकर्मानुष्ठानात् अशुद्धिक्षये सति कायेन्द्रियाणां ज्ञाननिष्ठायोग्यतालक्षणां संसिद्धिं लभते प्राप्नोति नरः अधिकृतः पुरुषः । किं स्वकर्मानुष्ठानतः एव साक्षात् संसिद्धिः ? —न । कथं तर्हि ? स्वकर्मनिरतः सिद्धिं यथा येन प्रकारेण विन्दति तत् शृणु ॥

45.1. Zealously devoted to the works whose distinctions have already been set forth, man, the eligible candidate, wins perfection—the competence to devote himself to the discipline of knowledge after destroying the impurities of body and senses through the performance of his works. Can perfection be won directly through the performance of works alone? No. How, then? Listen how, being devoted to one's works, one wins perfection.

यतः प्रवृत्तिर्भूतानां येन सर्वमिदं ततम्।
स्वकर्मणा तमभ्यर्च्य सिद्धिं विन्दति मानवः ॥४६॥

46. Through the performance of his works as worship man wins perfection—worshipping Him from whom all beings have proceeded and by whom all this has been pervaded.

46.1. यतः इति ॥ यतः यस्मात् प्रवृत्तिः उत्पत्तिः चेष्टा वा यस्मात् अन्तर्यामिणः ईश्वरात् भूतानां प्राणिनां स्यात्, येन ईश्वरेण सर्वं इदं ततं जगत् व्याप्तं, स्वकर्मणा पूर्वोक्तेन प्रतिवर्णं तं ईश्वरं अभ्यर्च्य पूजयित्वा आराध्य केवलं ज्ञाननिष्ठायोग्यतालक्षणां सिद्धिं विन्दति मानवः मनुष्यः ॥

यतः एवं अतः—

46.1. That inner controller, God, from whom all living beings have originated and by whom all the world has been pervaded—by merely worshipping Him through the performance of each man's works according to his class, man wins perfection consisting in the eligibility for the discipline of knowledge.

Such being the case,

श्रेयान् स्वधर्मो विगुणः परधर्मात् स्वनुष्ठितात्।
स्वभावनियतं कर्म कुर्वन्नाप्नोति किल्बिषम् ॥४७॥

47. One's own law of righteousness, though defective, is better than that of another though well-observed. None incurs sin by doing the work ordained by his own nature.

47.1. श्रेयान् इति ॥ श्रेयान् प्रशस्यतरः स्वः धर्मः स्वधर्मः विगुणः अपि—इति अपिशब्दः द्रष्टव्यः—परधर्मात् स्वनुष्ठितात् । स्वभावनियतं स्वभावेन नियतं, यत् उक्तं स्वभावजम् इति तदेव उक्तं स्वभावनियतं इति—यथा विषजातस्य इव कृमेः विषं न दोषकरं, तथा स्वभावनियतं कर्म कुर्वन् न आप्नोति किल्बिषं पापम् ॥

47.1. 'One's own law' (of righteousness), though defective, is better than another's law however well-observed. The term 'though' is understood here. Doing the work that nature has made obligatory (vide verses 43, etc.), none incurs sin, just as a worm born of a poisonous stuff is not injured by that poison.

48.0. स्वभावनियतं कर्म कुर्वाणः, विषजः इव कृमिः, किल्बिषं न आप्नोति इति उक्तम्; परधर्मश्च भयावहः इति, अनात्मज्ञश्च 'न हि कश्चित् क्षणमपि अकर्मकृत् तिष्ठति' [३.५.] इति । अतः—

48.0. It was observed that one doing work dictated by nature does not incur sin on the analogy of the poison-bred worm; also that an alien law is a menace. Besides, in 3.5, it has been affirmed that a non-knower of the Self cannot remain for a moment without doing work. Therefore,

सहजं कर्म कौन्तेय सदोषमपि न त्यजेत् ।
सर्वारम्भा हि दोषेण धूमेनाग्निरिवावृताः ॥४८॥

48. Son of Kunti! work determined by nature, though defective, one shouldn't abandon; for all activities are shrouded in flaws as fire is by smoke.

48.1. सहजं इति ॥ सहजं सह जन्मना एव उत्पन्नं—किं तत् ? कर्म कौन्तेय ! सदोषम् अपि त्रिगुणात्मकत्वात् न त्यजेत् । सर्वारम्भाः आरभ्यन्ते इति आरम्भाः, सर्वकर्माणि इत्येतत्—प्रकरणात् ये केचित् आरम्भाः स्वधर्माः परधर्माश्च—ते सर्वे हि यस्मात्—त्रिगुणात्मकत्वं अत्र हेतुः—त्रिगुणात्मकत्वात् दोषेण, धूमेन सहजेन अग्निः इव, आवृताः । सहजस्य कर्मणः स्वधर्माख्यस्य परित्यागेन परधर्मानुष्ठानेऽपि दोषात् नैव मुच्यते; भयावहश्च परधर्मः । न च शक्यते अशेषतः त्यक्तुं अज्ञेन कर्म यतः, तस्मात् न त्यजेत् इत्यर्थः ॥

48.1. What is 'determined by nature' is what is born with oneself. What is that? Work, though defective as it partakes of the three constituents, should not be given up. All works that are initiated—the context shows this means both one's duties and those of others —, being made up of the stuff of the three constituents, are engulfed by defects, just as fire is covered by smoke. Thus giving up one's duties, even if accompanied by the adoption of others' duties, does not help one to get rid of flaws. Besides, others' duties are a source of fear. Nor is it possible for the ignorant to give up work altogether. So don't reject work.

48.2. किं अशेषतः त्यक्तुं अशक्यं कर्म इति न त्यजेत् ? किं वा सहजस्य कर्मणः त्यागे दोषः भवति इति ?

किं च अतः ?—

यदि तावत् अशेषतः त्यक्तुं अशक्यं इति न त्याज्यं सहजं कर्म, एवं तर्हि अशेषतः त्यागे गुणः एव स्यात् इति सिद्धं भवति ।

सत्यं एवं; अशेषतः त्यागः एव न उपपद्यते इति चेत्—किं नित्यप्रचलितात्मकः पुरुषः, यथा सांख्यानां गुणाः ? किं वा क्रिया एव कारकं, यथा बौद्धानां स्कन्धाः क्षणप्रध्वंसिनः ? उभयथाऽपि कर्मणः अशेषतः त्यागः न सभवति ।

अथ तृतीयोऽपि पक्षः—यदा करोति तदा सक्रियं वस्तु । यदा न करोति, तदा निष्क्रियं तदेव । तत्र एवं सति शक्यं कर्म अशेषतः त्यक्तुम् । अयं तु अस्मिन् तृतीये पक्षे विशेषः—न नित्यप्रचलितं वस्तु, नापि क्रिया एव कारकं—किं तर्हि ?—व्यवस्थिते द्रव्ये अविद्यमाना क्रिया उत्पद्यते, विद्यमाना च विनश्यति । शुद्धं तत् द्रव्यं शक्तिमत् अवतिष्ठते—इति एवं आहुः काणादाः, तदेव च कारकं इति । अस्मिन् पक्षे को दोषः इति ?

48.2. "What is the reason for non-rejection of work? Is it that—work cannot be wholly given up; or is it that—it is wrong to give up innate work?" What follows? "If the first is accepted, it will follow that total rejection of works is meritorious." This is true. But the idea of a total rejection itself is unreasonable. Whether man (the spirit that is man) like the Sāṁkhyan constituents, is deemed an eternal flux, or whether, like the Buddhist *skandhas* (or groups), they perish instantaneously, the idea of a total rejection of works is unreasonable. Or, a third alternative may be considered:

When work is being done an entity is active; when this is not the case, that entity is inactive. In this alternative it is possible to give up work altogether. But what distinguishes it is that the entity is not a flux in itself and its activity is not self-generated, but that a non-existent activity springs up in a stable entity and an existent activity ceases to be. That pure entity remains potent. This is the Vaiśeṣika view. It may be asked—what is the flaw in this position?

48.3. अयम् एव तु दोषः यतः अभागवतं मतं इदम् । कथं ज्ञायते ? यत. आह भगवान् 'नासतो विद्यते भावः' [२.१६.] इत्यादि । काणादानां हि असतः भावः, सतश्च अभावः, इति इदं मतं अभागवतम् ।

अभागवतम(त्वे)पि न्यायवच्चेत् को दोषः ? इति चेत्—

उच्यते—दोषवत्तु इदं सर्वप्रमाणविरोधात् । कथं ?— यदि तावत् द्व्यणुकादि द्रव्यं प्राक् उत्पत्तेः अत्यन्तम् एव असत्, उत्पन्नं च स्थितं कंचित् कालं पुनः अत्यन्तम् एव असत्त्वं आपद्यते, तथा च सति असदेव सत् जायते, सदेव असत्त्वं आपद्यते, अभावः भावः भवति, भावश्च अभावः भवति; तत्र अभावः जायमानः प्राक् उत्पत्तेः शशविषाणकल्पः समवाय्यसमवायिनिमित्ताख्यं कारणं अपेक्ष्य जायते इति । न च एवं अभावः उत्पद्यते, कारणं च अपेक्षते, इति शक्यं वक्तुं; असतां शशविषाणादीनां अदर्शनात् । भावात्मकाश्चेत् घटादयः उत्पद्यमानाः, किंचित् अभिव्यक्तिमात्रे कारणं अपेक्ष्य उत्पद्यन्ते इति शक्यं प्रतिपत्तुम् ।

किंच—असतश्च सद्भावे सतश्च असद्भावे न क्वचित् प्रमाणप्रमेयव्यवहारेषु विश्वासः कस्यचित् स्यात्; 'सत् सदेव, असत् असदेव' इति निश्चयानुपपत्तेः ॥

किंच—उत्पद्यते इति द्व्यणुकादेः द्रव्यस्य स्वकारणसत्तासम्बन्धं आहुः । प्राक् उत्पत्तेश्च असत्, पश्चात् कारणव्यापारं अपेक्ष्य स्वकारणैः परमाणुभिः सत्तया च समवायलक्षणेन सम्बन्धेन सम्बध्यते । सम्बद्धं सत् कारणसमवेतं सत् भवति । तत्र वक्तव्यं कथं असतः स्वं कारणं भवेत्, सम्बन्धः वा केनचित् स्यात् ? न हि वन्ध्यापुत्रस्य स्वं कारणं, सम्बन्धः वा केनचित्, प्रमाणतः कल्पयितुं शक्यते ॥

48.3. The flaw, indeed, is that this alternative contradicts the Lord's teaching. How? He has taught that the non-existent cannot come into being, etc., (vide 2.16). But the Vaiśeṣikas hold the exactly contrary view—the non-existent comes into existence and the existent lapses into non-existence. But if reason supports that view, what does it matter even if it contradicts the Lord's view? The answer is that the Vaiśeṣika view is faulty, being contrary to all means of right cognition.

To explain: If substances like the dyad are absolutely non-existent before their origination and after a brief existence, they lapse into non-existence, it follows that the existent becomes non-existent and that the non-existent emerges into existence. Before origination which depends on the material, immaterial and efficient causes, those substances like the dyad were like a hare's horn. One, then, cannot really say that non-existence orignates depending on causes. Such a phenomenon is never experienced in regard to things like the hare's horn. As for positive entities like the pot, they may causally depend on something for the sole purpose of manifestation. Besides, if novel existents come into being and the existents fall into non-being, one cannot rely anywhere on the validity of the means of right cognition or of objects cognised. There will thus be no basis for the conviction regarding existents and non-existents. To say that a dyad originates is to assert its connection with causes. It is non-existent before its origination; then, through the operation of causes it gets related to them, viz., atoms and existence, the link being *samavāya*. After such relation it comes to inhere in its causes. How can a non-existent entity have *its* cause? With what can it be related? A barren woman's son has no cause of his own; nor does he get related in any valid sense of these terms.

48.4. ननु नैवं वैशेषिकैः अभावस्य सम्बन्धः कल्प्यते । द्व्यणुकादीनां हि द्रव्याणां स्वकारणसमवायलक्षणः सम्बन्धः सताम् एव उच्यते इति ॥
न; सम्बन्धात् प्राक् सत्त्वानभ्युपगमात् । न हि वैशेषिकैः कुलालदण्डचक्रादिव्यापारात् प्राक् घटादीनां अस्तित्वं इष्यते । न च मृदः एव घटाद्याकारप्राप्ति इच्छन्ति । ततश्च असतः एव सम्बन्धः पारिशेष्यात् इष्टः भवति ॥

48.4. *Objection:* "The Vaiśeṣikas do not thus relate non-existence. What they assert is the relation of existent dyads etc., with their causes viz., Samavāya." *Reply:* "No, they do not grant that the dyads, etc. exist before getting related to their causes. They negate the existence of effects like pots before the operation of causal factors like the potter, wheel, and so forth. They do not hold that clay itself assumes the form of pots, etc. This implies that what is related, in their view, is the non-existent pot, etc."

48.5. ननु असतः अपि समवायलक्षणः सम्बन्धः न विरुद्धः ।

न; वन्ध्यापुत्रादीनां अदर्शनात् । घटादेः एव प्रागभावस्य स्वकारणसम्बन्धः भवति, न वन्ध्यापुत्रादेः, अभावस्य तुल्यत्वेऽपि, इति विशेषः अभावस्य वक्तव्यः । एकस्य अभावः, द्वयोः अभावः, सर्वस्य अभावः, प्रागभावः, प्रध्वंसाभावः, इतरेतराभावः, अत्यन्ताभावः इति लक्षणतः नः केनचित् विशेषः दर्शयितुं शक्यः । असति च विशेषे घटस्य प्रागभावः एव कुलालादिभिः घटभावं आपद्यते, सम्बध्यते च भावेन कपालाख्येन स्वकारणेन, संबद्धश्च सर्वव्यवहारयोग्यश्च भवति, न तु घटस्य एव प्रध्वंसाभावः अभावत्वे सत्यपि, इति प्रध्वंसाद्यभावानां न क्वचित् व्यवहारयोग्यत्वं, प्रागभावस्य एव द्व्यणुकादिद्रव्याख्यस्य उत्पत्त्यादिव्यवहारार्हत्वं इत्येतत् असमञ्जसं; अभावत्वाविशेषात् अत्यन्तप्रध्वसाभावयोः इव ॥

ननु नैव अस्माभिः प्रागभावस्य भावापत्तिः उच्यते ।

भावस्य एव तर्हि भावापत्तिः; यथा घटस्य घटापत्तिः, पटस्य वा पटापत्तिः । एतदपि अभावस्य भावापत्तिवत् एव प्रमाणविरुद्धम् ॥

48.5. *Objection:* "But it is not wrong to relate the non-existent by means of *samavāya* or inherence." *Reply:* "No; non-existents like the barren woman's son are not seen to be so related. You may say that the prior non-existence of pot, etc. alone gets related to their causes, and not absolute non-existents like the barren woman's son and so forth, though both are forms of non-existence. Thus a distinction has to be drawn among forms of non-existence. But this leads to a list of non-existences—of prior non-existence, post non-existence, mutual non-existence, absolute non-existence, etc. Now no factual distinction is available among these non-existences, as such. In the absence of such distinction, it has to be maintained that the prior non-existence of the pot alone becomes the pot via the activities of the potter, etc., and gets related to the existent particles of clay that form the cause of the pot; then it serves various purposes. Such a thing does not happen to the past non-existence of this very pot. This kind of distinction, according to us, is unreasonable, no essential distinction being available among forms of non-existence. The Vaiśeṣika may reply; 'The prior non-existence of a pot does not become a pot.'

Then, it may be questioned: Are you holding that one existence becomes another?—that a pot becomes a pot or a cloth?" This view is opposed to valid criteria, just like your earlier view, viz., non-existence becomes existence.

48.6. सांख्यस्य अपि यः परिणामपक्षः सोऽपि अपूर्वधर्मोत्पत्तिविनाशाङ्गीकरणात् वैशेषिकपक्षात् न विशिष्यते । अभिव्यक्तितिरोभावाङ्गीकरणेऽपि अभिव्यक्तितिरोभावयोः विद्यमानत्वाविद्यमानत्वनिरूपणे पूर्ववत् एव प्रमाणविरोधः ॥

एतेन कारणस्य एव संस्थानं उत्पत्त्यादि इत्येतत् अपि प्रत्युक्तम् ॥

पारिशेष्यात्—सत् एकम् एव वस्तु अविद्यया उत्पत्तिविनाशादिधर्मैः अनेकधा नटवत् विकल्प्यते इति । इदं भागवतं मतं उक्तं 'नासतो विद्यते भावः' [२.१६.] इत्यस्मिन् श्लोके, सत्प्रत्ययस्य अव्यभिचारात्, व्यभिचारात् च इतरेषां इति ॥

48.6. The Sāṁkhyan view of transformation also, in so far as it affirms the origination of novel attributes and their destruction, is no better than the Vaiśeṣika view. The affirmation of appearance and disappearance (of attributes) is, as shown earlier, opposed to all means of right cognition, since it involves the question whether *this* appearance and *this* disappearance had prior existence or not. Thus stands refuted the view that appearance, etc., are only the states of the cause. By this process of elimination the conclusion follows that reality is one only, which, like an actor, plays numberless roles, assuming attributes like appearance and disappearance due to nescience. This is the Lord's view as stated in 2.16. The awareness of existence persists throughout, while that of all other factors fluctuates.

48.7. कथं तर्हि आत्मनः अविक्रियत्वे अशेषतः कर्मणः त्यागः न उपपद्यते इति ॥

यदि वस्तुभूताः गुणाः, यदि वा अविद्याकल्पिताः, तद्धर्मः कर्म । तत् आत्मनि अविद्याऽध्यारोपितम् एव अविद्वान् 'न हि कश्चित् क्षणमपि अशेषतः त्यक्तुं शक्नोति' [३.५.] इति उक्तम् । विद्वांस्तु पुनः विद्यया अविद्यायां निवृत्तायां शक्नोति एव अशेषतः कर्म परित्यक्तुं, अविद्याऽध्यारोपितस्य शेषानुपपत्तेः । न हि तैमिरिकदृष्ट्या अध्यारोपितस्य द्विचन्द्रादेः तिमिरापगमेऽपि शेषः अवतिष्ठते । एवं च सति इदं वचनं उपपन्नं 'सर्वकर्माणि मनसा' [५.१३.] इत्यादि, 'स्वे स्वे कर्मण्यभिरतः संसिद्धिं लभते नरः' [१८.४५.], 'स्वकर्मणा तमभ्यर्च्य सिद्धिं विन्दति मानवः' [१८.४६.] इति च ॥

48.7. Thus if the Self is immutable, it is not unreasonable to maintain that activities must be renounced wholly. Whether the constituents are existent reals or set up due to nescience, action is their attribute. Through nescience it is superimposed on the Self. The ignorant man can't wholly give it up (3.5). But the wise man, once nescience is dispelled through knowledge, can indeed do so; for, there is no residue for an ignorantly precipitated super-imposition. The double moon, seen with the diseased eye, is not seen, once the disease is cured. Such being the case, the utterance in 5.13 may also be seen to be eminently reasonable, just as also others like 18.45-46.

49.0. या कर्मजा सिद्धिः उक्ता ज्ञाननिष्ठायोग्यतालक्षणा, तस्याः फलभूता नैष्कर्म्यसिद्धिः ज्ञाननिष्ठालक्षणा च वक्तव्या इति श्लोकः आरभ्यते—

49.0. This verse sets down the attainment of that perfection which results from works and which consists in the fitness for the discipline of knowledge. The fruit of this is the winning of worklessness which is a feature of the discipline of knowledge. Both these concepts call for affirmation.

असक्तबुद्धिः सर्वत्र जितात्मा विगतस्पृहः ।
नैष्कर्म्यसिद्धिं परमां संन्यासेनाधिगच्छति ॥४९॥

49. He whose intellect is unattached to objects, whose self is disciplined, and from whom all desires have departed, wins the supreme perfection of worklessness by means of renunciation.

49.1. असक्तबुद्धिः इति ॥ असक्तबुद्धिः असक्ता सङ्गरहिता बुद्धिः अन्तःकरणं यस्य सः असक्तबुद्धिः सर्वत्र पुत्रदारादिषु आसक्तिनिमित्तेषु, जितात्मा जितः वशीकृतः आत्मा अन्तःकरणं यस्य सः जितात्मा, विगतस्पृहः विगता स्पृहा तृष्णा देहजीवितभोगेषु यस्मात् सः विगतस्पृहः, यः एवम्भूतः आत्मज्ञः सः नैष्कर्म्यसिद्धिं निर्गतानि कर्माणि यस्मात् निष्क्रियब्रह्मात्मसम्बोधात् सः निष्कर्मा तस्य भावः नैष्कर्म्यं, नैष्कर्म्यं च तत् सिद्धिश्च सा नैष्कर्म्यसिद्धिः, निष्कर्मत्वस्य वा निष्क्रियात्मरूपावस्थालक्षणस्य सिद्धिः, निष्पत्तिः, तां नैष्कर्म्यसिद्धिं परमां प्रकृष्टां कर्म-

जसिद्धिविलक्षणां सद्योमुक्त्यवस्थानरूपां संन्यासेन सम्यग्दर्शनेन, तत्पूर्वकेन वा सर्वकर्मसंन्यासेन, अधिगच्छति प्राप्नोति । तथा च उक्तं—सर्वकर्माणि मनसा सन्न्यस्य नैव कुर्वन्न कारयन्नास्ते' [५.१३.] इति ॥

49.1. He whose intellect or inner sense is unattached to objects like children, wife and so forth which usually claim attachment, whose self, i.e., the inner self, is disciplined, whose clinging to body, life and enjoyments has departed—such a Self-knower wins the status of a total renouncer, all of whose works have left him due to the knowledge of the quiescent Brahman. This status is the perfection Naiskarmya-siddhi mentioned in this verse. Or, it may mean the emergence of the status of the actionless Self. This gain is different from the work-born perfection mentioned earlier. It is the same as instantaneous liberation, and won through renunciation—a right perception, leading to the giving up of all activities. This has been mentioned in 5.13.

50.0. पूर्वोक्तेन स्वकर्मानुष्ठानेन ईश्वराभ्यर्चनरूपेण जनितां प्रागुक्तलक्षणां सिद्धिं प्राप्तस्य उत्पन्नात्मविवेकज्ञानस्य केवलात्मज्ञाननिष्ठारूपा नैष्कर्म्यलक्षणा सिद्धिः येन क्रमेण भवति तत् वक्तव्यम् इति आह—

50.0. Now is set forth the sequence of steps leading the man of discriminative Self-knowledge to the perfection of quietude —the man who started from the initial fitness born of the performance of his duties as the worship of God:

सिद्धिं प्राप्तो यथा ब्रह्म तथाऽऽप्नोति निबोध मे ।
समासेनैव कौन्तेय निष्ठा ज्ञानस्य या परा ॥५०॥

50. Know from Me briefly how one, made fit (for the discipline of knowledge), reaches Brahman—the supreme consummation of knowledge, O Arjuna!

50.1. सिद्धिं इति ॥ सिद्धिं प्राप्तः स्वकर्मणा ईश्वरं समभ्यर्च्य तत्प्रसादजां कायेन्द्रियाणां ज्ञाननिष्ठायोग्यतालक्षणां सिद्धिं प्राप्तः—'सिद्धिं प्राप्तः, इति तदनुवादः

उत्तरार्थः । किं तत् उत्तरं, यदर्थः अनुवादः इति ? उच्यते—यथा येन प्रकारेण ज्ञाननिष्ठारूपेण ब्रह्म परमात्मानं आप्नोति, तथा तं प्रकारं ज्ञाननिष्ठाप्राप्तिक्रमं मे मम वचनात् निबोध त्वं निश्चयेन अवधारय इत्येतत् । किं विस्तरेण ? न इति आह—समासेन एव संक्षेपेण एव हे कौन्तेय ! । यथा ब्रह्म प्राप्नोति तथा निबोध इति अनेन या प्रतिज्ञाता ब्रह्मप्राप्तिः तां इदंतया दर्शयितुं आह—'निष्ठा ज्ञानस्य या परा' इति । निष्ठा पर्यवसानं परिसमाप्तिः इत्येतत् । कस्य ? ब्रह्मज्ञानस्य या परा । कीदृशी सा ? —यादृशं आत्मज्ञानम् । कीदृक् तत् ? —यादृशः आत्मा । कीदृशः सः ? —यादृशः भगवता उक्तः (१८.१७) उपनिषद्वाक्यैश्च, न्यायतश्च ॥

50.1. The seeker after perfection has won the fitness of the body and the senses for the discipline of knowledge—a fitness born of the grace of God due to His worship by the doing of one's works. The reference here is to the initial fitness and not to the final attainment. It is only an introduction to the steps for the final attainment stated hereafter. This affirmation refers to the manner in which, through the discipline of knowledge, one attains Brahman, the supreme Self. Learn from My words the steps leading to the final consummation of knowledge, the establishment in the discipline of knowledge. It is but briefly that I shall speak. The attainment of Brahman promised above is directly specified in the words 'the supreme discipline of knowledge.' *Niṣṭhā* or discipline of knowledge refers to a definitive achievement and a goal. Goal of what? The supreme goal of Brahman-knowledge. What is this goal like? It is like the knowledge of the Self. And what is *this* like? 'It is like the Self'. 'What is the Self like?—Like what has been elucidated by the Lord (cf.BG 18.17), is affirmed by the Upaniṣads, and is in accordance with reason.

50.2. ननु विषयकारं ज्ञानम् । न ज्ञानविषयः, नापि आकारवान् आत्मा इष्यते क्वचित् ।

ननुः 'आदित्यवर्णम्' [श्वे. उ. ३.८.], 'भारूपः' [छां. उ. ३.१४.२.], 'स्वयंज्योतिः' [बृ. उ. ४.३.९.] इति आकारवत्वं आत्मनः श्रूयते ।

न; तमोरूपत्वप्रतिषेधार्थत्वात् तेषां वाक्यानाम्—द्रव्यगुणाद्याकारप्रतिषेधे आत्मनः तमोरूपत्वे प्राप्ते तत्प्रतिषेधार्थानि 'आदित्यवर्णं' इत्यादीनि वाक्यानि । 'अरूपं' [कठ. उ. ३.१५.] इति च विशेषतः रूपप्रतिषेधात् । अविषयत्वाच्च—'न संदृशे तिष्ठति रूपमस्य न चक्षुषा पश्यति कश्चनैनं' [श्वे. उ. ४.२०.], 'अशब्दमस्पर्शं'

[कठ. उ. ३.१५.] इत्यादेः । तस्मात् आत्माकारं ज्ञानं इति अनुपपन्नम् ॥

कथं तर्हि आत्मनः ज्ञानम् ? सर्वं हि यद्विषयं यत् ज्ञानं, तत् तदाकारं भवति । निराकारश्च आत्मा इति उक्तम् । ज्ञानात्मनोश्च उभयोः निराकारत्वे कथं तद्भावनानिष्ठा इति ?

नः अत्यन्तनिर्मलत्वातिस्वच्छत्वातिसूक्ष्मत्वोपपत्तेः आत्मनः । बुद्धेश्च आत्मवत् (–त्मसम–) नैर्मल्याद्युपपत्तेः आत्मचैतन्याकाराभासत्वोपपत्तिः । बुद्ध्याभासं मनः, तदाभासानि इन्द्रियाणि, इन्द्रियाभासश्च देहः । अतः लौकिकैः देहमात्रे एव आत्मदृष्टिः क्रियते ।

50.2. *Objection:* "Knowledge implies that the mind assumes the form of the object. But nowhere is the Ātman held to be an object of knowledge; neither has Ātman a form." *Tentative reply:* "But look at the affirmations of *śruti*: 'The sun-coloured', (BU 4.2.9). These teach that the Self has a form." *Objection:* "No, the purpose of these affirmations is to state that the Self is not mere darkness. When the Self is denied as a substance, quality, etc., there arises the contingency that it is mere darkness—*this* is denied in the statements quoted above from SU etc. KU.3.15 specifically affirms that the Self is formless. Also It is said to be no object. Vide: 'Its form is not seen; none sees It with the eye, (ŚU.4.20); soundless, touchless' (KU.3.15), etc. Therefore with reference to the Self the statement that knowledge conforms to Self's form is erroneous. Then how does the knowledge of the Self arise? All kinds of knowledge conform to their objects. But the Self is held to be formless. If both Self and knowledge are formless, how can there be a discipline of contemplation on either?" *Final reply:* This is no valid objection; for reasoning shows that the Self is absolutely pure, supremely transparent, and wholly subtle. The intellect may reasonably resemble this Self in these respects and share with It Its conscious nature. Further, the mind reflects the intellect; the senses reflect the mind, and the body reflects the senses. Therefore worldly folk look upon the body itself as the Self.

50.3. देहचैतन्यवादिनश्च लोकायतिकाः 'चैतन्यविशिष्टः कायः पुरुषः' इत्याहुः । तथा अन्ये इन्द्रियचैतन्यवादिनः, अन्ये मनश्चैतन्यवादिनः, अन्ये बुद्धिचैतन्यवादिनः ।

ततोऽपि आन्तरं अव्यक्तं अव्याकृताख्यं अविद्यावस्थं आत्मत्वेन प्रतिपन्नाः केचित् । सर्वत्र बुद्ध्यादिदेहान्ते आत्मचैतन्याभासता आत्मभ्रान्तिकारणं इत्यतश्च आत्मविषयं ज्ञानं न विधातव्यम् । किं तर्हि ?— नामरूपाद्यनात्माध्यारोपणनिवृत्तिः एव कार्या, न आत्मचैतन्यविज्ञानं कार्यम्, अविद्याऽध्यारोपितसर्वपदार्थाकारैः एव विशिष्टतया दृश्यमानत्वात् इति । अत एव हि विज्ञानवादिनः बौद्धाः विज्ञानव्यतिरेकेण वस्तु एव नास्ति इति प्रतिपन्नाः, प्रमाणान्तरनिरपेक्षतां च स्वसंविदितत्वाभ्युपगमेन । तस्मात् अविद्याऽध्यारोपितनिराकरणमात्रं ब्रह्मणि कर्तव्यं, न तु ब्रह्मविज्ञाने यत्नः, अत्यन्तप्रसिद्धत्वात् । अविद्याकल्पितनामरूपविशेषाकारापहृतबुद्धीनां अत्यन्तप्रसिद्धं सुविज्ञेयं आसन्नतरं आत्मभूतम् अपि, अप्रसिद्धं दुर्विज्ञेयं अतिदूरं अन्यत् इव च प्रतिभाति अविवेकिनाम् । बाह्याकारनिवृत्तबुद्धीनां तु लब्धगुर्वात्मप्रसादानां न अतः परं सुखं सुप्रसिद्धं सुविज्ञेयं स्वासन्नतरं अस्ति । तथा च उक्तम्—'प्रत्यक्षावगमं धर्म्यम्' [९.२.] इत्यादि ।

50.3. "The materialists, *lokāyatikas*, for whom the body is intelligent, aver man is body qualified by intelligence. So also are there others who declare that the senses are intelligent; for still others the intellect is intelligent. Other than those are the thinkers for whom an inner principle, the unmanifest called the un-differentiated (*avyākṛtam*) sunk in nescience, is the self. In all these cases, from the intellect down to the body, the cause of the delusion, that the body etc. form the Self, is the reflection of the Self's intelligence in them. Hence in all these cases, it is not right to enjoin a knowledge of the Self. Rather, what is to be achieved is an abolition or sublation of the superimposed name and form that are other than the Self and not the knowledge of intelligence that is the Self; for the Self appears, in all these cases, as qualified by the objects superimposed on It. This indeed is the reason why the idealistic Buddhists aver that nothing is real except cognitions. This knowledge does not depend on an independent means of cognition, for each cognition is self-cognised. Therefore, as regards Brahman, what is to be aimed at is only the repudiation of objects superimposed through nescience; no effort is needed to secure knowledge of Brahman that is absolutely evident. To those, however, who lack discrimination, who are distracted by appearances associated with name and form, the self-evident Brahman seems to be remote; though effortlessly known, seems hard to know; though the closest being, the very Self, seems alien. On the contrary, for those who have withdrawn their intellect from external objects, who have won the grace of their teacher, and whose mind has attained serenity, nothing is easier to understand or is closer than Brahman. Vide BG 9.2. etc.

50.4. केचित्तु पण्डितंमन्याः 'निराकारत्वात् आत्मवस्तु न उपैति बुद्धिः । अतः दुःसाध्या सम्यग्ज्ञाननिष्ठा' इति आहुः ।

सत्यं, एवं गुरुसम्प्रदायरहितानां अश्रुतवेदान्तानां अत्यन्तबहिर्विषयासक्तबुद्धीनां सम्यक्प्रमाणेषु अकृतश्रमाणाम् । तद्विपरीतानां तु लौकिकग्राहकद्वैतवस्तुनि सद्बुद्धिः नितरां दुःसम्पाद्या, आत्मचैतन्यव्यतिरेकेण वस्त्वन्तरस्य अनुपलब्धेः, यथा च एतत् एवम् एव, न अन्यथा इति अवोचाम; उक्तं च भगवता 'यस्यां जाग्रति भूतानि सा निशा पश्यतो मुनेः' [२.६९.] इति । तस्मात् बाह्याकारभेदबुद्धिनिवृत्तिः एव आत्मस्वरूपावलम्बनकारणम् । न हि आत्मा नाम कस्यचित् कदाचित् अप्रसिद्धः प्राप्यः, हेयः, उपादेयः वा । अप्रसिद्धे हि तस्मिन् आत्मनि, स्वार्थाः सर्वाः प्रवृत्तयः व्यर्थाः प्रसज्येरन् । न च देहाद्यचेतनार्थत्वं शक्यं कल्पयितुम् । न च सुखार्थं सुखं, दुःखार्थं दुःखम् । आत्मावगत्यवसानार्थत्वाच्च सर्वव्यवहारस्य [ब्र. सू. ३.४.२६, २७.] तस्मात् यथा स्वदेहस्य परिच्छेदाय न प्रमाणान्तरापेक्षा, ततोऽपि आत्मनः अन्तरतमत्वात् तदवगतिं प्रति न प्रमाणान्तरापेक्षा । इति आत्मज्ञाननिष्ठा विवेकिनां सुप्रसिद्धा इति सिद्धम् ॥

50.4. However, some self-styled scholars maintain that the Self, being formless, is unamenable to understanding and so the discipline of knowledge is difficult to acquire. This is true only of people devoid of the advantages of the right tradition established by a real teacher; who have not been schooled in Upaniṣadic wisdom; who are the thralls of the realm of objects and are untrained in the employment of the means of right cognition. But those who are of the opposite type (Advaitins) would find it very hard to deem as real the objects which lure the worldly minded; they don't cognise anything other than pure consciousness that is the Self. We have already explained how this is so. The Lord too has declared:- 'To the sage . . . . . the wakeful state is night' (2.69). Therefore what makes one resort to the Self's essence is the mind's withdrawal from the realm of objects. To none indeed, at any time, is the Self an alien, to be attained or rejected or accepted. Were that

Self unknown, all self-regarding activities would turn out to be pointless. They cannot be supposed to subserve inert things like the body. Pleasure and pain don't subserve themselves. All activities must ultimately subserve Self-knowledge (vide BSB 3.4.26,27). Hence just as there is no need to resort to a *pramāṇa* to know one's body, there is no need for a *pramāṇa* to know the Self that is far more intimate than the body. So, to the discriminating, the discipline of knowledge is very well-known indeed.

50.5. येषाम् अपि निराकारं ज्ञानं अप्रत्यक्षं, तेषाम् अपि ज्ञानवशेन एव ज्ञेयावगतिः इति ज्ञानं अत्यन्तप्रसिद्धं सुखादिवत् एव इति अभ्युपगन्तव्यम् ॥

जिज्ञासानुपपत्तेश्च—अप्रसिद्धं चेत् ज्ञानं, ज्ञेयवत् जिज्ञास्येत । यथा ज्ञेयं घटादिलक्षणं ज्ञानेन ज्ञाता व्याप्तुं इच्छति, तथा ज्ञानम् अपि ज्ञानान्तरेण ज्ञाता व्याप्तुं इच्छेत् । न च एतत् अस्ति । अतः अत्यन्तप्रसिद्धं ज्ञानं, ज्ञाताऽपि अतः एव प्रसिद्धः इति ॥

तस्मात् ज्ञाने यत्नः न कर्तव्यः, किंतु अनात्मनि आत्मबुद्धिनिवृत्तौ एव । तस्मात् ज्ञाननिष्ठा सुसम्पाद्या ॥

50.5. Even those who hold that formless cognition is not immediate must admit that the object of knowledge is known through that knowledge; so, like pleasure, etc., knowledge is immediately experienced. Nor can a desire to know knowledge be admitted. Were knowledge not directly known, it would be sought after like any other unknown object. As a pot, etc., is sought to be encompassed by knowledge, knowledge would have become an object of pervasion by another knowledge. But this is not so, in fact. Hence knowledge is most readily apprehended; so too is the knower. No effort is necessary to know knowledge. The effort is directed to get rid of the notion that non-self is Self. Thus the discipline of knowledge is easily cultivated.

51.0. सा इयं ज्ञानस्य परा निष्ठा उच्यते, कथं कार्या इति ?—

51.0. How is the supreme discipline of knowledge to be accomplished?

बुद्ध्या विशुद्धया युक्तो धृत्याऽऽत्मानं नियम्य च ।
शब्दादीन् विषयांस्त्यक्त्वा रागद्वेषौ व्युदस्य च ॥५१॥

51. Conjoined to the purified intellect, restraining the self with resolution, rejecting objects like sounds, and setting aside attachment and aversion;

51.1. बुद्ध्या इति ॥ बुद्ध्या अध्यवसायलक्षणया विशुद्धया मायारहितया युक्तः सम्पन्नः, धृत्या धैर्येण आत्मानं कार्यकरणसङ्घातं नियम्य च नियमनं कृत्वा वशीकृत्य, शब्दादीन् शब्दः आदिः येषां तान् विषयान् त्यक्त्वा—सामर्थ्यात् शरीरस्थितिमात्रहेतुभूतान् केवलान् मुक्त्वा ततः अधिकान् सुखार्थान् त्यक्त्वा इत्यर्थः—शरीरस्थित्यर्थत्वेन प्राप्तेषु रागद्वेषौ व्युदस्य परित्यज्य च ॥

ततः—

51.1. 'Conjoined' or united with the intellect, the faculty of decision that has been purged of all guile; restraining with resolution 'the self' or the intellect and the psycho-physical organism, i.e. subduing it, rejecting objects like sound and reducing them to their indispensable limits, i.e. not seeking pleasure in objects; and 'setting aside attachment and aversion' to everything except in regard to the minimum needed to support life in the body; then,

विविक्तसेवी लघ्वाशी यतवाक्कायमानसः ।
ध्यानयोगपरो नित्यं वैराग्यं समुपाश्रितः ॥५२॥

52. Cultivating solitude; eating lightly; speech, body and mind controlled; ever intent on the Yoga of meditation; resorting to dispassion;

52.1. विविक्त इति ॥ विविक्तसेवी अरण्यनदीपुलिनगिरिगुहादीन् विविक्तान् देशान् सेवितुं शीलं अस्य इति विविक्तसेवी, लघ्वाशी लघ्वशनशीलः—विविक्तसेवालघ्वशनयोः निद्रादिदोषनिवर्तकत्वेन चित्तप्रसादहेतुत्वात् ग्रहणम्—यतवाक्कायमानसः वाक् च कायश्च मानसं च यतानि संयतानि यस्य ज्ञाननिष्ठस्य सः ज्ञाननिष्ठः

यतिः यतवाक्कायमानसश्च स्यात् । एवं उपरतसर्वकरणः सन् ध्यानयोगपरः ध्यानं—आत्मस्वरूपचिन्तनं, योगः—आत्मविषये एकाग्रीकरणं, तौ ध्यानयोगौ परत्वेन कर्तव्यौ यस्य सः ध्यानयोगपरः नित्यं—नित्यग्रहणं मंत्रजपाद्यन्यकर्तव्याभावप्रदर्शनार्थम्—वैराग्यं विरागस्य भावः दृष्टादृष्टेषु विषयेषु वैतृष्ण्यं समुपाश्रितः सम्यक् उपाश्रितः नित्यम् एव इत्यर्थः ॥

किंच—

52.1. Habitually resorting to solitary spots like woods, riverbanks, hills and caves; 'eating lightly'—these two traits are mentioned as they diminish flaws like sleep and promote mind's clarity—and having controlled speech, body and mind —the ascetic should be firm in the discipline of knowledge. Thus with all the instrumental senses stilled, he will be engaged in contemplation or investigation into the essential nature of Self and Yoga. Thus he will be dispassionate. Other activities like *japa* are ruled out in his case. He has resorted to unwavering dispassion or non-craving for objects, seen or unseen.

And,

अहङ्कारं बलं दर्पं कामं क्रोधं परिग्रहम् ।
विमुच्य निर्ममः शान्तो ब्रह्मभूयाय कल्पते ॥५३॥

53. Renouncing egoism, force, pride, lust, wrath, and possessions, rid of the sense or ownership and tranquil, one becomes fit for the Status of Brahman.

53.1. अहङ्कारं इति ॥ अहङ्करणं अहङ्कारः देहादिषु तं, बलं सामर्थ्यं कामरागसंयुक्तं—न इतरत् शरीरादिसामर्थ्यं, स्वाभाविकत्वेन तत्त्यागस्य अशक्यत्वात्—दर्पं, दर्पो नाम हर्षानन्तरभावी धर्मातिक्रमहेतुः 'हृष्टो दृप्यति दृप्तो धर्ममतिक्रामति' [आप. ध. १.१३.४.] इति स्मरणात्; तं च, कामं इच्छां, क्रोधं द्वेषं, परिग्रहं, इन्द्रियमनोगतदोषपरित्यागेऽपि शरीरधारणप्रसङ्गेन धर्मानुष्ठाननिमित्तेन वा बाह्यः परिग्रहः प्राप्तः, तं च विमुच्य परित्यज्य, परमहंसपरिव्राजकः भूत्वा देहजीवनमात्रेऽपि निर्गतममभावः निर्ममः, अतः एव शान्तः उपरतः, यः संहृतहर्षायासः यतिः ज्ञाननिष्ठः ब्रह्मभूयाय ब्रह्मभवनाय कल्पते समर्थः भवति ॥

अनेन क्रमेण—

53.1. 'Egoism' consists in treating the non-self such as the body as Self. 'Force' is capacity based on lust and greed and not the natural competence of body, etc. This latter, being natural, can't be given up. 'Pride' is what, in the wake of joy, makes one transgress righteousness. Vide Ap.D.S. 1.13.4: "One delighted grows proud; the proud transgresses righteousness." 'Lust' is desire; wrath, is anger; also possession—even after giving up the flaws of the senses and the mind, one may have to maintain external possession to support bodily life and practise righteousness; this too has to be given up. In other words, becoming a mendicant of the Paramahamsa Order, discarding the sense of possession in respect of the means of supporting the body, and becoming tranquil, the asectic arrests all forms of turbulence, becomes disciplined in knowledge, and acquires fitness for the Brahman-status:

By this process,

ब्रह्मभूतः प्रसन्नात्मा न शोचति न काङ्क्षति ।
समः सर्वेषु भूतेषु मद्भक्तिं लभते पराम् ॥५४॥

54. Becoming Brahman, with a tranquillized mind, he neither grieves nor desires. The same towards all beings, he wins supreme devotion to Me.

54.1. ब्रह्मभूतः इति ॥ ब्रह्मभूतः ब्रह्मप्राप्तः प्रसन्नात्मा लब्धाध्यात्मप्रसादस्वभावः न शोचति, किंचित् अर्थवैकल्यं आत्मनः वैगुण्यं वा उद्दिश्य न शोचति न सन्तप्यते, न काङ्क्षति । न हि अप्राप्तविषयाकांक्षा ब्रह्मविदः उपपद्यते; अतः ब्रह्मभूतस्य अयं स्वभावः अनूद्यते 'न शोचति न काङ्क्षति' इति । 'न हृष्यति' इति वा पाठान्तरम् । समः सर्वेषु भूतेषु, आत्मौपम्येन सर्वभूतेषु सुखं दुःखं वा सममेव पश्यति इत्यर्थः । न आत्मसमदर्शनं इह, तस्य वक्ष्यमाणत्वात् 'भक्त्या मामभिजानाति' [१८.५५.] इति । एवंभूतः ज्ञाननिष्ठः मद्भक्तिं मयि परमेश्वरे भक्तिं भजनं परां उत्तमां ज्ञानलक्षणां चतुर्थीं लभते, 'चतुर्विधा भजन्ते मां' [७.१६.] इति हि उक्तम् ॥

54.1. Having risen to Brahman's status and won serenity of mind, he does not grieve when some material concern gets upset or deterioration (*vaigunya*) supervenes; neither does he seek anything. A Brahman-knower can't desire any ungained object. So the phrase 'does not grieve nor desire' is just a statement of fact about him. An alternative reading is 'delights not'. On the basis of equality with the self, he sees others' pleasures and pains as his own. Here what is meant is not the vision of the one Self in all. It will be mentioned in the next verse. This disciplined knower attains the highest devotion to Me, the supreme Lord, devotion marked by knowledge, i.e., of the fourth kind of devotees (vide 7.16).

55.0. ततः ज्ञानलक्षणया—

55.0. By means of this devotion marked by knowledge,

भक्त्या मामभिजानाति यावान् यश्चास्मि तत्त्वतः।
ततो मां तत्त्वतो ज्ञात्वा विशते तदनन्तरम् ॥५५॥

55. He comprehends Me—what My extent is, who I am. Thus knowing Me in truth, he enters (into Me).

55.1. भक्त्या इति ॥ भक्त्या मां अभिजानाति यावान् अहं उपाधिकृतविस्तरभेदः, यः च अहं अस्मि विध्वस्तसर्वोपाधिभेदः उत्तमः पुरुषः आकाशकल्पः, तं मां अद्वैतं चैतन्यमात्रैकरसं अजरं अभयं अनिधनं तत्त्वतः अभिजानाति। ततः मां एवं तत्त्वतः ज्ञात्वा विशते तदनन्तरं मामेव ज्ञानानन्तरम्। नात्र ज्ञानान्तरप्रवेशक्रिये भिन्ने विवक्षिते 'ज्ञात्वा विशते तदनन्तरं' इति। किं तर्हि?— फलान्तराभावात् ज्ञानमात्रमेव, 'क्षेत्रज्ञं चापि मां विद्धि' [१३.२.] इति उक्तत्वात् ॥

55.1. By means of devotion he knows Me—what My extent is, My extent being due to multifarious adjuncts, and who I am, i.e., as the supreme Spirit I am devoid of all adjuncts whatsoever, like the sky. He truly knows Me who am non-dual, whose sole essence is consciousness, unaging, fearless, endless. Thus knowing Me, he enters into Me immediately. Two activities are not meant here—those of knowing and entering; for, there are not two results. Pure knowledge is what is meant. Vide 13.2 "Know Me also to be the field-knower."

55.2. ननु विरुद्धं इदं उक्तं "ज्ञानस्य या परा निष्ठा तया मां अभिजानाति" इति । कथं विरुद्धं इति चेत्, उच्यते—यदैव यस्मिन् विषये ज्ञानं उत्पद्यते ज्ञातुः, तदैव तं विषयं अभिजानाति ज्ञाता इति न ज्ञाननिष्ठां ज्ञानावृत्तिलक्षणां अपेक्षते इति; अतश्च ज्ञानेन न अभिजानाति, ज्ञानावृत्त्या तु ज्ञाननिष्ठया अभिजानातीति ॥

नैषः दोषः; ज्ञानस्य स्वात्मोत्पत्तिपरिपाकहेतुयुक्तस्य प्रतिपक्षविहीनस्य यत् आत्मानुभवनिश्चयावसानत्वं तस्य निष्ठाशब्दाभिलापात् । शास्त्राचार्योपदेशेन ज्ञानोत्पत्तिपरिपाकहेतुं सहकारिकारणं बुद्धिविशुद्धत्वादि अमानित्वादिगुणं च [१३.७.] अपेक्ष्य जनितस्य क्षेत्रज्ञपरमात्मैकत्वज्ञानस्य कर्तृत्वादिकारकभेदबुद्धिनिबन्धनसर्वकर्मसंन्याससहितस्य स्वात्मानुभवनिश्चयरूपेण यत् अवस्थानं, सा परा ज्ञाननिष्ठा इति उच्यते । सा इयं ज्ञाननिष्ठा आर्तादिभक्तित्रयापेक्षया परा चतुर्थी भक्तिरिति उक्ता [७.१७.] । तया परया भक्त्या भगवन्तं तत्त्वतः अभिजानाति, यदनन्तरमेव ईश्वरक्षेत्रज्ञभेदबुद्धिः अशेषतः निवर्तते । अतः ज्ञाननिष्ठालक्षणया भक्त्या मां अभिजानातीति वचनं न विरुध्यते । अत्र च सर्वं निवृत्तिविधायि शास्त्रं वेदान्तेतिहासपुराणस्मृतिलक्षणं अर्थवत् भवति—'विदित्वा ... व्युत्थायाथ भिक्षाचर्यं चरन्ति' [बृ. उ. ३.५.१.], 'तस्मान्न्यासमेषां तपसामतिरिक्तमाहुः' [महान. उ. २४.१.], 'न्यास एवात्यरेचयत्' [महाना. उ. २१.२.] इति । 'संन्यासः कर्मणां न्यासः' [१८.२.], 'वेदानिमं च लोकममुं च परित्यज्य' [आप. ध. २.२३.१३.], 'त्यज धर्ममधर्मं च' [शां. प. ३२९.४०; ३३१.४४.] इत्यादि । इह च [५.१३.] प्रदर्शितानि वाक्यानि । न च तेषां वाक्यानां आनर्थक्यं युक्तम्; न च अर्थवादत्वं, स्वप्रकरणस्थत्वात्, प्रत्यगात्माविक्रियस्वरूपनिष्ठत्वाच्च मोक्षस्य । न हि पूर्वसमुद्रं जिगमिषोः प्रातिलोम्येन प्रत्यक्समुद्रजिगमिषुणा समानमार्गत्वं संभवति । प्रत्यगात्मविषयप्रत्ययसन्तानकरणाभिनिवेशश्च ज्ञाननिष्ठा । सा च प्रत्यक्समुद्रगमनवत् कर्मणा सहभावित्वेन विरुध्यते । पर्वतसर्षपयोः इव अन्तरवान् विरोधः प्रमाणविदां निश्चितः । तस्मात् सर्वकर्मसंन्यासेनैव ज्ञाननिष्ठा कार्या इति सिद्धम् ॥

55.2. *Objection:* "Is this not self-contradictory?—to say that by the firm establishment in Knowledge through disciplines like repetition (cf. 18.50), one comes to know Me. To explain: The moment one acquires knowledge of an object, the knower knows it immediately; there is no further need for a discipline of knowledge consisting in the repetition of that knowledge. Here however is affirmed not that by knowledge one knows, but by its repetition, by the discipline of knowledge." *Reply*: "This is no flaw. By discipline what is meant is the definitive consummation of the experience of the Self, which is no longer exposed to doubts of any kind; for, it is the final fruit of the rise of Self-knowledge. The supreme discipline of knowledge that is relevent may be pin-pointed: it is the status of certitude of Self-experience accompanied by the renunciation of all works, consequent on the disappearance of plurality among accessories of action such as agent, instruments, etc. Of course, this follows from the perception of identity between the field-knower and the supreme Self, brought about by the instructions of the *śāstras* and the teacher, and the cooperation of causal factors listed in 13.7 and the purity of intellect, etc. This discipline has also been styled in 7.17 as the fourth variety of devotion distinct from devotions marking the sufferer, the seeker of knowledge and the pursuer of possessions. By this supreme form of devotion, one knows the Lord truly, immediately after which the idea of difference between God and the field-knower vanishes. Therefore, there is no contradiction in the statement quoted above ('by which one knows Me')." In the light of this interpretation alone, all *śāstraic* injunctions bidding cessation from work, in Vedānta, Itihāsa, Purāna and Smṛtis can be seen to be consistent with reasoning and therefore significant. "Knowing . . . . . go forth and become mendicants" (BU. 3.5.1) ; "So they say that renunciation excels all these austerities" (Maha.Nā.U. 24.1) ; "Renunciation alone excelled" (ibid.10.62.12) ; "Relinquishment of voluntary works is *sannyasa*"(18.2); "Giving up Vedas, this world and that" (AP.D. S.2.23.13) ; "Give up righteousness and unrighteousness" (Sānti.329. 40 ; 331.44), etc. In the Gītā also such affirmations have been made (5.13). It is unreasonable to hold that these affirmations are futile. Nor are they merely glorificatory ; for, they occur in their autonomous contexts. Besides, liberation hinges on the immutability of the inner Self. Of course, he who wishes to reach the eastern sea cannot follow the same route as he who wishes to reach the western sea. Discipline of knowledge is the zeal for the unbroken contemplation of the inner Self. It conflicts with work just as the routes leading west and east. Their contrast is similar to that between a hill and a mustard seed, as all epistemologists recognise. Therefore, it follows that the discipline of knowledge must be achieved by means of the renunciation of all works.

56.0. स्वकर्मणा भगवतः अभ्यर्चनभक्तियोगस्य सिद्धिप्राप्तिः फलं ज्ञाननिष्ठा-योग्यता, यन्निमित्ता ज्ञाननिष्ठा मोक्षफलावसाना । सः भगवद्भक्तियोगः अधुना स्तूयते शास्त्रार्थोपसंहारप्रकरणे शास्त्रार्थनिश्चयदाढर्याय—

56.0. The gaining of 'perfection', i.e., of the fitness for the discipline of knowledge, is the fruit of the Yoga of devotion consisting in divine worship in the form of the performance of one's allotted works ; this fitness leads to the discipline of knowledge and culminates in liberation. Now this Yoga of devotion to the Lord (consisting in the performance of one's allotted work as worship of Him) is extolled in this concluding portion of the Gītā, the aim being the strengthening of the conviction regarding its doctrines.

सर्वकर्माण्यपि सदा कुर्वाणो मद्व्यपाश्रयः ।
मत्प्रसादादवाप्नोति शाश्वतं पदमव्ययम् ॥५६॥

56. Though performing all works continuously, in total dependence on Me, due to My grace, one achieves the eternal and immutable status.

56.1. सर्वकर्माणि इति ॥ सर्वकर्माणि अपि प्रतिषिद्धानि अपि सदा कुर्वाणः अनुतिष्ठन् मद्व्यपाश्रयः अहं वासुदेवः ईश्वरः व्यपाश्रयो व्यपाश्रयणं यस्य सः मद्व्यपाश्रयः, मय्यर्पितसर्वभावः इत्यर्थः । सोऽपि मत्प्रसादात् मम ईश्वरस्य प्रसादात् अवाप्नोति शाश्वतं नित्यं वैष्णवं पदं अव्ययम् ॥

यस्मात् एवम्—

56.1. Though doing all works, even forbidden ones, depending on Me, the Lord Vāsudeva, all his emotional attitudes being oriented towards Me, he will, due to My grace, attain the eternal and immutable status of Viṣṇu.

This being the case,

चेतसा सर्वकर्माणि मयि संन्यस्य मत्परः ।
बुद्धियोगमुपाश्रित्य मच्चित्तः सततं भव ॥५७॥

57. Mentally surrendering all works to Me, setting Me above all, and resorting to concentrated understanding, fix your mind unceasingly on Me.

57.1. चेतसा इति ॥ चेतसा विवेकबुद्ध्या सर्वकर्माणि दृष्टादृष्टार्थानि मयि ईश्वरे संन्यस्य 'यत् करोषि यदश्नासि' [९.२७.] इति उक्तन्यायेन, मत्परः अहं वासुदेवः परः यस्य तव सः त्वं मत्परः सन् मय्यर्पितसर्वात्मभावः बुद्धियोगं समाहितबुद्धित्वं बुद्धियोगः तं बुद्धियोगं अपाश्रित्य (उपाश्रित्य) अपाश्रयः अनन्यशरणत्वं मच्चित्तः मयि एव चित्तं यस्य तव सः त्वं मच्चित्तः सततं सर्वदा भव ॥

57.1. 'Mentally' means through discrimination; 'surrendering', in the spirit of verse 9.27 'all works' aimed at results, seen and unseen, to 'Me', the Lord; 'setting Me,' Lord Vāsudeva, above all, i.e. having spiritual attitudes directed to Me; 'resorting to concentrated understanding'—fix your mind, at all times, exclusively on Me, since I am your sole refuge.

मच्चित्तः सर्वदुर्गाणि मत्प्रसादात्तरिष्यसि ।
अथ चेत्त्वमहङ्कारान्न श्रोष्यसि विनङ्क्ष्यसि ॥५८॥

58. With your mind fixed on Me, you will overcome all obstacles due to My grace; but if, egoistically, you pay no heed, you will perish.

58.1. मच्चित्तः इति ॥ मच्चित्तः सर्वदुर्गाणि सर्वाणि दुस्तराणि संसारहेतुजातानि मत्प्रसादात् तरिष्यसि अतिक्रमिष्यसि । अथ चेत् यदि त्वं मदुक्तं अहङ्कारात् 'पण्डितः अहं' इति नं श्रोष्यसि न ग्रहीष्यसि, ततः त्वं विनङ्क्ष्यसि विनाशं गमिष्यसि ॥

58.1. With your mind fixed on Me you will, due to My grace, overcome all obscacles that are hard to overcome, i.e., the causes of this transmigratory life, in their totality. If, however, 'egoistically' thinking 'I am wise', you pay no heed to what has been said—do not accept and act on it—you will perish, come to ruin.

59.0. इदं च त्वया न मन्तव्यं 'स्वतन्त्रः अहं, किमर्थं परोक्तं करिष्यामि ?' इति—

59.0. Don't imagine "I am free; why should I do what another bids?"

यद्यहङ्कारमाश्रित्य न योत्स्य इति मन्यसे।
मिथ्यैष व्यवसायस्ते प्रकृतिस्त्वां नियोक्ष्यति ॥५९॥

59. If egoistically you maintain 'I will not fight', this decision of yours is erroneous; your nature will constrain you.

59.1. यद्यहङ्कारं इति ॥ यदि चेत् त्वं अहङ्कारं आश्रित्य न योत्स्ये इति न युद्धं करिष्यामि इति मन्यसे चिन्तयसि निश्चयं करोषि, मिथ्या एषः व्यवसायः निश्चयः ते तव; यस्मात् प्रकृतिः क्षत्रियस्वभावः त्वां नियोक्ष्यति ॥
यस्माच्च—

59.1. Resorting to egoism if you think 'I will not fight'—if you resolve thus—this resolve of yours is erroneous. 'Nature'—your nature as a *kṣatriya*—will constrain you to fight.
Also because,

स्वभावजेन कौन्तेय निबद्धः स्वेन कर्मणा।
कर्तुं नेच्छसि यन्मोहात् करिष्यस्यवशोऽपि तत् ॥६०॥

60. Son of Kuntī! What, through delusion you don't desire to do, bound by your own work, born of nature, you will inevitably do.

60.1. स्वभावजेन इति ॥ स्वभावजेन शौर्यादिना यथोक्तेन कौन्तेय ! निबद्धः निश्चयेन बद्धः स्वेन आत्मीयेन कर्मणा कर्तुं न इच्छसि यत् कर्म मोहात् अविवेकतः करिष्यसि अवशः अपि परवशः एव तत् कर्म ॥
यस्मात्—

60.1. Arjuna! swayed by heroism, etc., 'born of your nature' as already explained, and 'bound by your work' which, due to 'delusion' or non-discrimination, you don't desire to do—you will do that unavoidably.

For,

ईश्वरः सर्वभूतानां हृद्देशेऽर्जुन तिष्ठति।
भ्रामयन् सर्वभूतानि यन्त्रारूढानि मायया ॥६१॥

61. God is in the heart of all beings, Arjuna! causing them all to revolve through māyā, as though they are mounted on a machine.

61.1. ईश्वरः इति ॥ ईश्वरः ईशनशीलः नारायणः सर्वभूतानां सर्वप्राणिनां हृद्देशे हृदयदेशे अर्जुन शुक्लान्तरात्मस्वभाव ! विशुद्धान्तःकरण—'अहश्च कृष्ण-महरर्जुनं च' [ऋ. सं. ६.९.१.] इति दर्शनात्—तिष्ठति स्थितिं लभते । तेषु सः कथं तिष्ठतीति ? आह—भ्रामयन् भ्रमणं कारयन् सर्वभूतानि यन्त्रारूढानि यन्त्राणि आरूढानि अधिष्ठितानि इव—इति इवशब्दः अत्र द्रष्टव्यः—यथा दारुकृतपुरुषादीनि यन्त्रारूढानि । मायया छद्मना भ्रामयन् तिष्ठति इति सम्बन्धः ॥

61.1. O Arjuna! Mighty God-Nārāyaṇa dwells in the hearts of all beings. Arjuna is so called because his inner self is 'white—pure'. Vide 'The day black and the day white' (RV 6.9.1). How does He dwell there? Causing all those beings to revolve as though they are mounted on machines. The phrase 'as though' *iva* must be understood here. They resemble wooden puppets set on machines, caused to revolve through Maya or illusion. Thus it has to be construed.

तमेव शरणं गच्छ सर्वभावेन भारत।
तत्प्रसादात्परां शान्तिं स्थानं प्राप्स्यसि शाश्वतम् ॥६२॥

62. O Bhārata! seek refuge in Him alone with all your heart and all your soul. Due to His grace you will win peace supreme and status eternal.

62.1. तमेव इति ॥ तम् एव ईश्वरं शरणं आश्रयं संसारार्तिहरणार्थं गच्छ आश्रय सर्वभावेन सर्वात्मना हे भारत ! । ततः तत्प्रसादात् ईश्वरानुग्रहात् परां प्रकृष्टां शान्तिं उपरतिं स्थानं च मम विष्णोः परमं पदं प्राप्स्यसि शाश्वतं नित्यम् ॥

62.1. Seek refuge with all your heart and all your soul—in your entirety. Rest in Him alone to save yourself from the sufferings of transmigratory life, O Arjuna! Then, due to His grace—divine blessings—you will win supreme peace or withdrawal and the eternal status of Viṣṇu.

इति ते ज्ञानमाख्यातं गुह्याद्गुह्यतरं मया ।
विमृश्यैतदशेषेण यथेच्छसि तथा कुरु ॥६३॥

63. Thus has been declared to you knowledge most secret by Me. Taking full account of it, do as you deem fit.

63.1. इति इति ॥ इति एतत् ते तुभ्यं ज्ञानं आख्यातं कथितं गुह्यात् गोप्यात् गुह्यतरं अतिशयेन गुह्यं रहस्यं इत्यर्थः, मया सर्वज्ञेन ईश्वरेण । विमृश्य विमर्शनं आलोचनं कृत्वा एतत् यथोक्तं शास्त्रं अशेषेण समस्तं यथोक्तं च अर्थजातं यथा इच्छसि तथा कुरु ॥

63.1. Thus has this knowledge been declared—an extreme secret, a mystery—by Me, the omniscient Lord. Taking full account of it and pondering over this mandate—i.e., this group of ideas in its entirety as set forth—do as you think fit.

64.0. भूयोऽपि मया उच्यमानं शृणु—

64.0. Listen again to what is going to be said:

सर्वगुह्यतमं भूयः शृणु मे परमं वचः ।
इष्टोऽसि मे दृढमिति ततो वक्ष्यामि ते हितम् ॥६४॥

64. Again listen to My supreme word—the most exalted

mystery; for you are indeed dear to Me. So I shall say what is good for you.

64.1. सर्वगुह्यतमं इति ॥ सर्वगुह्यतमं सर्वेभ्यः गुह्येभ्यः अत्यन्तगुह्यतमं अत्यन्त-रहस्यं उक्तम् अपि असकृत् भूयः पुनः शृणु मे मम परमं प्रकृष्टं वचः वाक्यम् । न भयात् नापि अर्थकारणाद्वा वक्ष्यामि; किं तर्हि ? इष्टः प्रियः असि मे मम दृढं अव्यभिचारेण इतिं कृत्वा ततः तेन कारणेन वक्ष्यामि कथयिष्यामि ते तव हितं परमं ज्ञानप्राप्तिसाधनम्, तत् हि सर्वहितानां हिततमम् ॥

64.1. Listen to My supreme word, the most exalted mystery, the greatest secret, though often it has been declared. Not out of fear nor due to desire to gain some end, do I speak but because you are consistently dear to Me indeed. I shall say what is good—the best means of securing knowledge. This knowledge is the highest good indeed.

65.0. किं तत् इति ? आह—

65.0. What is that? Says the Lord—

मन्मना भव मद्भक्तो मद्याजी मां नमस्कुरु ।
मामेवैष्यसि सत्यं ते प्रतिजाने प्रियोऽसि मे ॥६५॥

65. Set your mind on Me; be My devotee; sacrifice unto Me; prostrate before Me; you will surely attain Me. Truly do I promise thus, for you are dear to Me.

65.1. मन्मनाः इति ॥ मन्मनाः भव मच्चित्तः भव । मद्भक्तः भव मद्भजनः भव । मद्याजी मद्यजनशीलः भव । मां नमस्कुरु नमस्कारं अपि ममैव कुरु । तत्र एवं वर्तमानः वासुदेवे एव समर्पितसाध्यसाधनप्रयोजनः माम् एव एष्यसि आग-मिष्यसि । सत्यं ते तव प्रतिजाने, सत्यां प्रतिज्ञां करोमि एतस्मिन् वस्तुनि इत्यर्थः; यतः प्रियः असि मे । एवं भगवतः सत्यप्रतिज्ञत्वं बुद्ध्वा भगवद्भक्तेः अवश्यम्भावि मोक्षफलं अवधार्य भगवच्छरणैकपरायणः भवेत् इति वाक्यार्थः ॥

65.1. Set your mind on Me; be My devotee—love Me. Sacrifice unto me habitually. Prostrate before Me—pay obeisance unto Me alone. Thus doing—seeing goals, means and profit in Vāsudeva exclusively,—'you will attain Me'—come to Me. I promise you this truly in regard to this matter of spiritual concern; for, you are dear to Me. The idea is that, knowing the Lord's promise to be certainly true and the fruit of liberation sure to follow, one should dedicate oneself exclusively to the Lord.

66.0. कर्मयोगनिष्ठायाः परमरहस्यं ईश्वरशरणतां उपसंहृत्य अथ इदानीं कर्मयोगनिष्ठाफलं सम्यग्दर्शनं सर्ववेदान्तसारविहितं वक्तव्यम् इति आह—

66.0. Having thus concluded the supreme secret of the discipline of Karma Yoga, namely, self-dedication to the Lord, He declares now the fruit of the discipline of Karma Yoga, or right perception which forms the quintessence of all Upaniṣads.

सर्वधर्मान् परित्यज्य मामेकं शरणं व्रज ।
अहं त्वा सर्वपापेभ्यो मोक्षयिष्यामि मा शुचः ॥६६॥

66. Giving up all Dharma (acts of righteousness), seek refuge in Me, alone; I shall liberate you from all sins; grieve not.

66.1. सर्वधर्मान् इति ॥ सर्वधर्मान् सर्वे च ते धर्माश्च सर्वधर्माः तान्—धर्मशब्देन अत्र अधर्मः अपि गृह्यते, नैष्कर्म्यस्य विवक्षितत्वात्, 'नाविरतो दुश्चरितात्,' [कठ. उ. २.२४.], 'त्यज धर्ममधर्मं च' [शां. प. ३२९.४०; ३३१.४४] इत्यादिश्रुतिस्मृतिभ्यः—सर्वधर्मान् परित्यज्य संन्यस्य सर्वकर्माणि इत्येतत् । मां एकं सर्वात्मानं समं सर्वभूतस्थितं ईश्वरं [अच्युतं गर्भजन्मजरामरणविवर्जितं] 'अहमेव' इत्येवं एकं शरणं व्रज, न मत्तः अन्यत् अस्ति इति अवधारय इत्यर्थः । अहं त्वा त्वां एवंनिश्चितबुद्धिं सर्वपापेभ्यः सर्वधर्माधर्मबन्धनरूपेभ्यः मोक्षयिष्यामि स्वात्मभावप्रकाशीकरणेन । उक्तं च 'नाशयाम्यात्मभावस्थो ज्ञानदीपेन भास्वता' [१०.११.] इत्यतः मा शुचः शोकं मा कार्षीः इत्यर्थः ॥

66.1. 'All Dharma or acts of righteousness'— Dharma (righteousness) here includes Adharma (unrighteousness) also. What is sought to be conveyed is the idea of freedom from all works. (Dharma here means Karma). From pronouncements in *śruti* and *smṛti* like the following it is clear that the sense is the renunciation of all works. "Without withdrawing from evil conduct", KU.2.24; "Give up righteousness and unrighteousness", (Sānti P. 329.40; 331.44). 'In Me alone, in the Self of all, the same dwelling in all, God (the Unlapsing, beyond conception, birth, old age, and death)—seek refuge' with the idea: "There is nothing but I," "Know for certain nothing exists other than Me." If you are firm in this intellectual conviction I shall liberate you 'from all sins'—from the bonds of righteousness and unrighteousness (i.e. the bondage of all Karma) by revealing My status as the Self of all. In 10.11 it has already been affirmed— established as Self, with the shining lamp of knowledge I destroy the darkness of nescience. Therefore do not grieve. This is the sense.

66.2. किं अस्मिन् गीताशास्त्रे परं निःश्रेयससाधनं निश्चितम् ?— किं ज्ञानं, कर्म वा ? आहोस्वित् उभयम् इति ?

कुतः संशय—?

'यत् ज्ञात्वाऽमृतमश्नुते' [१८.१२.], 'ततो मां तत्त्वतो ज्ञात्वा विशते तदनन्तरं' [१८.५५.] इत्यादीनि वाक्यानि केवलज्ञानात् निःश्रेयसप्राप्तिं दर्शयन्ति । 'कर्मण्येवाधिकारस्ते' [२.४७.], 'कुरु कर्मैव' [४.१५.] इत्येवमादीनि कर्मणां अवश्यकर्तव्यतां दर्शयन्ति । एवं ज्ञानकर्मणोः कर्तव्यत्वोपदेशात् समुच्चितयोः अपि निःश्रेयसहेतुत्वं स्यात् इति भवेत् संशयः ।

66.2. *Question:* "In this science of the Gītā what is established as the means of attaining the supreme good or *mokṣa*? Is it knowledge, work, or both of them together?" *Reply* (tentative): "Why entertain this doubt at all? Witness statements like the following: 'Knowing which one experiences immortality', (13.12); 'Then knowing Me truthfully one immediately enters into Me,' (18.55). These reveal attainment of immortality from unaided knowledge. There are other statements of an opposite nature: 'Only to the performance of works have you the right,' (2.47); 'Do only work' (4.15) etc.— These show that works have necessarily to be performed. Thus, since both knowledge and work have been ordained it is possible that their combination may liberate. Hence the doubt mentioned above is in order."

66.3. किं पुनः अत्र मीमांसाफलम् ?

ननु एतत् एव—एषां अन्यतमस्य परमनिःश्रेयससाधनत्वावधारणं; अतः विस्तीर्णतरं मीमांस्यं एतत् ॥

आत्मज्ञानस्य तु केवलस्य निःश्रेयसहेतुत्वं, भेदप्रत्ययनिवर्तकत्वेन कैवल्यफलावसायित्वात् । क्रियाकारकफलभेदबुद्धिः अविद्यया आत्मनि नित्यप्रवृत्ता—'मम कर्म, अहं कर्ता, अमुष्मै फलाय इदं कर्म करिष्यामि'—इति इयं अविद्या अनादिकालप्रवृत्ता । अस्याः अविद्यायाः निवर्तकं—'अयं अहं अस्मि केवलः अकर्ता अक्रियः अफलः; न मत्तः अन्यः अस्ति कश्चित्'—इत्येवंरूपं आत्मविषयं ज्ञानं उत्पद्यमानं कर्मप्रवृत्तिहेतुभूतायाः भेदबुद्धेः निवर्तकत्वात् । तुशब्दः पक्षद्वयव्यावृत्त्यर्थः—न केवलेभ्यः कर्मभ्यः, न च ज्ञानकर्मभ्यां समुच्चिताभ्यां निःश्रेयसप्राप्तिः इति पक्षद्वयं निवर्तयति । अकार्यत्वाच्च निःश्रेयसस्य कर्मसाधनत्वानुपपत्तिः । न हि नित्यं वस्तु कर्मणा ज्ञानेन वा क्रियते ।

66.3. *Question:* "What will be the result of this proposed inquiry?" *Reply:* "It is the conviction that one of the three alternatives is the means to the achievement of the summum bonum". Therefore the question demands a wide-ranging investigation.

"Only the unaided knowledge of the Self is the cause of liberation", as it dispels all notions of plurality and produces the fruit of liberation. Nescience, the sense of difference among works, accessories and fruits, has always prevailed in regard to the Self, taking the form 'my work', 'I am the agent', 'I do this work for that specific fruit'. etc. This nescience has been active from beginningless time. Its dispeller is Self-Knowledge whose content is—Here I am, alone, a non-agent; without work of any kind or fruit; there is none other than me." It dispels nescience, because it abolishes the idea of differences that conditions all activity. *Tu* (or 'only' given at the beginning of this para)—serves to rule out two of the three alternatives mentioned above. *Mokṣa* or liberation results neither from works alone nor from a combination of knowledge and works. As *mokṣa* is not a product, it is unreasonable to hold that its means is works. An eternal entity cannot be produced either by works or knowledge.

66.4. केवलज्ञानम् अपि अनर्थकं तर्हि ?
न, अविद्यानिवर्तकत्वे सति दृष्टकैवल्यफलावसानत्वात् । अविद्यातमोनिवर्तकस्य ज्ञानस्य दृष्टं कैवल्यफलावसानत्वं, रज्ज्वादिविषये सर्पाद्यज्ञानतमोनिवर्तकप्रदीपप्रकाशवत् । विनिवृत्तसर्पादिविकल्परज्जुकैवल्यावसानं हि प्रकाशफलम्; तथा ज्ञानम् । दृष्टार्थानां च छिदिक्रियाग्निमन्थनादीनां व्यापृतकर्त्रादिकारकाणां द्वैधीभावाग्निदर्शनादिफलात् अन्यफले कर्मान्तरे वा व्यापारानुपपत्तिः यथा, तथा दृष्टार्थायां ज्ञाननिष्ठाक्रियायां ['निष्क्रियायां ज्ञाननिष्ठाक्रियायां' इति, 'निष्क्रियायां ज्ञाननिष्ठायां' इति च पाठौ.] व्यापृतस्य ज्ञात्रादिकारकस्य आत्मकैवल्यफलात् कर्मान्तरे प्रवृत्तिः अनुपपन्ना इति न ज्ञाननिष्ठा कर्मसहिता उपपद्यते ।
भुज्यग्निहोत्रादिक्रियावत् स्यात् इति चेत्—
न; कैवल्यफले ज्ञाने क्रियाफलार्थित्वानुपपत्तेः । कैवल्यफले हि ज्ञाने प्राप्ते, सर्वतःसंप्लुतोदकफले कूपतडागादिक्रियाफलार्थित्वाभाववत्, फलान्तरे तत्साधनभूतायां वा क्रियायां अर्थित्वानुपपत्तिः । न हि राज्यप्राप्तिफले कर्मणि व्यापृतस्य क्षेत्रमात्रप्राप्तिफले व्यापार उपपद्यते, तद्विषयं वा अर्थित्वम् । तस्मात् न कर्मणः अस्ति निःश्रेयससाधनत्वम् । न च ज्ञानकर्मणोः समुच्चितयोः । नापि ज्ञानस्य कैवल्यफलस्य कर्मसाहाय्यापेक्षा, अविद्यानिवर्तकत्वेन विरोधात् । न हि तमः तमसः निवर्तकम् । अतः केवलम् एव ज्ञानं निःश्रेयससाधनं इति ।

66.4. *Objection*: "Then, is not unaided knowledge also pointless?" *Reply*: "No; for it abolishes nescience and is seen to culminate in liberation. Knowledge that abolishes the darkness of nescience is experienced as culminating in the fruit of *mokṣa.* It resembles the light of a lamp that dispels ignorance about the rope-snake, etc. The fruit of the lamp-light is the residual existence of the rope after the abolition of the superimposed snake. Similar is the case of knowledge. Other examples too are available in this context. Activities like cutting of the wood and churning it for producing fire, in which the accessories like the agent operate, do not lead to any result other than separation of parts, blazing forth of fire, etc. (These results are immediately visible) Such is the case with the discipline of knowledge. Its result is immediate and excludes all further object-directed operations. Here the knower is not involved in any of the further irrelevant activity; he is confined to the fruit of liberation solely. So the discipline of knowledge is unaccompanied by work of any kind." *Objection*: "Why not hold that this discipline is like the activity of eating or the performance of the fire-sacrifice (in which other consequent and collateral activities find a place?)" *Reply*: "No, the fruit of knowledge is *mokṣa* and the knower cannot reasonably look for any other fruits at all. When knowledge, whose fruit is but *mokṣa*, has been won, the position is as has been described in 2.46—no activity aimed at lesser ends is conceivable. None striving to secure an empire will waste his energy in seizing a petty field; his goal can't be the ownership of that field." Therefore work is no means to emancipation. Nor may combined work and knowledge prove a means. Again, knowledge bearing *mokṣa* as its fruit needs no assistance from work; for, as the sublater of nescience there is conflict between knowledge and work. Darkness does not abolish darkness. Therefore only pure knowledge is means to *mokṣa*.

66.5. न—नित्याकरणे प्रत्यवायप्राप्तेः, कैवल्यस्य च नित्यत्वात् । यत् तावत् केवलज्ञानात् कैवल्यप्राप्तिः इत्येतत्, तत् असत्; यतः नित्यानां कर्मणां श्रुत्युक्तानां अकरणे प्रत्यवायः नरकादिप्राप्तिलक्षणः स्यात्—

ननु एवं तर्हि कर्मभ्यः मोक्षः नास्ति इति अनिर्मोक्षः एव ।

नैष दोषः; नित्यत्वात् मोक्षस्य । नित्यानां कर्मणां अनुष्ठानात् प्रत्यवायस्य अप्राप्तिः, प्रतिषिद्धस्य च अकरणात् अनिष्टशरीरानुपपत्तिः, काम्यानां च वर्जनात् इष्टशरीरानुपपत्तिः, वर्तमानशरीरारम्भकस्य च कर्मणः फलोपभोगक्षये पतिते अस्मिन् शरीरे देहान्तरोत्पत्तौ च कारणाभावात् आत्मनः रागादीनां च अकरणे स्वरूपावस्थानं कैवल्यम् इति अयत्नसिद्धं कैवल्यं इति ।

अतिक्रान्तानेकजन्मान्तरकृतस्य स्वर्गनरकादिप्राप्तिफलस्य अनारब्धकार्यस्य उपभोगानुपपत्तेः क्षयाभावः इति चेत्—

न; नित्यकर्मानुष्ठानायासदुःखोपभोगस्य तत्फलोपभोगत्वोपपत्तेः । प्रायश्चित्तवद्वा पूर्वोपचितदुरितक्षयार्थं नित्यं कर्म । आरब्धानां च कर्मणां उपभोगेन एव क्षीणत्वात् अपूर्वाणां च कर्मणां अनारम्भे अयत्नसिद्धं कैवल्यम् इति ।

66.5. *Objection:* 'No; the non-performance of obligatory works entails the sin of omission whereas *mokṣa* is eternal. The Advaitic proposition that the achivement of *mokṣa* is through pure knowledge is wrong; for the non-doing of obligatory works ordained by *sruti* entails the sin of omission leading to hell, etc. Further, if *mokṣa* does not result from works, there arises the contingency of non-emancipation. *Reply*: No such flaw needs to be feared. *Mokṣa* is eternal. Through the performance of obligatory works the sin of omission may be averted; through the non-performance of forbidden works unwanted embodiments may be warded off; through the non-performance of voluntary works, desirable embodiments also may be stopped. When the works that led to the present embodiment get exhausted through the due experience of their fruits, the body will fall. No fresh embodiment will follow. Emotions like attachment won't be there and the Self will abide in Itself. This is *mokṣa* and it is effortlessly won. *Objection*: But it may be argued that the accumulated works of the past many lives won't dwindle away without their agent experiencing their fruits. *Reply*: Such an apprehension is not in order; for, the troubles taken in the performance of obligatory works may be equated with the reaping of the fruits in question. This case is similar to the performance of expiatory rites. Obligatory works cause the dwindling of sins committed in the past. Works which have started to yield fruits will wear away through their experience itself. No fresh works will be undertaken. Thus effortlessly will *mokṣa* follow.

66.6. न; 'तमेव विदित्वाऽतिमृत्युमेति नान्यः पन्था विद्यतेऽयनाय' [श्वे. उ. ३.८.] इति विद्याया अन्यः पन्थाः मोक्षाय न विद्यते इति श्रुतेः, चर्मवदाकाशवेष्टनासम्भववत् अविदुषः मोक्षासम्भवश्रुतेः [श्वे. उ. ६.२०.], 'ज्ञानात् कैवल्यमाप्नोति' इति च पुराणस्मृतेः [?] अनारब्धफलानां पुण्यानां कर्मणां क्षयानुपपत्तेश्च । यथा पूर्वोपात्तानां दुरितानां अनारब्धफलानां स्यात् सम्भवः, तथा पुण्यानां अनारब्धफलानां स्यात् सम्भवः । तेषां च देहान्तरं अकृत्वा क्षयानुपपत्तौ मोक्षानुपपत्तिः । धर्माधर्महेतूनां च रागद्वेषमोहानां अन्यत्र आत्मज्ञानात् उच्छेदानुपपत्तेः धर्माधर्मोच्छेदानुपपत्तिः । नित्यानां च कर्मणां पुण्यफलत्वश्रुतेः, "वर्णा आश्रमाश्च स्वकर्मनिष्ठाः" [गौ. ध. सू. ११.२९.] इत्यादिस्मृतेश्च कर्मक्षयानुपपत्तिः ।

66.6. *Final Reply*: All this is erroneous. *Śruti* clearly teaches

that no road other than knowledge leads to *mokṣa* Vide: "Knowing Him alone one conquers death; no other road is available for going there" (ŚU.3.8).
Further, 6.20 (ibid) teaches that the non-knower's achievement of *mokṣa* is as impossible as the folding up of the sky like a hide. Purāṇas, too, teach that *mokṣa* is won through knowledge. Note also that without knowledge meritorious works that have yet to bear fruits will not dwindle at all. The meritorious and sinful acts producing their respective fruits stand on the same footing as far as *Mokṣa* is concerned. The possibility of meritorious works remaining without bearing happy fruits is as likely as that of the unmeritorious works with their unhappy fruits. These meritorious works should lead to fresh embodiment and *mokṣa* will remain unrealised. The extermination of attachment, aversion and delusion which issue from righteousness and unrighteousness cannot be achieved except through self-knowledge. Thus will *dharma* and *adharma* survive in the absence of Self-knowledge. Besides *Śruti* teaches obligatory works to bear meritorious fruits; *smṛtis* too do it (GDS. 11.29). Thus works will survive undwindled.

66.7. ये तु आहुः—नित्यानि कर्माणि दुःखरूपत्वात् पूर्वकृतदुरितकर्मणां फलमेव, न तु तेषां स्वरूपव्यतिरेकेण अन्यत् फलं अस्ति, अश्रुतत्वात्, जीवनादिनिमित्ते च विधानात् इति ।

न; अप्रवृत्तानां कर्मणां फलदानासम्भवात्; दुःखफलविशेषानुपपत्तिश्च स्यात् । यत् उक्तम्—पूर्वजन्मकृतदुरितानां कर्मणां फलं नित्यकर्मानुष्ठानायासदुःखं भुज्यते इति—तत् असत् । न हि मरणकाले फलदानाय अनङ्कुरीभूतस्य कर्मणः फलं अन्यकर्मारब्धे जन्मनि उपभुज्यते इति उपपत्तिः । अन्यथा स्वर्गफलोपभोगाय अग्निहोत्रादिकर्मारब्धे जन्मनि नरकफलोपभोगानुपपत्तिः न स्यात् । तस्य दुरित-दुःखविशेषफलत्वानुपपत्तेश्च—अनेकेषु हि दुरितेषु सम्भवत्सु भिन्नदुःखसाधनफलेषु नित्यकर्मानुष्ठानायासदुःखमात्रफलेषु कल्प्यमानेषु द्वन्द्वरोगादिबाधनं निर्निमित्तं न हि शक्यते कल्पयितुं, नित्यकर्मानुष्ठानायासदुःखम् एव पूर्वोपात्तदुरितफलं न शिरसा पाषाणवहनादिदुःखम् इति । अप्रकृतं च इदं उच्यते—नित्यकर्मानुष्ठानायासदुःखं पूर्वकृतदुरितकर्मफलं इति । कथम्?— अप्रसूतफलस्य हि पूर्वकृतदुरितस्य क्षयः न उपपद्यते इति प्रकृतम् । तत्र प्रसूतफलस्य कर्मणः फलं नित्यकर्मानुष्ठानायास-दुःखं आह भवान्, न अप्रसूतफलस्य इति । अथ सर्वमेव पूर्वकृतं दुरितं प्रसूतफलम् एव इति मन्यते भवान्—ततः नित्यकर्मानुष्ठानायासदुःखम् एव फलं इति विशेषणं

अयुक्तम् । नित्यकर्मविध्यानर्थक्यप्रसङ्गश्च, उपभोगनैव प्रसूतफलस्य दुरितकर्मणः क्षयोपपत्तेः । किंच—श्रुतस्य नित्यस्य दुःखं चेत् फलं, नित्यकर्मानुष्ठानायासात् एव तत् दृश्यते व्यायामादिवत्; तत् अन्यस्य इति कल्पनानुपपत्तिः । जीवनादि-निमित्ते च विधानात्, नित्यानां कर्मणां प्रायश्चित्तवत् पूर्वकृतदुरितफलत्वानुपपत्तिः । यस्मिन् पापकर्मणि निमित्ते यत् विहितं प्रायश्चित्तं, न तु तस्य पापस्य तत् फलम् । अथ तस्य एव पापस्य निमित्तस्य प्रायश्चित्तदुःखं फलं, जीवनादिनिमित्तेऽपि नित्य-कर्मानुष्ठानायासदुःखं जीवनादिनिमित्तस्य एव फलं प्रसज्येत, नित्यप्रायश्चित्तयोः नैमित्तिकत्वाविशेषात् । किंच अन्यत्—नित्यस्य काम्यस्य च अग्निहोत्रादेः अनुष्ठा-नायासदुःखस्य तुल्यत्वात् नित्यानुष्ठानायासदुःखम् एव पूर्वकृतदुरितस्य फलम्, न तु काम्यानुष्ठानायासदुःखं इति विशेषः न अस्तीति तदपि पूर्वकृतदुरितफलं प्रसज्येत । तथा च सति नित्यानां फलाश्रवणात् तद्विधानान्यथानुपपत्तेश्च नित्यानुष्ठानाया-सदुःखं पूर्वकृतदुरितफलं इति अर्थापत्तिकल्पना च अनुपपन्ना । एवं विधानान्यथानु-पपत्तेः अनुष्ठानायासदुःखव्यतिरिक्तफलत्वानुमानाच्च नित्यानाम् । विरोधाच्च; विरुद्धं च इदं उच्यते—नित्यकर्मणा अनुष्ठीयमानेन अन्यस्य कर्मणः फलं भुज्यते इति अभ्युपगम्यमाने स एव उपभोगः नित्यस्य कर्मणः फलं इति, नित्यस्य कर्मणः फलाभावः इति विरुद्धं उच्यते । किंच—काम्याग्निहोत्रादौ अनुष्ठीयमाने नित्यम् अपि अग्निहोत्रादि तन्त्रेण एव अनुष्ठितं भवतीति तदायासदुःखेन एव काम्याग्नि-होत्रादिफलं उपक्षीणं स्यात्, तत्तन्त्रत्वात् । अथ काम्याग्निहोत्रादिफलं अन्यत् एव स्वर्गादितदनुष्ठानायासदुःखम् अपि भिन्नं प्रसज्येत । न च तत् अस्ति, दृष्टविरोधात् । न हि काम्यानुष्ठानायासदुःखात् केवलनित्यानुष्ठानायासदुःखं भिन्नं दृश्यते । किंच अन्यत्—अविहितं अप्रतिषिद्धं च कर्म तत्कालफलं, न तु शास्त्रचोदितं प्रतिषिद्धं वा तत्कालफलं भवेत् । तदा स्वर्गादिषु अपि अदृष्टफलशासनेन उद्यमः न स्यात्—अग्निहोत्रादीनाम् एव कर्मस्वरूपाविशेषे अनुष्ठानायासदुःखमात्रेण उपक्षयः नित्यानां; स्वर्गादिमहाफलत्वं काम्यानां—अङ्गेतिकर्तव्यताद्याधिक्ये तु असति—फलकामित्व-मात्रेण इति । तस्माच्च न नित्यानां कर्मणां अदृष्टफलाभावः कदाचित् अपि उपपद्यते ।

66.7. Wrong is the argument of those who say, Obligatory works, being troublesome, constitute the fruit of evil works done in past; they bear no fruit other than their essential nature of entailing trouble. But the *Śruti* does not teach such a doctrine; they have been ordained to coexist with the entire life-period. It is not possible for works that cannot by nature bear fruits, yield any fruit. Further this doctrine does not explain how specific troubles accrue from obligatory works. The statement that evil done in the past causes the sufferings involved in the doing of obligatory works, is not fair. It is unreasonable to hold that in a life resulting from other causes is experienced the result of works that have not yet started yielding fruits. Otherwise there would be nothing illogical if, in a life begun to yield the fruits of heavenly life, there occurred hellish sufferings. Nor can the troubles entailed in the doing of obligatory works be treated as the exclusive fruit of past evils. Such evils are numerous, of course. How can they all be held to cause just these troubles associated with the doing of obligatory works? This will keep unexplained numerous other ills of life. The sufferings of a prisoner condemned to hard labour will, for instance, remain unintelligible. Besides, such contentions as these are irrelevant. How? What is relevant is the view that, without yielding their proper fruits, past evils won't dwindle away. What you aver is that the pains entailed in obligatory works are the fruits of works that have started to bear fruits, and not those of works not yet yielding fruits. Or, do you contend that all past evil deeds have begun to yield their fruits? Then the specification 'troubles entailed by obligatory works' becomes meaningless. Also, in this case arises the contingency that obligatory works have been unnecessarily prescribed; for, all past evils of course will get exhausted through the experience of their logical consequences i.e. their fruits. As the strain of exercises is fully explained by the very exercises, the troubles of obligatory works also are explicable fully by their performance—there is no need to refer them to past evils of any kind. The obligatory works have been ordained to co-exist with life; it is improper to refer them, as expiatory rites are, to past evils. If the pains of expiatory works flow from these very works and their occasions, those involved in obligatory works will have to be referred to the causes of life itself; for, both obligatory and expiatory works are equally occasional—i.e. *naimittika*. One more point may be noted: since the troubles involved in obligatory and optional fire-churning rite are identical, what is the reason for referring the former alone to past evils? No such reason is forthcoming. However, there is room for inferring that obligatory works bear fruits other than the troubles they entail. Also, a contradiction is involved here: through the performance of obligatory works are reaped the results of entirely different prior acts. Experience of the troubles is the result of the mere performance of those works, which are at the same time held to be fruitless. Further, when the optional variety of obligatory works is done, obligatory work, as such, of course also gets done, *tantreṇa*, technically. The troubles undergone in this connection will exhaust the fruit of the obligatory work. It may not be argued that the results of the optional variety of the obligatory work, heaven, etc., are different. Were they different, the troubles also would have been differently experienced. This of course is not the fact. A work that is unprescribed and unforbidden yields only a temporary result; what the *śāstras* prescribe and forbid will not yield temporary results. Otherwise who would seek to secure heaven, etc., yielded by the supernatural force of *śāstraic* works? No special pleadings may redeem this position. Therefore it is not reasonable to maintain that obligatory works never yield fruits through the forces of *adṛṣṭa* (unseen efficiencies) released by them.

66.8. अतश्च अविद्यापूर्वकस्य कर्मणः विद्या एव शुभस्य अशुभस्य वा क्षयकारणं अशेषतः, न नित्यकर्मानुष्ठानम्; अविद्याकामबीजं हि सर्वमेव कर्म । तथा उपपादितं अविद्वद्विषयं कर्म, विद्वद्विषया सर्वकर्मसंन्यासपूर्विका ज्ञाननिष्ठा—'उभौ तौ न विजानीतः' [२.१९.], ''वेदाविनाशिनं नित्यं' [२.२१.], 'ज्ञानयोगेन साङ्ख्यानां कर्मयोगेन योगिनां' [३.३.], 'अज्ञानां कर्मसङ्गिनां' [३.२६.], 'तत्त्ववित्तु महाबाहो...गुणा गुणेषु वर्तन्ते इति मत्वा न सज्जते' [३.२८.], सर्वकर्माणि मनसा संन्यस्यास्ते' [५.१३.], 'नैव किञ्चित् करोमीति युक्तो मन्येत तत्त्ववित्' [५.८.] —अर्थात् अज्ञः 'करोमि' इति; आरुरुक्षोः कर्म कारणं, आरूढस्य योगस्थस्य शम एव कारणं [६.३.]; 'उदाराः' त्रयोऽपि अज्ञाः—'ज्ञानी त्वात्मैव मे मतं' [७.१८.]; अज्ञाः कर्मिणः 'गतागतं कामकामा लभन्ते' [९.२१.]; 'अनन्याश्चिन्तयन्तो मां नित्ययुक्ताः यथोक्तं आत्मानं आकाशकल्पं अकल्मषम् उपासते' [९.२२.]; 'ददामि बुद्धियोगं तं येन मामुपयान्ति ते' [१०.१०.]—अर्थात् न कर्मिणः अज्ञाः उपयान्ति । भगवत्कर्मकारिणः ये युक्ततमाः अपि कर्मिणः अज्ञाः ते उत्तरोत्तरहीनफलत्यागावसानसाधनाः [१२.६.-११.] ॥

अनिर्देश्याक्षरोपासकास्तु 'अद्वेष्टा सर्वभूतानाम्' [१२.१३-२०.] इति आ अध्यायपरिसमाप्ति उक्तसाधनाः क्षेत्राध्यायाद्यध्यायत्रयोक्तज्ञानसाधनाश्च [१३.७-११; १४.२२-२६; १५, ३-५] । अधिष्ठानादिपञ्चकहेतुकसर्वकर्मसंन्यासिनां [१८.१४.] आत्मैकत्वाकर्तृत्वज्ञानवतां परस्यां ज्ञाननिष्ठायां वर्तमानानां भगवत्तत्त्वविदां अनिष्टा-

दिकर्मफलत्रयं [१८.१२.] परमहंसपरिव्राजकानाम् एव लब्धभगवत्स्वरूपात्मैकत्व-शरणानां न भवति; भवति एव अन्येषां अज्ञानां कर्मिणां असंन्यासिनां—इत्येषः गीताशास्त्रोक्तकर्तव्यार्थस्य विभागः ॥

66.8. For the following reason also only knowledge can bring about the total dwindling of good and evil works born of nescience, and never the performance of obligatory work. Indeed, all work emanates from nescience and desire. This has already been explicated earlier, namely that works are done by the nescient while the discipline of knowledge is under-taken by the knowers who have renounced all works. Vide 2.19,21; 3.3,26,28; 5.8,13; 6.3; 7.18; 9.21,22; 10.10; 12.6-11. The discipline of the devotees of the Immutable may be found set forth in 12. 13-20; 13.7-11; 14.22-26; and 15.3-5. The three kinds of works' fruits—favourable, unfavourable, and indifferent—cannot accrue to the renunciants of the *Param-ahaṁsa* Order who have sought exclusive refuge in the Self, who possess the knowledge of the non-agency of that non-dua Self and who also are cognizant of the real nature of God. Only to the non-renouncing and nescient agents of activities can they accrue. Such is the broad divisions of the duties taught in the B.G.

66.9. अविद्यापूर्वकत्वं सर्वस्य कर्मणः असिद्धम् इति चेत्—

न; ब्रह्महत्यादिवत्। यद्यपि शास्त्रावगतं नित्यं कर्म; तथाऽपि अविद्यावतः एव भवति। यथा प्रतिषेधशास्त्रावगतम् अपि ब्रह्महत्यादिलक्षणं कर्म अनर्थकारणं अविद्याकामादिदोषवतः भवति—अन्यथा प्रवृत्त्यनुपपत्तेः—तथा नित्यनैमित्तिककाम्यानि अपि इति ॥

देहव्यतिरिक्तात्मनि अज्ञाते प्रवृत्तिः नित्यादिकर्मसु अनुपपन्ना इति चेत्—न; चलनात्मकस्य कर्मणः अनात्मकर्तृकस्य 'अहं करोमि' इति प्रवृत्तिदर्शनात् ॥ देहादिसङ्घाते अहंप्रत्ययः गौणः, न मिथ्या इति चेत्—

न; तत्कार्येष्वपि गौणत्वोपपत्तेः। आत्मीये देहादिसंघाते अहंप्रत्ययः गौणः; यथा आत्मीये पुत्रे 'आत्मा वै पुत्रनामाऽसि' [तै. सं. २.११.] इति, लोके च 'मम प्राण एव अयं गौः' इति, तद्वत्। नैवं मिथ्याप्रत्ययः। मिथ्याप्रत्ययस्तु स्थाणु-पुरुषयोः अगृह्यमाणविशेषयोः। न गौणप्रत्ययस्य मुख्यकार्यार्थता, अधिकरणस्तुत्य-र्थत्वात् लुप्तोपमाशब्देन। यथा 'सिंहो देवदत्तः', 'अग्निः माणवकः' इति सिंह इव, अग्निरिव क्रौर्यपैङ्गल्यादिसामान्यवत्त्वात् देवदत्तमाणवकाधिकरणस्तुत्यर्थम् एव, न

तु सिंहकार्यं अग्निकार्यं वा गौणशब्दप्रत्ययनिमित्तं किंचित् साध्यते; मिथ्याप्रत्ययकार्यं तु अनर्थं अनुभवति इति । गौणप्रत्ययविषयं जानाति 'नैष सिंहः देवदत्तः', 'नायं अग्निः माणवकः' इति । तथा गौणेन देहादिसंघातेन आत्मना कृतं कर्म न मुख्येन अहंप्रत्ययविषयेण आत्मना कृतं स्यात् । न हि गौणसिंहाग्निभ्यां कृतं कर्म मुख्यसिंहाग्निभ्यां कृतं स्यात् । न च क्रौर्येण पैङ्गल्येन वा मुख्यसिंहाग्न्योः कार्यं किंचित् क्रियते, स्तुत्यर्थत्वेन उपक्षीणत्वात् । स्तूयमानौ च जानीतः 'न अहं सिंहः', 'न अहं अग्निः' इति; न हि 'सिंहस्य कर्म मम, अग्नेश्च' इति । तथा 'न संघातस्य कर्म मम मुख्यस्य आत्मनः' इति प्रत्ययः युक्ततरः स्यात्, न पुनः 'अहं कर्ता, मम कर्म' इति । यच्च आहुः 'आत्मीयैः स्मृतीच्छाप्रयत्नैः कर्महेतुभिः आत्मा कर्म करोति' इति—न, तेषां मिथ्याप्रत्ययपूर्वकत्वात् । मिथ्याप्रत्ययनिमित्तेष्टानिष्टानुभूतक्रियाफलजनितसंस्कारपूर्वकाः हि स्मृतीच्छाप्रयत्नादयः । यथा अस्मिन् जन्मनि देहादिसंङ्घाताभिमानरागद्वेषादिकृतौ धर्माधर्मौ तत्फलानुभवश्च, तथा अतीते अतीततरेऽपि जन्मनि इति अनादिः अविद्याकृतः संसारः अतीतः अनागतश्च अनुमेयः । ततश्च सर्वकर्मसंन्याससहितज्ञाननिष्ठया आत्यन्तिकः संसारोपरमः इति सिद्धम् । अविद्यात्मकत्वाच्च देहाभिमानस्य, तन्निवृत्तौ देहानुपपत्तेः संसारानुपपत्तिः । देहादिसंघाते आत्माभिमानः अविद्यात्मकः । न हि लोके 'गवादिभ्यः अन्यः अहं, मत्तश्च अन्ये गवादयः' इति जानन् तान् 'अहं' इति मन्यते कश्चित् । अजानंस्तु स्थाणौ पुरुषविज्ञानवत् अविवेकतः देहादिसंघाते कुर्यात् 'अहं' इति प्रत्ययं, न विवेकतः जानन् । यस्तु 'आत्मा वै पुत्रनामाऽसि' [तै. सं. २.११.] इति पुत्रे अहंप्रत्ययः, स तु जन्यजनकसम्बन्धनिमित्तः गौणः । गौणेन च आत्मना भोजनादिवत् परमार्थकार्यं न शक्यते कर्तुम्, गौणसिंहाग्निभ्यां मुख्यसिंहाग्निकार्यवत् ॥

66.9. *Objection:* Though obligatory work is inculcated by the *śāstras*, it is operative only in the case of the nescient. Slaughter of holy men etc. are referred to as sources of sins in the prohibitions laid down in the *śāstras*; they are committed only by those who are smitten by flaws like nescience, lust and so forth; without these flaws none would perpetrate them. Similar is the case with obligatory, occasional and voluntary activities.

The argument that without the knowledge of a transcendent Self none would address himself to obligatory works, etc., is defective; for, work whose essence is movement, is found egoistically associated with non-selves like the body. But the treatment of the body etc., as self or 'I', is not false or *mithyā*; it is only secondary or *gauṇa*''. No, one must discrimate here. The treatment of the body complex as 'I' is secondary even as those of one's son as one's self is (Vide:- your son is yourself—T.S. 2.11; this bull is my very self.) An error is entirely different. This occurs when there is failure to distinguish between two entities like a post and a man. Secondary notions don't produce real consequences; they are meant only to commend by means of implied similes. cf: Devadatta is a lion; the student is fire—these mean fierce and tawny like lion and fire. Those statements are not taken literally. Where errors occur troubles follow. In secondary usage there is no real confusion as between self and body. Even where praise is conveyed, the praised ones know: 'I am no lion; I am no fire.' In the case of errors the work of the body is claimed by the self as its own. Wrong is the assertion that the self works due to the causes like memory, desire, exertion, etc.; these are consequences of prior errors, results of impressions of pleasant and unpleasant experiences. Just as in this birth righteousness and unrighteousness and their consequences are products of conceit in the body-complex, attachment, aversion, etc., in prior lives too, the case was similar. Thus transmigratory lives in the past and future are beginningless and nescience-born. Therefore, the definitive dwindling away of transmigratory life is possible only through the discipline of knowledge accompanied by total renunciation. Note that conceit in the body-complex is essentially nescience. When this nescience is sublated, embodiment will cease and so too the transmigatory life. Treating the body-complex as self is obviously an act of nescience. One that knows himself as different from his possessions like cattle, etc, never mistakes them for his self—his 'I'. Ignorant of this distinction due to non-discrimination, as of the post from a man, one may mistake the body-complex for self. Of course, treatment of one's son as one's self is secondary, because they are related as the begetter and the begotten. Of course one can't eat through one's son, etc., just as the student can't operate like the lion and the fire.

66.10. अदृष्टविषयचोदनाप्रामाण्यात् आत्मकर्तव्यं गौणैः देहेन्द्रियात्मभिः क्रियते एव इति चेत्—

न; अविद्याकृतात्मकत्वात् तेषाम् । न गौणा: आत्मान: देहेन्द्रियादय:; किं तर्हि ?— मिथ्याप्रत्ययेन एव अनात्मान: सन्त: आत्मत्वं आपाद्यन्तें, तद्भावे भावात्, तदभावे च अभावात् । अविवेकिनां हि अज्ञानकाले बालानां दृश्यते 'दीर्घ: अहं', 'गौर: अहं' इति देहादिसंघाते अहंप्रत्यय: । न तु विवेकिनां 'अन्य: अहं देहादिसंघातात्' इति जानतां तत्काले देहादिसंघाते अहंप्रत्यय: भवति । तस्मात् मिथ्याप्रत्ययाभावे अभावात् तत्कृत: एव, न गौण: । पृथग्गृह्यमाणविशेषसामान्ययो: हि सिंहदेवदत्तयो: अग्निमाणवकयो: वा गौण: प्रत्यय: शब्दप्रयोग: वा स्यात्, न अगृह्यमाणविशेषसामान्ययो: । यत्तु उक्तं 'श्रुतिप्रामाण्यात्' इति—तत् न, तत्प्रामाण्यस्य अदृष्टविषयत्वात् । प्रत्यक्षादिप्रमाणानुपलब्धे हि विषये अग्निहोत्रादि-साध्यसाधनसम्बन्धे श्रुते: प्रामाण्यं, न प्रत्यक्षादिविषये, अदृष्टदर्शनार्थविषयत्वात् प्रमाण्यस्य । तस्मात् न दृष्टमिथ्याज्ञाननिमित्तस्य अहंप्रत्ययस्य देहादिसंघाते गौणत्वं कल्पयितुं शक्यम् । न हि श्रुतिशतमपि 'शीत: अग्नि:, अप्रकाशो वा' इति ब्रुवत् प्रामाण्यं उपैति । यदि ब्रूयात् 'शीत: अग्नि:, अप्रकाशो वा' इति, तथाऽपि अर्थान्तरं श्रुते: विवक्षितं कल्प्यम्, प्रामाण्यान्यथाऽनुपपत्ते:, न तु प्रमाणान्तरविरुद्धं स्ववचनविरुद्धं वा कल्प्यम् ॥

66.10. Vain is the insistence that due to the validity of Vedic injunction aimed at the generation of the force of *apūrva*, one's works may very well be performed by the body-complex. The body-complex functions as self not due to secondary use of words like *ātmā vai putra nāmāsi*, but due to error which makes these non-selves appear as self. Only as long as the error lasts such functioning lasts. Ignorant children aver 'I am tall, white', etc., mistaking the body for the self; not so those who discriminate. A secondary usage is admissible only where the distinction between the particular and the universal is clearly grasped. This is the case in regard to the lion and Devadatta; the fire and the student. Where such distinction is not grasped, the secondary usage is not in order. The appeal to the infallibility of the Vedic injunction is misconceived. The infallibility in question refers only to the unseen force or *apūrva*, and is admissible only in regard to matters not confined to the sphere of direct perceptions, etc. The said infallibility is relevant to matters unseen. Therefore, the explanation of the conceit of 'I' in regard to the body-complex—a matter of error—has nothing to do with secondary usage. Even a hundred statements of *sruti* to the effect that fire is cold and non-luminous won't prove valid. If it does make such a statement, its import will have to be interpreted differently. Otherwise, validity won't attach to it. Nothing in conflict with the means of valid cognition or with its own statements may be imputed to *śruti*.

66.11. कर्मणः मिथ्याप्रत्ययवत्कर्तृकत्वात् कर्तुः अभावे श्रुतेः अप्रामाण्यम् इति चेत्— न; ब्रह्मविद्यायां अर्थवत्त्वोपपत्तेः ॥

कर्मविधिश्रुतिवत् ब्रह्मविद्याविधिश्रुतेः अपि अप्रामाण्यप्रसङ्गः इति चेत्— न; बाधकप्रत्ययानुपपत्तेः । यथा ब्रह्मविद्याविधिश्रुत्या आत्मनि अवगते देहादिसंघाते अहंप्रत्ययः बाध्यते, तथा आत्मनि एव आत्मावगतिः न कदाचित् केनचित् कथंचित् अपि बाधितुं शक्या, फलाव्यतिरेकात् अवगतेः यथा अग्निः उष्णः प्रकाशश्च इति । न च एवं कर्मविधिश्रुतेः अप्रामाण्यं, पूर्वपूर्वप्रवृत्तिनिरोधेन उत्तरोत्तरापूर्वप्रवृत्तिजननस्य प्रत्यगात्माभिमुख्येन प्रवृत्त्युत्पादनार्थत्वात् । मिथ्यात्वेऽपि उपायस्य उपेयसत्यतया सत्यत्वम् एव स्यात्; यथा अर्थवादानां विधिशेषाणाम्, लोकेऽपि बालोन्मत्तादीनां पयआदौ पाययितव्ये चूडावर्धनादिवचनम् । प्रकारान्तरस्थानां च साक्षात् एव प्रामाण्यं सिद्धं, प्राक् आत्मज्ञानात् देहाभिमाननिमित्तप्रत्यक्षादिप्रामाण्यवत् ॥

66.11. *Objection:* "Since works are enjoined on agents subject to error, they will cease to be agents on the dawn of knowledge and '*śruti*' will prove invalid".

Answer: "No; the validity of '*śruti*' will hold good in regard to the knowledge of Brahman. There is no danger that as in respect of prescriptions of work, in respect of the knowledge of the Brahman also it will break down, for, in respect of the knowledge of the Brahman no sublating cognition is available. Once the Self is known by virtue of Brahman-knowledge, the error of treating the body-complex as Self is abolished. Such abolition however cannot be shown, by anyone, at any time, in any manner whatsoever, to apply to the knowledge of the real Self as Self; for, there is total correspondence between fact and cognition, exactly as in the case of the cognition 'fire is hot and luminous'. Neither does this explanation entail the invalidity of scripture enjoining works; for, these mandates are meant only to arrest lower works and promote higher ones, to induce activity aimed at the realisation of the inner Self. The means may very well be erroneous; but what is sought after is true. Thus even the means turn out to be true. Cf. glorificatory passages subject to mandates. In empirical life, too, unveridical praise is employed to induce the ignorant and the sick to undergo medical treatment. In contexts other than that of Self-knowledge the validity of mandates is direct, just as sense-perception, etc., are valid before the dawn of self-knowledge.

66.12. यत्तु मन्यसे—स्वयं अव्याप्रियमाणोऽपि आत्मा संनिधिमात्रेण करोति, तदेव मुख्यं कर्तृत्वं आत्मनः, यथा राजा युध्यमानेषु योधेषु युध्यते इति प्रसिद्धं स्वयं अयुध्यमानोऽपि सन्निधानात् एव जितः पराजितश्चेति, तथा सेनापतिः वाचैव करोति; क्रियाफलसम्बन्धश्च राज्ञः सेनापतेश्च दृष्टः । यथा च ऋत्विक्कर्म यजमानस्य, तथा देहादीनां कर्म आत्मकृतं स्यात्, फलस्य आत्मगामित्वात् । यथा वा भ्रामकस्य लोहभ्रामयितृत्वात् अव्यापृतस्य एव मुख्यम् एव कर्तृत्वम्, तथा च आत्मनः इति ।

तत् असत्; अकुर्वतः कारकत्वप्रसङ्गात् ।

कारकं अनेकप्रकारम् इति चेत्—

नः, राजप्रभृतीनां मुख्यस्य अपि कर्तृत्वस्य दर्शनात् । राजा तावत् स्वव्यापारेण अपि युध्यते; योधानां च योधयितृत्वे धनदाने च मुख्यम् एव कर्तृत्वं, तथा जय-पराजयफलोपभोगे । यजमानस्य अपि प्रधानत्यागे दक्षिणादाने च मुख्यम् एव कर्तृत्वम् । तस्मात् अव्यापृतस्य कर्तृत्वोपचारः यः सः गौणः इति अवगम्यते । यदि मुख्यं अन्यत् कर्तृत्वं स्वयव्यापारलक्षणं न उपलभ्येत राजयजमानप्रभृतीनां, तदा सन्निधिमात्रेण अपि कर्तृत्वं मुख्यं परिकल्प्येत; यथा भ्रामकस्य लोहभ्रमणेन, न तथा राजयजमानादीनां स्वव्यापारः नोपलभ्यते । तस्मात् सन्निधिमात्रेण कर्तृत्वं गौणम् एव । तथा च सति तत्फलसम्बन्धोऽपि गौणः एव स्यात् । न गौणेन मुख्यं कार्यं निर्वर्त्यते । तस्मात् असदेव एतत् गीयते 'देहादीनां व्यापारेण अव्यापृतः आत्मा कर्ता भोक्ता च स्यात्' इति । भ्रान्तिनिमित्तं तु सर्वं उपपद्यते, यथा स्वप्ने; मायायां च एवम् । न च देहाद्यात्मप्रत्ययभ्रान्तिसन्तानविच्छेदेषु सुषुप्तिसमाध्या(-धाना-)दिषु कर्तृत्वभोक्तृत्वाद्यनर्थः उपलभ्यते । तस्मात् भ्रान्तिप्रत्ययनिमित्तः एव अयं संसारभ्रमः, न तु परमार्थः, इति सम्यग्दर्शनात् अत्यन्तः एव उपरमः इति सिद्धम् ॥

66.12. Now the objector may argue as follows: the inactive Self may accomplish works by mere presence. This may be understood as Self's agency, just as a king, though not fighting literally, is held to fight when his soldiers alone in fact fight. He is thus said to win or lose. A general operates through commands issued. Both the king and the general are related to the final victory or defeat. This is like the actual work of priests being credited to the performer of a sacrifice. Thus the work of the body-complex may be held to be done by the Self. Or, this is like the operation of a magnet; inactive physically, it produces results. This line of argument is false; for what does not operate at all is treated as an accessory of work. 'Are there not different kinds of accessories?' The answer is that the king, etc., do have full-fledged activity also in regard to works. He can and does actually fight also. In causing his soldiers to fight, in remunerating them, etc., his agency is primary. Hence in the example cited above he is an agent only figuratively; it is secondary. If it were known that he could not be an agent in any other way, his mere presence could have been equated with his agency, as in the case of the magnet. This of course is not the case in regard to the king and the general. Therefore agency through mere presence is only secondary, in which case ownership of the results of such agency would also have to be secondary. The secondary agency cannot explain primary results. Hence the entire argument—that the activities of the body-complex may make an inactive Self agent and experiencer—is invalid. On the other hand, all this may be explained on the basis of an illusion, as the phenomena in a dream or magic show are. When such illusions are broken up in states of concentration or deep sleep, the vexations of agency, etc., are not experienced at all. The conclusion is that the illusion of transmigratory life is caused by an error; it is not real. Through right perception the said illusion will, once for all, dry up.

67.0. सर्वगीताशास्त्रार्थं उपसंहृत्य अस्मिन् अध्याये, विशेषतश्च अन्ते इह शास्त्रार्थदार्ढ्याय संक्षेपतः उपसंहारं कृत्वा, अथ इदानीं शास्त्रसंप्रदायविधिम् आह—

67.0. Having concluded the teachings of the Gītā and reiterated them, the traditions of the *śāstra* are explained finally to strengthen these teachings.

इदं ते नातपस्काय नाभक्ताय कदाचन।
न चाशुश्रूषवे वाच्यं न च मां योऽभ्यसूयति ॥६७॥

67. Don't impart this to a non-ascetic (one without control of the senses), a non-devotee, at any time, nor, again, to one who seeks it not and to one who reviles Me.

67.1. इदं इति ॥ इदं शास्त्रं ते तव हिताय मया उक्तं संसारविच्छित्तये अतपस्काय तपोरहिताय न वाच्यं इति व्यवहितेन सम्बध्यते । तपस्विनेऽपि अभक्ताय गुरौ देवे च भक्तिरहिताय कदाचन कस्यांचित् अपि अवस्थायां न वाच्यम् । भक्तः तपस्वी अपि सन् अशुश्रूषुः यः भवति तस्मै अपि न वाच्यम् । न च यः मां वासुदेवं प्राकृतं मनुष्यं मत्वा अभ्यसूयति आत्मप्रशंसादिदोषाध्यारोपणेन ईश्वरत्वं मम अजानन् न सहते, असौ अपि अयोग्यः, तस्मै अपि न वाच्यम् । भगवति अनसूयायुक्ताय तपस्विने भक्ताय शुश्रूषवे वाच्यं शास्त्रं इति सामर्थ्यात् गम्यते । तत्र 'मेधाविने तपस्विने वा' [?] इति अनयोः विकल्पदर्शनात् शुश्रूषाभक्तियुक्ताय तपस्विने तद्युक्ताय मेधाविने वा वाच्यम् । शुश्रूषाभक्तिवियुक्ताय न तपस्विने नापि मेधाविने वाच्यम् । भगवति असूयायुक्ताय समस्तगुणवतेऽपि न वाच्यम् । गुरुशुश्रूषाभक्तिमते च वाच्यं इत्येषः शास्त्रसंप्रदायविधिः ॥

67.1. This *śāstrā*, imparted to you for your good—for terminating your transmigratory travails—, don't impart, in any circumstance to a non-ascetic. '*Na vācyam*', not to be imparted, must be read here, though remotely placed in the verse. To be an ascetic is not enough; one must also be a devotee—have devotion to God and teacher. Even asceticism and devotion don't suffice, one must also have the desire to heed. The seeker should not, again, be a reviler, taking Me, Vāsudeva, to be a mere man, accusing Me of boastfulness and other faults, not tolerating, through ignorance, My Godhood. He too is unfit to receive this instruction. Its fit recipient is a non-reviling ascetic devotee, anxious to listen to it. An alternative reading uses the expressions, 'to an intelligent or ascetic person'. The right tradition here insits that the candidate, no matter how richly endowed, shall not be a reviler of God or one without devotion and yearning to learn. Teach one who has the yearning and devotion to God and teacher.

68.0. सम्प्रदायस्य कर्तुः फलं इदानीं आह—

68.0. Now is set forth the fruit accruing to one who follows the right tradition:

य इमं परमं गुह्यं मद्भक्तेष्वभिधास्यति ।
भक्तिं मयि परां कृत्वा मामेवैष्यत्यसंशयः ॥६८॥

68. He who imparts this transcendent secret to My devotee, nurturing utmost devotion to Me, will doubtlessly attain Me.

68.1. य इमं इति ॥ यः इमं यथोक्तं परमं परमनिःश्रेयसार्थं केशवार्जुनयोः संवादरूपं ग्रन्थं गुह्यं गोप्यतमं मद्भक्तेषु मयि भक्तिमत्सु अभिधास्यति वक्ष्यति, ग्रन्थतः अर्थतश्च स्थापयिष्यति इत्यर्थः, यथा त्वयि मया । भक्तेः पुनर्ग्रहणात् भक्तिमात्रेण केवलेन शास्त्रसम्प्रदाने पात्रं भवति इति गम्यते । कथं अभिधास्यति इति ? उच्यते—भक्तिं मयि परां कृत्वा 'भगवतः परमगुरोः अच्युतस्य शुश्रूषा मया क्रियते' इत्येवं कृत्वा इत्यर्थः । तस्य इदं फलम्—माम् एव एष्यति मुच्यते एव । असंशयः अत्र संशयः न कर्तव्य ॥ किंच—

68.1. This 'transcendent secret dialogue' between Kṛṣna and Arjuna which yields the summum bonum—whoever imparts it to My devotee, both in letter and spirit, as I did in your case, will attain Me indeed. How is it to be imparted?—'Nurturing the utmost devotion to Me', i.e., in the spirit of service done to the Supreme Teacher, the unlapsing God. No doubt about this need be entertained. Reference to devotion a second time in the second half of this verse shows that eligibility for cultivating this *śāstrā* is bound up with devotion to God alone. Also,

न च तस्मान्मनुष्येषु कश्चिन्मे प्रियकृत्तमः ।
भविता न च मे तस्मादन्यः प्रियतरो भुवि ॥६९॥

69. None among men, other than he, does a deed dearer to Me; nor is there in the world one dearer to Me.

69.1. न च इति ॥ न च तस्मात् शास्त्रसम्प्रदायकृतः मनुष्येषु मनुष्याणां मध्ये कश्चित् मे मम प्रियकृत्तमः अतिशयेन प्रियकरः, अन्यः प्रियकृत्तमः, नास्त्येवं इत्यर्थः वर्तमानेषु । न च भविता भविष्यत्यपि काले तस्मात् द्वितीयः अन्यः प्रियतरः प्रियकृत्तरः भुवि लोकेऽस्मिन् न भविता ॥ योऽपि—

69.1. Among men, now, none does a deed dearer to Me than he who transmits the tradition of this *śāstra*. Nor, in future, will there be another in this world who does aught dearer to Me.

He, too,

अध्येष्यते च य इमं धर्म्यं संवादमावयोः ।
ज्ञानयज्ञेन तेनाहमिष्टः स्यामिति मे मतिः ॥७०॥

70. Whoever shall study this righteous dialogue between us shall have offered Me a sacrifice wrought with knowledge—this is My view.

70.1. अध्येष्यते इति ॥ अध्येष्यते च पठिष्यति यः इमं धर्म्यं धर्मादनपेतं संवादरूपं ग्रन्थं आवयोः, तेन इदं कृतं स्यात् । ज्ञानयज्ञेन—विधिजपोपांशुमानसानां यज्ञानां ज्ञानयज्ञः मानसत्वात् विशिष्टतमः इत्यतः तेन ज्ञानयज्ञेन गीताशास्त्रस्य अध्ययनं स्तूयते; फलविधिः एव वा, देवतादिविषयज्ञानफलतुल्यं अस्य फलं भवतीति —तेन अध्ययनेन अहं इष्टः पूजितः स्यां भवेयं इति मे मम मतिः निश्चयः ॥

70.1. Whoso shall study this righteous dialogue between us shall have offered Me a sacrifice consisting of knowledge. Among the many forms of sacrifice—ritual, muttering either aloud or in a low tone, and mental—the most sacred is mental. The study of the Gītā is exalted as being equal to a mental sacrifice. Or, this may be taken to point to the fruit of such study. This fruit is equal to what is obtained by worship of deities. To study the Gītā is to sacrifice unto Me most excellently. I am sure it is so.

71.0. अथ श्रोतुः इदं फलम्—

71.0. The fruit of listening to the Gītā is set forth here:

श्रद्धावाननसूयश्च शृणुयादपि यो नरः।
सोऽपि मुक्तः शुभाँल्लोकान् प्राप्नुयात्पुण्यकर्मणाम् ॥७१॥

71. Endowed with faith and unreviling, whoever listens to the Gītā will be liberated, he will reach the happy realms reserved for the meritorious.

71.1. श्रद्धावान् इति ॥ श्रद्धावान् श्रद्दधानः अनसूयः च असूयावर्जितः सन् इमं ग्रन्थं शृणुयात् अपि यः नरः—अपिशब्दात् किमुत अर्थज्ञानवान् ? सः अपि पापात् मुक्तः शुभान् प्रशस्तान् लोकान् प्राप्नुयात् पुण्यकर्मणां अग्निहोत्रादिकर्मवताम् ॥

71.1. Faithful and unreviling, whoso shall at least listen to this work will be liberated from sins and will reach realms reserved for the performers of rites like the *agnihotra*. *Api*—at least—shows what excellent fruits await him who understands also its sense.

72.0. शिष्यस्य शास्त्रार्थग्रहणाग्रहणविवेकबुभुत्सया पृच्छति । तदग्रहणे ज्ञाते पुनः ग्राहयिष्यामि उपायान्तरेण अपि इति प्रष्टुः अभिप्रायः । यत्नान्तरं च आस्थाय शिष्यस्य कृतार्थता कर्तव्या इति आचार्यधर्मः प्रदर्शितः भवति ।

72.0. The (following) question is meant to find out whether the disciple has grasped the contents of the *śāstra.* If he has failed, he may be instructed again—such is the idea of the teacher. This also shows what the duty of a real teacher is.

कच्चिदेतत् श्रुतं पार्थ त्वयैकाग्रेण चेतसा।
कच्चिदज्ञानसम्मोहः प्रनष्टस्ते धनञ्जय ॥७२॥

72. Have you, Arjuna! with concentrated mind listened

to this? Wealth-winner! has your confusion, wrought by ignorance, been dispelled?

72.1. कच्चित् इति ॥ कच्चित् किं एतत् मया उक्तं श्रुतं श्रवणेन अवधारितं पार्थ! त्वया एकाग्रेण चेतसा चित्तेन? किं वा अप्रमादतः? कच्चित् अज्ञानसम्मोहः अज्ञाननिमित्तः सम्मोहः अविविक्तभावः [विचित्तभावः] अविवेकः स्वाभाविकः किं प्रनष्टः?— यदर्थः अयं शास्त्रश्रवणायासः तव, मम च उपदेष्टृत्वायासः प्रवृत्तः—ते तव हे धनञ्जय! ॥

72.1. Have you grasped with concentrated mind what I have told you? Arjuna! Has your native non-discrimination, born of nescience, perished? It was for this that you took the trouble to listen to Me and I to impart this *śāstra*.

अर्जुन उवाच:

नष्टो मोहः स्मृतिर्लब्धा त्वत्प्रसादान्मयाऽच्युत।
स्थितोऽस्मि गतसन्देहः करिष्ये वचनं तव ॥७३॥

Arjuna said:

73. Lord! Confusion has been dispelled, and memory (of truth) regained due to Your grace. I abide, unassailed by doubts. I shall do Your bidding.

73.1. नष्टः इति ॥ नष्टः मोहः अज्ञानजः समस्तसंसारानर्थहेतुः, सागरः इव दुस्तरः। स्मृतिः च आत्मतत्त्वविषया लब्धा—यस्याः लाभात् सर्वहृदयग्रंथीनां विप्रमोक्षः—त्वत्प्रसादात् तव प्रसादात् मया त्वत्प्रसादं आश्रितेन अच्युत। अनेन मोहनाशप्रश्नप्रतिवचनेन सर्वशास्त्रार्थज्ञानफलं एतावत् एव इति निश्चितं दर्शितं भवति, यतः ज्ञानात् मोहनाशः आत्मस्मृतिलाभः च इति। तथा च श्रुतौ 'अनात्मवित् शोचामि' इति उपन्यस्य आत्मज्ञानेन सर्वग्रंथीनां विप्रमोक्षः उक्तः—[छां. उ. ७. १. ३; २६.२.]। 'भिद्यते हृदयग्रन्थिः' [मुं. उ. २.२.८.], 'तत्र को मोहः कः शोकः एकत्वमनुपश्यतः' [ई. उ. ७.] इति च मन्त्रवर्णः। अथ इदानीं त्वच्छासने स्थितः अस्मि गतसन्देहः मुक्तसंशयः। करिष्ये वचनं तव। अहं त्वत्प्रसादात् कृतार्थः, न मे कर्तव्यं अस्ति इत्यभिप्रायः ॥

73.1. Destroyed is the nescience-born confusion, the cause

of all transmigratory ills—a veritable sea, hard to cross. Won is the memory of the Self's truth by virtue of which all knots of the heart have been rent. All this has been due to Your grace, on which alone I depended, O Lord! This expression proves that the fruit of mastering this *śāstra* is the destruction of confusion and the winning of the memory of the Self. The *śruti*, after mentioning, 'I, a non-knower of Self, am grieving,' proceeds to show freedom from all bonds through Self-knowledge:—

CU.7.1.3; 26.2. MU.3.2.8; IU.7. Now subject to Your discipline, I am no longer assailed by doubts. I shall do your bidding. I have fulfilled all my duties due to Your grace. Nothing more remains to be achieved.

74.0. परिसमाप्तः शास्त्रार्थः । अथ इदानीं कथासम्बन्धप्रदर्शनार्थं संजयः उवाच—

74.0. Completed is the import of the *śāstra*. Now its relation to the epic story is set forth by Sañjaya:

सञ्जय उवाच :

इत्यहं वासुदेवस्य पार्थस्य च महात्मनः ।
संवादमिममश्रौषमद्भुतं रोमहर्षणम् ॥७४॥

Sañjaya said:

74. Thus have I listened to this dialogue between Vāsudeva and the high-souled Arjuna—a dialogue marvellous and thrilling.

74.1. इत्यहं इति ॥ इति एवं अहं वासुदेवस्य पार्थस्य च महात्मनः संवादं इमं यथोक्तं अश्रौषं श्रुतवान् अस्मि अद्भुतं अत्यन्तविस्मयकरं रोमहर्षणं रोमाञ्चकरम् ॥ तं च इमम्—

74.1. Thus have I, as set forth above, listened to the dialogue between Kṛṣṇa and the high-souled Arjuna—extremely wonderful and hair-raising. And this,

व्यासप्रसादाच्छ्रुतवानिमं गुह्यतमं परम् ।
योगं योगेश्वरात्कृष्णात्साक्षात्कथयतः स्वयम् ॥७५॥

75. Due to the grace of Vyāsa, I heard of this most secret and supreme Yoga, directly from Kṛṣṇa Himself, the Master Yogin who elucidated it.

75.1. व्यास इति ॥ व्यासप्रसादात् ततः दिव्यचक्षुर्लाभात् श्रुतवान् इमं संवादं गुह्यतमं परं योगं—योगार्थत्वात् ग्रन्थोऽपि योगः—संवादं इमं योगम् एव वा योगेश्वरात् कृष्णात् साक्षात् कथयतः स्वयं, न परम्परया ॥

75.1. Due to the favour of Vyāsa, through the gift of the divine sight, I heard this dialogue, and of this most secret Yoga—the text which teaches this Yoga being itself Yoga. I heard it from Kṛṣṇa, the master of Yoga, who spoke it forth directly, and not indirectly through disciples, etc.

राजन् संस्मृत्य संस्मृत्य संवादमिममद्भुतम् ।
केशवार्जुनयोः पुण्यं हृष्यामि च मुहुर्मुहुः ॥७६॥

76. O King! Calling to mind again and again this wonderful and holy dialogue between Kṛṣṇa and Arjuna, I repeatedly rejoice.

76.1. राजन् इति ॥ हे राजन् धृतराष्ट्र ! संस्मृत्य संस्मृत्य प्रतिक्षणं संवादं इमं अद्भुतं केशवार्जुनयोः पुण्यं इमं श्रवणेन अपि पापहरं श्रुत्वा हृष्यामि च मुहुर्मुहुः प्रतिक्षणम् ॥

76.1. King Dhṛtarāṣṭra! recalling this dialogue every moment, wonderful and holy, of Kṛṣṇa and Arjuna—merely to hear it is to dispel all sins— I repeatedly rejoice.

तच्च संस्मृत्य संस्मृत्य रूपमत्यद्भुतं हरेः ।
विस्मयो मे महान् राजन् हृष्यामि च पुनः पुनः ॥७७॥

77. Repeatedly calling to mind that most wonderful form of Kṛṣṇa, my amazement, O king! waxes; I rejoice without measure.

77.1. तच्च इति ॥ तत् च संस्मृत्य संस्मृत्य रूपं अत्यद्भुतं हरेः विश्वरूपं विस्मयः मे महान् राजन्! हृष्यामि च पुनः पुनः ॥

किं बहुना—

77.1. Recollecting again and again that most marvellous form—the cosmic form—of Kṛṣṇa, O King! my amazement waxes; I rejoice again and again.

Why dilate!

यत्र योगेश्वरः कृष्णो यत्र पार्थो धनुर्धरः।
तत्र श्रीर्विजयो भूतिर्ध्रुवा नीतिर्मतिर्मम ॥७८॥

78. Where the master Yogin Kṛṣṇa is, where the bowman Arjuna is, there, I deem, dwell glory, victory, prosperity and stable order.

इति श्रीमहाभारते शतसाहस्र्यां संहितायां वैयासिक्यां भीष्मपर्वणि योगशास्त्रे श्रीकृष्णार्जुनसंवादे मोक्षसंन्यासयोगो नाम अष्टादशोऽध्यायः ॥

78.1. यत्र इति ॥ यत्र यस्मिन् पक्षे योगेश्वरः सर्वयोगानां ईश्वरः—तत्प्रभवत्वात् सर्वयोगबीजस्य—कृष्णः, यत्र पार्थः यस्मिन् पक्षे धनुर्धरः गाण्डीवधन्वा, तत्र श्रीः तस्मिन् पाण्डवानां पक्षे श्रीः विजयः, तत्रैव भूतिः श्रियः विशेषः विस्तारः भूतिः ध्रुवा अव्यभिचारिणी नीतिः नयः, इत्येवं मतिः मम इति ॥

78.1. To the side where the master Yogin Kṛṣṇa is—of whom are born all forms of Yoga—, and also Arjuna, the bearer of the bow Gāṇḍīva, is will go fame, victory, affluence, vast glory—and stable order. Order means State-policy. This is my conclusion.

इति श्रीमत्परमहंसपरिव्राजकाचार्यगोविंदभगवत्पूज्यपादशिष्य श्रीमच्छङ्करभगवतः कृतौ श्रीमद्भगवद्गीताभाष्ये मोक्षसंन्यासयोगो नाम अष्टादशोऽध्यायः ॥१८॥

श्रीमद्भगवद्गीताश्लोकाद्यचरणप्रतीक-वर्णानुक्रमः